THE ESSENTIAL SOCIOLOGIST

An Introduction

Beth B. Hess
County College of Morris

Peter J. Stein
William Paterson University

Susan A. Farrell
Kingsborough Community College

Foreword by
Judith Lorber
Brooklyn College and Graduate School, CUNY

Roxbury Publishing Company
Los Angeles, California

NOTE TO INSTRUCTORS: A comprehensive *Instructor's Manual/ Testing Program* and a <u>free</u> *Student Study Guide* are available from the publisher. There is also a dedicated *Web Site* for this text at http:// www.roxbury.net/esbindex.html.

Library of Congress Cataloging-in-Publication Data
Hess, Beth B., 1928–
The essential sociologist: an introduction / Beth B. Hess, Peter J. Stein, Susan A. Farrell.
    p. cm.
Includes bibliographical references and index.
ISBN 1-891487-49-3
1. Sociology. I. Stein, Peter J., 1937– II. Farrell, Susan A. III. Title.
HM586.H47 2001
301—dc21   00-032348
                                                                CIP

THE ESSENTIAL SOCIOLOGIST: AN INTRODUCTION

Publisher: Claude Teweles
Managing Editor: Dawn VanDercreek
Production Editor: Jim Ballinger
Copyeditor: Arlyne Lazerson
Graphics Editor: Bonnie Gillespie
Proofreaders: David Marion, Roger Mensink
Production Assistant: Susan Ivanoff-Renteria
Typography: Synergistic Data Systems
Cover Design: Marnie Kenney

Printed on acid-free paper in the United States of America. This book meets the standards for recycling of the Environmental Protection Agency.

ISBN 1-891487-49-3

Roxbury Publishing Company
P.O. Box 491044
Los Angeles, California 90049-9044
Tel.: (310) 473-3312 • Fax: (310) 473-4490
E-mail: roxbury@roxbury.net
Web Site: www.roxbury.net

Contents

Part I

Self in Society

Part II

Structures of Inequality

Part III

The Institutional Order

Part IV

Modern Dilemmas

Foreword

*by Judith Lorber, Brooklyn College
and Graduate School, CUNY*

When I taught my first introductory sociology classes thirty years ago, I turned up my nose at the standard texts. Based on a view of sociology that was number-driven, functionally oriented, and consensual, they were, to me, too standard. My graduate education in the 1960s was at a school that stressed qualitative analysis of what people did rather than tabulations of what they said they did. I was completely sold on the social construction view that societies were made by people who may have gotten locked into institutionalized patterns of norms and expectations, but had the wiggle room to resist and rebel. The sociological readings I assigned recognized that social orders are not fixed in place by consent, but fragilely maintained by power and suppression of dissenting voices.

The political and social struggles recognized by the new sociological thinking was actually taking place both in and out of the classroom. The semester I began teaching, Spring 1970, was cut short by the nationwide student strike over the killing of four Kent State University students who were protesting against the Vietnam War. The informal discussions with students in the cafeteria were some of the best sociology classes I ever had.

I didn't teach introductory sociology for much of the 1980s. When I began to again in the 1990s, there was a text that was ideal for me. It was by Beth Hess, Peter Stein, and Elizabeth Markson. Their book *Sociology* reflected what I felt sociology should be for students—a way of looking at their world that took nothing for granted.

During this time I worked closely with Susan Farrell, first on her Ph.D. dissertation, then as managing editor of *Gender & Society,* and finally as coeditor of *The Social Construction of Gender.* I knew that the introduction to sociology that Beth, Peter, and Susan would write would be iconoclastic, critical, social constructionist, multicultural, multigendered, and multisexual. And so it is!

The Essential Sociologist presents the student with thoroughgoing information and the conceptual tools to make sense of it. The text lays out the constricting patterns of stratification, large-scale bureaucracies, and institutionalized inequality, but also shows how individuals shape society as much as society shapes individuals. It is a rich picture of a complex field with a history, competing schools of thought, and interdisciplinary roots. As the authors state at the beginning, sociology is not for children, but for young adults who look around their world with the clear eyes of those coming of age in a new century, with new sources of knowledge and new ways of thinking. It gives students the ideas and sources to make sense of their twenty-first century world—and perhaps to shape it for the better. ✦

Preface

Welcome! You are about to read the First Edition of a brand-new undergraduate sociology text, titled *The Essential Sociologist: An Introduction.* Although the text is new, Hess and Stein are the authors of five editions of *Sociology,* coauthored with Elizabeth Markson and published by Macmillan in 1982, 1985, 1988, 1993, and by Allyn & Bacon in 1996. Hess and Stein have been joined by Susan Farrell in the writing of this new text.

One of the strengths of *The Essential Sociologist* is its treatment of gender, race, and class as elements of social structure, and the integration of these important variables into the substantive chapters as well as chapters specifically focused on them.

We used the most recent data and research findings available at the time of writing. This task has been made considerably easier by the proliferation of information and web sites on the Internet, resulting in fewer trips to local libraries.

We bring to *The Essential Sociologist* many decades of teaching in various settings, including at a community college, a four-year state university, and a major research university. Our collaboration on the text has strengthened our friendship and reinforced our commitment to the discipline of sociology.

Distinctive Features of *The Essential Sociologist*

These distinctive features of the text are designed to make the text as "user friendly" as possible:

Chapter openers. Each chapter begins with a short outline of its content and moves into a timely, thought-provoking discussion of the topics to be covered. These are intended to spark the interest of students and provide a road map for the reader.

Key definitions. All key terms are defined to reinforce the concepts presented in the body of the text. Students report that these highlighted definitions are very useful for chapter review. An alphabetical listing of all key terms appears in the glossaries at the end of each chapter.

Boxed material. Boxed case studies expand concepts and themes of the core material with the most recent research and up-to-date applications. The boxes are clearly linked to the text.

Surfing the Sociological Web. The text has exciting web sites in each chapter. There are 10 to 15 sites for each of the 16 chapters and many are interactive as well as scholarly and research oriented. These addresses will lead students to cutting-edge research in sociology as well as government sites packed with statistics and data on the subjects in each chapter.

The Sociology Café. This is an interactive site where students can communicate with other students about sociological topics, issues, and research.

Summaries. A summary of important themes and concepts at the end of each chapter helps students review the material.

Illustrations: Photographs, graphs, charts, and tables. These expand the learning process for students by illustrating recent social developments in the United States and other countries. The captions for the photos in every chapter address stimulating, critical-thinking issues that integrate text and illustrations. Clear and lively charts, graphs, and tables present the most recent information available on societal trends.

Recent sociological studies and research. Sociology is constantly reviewing and renewing itself, and in *The Essential Sociologist* we have combined classical tradition with the latest research. We have systematically reviewed all major sociological journals and recent publications to provide an accurate and current portrait of sociology.

Inclusive treatment of gender, race, and social class. The crucial sociological concepts of gender, race, and social class are not only addressed in separate chapters but treated centrally throughout the text, demonstrating how intrinsic gender, race, and social class are to social structure and their impact on all aspects of social life.

A global outlook. Chapters include rich comparative material exploring the social diversity of the world. We have included material from different cultures ranging from small, traditional societies to large, developing and industrialized societies. Students will learn how social trends in the United States are affected by developments in other lands and, in turn, how our social patterns and social policies influence other societies around the globe.

A balanced theoretical approach. The major sociological frameworks—functional, conflict, and interpretive analysis—are introduced in chapter 1 and systematically applied throughout the text. Key concepts of other frameworks—humanist, feminist, and exchange—will help students understand diverse social systems and social interaction.

Writing styles. *The Essential Sociologist* is a highly readable text with a fresh, informal writing style that will engage and sustain student interest with its student-friendly tone. Theoretical and factual knowledge is presented simply and examples abound.

The Organization of *The Essential Sociologist*

The text is divided into four parts, each of which develops a major sociological theme.

Part I: Self in Society defines and provides an overview of the study of society and its special subject matter; introduces the methods by which it is studied; describes culture and social structure; and covers the process by which individuals become social through the process of socialization and learn about their sexual identities.

Chapter 1: What Is Sociology and How Do You Do It?

Chapter 2: How Is Society Possible? Culture and Social Structure

Chapter 3: Becoming Social: Conformity and Deviance

Chapter 4: Sexualities: How Many?

Part II: Structures of Inequality focuses on the distribution of resources in our society; the consequences of structured inequality; and opportunities for social mobility. It examines the experiences of various racial, ethnic, and religious minorities and compares the experiences of women and men.

Part III: The Institutional Order focuses on major institutions that provide socially constructed norms and behaviors essential to the survival of individuals and societies. These institutional spheres center on the complex arenas of family life, work and economic activity, politics, education, belief systems, crime and punishment, and health and healthcare systems.

Part IV: Modern Dilemmas focuses on populations and the environment including population trends and changes in the natural environment. It concludes with a look at social change and new technology and how cultures have been affected by contact with other societies.

Supplements

The Essential Sociologist is supported by a learning package of instructional ancillaries. These have been developed by Professor Susan Lachman of Kingsborough Community College, along with Susan Farrell and Peter Stein.

Website: The authors have created a website for students at http://www.roxbury.net/esbindex.html.

Instructor's Manual: The Instructor's Manual offers:

- Discussion questions.
- Key concepts and ideas.
- In-class exercises.
- Out-of-class projects.
- Media resources (relevant films and videos).

Free Student Study Guide: The Student Study Guide is provided *free* to students upon request. It provides chapter outlines, learning objectives, definitions, sample test questions, glossary terms, exercises, and other techniques to help students master sociology.

Test Bank: The Test Bank for this edition has been prepared by Susan Lachman and consists of approximately 1,500 test items, all carefully selected to test the full range of material presented in this text. It contains true-false, multiple choice, and essay questions, with answers to all questions page-referenced to the text. The Test Bank is available in print or on disk. ✦

Acknowledgments

The Hess-Stein-Farrell team had the benefit of a very supportive Roxbury staff—Jim Ballinger, Project Editor, Arlene Lazerson, Copyeditor, Bonnie Gillespie, Graphics Editor, and David Marion and Roger Mensink, Proofreaders. We are especially grateful to Claude Teweles, Publisher, for his interest in this project and his ongoing encouragement.

We also want to acknowledge our debt to the many colleagues who reviewed the manuscript. Their guidance and suggestions proved to be very useful: Debbie Abowitz (*Bucknell University*), Sara L. Crawley (*University of Florida*), Pat Dorman (*Boise State University*), Anne Hastings (*University of North Carolina at Chapel Hill*), Jon E. Iannitti (*SUNY-Morrisville College*), Peter Kivisto (*Augustana College*), Michelle Newton (*Averett College*), Scott Sernau (*Indiana University at South Bend*), Theresa Sullivan (*University of Texas at Austin*), Kathleen Tiemann (*University of North Dakota*), Robert E. Tournier (*The College of Charleston*), and Mark A. Winton (*University of Central Florida*).

We wish to thank a number of sociologists at various colleges and universities especially colleagues at William Paterson University, Kingsborough Community College, and to members of Sociologists for Women in Society for their helpful comments and suggestions. Included in this supportive groups are William Paterson University Professors Bob Alexander, Maboud Ansari, Mary Pat Baumgartner, Mark Ellis, Michael Elsner, Charley Flint, Lou Gaydosh, Ron Glassman, Kathleen Korgen, Howard Lune, Clyde Magarelli, James Mahon, Rosanne Martorella, Patrick McMannomen, Vincent Parrillo, Enrique Pumar, Susanne Tardi, Gabe Wang and Bill Willis, Celine Kraus at Kean University, and Carla Howery of the American Sociological Association. We are grateful to colleagues at Kingsborough Community College, City University of New York, William Burger, Chair of the Behavioral Sciences and Human Services Department, Susan Ednie, Anna Karpathakis, Susan Lachman, Ailene Nusbacher, Julian Schtierman, Franceska Smith, Barbara Walters, Sydelle Basile, Joyce Magenheim, and Barbara Manzo for their advice and support.

Special thanks go to our support staff, Rosanne Anello and Tina Berrian, for their research skills and organizational acumen, and to Diane Anderson for facilitating communication. ✦

About the Authors

Beth B. Hess is Professor Emerita of Sociology at County College of Morris where she has taught introductory courses for a number of years. A graduate of Radcliffe and Rutgers University, she joined the team assembled by Matilda White Riley to produce three volumes of *Aging and Society* (Russell Sage, 1968, 1970, 1972). She has published extensively in the areas of gender, including three editions of *Controversy and Coalition: The New Feminist Movement* (1984, 1994, 2000), written with Myra Marx Ferree, *Analyzing Gender* (1987), edited with Myra Marx Ferree, and *Revising Gender* (1999), with Myra Marx Ferree and Judith Lorber. She has also published extensively in the area of social gerontology, including five editions of *Growing Old in America* (edited with Elizabeth W. Markson) and in introductory sociology with five editions of *Sociology* with Peter Stein and Elizabeth Markson. Beth Hess has devoted considerable time and energy to professional organizations, serving as the Secretary of the American Sociological Association and as President of Eastern Sociological Society, The Association of Humanist Sociology, Sociologists for Women in Society, and the Society for the Study of Social Problems. Honors include awards for teaching, mentorship, and career achievements, most recently the 2000 Lee Founders award from the Society for the Study of Social Problems.

Peter J. Stein is Professor of Sociology at William Paterson University. He received his B.A. at the City College of New York and his Ph.D. in sociology from Princeton University. Stein has taught a number of undergraduate and graduate courses including Introduction to Sociology, Marriage and the Family, Gender in Contemporary Society, Contemporary Issues in the Workplace, and Sociology of Genocide and the Holocaust. His published articles focus on work and family issues, single adults, and diversity in the workplace. His books include: *Single*; *Single Life*; *Unmarried Adults in Social Context*; *The Family: Functions, Conflicts, and Symbols* (with Judith Richman and Natalie Hannon); and *The Marriage Game: Understanding Marital Decision Making* (with Cathy Greenblat and Norman Washburne), and five editions of *Sociology*, with Beth Hess and Elizabeth Markson. He has been active in professional organizations and has served as vice president of the Eastern Sociological Society; chair of the Family Division of the Society for the study of Social Problems; and as Council member of the Sex and Gender section of the American Sociological Association. He served as the chair of ASA's Committee on Teaching. Currently he is involved in diversity training programs for several organizations.

Susan A. Farrell is Associate Professor of Sociology and coordinator of the sociology area in the Behavioral Sciences and Human Services Department at Kingsborough Community College, CUNY. She received her B.A. from Queens College, her M.A. in Religious Studies from St. John's University, and her Ph.D. in sociology from the City University of New York. Susan Farrell teaches Introductory Sociology, Sociology of Gender, Sociology of the

Family, and Human Service Organizations. Farrell served as Managing Editor of *Gender & Society* and was Chair of the SWS publications committee. With Judith Lorber, Susan Farrell edited *The Social Construction of Gender*, which includes her research on women in the Roman Catholic Church. She coedited *The Power of Gender in Religion* with Georgie Ann Weatherby and is the coauthor of *Family Sociology: Integrating Macro and Micro Systems Across the Life Cycle* with Marvin I. Shapiro. Other articles and chapters in books cover feminist methodology in the social sciences, the social construction of feminist ethics, and the development of Women-Church in Roman Catholicism. Farrell currently serves on the executive committee for the Eastern Sociological Society. ✦

Part I
Self in Society

What Is Sociology and How Do You Do It?

In this chapter you will learn:

- The definition of sociology.
- The scope of the field and of this book.
- The history and development of sociology.
- The founders and early sociological theories and practitioners.
- Modern sociological theories.
- How to conduct scientific studies of social life.

> Só-ci-oĺ-o-gy (noun).
> The systematic study of human social behavior.

This definition looks very straightforward, but it will take the rest of the book to tell you about all the topics covered by these seven words. It is best to begin by examining the basic concepts in the definition itself:

"Systematic" because sociologists use the methods of science to examine and interpret this behavior, as is described in the second part of this chapter.

"Human" because, although people's closest ancestors, the great apes, also live in well-defined groups and learn from one another, there are differences that set us apart. Most importantly, humans have complex language skills, a self-conscious mind that has replaced instinct as the trigger to behavior, and the ability to create an endless number of items of beauty and usefulness and to pass them on from generation to generation (see chapter 2).

"Social" because the very course of evolution that produced our species—*Homo sapiens*, the thinking creature who can invent languages, control impulses, write symphonies, and build places of worship—also made us dependent on one another for safety, support, and personal satisfaction. To be human is to be social, to be a member of a variety of **collectivities** (sets of individuals) from friendship groups to a college class, from a family to society as a whole. The distinction between collectivity and group is that in a group, the members know and are aware of one another, whereas a collectivity of individuals share an identity but do not necessarily interact. Thus, your college alumni association is a collectivity, but your English class is a group.

"Behavior" because the whole point of sociology is that our thoughts and actions are primarily determined by these group memberships. 1

Aha! you may say, but what about biological forces? Isn't much of my behavior coded into my genes, a product of general evolution and particular inheritance? Perhaps, but these are not very accurate predictors of either history or individual behavior. Yes, there may be an aggressive component in human nature, but it cannot explain the Vietnam War. And, yes, you may have inherited perfect pitch from a parent, but if your parents could not pay for music lessons, you will not become a concert artist.

Your biological makeup has provided you with a variety of emotions and impulses to act on these emotions, but in order to live in human groups, individuals must be able to control their impulses. Even chimpanzees expect as much of one another. No matter how angry you may feel, you will rarely strike the first person you see, and if you do, you'll be locked up as a menace to public order. Similarly, sexual urges are common, but people do not jump up and put their arms around the person next to them. Quite the opposite; most of you are probably very selective. You have learned when, with whom, and under what circumstances sexual expressions are acceptable and lawful. If you cannot control yourself, you will be locked up as a sex offender.

OK, you might now be asking, "But what about my feelings and attitudes, don't they influence my behavior?" To some extent, but those attitudes and feelings did not spring up spontaneously; they are a product of your past experiences in human groups and your understanding of the immediate situation, an understanding that you have learned from others. It is very difficult to convince American students that they do not act out of some psychological necessity, but there is not much evidence that psychological profiles are predictive of behavior. Indeed, it is usually *after* someone has done something exceptional that psychologists find a background factor that might explain it. For someone to predict your behavior for the next hour or so, knowing your emotional state will not be nearly as helpful as knowing where you will be and with whom.

It is often thought that early life experiences determine adult behavior, but most research indicates that people are influenced by more recent relationships and events. It is both the glory and agony of being human that very little, if anything, is predetermined by our genes or psyche (Katz Rothman 1999). We are the creatures who can invent and reinvent ourselves, and who can create and destroy social order. Thus, although some of what we are, the traits that make each of us unique, have genetic and psychological origins, such tendencies are played out in social groups, where there is no fixed outcome. It is precisely this lack of certainty that makes us anxious and leads us to blame forces beyond our control, as in "I can't help it; my hormones made me do it."

This emphasis on the context rather than the individual and on possibilities rather than certainties is one reason why sociology is not regularly taught in high schools, because these ideas are quite difficult for young people to understand. The other reason why sociology is primarily for college students is that it challenges authority. By showing you how most of what you take for granted as eternal and necessary is really a product of social forces rather than of divine intervention or "human nature," sociologists ask you to rethink all the accepted ideas you grew up with. This is probably the last thing that school authorities want to encourage or that many of you have thought about until now. But questioning the taken-for-granted world is what college is all about, even the realization that social life is a human creation and a human necessity. So, welcome to what we authors hope will be the most eye-opening intellectual experience of your college years.

Scope of the Field and This Book

As you may have gathered, sociologists tend to be very imperial, applying their insights to everything from dating relationships to world wars. Whenever more than one person is involved, there is something social; that is, what one person does is influenced by the other, and the relationship has characteristics of its own, which do not belong to the particular individuals

❖ ❖ ❖ ❖   involved. A family, for example, has a division of labor that is not a character-istic of any one member but is found in the way they all relate to one another. It is these characteristics of social groups that sociologists study—how each member contributes to the larger unit and how that unit influences each per-son's behavior. In the sociological perspective, you are the sum of your group memberships, as you participate in an endless series of social activities.

Sociology is the study of human behavior as shaped by collective forces and the ways in which people give meaning to their experiences.

The remainder of this chapter briefly reviews the emergence of sociology as a field of study and introduces you to some of its leading historical figures. The chapter ends with a quick run-through of techniques for "doing sociol-ogy" that you will need both to appreciate how sociologists work and to undertake some of the relatively simple research projects suggested through-out the textbook. Unfortunately, students often find these introductory top-ics—theory and methods—somewhat slow going, but they form a necessary base for understanding the rest of the book. However, many of you might pre-fer to read chapter 2 at this point and then return to these pages.

Chapter 2 is the heart of the sociological perspective. The concepts of *structure* (forms) and *culture* (way of life) refer to the contexts within which we go about our daily tasks. We do not reinvent the world every morning. Rather, we fit into preexisting patterns of behavior and sets of beliefs, we use objects already available to us, we perceive ourselves as members of particu-lar groups. Across the life course, we may enact or witness changes in these patterns; new objects will be invented and created, and new ideas will enter the society, all of which become the culture and structures confronted by the next generation. It is in this sense that society has a reality of its own even as some members die and others are born.

Newborns, of course, are not immediately aware of culture and social structure. As discussed in chapter 3, although human babies are equipped to master any language and learn any customs, it takes many years of *socializa-tion* to the ways of the group before a child is a competent participant. Because language and custom limit group members' degree of freedom in thought and action, they tend to have many similarities. Nonetheless, social-ization is never so complete that individual differences and nonconforming ("deviant") behaviors do not occur, some of which are tolerated and others not. Also, because we are not born with knowledge of who and what we are, a person's sense of self is developed in the course of socialization and is modi-fied across the life course.

Similarly, as difficult as this may be to understand now, sexual identity, or the *sexual self,* is also a social product, as discussed in chapter 4. The chapter also deals with changing patterns of sexual behavior in the United States, from teenagers to mature adults. Of special interest should be the section on the social construction of heterosexuality and homosexuality. The title of part 1, after all, is "Self in Society."

Part 2 deals with another fundamental characteristic of social groups, the tendency toward *stratification*, or inequality in the distribution of societal resources. Chapter 5 describes the basic processes through which inequality is generated and maintained, processes whereby certain kinds of people are judged superior or inferior to others and therefore entitled to more or less of the collective goodies. Chapters 6 and 7 focus on race, ethnicity, and gender as major dimensions of stratification in the United States.

The first five chapters in part 3 examine major areas of structured activity—family, economics, politics, education, and religion. Each area can be studied as a pattern of rules and behaviors quite apart from actual people. For example, "the family system" of the United States, as an abstraction, is based on heterosexual marriage to one person at a time, in which the couple lives apart from other relatives and focuses on raising children and maintaining the emotional well-being of its members. Looking at the family system from this perspective is called macro-level analysis. Literally, "macro" means big, in the sense of the broad outline.

At the same time, each area can be studied at the level of everyday life—or micro-level—for example, the Jones family, composed of real-life people interacting with one another, who may or may not live up to the ideals of "the" American family. Literally "micro" means small, as in microscope, looking intensely at a limited set of objects. These five chapters move from micro to macro, from the personal to the societal, because we all encounter society originally through daily experience. For example, the American educational system is something first met in preschool, and the economic system becomes real when a person gets that first job.

The other two chapters in part 3 deal with topics of immediate public interest: crime and punishment and health and health care.

Part 4 covers two areas of broader current and future concern: human ecology, including environmental issues, and the future of American cities and suburbs. The book ends with a chapter on "Technology and Social Change." Throughout this course you will be exposed to ideas and information that cry out for someone to do something! But just who can do what effectively is another question, and so various chapters include a list of organizations and websites that can give you a deeper understanding of the issues. Most major changes in a society, however, require a degree of organized effort, and inevitably there will be powerful forces that organize to resist change. You will meet them both in chapter 16.

This outline covers the bare essentials of sociology. But as the old saying goes, "the devil is in the details," and the details comprise the rest of this book.

What Do Sociologists Know and When Did They Learn It?

One of those "taken-for-granted" assumptions with which you began this course is probably the belief that important ideas exist in some pure form out there just waiting to be discovered. Ideas, however, are discovered only at particular historical moments, when the time is ripe, and usually only by people with the required education and social support. The study of how ideas are grounded in time and the social context of thinkers is called the **sociology of knowledge**. In essence, what we know as members of a society and when we know it depend on what those in power tell us is "the truth."

The Historical Roots of Sociology

In this spirit, we authors must here apply the sociology of knowledge approach to sociology itself. While questions about human behavior have been asked since the beginning of recorded time, we can date the systematic examination of social life to a particular moment in Western history, namely, the period called the *Age of Reason* or the *Enlightenment*, beginning in the 1720s. As the word "enlightenment" suggests, it was as if a window were opened, letting in the sunlight of reason to banish the Dark Ages of medievalism in Europe. Scientific knowledge began to replace superstition and blind faith; absolute monarchs came under the rule of law; and religious leaders were challenged by people seeking well-being in this world rather than waiting for rewards in the next one. As traditional sources of authority lost their legitimacy and were replaced by the power of rational thought, nothing was exempted from the light of scientific investigation.

Early thinkers. By the 1850s, the term "sociology" had been coined by the French philosopher **Auguste Comte** (1798–1857) to describe the systematic study of group life. For Comte, the social unit, from two people to an entire society, had a reality in its own right that could be discovered by objective observations. But even before Comte gave it a name, two remarkable women had already engaged in the scientific study of social life: **Sophie Germain** (1776–1831) in France and **Harriet Martineau** (1802–1876) in England. Germain developed a philosophy of **positivism**, the idea that observers could be impartial and free of personal bias in their observations of social phenomena. Martineau actually carried out research on work and family life 150 years before the current concern with this issue. So also was her recognition of race, gender, and class inequalities way ahead of its time.

Karl Marx (1818–1883). The emergent field also owes much to the pioneering work of **Karl Marx**, an economist and political theorist whose insights into the workings of society have shaped the sociological perspective to this day. A true child of the Enlightenment, Marx firmly believed that real-life (*material*) conditions were more important than abstract ideas or spiritual values in determining human history. The important questions for Marx were: (1) How are goods and services produced? (2) Who owns the tools, weapons, and knowledge needed for production? and (3) How are the products distributed within the society? In this view, economic factors are basic, and all else flows from how resources are divided among competing groups. Those who end up with most property and power, by whatever means, also produce beliefs that justify their dominance, as seen in the many theories of white superiority that legitimated colonialism, slavery, and racial separation even now. In other words, ideas are social constructions designed to serve the interests of the people who produce and impose them.

Marx's most immediate problem, however, was to make sense of the conditions of most workers in the early years of the Industrial Revolution. People who had lost their farms to hereditary landowners flocked to the cities, where they were paid pennies for 12-hour workdays, seven days a week, in unsanitary and unsafe factories. A vast gap emerged between the poverty of those who actually produced goods and the great wealth of those who profited from their labor. Marx predicted that the entire system would collapse once the workers could organize in their own interests. The greater the inequality within a society, the more unstable its social order, he reasoned; therefore, the more resources given to the masses, the greater the public good.

Above all, Marx is responsible for one of the more important insights of sociology: that the various parts of a society—its economy, political system, family patterns, educational programs, and religious beliefs—all tend to be mutually reinforcing and together form the unique culture and social structure of that society at a particular historical moment. In addition, for many contemporary sociologists, Marx's emphasis on the destructive societal effects of extreme inequality remains an abiding concern.

Yet as soon as sociology became a recognized academic discipline, with its claim to scientific rigor, gifted outsiders such as Germain, Martineau, and Marx were replaced by men with the proper credentials and university appointments. In general, the prestige of any field was diminished when women entered it, so it became important to the founders of sociology to limit graduate studies admission to men of good reputation.

The 'Big Three' of Classical Sociology

Emile Durkheim (1858–1917). The idea of society as a reality in its own right was central to the work of the French sociologist Emile Durkheim, who also spoke of a "collective consciousness" representing the shared beliefs of members of a social unit. That is, despite the variety of people within the society and the fact that some die off and others are born, there is an order that exists above and beyond its specific components at any given time. Moreover, this order can be examined scientifically, through the collection of observations. Such observations produce social statistics, or **social facts**, numbers that characterize a collectivity. Although composed of thousands of individual behaviors, a birthrate is a single number, a social fact at the level of the society as a whole. Above all, Durkheim insisted that *social facts must be explained by other social facts* and not reduced to either individual psychology or biology.

Durkheim's emphasis on statistics reflects his personal concern to make sociology respectable to the ruling intellectual elites of his day. Then, as now, the aura of "science," of pure facts represented numerically, implies far greater certainty than do nonstatistical descriptions. It was important, therefore, in order to achieve prestige in the university, to distinguish the scientific study of society and human behavior from the fields of philosophy and social work. In addition to establishing sociology as a social science, Durkheim also

❖ ❖ ❖ ❖   made important contributions to a number of subfields—crime, religion, family, education, and suicide—that are dealt with in the chapters to follow.

Max Weber (1864–1920). The German sociologist Max Weber focused on a different set of concerns. Like Marx, Weber looked at the broad sweep of history and the interplay between material conditions and ideas, but, unlike Marx, Weber saw ideas as being more than a set of justifications for economic inequality. Rather, the major world religions had a special effect on economics and politics, producing different types of societies. For example, for reasons covered in later chapters, Protestant countries were able to industrialize much earlier than the Catholic nations of Europe, even though the societies were similar in other respects.

For Weber, the master trend of industrial capitalism is toward increasing *rationalization*, that is, the dominance of rational calculations, of technology, of breaking tasks into smaller and smaller components. In this process, modern individuals lost a sense of the wonder and mystery of life, the anchorage of traditional values, and the warmth of community. The consequence, said Weber, is a feeling of *disenchantment*, a disconnect between self and others, where everything is judged by its contribution to each individual's own satisfactions. Sound familiar?

With Durkheim and Germain, Weber saw the necessity for sociologists to attempt to be as objective, or *value-free*, as possible, knowing that such an ideal was probably impossible. Not only will personal values intrude, but the very nature of social studies is different from that of the physical sciences because people, unlike a chemical or even a lab rat under study, are extremely varied, complex, and changeable. In addition, no amount of observation or questioning can really get one person into the mind of another; for this, one needs to make an imaginative leap and try to see the world through the eyes of someone else—a form of empathy that Weber called *Verstehen* (a German word for "understanding").

Georg Simmel (1858–1916). Perhaps because he was not part of the inner circle of German academic sociologists but was highly influenced by people in the humanities and artistic world, Simmel took a different view of how to study social life. In contrast to those who focused on society as an abstraction, governed by impersonal forces, Simmel claimed that sociology must start with the personal. What regularities in everyday interactions can be identified as the basic patterns that underlie a variety of relationships? What, he asks, are the most essential components of competition, of being an outsider, of keeping a secret (just think Monica Lewinsky), and so forth? For example, how does the very size of a group affect the behavior of its members? Think of how different it is when there are only three of you rather than six. For Simmel, the study of social forms should begin from the bottom up rather than from the top down. 2

Research Issues

As Comte went to great pains to point out, the crucial feature that distinguishes sociology from earlier philosophical traditions is the application of the **scientific method**. Unlike philosophers, sociologists do not discover universal laws by staring at their own navels; nor, like social workers, do they administer direct service to the needy. Rather, a sociologist is a systematic observer who looks for patterned regularities in social behavior.

Ideally, the choice of research subject, the gathering of information, and the reporting of findings should be done objectively, without bias and free of personal values. But research is not an unguided missile. Sociologists are drawn to particular topics by their own interests or by those of the people paying for the study. Indeed, as research techniques become increasingly sophisticated and statistically complex, large-scale projects require outside funding, usually from government departments or private corporations, each with its own agenda.

Also important is the researcher's theoretical framework, or **paradigm**, the conceptual model of how the world works that each person has in his or her head. Because each of us views the world as following certain rules—for example, that people get what they deserve, or that skin color is associated with particular abilities—we can make sense of our observations and experiences. Similarly, sociologists work with a set of paradigms that lead them to ask certain questions and help them to interpret their findings. Because sociology is a multiparadigm discipline, the same phenomenon can be looked at from different directions, with greater attention to some details than to others.

A few of the dominant theoretical models in sociology are briefly described in the following section, where, applying the *sociology of knowledge* model, the authors attempt to locate each perspective in its particular historical frame.

How Do Sociologists Know What It Means? Contemporary Social Theory

If you have seen an episode of the TV series *Father Knows Best*, you have a taste of the self-satisfaction and optimism that characterized the United States during the two decades following the end of World War II in 1945. It seemed that God was in His heaven, Dad was moving up the corporate ladder, Mom was cleaning, cooking, and caring for their 3.5 children, and all was right with the world—at least for white, middle-class America. It should not be a surprise, then, that the most influential theoretical model of that period, functional theory, emphasized balance and harmony among the parts of any social system.

Functional Analysis

According to functional theory, collectivities, including entire societies, are structured in such a way that, over time, the various parts come to reinforce one another. For example, the individualism of Protestantism, the dominant American religion, "fits" the success orientation of a capitalist economic system, as well as the one-person, one-vote model of democracy and an educational system that pits one child against the others for best grades. When analyzing more micro-level phenomena, such as the family, workplace, or classroom, functional theory focused on the division of labor that kept the system going with minimal friction.

A prime example of **functional analysis** is the influential work of **Talcott Parsons** (1902–1979) on the American family, published in the mid-1950s. Parsons extolled the stability of the family unit composed of husband, wife, and minor children, based on the husband/father being the link to the outside world of work and civic duty, and the wife/mother maintaining the home and children. In this view, the arrangement worked because the adults *complemented* one another rather than competing inside or outside the home, to the satisfaction of all concerned. We know now that the wife and mother was quite likely to feel imprisoned in her home and that the children so lovingly cared for became the rebels of the 1960s. Parsons had mistaken a limited moment in middle-class white American experience for a timeless ideal.

The functional perspective focuses on the relationship between society and its various institutions, such as the economy, education, and religion. Religious ceremonies based on beliefs and rituals bind people to one another and reinforce their sense of community.

Other functionalists, such as **Robert K. Merton** (b. 1910) were more sensitive to the potential for social patterns to produce problems as well as solutions. No social act has only one outcome; there are always unintended and often undesirable consequences. What is functional for some people or groups may be *dysfunctional* for others. For example, military officers benefit from wars, which provide opportunities for promotion; foot soldiers run the risk of injury and death. One must always ask "functional for what and whom, and under what circumstances?" The Parsonian family was wonderfully functional for men and the corporations that hired them but less so for other family members. You can make a similar analysis of your college or workplace or peer group. There are many social phenomena that can be illuminated by asking what functions are served by that arrangement. What goals are met for individuals and groups? And how does that arrangement fit into a larger picture? For example, what are the functions and dysfunctions of spending a university's funds on a bigger and better stadium for its football team?

Conflict Analysis

After two decades of prosperity and self-congratulation, from 1945 to 1965, it became clear that there were many Americans who felt left out—African Americans, women, gay men, and lesbians—and others who felt smothered by smugness and conformity—college students and young adults seeking greater self-expression. Rather than assuming a natural tendency toward harmony in social systems, with a few unfortunate glitches that needed repair, a new generation of sociologists began with the opposite assumption: That it is the nature of social systems to be in a state of tension, with unrest as the basic condition, punctuated by rare moments of harmony.

The **conflict analysis** approach assumes that because the scarce resources of any society or group cannot be distributed in a way to please all members, some level of conflict is normal. In the 1960s and 1970s, one had only to look out of a classroom window to see the evidence: students demanding freedom of speech, civil rights marchers, antiwar protesters, feminists, and gay male and lesbian activists. Today, despite the relative quiet in the streets, the dominance of conservative politics, the rise of antifeminism, and the abandonment of desegregation efforts on campus and in the wider society in the 1990s, the conflict approach continues to characterize large areas of sociology. The key question for a conflict theorist is "who benefits?" from the dominant ideas and social patterns, and it can be asked under any circumstances.

Both the functional paradigm and the conflict paradigm illuminate certain areas of sociological interest, and the authors will employ whichever is most appropriate throughout this book. In general, functional and conflict models work best at the macro-level, that is, in explaining fairly general and abstract relationships. But you will remember that sociologists are also interested in the face-to-face interactions of everyday life, the micro-level. For the analysis of these phenomena, researchers often apply models that are called **interpretive** because they deal with how people talk to and make sense of one another, and how, through their joint activity, they impose meaning on their shared world. Another term used for these paradigms is the **social construction** of reality.

Interpretive and Social Construction Models

There are a number of these models, each with a fancy name, but the underlying point is the same. Because to be human is to be without preexisting knowledge of self and the world, we must continually work at making sense of it all. We do this through interpreting the words and gestures of those with whom we interact, and they are using us for the same purpose. Reality is a joint project.

Symbolic interaction refers to the two essential aspects of being human: (1) We communicate through language and gestures, the meaning of which depends on the groups' agreement. As set out in chapter 2, language is a set of symbols because the sounds and written lines have no built-in meaning but stand for something else, and just what that something else is varies from one society to another. (2) To be human is to be in constant interaction; even

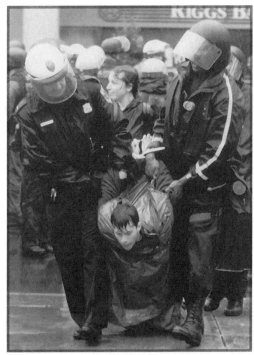

The conflict perspective assumed that because the scarce resources of any society are not distributed equally, some level of conflict is normal. A number of demonstrators in Washington, DC, protested what they perceived as the exploitation of poor nations by the International Monetary Fund and World Bank meeting in Washington, DC.

when other people are not there physically, they are in your head. It is through these conversations that the world "out there" is filtered and reaffirmed or changed (Blumer 1969). For example, one can speak of the American family in the abstract because individual women and men decided to marry, raise children, and behave according to the rules. But if you compare the idea of "family" a hundred years ago and today, you can see that vast changes have taken place, as real-life men and women change the rules. The social construction of reality is a major theme of this textbook.

Dramaturgy. As the word clearly proclaims, this model treats social interaction as a series of mini-dramas (Goffman 1959). The world is indeed a stage, and we play parts in an ongoing soap opera in which our self-image is always at risk. At the same time we are someone else's audience, so that much of what goes on in everyday life involves trying to manipulate one another's reactions. Just think of the last time you went to a party and met new people; how did you manage the impression you wanted to give off? And how did you treat their attempts to impress you? How much did you really risk? What if they had not taken you for the person you presented? It is a bit scary when your presenting self gets the cold shoulder.

In keeping with the analogy of a theater performance, remember how embarrassing it was when you walked onto the wrong stage or flubbed your lines or wore an inappropriate costume? Being hissed off the stage is a frightening experience, and so we try to appear before audiences that will appreciate our performance. In turn we offer to accept their presentations. Relationships end when this mutual agreement is broken.

Ethnomethodology. Although quite a mouthful, this is essentially a technique for looking under the "taken-for-granted" surface of daily life by doing something that turns the taken-for-granted world upside down in order to reveal an unspoken reality (Garfinkel 1967). For example, you have probably been brought up to believe that it is a sign of respect for a man to open a door for a woman. But think of the other people for whom any of us would hold open a door—children, the aged, and the disabled—all relatively powerless. Could control over the door be an expression of superiority? Several years ago, an ethnomethodologist conducted a study at a downtown office building in which young women rushed to hold open the door for male executives, several of whom struggled to regain control of the door, while others left to find another entrance (Richardson 1974). You might want to keep your eye on who opens the

We constantly interpret the gestures of those with whom we interact and they use us for the same purpose. When U.S. President Bill Clinton met with Israeli Prime Minister Ehud Barak (on the right) and Palestinian President Yassar Arafat (in the middle) to pursue peace in the Middle East, both Arafat and Barak insisted that the other proceed through the door first. Why would that matter?

door for whom at work or school. Another ethnomethodological exercise would involve men asking their dates to pay half the evening's expense, and women insisting on doing so. You may just uncover the hidden meaning of being a guest.

Sociology of emotions. Feelings are also socially constructed; they are aroused by certain environmental cues and expressed in socially learned ways. Here again, reverse your thinking and see emotions as shaped by cultural and situational forces rather than internal psychological states. Each society has a set of **feeling rules** for how, when, where, and with whom emotions can be shown (Hochschild 1983). Love, hate, jealousy, shame, guilt, sympathy, fear—all are aspects of social relationships. As such, they can be managed and manipulated. For example, many occupations, typically those dominated by women, require a lot of smiling—cocktail hostess, flight attendant, hair dresser, salesperson, receptionist—designed to make clients feel good.

Love is perhaps the most manipulated of all emotions. Think of all the false claims to love and be loved that you have heard. Remember, also, that surge of pride in being loved and the pain of rejection. But other emotions are also easily manipulated. Just call an American teenage boy "wuss" and watch the immediate arousal of fear and anger. Shame is another readily manipulated feeling, especially in societies where family reputation is very important. In Japan, for example, shame is the most powerful tool of crime control and is thought to account for the very low rates of homicide and imprisonment. At the same time, suicide rates are high—better death than to disgrace one's family!

What Is New in Social Theory?

Reflecting the historical era, the newest developments in social theory center on current controversies in the society at large.

Humanist sociology. Humanist sociology carries on the social reform tradition of the 1960s and 1970s, based on the belief that a value-free sociology is impossible and that academic sociological research only reinforces existing inequalities and injustice. In this view, sociologists have an obligation to become actively engaged in finding solutions to social problems (Tiemann 1999). Just presenting data and pointing fingers is not enough.

Feminist sociology. Feminist sociology also questions the traditional claim to objectivity, noting that positivism is primarily a male mode of thinking in which the researcher stands apart from the object of study. Far from being value-free, sociological theory and research before the 1970s reflected the very narrow view of reality of Western, white, middle-class men. Women and nonwhites were assumed to share these perceptions and then were judged morally or mentally deficient if they did not think and act accordingly.

The influx of women into higher education and graduate schools from 1965 on, however, has brought a major rethinking of knowledge that has transformed one academic field after another. In sociology, feminist theory and research have not only brought women back into the picture but have also changed the way in which both sex and gender are understood (Lorber 1994). Indeed, the very concept "gender" gave a name to assumptions that had been taken for granted but that were now open to systematic analysis.

✦ ✦ ✦ ✦   The importance of gender as an element of social structure rather than as a characteristic of individuals is discussed in chapter 6.

Rational choice theory. Not all the new thinking challenges tradition in ways that broaden the sweep of the sociological imagination. The rational choice, or exchange model, is primarily a narrow economic view of behavior in which people and organizations tend to do that which brings the most benefit at the least cost (Coleman 1992). This type of theory has always had great appeal to Americans because of the focus on rational individuals, but, by the same token, it strikes others as very nonsociological because little attention is paid to context. In real life, decisions are rarely made in a vacuum; participants enjoy varying levels of power and no person or organization behaves in a fully rational way all the time.

At the micro-level, however, the exchange perspective can be very illuminating. If you think about the last person you stopped dating, it was probably because you figured that what you were getting back from the relationship was not worth the time and effort you were putting into it. Think also of the situations you have avoided because the risk of loss was more than you thought you could afford. Your mind often works as if it were a cost/benefit calculator.

Data can be gathered through quantitative or qualitative methods, depending on the research question. For example, if the research question has to do with trends in the divorce rates, the researcher would go directly to the numbers collected and published by the government.

Evolutionary psychology. Although exchange models reduce complex behaviors to rational calculation, other theories are even less sociological in that they seek the roots of social behavior in evolutionary forces. The basic idea behind evolutionary models is that through the million years of human and prehuman evolution, the forces of natural selection favored certain traits, and these were then passed down genetically from one generation of survivors to another. Although this can be shown for some physical characteristics, the leap to social behavior is based largely on guesswork (Greene 1999). At best, evolutionary psychology can explain only the most general patterns, such as the observation that women invest more time in child rearing than do men or that men tend to marry women younger than themselves—both of which are excellent survival tactics but not necessarily hardwired into the species. What is of paramount interest to a sociologist is the range of variations in these patterns, the great *differences* historically and from one society to another and from one group to another within a society. It is this vast variety that testifies to the remarkable flexibility of human behavior and the influence of society and culture. What possible differences in biological make-up, for example, could account for the fact that almost all running backs in professional football in the United States are black, while all but a few quarterbacks are white?

It would be a mistake to dismiss biology altogether; the human body does set limits, and its impulses are ever present. Currently, there are several attempts to develop theories that integrate biological and sociological factors, called *biosocial* or *biocultural* models. For example, studies have shown that while levels of the male hormone testosterone tend to rise before a competition, they rise even faster after the game among the winners and decline among the losers (Mazur et al. 1992). In other words, hormone levels are responsive to the social context.

Postmodern social thought. As the twenty-first century begins, it appears that the grand goal of the Enlightenment—the ultimate triumph of reason—remains a distant dream. We may glory in technological wonders, but it would be difficult to argue that there has been a vast improvement in the human spirit. Inequality and injustice remain unchecked; world peace continues to elude us; one-third of the world's children are close to starvation. Some bemoan the end of Western domination of the globe. Still, few would question the basic foundation of modern thought, namely, that there is an underlying reality that can be discovered by the scientific method.

Now, however, even that shred of Enlightenment philosophy has been challenged. Suppose that there is no "there" there, no enduring truth waiting to be uncovered, that what is "real" is only what those in power want us to believe? These questions lead to a perspective called **postmodernism**, in which all claims to "the truth" are suspect because they are based on the meanings given to words in that society at that historical moment (Wood and Foster 1997). Meaning is encoded in language; it is the words that define what is real. Thus, one era's truth is another era's superstition, and one society's Gods are another society's mythology. And the idea that there is an eternal and universal truth may be the most powerful myth of all.

The technique favored by postmodernists is called *deconstruction*—literally, to pull the words apart. For example, once such seemingly self-evident concepts as "normal sexuality" are deconstructed, with every assumption carefully examined, one can see how political these definitions are. What is "normal" usually turns out to be what is done by those with the power to define normalcy. This is where whiteness, maleness, and being middle class come into play and why the postmodern perspective appeals to feminists and to gay male and lesbian scholars. Indeed, **queer theory** is the most recent variation on postmodernism, with its emphasis on the deconstruction of "masculine/feminine" and "female/male" (Seidman 1997). As you will see in chapters 4 and 7, putting people in one box or the other hides the overlap and fluidity of these categories.

No one paradigm can explain everything, and each of these theories illuminates some aspects of social life. Table 1.1 summarizes the theories. Throughout this volume, the authors apply the model that offers the most complete understanding of the topic under consideration. Each perspective provokes particular questions, and in the course of providing answers, suggests particular types of research. 🖥 3

Table 1.1 Models of Contemporary Social Theories		
Theory	**Focus**	**Level of Analysis**
Functionalism	Parts of society reinforce each other for a complementary fit with minimal friction	Macro-Level
Conflict	Society is in a state of tension and unrest due to unequal access to scarce resources	Macro-Level
Interpretive/ Constructionist	Communication and interaction create social reality	Micro-Level
a. Dramaturgy	Interaction as a series of mini-dramas	
b. Ethnomethodology	Examines the taken-for-granted aspects of social life	
c. Sociology of Emotions	Emotions and feelings are shaped by cultural and social forces	
Humanist Sociology	Analysis of society in order to change it for the better	Macro-Level
Feminist Sociology	Bringing women into research and analysis and understands gender as an element of social structure	Macro- and Micro-Levels
Rational Choice	Analyzes social interaction as a cost-benefit analysis	Micro-Level
Evolutionary Psychology	Behavior is rooted in evolutionary and biological forces	Macro-Level
Postmodern	Meaning and "truth" are relative and change over time	Micro-Level

Why and How Do Sociologists Do Sociology?

Throughout this book, you will be asked to check out the taken-for-granted world, to go outside the classroom and find out for yourself. The Workbook that accompanies this textbook suggests other kinds of research that can be done on the web or in the library. This section briefly reviews a number of techniques for gathering *data* (the plural of *datum*, a single piece of information) in order to test one's perceptions of reality.

As it turns out, you may find that much of what you have assumed to be real is not borne out by the evidence. A few recent examples of mistaken assumptions include the belief that welfare encourages women to have more children; that old people are dumped into nursing homes by uncaring kin; that the death penalty deters homicides; and that divorce rates continue to climb. Yet because Americans believe these statements, politicians get elected, laws are passed, and people's lives are affected. This point illustrates the basic sociological concept of the **definition of the situation**, that what people believe to be real is real in its consequences (Thomas and Thomas 1928). In fact, two of the most notorious events of the 1960s never took place. No feminist ever burned her bra in Atlantic City, and there is no evidence to support the story of protesters spitting on returning Vietnam veterans (Lembcke 1998). Yet think of the mileage antifeminists and war supporters got from these myths. Sometimes, even when disproving data are widely circulated, the false belief persists because it resonates to some deep need people have to believe that the world is a just place in which sinners are punished and virtue rewarded.

Definitions of the situation also allow people to identify and label new and strange behaviors, such as "road rage" or "going postal," when a relatively few cases become defined as a trend that requires intervention by government or mental health experts (Glassner 1999). Alas, the world is more imperfect and the meaning of events more ambiguous than we would like to think, which makes it even more important that public policy be informed by accurate data.

Data can be gathered through either **quantitative** or **qualitative research** methods, depending on the research question. For example, if the research question has to do with trends in divorce rates, you would go directly to the numbers collected and published by the government (quantitative). But if you wanted to know how people on the edge of divorce deal with one another, you need to record their words and gestures (qualitative).

The choice between number-crunching and descriptive studies is also colored by gender and prestige issues. In general, quantitative methods are thought to be more like real science and therefore worthy of academic respect, which is the basis for the term "social scientists." In contrast, qualitative studies are often dismissed as being closer to art than science. Because numbers represent "hard" data and descriptions are considered "soft," quantitative sociology has an aura of intellectual toughness, or masculinity, in contrast to verbal descriptions, at which women are thought to excel. It does happen that qualitative work is favored by many women sociologists, both because of the topics they choose to study but also as a matter of principle, to erase the dehumanizing distance between observed and observer. To date, however, academic rewards have gone primarily to sociologists engaged in the most abstract quantitative studies, using the most advanced statistical skills. Yet, how is a videotaped encounter any less "exact" than a divorce rate? Indeed, only the qualitative approach can uncover the *how* and *what* of "lived existence" (Gubrium and Holstein 1997). The rules of the scientific method can be followed by both types of researcher.

The **scientific method** is a set of procedures, developed in the natural sciences, for gathering information and testing theory. These procedures are specifically designed to minimize personal bias, so that other researchers using the same techniques should come to similar conclusions. The scientific method includes these key elements:

- Objectivity—eliminating personal feelings and expectations.
- Precise design, measurement, and analysis.
- Disclosure of findings and methods.

When used to explore the physical world, the method has been remarkably productive, although never perfect. When applied to the study of social life, however, trying to measure the opinions and behaviors of living, acting, and reacting persons is extremely difficult. People change from one measurement to another, and they do not always tell the truth. It is also nearly impossible to keep personal values out of social science, in scholars' choice of subfield, of research topics, and how they interpret the findings.

Another major problem in social research is that what researchers observe and count is usually only an indirect measure of what they are really looking for. Confusing? Yes, indeed, and not just for students. What a researcher really wants to examine is often an abstraction that cannot be measured directly—for example, "economic efficiency," "crime wave," "satisfaction in marriage," or "modernization." The researcher has to pick something that is visible to stand for the abstract concept. That concrete something is an **empirical referent**, an observable item that represents the abstraction. For example, how many of what types of crime constitute a "crime wave" in contrast to ordinary variations in rates?

It is always possible that critics will object to a researcher's choice of referents, claiming that they do not really measure what is claimed (the problem of *validity*) or do not do it very accurately (the problem of *reliability*). This is one reason why full disclosure is so important to the scientific enterprise. Only by letting others know exactly what you did can they repeat the research and establish its accuracy or point to questions for further study. Science proceeds by small steps, and the data from repeated trials become cumulative, leading to the next step, and so forth.

What to Study

As already noted, sociologists are less interested in individuals than in the **social facts** that describe the collectivity. Individuals jump off bridges, but the suicide rate is a characteristic of the society, not the jumper. Social facts rarely remain constant but vary from one place and time and one subgroup to another; that is, they are *variables,* factors that differ from one collectivity or group to another and that change over time. Other variables characterize individuals, such as race, gender, ethnicity, and sexual preference, or occupation, education, and income—all traits that are assumed to have particular social outcomes.

What fascinates sociologists is *the relationship between or among variables*, how one influences another. For example, think of two variables that you assume are related in some predictable way, say, educational levels (variable A) and birthrates (variable B). Ideally, researchers begin with a theoretical model that suggests how the two are related; in this example, you probably see education as the prior and more powerful variable, and birthrates as being affected by a person's educational level. In technical terms, education is the **independent variable**—the one that has an effect on the other—and birth rates are the **dependent variables**, the value of which varies systematically with changes in the independent variable.

This relationship, an expected **correlation** between the two variables, is expressed in a testable **hypothesis**, your guess about what you would find when you gathered the appropriate data: "As the educational level of a collectivity or subgroup rises, its birth rates will decline." Data reporting education and birth rates are readily available from various government departments, and you would, indeed, find a correlation between education and birth rates.

The relationship is so strong that a recent world conference on population concluded that the surest way to reduce population growth was not to flood the country with condoms but rather to see that girls and women were allowed to be educated.

Notice, however, that an alternative theoretical model would predict a cause-and-effect relationship between these two variables that goes the other way: "The smaller the family, the more likely its children are to enter college"—a hypothesis that is also supported by the data. The important point is that the numbers do not speak for themselves but take on meaning from the theory that led to the hypothesis that the data are used to test.

Participant observation is a sociological method for research on groups not easily accessible to observation, such as motorcycle gangs. How could you study such groups?

How to Go About Doing It

Depending on characteristics of the research question, you must make a number of choices: One factor is the *time frame:*

1. If your hypothesis focuses on a correlation at one time only, a **cross-sectional design** is appropriate, similar to a snapshot, or a slice of life in which different levels of your variables can be compared.

2. But if your hypothesis is about changes over time, then you need to use a panel or **longitudinal framework**, in which the same people or variables are followed over several years.

Another factor is whether your answer requires *new data or old:* Some research can be done by reworking existing data, such as government publications, historical records, and diaries and letters. This **secondary analysis** involves material prepared for other uses. One common form of secondary research is called *content analysis*, in which the contents of publications are counted and categorized. Another is *comparative analysis*, in which different societies are compared to see which patterns are universal and which unique. But because secondary analysis uses information originally gathered for another purpose, many researchers prefer to gather original data, even though it is usually more expensive and time consuming.

Primary material refers to new information gathered specifically for a particular research project. Methods for producing primary material range from the most distant, such as a mail-in questionnaire, to the most intimate, as when the researcher takes part in the interactions under study.

Survey research. How can you get a lot of information from a large number of people in a short time? Not very easily. Mail-in questionnaires are usually thrown away, so the results can be generalized only to people who did not use their wastebaskets and who bothered to fill it out. Knocking on doors would increase the response rate but bust the budget. Thus, most large-scale attempts to derive new data depend on telephone surveys. In order to be able to say that the survey findings accurately represent all citizens, or women, or taxpayers, or whomever, either you must contact every member of that category or else select a smaller number, a *sample*, in such a way that the laws of statistics allow you to make a claim to representing them all. Just standing on a street corner and handing out questionnaires would not do.

Random sampling is the technique for selecting a manageable number of cases that, within statistical limits, can be said to stand for the entire category. The key is that everyone in the category should have the same likelihood of being selected. Putting names in a hat and drawing out one or two meets the criterion—each name had the same probability of being picked. State lotteries operate the same way when numbered balls are rotated in a machine that pops them up by chance.

For large-scale social science surveys, including political polling, you need only a few thousand computer-generated ten-digit phone numbers to select a sample that could accurately represent all 105 million U.S. households. The laws of probability will tell you how many times in a hundred the same size sample would produce the same distribution of households by region, age of householder, income level, and so forth. This statistical variation is what reporters refer to when they give a margin of error of plus or minus a certain number of percentage points. Chapter 15 reviews the debate on sampling to correct for undercounts in the U.S. Census.

Care must be taken in *constructing the questionnaire*. While the sample can be scientifically above reproach, the same cannot always be said of the schedule of questions, or the survey *instrument*. The sequence and wording of questions has an effect on the answers. There are loaded questions such as "Do you approve of reckless spending by Congress?" There are "red flag" issues such as "Do you think that government welfare policy should encourage poor women to have more children?" In one survey, respondents answering one question said "too much was spent on welfare," but at a later point in the interview thought the government should "increase assistance to poor people." In addition, characteristics of the researcher also influence responses, as when opinions on race relations vary by whether respondents thought they were talking to a white or African-American phone interviewer.

Even allowing for sampling error and problems in constructing value-free questionnaires, the large-scale survey is a relatively cost-effective way to gather information on public opinion and even some behaviors, at least those that respondents are willing to talk about on the phone with a stranger. For more intimate matters, however, interviews may have to be face-to-face, an expensive procedure that often limits the number of respondents. The face-to-face data, however, are richer and probably far more accurate than those from telephone interviews. Thus, survey research provides information only on what respondents say that they believe or do; no survey, however accurate, can tell us much about how people actually interact with one another.

Observational techniques. To study real-life behaviors, you have to get out in the field and take notes, and do it systematically. If, for example, you are researching consumer behavior, you would have to station yourself in the same place in the same store for many days to make sure that your original observations were not unique. You might want to vary the time of day since different kinds of people shop at different times; then you could do the same in other types of stores. All the time you are observing, you must make sure that the people you are observing do not notice you, which might cause them to react to your presence rather than going about their ordinary business. Pure observation is enormously time consuming and requires intense attention to details, which limits its usefulness as a research technique.

Participant observation is a favorite method for research on groups not easily accessible to pure observation, such as a motorcycle gang, bar patrons, or farm laborers. As the name indicates, the researcher becomes part of the group under study. This technique is very tricky ethically and practically. The practical problem is that researchers typically come from social backgrounds very different from those of the people under study, so giving an acceptable reason for being there often involves some deception. The ethical problem is that the researcher uses other people's willingness to accept the deception in order to advance her or his own career. One solution to both problems is to be open about the whole enterprise from the start, but this might influence the very interactions under observation. Another solution is to "debrief" the subjects as soon as possible after the project is completed. Some participant observers have even invited their new friends to help write up the research report.

Experimental designs. Used primarily by psychologists and social psychologists (researchers who study small-group interaction), experiments are typically carried out under carefully controlled conditions. That is their main advantage and disadvantage. The advantage is that all variables remain unchanged except for the ones under study, which means that the findings are the result of whatever variable is being manipulated and not of some outside factor. The disadvantage is that the laboratory is an artificial environment; the real world is a much messier place, where control over variables is impossible and behavior itself is modified in the course of interacting. Nonetheless, experimental research has uncovered important processes in the study of stratification (Ridgeway 1999), following orders (Milgram in chapter 2), and identity formation (Zimbardo in chapter 3).

Field experiments take place outside the laboratory, where some aspect of the environment can be manipulated to influence the responses of unaware (naïve) subjects. The television program *Candid Camera* is a series of field experiments. Our favorite is the one in which people entering an elevator see that everyone in the car is facing the rear, and, without exception, the new passengers immediately turn around, even though the elevator has only one door.

A more serious type of field experiment is designed to measure helping behavior, for example, staging an accident in order to see which bystanders will come to the aid of an injured person. As it turns out, helpers are not very different from nonhelpers on any personality dimensions. What makes a difference is the *situation itself*. For example, the more witnesses there are to the accident, the less likely is any one of them to offer assistance; also, the more seriously hurt the "victim," the fewer the number of bystanders willing to help. In other words, naïve subjects are responding to the *definition of the situation* rather than to the actual events or their own internal impulses.

These are the bare outlines of the basic research techniques that you can employ to answer questions posed in many of these chapters and in the Workbook.

Understanding the Numbers

Throughout this book, data are presented in the form of tables and graphs. It is important that you be able to read these accurately and quickly, not only to get through this course but to become a smart consumer of other people's numbers. You live in a society that is increasingly obsessed with measurement and statistical sophistication. If you do not want to be at the mercy of the next person in a white coat with a clipboard, you should become familiar with the basic statistics and techniques for interpreting tables and figures, and an introductory sociology course is an excellent place to begin because it does not get much more basic.

Basic statistics. The most familiar and common statistic is the **percentage**, or how many of a given item there are in every 100 cases. Percentages allow us to compare units of different size. For example, although the population of the United States is 1,000 times larger than that of Iceland, we can compare data on women's employment in the two countries by using percents; in this case the smaller country has the higher percentage of its female population in the labor force (over 82 percent compared to about 73 percent for U.S. women). The term proportion is often used interchangeably with percentage.

Rates, like percentages, tell us how many times a given item appears in a population, but the base is usually greater than 100, such as 1,000 or 100,000. For example, the birthrate, or number of births per 1,000 Americans, is about 14.5 today, compared to 25.0 during the baby boom of the mid-1950s.

Ratios permit us to compare one subpopulation with another, such as the ratio of men to women, or of married to unmarried mothers. For example, the number of American males compared to the number of American females, or *sex ratio*, varies with age. Nature has provided for 110 males to be conceived for every 100 females, but because males have higher death rates at all ages and stages (even in the womb), the sex ratio at birth is 104/100, dropping to 97/100 for people aged 25 to 44. By age 85, there are fewer than 40 men for every 100 women. The reasons for these ratios are discussed in chapters 13 and 14, but there are a combination of biological and social factors that lead to variation in sex ratios historically and cross-culturally.

Measures of central tendency are single numbers that summarize an entire set of data. For example, a printout of the income of each American household would have 105 million entries and probably spread across several miles, but there are three measures of central tendency that could describe these data:

The **mean**, or *average*, is derived by dividing the total by the number of units. For example, dividing the total income of all U.S. households in 1998 by the number of households produced a single number—the mean—that was slightly over $47,000. One can then compare that with the average for

other years, or break down the data further and compare means for blacks
and whites, or households in different parts of the country.

A major problem with averages, especially when measuring income, is
that a few cases at the extremes, such as billionaires or teenage mothers, will
skew the average upward or downward. If you have a population in which a
small number of households had incomes in the million-dollar range and all
the others had earnings of no greater than $30,000, you could end up with an
inflated average of about $47,000, which obscures the relatively low income
of most households in that society.

The **median**, or *midpoint in a distribution*, is a statistic that deals with the
problem of extremes. To derive the median income of American households,
one would arrange the data in an array from highest to lowest and then find
the point at which 50 percent of all households fall below and 50 percent are
above that number. Each household is one case regardless of the size of its
income, with the middle case as the median, which was about $38,900 in
1998, considerably lower than the mean but closer to reality.

The **mode** is the single most common case in the collected data; with U.S.
income in 1998, arranged in steps of $10,000, the modal category was
$15,000–24,999, but this really covered only about 15 percent of households.
Although not very helpful for measuring income, the mode is better than the
mean for something like family size, where an average would give us something like 2.6 persons. 🖳 4

Reading a table. Here are a few helpful hints for reading tables and
graphs.

1. Read the table title or figure legend to find out what it is about.
2. Identify the statistics being used.
3. Identify the independent and dependent variables.
4. Then go to the actual data in the body of the table or figure.
5. Figure out what stories are being told by the numbers.

Table 1.2 Educational Attainment in the United States: 1998
(In percents for persons age 25 and over in each category)

	White	Black	Hispanic[a]	Asian
Race and Ethnicity				
Completed 4 years of high school or more				
1960	43.2	20.1	—	—
1980	68.8	51.2	44.0	—
1997	83.0	74.9	54.7	84.9
Completed 4 years of college or more				
1960	8.1	3.1	—	—
1980	17.1	6.4	7.6	—
1997	24.6	13.3	10.3	42.2

[a] Hispanics can be of either race

Source: *Statistical Abstract of the United States 1999*, p. 169.

6. Interpret the data—that is, try to explain the stories in the numbers.

This will get easier as you work your way through the book and learn more and more sociology.

Let's walk through Table 1-2:

Step 1: What is it about? Educational attainment (last grade completed).

Step 2: The statistic is a percentage of adults in each education category.

Step 3: Identifying variables. If independent variables predict the dependent ones, then race and year are independent, while last grade completed is dependent. Think of it this way: You cannot argue that people's educational level will affect what year it is or their skin color, but you can clearly say that how long a person stays in school depends on the year and one's race and ethnicity.

Steps 4 and 5: As the cells of the table indicate, there are many stories here: (1) the changes over time; (2) the relative gains for whites and blacks; (3) the high attainment levels of Asian Americans and the lag for Hispanics. Incidentally, the blank cells indicate only that no one was counting these categories in those years, which is interesting in itself.

Step 6: What accounts for these trends is discussed in chapter 10, but you could probably make some educated guesses right now.

Figures and Graphs. Some of these data can also be presented in more graphic form such as a bar graph, as shown below.

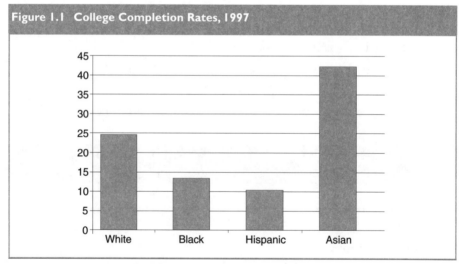

Figure 1.1 College Completion Rates, 1997

Source: *Statistical Abstract of the United States 1998*, p. 167.

Conclusion

You have had a very quick run-through of material that typically takes twice the space in introductory textbooks, but all the major points are here. You can recognize sociology as distinct from other social sciences, especially psychology, because of its special focus on the collectivity rather than the individual, on interaction rather than internal emotional states, and on the situations in which thought and behavior take place.

In the section on scope of the field and this book, the whole of sociology was laid before you, but only in bare outline. The best is yet to come.

You have learned to put theories in their historical and intellectual context, and you have seen the link between theory, hypotheses, and various research tools. All this now puts you in position to gain in mastery, not only over sociology but the very society in which you will spend the rest of your life. Far better to understand how it works than to leave yourself open to the manipulation of those who do.

❖ ❖ ❖ ❖

Surfing the Sociological Internet

Monitor screens 💻 in the text alert you to websites that can be used for further reading and research. The websites are working as of publication, but sometimes web addresses change, are under construction, or are being reconstructed. Updates will be available on the Roxbury webpage: **www.roxbury.net.**

💻 1   There is a Sociology Café and glossary at:
      http://www.geocities.com/~sociology/
      For the social sciences in general:
      http://dir.yahoo.com/Social_Science/Sociology/

💻 2   Visit the Dead Sociologists' Society at:
      http://raven.jmu.edu/~ridenelr/DSS/DEADSOC.HTML

💻 3   Explore sociological theories at:
      http://www.geocities.com/Athens/Olympus/2147/ basetheory.html
      Click on sociologists to explore more sociological theorists and writers, dead and alive:
      http://www.geocities.com/Athens/Olympus/2147/ basesociologists.html
      http://www.mcmaster.ca/socscidocs/w3virtsoclib/index.htm

💻 4   For statistical data and research sources, see:
      http://www.geocities.com/Athens/Olympus/2147/ basestats.html
      http://www.usi.edu/LIBARTS/SOCIO/Stats.htm

Glossary

Collectivities Sets of individuals who share an identity but do not necessarily interact.

Conflict Analysis A theoretical approach that assumes social systems are in a state of tension, with unrest as the basic condition, as a result of the unequal distribution of scarce resources.

Correlation A relationship between two variables.

Cross-Sectional Design A research tool used when the hypothesis focuses on a correlation at one time only.

Definition of the Situation Sociological concept that what people believe to be real becomes real in its consequences.

Dependent Variable A variable influenced systematically by changes in the independent variable.

Dramaturgy A social construction model that treats social interaction as a series of mini-dramas.

Empirical Referent An observable item that can be measured and counted and that represents an abstraction.

Ethnomethodology A technique for looking under the taken-for-granted surface of daily life by turning it upside down to reveal an unspoken reality.

Evolutionary Psychology Theoretical approach that explains human behavior in evolutionary and biological terms.

Feeling Rules Behavior norms that guide where, when, and with whom emotions can be shown.

Field Experiments Experiments that take place outside the laboratory but where some aspect of the environment can be manipulated to influence the responses of unaware (naïve) subjects.

Feminist Sociology A theoretical approach that directs attention to women's experience and to the importance of gender as an element of social structure.

Functional Analysis A theoretical approach that views collectivities including entire societies as structured in such a way that, over time, the various parts come to reinforce one another.

Humanist Sociology A theoretical approach based on the belief that a value-free sociology is not possible and that attempts at employing one only reinforce existing inequalities and injustice.

Hypothesis A testable guess, derived from theory, about relationships among variables.

Independent Variable In research studies, the independent variable has the greatest impact, comes first in the chain of events, is relatively fixed, and/or affects dependent variables.

Interpretive/Social Construction Models These theoretical approaches focus on communication and shared understandings created through social interaction.

Longitudinal Framework A research method in which the same people or variables are followed over several years.

Macro-Level This form of analysis focuses on the broad outline or larger picture of society and social institutions.

Mean A statistic whereby the average is derived by dividing the total by the number of units.

Measures of Central Tendency These are single numbers that summarize an entire set of data.

Median The median is the midpoint in a distribution; it is a statistic that deals with the problem of extremes.

Micro-Level This form of analysis focuses on the smaller aspects of society and social interactions, looking intensely at a limited set of objects.

Mode A statistic that pinpoints the single most common or frequent item in an array of data.

Paradigm A conceptual model of how the world works.

Participant Observation A research method in which the researcher becomes part of the interaction under study.

Percentage A statistic that shows how many of a given item there are in every 100 cases.

Positivism The idea that observers can be impartial and free of personal bias in their observations of social phenomena.

Postmodernism A theoretical approach that views all claims to "the truth" as suspect because they are based on the meanings given to words in one society at a given historical moment.

Primary Material New information gathered specifically for a particular research project.

Qualitative Research A research method that relies primarily on interpretive description rather than on statistics.

Quantitative Research A research method that uses the features of scientific objectivity, including complex statistical techniques.

Queer Theory A recent variation on postmodernism that emphasizes the deconstruction of "masculine/feminine" and "female/male."

Random Sampling A research technique for selecting a manageable number of cases that, within statistical limits, can be said to stand for an entire category.

Rate A measure of how many times a given item appears in a population; the base is usually greater than 100, such as 1,000 or 100,000.

Rational Choice Theory A theoretical approach based on a narrow economic view of behavior in which people and organizations tend to do that which brings the most benefit at the least cost.

Ratio A statistic that permits comparison of one subpopulation with another, such as the ratio of men to women.

Scientific Method A set of procedures, developed in the natural sciences, consisting of objective observations, precise measurement, and full disclosure of results.

Secondary Analysis Research done by reworking existing data, such as those found in government publications, historical records, and diaries and letters.

Social Facts Patterned regularities that characterize a collectivity.

Sociology The systematic study of human social behavior.

Sociology of Emotions A theoretical approach that analyzes feelings as socially constructed and expressed in socially learned ways, shaped by cultural and situational forces.

Sociology of Knowledge A theoretical approach that studies how ideas are grounded in historical time and the social context of thinkers.

Symbolic Interaction A social construction model that focuses on communication through shared understandings and on humans' constant interaction with others. ✦

How Is Society Possible?
Culture and Social Structure

❖ ❖ ❖ ❖   Why is the week seven days long? There is nothing in nature that has a seven-day cycle. Actually, three ten-day weeks would also reflect the monthly phases of the moon. The beauty of the seven-day week is precisely that it is an artificial, arbitrary division of time that imposes order on nature (Zerubavel 1985). Once in place, notice how the rhythms of your life adapt to it; Monday really is different from Friday. The seven-day week is an example of the triumph of the social—of culture and social structure—over nature, mind, and body. In this chapter you will be introduced to many of the basic concepts of sociology.

- Culture: universals and variations.
- Norms, values, and sanctions.
- Ethnocentrism and cultural relativism.
- Social structure.
- Status and role.
- Primary and secondary groups.
- Social networks and processes.
- Formal organizations.

These are the building blocks of sociological analysis, and once you have mastered them you will never look at your social world in the same way as before. Sociology is really a way of looking—a perspective—in which familiar things are viewed from a new angle, as products of culture and social structure.

Take today, for example. What do you expect to do? Attend classes, work at a part-time job, go to the movies? Or maybe hunt for giraffe, cook turtle eggs, build a canoe? It all depends on the society into which you were born. Its way of life becomes your reality, the only ideas and behaviors you know. This is **culture**, ways of thinking, believing, and acting that are shared by members of a society. Culture is learned through experience and language, and is never fixed but is always changing. Sometimes it changes so slowly that it seems time has stood still, and in other places, so rapidly that parents and children appear to have little in common.

Whatever your daily routine, the activities that make up that routine are possible only because certain patterns already exist. In your case, the college was in place before your admission and will most likely be there after your graduation. Your day is spent moving through a variety of preexisting places and relationships. These are **social structures**, and because you have a pretty clear idea of how you fit into these structures, your day unfolds with minimal difficulty. But if you were to wake up each morning without the assurance that the world outside your bedroom is structured, patterned, and predictable in ways you are familiar with, you would be frozen by anxiety and unwilling to get out of bed, much less go through the rest of the day.

Cultures and structures do not appear by magic; they are social constructions, produced by people who share a language, live together, and cooperate in devising the rules that allow the group to survive over time. Sociology is the study of how these outside forces determine how you think, feel, and behave. The key to understanding self and society, remember, is the fact that we do not act as individuals in a vacuum but as members of various collectivities and groups.

Culture

Around two million years ago, chimpanzees and humans split off from a common ancestor and went their own ways. You can see the chimps today in a few places such as Central Africa and the Central Park Zoo, but the humans are everywhere, even on expeditions to study the chimpanzees. Such studies have found that geographically separated bands of chimpanzees vary greatly in a number of behaviors that were not genetically programmed and that therefore had to be handed down from adults to infants (Whiten et al. 1999). In other words, along with some built-in responses, the chimps had culture! Humans, however, have *only* culture, those learned patterns that allow us to survive, to accumulate knowledge, and to create objects of usefulness and beauty.

How Humans Got Culture

Over the several million years of evolution from ape-like to humanoid, the most important development was the gradual replacement of instinctual drives by the workings of a mind that can reflect on itself—the triumph of thought over impulse. It all began about 3.5 million years ago when a climate shift forced some tree-living apes to come down to earth, where they needed to look over tall grasses to find food and to escape from enemies. The prehumans who were able to stand on two feet (**bipedalism**) had a survival advantage, and with upright posture came many other body changes over the next million years or so: (1) the birth canal narrowed so that typically one child is born at a time, and at a relatively early stage in its physical development, before the skull is fully shaped, when it can slip easily down the canal; (2) the hands, no longer needed for knuckle-walking, could be used to hold objects, which led to the development of the brain areas that control hand-eye coordination; (3) sexual intercourse started to take place face-to-face, so that some emotional closeness could be established; and (4) the head now sat atop the spinal cord, leaving room in the throat for a voice box. At the same time, changes in diet reduced the need for large teeth and jawbones, freeing even more area in the skull for brains and making the human face more expressive.

All these gradual and mutually reinforcing changes made it necessary to forge stable ties with other humans for affection, child rearing, conversation, and cooperation in gathering food and protection. This is not a world in which a chimpanzee,

Culture includes many different artifacts including material such as pottery. Here a Korean craftsperson carves a ceremonial horse.

❖ ❖ ❖ ❖   much less a human being, could survive alone. Thus, from the very beginning, *to be human is to be social*—dependent upon and responsible for one another, sharing and cooperating. The helpless infant cannot stay alive without the care of adults, who, in turn, need one another for emotional well-being and personal safety. Furthermore, the human infant is born before the brain is fully developed; the hard wiring of brain circuits comes *after* birth, in social settings. The basic point is that human beings *must* learn how to behave and can do so because they have the necessary brain power and self-control.

The prehumans most likely to succeed had to figure out how to create peaceable communities. Aided by that evolving voice box and complex brain, each group created a unique language through which they were able to make rules and to pass along the accumulated wisdom of the group to their newborns. So wondrously inventive are humans that they have devised ways to adapt to widely different climates and places—to hunt seals off the tip of South America, herd caribou in the Arctic, or grow yams on a Pacific Island. The flexibility, adaptability, and sheer variety of human cultures make us different from all other species. The chimps, with whom we share 98.4 percent of genetic material, can devise a dozen different ways to attack an ant hill, but only humans have built cathedrals.

The creatures that remained trapped in biologically programmed responses, unable to change their ways, gradually disappeared in favor of more clearly human-like types. Finally, about 300,000 years ago, early members of our species, *Homo sapiens* (the thinking creature), called Neanderthals, made their appearance. Then, around 100,000 years ago, Neanderthals begin to disappear, eventually replaced by a more "modern" type—Cro-Magnon or *Homo sapiens sapiens* (with a double emphasis on thinking)—who, in jeans and a T-shirt, would look just like anyone else in your sociology class. And by 50,000 years ago, thanks to the development of language and the manufacture of stone tools, groups of people who think and act just like you began to move out of their original home in East Africa and gradually populated the entire globe (Klein 1999). 1

Elements of Culture

Culture is often described as the blueprint for living of people who share a language, territory, and identity. Culture consists of (1) solutions to the problem of survival; (2) values that shape rules of behavior; and (3) artifacts, material items such as pottery, tents, or spears. The key to any culture is its language, that is, the words and gestures and their meanings that are unique to that society.

Language: the ultimate symbol system. The origins of culture are lost in the mists of time, when those first prehumans took grunting and arm-waving a step further, developing increasingly subtle sounds and gestures, thanks to their voice box and evolving brain. These body changes are essential for the capacity to think symbolically. A symbol is something that may signify nothing in and of itself but that is *given meaning by the agreement of group members*. A six-pointed star, for example, has great emotional significance for Jews but could be just an interesting design in another culture.

The ultimate symbol system is language itself, the meanings given to sounds and words based on a common understanding among the speakers. *All human communication is symbolic*, and because languages are unique to particular societies, it can be argued that each language creates a unique world of meaning and that you cannot understand a culture without being familiar with its language. It is through the words and the gestures of your caregivers that you are first introduced to the culture and begin to see the world in a certain way. Language is a screen through which reality is filtered; we never confront the world directly but only through the lens of culture.

It follows, then, that what you might have thought of as basic realities, such as time, color, or space, are actually experienced quite differently by members of other societies. People in the Amazon rain forest may not have a different name for days of the week—all days are much the same—yet can identify hundreds of different plants that look alike to us. Even in the same society, distance can be measured differently, as when children who walk to school count the number of blocks they take, while those who ride measure distance in terms of time on the bus. Human language is also characterized by the variety of sounds made possible by that voice box, from the clicking rhythms of the !Kung San to the sharp inflections of Asian speech to the smoothness of French vowels.

Each culture has ideas about appropriate 'bubbles of personal space' to which a person is entitled. Breaking that norm can get you into trouble as seen in this confrontation between an umpire and a baseball coach.

In addition to spoken language, aspects of culture are conveyed through gestures. The study of nonverbal communication, called **kinesics**, reinforces the concept of cultural variability, even though smiles and frowns appear to have universal meaning. For example, each culture has ideas about privacy and the "bubble of personal space" to which you are entitled. Arabs talk head-to-head; Americans stand about two feet apart. The bubble will also vary by gender and power. Next time you are in the library, observe who is most likely to move into the space of someone else, who has the most privacy and who the least.

Cultural universals. Communication, however, does not automatically ensure survival of the group over time. No band of people is going to last very long unless it can produce enough food to feed its members, make rules and maintain order, pair off individuals for sexual satisfaction and child rearing, transmit its ways to infants, and instill a sense of shared identity and responsibility. And no two groups are going to come up with the same solutions. Over time, in any society, each of these solutions becomes patterned, or *institutionalized*, as "the" way we do things. These patterns are summarized in Table 2.1.

Table 2.1	Cultural Universals
Survival Need	**Institutionalized Solution**
To produce and distribute food and other essentials of physical survival	Economic system
To create rules for dividing labor and ensuring that necessary tasks are done	Political system/order keeping functions
To pair off people for orderly reproduction and minimize sexual jealousy	Courtship, marriage, and family rules
To transmit the culture	Socialization/educational practices
To create a shared identity and sense of responsibility for one another	Religious beliefs and rituals

These five essential elements of culture are universal; that is, they are found in every society from the small gathering bands of the Amazon rain forest to the United States of America, and all stops in between. But the content of each of these elements will vary from one society to another and within the same society historically. For example, some evolutionary biologists claim that humans are programmed to invent something like marriage, but nothing in nature could possibly explain the enormous cultural variability in patterns of courtship, marriage, and family relationships (see chapter 8). The one factor that appears to account for similarities in culture is not biology but the economic base of the society. Patterns of production, land use, and ownership tend to produce certain political, family, and religious systems, just as Marx suggested.

Norms. Another essential element of culture is the rules—or norms—that regulate behavior and ensure social order. Some norms tell us how we should behave ("thou shalt," or *prescriptive norms*) and others how not to ("thou shalt not," or *proscriptive norms*). Just think of the Ten Commandments, which are as perfect a set of proscriptive and prescriptive norms as could be devised to ensure social order in any society: obey authority; control sexuality, envy, and aggression; do not give false testimony; honor property rights; and recognize your shared identity as worshippers of a particular God.

Not all norms reach the level of universal necessity. Some are simply folkways, or matters of custom and habit passed on as "the way we do things here," without any important social consequences. Examples include eating with chopsticks, fingers, or forks; the customs that regulate cleanliness; or clothing styles. Other norms, called mores (always plural), cover matters of some moral or ethical importance, such as courtship conduct or showing respect to ancestors. The most essential rules, those that cover activities central to the well-being of the collectivity are enshrined in laws, written and unwritten. The laws cover all members of the society and are strictly enforced. Indeed, one can tell the strength of a norm by the severity of the reaction to its violation.

These reactions, or **sanctions**, express the approval or disapproval of the collectivity and are imposed by specific members of society. Violations of the folkways are typically dealt with informally, by friends or family—a slap on the wrist, a cold shoulder, something immediate that lets you know you had better shape up. Those who disobey the mores are subject to more severe sanctions, such as being shunned or disinherited or excommunicated. Breaking the law, however, is a very serious threat to social order, calling for *formal sanctions* administered by officials charged with maintaining conformity—judges, police, and the people who staff prisons and asylums.

The idea of "normative" also extends to appearance and expectations of behavior. People who do not "fit in" are subject to informal sanctions every bit as painful as official ones. In addition, definitions of normative change over time, as you can see by comparing ideals of beauty in women's magazines from the 1890s and today.

Precisely because we are not born knowing how to behave, there are bound to be moments when we do not know what to do, situations for which no norms have been worked out or in which appropriate responses are unclear. **Anomie** (pronounced ah-no-me) is a French word, originally used by Durkheim to refer to those moments when normative guidance is lacking or ambiguous. Anomie is emotionally uncomfortable. Remember the wave of panic you felt when you didn't know how to react to some situation for which you were unprepared—a sudden change in plans, being let down by someone you trusted, entering the wrong room. After the initial state of confusion, order is restored when you and your role partners come up with an acceptable definition of the situation and the attached norms. Whew! To be human is to need the norms.

Values. Norms typically reflect some deeper sense of ultimate worthiness, of right and wrong, good and bad—**values**, or standards against which the norms can be judged. The fit between values and norms is not always direct. For example, "Thou shalt not kill" is a fairly universal norm, reflecting the value of life itself and the need to control blood feuds, but in reality, the proscription applies only to members of your society; killing enemies will win you a medal.

The American 'Work Ethic'

The closest to an American value system, with its emphasis on the individual, comes to us from the English settlers seeking religious freedom in the New World almost 400 years ago. They brought with them a set of values forged during the Protestant Reformation of the sixteenth century, values that freed individuals from the oppression of hereditary monarchs and religious authorities. These values also allowed an emergent merchant class to accumulate wealth, hold on to profits, and lay the foundation of modern capitalism (see chapter 8 for a full discussion of capitalism).

The link between the values of early Protestantism and the emerging capitalist economic system in Western Europe was first described by Max Weber (1904–5/1976) and many of his insights are still on target. What Weber called the Protestant Ethic is now referred to simply as the "work ethic," to which all Americans are exposed regardless of their religion. There are three aspects of the ethic that continue to shape American values and how you judge yourself and others.

Work as a 'calling.' A "calling" is a sacred task. Throughout most of human history, daily labor was simply what you did in order to survive. To define work as something ordained by God is a very different thing and a powerful motive to keep at the task. Notice how difficult it is for Americans to enjoy their leisure unless they feel it has been earned; that beer is yours only after the cattle are back in the corral. In addition, if work is a sacred task, nonwork can only be an invitation to sin: "Idle hands are the devil's workshop." And think of the words so often used to describe the unemployed, as in "good-for-nothing lazy bum." This is not a description so much as a value judgment.

Success as a sign of grace. It follows, then, that doing especially well at your work must be a sign of divine favor and inner virtue. The American tendency to worship success, regardless of how it is achieved, is on display on every magazine rack. By the same reasoning, failure is taken as a sign of some deep character flaw. The logic argues that if your success is due to innate virtue, then the less successful must, by the same standards, be less virtuous.

Individual responsibility for one's actions. It is here that extreme individualism kicks in. The Protestant revolt against the Catholic Church in sixteenth century Europe was largely an effort to eliminate the layers of churchly authority that interfered with a believer's direct communication with God. You alone are responsible for what you do with your life—no deathbed absolution, no wiping away of sin. It is your conduct in this world that counts, but you can never be totally certain of salvation. Intense anxiety and fear of eternal damnation keep the good Puritan on the straight and narrow.

How have these ideas played out in the United States? If you can convince workers that laboring all day every day in filthy factories for survival wages is God's will and their lot in life, can they really complain or unionize? It takes much less to convince the employers that they are not exploiting workers but, rather, doing the Lord's work. And, of course, if your success reflects moral superiority, other people's failures must be due to some moral deficit. Thus, if the poor have brought their troubles upon themselves, then the rest of us are not really responsible. Indeed, "handouts" from government will only encourage their irresponsibility, although we may choose to offer assistance through charity. Sound familiar? These ideas come pretty close to the sentiments expressed by most Americans and members of Congress during the 1996 debate on welfare programs.

Curiously, in Europe, where these ideas originated and had great force in the Protestant nations, the outcome is opposite than that seen in the United States. Europe has the most generous and extensive social welfare policies in the twentieth century. What is unique about the United States that makes our social welfare system the least generous of all modern societies? The answer to this question is in chapter 5, but you may be able to figure it out already.

Worldly asceticism. One last aspect of the work ethic deserves attention. Originally, the early Protestants stressed simplicity in life style, or **worldly asceticism**, that is, to live in this world as if one had taken a vow of poverty (think of those unsmiling Puritans in their plain black clothes). Asceticism was very important in the first stages of modern economic development, because if you work hard, save the profit, do not have to give it to the king or the church, and cannot spend it on frills for yourself, it becomes available for investment in new businesses, machines, and factories.

Although worldly asceticism was essential for the accumulation of capital needed to fund new enterprises, the continued success of profit-making business required ever higher levels of demand for their products. In other words, asceticism had to be replaced by its exact opposite, an unending desire for goods and services. Success was no longer measured by an inner sense of virtue, shared only with God, but by outward displays of wealth, designed to impress other people. And so a "culture of materialism," the need to prove your worth through accumulating objects of value, became part of the American value system. Indeed, the more goods and services that people can buy and waste, the more they are respected. Over a hundred years ago, the American economist Thorstein Veblen (1899) coined the term conspicuous consumption to describe these lavish displays of wastefulness, and he hadn't even heard of Donald Trump. As long as people judge themselves and one another by how many things they own, the economic system will keep rolling along.

Cultural Development

Only a few societies can be called "modern" or "industrial." Of the thousands of different cultures across the globe today, there are still some that have been so isolated that they practice the same way of life as they did hundreds of years ago. Others have changed more or less thoroughly, each with its own unique history. But some general patterns can be found. Over the past 100,000 years, our species has gradually accumulated tools and weapons, discovered fire and the wheel, painted on cave walls, learned to grow crops, invented writing, imagined gods, built factories, and created philosophies—to name but a few of our enduring accomplishments. In general, the trend between and within societies is from simple to increasingly complex, in terms of the amount of knowledge and number of artifacts.

As new ways of providing food are added to the group's economic base—for example, when hunters also plant crops or learn to herd cattle—more people can be supported. But an increase in population creates problems of order and coordination, leading to ever more elaborate political and educational systems, while family and religious organizations tend to lose power and complexity.

Figure 2.1 is a greatly simplified overview of cumulative cultural change from the earliest gathering band to a modern industrial society. Some historical moments are watersheds, forever separating past from future. One such period involved the development of plow agriculture, which led to large permanent settlements; written language to keep track of business transactions; and widespread trade with other societies. More recently, the emergence of industrialization, democratic governments, and near-universal education radically changed the course of history and the nature of society across the globe.

Over tens of thousands of years, societies have come and gone. Historically, each occupies a segment of Figure 2.1 (see also Lenski and Lenski 1991). Some rose and fell very quickly (Biblical tribes). Others have endured

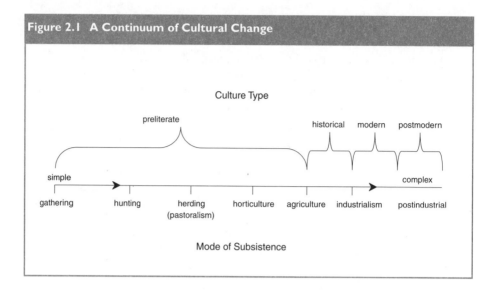

Figure 2.1 A Continuum of Cultural Change

for many generations with minimal change (Amazon tribes); some will last for thousands of years, adapting to all sorts of external influences (Egypt); and still others emerged only a few centuries ago, on the verge of the Industrial Age (the United States). Added together, all these trajectories can be plotted along the path to increasing the size and complexity of the culture base of a society. Cultural complexity, however, should not be equated with cultural superiority.

Ethnocentrism. Actually, the members of any society think that their way of life is the only, truest, best, most natural, divinely ordained, or whatever makes it worth defending. This attitude is called **ethnocentrism** (from ethnos = nation), and, although it does not make for friendly relations with outsiders, ethnocentrism is clearly functional for social solidarity. If you did not think your culture was superior to all others, you would not be so eager to obey its laws or sacrifice yourself in time of war. In this sense, ethnocentrism is functional for group morale but dysfunctional for a peaceful world.

Ethnocentrism in modern industrial societies also produces a sense of intellectual superiority, the belief that we Americans are somehow more advanced in mental functioning than are the "poor" natives in what is often described as the Third World. There is no evidence to support this claim however; we appear bigger and better only because we stand on the accumulated knowledge of Western civilization. It is the size of the culture base rather than innate abilities that makes the difference, and who is to say who is happier—members of a small hunting band or some of your friends?

Cultural relativism. In contrast to ethnocentrism, **cultural relativism** refers to the ability to appreciate the content of other cultures without making value judgments. The basic assumption is that each society's solutions to the problems of survival are as valid as any other, however unappealing they may appear to us. The trick is to see how that trait or behavior fits into the culture as a whole and how it is interpreted within that society—a great leap of the imagination, certainly, but one that stretches the mind. 💻 2

Subcultures

Just as culture provides values, norms, and a history for the nation, so, too, within the larger collectivity, **subcultures** provide social support to groups that differ from the majority. Most societies are fairly **homogeneous** (containing people who are similar) in terms of race, religion, and ethnic background, although age and sex will always distinguish some members from others. Other societies are **heterogeneous**, containing sizable numbers of citizens who worship different gods or are of varying skin colors and national origins. Whenever these differences lead to differing experiences of the general culture, to exclusion or discrimination, subcultures develop as a protective envelope, shielding members from others' negative attitudes.

Subcultures often characterize groups that do not experience discrimination yet differ from the mainstream enough to generate a "we" feeling, a sense of separateness and a need to establish a boundary that excludes non-members. Examples include police officers, physicians, or college professors, or any subgroup with its special language and customs. Subcultures typically consist of variations on dominant values and norms, close enough to remain under the societal umbrella but different enough to reflect the unique experience of subgroup members.

Thus, in the United States today, there is a distinct subculture of teenagers, of urban African Americans, of military officers, of medical staff, of sociologists, and so forth. Each group has a special way of talking or dressing so that insiders recognize one another while keeping outsiders out. Once you have learned the vocabulary of sociology you, too, can join our subculture. 💻 3

Culture Change

Trends in American institutions are discussed in the relevant chapters throughout the book, and the future of postindustrial societies is dealt with in chapter 16. But we can ask here if there are signs of major culture change in the United States? In the 1960s it appeared that materialistic values were being challenged by young people concerned with personal fulfillment and sexual liberation, along with a commitment to social justice. The 1960s and 1970s did leave a legacy of openness to new experience, a concern for the environment, and support for the civil rights of women, racial and ethnic minorities, and homosexuals.

More recently, increased resistance to these changes has emerged, a backlash movement toward more conservative positions on civil rights, feminism, sexuality, and the environment. This development has led to what is described as the *culture wars* between the lingering values of the 1960s and a renewed traditionalism. These tensions are reflected in data on the entering college class of 2004, which find students taking basically liberal positions on social issues (environment, women's rights, reproductive choice) but also more likely than students in the past to call themselves politically conservative. Also in contrast to the 1960s and 1970s, students today are more likely to value their college degree as a means to economic security rather than as a means to personal growth (American Council on Education 2000).

Do these data mean a return to the old ethic? Or are today's students forging a new synthesis of more open personal relationships with the older tradition of material success? How would you describe the value systems of your friends or the student body as a whole?

Social Structure

Social structure can be thought of as the relatively enduring institutions and relationships through which the culture is realized. These structures refer to a collective reality that cannot be reduced to its various parts, from a dating couple to the society as a whole to the world economic system.

Levels of Social Structure

At the very personal level, or **micro-level**, structure emerges from everyday interactions. If you think about the group of friends with whom you hang out, although it may seem that your interactions are purely spontaneous, a closer look should uncover fairly regular patterns. Typically, there will be a "task leader," the one who settles disputes, and a "joker," the one who defuses tension by doing something goofy. Over time, you will develop decision-making mechanisms, a division of labor, and some way to draw a boundary around the group, to signify who is in and who is out—a handshake, an item of clothing, or special words.

Personal agency is the ability to affect one's environment. Marla Runyon, a legally blind runner (#796), qualified for the U.S. Olympic track team and finished eighth in the 1500 meter finals in Sydney, Australia, 2000.

At the highest level of abstraction, the **macro-level**, the focus is on the society as a whole and its institutionalized parts. The solutions to the problems of survival listed in Table 2.1 are realized through concrete structures. That is, there is a pattern of relationships among variables and individuals that can be called an economic system, whether it involves gathering berries or manufacturing jelly. There is a set of norms that defines the political and family systems of a given society, and a set of beliefs and rituals that compose its religion. Each of these institutional spheres is the subject of an entire chapter in part III of this book.

There is also an intermediate level of sociological analysis—the **meso-level** of organizational activity. Somewhere between the abstraction, educational structure, and the actual classroom as an interactive system, there is a particular school. Between the economy as a whole and the shop floor is the factory, and so forth.

Table 2.2   Levels of Social Structure

Level of Analysis	Level of Abstraction	Focus	Examples
Macro-Level	Highest	Society and its institutions	Economic system Political system Marriage and family rules Educational system
Meso-Level	Intermediate	Organizational activities	Factories and offices Schools, colleges, and universities Political parties Churches, synagogues, and mosques Community groups
Micro-Level	Lowest	Patterns of everyday interactions	Your ability to affect your environment (decision making) Your interaction with others in various social settings

Each of these structural levels provides a context for learning the rules and meanings that govern it. But context, while limiting, is not a straitjacket. Because social structures are products of trial-and-error attempts to sustain the collectivity, they can also be changed through **personal agency**, one's ability to affect one's environment. The give-and-take between existing structures and the intentional or accidental forces that modify social conditions adds a dynamic dimension to social life. Yes, you are a creature of your time and place, but you can also leave your mark, and even join with others to create major changes (see chapter 16).

Components of Social Structure: Systems, Statuses, and Roles

System. Technically, a system is a whole composed of interdependent parts. An automobile engine is a system that works only when the various parts are put together in a particular way. Similarly, some butter, flour, baking powder, and an egg are only ingredients that, depending on how they are combined, could end up as a cake, cookie, or gooey mess. Furthermore, what makes the cake a birthday cake is not something in the object itself but a product of how it is defined by the group and symbolized by special decorations. Meaning, remember, is *socially conferred*, and that is what makes a birthday candle different from other candles.

At the macro-level, the parts that comprise the social system of the society as a whole are those institutionalized survival patterns in Table 2.1: the economic, political, family, educational, and religious subsystems.

At the meso-level, any collectivity or group must meet the same needs—keeping members alive physically, maintaining order, recruiting new members, transmitting the culture, and generating solidarity. Your college, for example, has dormitories and cafeterias to house and feed you, campus rules and security to enforce the norms, an admissions office to find new students, orientation programs, and the college songs and rituals (graduation, homecoming) to reinforce loyalty. The same challenges must be met by the Jones family, the First Baptist Church, Sam's Autobody Shop, and the U.S. Senate.

Status. As an individual, you may be involved in a number of such systems, or, more accurately, a part of you is engaged in each one. In sociological terms, you have a **status**, or position in a social system: student, son or daughter, patron, date, friend, employee, worshipper, and so forth. Your status determines how everyone in the system should treat you and how you should deal with them. These rules of conduct are learned, and you violate the norms at a cost. Workers can be fired, students expelled, wives and husbands divorced, and heretics burned at the stake.

Role. At the micro-level of everyday interactions, the behavior attached to each status is called **role**. Most of what you do in the course of a day, every day of your life, is role enactment, literally reading off the script provided by your culture. And what a versatile actor you are! Keep a log of just one day's performances, and you will be amazed at how many different "yous" there are in one body.

Table 2.3 illustrates the various components of social structure.

Table 2.3	Components of Social Structure			
		Society		
		Composed of five institutional spheres		
I. Politics	II. Economics	III. Religion	IV. Family	V. Education

Components of Each Institutional Sphere

Macro	A. Organization structure
	1. Organizations (larger, more formal groups)
↓	2. Groups (two or more interacting people, sharing in identity)
	3. Statuses (positions within an organization or group)
	4. Roles (behavior attached to status)
Micro	B. Institutionalized moral beliefs and behavioral rules that support structure
	5. Values (moral beliefs)
	6. Norms (rules of behavior based on moral beliefs)

Source: Janice M. Saunders, "Relating Social Structure Abstractions to Sociological Research," *Teaching Sociology* 19 (1991): 270–271. Reproduced by permission of the American Sociological Association with Janice M. Saunders.

Ascribed and achieved statuses. Some positions in social systems are **ascribed**; that is, they are assigned because of who you are by birth and are therefore more or less unchangeable. Race, sex, nationality, age, religion, and family social standing are major bases of ascription. Depending on the social value attached to the status, people can try to change, hide, or disguise these traits.

Other status characteristics are less fixed—education, income, and occupation, for example, These are **achieved** statuses because they are thought to be gained by one's own effort. By definition, achieved statuses are more flexible than ascribed positions. An employee can be fired and students can drop out, but it is extremely difficult to become an ex-son or ex-daughter or former Italian-American.

Master status. Because the human mind can take in only a limited number of impressions at one time, you tend to focus on a few very visible traits in order to "locate" people in social systems, so that you know how to treat them—as an equal, inferior, or superior. A **master status** is the trait with the strongest impact on how you appear to others. Race, sex, and age are powerful master statuses; just knowing that someone is male or female, or age 75, or Asian American is connected in your mind with all kinds of other traits. Body size is another master status; notice your differing expectations of someone who is either extremely large or small and how these expectations also vary by whether that person is male or female.

Role strain, conflict, and overload. Because a status is a position in a social system and is therefore linked to all the other participants, statuses and roles are always *relational*, organizing the behavior of all participants in the system. Roles cannot be studied in a vacuum but only in relation to one's **role partners**. One cannot be a father without a child or a minister without a

In young adulthood the number of roles most people occupy expands, including employment, family obligations, community volunteer work, and a commitment to influence one's world.

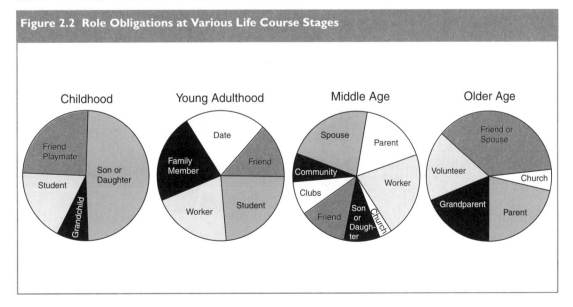

Figure 2.2 Role Obligations at Various Life Course Stages

❖ ❖ ❖ ❖

flock. For the sociologist, the individual is a bundle of roles that contracts and expands at various points in the life course. Your life space is parceled out among the various systems in which you occupy a status and have role obligations. Try visualizing yourself as a pie with slices of differing size.

As a child, your set of statuses is rather limited. As a teenager, you will add some big slices, but the big crunch comes in young adulthood, with marriage, parenthood, committed worker, community volunteer, and church member, in addition to friend and child to your own parents. Old age brings status and role losses, so that the pie becomes smaller and less varied. In addition, as the occupant of a single status, one of those slices—college student, for example—you have obligations to a variety of role partners—your **role set**—and they, in turn, have obligations to you. When you think of yourself as one big pizza pie and then look at all the role sets attached to each slice, you can immediately see why you feel stressed or tugged in different directions.

Role conflict involves competing expectations of role partners. As a college student, for example, you have probably noticed that parents and friends are often at odds: one wants you to "stay in and study hard," the other says "you've earned a good time, let's party." But it is as a mature adult that the most severe role conflicts will be experienced, most notably the tension between obligations to an employer and those to spouse and children. The reason that the conflict between work or education and family is especially acute for women is that they are still expected to make home-based roles primary, whereas men can meet their family obligations by being good earners.

Another form of role conflict occurs when you receive incompatible messages from the same partner. Remember when your parents told you to "have a good time" but also to "behave yourself"? Similarly, young women and men today face potentially conflicting expectations from dating partners, such as "be independent but feminine" or "be strong but sensitive."

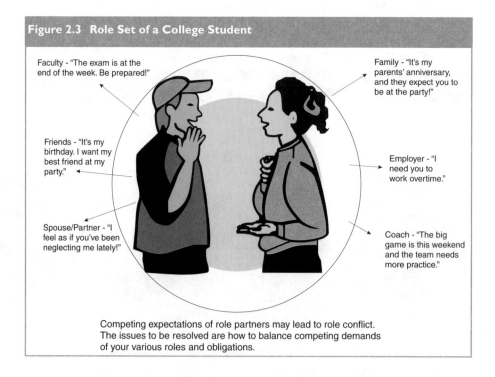

Figure 2.3 Role Set of a College Student

Faculty - "The exam is at the end of the week. Be prepared!"

Family - "It's my parents' anniversary, and they expect you to be at the party!"

Friends - "It's my birthday. I want my best friend at my party."

Employer - "I need you to work overtime."

Spouse/Partner - "I feel as if you've been neglecting me lately!"

Coach - "The big game is this weekend and the team needs more practice."

Competing expectations of role partners may lead to role conflict. The issues to be resolved are how to balance competing demands of your various roles and obligations.

Sometimes the conflict comes from within, as when you are asked to do   ❖ ❖ ❖ ❖
something that deeply offends your sense of right and wrong. For example,
while most of us think that we are incapable of consciously inflicting pain on
another person, researchers had little difficulty constructing a laboratory
experiment in which a majority of naïve subjects did just that, as described in
Box 2.1.

Box 2.1

Shocking Behaviors

At the end of World War II, when the full extent of the Nazi death camps became
known, social scientists asked how so many seemingly well-civilized Germans
could either take part or sit by quietly while their neighbors were taken away to gas
chambers. Was there something in the German personality or upbringing—harsh
fathers and overprotective mothers—that made them especially cruel? Not really. It
seems any of us could push a button to administer what we think is a dangerous
electric shock to someone else—under certain conditions.

In the 1960s, psychologist Stanley Milgram (1965) devised a series of laboratory
experiments in which naïve subjects were asked to take part in a "learning study"
that involved administering electric shocks to "learners" who gave an incorrect answer. The subjects sat before a console with a voltage dial numbered from 15
("Slight Shock") to 450 ("Danger: Severe Shock") and received orders from the ex-
perimenters about when and what voltage to apply. (No shocks were actually administered; the console was a dummy.)

Before the experiment, psychiatrists had estimated that about 1 percent of subjects would administer the highest voltage and that those people would undoubtedly have some emotional abnormality. As it turned out, over 60 percent of all subjects—women as well as men, old or young, college-educated or not—could and did
obey the teacher right up to the "danger" point of 450 volts!

What distinguished levels of obedience was not any particular personality trait
but, rather, variations in the experimental situation. Milgram manipulated the conditions in a number of ways, but the most crucial appeared to be (1) whether the
subject saw the learner enter the booth; (2) the loudness of moans coming from the
learning room; (3) the subject's belief that earlier subjects had followed orders; and
(4) the closeness of the teacher to the subject. When orders are given by an authority figure standing at your side, you are very likely to obey. When instructions come
from a distance, via headphones or a public address system, obedience is more
problematic.

These were not unusually cruel or disturbed subjects, only ordinary men and
women who believed that the situation required obedience to legitimate authority.
Alas, under certain conditions, many of us could become good concentration camp
guards.

In general, role sets become more complex with age, peaking in mid-life,
before contracting again in old age. It is the middle-aged who are most likely
to experience **role overload** in the sheer number of roles that must be juggled
simultaneously. If you think your life is complicated now, just wait! Role overload has negative consequences at both the personal and organizational level.
Unhappy and stressed-out people do not perform well at home or at work.
Overload can be handled in a number of ways, including becoming emotionally or physically ill enough to be released from everyday responsibilities (the
"sick role"). Other solutions range from setting clear priorities among obligations to exiting from the status altogether—ending a friendship, leaving the
church choir, quitting a job, or divorcing.

As distressing as conflict, strain, and overload can be, they are the price
individuals pay for the enormous range of choices available in modern societ-

ies, in contrast to the limited statuses of young people in other cultures dominated by ascription and tradition.

Groups and Interaction Patterns

A group, remember, is not simply a collection of individuals who happen
to be in the same place at the same time. Sociologically, a **group** has certain
properties: (1) its members have a distinctive way of relating to one another;
(2) they are aware of their interdependence; (3) and they have a sense of
shared identity, or a "we" feeling. Groups vary in size, intensity, and stability
over time, but all are based on mutual awareness of and responsiveness to
role partners

Primary and secondary groups. A basic distinction is made between
small, close-knit, intimate groupings, or **primary groups**, on the one hand,
and larger, more impersonal, formal groupings, or **secondary groups**, on the
other. Table 2.4 lists the essential difference between the two types.

Table 2.4 Comparison of Primary and Secondary Groups			
Structural Characteristics	**Processes**	**Sample Relations**	**Sample Groups**
Primary Groups			
Physical proximity	Whole person relationships	Husband-wife	Family
Small number of members	Spontaneity	Parents-children	Neighborhood
Long duration	Informal social control	Close friends	Work team
Shared norms and values	Expressive behavior	Close work group	
Shared goals			
Secondary Groups			
Large number of members	Segmented role relationships	Student-teacher	College freshmen
Limited sharing of norms and values	Formality	Officer-subordinate	Army
Limited shared goals	More formal social control	Boss-worker	Corporation
No physical proximity necessary	Instrumental behavior		Alumni association
Contacts of limited duration			

Primary group relationships tend to be highly personalized, or **expressive**, valued in their own right. We hang out with our friends for the sheer
pleasure of being with them; belonging is an end in itself. And while family
relationships may not always be so pleasurable, members are valued just for
being who they are.

Secondary group relationships, in contrast, are largely **instrumental**,
maintained as a means to another goal. Many students stay in school only to
receive the diploma that will enhance their earning power, just as many work-

❖ ❖ ❖ ❖

ers stay on the job for the paycheck that buys pleasurable things. But as these examples suggest, expressive and instrumental goals are not necessarily incompatible. Some students derive great pleasure from the sheer delight of learning something new, and, with luck, they may even find employment that is personally satisfying along with affording a nice income.

The two types of relationship can also be combined when primary groups form within the instrumental settings. Friendship circles, or *cliques* (pronounced kleeks), are common in the workplace, offering warmth in a cold climate. As an extreme example, one of the most important findings from studies of combat troops is that their behavior is driven, not by patriotism or hatred of the enemy, but by loyalty to the unit, the band of interdependent buddies. And the military knows this.

The difference between primary and secondary groups is also captured in the distinction made by German sociologist Ferdinand Toennies (1853–1936) between *Gemeinschaft* (community) and *Gesellschaft* (society). The very word "community" evokes the image of a warm and comforting environment. "Society," in contrast, is much colder and impersonal, where social ties are voluntary, temporary, and based on self-interest.

The *Gemeinschaft* is typically associated with family, neighborhood, small town, or the tribe as a whole, a vanished world overtaken by the *Gesellschaft*, the modern way of life. However, probably both the supportiveness of traditional groups and the heartlessness of industrial society have been exaggerated. Many young people are not eager to spend the rest of their lives in a small town, where everyone knows what everyone else is doing. But the price of independence and privacy in the larger world will be a sense of isolation and loneliness. One of your life tasks will be precisely to find and nurture circles of intimacy within the *Gesellschaft* of modern America.

Ingroups and outgroups. Groups need boundaries, some way of distinguishing who is in and who is out. The clearer the boundary markers, the tighter, more cohesive is the group. The less clear and more leaky the boundaries, the weaker are the ties that bind members but the freer they are to join a variety of groups and enlarge their personal network.

As originally described by the American sociologist William Graham Sumner (1840–1910), the distinction between "us" and "them" generates a high level of solidarity, or togetherness, within a group while also encouraging negative feelings toward outsiders. Surely, you must have noticed how much nicer and smarter members of your campus clubs are in comparison with members of other clubs.

Because the need for group solidarity is greatest under conditions of competition and threat, when people become increasingly dependent on the group as a whole, the level of out-group hostility rises accordingly, as seen in the boys–camp experiment, described in Box 2.2.

Box 2.2

Ins and Outs

Back in the 1950s, before social science had strict rules about the treatment of human subjects, researchers into group dynamics conducted a famous field experiment. Eleven- and twelve-year-old boys, unknown to each other but similar on all social background characteristics, were recruited to attend a summer camp. For ☞

the first few days, the boys engaged in spontaneous games and unstructured play, after which they were asked to list the names of best friends at camp. The researchers then divided the boys into two teams, Eagles and Rattlers, separating previous cross-choices of "best friend."

Each team was then given a set of problems to solve that required cooperation, so that strong in-group loyalties were formed. After a few days of this exercise, the boys were asked again to list their best friends. This time, regardless of the spontaneous friendships of only a few days earlier, the boys almost unanimously selected teammates. This illustrates a major social psychological principle: the more that individuals need to cooperate to achieve a goal, the closer they become, and the better they like one another.

The researchers then introduced a series of competitions between the teams, so that the success of one team came at the expense of the other. It did not take long before the boys displayed high levels of out-group hostility, and as these feeling intensified, so did the strength of in-group solidarity. In fact, the situation almost got out of hand, and the researchers had to devise ways of reducing *inter* (between)-group conflict.

How would you go about restoring *intra* (within)-camp harmony? One solution would be to compete against another camp that the boys could unite in hating, but this was not the way the researchers wanted to end the summer. The chosen solution was to devise projects that involved cooperation among all campers. (Sherif et al. 1961).

Throughout history, when it seemed that social order was collapsing, political leaders have tried to unite their citizens by directing hostility onto "outsiders"—not only foreigners, but often the Jews, Gypsies, and gays who may live next door.

Social Networks

A **social network** is the sum total of your group memberships and, therefore, of your interpersonal resources, or "social capital," namely the number and type of people you can call on for support. Networks have both structural and interactive dimensions: (1) Structural dimensions include *range* (how many groups), *density* (how many overlapping relationships), and *diversity* (how many different kinds). (2) Interactive dimensions include *frequency* of contact, *strength* of the bonds, their *duration*, and *how willing you are to seek assistance.*

Cooperation is a form of interaction that involves pooling the group's assets in order to achieve a common goal. Here members of the Amish community and outsiders work together to raise a barn.

Another structural dimension is the number of persons in a particular network. You act very differently when you are with one or two people than you do when in a larger group. Just the addition of a single other person can change the dynamics of a

group. For example, the smallest unit of sociological analysis, the dyad, or ❖ ❖ ❖ ❖
two-person group, permits the closest intimacy but is at the same time the
most fragile of bonds because all it takes to destroy a dyad is one person leaving. This may explain why your most emotionally intense relationships are
also the most anxiety-ridden.

Adding a third person creates a triad, which is less intimate and more stable than the dyad. Triads can be maintained as long as the same two members
do not constantly unite against the third. Think of the triads to which you
belong and the ways in which the three of you try to avoid the "ganging up"
problem.

Interaction Processes

There are a limited number of ways in which group members can set
goals, organize behavior, and distribute resources:

- *Competition* occurs when the resources are distributed on a winner-
  takes-all basis. As long as the contest is considered fair, losers can accept the outcome.

- *Cooperation* involves pooling the group's resources in order to achieve
  a common goal. Although individuals must be satisfied, the greater
  good is that of the group as a whole.

- *Compromise* requires that participants give up some of their demands
  and agree to settle for more limited goals. Although no one faction will
  be completely satisfied, none will be empty-handed.

- *Conflict* breaks out when members cannot agree on the rules of the
  game; social order breaks down, and the factions are left to fight it out.

- *Cooptation* is a way to reduce conflict by incorporating real or potential trouble-makers into the mainstream, as when women were permitted to vote or students are given representation on the College
  Council.

- *Coercion* is the application of force to settle disputes and get other people to agree to your terms.

Any given group may engage in a variety of processes to maintain itself
over time. In general, however, those groups and collectivities that develop
cooperative mechanisms for setting goals and working toward them last the
longest and rank highest on participant well-being (Orbell and Dawes 1993).

Within-Group Processes

In any small group, a division of labor tends to emerge in which some
individuals assume the *instrumental roles* needed for keeping an eye on the
goal and making sure that all necessary steps are taken. Other members take
on the more *expressive roles* of joker or healer, who relieves the tension and
binds up the wounds generated by instrumental leaders.

The *dramaturgical model* described in chapter 1 is especially useful in the
analysis of small-group interaction, where each encounter is a mini-drama
with one's identity at stake. The performance can be sustained only as long as
players agree to accept each other's claims. The next time you meet new peo-

ple at a party, pay attention to all the cues you send out to let them know just who you wish to be taken for; how attentive you are to their reactions; and then how you do the same to their presentations of self.

Interactions can also be analyzed in terms of the *exchange model*. People remain in relationships in which they feel that what they get back is a fair trade for what they give up, including using the time to do something else ("opportunity costs"). What is considered a fair exchange depends on each person's needs, resources, and alternative suppliers. If you have ever wondered "What does she see in him?" or "Why is he still going out with her?" ask yourself what each is giving and getting, why it might seem a fair trade-off to them, and what their alternatives are.

Formal Organizations

At the other end of the structural spectrum from the *Gemeinschaft* of the small group is the **formal organization**, the defining feature of the *Gesellschaft*. The following characterize formal organizations:

- Clearly defined rules for each status.

- Ranked statuses, from many below to few at top.

- Large size and complex division of labor.

- Duration longer than current members.

You will spend much of your life as a member of or being processed by formal organizations, including school systems, businesses, hospitals, and government agencies. The formal organization is here to stay because it is an efficient way to handle a large-scale task that needs to coordinate a lot of workers doing different things.

The most familiar type of formal organization in modern societies is the **bureaucracy**, a set of offices arranged in levels, broader at the base than the top, as shown in Figure 2.4. This type of triangular structure—a set of ranked status from least to most powerful—is called a **hierarchy**.

Here are some characteristics of a bureaucracy:

- Division of labor with all on same level doing comparable tasks.

- Each level reporting to next higher and supervising the lower level.

- Governed by impersonal rules applying to all at same level.

- Employment based on tested skills and promotion by merit.

- Records kept of all transactions.

- Impartial treatment—without fear or favor—within the bureaucracy and toward clients.

In other words, it should make no difference exactly who is sitting behind the desk as long as the person does the specific job assigned to the office. Although one may think of the bureaucracy as a peculiarly modern invention, its history goes back to the large-scale projects of ancient China and Egypt. Suppose that Pharaoh had asked you to build a pyramid; how would you

Figure 2.4 Organizational Chart of a Typical College

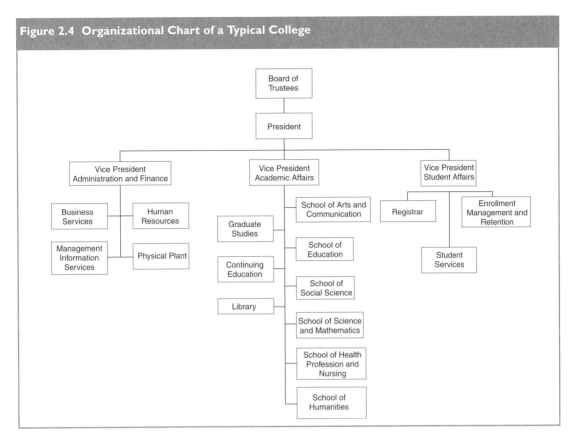

organize the vast numbers of different kinds of workers? You might end up with a chain of command not all that different from that of General Motors.

The bureaucracy with which you are most familiar, however, is probably your state motor vehicle division, a source of great annoyance for the very reasons that make bureaucracies work. Impartiality rules when the clerk behind the grille is nasty (or nice) to everyone. The thing to avoid is having the clerks hand out licenses on the basis of personal whim, only to blue-eyed

applicants, for example. You may also have complained about the number of forms to be filled out, but how would you feel if you lost your driver's license and no one could find any record of it?

The major dysfunction of formal organizations, however, is **goal displacement**, when the original purpose of the organization is replaced by the need to protect the jobs of the office holders. For example, when the March of Dimes, created to find a

You will spend much of your life being processed by formal organizations including school systems, businesses, hospitals, and government agencies. Good luck!

❖ ❖ ❖ ❖   cure for infantile paralysis, was rendered obsolete by the vaccines that effectively wiped out the disease, the organization did not fade away. The officers,
offices, and know-how just changed their mission—to deal with birth defects.

As discussed in chapter 9, the shift in modern economic systems from
manufacturing goods to producing information and services (education,
health care, crime control) could make the hierarchical model obsolete.
Designing software, for example, can best be done by a small group of status
equals assembled for that specific task, who then disband and reassemble in
other combinations depending on the job, following their thoughts rather
than a boss's orders. Even in the manufacturing sector, employers are finding
that cooperative work groups are often more productive than the traditional
top-down system. The new key to effective organization will be collaboration
among equals rather than top-to-bottom hierarchy (Rothschild 2000). Think
of the job you hope to have 20 years from now and how it might be organized
for maximum efficiency and personal satisfaction. 🖳4

Conclusion

In this chapter, you have been introduced to the twin pillars of sociological analysis: culture and social structure. Culture is the distinctive mix of
knowledge, beliefs, norms, traditions, and art that constitute a society's "way
of life." Social structure consists of both the institutions that ensure survival
and the patterns of relationships through which the culture is enacted in
everyday life.

You have also learned many other key terms: symbols, cultural universals, norms, sanctions, values, the work ethic, materialism, ethnocentrism,
cultural relativism, social system, status, role and its variations, primary and
secondary groups, expressive and instrumental behavior, social network, formal organization, and bureaucracy. These are the building blocks for understanding the chapters that follow. Many of these words have also become part
of the general vocabulary of educated persons, so you may also use them in
other contexts.

Surfing the Sociological Internet

🖳1   For a global trip of the world's cultures, visit:
       http://curry.edschool.virginia.edu/go/multicultural/
       http://dir.yahoo.com/Society_and_Culture/Cultures_and_
       Groups/Cultures/ or
       http://www.wsu.edu:8080/~dee/WORLD.HTM

🖳2   Promoting cultural relativism and combating ethnocentrism,
       see:
       http://www.primarysource.org/ which tries to bring American
       history and world cultures to life.

🖳3   For the sociology of culture and subcultures, visit:
       http://www.geocities.com/CollegePark/Quad/5889/cul-
       ture.htm
       http://dir.yahoo.com/Society_and_Culture/Cultures_and_

Groups/
Visit the following sites for examples of two different subcultures:
http://www.800padutch.com/amish.htm describes the Amish subculture and
http://members.aol.com/maggyblu/rocky1.htm to see how one sociologist studied the subculture of *The Rocky Horror Picture Show*.
View a new subculture in the making, cyberculture, at:
http://www.otal.umd.edu/~rccs/intro.html

🖥 4 Bureaucracy
Find out how the U.S. government bureaucracy works at:
http://encarta.msn.com/find/Concise.asp?ti=00339000

Glossary

Anomie A feeling of bewilderment when normative guidance is lacking or ambiguous.

Artifacts Material items such as pottery, tents, or spears.

Achieved Status Statuses that are thought to be gained by a person's own effort (e.g., education, income, and occupation).

Ascribed Status Statuses assigned because of who you are at birth.

Bipedalism Ability to walk on two feet.

Bureaucracy A formal organization characterized by rationality and efficiency, so that large-scale tasks can be accomplished.

Conspicuous Consumption The open display of wastefulness designed to impress others.

Cultural Relativism The ability to appreciate the content of other cultures without making value judgments.

Cultural Variability The variety of customs, beliefs, and artifacts devised by humans to meet universal needs.

Culture The ways of thinking, believing, and acting that are shared by members of a society.

Dyad A two-person group.

Ethnocentrism The belief that one's own culture is the best and therefore the standard by which other cultures are judged.

Expressive Relationships Relationships that are valued in their own right.

Folkways Norms that are a matter of custom of habit.

Formal Organization A social structure characterized by impersonality, ranked positions, large size, relative complexity, and long duration.

Gemeinschaft A way of life characterized by small, traditional communities, primary-group relationships, and intergenerational stability.

Gesellschaft A way of life common in large modern cities, involving contractual relationships, voluntary social bonds based on rational self-interest, and instrumental behavior.

Goal Displacement Occurs when the original purpose of an organization is replaced by the need to keep the organization going at all costs.

Group A group is characterized by a distinctive set of relationships, interdependence, and a sense of membership.

Hierarchy A set of ranked statuses from least to most powerful.

Heterogeneous Societies Made up of sizable numbers of citizens who worship different gods and are of varying skin colors and national origins.

Homogeneous Societies Made up of people who are similar in terms of race, religion, and ethnic background.

Instrumental Relationships Relationships that are maintained as a means to another goal.

Kinesics The study of nonverbal communication.

Laws Norms that govern behavior considered essential to group survival.

Master Status The trait with the strongest impact on how you appear to others.

Macro-Level Sociology Focuses on society as a whole or on social systems at a high level of abstraction.

Materialism The need to prove one's worth through accumulating objects of value.

Meso-Level Sociology Focuses on intermediate-level analysis such as organizational activity.

Micro-Level Sociology Focuses on smaller units of social systems, such as face-to-face interactions.

Mores Norms governing matters of moral and ethical importance, such as courtship conduct or showing respect to ancestors.

Norms Rules that regulate behavior and ensure social order.

Personal Agency The ability to affect one's own environment.

Primary Groups Close-knit, intimate groupings of individuals.

Role Behavior attached to each status.

Role Conflict Competing and conflicting demands stemming from a role set.

Role Overload Occurs when the total of role requirements overwhelm one's ability to fulfill them.

Role Partners People with whom one interacts in systems.

Role Set The collection of role partners.

Sanctions Reactions that convey approval or disapproval.

Secondary Groups Groupings that are more formal and impersonal than primary groups.

Social Network The sum total of an individual's group memberships.

Social Structure A collective reality that exists apart from individuals and forms the context in which people interact.

Status An individual's position in a social system.

Subculture Consist of variations of values, beliefs, norms, and behavior among social subgroups.

Symbol Signifies nothing in and of itself but which is given meaning by the agreement of group members.

Triad A three-person group.

Universals Elements of culture found in every society from the small gathering bands of the Amazon rain forest to the United States.

Values Refers to the central belief of a culture that provides standards against which norms can be judged.

Worldly Asceticism To live in the world as if one had taken a vow of poverty. ✦

Chapter 3

Becoming Social: Conformity and Deviance

❖ ❖ ❖ ❖   How do the majority of Japanese children become extremely law-abiding adults while many Jivaro boys grow into skilled headhunters and too many American infants end up as self-absorbed teenagers and adults? The socio-logical answer is the process called **socialization**, whereby the raw material of infancy is shaped into a functioning member of society. In addition, as in-dividuals internalize the culture in infancy and childhood, they are also learning about a "self"—who and what kind of person they are. This chapter covers such basic aspects of socialization as:

- How you become social.

- How you develop a self.

- Cultural and structural pressures to conform.

- Nonconformity (deviance) and its consequences.

Each society has a unique culture and social structure that provides the environment in which people become social. Since no one is born with knowledge of this environment, it must be learned. What *Homo sapiens* does have at birth is a wonderfully complex, reflexive mind that allows us to create culture and to adapt to all kinds of conditions. The key here is the physical helplessness of the human infant, born long before the brain and nervous sys-tem are fully wired and thus dependent on nurturing adults. This dependency creates a basic sensitivity to the expectations of others that never leaves you, although the objects of that sensitivity will change—from parents to peers, to lovers, to colleagues, to your own children.

Although the infant's body is relatively helpless, the growing brain is spin-ning with activity, registering sensations and processing information. Grad-ually, you realize that you are both separate from and connected to others; that what you do has an effect on them and vice versa; that a gurgle brings oh's and ah's, while a whine can lead to harsh words. But it is also part of the human condition that the mind that reflects on itself is never altogether cer-tain. And so you ask, over and over again, "Who am I?" "Am I loved?" "Am I doing the right thing?" And because you will never know for certain, you must depend on other people for reassurance and guidance. Identity is a pro-cess, not an endpoint.

What, then, would happen to an infant deprived of all but minimal social contact? What kind of speech and behavior would arise spontaneously? For-tunately, examples of **extreme isolation** are very rare, although they tell soci-ologists a great deal about human development, as illustrated in the case of Genie (Rymer 1993).

An apparently normal baby at birth, Genie spent her first 13 years in a small dark room, was rarely spoken to, fed only baby food, and often beaten by her father. In 1970, Genie and her almost incompetent mother escaped and came to the attention of welfare workers and social scientists. Genie knew only a few words and was unable to control her body movements. Clearly, neither mental nor physical growth unfolds automatically; babies eventually master language and walking only with the help of supportive adults. Genie's new caregivers—social workers and academics—had little success in teaching her language and self-care, while they fought endlessly among themselves over who was in charge of the case. After years of shuttling between foster homes and institutions, Genie lives today in a home for the retarded, still almost wordless and isolated. But she left a legacy of insights, namely that sustained nurturing is essential to mental and physical development and that *language is the key to humanness*.

In adulthood, also, extreme isolation has severe negative consequences. Solitary confinement is cruel (if not always unusual) punishment precisely because we need to talk to other people in order to remain sane. Otherwise we lose our sense of time, identity, and reality. Among survivors of German concentration camps, for example, it was the most isolated prisoners who suffered the greatest loss of mental stability (Goldhagen 1996). Because reality is socially constructed, it must be continually tested and verified against the perceptions of others. 🖥 1

The essential point is that to be human is to be social. You cannot survive and grow as an infant without being nurtured, and it is difficult to stay sane as an adult in isolation. In addition, social networks provide three other inputs essential to well-being across the life course:

1. **Affection**—the sense of being loved for yourself alone. How many times have you asked, "Do you really love me?" followed by "Really, really?" You can never be told often enough.

2. **Approval**—the knowledge that your behavior is normative. "How am I doing?" is another eternally asked question.

3. **Validation of self**—reassurance that you are who you claim to be.

The people whose affection, approval, and validation are most crucial to your emotional well-being are those whose rejection will hurt the most, which gives them great power over you. By the same token, you can accept or reject people who are dependent on your good will. Throughout life, we are especially sensitive to the threat of the withdrawal of affection by important role partners.

At this point, you may be asking, "Is the process entirely social? Are there no individual differences, no unique characteristics that set me off from everyone else?" Yes, there are. Each infant is a distinct mix of inherited tendencies toward certain types of behavior or appearance. Some will learn faster than others; some will be slower on their feet; some will be slim, others heavy; some calm, others fidgety, and so forth through a long list of traits with some inherited biological—genetic—basis. But these are only *predispositions*, tendencies that may or may not be fully developed. It is the interaction between biology (nature) and society (nurture) that produces the person. Even people born with great talent, such as those with perfect pitch, will not realize their potential as musicians without encouragement and training. The route to the concert hall remains "practice, practice, practice."

The family unit is a major source of affection, approval, and validation of the self.

Yet despite individual uniqueness and impulses that may not be fully
socialized, members of a given society do, to varying degrees, share a culture
and social structure, learn appropriate norms, and for the most part behave
within the society's acceptable limits. Only thus is society possible.

Socialization

Socialization is the process whereby you learned a single world of meaning as the one and only way to see things and interpret your experiences
(Berger and Luckmann 1966). Depending on the accident of birth, you could
have become a cannibal or a Calvinist, sexually chaste or promiscuous, war-
like or peaceable. There is no universal "human nature," only a flexible set of
responses to cultural demands, capable of change over time.

Developing from infant to child to adult is a process whereby you literally
"learn your place," including the statuses you will occupy and the roles
attached to those positions in social systems. Learning one's place involves
receiving the necessary information and having opportunities to rehearse the
role. **Anticipatory socialization** occurs when you practice the role in
advance of assuming the status, as when children play at being grown-ups or
when employees expecting a promotion dress more carefully. A related phenomenon is **role modeling**, where you copy the dress and manner of someone you admire, such as a teacher or media star.

Roles are performed before an audience of role partners, whose reactions
will affect your next move. They may react with **positive sanctions**,
responses that let you know how well you are doing, or with **negative sanctions**, which, like a bad review that pans your performance, may threaten
your self-esteem. Your reactions, in turn, will depend on how much you want
the approval and affection of that particular audience. Your choices are limited, however, typically either to changing your behavior or your role partners
or to convincing yourself that your partners do not really matter. Most people
find it easier to change their behavior than to continue to receive negative
feedback.

Socialization across the life course is a series of status entries and exits
that require **desocialization**, giving up the old, accustomed ways of thinking
and acting, and **resocialization**, learning new ones. Both processes go more
smoothly when you have a network of supportive friends and relatives. In
general, the research suggests that the wider and more varied your social circles, the more successful you will be in dealing with change and stress
(Turner, Wheaton, and Lloyd 1995).

Agents of Socialization

Networks of role partners function as **agents of socialization**, charged
with transmitting the culture and its rules. In more complex societies, more
agents of different kinds are needed to transmit all the information individuals need to function as adults. In a simple society, parents and peers would
suffice, but today, young people can use all the resources of an extended formal education, a variety of friendship circles, clubs and church groups, occupational mentors, and even the mass media.

Parents.   The first agents of socialization are the nurturers of infants. Usually, these are the biological parents, but the flexibility of *Homo sapiens* makes it possible for infants to relate to nonbiological parents and for other adults to take on the role of caregiver. This flexibility has served as an essential survival mechanism through the thousands of years of high maternal death rates. The fear of losing this most vital source of food and comfort makes an infant sensitive to every whim of his or her early nurturers, just as the caretakers learn to interpret the baby's gestures. Further, the quality of these interactions—the way in which the baby is held and cared for—can be as important as feeding or changing. Through these experiences, infants begin to develop the capacity for *empathy*, to put themselves in the place of others and imagine how they feel. 💻 2

Your culture was *internalized* (brought into your consciousness) when caregivers' expectations became part of your own thinking and when fear of letting them down became a prime motivator of your actions. To be sure, not all socialization is one-way. In a complex society characterized by rapid social change, children can be a source of information for parents. Consider the generations of immigrant children who translated English for their elders, and the many teenagers today who help their parents program the VCR and master the Internet. **Reciprocal socialization** takes place when the generations mutually influence the attitudes and knowledge base of one another.

As important as parents are in early socialization, they are not all-powerful. The belief that the first three years are the most crucial is being questioned today by psychologists as well as by sociologists (Kagan 2000). There is a long span between age three and adulthood in which all kinds of experiences and interventions take place, with profound impact on a person's emotions and behaviors. Current research also suggests that even in childhood, friendship groups of age-mates are as important as parents, if not more so, in the socialization process (Corsaro 1997; Harris 1998).

Peers.   **Peers** are equals, and the term peer group typically refers to those equal in age. In childhood and adolescence, peers are also status equals, in contrast to parents, who are superiors in terms of power. The inequality of parent-child relations makes some kinds of learning difficult, such as how to deal with other children or how to approach the opposite sex. Friends can tease and tolerate flawed role performances without the heavy emotional baggage of parental intervention. With peers, children create worlds of meaning, cultures in which they

The term peer group usually refers to people of the same age. In adolescence, peers become a major source of socialization. These teenagers are learning about trust in this circle activity.

❖ ❖ ❖ ❖

become active agents in their own socialization (Corsaro 1997). In adulthood, peers are essential agents of socialization to marriage, parenthood, retirement, and widowhood. But it is the peer groups of adolescence that have received most popular and scientific attention, largely negative.

Despite the anxiety they often produce, the peer groups of adolescence provide the necessary support for the difficult journey from dependent childhood to independent adulthood, from being judged by the particular values of one's ascribed status in the family to meeting universal standards of performance in achieved statuses. In other words, your friends help you grow up and out of the family nest. Most teenagers have figured out how to divide the socialization labor, with parents providing guidance on long-term goals while peers influence immediate lifestyle choices.

Teachers. There is a vast store of information and technical skills that you will need in the new millennium, which neither parents nor peers can convey. For this, you need increasingly longer years of formal education under the guidance of professionals. Teachers not only transmit knowledge but also can serve as models for responsible adulthood. Some may even pass along the sheer excitement of learning, of cultivating the life of the mind as an end in itself. These will be the ones you never forget. 💻 3

Media. The mass media consist of print and electronic channels of information and entertainment: newspapers, magazines, books, radio, television, recordings, and, most recently, the Internet. Contrary to popular opinion, there is little scientific evidence of a direct, consistent link between media exposure and subsequent behavior. Media effects are filtered through the social context in which you read and listen. What the media do accomplish, and quite powerfully, is to set the public agenda, the set of issues that grab our attention. With regard to socialization, the mass media provide a storehouse of role models, life styles, and vicarious experiences. Increasingly, also, the Internet, with its chat rooms and bulletin boards, provides an arena for role playing (see chapter 16). 💻 4

Subcultural Differences

Socialization is not a uniform process. It will vary by such ascribed variables as sex, race, religion, and ethnicity, as well as by the achieved statuses of parental education, income, and occupation. 💻 5 This brief overview mentions the two most powerful differences: parental occupation and the child's gender.

Parents' occupation. The work experience of parents has a strong effect on what and how they teach their children (Kohn and Slomczyski 1990). The major distinction is between (1) jobs that deal with people and ideas (typically, "white-collar") and (2) those that deal with machines and other inanimate objects (most often "blue-collar"). Although computer work straddles these categories—machines operated by white-collar workers—the crucial distinction is between more creative and more routine tasks. The first type of occupation often requires imaginative problem solving, verbal skills, and self-direction. As a consequence, these parents will value self-control, flexibility, and intellectual curiosity, even to the point of allowing the child to question parental authority. To achieve these goals, white-collar parents tend to use subtle psychological and verbal disciplining techniques that emphasize achievement motivation and self-reflection.

In contrast, most blue-collar work requires that one strictly follow orders, be punctual, and ask few questions. Based on their experiences, these parents will try to instill in their children respect for authority, conformity to parental norms, and mastery of technical skills. Disciplining is most often direct and physical, based on fear and designed to produce outward conformity and no sassing.

Thus, the nature of work—a structural variable—affects values that, in turn, influence disciplining techniques and ultimately the personality of the child. The more psychological approach tends to encourage creativity, internalized controls, and high achievement expectations. To a very great extent, these differences in child rearing contribute to the school performance and ultimate occupational choices of the children.

Box 3.1

Spare the Rod and Save the Child (and the Adult)

Perhaps the most important piece of advice that we authors can offer for when you become a parent is this, "Never hit a child." As most psychology textbooks will agree, physical punishment is probably the least effective way of changing behavior; it works only in the short run, if at all, and only when administered immediately and in proportion to the offense. Far more powerful and long lasting is the careful manipulation of rewards, especially affection and approval.

Not only is hitting a child relatively ineffective, but such punishments have many negative outcomes, especially a child's feelings of powerlessness, resentment, and lowered motivation to succeed in school or work (Straus 2000). Low grades and low self-esteem combine to limit occupational goals. For men, the more frequent the punishment as a child, the lower the income in adulthood. Boys become aggressive and girls depressed, and both are likely to experience continued family violence as adults (Swinford et al. 2000). The lessons learned by the child are that big people can hit little ones; that those who say they love you can hurt you; and that hitting is an acceptable way to resolve conflicts. It is very difficult to teach self-control to children when you have just lost your own.

As a parent, there will be many occasions when it will seem easier to strike out at a child than to make the effort to find a nonviolent resolution, but it will be well worth it if you want a creative, curious, self-confident daughter or son. Always ask, "What is it I really want my child to learn?" Physical violence does not work any better on adults. Hitting people who are weaker than you does not add much to the self-worth of either.

Gender differences. There is no doubt that agents of socialization have different expectations of girls and boys, based on what are assumed to be their major roles in adulthood—marriage and motherhood for females, paid employment for males—and act accordingly. In most families, for example, girls are still kept close to home, which may enhance their verbal skills but limits opportunities to explore the big world beyond and to develop the kind of abstract thinking necessary for mastering math and sciences (Entwisle et al. 1994). In contrast, sons are encouraged to wander far afield, where they can explore nature, take risks, meet other people, and develop a sense of independence. In many homes, the division of household labor still follows this pattern: girls get the inside chores, boys the outside ones.

As you may have experienced in grammar school and high school, a boy's popularity is often based on active, achieved statuses such as athletic ability and toughness, while a girl is rated on such passive, ascribed traits as appearance and family social position. These differences appear to persist even after three decades of increased opportunities for girls and women to achieve on their own merits (Eder, Evans, and Parker 1995; Adler and Adler 1998).

Learning language, rules, and roles is only one aspect of the socialization process. At the same time that you internalize the culture, and through the very same experiences, you also construct a sense of identity, a *self*, your self.⌨6

The Social Self

The **self**, for sociologists, is a set of perceptions about who and what kind of person you are. We also use the terms "self-concept" or "identity" to convey the sense of a socially constructed aspect of personality, never firmly fixed but developed through countless interactions. Because these messages are conveyed through face-to-face encounters, the study of the social self has been a special focus of symbolic interaction theorists.

James, Cooley, and the Social Self

The concept of the social self was introduced by the psychologist William James (1842–1910), who stated that you have as many selves as there are people who carry an image of you in their minds. In other words, there are many you's, one for each role partner. An interesting exercise would be to ask friends and acquaintances to pick three words to describe their impression of you and then see how many of these overlap.

Building on James' insight, social psychologist Charles Horton Cooley

The 'looking glass self' refers to the fact that we never see ourselves directly but only as a reflection of the impressions we make on other people.

(1864–1929) proposed that the self consists of a basic self-feeling shaped through interactions in primary groups. Cooley is best known for his concept of the **looking-glass self**. Just as a mirror reflects a reverse image, you can never see yourself directly but only as a reflection of the impressions you make on other people. Perceptions about identity, then, are based on: (1) how we think we appear to others; (2) how we perceive their judgments; and (3) how we feel about it. In this view, the self is never a finished object but a work in progress, as you actively manipulate your appearance and process the reactions of others (Cooley 1909).

Mead and the Interacting Self

A more elaborate analysis of the social self was the life work of George Herbert Mead (1863–1931). For Mead, the essential process is "taking the role of the other toward oneself." What this means is that the reflexive mind allows you to imagine how you appear to another person and to predict that person's response so that you can adjust your behavior accordingly. We internalize the norms of our society as we enact roles. Thus, mind, self, and society are all mutually constructed (Mead 1934).

Play and games. The imaginative leap into the mind of another person, so central to the development of self-concept, is an ability that matures throughout childhood as you enter increasingly complex role systems. For Mead, the infant's **play** is very serious business; it is the child's introduction to acting out roles such as daddy, doctor, or police officer. The child who says "naughty girl" to herself has taken on the role of the other in judging her own actions.

Games involve a much more sophisticated level of mental and physical abilities than simple play. Animals will roughhouse but they can never play games, because games are social constructions, with structure and rules. Players must internalize the entire system of roles. You do not learn how to be a shortstop in isolation from your relationship to all the other players on the team. This early exposure to complex systems is boot camp for all the secondary groups you join throughout life; it is an advantage more often encouraged for boys than for girls, although the gap has narrowed somewhat in recent years (Coltrane 1998).

The 'I' and the 'Me.' Mead's "self" is not a mere passive reflection of internalized norms but a dynamic construction of perceptions. The self emerges out of a conversation in your mind between a spontaneous, creative aspect that Mead called the "I" and the socialized "me," based on internalized attitudes of others. For example, right now, your "I" is probably longing to be free of this chapter, but your "me" is telling you that your instructor expects you to keep reading and you had better do so if you want to pass the course. Sometimes, the "I" wins and you drop the book for an evening with friends; other times, the "me" triumphs as you remember the long-range goal of graduating.

Significant and generalized others. Not all internalized expectations carry the same weight. Mead distinguished the influence of **significant others**, those persons whose affection, approval, and validation you most desire, from the strength of societal norms applied to anyone in a particular role, or the **generalized other.** Although both sets of expectations are in your mind, significant others are in a position to sanction behavior directly, hence their "significance."

Goffman and the Presentation of Self

For Erving Goffman (1922–1983), a key element in the interactionist model is *self-presentation*, or managing the impression we give to others. In this view, the presenting self is always at risk of rejection, so every encounter becomes a mini-drama in which each party tries to impress the other and gain control of the interaction. Think of your last job interview or blind date.

Role distance. Goffman spoke of a **virtual self** that awaits us in every role, the perfect embodiment of expectations for anyone occupying that status—the devoted homemaker, mad artist, or absent-minded professor. But some virtual selves may not be very appealing to our self-image. A college student with a part-time job at a fast-food outlet, for example, may resist the virtual self of "hamburger helper" and take every opportunity to let people know his true status, including bringing textbooks to work, in effect saying, "I am a prince, not a frog!" Other roles offer a virtual self so appealing that you eagerly become the person awaiting you in the role—for example, steady date.

Role distance refers to the space between self and self-in-the-role, ranging from *embracement* (literally, like young lovers, disappearing into the virtual self) to *rejection* (total denial of the virtual self, usually accomplished by exiting the status). Between these two are all shades of distance. Make a list of the statuses you occupy in the course of a day, evaluate the distance between self and the one that awaits you in each role, and then identify the distancing techniques you employ. In some situations, however, you may have little choice but to become the virtual self, regardless of your feelings, as shown in the "prison" study described below.

Box 3.2

The Mind as Jailer

In a famous experiment, Philip Zimbardo and his colleagues (1973) found that the line between self and self-in-role could be erased in a very short time under extreme conditions. The researchers placed an ad in a college paper for volunteers for a "study of prison life." Twenty-one young men, screened for physical health and emotional maturity, were randomly assigned the status of guard or prisoner in a carefully designed fake prison. With minimal formal instruction, stripped of their civilian identity and outfitted accordingly—shaved heads and ill-fitting clothes for prisoners, khaki uniforms and nightsticks for the guards—it took only a few days for the men to *disappear into the virtual self awaiting them in the role*. The guards quickly learned to enjoy unchecked power, and the prisoners acted in ways that invited further humiliation. The prisoners broke down mentally and physically so quickly that the entire experiment was called off before the week was out.

The researchers were astounded at the speed and ease with which assigned roles and the definition of the situation affected men who had been found emotionally fit only a few days earlier. Although the experiment was designed by psychologists, there was nothing in the men's personality profiles to explain their behavior. Rather, the researchers concluded with a ringing endorsement of the sociological perspective: *situational forces are stronger than personality factors*.

Other Views on Self Development

Some social scientists have found the concept of the social self much too limited in explaining the wide range of individual differences among people who have been brought up similarly. This *oversocialized* perspective has been criticized for minimizing the effects of biological and psychological components of personality and behavior (Wrong 1961). Other critics object to the sociological model's emphasis on flexibility and change, arguing that some aspects of self are relatively stable across the life course, such as friendliness, anxiety level, resistance or openness to change, and the ability to plan ahead (Costa et al. 1987; Clausen 1993). For most people and most traits, however, even feelings of satisfaction, well-being, and connectedness are strongly influenced by immediate experiences. In general, predicting adult personality on the basis of childhood traits is very risky business (Settersten 1999; Kagan 2000).

Nonetheless, sociologists are increasingly attentive to the **affective** (emotional) and **cognitive** (thinking) dimensions of the development of self. The work of several leading figures is briefly reviewed in the following section.

Sigmund Freud and the Control of Impulse

One of the most influential thinkers of the twentieth century, Sigmund Freud (1856–1939), established the medical specialty of psychoanalysis, which involves the study of unconscious motivations and the treatment of emotional distress resulting from tension between these impulses and the requirements of being socialized. Although many of his ideas reflect the world of upper-middle-class Europeans in the late nineteenth century, several of Freud's insights are also major contributions to the sociological perspective.

The conflict between self and society. In *Civilization and Its Discontents* (1930), Freud examines, from a psychological perspective, the same assumption that underlies sociology: *Society is possible only when individual actions are brought under control of social norms.* What Freud meant by "civilization" is what we have been calling "culture," the rules that limit the expression of personal desire in the interests of group survival. But because basic biological drives can never be fully socialized, a dynamic tension exists between the individual seeking instant gratification and the collective good. Social order, therefore, depends on everyone's willingness to forgo immediate pleasures in order to establish stable relationships. Civilization/culture is based on the control of impulse by the reflexive mind, and socialization is the progressive renunciation of sources of instant gratification.

Stages of development. These renunciations take place in a series of emotionally stressful episodes in infancy and childhood. The first of these comes when you must give up the all-embracing comfort of being cuddled and fed at the same time. Being weaned from breast or bottle generates a lot of anger that cannot be directly expressed for fear of losing the affection of caregivers. The best you can do is throw a minor fit, spill your food, and bury the anger deep in the unconscious mind. But you will have learned the first two lessons of social life: Rules are made by the more powerful, and life is full of hard knocks.

In the next stage, you are asked to control bladder and bowels, to become toilet trained and to deal with this loss of personal freedom. Eventually you give up the unequal struggle for control of your body and send another deposit of anger to the subconscious. The third critical period, in late childhood, involves dealing with strong and disturbing feelings of intense desire and hostility directed toward your parents. These tensions are resolved by renouncing the possibility of sexual gratification within the family and by directing sexual feelings toward members of the opposite sex who are not family members.

Although Freud emphasized the turmoil within the child's mind (psyche), the events he describes are social processes, interactions between the individual and adults representing the social order. As with any socialization experience, fear of losing affection and approval motivates conformity. The norms are internalized, the dream of complete fulfillment given up, and order is restored. But those unfulfilled desires and deposits of anger are never fully repressed; they can bubble up from the unconscious and cause mental distress.

The ego and its defenses.   It is the fear of losing control that leads us to develop protective mechanisms called **ego defenses** (Swanson 1988). Defenses are techniques for dealing with unacceptable impulses, and include outright denial, blaming others, finding scapegoats, and inventing excuses (rationalizations). From the societal viewpoint, the defenses protect the group from the threat of individuals who might become so distressed that they "lose it."

The ego is but one element in Freud's scheme of the psyche, which has three aspects: (1) the *id*, representing impulsive desires; (2) the *superego*, consisting of internalized norms that restrict behavior; and (3) the *ego*, that part of the self that moderates between desire and control. As central as the concept was, Freud never really clarified his understanding of ego functions. This was left to later theorists, such as Erik Erikson.

Erikson and Ego Development

The idea of *psychosexual development* has been elaborated by contemporary psychologists who depart from Freud in two directions. First, the stages of personality growth have been extended to cover the entire life course, and, second, the emphasis has shifted exclusively to the ego as a set of self-perceptions, with little attention to id (innate impulses) or superego (repressive norms).

Today, as in the 1940s, in adolescence, the developmental task is that of identity formation, a sense of selfhood, often aided by one's peer group.

The most influential of these post-Freudian formulations is that of Erik Erikson (1902–1990) who proposed that at various moments in the life course, individuals face particular challenges that can lead to a more complex organization of self-perceptions and, hence, ego growth, or, in case of failure, to arrested development.

Erikson (1959) described eight stages of self-development in psychological terms, but you can easily see that he is also describing major life cycle transitions in statuses and roles. That is, what Erikson sees as internal growth actually reflects changes in the social world of the individual who is exiting and entering status/role systems.

- *Stage 1.*   From early experiences with caregivers, the infant develops a sense of either basic *trust* or *mistrust* in its social environment.

- *Stage 2.* In the next few years, the child learns new skills and emerges with a feeling of *autonomy* (self-direction) or *doubt* and *shame* over inability to cope.

- *Stage 3.* The 4- to 5-year-old's exploration of the environment and dealing with peers produces either self-confidence (*initiative*) or *guilt* over failure.

- *Stage 4.* Between ages 6 and 13, the focus shifts from home to school, where the child develops either *industriousness* (task achievement) or feelings of *inferiority*.

- *Stage 5.* In adolescence, the developmental task is that of *identity formation*, a firm sense of selfhood, in contrast to *identity confusion*.

- *Stage 6.* The great challenge of young adulthood is that of establishing stable love relationships, with either *intimacy* or *isolation* as the outcome.

- *Stage 7.* Work, parenthood, and community responsibilities are the major concerns of mature adulthood, characterized by *generativity* (active involvement) or its opposite, *self-absorption* and personality *stagnation* of those who do not contribute to the well-being of others and society as a whole.

- *Stage 8.* Even the last stage of the life course poses a developmental challenge: finding continuity and meaning in one's life choices—*integrity*—or, unable to break out of self-absorption, giving way to *despair*.

Erikson's alternatives represent the very best or worst outcomes. Few people go through these experiences at just the right ages and with only one result; most of us meet life's expected and unexpected challenges with only partial success—some self-confidence, many doubts, general satisfaction, and lingering anxiety. From the sociological perspective, Erikson's stages coincide with major transitions in status and role sets that require a reorganization of self-perceptions precisely because situations, role partners, and societal expectations have changed.

Piaget and Cognitive Development

In addition to affective factors that play a part in development, social scientists are concerned with changes in the way the mind works, or **cognitive** factors. A leading figure in this field was the Swiss psychologist, Jean Piaget (pronounced pea-ah-jay) (1896–1980). From his observations and conversations with children at play and school, Piaget found that the brain processes information differently depending on the age and social experiences of the child. For example, in the game of marbles, the youngest players accepted the rules as carved in stone, while slightly older ones realized that rules can be modified to fit the circumstances, and even more mature youngsters discovered that they could invent entirely new games. For Piaget, each stage represented a higher form of mental functioning, from unquestioned obedience to self-direction. For the sociologist, what the mature children discovered was the central insight that the rules (norms) are social constructions, not given from on high but worked out by the players in the system.

❖ ❖ ❖ ❖   ## Kohlberg and Moral Development

Building on Piaget's model, the American psychologist Lawrence Kohlberg proposed a six-stage theory of moral development—of knowing "right" from "wrong." The stages run from a "premoral" state in which the child acts out of fear of punishment or a desire to please significant others to the highest level, where one acts out of an autonomous commitment to universal principles of justice and human dignity (Kohlberg 1981). This model has been faulted for its ethnocentric bias in assuming that mid-twentieth-century liberal American values represented the highest good.

A more serious problem is that, as with most psychological theorizing, the claim to discover universal processes fails to account for variations by race, sex, income, and education. White, middle-class, male development becomes the standard, and those who fall short are considered morally deficient. It is not surprising, then, that the sons of white-collar families did best on Kohlberg's tests. What he was really measuring were the effects of socialization to a particular subculture.

Gilligan and 'Different Voices'

When researchers found that girls and women answered their questions differently from boys and men, they assumed that female levels of moral functioning were naturally inferior to those of males. It was left to one of Kohlberg's students, Carol Gilligan (1982), to point out that gender differences need not signify superiority and inferiority but, rather, reflected different ways of approaching moral dilemmas. Because of their more dependent upbringing and their family-based responsibilities, girls and women tend to see problems in terms of personal relationships. Boys and men, in contrast, are encouraged to break away from dependency on their mother, to reject things feminine, and to see themselves as independent actors who judge dilemmas in terms of universal abstractions such as "truth" and "justice." In adulthood, these processes produce men who fear attachment and women who fear abandonment. You may have noticed this already.

For Gilligan and other contemporary scholars, neither mode of problem solving is innate. Moral reasoning is deeply influenced by socialization practices and by structural factors that assign infant care exclusively to women. This suggests that if men were to be deeply involved in child rearing, they, too, might be sensitive to relationships (Risman 1998); also, if women were fully involved in work and politics, they would tend to think the way most men do.

In any event, socialization is the basic process through which you learn to function in society and gradually form a self-concept. From the society's standpoint, socialization is the most powerful guarantee of social order. Once the norms are internalized, you become your own monitor. Yet none of us is so fully socialized that we follow all the rules all the time. Deviation from the norms is the subject of the following section.

Deviance and Social Control

Because conformity to norms is the bedrock of social order, all societies have powerful techniques for ensuring that most people do what is expected of them most of the time. The intensity of infant socialization is the first and most effective line of defense against violations of the normative order. **Deviance** refers to acts that fall outside the socially constructed limits of acceptable behavior. Actually, deviant behavior is constructed whenever a norm is defined; by describing what is appropriate (normative), we automatically create a category of "non-normative."

Durkheim and the Societal Reaction Model

Although it is always tempting to locate deviance within the individual— a moral flaw or "bad seed"—most sociologists follow Durkheim (1912/1961) in viewing deviance as a matter of definition, that is, how an act is interpreted. What makes it deviant is the societal reaction; the same behavior could be excused under some circumstances, honored under other conditions, or heartily condemned. For example, killing someone can be "justifiable homicide" if done in self-defense, "heroic" if done in wartime, and plain old "murder" under other circumstances. Same act, different contexts.

It also matters who does it. In many societies, husbands who kill adulterous wives are defending their honor, but wives who attack a philandering husband are prosecuted because women have no personal honor to defend. Same act, different gender norms. Similarly, if a wealthy woman and her maid were each caught shoplifting, would their actions be similarly defined and prosecuted? One suspects that Mrs.Van Arsdale's attorney would plead mental distress, whereas Maisie, the maid, is clearly a thief and would be dealt with accordingly. Same act, different degrees of social power.

These examples illustrate a key insight of sociology: *All social action must be interpreted in context: who does what to whom under which circumstances.* In addition, because deviance is a social construction, perceptions of what falls within or outside normative boundaries are always shifting. Sometimes, it depends on where the activity takes place. In several Southern states, for example, gambling is fine when done in the church bingo hall but the Devil's work when conducted by the state. The historical period also matters, as illustrated by the history of cigarette smoking in America. In the 1920s, a period of great cultural liberation, smoking in public became a symbol of modern sophistication and equality for women. If you watch movies from the 1930s and 1940s, you can barely see the actors for all the smoke. And for the next two decades, a nonsmoker was considered a bit "square." But as information on the health hazards of smoking became widely known, the normative was transformed into the deviant. Today, it is the smokers who violate the norms, forced to huddle outside their office building to engage in their vice, perceived as people unable to control their impulses. Smoking has now been redefined by the American Psychiatric Association as Nicotine Dependence Disorder and has been added to the list of addictive diseases requiring psychiatric treatment—the ultimate step in the social construction of deviance (*Diagnostic and Statistical Manual* 1994).

Social Functions of Deviance

Although deviance is typically viewed as a threat to social order, Durkheim also pointed out that it serves a number of positive functions. Not only is it impossible to wipe out all nonconformity, it may not be desirable. Acts that may offend you personally can have positive effects for the group as a whole.

Deviance as a unifying force. Whenever you join in condemning the deviant, you actually reaffirm and strengthen the group's commitment to the rules and to one another. Uniting in righteous anger, we come together and create what Durkheim called the **public temper,** a set of shared ideas of right and wrong. When Americans joined in condemning Iraq's invasion of Kuwait, enveloping the nation in a sea of yellow ribbons, our common identity was reaffirmed and woe to anyone who dissented.

Deviance as a boundary marker. Particularly in periods of shifting norms, the public identification and punishment of offenders serves to draw a clear line between what is acceptable and what is not, between "us" the virtuous and "them" the wrong-doers. Such **boundary setting** reduces confusion and reinforces the normative consensus. In other words, the violators let the rest of us know just how far we can go.

Deviance as a safety valve. All societies must deal with potentially disruptive human impulses. Anger, frustration, and inappropriate sexual urges must be siphoned off in relatively harmless ways so as not to disturb such basic systems as family, workplace, and school. Some deviance, then, will be permitted because it serves to release unacceptable impulses under controlled conditions. This is the **safety valve** function of "red light" districts, where prostitution and adult sex shops are located, far from home, workplace, and school. Even as we unite in righteous anger at immorality, we often wink. Notice that brawling is often tolerated as long as it is confined to the parking lot outside the bar or to the cheap seats at sporting events (Kivel 1999).

Deviance as the cutting edge of social change. A society without deviance would be one in which nothing new ever happened, a clearly dysfunctional situation. Just as flexibility and adaptability are the keys to human evolution and survival, so, too, is the ability to undergo change peaceably a requisite for the survival of a society. In this sense, some forms of deviance, such as political protests, can be the cutting edge of social change (chapter 16).

In most societies, young adults are in the forefront of demonstrations against the existing order. Because they are not yet fully integrated into mainstream institutions, college youth have greater freedom to challenge the norms. There is nothing like a family, mortgage, and full-time job to dampen revolutionary fervor. Most movements for social change throughout the world today are largely fueled, if not led, by college students—but rarely in the United States. The one time that large numbers of American students had an effect on public policy was in the 1960s protests against the Vietnam War. However, the sight of unruly students burning flags and occupying college buildings led other Americans to close ranks in defense of existing norms; blue-collar workers in hardhats broke up student demonstrations; college officials called in the local police; parents and politicians deplored the selfish ingratitude of youth; and the National Guard fired real bullets at Kent State and Jackson State Universities. Order was quickly restored and traditional values reaffirmed. Although the protests probably changed some aspects of the campus, the long-term result was to reinforce the power of the school administration. The long hair and sloppy clothing, even the loosening of sexual norms, could be tolerated, but not the challenge to authority.

Other expressions of discontent are carefully organized efforts to enact crucial changes in existing laws and customs. These **principled challenges to the norms** often involve the risk of arrest and prosecution. For example, the African-American college students who defied law and custom in the 1960s by sitting down at a department store lunch counter were making a principled challenge to the practice of racial segregation. Their deviance began a chain of events that ultimately changed the face of the nation and its legal structure (Morris 1984; McNair Barnett 2000).

Principled challenges today can be found among antinuclear activists, animal rights crusaders, and on both sides of the great debate over abortion in the United States. Defying the law carries great risks—not only the scorn typically heaped on deviants but also the full force of agents of social control.

Keeping You in Line: Mechanisms of Social Control

The term **social control** refers to all the pressures on you to conform. Group survival, remember, depends on most members doing what is expected of them most of the time. Predictability is the basis of social order, which is why socialization is so crucial. But we would be robots and not humans if we did not violate some norms some of the time. Some nonconformity will simply go unnoticed, while other actions come to the attention of **agents of social control**, those charged with enforcing the norms.

Minor infractions are typically dealt with through **informal controls**, expressions of disapproval from significant others. A raised eyebrow or cold shoulder is enough to tell you that you risk their affection and approval. If their response is important to your sense of well-being, you will probably change. But when informal sanctions fail, and your behavior is defined as a "problem," official agents may be called in.

Formal agents of social control occupy statuses that give them the power of official sanctioning. Such agents include mental health professionals, social workers, religious leaders, and those who make the laws and enforce them. It is they who decide whether your actions threaten social stability. People who do not conform are called "sick," while "healthy" is defined as conforming to expectations.

If the deviant behavior continues despite loss of support from significant others and the efforts of formal agents, the offender is simply removed from the community. This is the function of prisons and mental hospitals—to contain those who cannot control themselves. No society can afford to let its citizens do whatever they feel like doing whenever they want to.

Formal agents of social controls have official power to enforce laws.

Explaining Deviance

"Why do they do it?" is the first question most people ask, in the belief that a single cause will explain complex behavior of any kind, especially a cause that lies within the individual, in their genetic make-up or childhood experiences.

Biological Theories

Although some mental illnesses are clearly linked to some organic factor—brain damage, chemical imbalance, or genetic defect—the great majority of deviant behaviors cannot be directly related to a biological trait. The most that can be claimed is that several interacting genetic influences might produce a predisposition to act in a particular way (Fishbein 1990). In addition, some physical conditions such as learning disabilities, nervous system disorders, and physical handicaps can lead to rejection by "normal" people and thus reinforce deviant tendencies.

Nonetheless, the search for a single, easily identified marker for criminal deviance, in particular, has produced one discredited theory after another: head shape, body size, unusual chromosome patterns. For example, a flurry of speculation was set off in the 1970s by the finding that there was a higher than expected incidence of an extra "Y" (male) chromosome among prison inmates. Researchers speculated that somehow supermasculinity led to aggressive antisocial acts. In actuality, the chromosomal pattern turned out to be almost as common in the general population as among prisoners, and it was primarily associated with low intelligence and extreme tallness—precisely the kind of person likely to be identified by witnesses and caught by the police (Witkin et al. 1976).

Psychological Theories

The belief that deviance is caused by a moral flaw or personality disorder is as popular as ever. Contemporary psychiatry has replaced the "bad seed" with a more scientific vocabulary: psychopath, sociopath, or anti-social personality. But the reasoning here is often circular: How do you know John or Jane Doe is a sociopath? Because he or she has done something awful. Why has he or she done something awful? Because they are sociopaths. The true test of any theory is if it can predict *in advance* what kind of person will commit which act, and, as you learned from the fake prison (earlier in this chapter) and the Milgram experiments (chapter 2), psychological profiles are of little value in predicting behavior. Far more important was the immediate setting and the role players' definition of the situation.

The childhood factors with most predictive power are less psychological or biological than social and economic. Poverty, overcrowding, malnutrition, abusive families, ineffective schools, and dangerous neighborhoods are all far more important than personality traits in accounting for physical and emotional problems or criminality. Violent families and neighborhoods tend to breed violent children (McCord 1997; Rhodes 1997).

The interaction of social, emotional, and biological factors is illustrated by the example of lead poisoning. Children living in poorly built housing will be exposed to lead poisoning, which affects the nervous system, lowering IQ and the ability to control oneself. These effects lead to school failure and lowered employment opportunities, which then reduce the chances of success in marriage, and so forth (Denno 1990). The spiral of failure will lead some to drugs, others to madness, and still others to crime. Remaining in poverty means that the next generation of children will be exposed to dangerous lead levels, the cycle is repeated, and some researchers will claim to have evidence that deviance is inherited.

Sociological Models

The sociological study of deviance has produced a number of theoretical models and concepts. ⌨ 7 As summarized in Table 3.1, these can be arranged along two dimensions: (1) level of analysis—macro or micro, and (2) focus on the social context or on societal reactions.

Table 3.1 A Typology of Theories of Deviance		
	Focus	
Level	Social Origins	Social Reactions
Macro (societal level)	Disorganization Anomie Opportunity structure Poverty Deviant subcultures	Conflict models Social control models
Micro (individual's environment)	Social learning Differential association Group controls	Labeling Primary and secondary deviation Stigma Deviant career

From George S. Bridges, "Deviance Theories." Adapted with permission of Simon & Schuster/Macmillan Reference from *Encyclopedia of Sociology*, Edgar F. Borgatta, Editor in Chief. Volume 1, pp. 476–487. Copyright © 1992 by Edgar F. Borgatta and Marie K. Borgatta. Reprinted with permission.

Focus on contextual variables.   At the macro level, or "big picture," some researchers have focused on the **social disorganization** produced when communities are destroyed by trends in the wider society, as when small towns are isolated by superhighways or when the only factory in town is closed down or when jobs flee to the suburbs. Where local church and civic leaders have lost control, adults experience anomie, while gangs take over the lifespace of adolescents.

Another structural model looks at the "fit" between culturally valued goals and access to legitimate means of achieving them. In the United States, the major goal is economic success and the recognized path is through education and hard work. Robert K. Merton (1957) refined Durkheim's concept of **anomie** to describe what happens when the two sides of the equation—goals and means—do not fit: (1) People who accept the goals and can achieve them legitimately tend to uphold the norms (*"conformists"*). (2) In contrast, those

✦ ✦ ✦ ✦   who desire worldly success but cannot get a decent education or find challenging employment will devise new and probably illegal ways to get ahead ("*innovators*"). (3) A third group, realizing that fame and fortune are out of reach, measures success by rigid conformity to the rules, as exemplified by the bureaucrat obsessed with details ("*ritualists*"). (4) Some individuals will reject both the goals and the approved means and drop out into alternative life styles, drugs, or mental illness ("*retreatists*"), while still others will attempt to replace the current system with new values and avenues of achievement ("*rebels*").

In the gap between high hopes and limited resources, deviant subcultures emerge to do what any subculture does—offer an alternative view of

reality, the friendship of peers, and protection from condemnation by outsiders (Cohen 1955). Faced with blocked opportunity structures, members of deviant subcultures define success in terms of what they can achieve, such as sexual conquests.

At the micro-level, theories about the origins of deviance examine the immediate context. The classic work of Edwin Sutherland (1939) proposes that deviant behavior is learned in the same

Some individuals reject both the goals and the approved means and drop out into alternative lifestyles or drugs.

way as any other behavior, namely, through peer interaction, or differential association. If you value money, you could become a stockbroker, bank robber, or physician, depending on the definitions of the situation and behavioral reinforcements of your primary groups.

Differential association is a variation of the social learning model that sees behavior as conditioned by cost-benefit calculations. You will do that which brings the most rewards (in affection, approval, material goods) at the least cost (in time, energy, risks to self-image). Fear of punishment is far less powerful than the ability of the deviant subculture to reward its members with the respect that the rest of society withholds.

A final micro-level focus on causal factors emphasizes group controls that stem from being integrated into mainstream institutions—family, school, work, and community (Gottfredson and Hirschi 1990). Individuals who are embedded in these conforming subcultures have a stake in the stability of these systems. When ties to conventional norms are broken—through divorce, job loss, or residential moves—people become "structurally available" for recruitment to a deviant subculture. Control theory assumes that you make a rational decision, weighing the relative benefits and costs of your actions, potential rewards and possible losses. It is the *certainty*, not the severity, of sanctions that has greatest weight. If the likelihood of being caught is very low, it matters little if the penalty is being hanged at dawn. In addition, people vary in their levels of self-control as well as opportunity structures, so that some will be more available than others for whatever trouble comes their way (Longshore 1998).

Focus on societal reaction. The study of societal reaction at the macro-level focuses on the question of "who has the power to define and enforce the norms?" Laws are typically made by people of some substance, whose behavior is then taken as the standard against which deviance is defined. In the United States, historically, definitions of deviance and efforts at social control have been directed at the activities of the poor and powerless (Liska 1992). Who else would loiter or spit in the street or hang out the laundry? Even today, penalties for dealing and using crack cocaine, favored by the urban poor, are many times harsher than for using powder cocaine, the preferred habit of the rich and powerful. Race and ethnicity also come into play; people who look different from the enforcers are likely to be seen as threatening, which is why police are more likely to shoot at a minority male than an equally violent white person (Liska and Yu 1992).

At the micro-level, societal reaction models are primarily concerned with the messages exchanged in face-to-face encounters. How do family, friends, and other agents of social control react? How do their reactions affect self-image and subsequent behavior? The key concept here is labeling, the process through which a given act or aspect of appearance is defined as deviant (Becker 1963). In essence, what is deviant is what the powers-that-be say it is. Not all violations of the norms become visible, in which case one can avoid the label. But once the label is applied, correctly or not, the process develops its own logic. Notice that it is not the original act but the reaction to it that matters.

Primary deviance refers to the original violation, which, even if noticed, can be overlooked or excused (Lemert 1972). Artists, for example, are expected to look and act in ways that would be deviant among stockbrokers. How many times have you driven over the speed limit because you needed to be on time for an appointment without ever seeing yourself as a "dangerous driver"? Yet, if you had been stopped and given a ticket by a police officer, you could no longer claim to be innocent of wrongdoing.

Secondary deviance occurs once you have been identified and labeled. The labeling affects how other people perceive and deal with you, and it enters into your self-image. If everyone thinks of you as a junkie, it is very hard to stay drug-free. Might as well have a snort since that is what they expect and they would not believe otherwise. In this way, labeling serves as a *self-fulfilling prophecy*, by setting in motion a chain of actions and reactions that make the original expectations come true (Merton 1968).

This process constitutes the deviant career, the last step of which involves seeking out others who share the label and joining the deviant subculture, where you will be accepted and protected. Heavy drinkers hang out at the neighborhood bar, drug users have their networks, couples without children socialize with other nonparents, and widows seek out other single women. The label serves as a master status through which all other perceptions are filtered. Notice how many other characteristics you assume about people who are overweight. Often these associations vary by gender, as when tall men are typically thought to be extremely competent, while tall women can seem intimidating.

❖ ❖ ❖ ❖   Some people escape the labeling process because their deviance goes unnoticed; others are considered relatively harmless "characters"; and still others are considered eccentric, strange but not threatening. Some eccentrics are tolerated because they are familiar (the town drunk) or are expected to be different (computer geeks) or are protected by powerful colleagues (womanizing politicians) or are so rich and famous that they are above ordinary standards (Ross Perot or Dennis Rodman). 🖥 8

The Medicalization of Deviance

A major issue in the sociology of deviance today is the medicalization of deviance, the tendency to define and treat deviant behaviors according to the medical model, that is, as diseases rather than as social constructions. 🖥 9 Thus, someone who combines masculine and feminine traits is now said to suffer from "gender identity disorder," when the problem is in society's inability to recognize more than two sexes or genders (see chapters 4 and 6). Since 1980, the number of mental disorders recognized by the American Psychiatric Association has tripled, from 106 to over 300. Because it is unlikely that 200 new diseases suddenly appeared, something else must be going on, namely the extension of control over new sets of patients and the money to study and treat them. This process is illustrated by the example of excessive drinking, now called "alcoholism," as seen in Box 3.3.

Box 3.3

Drinking and Deviance

Are alcoholics diseased? Yes, you can get sick from overdrinking, and, yes, some people get drunk faster than others, but is this a disease in the same way as measles? There is some evidence of a genetic influence—not a "drinking gene" but some combination of predispositions that affect only men whose overuse begins in adolescence (Pihl et al. 1990). For the vast majority of "problem drinkers," the social environment is key. Think of the times you have had just one more, not from any inner craving but because your friends insisted and you did not want to be the party pooper.

A major difficulty with medicalization is that the operative definitions, such as "overdrinking" or "problem drinker" are not medical judgments but sociological variables. "Overdrinking," for example, is a very relative term; what is ordinary alcohol consumption for Finnish men would put most Americans under the table. "Problem drinking" is an even more slippery concept. In general, drinking is defined as a problem not when it reaches some medical threshold but when it starts to interfere with family and work responsibilities (Roman 1991).

In addition, the most common "cure" for overdrinking is not medical but profoundly social. Alcoholics Anonymous and other 12-step programs provide a *supportive community* or subculture in which a new identity can be forged. Fear of losing the approval of these new significant others becomes the prime motive for behavior change. The medical vocabulary is designed to help the "addict" overcome guilt. It is far easier to live with a disease ("It happened to me") than with a moral flaw ("I did an awful thing") and one's family is also relieved of responsibility.

Despite the difficulties in the medical model, new behaviors are continually added to the list. No sooner had masturbation and homosexuality been removed from the index of mental illnesses than new ones took their place, such as Caffeine Intoxication and Oppositional Defiant Disorder ("argues with adults" and "intentionally annoys people"). Tobacco addiction and compulsive gambling have also been added, which probably has more to do with health insurance coverage than with science (Mirowsky and Ross 1989), especially now that doctors also get to treat "Nicotine Withdrawal Disorder" (*Diagnostic and Statistical Manual* 1994).

Conclusion

This chapter has examined the powerful forces that promote conformity, beginning with the internalization of norms in childhood to the influence of informal and formal agents of social control. You have also learned about the self-concept and the variations on the theme of the social construction of self. Yet, despite these pressures, all societies have to deal with nonconforming behaviors. The functions and dysfunctions of deviance and its control are discussed from a sociological perspective. Although biological and psychological factors are noted throughout the chapter, the major theme is the extent to which all these processes are structured at both the macro- and micro-levels.

Surfing the Sociological Internet

Socialization

1. http://www.nwmissouri.edu/nwcourses/martin/general/socialization/168108.html offers a slide show on socialization, the major theorists, and a discussion of the effects of isolation on children, including Genie.

2. For issues on children and health care, see: http://www.beritsbest.com/SeriousStuff/Health/index.shtml http://www.cyfc.umn.edu/ is the consortium for children, youth, and family well-being.

3. http://www.kidpower.org/ helps children and teens empower themselves at school and in their neighborhoods.
    Helping children become good citizens: http://www.hud.gov/kids/

4. For reports on media and development, see: http://www.cyfc.umn.edu/Media/effects.html
    and http://www.kff.org/content/1999/1535/

5. For international youth connections, go to http://www.yesintl.com/title2.htm

6. For more links related to children, see: http://dir.yahoo.com/Society_and_Culture/Cultures_and_Groups/Children/

 **_Deviance_**

🖥7   Sociological theories and perspectives on deviance can be found at:
http://www.hewett.norfolk.sch.uk/curric/soc/crime/crim.htm
http://www.geocities.com/CollegePark/Quad/5889/index.htm
A deviance map is available at: http://www.hewett.norfolk.sch.uk/curric/soc/crime/devmap.htm

🖥8   A selection of readings on deviance and links to other related sites can be found at:
http://www.extend.indiana.edu/courses/soc/socs320b/lesson1/disc1a.htm

🖥9   For links on deviance, mental illness, and stigmatized groups, see:
http://www.middlebury.edu/~sa288s97/devlks.html

Glossary

Affective   Emotional dimension of the development of self.

Agents of Social Control   Those charged with enforcing the norms.

Agents of Socialization   Individuals and organizations responsible for transmitting the culture.

Anomie   A person's sense of bewilderment in situations where norms are absent, unclear, or confusing.

Anticipatory Socialization   Practicing a role in advance of assuming the status.

Approval   The knowledge that one's behavior is acceptable.

Blocked Opportunity Structures   The absence of legitimate means to success.

Boundary Setting   Public identification and punishment of offenders makes clear what behavior is not acceptable.

Cognitive   The thinking dimension of the development of self.

Desocialization   Giving up the old, accustomed ways of thinking and acting.

Deviant Subcultures   Groups that offer an alternative view of reality, friendships, and protection from condemnation by outsiders.

Deviance   Acts that fall outside the socially constructed limits of acceptable behavior.

Deviant Career   Steps leading to joining the deviant subculture, where one is accepted and protected.

Differential Association   Model saying that deviant behavior is learned in primary groups and involves the same processes as the learning of nondeviant behavior.

Eccentric   Behavior that is strange but not threatening.

Ego Defenses   Techniques for dealing with unacceptable impulses; includes outright denial, blaming others, finding scapegoats, and inventing excuses.

Extreme Isolation   Deprivation of all but minimal social content.

Formal Agents of Social Control Those who occupy statuses that give them the power of official sanctioning, including mental health professionals, social workers, religious leaders, and law enforcement personnel.

Games Play that involve structures and rules that are socially constructed, requiring complex levels of mental and physical abilities.

Generalized Other Societal standards of acceptable behavior for everyone in the role.

Group Controls Control stemming from integration into mainstream institutions such as the family, school, and work.

Informal Controls Expressions of disapproval from significant others.

Labeling The process through which a given act or aspect of appearance is defined as deviant.

Looking-glass Self Seeing yourself as a reflection of the impressions you make on others.

Master Status Status through which all other perceptions are filtered.

Medicalization of Deviance The tendency to define and treat deviant behaviors according to the medical model; that is, as diseases rather than as social constructions.

Negative Sanctions Others' disapproval of one's role performance.

Peers Status equals.

Play Child's introduction to acting out roles.

Positive Sanctions Others' approval of one's role performance.

Primary Deviance The original violation, which can often be overlooked or excused.

Principled Challenges to the Norms Deliberate attempts to confront the norm setters and challenge current policy.

Public Temper A set of shared ideas of right and wrong.

Reciprocal Socialization When generations mutually influence the attitudes and knowledge base of one another.

Resocialization Learning new ways of thinking and acting.

Role Distance Relationship between self and self-in-the-role, ranging from embracement to rejection.

Role Modeling Copying the manners and dress of a person one admires.

Safety Valve Deviance that is permitted because it serves to release unacceptable impulses under controlled conditions.

Self A set of perceptions about who and what kind of person one is.

Secondary Deviance Occurs when one has been identified and labeled as a deviant.

Significant Others Persons whose affection, approval, and validation are most desired.

Social Control Mechanisms to ensure conformity to the norms

Social Disorganization Produced when communities are destroyed by economic and political forces in the wider society.

Socialization The process whereby the raw material of infancy is shaped into a functioning member of society.

Social Learning Model that sees behavior as conditioned by reactions from role partners.

Validation of Self Reassurance that one is who one claims to be.

Virtual Self Embodiment of the expectations for anyone occupying a particular status. ✦

Sexualities: How Many?

❖ ❖ ❖ ❖   The general belief about sexual behavior is summed up in the old musical comedy song as simply "doin' what comes naturally." But are your desires and actions all that natural? Or have they been shaped by culture and channeled by social structure? Since this is a sociology textbook, you can be sure that the authors are going to tell you that socialization has a great deal to do with the how, where, when, and with whom your sexual encounters take place, and with how you and others interpret such experiences. It is precisely because sexuality is such a powerful biological drive that it had to be brought under control of the group in order for humans to live peaceably with one another. Society and culture, as Freud reminded us, are possible only because people are able to control potentially disruptive impulses.

The problem with sexuality is that it is essential for reproduction and group survival, yet, if allowed full rein, it could threaten the stability of families and social order. Therefore, it is the biological function that has been most thoroughly shaped by social and cultural processes (Simon and Gagnon 1998). The earliest norms in human history were those that channeled sexual impulses into socially constructive directions, as, for example, in the rules forbidding sex between blood relatives (chapter 8) and in the Bible's commandments against adultery and envy. But controlling sexuality has never been totally successful. Also, by defining some aspects as "normal" and "natural," the norms create categories of sexual expression that come to be perceived as "abnormal" and "unnatural."

Thus, although sociologists are well aware of the evolutionary biological roots of sexual desire and actions, the focus in this text is on the ways in which such an elemental drive has been shaped by social forces. Humans are different from the birds and the bees, and even from some of our primate cousins. If you think about it for a moment, you do not blindly act on every hint of sexual arousal—otherwise, the classroom would be unmanageable. You wait and watch and think about what to say and how to act. The date is a ritual, with clear steps and limits. Human sexuality is a lot more complex than an automatic response to innate desires. This chapter is especially concerned with such current topics as:

- Sexual identities and scripts.
- Changing American norms and behavior.
- Adolescent sexuality.
- Reproductive technologies.
- Homosexualities.
- Sexual violence.

Sexual Identities and Scripts

The **sexual self** is the product of socialization and experiences that involve the three major dimensions of sexual identity: sex identity, gender identity, and erotic identity.

Sex identity refers to a basic definition of the self as male or female. This is usually clear at birth. Yet, in a small number of cases, the baby's genitals are ambiguous, and in most of these cases of intersexed infants, doctors and parents have chosen to raise the child as a girl because it is easier surgically to construct a female than a male (Turner 1999). With appropriate hormonal treatments, most of these individuals live quite natural lives as women, though unable to have children. In these cases, the socialized sex identity overrides chromosomal sex. Yet others are keenly aware that they are not female, but only recently have they spoken out and attempted to change the medical view that they were one of nature's "mistakes" in need of corrective surgery (Nussbaum 1999).

In other cases, even where there are no visible anomalies, a person feels that she or he is trapped in the wrong body. Some will undergo a long and painful set of surgical and hormone treatments so that their outward appearance matches their mental image of being male or female. The difficulties and rewards of such a *transsexual* transformation have been recorded by the economist Deirdre McCloskey (1999), who spent five decades as Donald McCloskey, raising a family and enjoying a high-profile academic reputation. (Interestingly, Deirdre's work has not achieved the same acceptance among economists as did Donald's.)

Gender identity refers to a sense of being appropriately feminine or masculine. As discussed in detail in chapter 7, this dimension is greatly influenced by culture and varies cross-culturally and historically. Just think of the difference between your definition of "feminine" and that of your grandparents. People who undergo sex change operations, such as Deirdre McCloskey, must construct a gender identity from scratch, endlessly observing and practicing how to walk and talk in a masculine or feminine manner. It does not come naturally, even with the added hormones, and often involves exaggerated gestures and appearance.

Erotic identity is based on the object of sexual attraction, whether of the opposite sex (heterosexual) or the same sex (homosexual). Because it is in the interests of most societies to encourage people to marry and raise children, heterosexuality is typically "compulsory," yet there are a number of historical and cross-cultural exceptions that are described later in this chapter.

For most people, most of the time, the three dimensions of the sexual self will tend toward consistency—for example, a feminine female attracted to men—because life is much easier that way. But you can see that there is a lot of room for inconsistency, and you probably know at least one very masculine male who is gay, as well as a relatively effeminate straight man. In addition, different situations will bring out different

Sexual scripts allow people to decide whether or not particular behaviors are appropriate.

aspects of the sexual self, a masculine streak under some circumstances and a softer feminine approach under others. An inconsistent sexual self can be a source of discomfort to people and their role partners, adding to the pressures to conform to cultural expectations.

Sexual Scripts

These expectations are codified in what sociologists call **sexual scripts** (Simon and Gagnon 1998). The scripts allow you to organize your feelings and behaviors in the appropriate way in different situations. For example, the classroom is defined as nonsexual, so although some flirting may go on, you manage to sit through the lectures, but when class is over and you go down to the local pub, another kind of script comes into play. Same people, but different places and different rules.

In this view, sexuality is a rather flexible set of responses that change from situation to situation. The possibility that sexuality is not some fixed quality is very upsetting to many people. Hence, the popularity of theories based on some biological master plan, such as the claim that "men are from Mars and women from Venus." Bringing order out of seeming chaos by placing people and things into two totally separate categories—"splitting and lumping" (Zerubavel 1997)—is one of the most basic human tendencies, but it obscures the degrees of overlap and variability and adaptability that are the essence of nature and of the human condition. In addition, the traditional scripts, especially those for women, have been powerful sources of social control.

As disruptive as uncontrolled male sexuality might be, the idea of sexually liberated women has been more frightening. With few exceptions, controlling female sexuality is a cultural constant—from keeping women out of sight to performing surgery. The easiest way, however, is to convince them that "good women" don't have sexual feelings (Groneman 2000). Right up to the 1960s, for example, most American women grew up believing that it was not only unladylike but also unnatural to have strong sexual desires, and such is the power of socialization that most were able to deny their feelings. But once the script was rewritten in the 1960s, it did not take long for women to become active seekers of sexual pleasure. Throughout our history, cultural and structural factors have transformed sexual norms and behaviors for women and men, straight and gay alike.

Historical Trends

The effect of social conditions on behavior, even that which is driven by powerful biological drives, is neatly illustrated by a very brief summary of 400 years of American sexual history (D'Emilio and Freedman 1997):

In the period from the 1600s to the mid-1800s, the nation needed a lot of new bodies, so sexuality was closely linked to reproduction. Strict norms of faithfulness in marriage were enforced by the community as a whole through public shaming.

Between 1840 and 1920, as the country became industrialized and urbanized with a growing middle class of educated city-dwellers, a new, more romantic conception of married love emerged, where a proper degree of sexual pleasure replaced stern duty. Towns and cities were also filled with single young people who had deserted the farms and villages in order to better themselves and to enjoy the promises and temptations of urban life, with its relaxed sexual norms. The cities also provided a social space for the emergence of a homosexual subculture, centered in bars and music halls, hidden from the larger society. As birthrates dropped and more young people engaged in nonmarried sex, religious leaders staged a powerful backlash, and by 1900, sex outside of marriage was once again condemned as dangerous to personal health and public order. The moral crusade against sexual "vices," including not only pornography but even pictures of nudes in art galleries, was primarily motivated by fears of unrestrained sexuality on the part of immigrants, which might corrupt the daughters and sons of the new urban business elites (Beisel 1997). Thus, the Puritan ethic that promotes hard work and clean living reappeared with a vengeance in late nineteenth-century America.

The new Puritanism did not last long. The 1920s ushered in another period of relative sexual freedom, especially for young women, as well as the triumph of the modern ideal of romantic love, preferably within the privacy of marriage. Women won the right to vote, and family planning became a public issue, although it would be another fifty years before women achieved legal equality and full access to a range of contraceptives. The 1920s were also influenced by the publication of Freud's work on the importance of a healthy sex life and the dangers of sexual repression, exactly the opposite of the Puritanism of the preceding decades. 🖥 1

Most recently, the liberating currents of the 1970s presented a strong challenge to the last vestiges of the nation's sexually repressive tradition: gender inequality and the fear of homosexuality. In this context, the Women's Movement and the Lesbian/Gay/ Bisexual/Transgender (LGBT) Rights Movement are a logical extension of the historical trend toward moving sexuality from the public to the private sphere and defining it as a source of personal fulfillment rather than as an unavoidable evil. In the process, however, some social critics fear that sex and love may have become uncoupled—that is, that much sexual activity, assisted by various medications and artificial enhancers, now takes place without deep personal commitment (Galston 1998). 🖥 2

Contemporary Patterns of Sexual Behavior

Collecting data on sexual activity is not easy, and once respondents agree to be interviewed, there is no way to check the accuracy of what they report. In general, men tend to exaggerate and women to minimize their sexual histories. The earliest systematic research was directed by Alfred Kinsey (Kinsey et al. 1948, 1953), who gathered sexual histories from anyone willing to be interviewed—not a very scientific sample. The results were considered quite shocking. It turns out that Kinsey's respondents did a lot of forbidden things, but it may be that only less inhibited people were willing to talk to him. 🖥 3

The best contemporary information comes from a large representative sample in the early 1990s (Laumann et al. 1994). The major finding was that both men and women are sexually active at increasingly earlier ages, over half by the time they finish high school. Because Americans are marrying at later ages than in the 1950s—typically in their mid- or late twenties—very few will enter marriage without sexual experience. The availability of reliable and inexpensive contraception has made sex before marriage less risky for women, allowing them to delay marriage. In addition, a woman's first partner is no longer someone to whom she is engaged or will eventually marry. For both men and women, the number of partners and the range of sexual expression have increased. Finally, attitudes toward contraception and sex before marriage have also changed to reflect what people are doing.

Yet in many other respects the respondents remain sexually conservative. High proportions continue to disapprove of adultery, and very few admit to having had extramarital affairs. The general finding from the mid-1990s is that close to 90 percent of married persons had had sex only with their husband or wife during the preceding year, and only 25 percent of husbands and 15 percent of wives admitted having been unfaithful. Furthermore, despite the belief that single people are enjoying a glorious, nonstop sex life, married people are twice as likely as the nonmarrieds to be satisfied with their sex life and to report having sex several times a week—they do not have to leave the house to find a partner. The researchers also found the expected differences by gender, with 54 percent of the men reporting that they think about sex every day compared to 12 percent for women. But the majority of both men and women indicate very conservative sexual tastes: Fewer than one in four had bought X-rated videos or had had oral sex—and even fewer claimed to have enjoyed the experience.

It appears, then, that much of the concern over a sexual revolution in America is greatly exaggerated. The major change has been in the years before marriage, thanks in large part to the contraceptive revolution that enlarged the range of life options for women. There is, however, one category of unmarried women whose sexual behavior remains a matter of societal concern if not outright condemnation—adolescents.

Adolescent Sexuality

All available data indicate that American teenagers are sexually active at increasingly younger ages. In 1996, for example, over half of women ages 15 to 17 had had sexual intercourse during the previous 12 months, compared with about 20 percent in 1972. However, there is evidence that these rates leveled off in the late 1990s, as a result of increased education and contraception use, coupled with less approval from one's peers, especially among girls (*Population Today* 2000).

Some teenagers are more likely to be sexually active than others. Hormones may play a part for some boys, but the stronger effects are social. A major variable is the *neighborhood context*. Regardless of race or ethnicity, young women in communities that offer few opportunities for success in school and work are particularly vulnerable to early sexual experiences (Brewster 1994). Racial segregation adds to the isolation from the mainstream of young black females and to their risk of teenage childbearing (Sucoff and Upchurch 1998). In addition, a large proportion of girls who had had sexual intercourse before age 15 reported that they had been unwilling partners (Abma, Driscoll, and Moore 1998).

For young men, the key variables associated with early and frequent sexual activity are living in a high-poverty neighborhood, having few successful adult role models, and holding traditional attitudes toward women. For

many of these young men, getting a girlfriend pregnant is a proxy for adult
status, perhaps the only visible sign of power about which they can boast to
friends (Little and Rankin 1998).

Early sexual activity is also associated with other risky behaviors, including delinquency, drug use, and exposure to sexually transmitted diseases, especially for those with multiple partners. Teenagers are not very careful or consistent users of contraceptives. Many men think it lessens their pleasure or insults
their masculinity, while many women find themselves in a "Catch-22": Using
contraceptives involves advance planning, but "good girls" do not plan in
advance to do something bad, so the only rationale is for the woman to be
swept off her feet, literally, by the passion of the moment, for which she is then
contraceptively unprepared. For every 1,000 sexually active teenage women,
about 220 will become pregnant, almost double the rate for all women
(Henshaw 1998).

Adolescent Pregnancy

Contrary to the public perception, however, even this pregnancy rate of
200 per 1,000 is well below that for 1970. Teenage pregnancies, like pregnancies for most other age groups of American women, have been on the decline
ever since the end of the baby boom in 1965, dropping sharply in the 1990s
(National Center for Health Statistics 2000).

About 54 percent of pregnant teenagers will give birth. Thirty percent of
the pregnancies will be intentionally terminated, and the remaining 15 percent
will be ended by miscarriage or infant death. Not surprisingly, when pregnancy
rates decline, so do the number of live births, which is exactly what has happened for four decades, as seen in Figure 4.1. While politicians have been leading a crusade against "a rising tide of teenage childbearing," the rates have
actually been falling, and quite dramatically despite a brief upswing in 1991.
The primary reason for the decline is increased use of condoms and implanted
contraceptives (e.g. Norplant)—and not greater reliance on abortion, the rates
for which have also dropped (Darroch and Singh 1999).

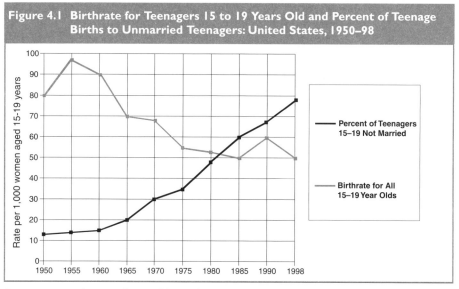

Figure 4.1 Birthrate for Teenagers 15 to 19 Years Old and Percent of Teenage Births to Unmarried Teenagers: United States, 1950–98

Source: National Center for Health Studies. 2000. *National Vital Statistics Report,* vol. 48, #6, April 24.

Teenage birthrates also vary widely by region of the country, with all the Southern states recording rates almost twice as high as every Northern state. The differences range from a high of almost 74 per 1,000 teenagers in Mississippi to a low of 27 in Vermont. Yet even Vermont's low is higher than almost anywhere else in the developed world. That is, despite America's high education and income levels, our teenagers have the highest rates of unintended pregnancies, births, and abortions of any modern society. Since the level of teen sexual activity is about the same in all these countries, the difference in pregnancy rates can be attributed to religious and political opposition to sex education in the schools and refusal to fund family planning services for teenagers. The irony is that the very people who condemn teenage mothers are the ones who vote against the programs that might have the greatest impact on decreasing unwanted childbearing (Schwartz 2000).

Adolescent Parenthood

The condemnation of teenage childbearing probably has less to do with the age of the mother than with the fact that she is likely today to be unmarried, in contrast to earlier periods when a high percentage of teenagers were married and no one complained about their pregnancies (see chapter 8).

Today's teenage mothers, however, are not only unmarried but also likely to be poor, not well educated, and with minimal job market skills. If the mother lives in a community without adequate health facilities, chances are that she will not have had prenatal care or a healthful diet or a stress-free environment. It is these negative conditions more than the mother's young age that account for relatively high infant mortality rates and severe health problems among the surviving babies, which only add to the stress on the mothers (Geronimus and Korenman 1993). Even though the baby may represent an island of warmth in a hostile environment, the mother will have difficulty trying to complete school or finding a job that pays enough for her to have child care or that provides health insurance. Her best bet, until 1996, was to become a welfare beneficiary with Medicaid coverage for herself and the child. Today, under the new welfare laws (chapter 5), unless she can pay the rent herself, she will have to move in with relatives and leave the child with someone while she works, typically for minimum wage. Medicaid is still technically available if she is aware of it and can negotiate the paperwork, which many cannot or have not.

Given these conditions, it is not surprising that three of ten pregnant teenagers will choose to end the pregnancy. The surprise is that so many will have found money to pay for the procedure, since Medicaid does not cover it in most states, and will have found a doctor, since only a few have received training and others have been harassed out of the field by militant antiabortion groups (Guttmacher Institute 2000). Most recently, an additional hurdle has been raised in many states, requiring teenagers to notify their parents and/or receive parental permission. The statutes have passed court review, provided that they include a "judicial bypass" whereby a young woman can try to convince a judge that she is competent to make the decision herself. The irony here is that the 14- or 15-year-old who is self-possessed enough to find a judge and be able to make her case is the one who can terminate the pregnancy, while the less competent youngster is forced to give birth.

But there is very little in the American abortion situation that can be separated from political and religious pressures. 🖥️4

Box 4.1

Abortion Politics: Whose Body? Whose Baby?

From the 1890s to 1973, state laws made it illegal for a woman to terminate a pregnancy voluntarily. This was less a religious crusade than a campaign by obstetricians to remove childbearing from the home and the care of midwives into a more "professional" environment, where the doctors could be assured of a steady stream of patients. Religious and medical groups had also successfully restricted access to contraceptives until a Supreme Court decision in 1965 carved out a space of privacy for married couples to decide how many children they wanted, which was followed by a 1972 decision extending the same rights to nonmarried couples. You may not have known that the contraceptive choices you take for granted have been available for only a few decades.

As you may suspect, wealthy women could work around the rules by finding willing physicians or by traveling abroad. An unknown number of women risked life and health by resorting to "back alley" abortionists. But by the late 1960s, a number of events converged to bring the issue into the public arena. An epidemic of measles had raised the risk of deformed fetuses, as had use of a drug called Thalidomide, prescribed for morning sickness among pregnant women. By this time, both the second wave of American feminism and the family planning movement had gained a strong following. As a result, several cases challenging the state prohibitions were working their way through the courts. The big moment came in 1973 when the Supreme Court announced its decision in the case of *Roe v. Wade*.

The Court interpreted the U. S. Constitution as providing an implied (never quite spelled out) right to privacy in intimate decisions, a space in which the state could not intrude unless it could prove a "compelling interest" in protecting the health and life of mother and child. Accordingly, the Court divided pregnancy and the right to privacy into three parts: (1) in the first three months, the states could not interfere with a woman's decision made in consultation with her physician; (2) in the second trimester, states could enact rules to protect the health of mother or fetus; and (3) in the last three months, when a fetus could survive outside the womb, the state could override the wishes of the mother. In essence, the Court limited the right to privacy with medical considerations that opened a back door for the states to regulate the procedure.

The number of legal abortions rose steadily from 1973 through 1980 before leveling off at 1.6 million a year through the 1980s, and then dropping to 1.3 million in the 1990s (Guttmacher Institute 2000). The drop is due to a number of factors, most crucially the lower pregnancy rate, which in turn reflects more effective contraception and the declining proportion of young women in the population as a whole. But much of the drop is due to the steady increase in legal barriers to abortion services raised by state legislatures and to the organized harassment of abortion providers.

The U.S. Supreme Court has gradually accepted most of the state-level restrictions without actually denying the right to privacy. In 1992, the Court announced a new standard for validation of state laws: whether the law constituted an "undue burden" on the woman seeking to exercise her rights, with the definition of "undue" left to the lower courts. In 1993, the Court decided that requiring a 14-year-old to get the written consent of both parents was not an undue burden. Currently the Court is dealing with the legality of very-late-term abortions, although only a very few—about one-half of one percent—of all abortions are performed after the sixth month. Over 90 percent of abortions take place in the first 12 weeks. And although the abortion rate for Catholic women is close to the national average, at about 22 percent of pregnancies, little seems to have slowed efforts to overturn *Roe v. Wade*.

Several states have recently declared that the fetus is a legal person from the moment of conception, with rights independent of the woman in whose womb it resides. This raises fascinating questions: Can there be two legal persons in one body? Which has precedence? Can the courts order a woman to give birth even though it might kill her? The questions are endless, and you will have to decide them every time you step into the voting booth.

Reproduction, Sexuality, and the Law

Questions about bodies and babies have taken on a completely new dimension with the development of reproductive technologies that separate every facet of reproduction. There are sperm donors; egg donors; mixing sperm and egg in a glass dish in the lab (*in vitro* fertilization); putting the fertilized egg into the uterus of a woman who has no relationship to either the egg or sperm; and having the resulting infant raised by another set of parents. Who is the mother? The egg donor, the one in whose body the fetus developed, or the woman who raises the child? Can there be a biological mother, a gestational mother, and a social mother? What happens to the more than 150,000 frozen embryos in laboratory refrigerators that have not been used or destroyed? Who owns them? How about the fertilized eggs that had not yet been implanted before a couple divorced? If, as in the case of Missouri, state law declares the fertilized egg to be a "preborn person," can any leftover eggs be destroyed? Who owns the eggs when the couple divorces? Can an ex-husband be forced to become an unwilling father? You may smile, but these issues have all appeared before the courts, with little consensus as yet.

Today contraceptives are readily available so that women and men can make informed decisions.

Many of these issues also reveal unspoken value judgments. For example, how would people you know react to a 70-year-old man who fathers a child with his very young third wife? How would they describe a 60-year-old woman who undergoes *in vitro* fertilization? These matters are further complicated by the American ambivalence over being paid for a labor of love, which seems to be appropriate only to women doing sex work. Why is it permissible for a woman to become a surrogate mother, carrying someone else's fetus, if she gets only medical expenses but against the law if she is given thousands of additional dollars?

Designer Genes

The money taboo, however, appears to dissolve completely in the case of egg donors. Your college newspaper probably carries at least one advertisement for a service that will pay bright, blonde female students up to $20,000 for an egg. If yours is an Ivy League school, the price in 1999 went up to $50,000 for a 5'10" athlete with SAT scores of at least 1400 and no family medical problems (Kolata 1999). Or you could try the website where women wanting to sell eggs advertise their good looks and top test scores. 📖5

As for men, sperm banks have existed for many years, stocked with the genetic material of tall, high-IQ, blonde donors, as well as the frozen sperm of powerful and wealthy men. One sperm bank in Virginia specializes in "Doctorate Donors" at a premium price (Stryker 2000). Today, a couple with enough money can pick both the male and female background characteristics of their offspring (and the woman to bear it). In contrast to adoption, there will be fewer surprises, but one wonders what will happen to the child who somehow fails to meet parental expectations (Katz Rothman 1999).

Overall, despite attempts to limit reproductive choices in the United States, the master trend of the past three decades in modern industrial societies has been toward extending the protection of privacy to intimate relationships and reproductive strategies. The same liberating currents that have transformed heterosexual behaviors and choice have also had a profound impact on the lives of American homosexuals.

Homosexualities: The Lesbian/Gay/Bisexual/ Transgender Experiences

The sexual script for Americans is decidedly, some might say oppressively, heterosexual. All our socialization, our laws, the teachings of religious authorities, and the pressure of peers direct desire toward persons of the opposite sex. Yet, throughout history, in most societies, some people will have been attracted to members of the same sex. How these desires and behaviors are defined and responded to is a cultural and historical variable (Nanda 2000).

Cross-Cultural and Historical Perspectives

Not all societies have been as fearful and condemning as the United States. Indeed, in many warrior cultures, intense bonds among men are considered superior to relationships with such inferior beings as women, although sexual intercourse with women is an unavoidable necessity for producing the next generation. Among the ancient Athenians, high-status men and their young male lovers formed an elite circle. The women of ancient Greece also enjoyed same-sex intimacies in addition to their wifely duties. The term "lesbian" derives from the name of the island Lesbos, where the poet Sappho spent time with her female companions. Similarly, in pre-Christian Rome, same-sex relationships were considered a private matter as long as men and women continued to do their civic duty to marry and have children (Boswell 1994).

With the triumph of Christianity in Europe, attitudes toward homosexuality became increasingly repressive, with some accused sinners being burned at the stake. The term "faggot" probably comes from the word for the small sticks used to start such a fire. When religious authority gave way to political leadership in Europe in the sixteenth century, homosexuals could still be persecuted, less as sinners than as criminals. In the twentieth century, the mental health establishment weighed in with its considered judgment that homosexuality was really a mental disorder, only to change its mind in the early 1970s. Nonetheless, American culture remains characterized by **homophobia**, an extreme fear of gay men and lesbians, as well as of bisexuals and the transgendered. 🖥6

In the United States, sexual relations are subject to state law, and about half the states, primarily in the South, still criminalize "unnatural sexual acts," often classified as **sodomy**, after the Biblical city of Sodom, destroyed by God because of the wickedness of its citizens. Sodomy statutes, which date from the eighteenth and nineteenth centuries, usually cover everything other than face-to-face heterosexual intercourse, but they are seldom invoked today except against homosexuals. In 1986, the Supreme Court refused to overturn the sodomy laws of Georgia, under which a homosexual couple were prosecuted for behavior in the privacy of their home. The Georgia law was voided by the state courts in 1998 and a similar Texas statute was overturned in 2000.

In the late 1990s, several well-publicized homicides illustrated the enduring strength of homophobia in the United States. In one case, a gay man was beaten and left to die tied to a fence in the bitter cold of Wyoming. The killers' unsuccessful defense was that they were in great fear because the victim had made an unwelcome advance in a bar. In another case, on a U.S. Army base, an enlisted man was beaten to death by drunken bunkmates for no other reason than that he was gay. When asked why the earlier harassment of the victim had not been stopped, the unit's sergeant said the "guys were having too much fun." Such fear tends to betray a rather fragile sense of the perpetrators' own manliness, which is probably why extreme homophobia is most common among men of limited educational and occupational attainment (Kimmel 1996). More successful men may also be homophobic, but they know better than to act out their fears. Even if most Americans are no longer openly homophobic, the culture remains dominated by **heterosexism**, or the belief that heterosexual desires and behaviors are superior and deserve a privileged status (Seidman 1996).

How Many Sexes Are There, Anyway?

Increasingly, scholars of sexuality believe that "homosexuality" is a concept that has meaning only in societies where just two sexes are recognized (Lorber 1994; Fausto-Sterling 2000). Yet, as noted in the case of **intersexed** infants, who are born with ambiguous genitals, nature provides a number of gradations from male to female. But because we have no category for such children, they are immediately subjected to surgery to transform them into a male or female (Kessler 1998). People who cross-dress—**transvestites**—similarly challenge our either-or, two-sex classification scheme, especially when they are not necessarily homosexual. Think of your first reaction to RuPaul, or "Pat" on *Saturday Night Live*. Not being able to put people in clear-cut boxes is mentally stressful, but rather than question the sex and gender system, it is easier for most people to dismiss nonconformists as sick or sinful.

The power of this two-category (*binary*) system is most strongly felt by the people who do not easily fit into its neat boxes. The term transgendered refers to all those individuals whose expressions of gender defy easy categorization, including the intersexed, transvestites, and persons at various stages of transformation from male-to-female or female-to-male (transsexuals). Most studies report that the transgendered are under enormous pressure, from self and others, to conform to strict role expectations, even as they resist having to make such stark choices (Gagne and Tewksbury 1998). 🖥7

Some cultures do recognize more than two sexes by having names for those who are neither male nor female, such as small children and the very old, often assumed to be sexually neutral. Some Native American tribes also recognized a special category of berdache, a third sex of relatively feminine men thought to have supernatural powers by virtue of combining male and female traits (Lang 1998). The social construction of sex and gender is especially evident in recent studies of transvestite prostitutes in Brazil (Kulick 1998) and Mexico (Prieur 1998), who quite literally "construct" a superfeminine appearance, thus reinforcing the gender norms while also deconstructing (untying) the links among sexual, gender, and erotic identities.

Box 4.2

Boy Wives and Female Husbands

A recent collection of research papers on the variety of sex/gender systems in contemporary Africa illustrates how questions of power affect the definition of the situation (Murray and Roscoe 1998). For example, in societies where power differences between men and women are crucial, homosexual men are referred to as "lesbians" because they tend to treat one another as equals (Gaudio 1998). By the same token, powerful men who take boys as sexual servants are not considered homosexual.

In yet another society, women who live together and love one another are not considered to be "having sex" because sex is possible only when the male penis is involved (Kendall 1998)—an attitude still shared by some Americans.

Although the number of transgendered persons is probably very small, it is generally estimated for modern societies that about 5 to 8 percent of men and a smaller proportion of women are almost exclusively involved in same-sex relationships. The number could be much higher, depending on how homosexuality is defined (Schwartz and Rutter 1998). Who really is gay? What about those individuals who are strongly attracted to someone of the same sex but never act on their feelings? Or those men and women who may have had a few homosexual encounters in an otherwise heterosexual life? Or inmates of single-sex institutions who find sexual satisfaction wherever they can? In addition to problems of definition, accurate information is difficult to gather, especially when the activities are considered illegal or deviant. The best guess from a number of recent studies is that over the life course, the proportion of Americans who will have some homosexual experience rises to 15 to 20 percent of men and 6 to 10 percent of women (Laumann et al. 1994).

Many of those who have had homosexual relationships are more accurately described as bisexual, able to enjoy sexual relations with both women and men (Esterberg 1997). Interestingly, in this category, women outnumber men. It appears that situational factors are important, with people seeking comfort and gratification from whoever is there for them. Notice, also, how bisexuality illustrates the distinctions between sex, gender, and erotic identities, with the same person (whose sex does not change) moving from same-sex to opposite-sex love objects with or without any changes in gendered presentation of self.

Being and Becoming Gay

It is always tempting to seek out a single direct cause for nonconforming behaviors; the favorites are genes, hormones, weak fathers, and domineering mothers. But none of these has much value in predicting homosexuality. There is evidence of a limited genetic influence for a small proportion of gay men and lesbians, but no one yet knows the precise mechanisms whereby genetic information affects behavior (Rice et al. 1999; Wickelgren 1991). Research on brain and nervous system differences between gays and straights is similarly inconclusive, including findings of no significant differences. Something as complex as human sexuality undoubtedly has many sources; biological tendencies interact with life experiences within a sociocultural context in a mutually reinforcing spiral. Whatever the roots of homosexuality, the process of being and becoming sexual are the same for all of us.

For a number of men and women, same sex relationships provide intimacy and support.

Thus, although some individuals might be more predisposed than others to becoming exclusively homosexual, whether or not they actually do so depends on a variety of other factors. As sociologists, our focus is on these other factors and the processes through which erotic identities are formed. In this view, the sexual self is constructed much like any other aspect of self, through interactions with role partners, labeling, internalization, and experiences that make some forms of sexual expression more comfortable than others. As with the presentation of self in general, erotic identities, for lesbians and gay males as well as for heterosexuals, are negotiated realities, created and recreated through the give-and-take of everyday life (Stein 1997).

Questions about the roots of homosexuality are not only of academic interest but have become deeply politicized in the debate about whether homosexuality is an orientation or a preference (Schwartz and Rutter 1998). Those who see erotic identity as an orientation believe that it is biologically based, an ascribed characteristic that is there from an early age and unchangeable. This is a very useful position for gay men and lesbians, who can then claim that they are who they are and no amount of therapy can change them. As an ascribed trait, similar to sex and race, homosexuality could be easily included in antidiscrimination legislation. This view should also reassure fearful heterosexuals that if it is not in their genes, they are protected from seduction.

In contrast, the idea that homosexuality is primarily a constructed identity, a lifestyle preference, is more sociological, but it is also the position of anti-gay activists who see homosexuals as sinners who refuse to change their sinful ways and who therefore do not deserve legal protection. Thus, from a political standpoint, the sociological view is harmful to the cause of gay rights. Yet, to deny personal agency in the construction of erotic identity is to give up responsibility for one's own lifestyle choices. The reality for many gay men and lesbians is that their sexuality is both given and chosen.

Among the general public, those who believe that homosexual tendencies cannot be changed are much more supportive of gay rights than are those who think of gayness as a lifestyle choice. At the same time that increasing numbers of Americans believe that homosexuality is inborn, and 84 percent say that gays should have equal job opportunities, a majority also feels that homosexuality is morally wrong and that gay couples should not marry or raise children (Berke 1998; Leland 2000). Ambiguity abounds and persists.

Organizing for Gay Rights

Because of the extreme stigma and threat of criminal prosecution throughout most of the past century, the vast majority of gay people have hidden their erotic identity—in their terminology, they have been *closeted*. The earliest organized efforts to reach homosexuals were largely concerned with helping them adapt to remaining in the closet. But with the sexually liberating currents of the 1960s and the emergence of the Civil Rights and Women's Movements, the climate seemed ripe for a nationally organized Gay Rights Movement (Marcus 1992). 🖥 8

The event that crystallized the shift from secrecy to militancy occurred in 1969 when the New York City police conducted one of their routine harassing raids on a gay bar, the Stonewall, and the patrons fought back instead of retreating. The symbolism of the Stonewall incident encouraged many gay men and lesbians to "come out" of the closet and publicly acknowledge their erotic identity. Today, Gay Pride events are common in the larger cities, and your college campus probably has at least one recognized student club for gays and their straight friends.

At the individual level, "coming out" remains a problem-filled choice. Fear of losing the affection of relatives and friends, as well as apprehension of being a target for harassment and occupational retaliation, exert powerful pressures to remain closeted (Woods 1993). Yet by not acknowledging their erotic identity, sexual nonconformists delay the day of full acceptance. When gay and transgendered people are visible in everyday life, their presence is "normalized." This means that many people can say, "Yes, I have a gay or transgendered friend, or aunt, or colleague, and he or she is not all that different from anyone else."

The 1970s and 1980s saw major gains in public tolerance. Several cities added "sexual orientation" to their antidiscrimination laws, and most Northern states changed their sex statutes to protect the sexual privacy of consenting couples. But this forward momentum was stalled by the AIDS epidemic of the late 1980s and the association of the disease with gay men. The devastation caused by the epidemic energized both gay rights organizations and anti-gay activists, with mixed results. In the 1990s, although some communities enacted gay rights legislation, others defeated such referendums on the grounds that the statutes would confer "special privileges."

Because of their willingness to leave the closet and their relatively high educational and income levels (Black et al. 1999), gay men and lesbians have been able to generate considerable political pressure in some states and cities. In other areas of the country, however, more traditional political and religious forces continue to define homosexuality as either evil or sick. You will undoubtedly have many opportunities to vote on public questions that affect the civil rights of lesbians, gay men, and other sexual nonconformists. The two institutional areas currently most affected by these tensions—the family and the military—are discussed in chapters 8 and 10.

Sexual Violence

The dark side of sexual expression is its capacity for harm. This situation arises from the power of the drive itself and also from all the social and cultural meanings attached to it, for men whose sense of self is bound up with their sexual exploits and for women who are judged by the power of the men they attract. Some men and women are driven by sexual desires that violate the norms, such as an attraction to children or to physically dangerous sex games. As noted in chapter 3, pornography and prostitution are found in many societies as a way to channel non-normative sexual impulses away from central institutions such as work and family. And, in all but a few societies, powerful norms operate to restrain the incestuous urges of closely related blood relatives.

On the contemporary scene, the same trends that have loosened traditional social controls may also have increased opportunities for acting out desires that involve inflicting harm upon another person. For a number of reasons, it is impossible to tell whether rates of sexual violence have risen because: (1) such things were not carefully recorded in the past; (2) few people report sex victimization in the first place; or (3) definitions of what is acceptable change from one situation to another and over time. For example, unwanted sexual demands that were once seen as a husband's prerogative are now defined by some as "marital rape."

As sociologists, we are not especially concerned with the personal characteristics of molesters, rapists, and the like. Some are undoubtedly mentally or physically ill; others will have grown up under appalling conditions; and still others will be overwhelmed by the passions of the moment or the influence of drugs or alcohol. Nor are we concerned with what consenting adults do in the privacy of their bedrooms. The questions we ask are: Are there common aspects to acts classified as sex crimes? When do personal problems become social issues? What do these acts tell us about the society and culture?

To take the two most publicized forms of sexual violence—child molesting and rape—the most obvious generalization is that the victims are relatively powerless, which suggests that control rather than sex *per se* is an important element. Because the victims often assumed that they had done something to provoke the attack, such acts tend to go unmentioned and unreported, especially when they involved family members. Under pressure from organizations representing women's rights and child protection, attitudes toward sexual violence have changed greatly, and what was once a private matter has become a matter of public concern.

❖ ❖ ❖ ❖

Violence Against Children

Concern over "threatened children" has been a major staple of American culture since the 1980s. Yet, as several sociologists have found, such concerns turn out to be based on very flimsy data (Best 1990; Glassner 1999). For example, take the furor over the tens of thousands of missing children whose faces adorn our milk cartons and who are thought to have been abducted by sexual perverts. The actual numbers are much smaller, and most will have been taken by a noncustodial parent. Others are runaways from violent homes, some of whom disappear into the urban subculture of drugs and prostitution, but few public funds have been spent on programs for their rehabilitation. Most money goes to the organizations that continue to make exaggerated claims of stranger-abductions, which are readily accepted and made even more alarming by the media (Glassner 1999).

This process of making claims on behalf of threatened children reached its peak in the late 1980s with reports of widespread sexual abuse of children in daycare centers. A decade later, after a number of trials and ruined reputations, few if any accusations have been proved in court. To the contrary, the lawyers for the state and parents not only accepted the children's wildest fabrications—including reports of satanism and cannibalism—but also urged the children to even greater imaginative heights. Parents, perhaps feeling guilty because of using child care, turned against the teachers with a vengeance. The media loved every carefully reported detail, and the children had a great time being the center of attention (Nathan and Snedeker 1995).

In fact, however, the most dangerous place for children is their own home. Eighty-six percent of sexual assaults of children under age 6 took place in the child's residence, and half these assaults were committed by a family member. Another 47 percent involved an acquaintance (U.S. Department of Justice 2000). Yet media attention has been focused almost exclusively on those rare but riveting cases of fatal sexual attacks by a stranger in the neighborhood. One New Jersey case has led to the enactment in most states of statutes ("Megan's Laws") requiring that released sex offenders register with the local police, who may then inform home owners that such a person resides in their neighborhood. Some lawmakers have proposed to go one step further and deny release altogether, even after the offender has completed a prison sentence. All kinds of questions are raised by these developments. How can one balance the rights of offenders, victims, and communities? Does the failure of states to provide effective treatment allow them to retain the offender indefinitely? Can sex offenders ever be rehabilitated?

Violence Against Women

In a society where only a wimp would let a woman boss him around, you can expect a high level of fear and resentment of women among men (Torr and Swisher 1999). One unintended consequence of the feminist movement's empowerment of women has been to heighten these fears. Keeping women in their place becomes more difficult as they fill classrooms and workplaces. By the same token, as women and men study and work together, opportunities for wanted and unwanted encounters also increase. The unwanted encounters range from minor forms of harassment to stranger rape, with a number of stops in between. Even so, the most dangerous place for women, as for children, has always been the home. The most recent nationwide data (Centers for Disease Control 1998) indicate that nearly 18 percent of American women say they have been the victim of a rape or attempted rape, almost half of the attacks before age 17, and most of these in or near the home. Half the women respondents in this survey also reported having been the victim of a physical assault with a fist or weapon. Three out of four of the victimized women identified their attacker as a current or former husband, a partner with whom they were living, or a date. For men, only 18 percent of victims identified the attacker as an intimate partner, male or female.

Sexual harassment. The very concept of sexual harassment is an example of the social construction of deviance. The behaviors—the teasing and touching and jokes and pornographic pictures—have always been there, but until recently there was no name for them, nor were they singled out as improper or illegal. The courts have decided that to the degree that such activities create a "hostile" environment, that interferes with the ability to perform a job for one sex but not the other, they violate the civil rights of students or employees (Kimmel 2000a). The unanswered question is whether this means that if everyone in the school or workplace harasses everyone else equally, the situation does not violate the law?

Although some men have sued successfully, the great bulk of complainants about harassment have been women suing their male superiors. These cases, which have swamped government agencies and the courts, are actually only the tip of the iceberg, since only a very few women bother to report harassing incidents. The charges are extremely difficult to prove, paper trails are rare, and misunderstandings abound. Many men are honestly surprised that what they thought of as a friendly gesture was not appreciated, while many women assume that they must have invited an unwanted advance (Guiffre and Williams 1994). The most important reason for not complaining, however, is fear of retaliation. Could you really prove that you were fired or given a poor grade because of revenge for refusing a sexual advance rather than as a result of your own sloppy work?

Sexual harassment by classmates in elementary and secondary schools is almost never reported because the victims are doubly powerless, as children and as girls or as boys suspected of being gay (Thorne 1993). The teasing and touching and horseplay are so much a part of accepted childhood schoolyard behavior that school authorities find it difficult to maintain a balance between protecting the girls or appearing silly when they punish a 6-year-old boy for giving unwanted kisses.

At the college level, even though they are no longer children, few victims lodge complaints against other students or instructors. In addition to all the usual factors that inhibit filing formal charges, colleges are caught in a bind between their commitment to free expression, on the one hand, and the need to provide a nonhostile learning environment for all students, on the other. As a result, most have a very carefully worded set of rules about appropriate expressions. Check out the policy at your school, and, if possible, find out how many charges of harassment were filed last year and how the cases were disposed of, formally or informally.

The ultimate key to reducing harassment at work and school is to define these spaces as nonsexual and safe for all participants. In general, also, rates of sexual harassment and any other form of violence toward women are lowest in societies with high levels of gender equality and tolerance of homosexuality, where girls and women feel good about themselves and are not treated as sex objects or trophies (Lepowsky 1993; Sanday 1990).

Sexual assaults. Since 1993, according to the Department of Justice's household surveys, the number of rapes and other sexual assaults has declined from about a half million to 332,000 in 1998 (U.S. Department of Justice 1999). Although a few men report being sexually assaulted, 93 percent of the victims were girls and women, almost all of whom were under age 25, including 8 percent of girls between 12 and 25. Comparing reports to police with the household data, one sees that only one in three sexual assaults is brought to the attention of authorities, despite changes in the rules of courtroom procedure and the creation of special units in police departments.

There is also a widespread belief that men are biologically programmed for sexual assaults, from visions of cavemen dragging women by the hair to the tough dudes of rap lyrics. This idea has recently received support from scholars who claim that there is an evolutionary drive to conquer and impregnate women (Thornhill and Palmer 2000). In other words, they suggest that rape really is about having sex and not about exercising control over women. In this view, because the evolutionary drive in men is to propagate their genes, those who cannot win young and fertile women by virtue of their high ascribed or achieved statuses will have to use force in order to spread their seed. Therefore, these scholars conclude, as deplorable as forced sex may be, there is a logic to the pattern.

Most sexual harassment consists of male superiors making unwanted advances towards female employees.

As with many biological and evolutionary theories, the imaginative leap from the distant past to contemporary behavior lacks empirical evidence. We do not yet know how the mechanisms work or if they have a strong or consistent effect on modern humans. Even if there had been a time when rape was adaptive for men, it will get you a long jail sentence today. It is the cultural variations on biological themes that interest sociologists. The fact that the American rape rate is the highest in the industrial world, twenty times higher than in Japan, says more about culture than about the evolutionary history of rape. In addi-

❖ ❖ ❖ ❖   tion, in the United States, a large proportion of rapes involve blood relatives, which is not a very adaptive behavior over the long run. As for the basic assumption of an evolutionary advantage to men who propagate most successfully, the odds will actually favor lower-status men, who tend to have larger families than those with more education and income, which may not be what the theorists had in mind as a long-term survival strategy for the society. As for rapes committed in wartime, these are clearly more about humiliating the enemy than about spreading one's seed, especially since the children will belong to the other side.

There is enough cultural encouragement to violent sex in the United States without the added rationale of acting out an evolutionary imperative. Athletes, from pro football players to suburban high school lettermen, are disproportionately involved in cases of sexual assault—perhaps because these incidents are widely publicized but also because there is something in the culture of male sports that encourages aggressive displays of competitive masculinity (Benedict 1998; Lefkowitz 1998). The men do not have to look far for partners, willing or not, in the sexually available "groupies" who follow them and compete for celebrity sex.

The issue of date rape is of concern on many campuses. Men and women come to the dating situation with very different attitudes and expectations that may not be interpreted very accurately (Fonow et al. 1992). The freedom of being away from home, the peer pressure from dormitory mates or fraternity brothers and sorority sisters, the heightened sexuality of young adulthood, all conspire to create situations that could easily lead to unwanted sexual encounters and to a reluctance to define them as rape (DeKeseredy and Schwartz 1998). The reluctance may extend to prosecutors and juries. Just think of the difference in your feelings toward the victim of an acquaintance rape in contrast to someone assaulted by a stranger. This being America, one must also be sensitive to matters of race and class. Rapes of nonwhite or poor women go largely unreported; those of white women receive more attention from police and media, especially if the victim is of high status and the perpetrator is black or Hispanic (Kennedy 1998). 🖳 9

Conclusion

This chapter has applied the sociological lens to various aspects of sex and sexuality. You have learned to distinguish between sex identity, gender identity, and erotic identity in the construction of the sexual self. You have also had a brief overview of the historical changes in American sexual behavior and attitudes, most recently the dramatic increase in sex before marriage. Problems of adolescent sexuality, pregnancy, and parenthood were discussed, as well as the dilemmas posed by the newest reproductive technologies. Just as there are many varieties of heterosexual behaviors, so also do gay men and lesbians display a range of sexual attitudes and activities within what remains a basically intolerant cultural context. The chapter closed with a discussion of sexual violence, most particularly toward children and women.

The overall trends in this century have been toward removing sexual behaviors from the public to the private sphere, and toward an emphasis on personal pleasure rather than religious duty. The decoupling of sex and reproduction that has led to the sexual liberation of women has had unintended consequences, such as increased opportunities for sexual exploitation and the single-minded pursuit of immediate satisfaction.

When Freud was asked the recipe for individual fulfillment, he answered "love and work." Historically, we have given women responsibility for love and men that for work, but now both women and men can combine the two and realize their full potential. When men and women meet as equals, worthy of mutual respect, it is likely that their personal relationships will be equally fulfilling. This is not an easy goal, which is why so many will fall short, but it is an increasingly attractive vision for Americans of all ages and most particularly those of college years. 🖥 10

❖ ❖ ❖ ❖

Surfing the Sociological Internet

🖥 1 Explore the history of sexuality at:http://www.historychannel.com/sex/

🖥 2 The International Lesbian and Gay Association is at http://www.ilga.org/default.htm
For Women, Feminism, and Sexuality: There are many links to sites dealing with sexual, gay/lesbian, and reproductive issues: http://www.feminist.com/repro.htm

🖥 3 The Society for the Scientific Study of Sexuality can be found at: http://www.ssc.wisc.edu/ssss
The Kinsey Institute is at: http://www.indiana.edu/~kinsey/

🖥 4 Go to The Allen Gutmacher Institute for the latest statistics, research, and information on procreation, contraception, and abortion: http://www.agi-usa.org and http://www.plannedparenthood.org/Library/SEXUALITYEDUCATION

🖥 5 Try http://www.ronsangels.com/ which advertises a service to buy eggs and sperm for infertility treatments.

🖥 6 For Gay, Lesbian, Bisexual, and Transgender Resources on the Web: http://www.ccp.arizona.edu/users/tallman/gay.htm

🖥 7 For discussion of and information on Transgender issues and the intersexed see: http://www.ifge.org/ and http://www.gendersanity.com/index.shtml as well as http://www.gender.org/resources/links.html, http://www.transfeminism.org/ and http://www.sonic.net/~cisae/

🖥 8 Websites on Gay Rights: http://www.actwin.com/eatonohio/gay/world.htm and http://www.taasa.org/library/gay_lesbian/gay_lesbian_rights.htm
Information document on the rights of lesbians: http://ffq.qc.ca/marche2000/en/di_lesbi/index.html
International Gay & Lesbian Human Rights Commission: http://www.iglhrc.org/

❖ ❖ ❖ ❖

💻9 Sites dealing with violence against women and children, rape, and sexual harassment:
http://www.ojp.usdoj.gov/vawo/about.htm
http://www.now.org/issues/violence/index.html
http://www.vix.com/pub/men/harass/harass.html
http://www.rainn.org/

💻10 For more information on sexual issues, visit these sites:
Get advice on sexual issues from http://www.msnbc.com/news/SEXPLORATIONH_Front.asp
On sexual Health: http://content.health.msn.com/living_better/sxy
http://www.sexhealth.org/
For fun and advice, Dr. Ruth is at:
http://webcenter.drruth.aol.com/DrRuth/
For general sex education and sex and disability, see the Sexuality Information and Education Council of the U.S.:
http://www.siecus.org/pubs/biblio/bibs0009.html

Glossary

Berdache A third sex of relatively feminine men thought by some Native American tribes to have supernatural powers by virtue of combining male and female traits.
Bisexual Able to enjoy sexual relations with both women and men.
Date Rape Nonconsensual sexual intercourse in the dating context.
Erotic Identity Based on the object of sexual attraction—persons of the opposite sex (heterosexual) or the same sex (homosexual).
Gay Rights Movement Organized efforts to extend full rights of citizenship to homosexuals.
Gender Identity A sense of being appropriately feminine or masculine.
Heterosexism The belief that heterosexual desires and behaviors are superior to homosexual ones and deserve a privileged status.
Homophobia An extreme fear of gay men and lesbians, as well as of bisexuals and the transgendered.
Intersexed Infants born with ambiguous genitals.
Sex Identity A basic definition of the self as male or female.
Sexual Orientation The view that erotic identity is biologically based from an early age and unchangeable.
Sexual Preference The view that erotic identity is shaped by lifestyle choices.
Sexual Scripts A set of expectations that organize our sexual perceptions and experiences.
Sexual Self The product of sex, gender, and erotic identities.
Sodomy Unnatural sexual acts as defined by laws.
Transgendered Individuals whose expressions of gender defy easy categorization.
Transsexuals People of various stages of transformation from male to female or female to male.
Transvestites People who cross-dress. ✦

Part II

Structures of Inequality

When Some Are More
Equal Than Others:
Social Stratification

As the guide in the novel *Animal Farm* (Orwell 1954) explains, "All animals are equal, but some animals are more equal than others." And so it is in the United States today, a society in which all are to be treated equally, but the outcome is that some are very much more equal than others. The mechanisms and ideology that account for this difference are described in this chapter. Here are some of the topics:

- Social stratification.
- Socioeconomic status (SES).
- Caste and class.
- Poverty and wealth in America.
- Social mobility and status attainment.
- Social status in everyday life.

By now, you have some idea of how culture and social structure form the reality within which your life unfolds—the water in your fishbowl. But you may not truly appreciate the strength of social forces until you study this chapter. Such is the power of the work ethic that most Americans still firmly believe that their success or failure is due to individual qualities and effort. In actuality, the likelihood of achievement in school and work is largely socially structured, less linked to personal abilities than to ascribed statuses and situational factors. The three chapters of Part II describe just how the process works, how ascription translates into achievement. This introductory chapter examines the general principles and processes of social stratification or the distribution of individuals and groups on the basis of their command over scarce societal resources.

Principles of Social Stratification

In any society, there are three kinds of valued resources:

1. Power—the ability to impose your will on other people.
2. Prestige—honor and respect.
3. Property—material goods.

In any society, people will also differ in the abilities and appearances that are culturally valued. That is, some individuals will be judged superior to others and therefore entitled to a greater share of those scarce resources. If the resources were evenly distributed, they would lose their value as signs of superiority.

The result is a **hierarchy**, a set of ranked statuses from high to low. Within the hierarchy, individuals and groups are arranged in layers, or *strata* (the plural of *stratum*), based on their claim to or control over societal goodies. The whole structure is called a **stratification system**. The major point of the three chapters in Part II is precisely this: *Your position in various systems of stratification is the most important determinant of your life choices and chances*, including how long you live, quality of marriage, probability of divorce, number of children, and even your health and happiness.

Theoretically, one can imagine a society in which all members are equally valued and hence equally rewarded. The closest to this ideal are the world's few remaining gathering bands, perhaps similar to the earliest human groups, in which both women and men, young and old, forage for food and care for infants. But once a division of labor takes place—for example, when men become hunters—some tasks will be considered more important than others and will be honored accordingly. At the very least, almost every known society is stratified on the basis of sex and age. The more complex the division of labor and the more diverse the population in terms of race, religion, and ethnic background, the more ways there are to evaluate people on the basis of what they do (achieved statuses) or are (ascribed traits), leading to a multiplicity of stratification systems.

Theoretical Perspectives

From the *functional perspective*, inequality in rewards is essential to getting the most talented people to use their skills for the public welfare (Davis and Moore 1945; Grimes 1991). The resulting hierarchy, based on a filtering process whereby those assumed to be most worthy rise to the top, is called a meritocracy, or the rule of the best and brightest. According to this view, stratification outcomes are the result of differences in human capital, the abilities, training, and social networks in which individuals have invested. For almost the entire history of the United States, this top stratum was exclusively composed of white males, primarily from economically comfortable backgrounds and graduates of elite schools (Domhoff 1998).

In contrast, the *conflict perspective* focuses on the processes whereby power and property are inherited, and the many less obvious ways in which the contest is rigged in favor of certain kinds of people (Feagin and Feagin 1994). Simply defining the type of person who would be a "good" worker immediately excludes entire categories of potential applicants. But as long as most Americans believe that the hierarchy reflects the real distribution of talent in a society where everyone has the same opportunity to excel, the system goes unchallenged. This is an example of ideological hegemony, or control over the production of ideas (*hegemony* means influence or power over). If you think about who produces ideas in our society—the people who run universities and think tanks, religious and political leaders, and owners of the media—you can see that they come from the more privileged strata. Therefore, it can be expected that they promote beliefs that justify their power and condemn as "radicals" anyone who questions the system, such as the organizers of trade unions in the 1930s (see chapter 16).

The two theoretical approaches can be reconciled by accepting that individual abilities, luck, and a willingness to take risks account for the origins of inequality. But once privileges are gained, every effort is made to pass them to one's children, regardless of the offsprings' talents. Thus, members of the next generation start from very different places, and the children of high-status families not only have a giant head start but also continue to build their lead through elite schooling and social networks, from which presumably lesser persons are excluded (Tilly 1998).

At the macro-level, it can be argued that the promise of great wealth and honor will ensure a vibrant economy, but the resulting inequality has high

❖ ❖ ❖ ❖   costs for the rest of the society, in human misery, unfair competition in future generations, a loss of shared concern for the common good, and the corruption of democratic politics (Wright 2000).

At the micro, interactive level, the accumulation of power, respect, and property is central to many Americans' self-image. The work ethic that underlies a capitalist economic system places a premium on *performance*, being first or best at whatever, so that, as Marx once remarked, "having replaces being" (Mannon 1997). Impressing others becomes a major goal of interaction, through which those with the most resources construct a reality in which their superiority is continually validated by status inferiors (Ridgeway et al. 1998).

Dimensions of Stratification in the United States Today

We will save the discussion of power until chapter 10, but the 2000 presidential election should serve as evidence of the unprecedented degree to which money translates into political power in the United States today.

In modern industrial society, prestige is usually linked to occupational status. In turn occupational status tends to be linked to income.

Prestige. Prestige, or *status honor*, is a purely sociological concept in being relational; that is, it depends on the respect that other people are willing to show. The importance of respect to self-image is amusingly illustrated by the comic Rodney ("I don't get no respect!") Dangerfield. But status honor is a valued resource for men at all levels of the society, as seen in the negative consequences of disrespecting ("dissing") among inner-city youth. Just what qualities are honored will vary from one society to another; some will value wisdom and the elderly, others will worship youth or warriors. In modern industrial society, prestige is typically linked to occupational status, although income is also important. For those with little money or job skills, interpersonal displays of physical intimidation are essential to gaining respect.

As you can see in Table 5.1, the top-ranked occupations are what Americans call **professions**, requiring many years of education and training. Professions are self-regulating in being able to control who and how many are allowed into the occupation and the circumstances under which they can be booted out. For example, the American Bar Association decides how many and which law schools are accredited as well as what is taught; supervises the examinations needed to practice law; and controls the procedures for disbarring members. By limiting the number of practitioners, professional associations keep competition low and fees high. At the other end of the prestige hierarchy, lowest rankings go to occupations requiring little formal education and typically involve "dirty work," such as emptying bedpans and clean-ing streets (Kelley and Evans 1993).

Table 5.1	Prestige Rankings of Occupations				
[Scores run from 100 (highest) to 1 (lowest)]					
Physician	86	Firefighter	53	Child care worker	35
Lawyer	75	Social worker	52	Bus driver	32
College professor	74	Mail carrier	47	Truck driver	30
Clergy	69	Secretary	46	Sanitation worker	28
Registered nurse	66	Bank teller	43	Waiter/waitress	28
High school teacher	66	Nurse's aid	42	Janitor	22
Police officer	60	Correctional officer	40		

Source: Davis and Smith, 1996.

In general, occupational status is linked to income, but not always. Col-lege professors, for example, have high prestige but relatively low salaries compared to lawyers and physicians. Conversely, some low-ranked workers benefit from union-negotiated wages and benefits. In addition, criminal activities are often well rewarded with income and respect in their communi-ties, while politicians, many of whom are both powerful and well-off, are fre-quently ranked below other white-collar jobholders.

Another interesting exception is the status of professional athletes and entertainers, who typically combine high income, low education, high pres-tige among some segments of the population, and not much political clout. The decisions that shape the nation are not made in left field or on a Las Vegas stage, but in Congress and on Wall Street, where black and Hispanic faces are rare. Yet, despite these variations, occupation is the single most powerful indicator of social rank because it is so closely linked to education and income.

Property. Every society has certain objects that signify success, such as the size of the pile of yams outside your hut, the number of your wives or chil-dren, or that Jaguar parked on your circular driveway. An individual's pros-perity can be measured either in terms of wealth or of income.

In the United States, we measure wealth by counting the money value of everything you own, including houses, bank accounts, stocks and bonds, insurance policies, retirement funds, artwork, and jewelry. But since wealthy people have many ways to hide their assets, total holdings are hard to mea-sure accurately. The best guess from official sources is shown in Table 5.2 which displays **net worth**, the value of all assets minus outstanding debt, of U.S. households in 1998 compared to the value in 1992. The data clearly illus-trate the relative stagnation in net worth for middle-income earners.

As the data in Table 5.2 indicate, most American households have very few assets. The bottom 15 percent own less than $4,000 worth of goods, and half of all households have a net worth of under $40,000, most of which is what they own of their home. The accumulation of assets for households with incomes under $75,000 is greatly limited by their high burden of debt—mort-gage, credit card, and automobile payments (Wolff 1998).

112 Part II ✦ *Structures of Inequality*

Table 5.2 Median Income and Median Net Worth of U.S. Households, 1992–1998				
By Income Level (in 1998 dollars)				
	1992		**1998**	
Median Income	**%**	**Median Net Worth**	**%**	**Median Net Worth**
Under $10,000	14.8	$2,900	12.6	$3,600
10,000–24,999	27.0	27,100	24.8	24,800
25,000–49,999	29.8	55,600	28.8	60,300
50,000–99,999	20.7	129,900	25.2	152,000
100,000 and over	7.6	481,900	8.6	510,800

Source: Federal Reserve Board, 2000.

When one counts individuals rather than households, there are now over 3 million Americans with a net worth in excess of $1,000,000—about 1.5 percent of U.S. adults. This 1.5 percent, however, owns over 40 percent of the total wealth of the nation, including half of all stocks and bonds (Federal Reserve Board 2000; Shapiro and Greenstein 1999). The share owned by the few at the top continues to grow, due to the rising value of stocks, tax cuts that benefit high-income earners, and the instant fortunes of Internet pioneers. The top 20 percent of households now owns close to 88 percent of the total wealth of America, leaving about 12 percent for all the others. And within the top 20 percent, three-fourths of that wealth is owned by just 1 percent of households (Krugman 1999). 1

These patterns of inequality can be seen in the data on income, which are more accurate and easier to compute than those on wealth. Median household income—the midpoint with 50 percent of all households above and 50 percent below—in the United States in 1998 was about $39,000. Table 5.3 summarizes the characteristics with greatest effect on household income: household composition, marital status, race/ethnicity, and sex. Clearly, it pays to be married, white, male, and well educated.

Table 5.3 Median Income by Selected Characteristics, 1998 (in dollars)	
Type of household	
Family households	
Married couple	$54,267
Female householder, no husband	24,393
Male householder, no wife	39,414
Nonfamily households	
Female householder	16,615
Male householder	30,414
Race and ethnicity	
Non-Hispanic white	42,439
Black	25,351
Hispanic origin (any race)	28,330
Education	
No high school diploma	15,500
High school diploma	29,200
Some degree	35,500
College degree	54,700
Earnings of full-time year-round workers	
Men	35,345
Women	25,662

Source: U.S. Bureau of the Census, P60-206, 1999: vi; Federal Reserve Board, 2000:5.

It should be noted that data on households will be different from that on families since many households contain only one person, usually someone very young or very old whose income is limited. Families are units composed of two or more persons related by blood, marriage, or adoption, and therefore likely to have more than one earner. In 1998, for example, the median annual income of American families was about $46,000 (compared to $39,000 for households). For a married couple, both full-time workers and without children, the median was over $73,000.

If all American households are divided into five categories—from the poorest 20 percent to the wealthiest 20 percent—the share of the aggregate income of the United States received by the top fifth, or *quintile*, rose from 43.8 percent in 1967 to 49.2 in 1998. This means that the shares received by the other four quintiles declined over the same period, especially those of the next two highest quintiles—the "shrinking middle" of the income distribution, as shown in Figure 5.1.

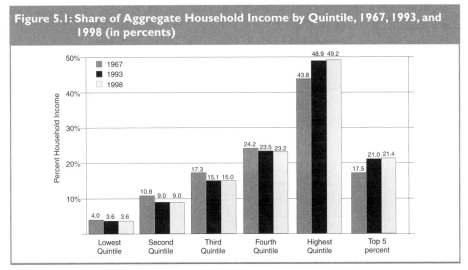

Figure 5.1: Share of Aggregate Household Income by Quintile, 1967, 1993, and 1998 (in percents)

Source: U.S. Census Bureau, *Current Population Survey*, March 1968, 1994, 1999.

Inequality in the United States

As the data on wealth and income clearly show, the gap between the very rich and everyone else, already the widest of all industrial nations and even greater than many Third World countries, continues to grow (Comai and Danziger 1997; United Nations 2000). In addition to favorable tax policies for the wealthy and a sharp decline in programs for the poor, here are some other explanatory factors (discussed further in chapter 9):

- Changes in the composition of the labor force as more women and entry-level baby boomers take low-wage positions.

- Escalating pay and benefit packages for the very few at the very top, e.g., chief executive officers (CEOs) and entertainment/sports stars.

- Declining power of unions to negotiate favorable wage and benefit packages for blue-collar workers or to attract white-collar employees.

- Relocation of manufacturing jobs to overseas or to low-wage anti-union states in the United States.

- Increased use of independent contractors and part-time employees without health and pension benefits.

- Growth in number of service jobs at the very lowest end of the skill and wage scale, e.g., fast food outlets and nursing homes.

The upside to some of these trends is that by the end of the 1990s, the demand for low-skill employees finally brought large numbers of hard-to-place workers into the labor force, so that the unemployment rate fell and household income among the poor stabilized. For the poor, this is good news and bad. The bad news is that full employment tends to create inflationary pressures that increase the cost of goods and services. The cure for inflationary pressures—the raising of interest rates, or the cost of borrowing—is especially disadvantageous to low-income earners, who will have difficulty getting loans, paying the mortgage, and even keeping their jobs.

Social Class and Social Order

Since people have varying positions in stratification hierarchies, sociologists have tried to simplify things by constructing a summary measure of social rank called **socioeconomic status (SES)**, based on occupational prestige, income, and educational level. SES is often used as the empirical referent for another abstraction, **social class**, which, along with race and gender, has a powerful effect on your life chances and choices.

Combining U.S. Bureau of the Census data on education, income, and occupation, Figure 5.2 reflects the authors' best guess about the social class distribution of Americans: a narrow band at the upper level; a vast middle that extends from college-educated managers to other white-collar workers; a working class that embraces blue-collar workers at various skill and pay levels; and a sizable segment of Americans disadvantaged along all dimensions of status. 🖥2

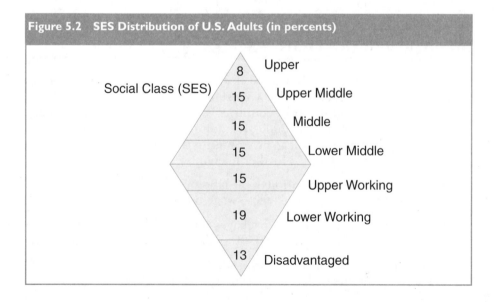

Figure 5.2   SES Distribution of U.S. Adults (in percents)

Social Class (SES)

- 8 Upper
- 15 Upper Middle
- 15 Middle
- 15 Lower Middle
- 15 Upper Working
- 19 Lower Working
- 13 Disadvantaged

Blue-collar work is also described as *manual*, literally involving "hands-on" labor with machines and other objects, in contrast to white-collar *nonmanual* labor involving work with people, ideas, and paper shuffling.

Another way of dividing the population by social class focuses on *relations of production*; namely, do you own your workplace or not, and do you control your labor or work for someone else (Wright 1985). In this perspective, very few are owners and bosses, with the bulk of the labor force really "working class," even though many carry briefcases rather than lunch pails. Nonetheless, most Americans and the media continue to use the term "middle class" to cover everyone except the very poor and the very wealthy. Thus, regardless of their objective position in a stratification hierarchy, most Americans locate themselves in the middle of the class system. In part, this reflects the *myth of classlessness*, a perfect example of ideological hegemony whereby children are brought up to believe that the system is open and fair, that the higher strata do not pursue class-based interests, and that, with hard work and a bit of luck, they, too, could become millionaires, just like Bill Gates, and he never completed college! As a consequence, although most Americans are aware of class-related distinctions, they do not make a big deal of it, unlike Europeans, for whom **class consciousness** is a central factor in political organizing and self-identity (Esping-Andersen 1990).

The myth of classlessness and the force of the work ethic go a long way toward explaining why the United States, with its rising levels of wage and wealth inequality, remains relatively stable. Inequality alone does not necessarily produce disorder, as long as most people perceive that the rules are fair and as long as they, too, enjoy an adequate standard of living (Bobo, Kluegel, and Smith 1997).

If you were to conduct a survey of Americans, asking which of the following reasons for poverty were very important, what do you guess you would find?

- Lack of thrift.

- Lack of effort.

- Lack of ability.

- Loose morals.

- Physical handicaps.

- Low wages.

- Lack of stable employment.

- Poor schools.

- Discrimination.

- Bad luck.

In fact, a majority of respondents will cite the first four items as most important, placing the blame for failure on individuals and making value judgments about the moral worth of the poor (Kluegel and Bobo 1994). In addition, beliefs about causes of poverty are also bound up with racial attitudes (Williams et al. 1999). Social structural factors—schools, wages, jobs, or race and ethnic discrimination—are barely considered. This is why it is so hard to teach sociology and why it is so important that you understand it.

Poverty in America

The debate over the causes of poverty—the importance of personal or structural variables—has real political outcomes. Conservatives explain persistent poverty in terms of behavioral problems such as bad work habits, family breakdown, single parenthood, and welfare dependency—a "culture of poverty" handed down from one generation to another (Herrnstein and Murray 1994). In contrast, most sociologists and political liberals focus on a lack of jobs paying a living wage, residential patterns that segregate the poor and minorities, outright discrimination in hiring and promotion, and a

About 35 million Americans live in poverty: a large majority are women and their children. Poverty can be found in both urban and rural areas.

shortage of stable wage-earners as marriage partners. In this perspective, the personality traits so often thought of as causes of poverty can also be seen as the consequences of living in a low-income neighborhood (Wilson 1996; Brooks-Gunn et al. 1997). Faced with such an environment—the crumbling schools, minimal job prospects, traffic in drugs, and disintegrating families—children have few options but to repeat the choices made by their parents.

How Is Poverty Measured?

Everyone uses the term "poverty level," but few know exactly what this means. The official poverty line, or threshold, is the dollar amount set by the federal government as the minimum needed to feed, house, clothe, and care for a household. 💻 3 The original formula was devised in the early 1960s, when, having found that a poor family spent about one-third of its income on food, an employee of the Department of Agriculture computed the cost of the least expensive nutritionally adequate diet for families of varying size (Orshansky 1965). The cost of that food basket, multiplied by three, became the poverty threshold. Each year, the poverty levels are adjusted for changes in the cost of living, but this adjustment only partly corrects for the fact that housing expenses have risen far more rapidly than expenses for food, which now take up only about 20 percent of the household income. For many fami-

lies, then, the choice is between rent and food, especially at the end of the
month (Edin and Lein 1997). Table 5.4 shows the poverty thresholds for 1999.

Table 5.4 Poverty Thresholds, 1999	
One person, under age 65	$8,667
One person, age 65 and older	7,990
Two persons, under age 65	11,156
Two persons, age 65 and older	10,070
Three people (1 adult, 2 children)	13,423
Four people (1 adult, 3 children)	16,954

Source: Bureau of the Census Online, 2000f.

How well could you and your two children live on $13,000 a year?

America's Poor: Who and How Many?

Figure 5.3 shows the trends in poverty from 1960 to 1998. As you can see,
contrary to public perception, the War on Poverty of the 1960s was a great
success, cutting the rate of poverty in half among all Americans, especially
the elderly, before hitting a plateau as the costs of the Vietnam War diverted
resources from domestic programs. Poverty rates increased with the recessions of the 1980s and then declined again in the late 1990s. Today's low rates
reflect the expansion of the lower-skill end of the job market as well as
changes in the welfare system that make it hard to count the poor.

Poverty is not evenly distributed by race or sex or age. Of the 35 million
officially poor Americans today, about 80 percent are women and their children. Although 46 percent of the poor are non-Hispanic whites, they represent less than 9 percent of that category, whereas about 24 percent of both
blacks and Hispanics (who can be of any race, so that there is some overlap)
lived in households below the poverty line. The predominance of women and
girls—from elderly widows to teenage mothers—is often referred to as the
feminization of poverty (Pearce 1985).

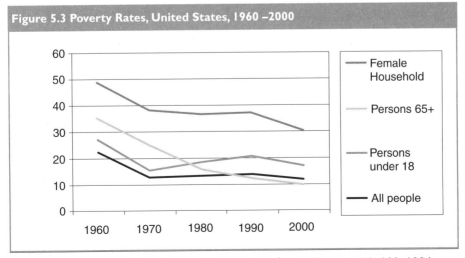

Figure 5.3 Poverty Rates, United States, 1960–2000

Source: U.S. Bureau of the Census, *Current Population Report*, p60–188, 1994.

More accurately, poverty is a problem for nonmarried women and their children. The proportion of children in poverty in the United States—one in five—is the highest by far of any industrial society (United Nations 2000). For black and Hispanic-American children, the proportion rises to 37 percent. Then, when one also adds the "near poor," those in households with an income only a few thousand dollars over the poverty threshold, we are talking about close to half of all children of black and Hispanic origin (Acs and Gallagher 2000). These numbers are worth thinking about, especially since poverty in childhood is associated with a number of negative outcomes for the children and for the society they enter as adults, such as delayed cognitive and physical development that affects school achievement and eventual earnings (Duncan et al. 1998). If poverty reproduces itself, it is not through socialization but through deprivation and limited life chances. No impoverished parent wishes to transmit her problems to her children, but the children have few alternatives.

Social Welfare Programs

With the exception of the Social Security legislation of the 1930s, reducing poverty or alleviating its effects has been considered a local and state responsibility. This decentralization of power is only one reason why, in contrast to other modern industrial societies, the United States never developed a comprehensive national system of social welfare. The other major reasons include the weakness of organized labor, the power of big business, the role of money in politics, and a streak of racism (Noble 1997).

Between 1945 and 1996, Congress did enact a few limited programs as a federal obligation, funded primarily from general taxes and subject to national guidelines, but left them to the states to administer. This minimal support system was defined as an "entitlement," open to anyone whose income fell below the poverty threshold or who met other basic criteria. The four major federal programs, of which only Medicaid and Food Stamps survived, were the following.

Medicaid—which reimburses doctors and hospitals for services to the poor. However, by 1995, the reimbursement rate was set so low that doctors turned patients away.

Food stamps—available to impoverished households and the unemployed, and supported by food merchants and legislators of farm states.

Supplemental Security Income (SSI)—which provided cash assistance to the elderly and to disabled Americans whose Social Security benefits fell below the poverty line. But by 1995, most states had lowered monthly payments and raised eligibility requirements so that fewer than half of those eligible received any SSI income. Especially hard hit were the parents of children with emotional and physical handicaps.

Aid to Families with Dependent Children (AFDC)—until it was ended in 1996, AFDC provided monthly benefits to unemployed single parents, almost all of whom were women. Here, too, by 1995, states had lowered benefit levels and raised eligibility standards; for example, a family could not be eligible if it owned items worth more than $1,000, excluding furniture and cooking utensils or a car valued at more than $1,500. Thus, more than half of

America's poor children were excluded from this program, as well as from Medicaid and food stamps.

Welfare myths and facts. Even the minimal efforts of those federal programs became perceived as "handouts" that encouraged dependency and antisocial behaviors and created a permanent underclass of recipients. Most Americans believed that welfare cheats were ripping off the system, that poor women had more children in order to increase their benefits, and that AFDC was a major contributor to the national debt.

In fact, none of these claims was supported by the evidence. Eighty-five percent of AFDC mothers were in the program for four years or less, with only 7 percent receiving benefits for eight or more consecutive years. In addition, AFDC mothers were less likely than other poor women to have additional children, with over 70 percent having only one or two. Unmarried teenage mothers—the most demonized of the poor—accounted for less than 10 percent of the AFDC caseload. And, finally, far from being a big drag on the budget, AFDC accounted for under 2 percent of the federal budget and under 5 percent of state outlays (Urban Institute 2000). 💻4

Indeed, it is precisely because the United States spends so little on social welfare programs that poverty persists; the benefits only made life a little less painful but were not sufficient to lift a household above the poverty line. In the rest of the industrialized world, the level of family supports is much higher, and the more generous the benefits, the more readily do families move out of poverty (Duncan 1994). Why then, have Americans taken exactly the opposite course, ending the concept of social entitlement as well as the federal role in establishing welfare policy? Certainly, the ideology of the work ethic plays a large part. So, also, does the electoral triumph of conservative Republicans pledged to dismantle all federal programs in favor of the states and private enterprise. And so, probably, does the fact that so many of the poor are nonwhite and female and sexually active—a triple whammy (Luker 2000).

From welfare to workfare. In 1996, President Clinton signed the Personal Responsibility and Work Opportunity Reconciliation Act which radically changed both the meaning and structure of social welfare in the United States. No longer an entitlement of those whose income fell below the poverty line and no longer subject to federal supervision, eligibility and benefit levels are now determined by each state. Where money had once been funneled from Washington for specific uses—housing, education, income supports— each state now receives a lump-sum payment, a **block grant** for Temporary Assistance to Needy Families (TANF), to be used in any way the state sees fit to lower the welfare rolls and reduce unmarried pregnancies (Watts 1997). The few federal guidelines emphasized that former recipients should be encouraged to find employment or lose all benefits. Immigrants, both legal and undocumented, were ineligible for participation in most programs. In addition, the legislation set time limits for receiving benefits—no more than five years during a lifetime, which the states could shorten—as well as a "family cap," permitting the states to deny benefits to unmarried teenage mothers or older women who have another child while enrolled in the program. Curiously, these proposals for using public policy to produce behavioral changes were proposed by the very politicians who claim to abhor "social engineering."

❖ ❖ ❖ ❖   The very title of the act—Personal Responsibility and Work Opportunity—reaffirms the work ethic. Echoes of our Puritan past resonate throughout the legislation—the fear of uncontrolled sexuality, condemnation of dependency, and the elevation of employment as the means to salvation (Astone 1997). As Mayor Giuliani of New York City advised the poor, "If you cannot get a job, start a small business. Start a little candy store. Start a little newspaper. Start a lemonade stand" (DeParle 1999, 88).

Between 1996 and 2000, welfare caseloads dropped dramatically across the nation, in part because of strict enforcement of TANF and in part because of the booming labor market. Overall, a high proportion of single mothers found employment, and most realized higher incomes than under welfare. Others remained untouched by the new policies, and a small minority were worse off than before TANF (Jencks and Swingle 2000). The aggregate data, however, obscure attempts by the states to lower welfare costs at the expense of the truly needy. In West Virginia, for example, much of the decline in welfare rolls occurred when SSI eligibility for families with disabled children was ended (Janofsky 1999a). In New York State, the statistics were inflated by the fact that being "employed" was defined as earning at least $100 in the three months after being dropped from welfare. In addition, many of the jobs assigned to TANF recipients place them in competition with other low-wage workers, lowering wages for all marginal workers (Hout 1996). As a result of such policies, most states have realized millions of dollars by not spending their full block grant, using unspent anti-poverty funds to finance large tax cuts for the middle class (Hernandez 2000).

Box 5.1

Welfare and Workfare in Minnesota

Few states have made as great an effort as Minnesota to find jobs for welfare mothers and to keep records on how this effort was succeeding. Realizing that bringing low-skilled parents into the labor force requires not only training for jobs but also providing child care and health insurance coverage, as well as continued income supports, the Minnesota Family Investment Program conducted a carefully monitored experiment with alternatives to welfare from 1994 through 1998 (Knox et al. 2000). The key element was the promise that going to work would not lower the family income, i.e., that work would pay and that the state would supplement earnings well above the poverty level. In addition, social services, job counseling, and child-care subsidies were provided. The results were surprising, even to the researchers: Not only did full-time employment rise, so also did yearly income, health insurance coverage, and home ownership. Most surprising was the effect on family formation and stability; marriage rates rose and divorce rates declined. There was also some evidence of positive effects on children's school performance and general behavior.

The cautionary note is that large numbers did not improve their circumstances, even in a period of full employment and in a state with a relatively high proportion of whites and high school graduates in the poverty population. As in most states, the easier-to-place workers were the first to move into employment, leaving the hard-to-place behind. Furthermore, because the price tag for the experimental program was the highest of any state, the Minnesota legislature modified the system in 1998 to reduce cash incentives, set more rigid time limits, and focus more exclusively on getting people into jobs. It appears that there are no free lunches, and much depends on the public's willingness to support the kinds of services needed to lift the really tough cases out of poverty.

How the Other 1.5 Percent Live

At the other end of the stratification hierarchy are those with net assets of at least one million dollars. Some of these are newly minted millionaires—high-tech geniuses, sports figures, entertainers—who have made instant fortunes. Until the late 1990s, however, most wealth in America was accumulated over a longer period, often over several generations.

Wealth and Class

There is a crucial distinction between "new" and "old" money. It takes more than a lot of dollars to join the "upper class," membership in which is based on family background (blood) as well as on inherited wealth. This is a very exclusive group consisting of fewer than 100,000 individuals and families who have maintained their position over time through careful marriages and the socialization of their children in private schools (Domhoff 1998). Old wealth tends to be less flashy than the new variety, although both the new and old rich today appear engaged in a frenzy of conspicuous consumption that has driven up the cost of luxury items and made it harder for everyone else simply to stay in place (Frank 2000).

Until recently, the upper stratum was almost exclusively composed of white, Anglo-Saxon (Dutch or British origins), Protestant families, hence the acronym WASP. It is still all white, but a few highly successful Jews and Catholics have managed to win acceptance—e.g., Henry Kissinger and the Kennedys. The WASP elite has lost ground, however, in its control over major corporations and financial institutions. While blood still counts in the prestige hierarchy, the wealthy class as a whole is much more varied than in the past, especially in terms of religion and social class origins. 🖥5

Old money is an exclusive group consisting of individuals and families who have maintained their position through marriages and the education of their children in private schools.

Staying on Top

Members of the upper strata benefit greatly from the tax system. Many pay few, if any, income taxes, and often at a rate lower than that of working class households (Johnson et al. 1999). In addition, the highest 1 percent of income earners reaped almost all the benefits from recent changes in the tax structure, especially the lowered rates on capital gains and the near-elimination of estate taxes. The wealthy are also the prime gainers from their own charitable giving, typically to the churches and elite schools they attend, private hospitals, conservative think tanks, and local cultural institutions such as museums and orchestras, and all contributions are written off as tax deductions (Wagner 2000). Even the national debt works to their advantage since the debt is funded by Treasury bonds purchased by the wealthy, with the interest coming from tax returns paid by all.

In addition, because most state legislators are fearful of raising income taxes, they raise money through state lotteries, gambling casinos, and sales and property taxes that actually penalize the less wealthy. It may sound fair that everyone pay at the same rate—a 5 percent sales tax, for example—because people who can buy more will pay more. But when you look at it in terms of percentage of income, the poor pay more. This is so because families with limited income will probably spend it all on the necessities of living and thus pay the sales tax on all of their disposable income. Wealthy people, however, spend only a fraction of their earnings on consumer goods and therefore pay taxes on a smaller proportion of total income. Such fixed-rate taxes are considered *regressive* because they take a bigger bite from the less well-off, in contrast to a *progressive* tax structure that would apply higher rates to higher incomes.

Despite the growing gap between the very rich and everyone else, few Americans express a sense of outrage. Indeed, politicians favoring a flat tax and other programs that benefit the wealthy have been very successful in recent elections. It appears that most voters feel that the system is fair and that with a little more hard work and luck, they or their children can join the ranks of the rich if not the upper class itself.

Just what are your chances for upward movement in the stratification system?

Social Mobility

Social mobility refers to movement upward or downward across stratification lines. Societies vary in the extent to which movement is possible. In a **caste system**, based on ascription, there is minimal mobility since a person's social status is fixed at birth. The caste into which you are born determines whom you marry, how much schooling you get, and what occupations you can enter. With a few exceptions for unusually lucky or talented individuals, the system reproduces itself from generation to generation.

For example, although legally abolished, the caste system of modern India remains powerful, with Brahmins at the top and the Untouchables at the bottom. In South Africa, until a decade ago, the system of rigid segregation between whites and people of color, called **apartheid**, assured white dominance even though whites were vastly outnumbered. Similar laws existed in the United States right up to the late 1960s, forbidding cross-race marriage, segregating school children, and denying voting rights. Some would argue that our society still has elements of a caste structure at the very top and bottom. It is the rare child of great wealth who ends up in a homeless shelter. It is also the case that very few families at the bottom of the stratification system will get rich (Gottschalk and Danziger 1998). The exceptions—a handful of sports or entertainment figures, and perhaps a lottery winner or two—do little to change the reality for the majority of the disadvantaged.

Open class systems, based primarily on achieved rather than ascribed statuses, permit individuals and groups to cross class boundaries. **Upward**

mobility involves improving one's position, while downward mobility represents status loss. Horizontal mobility refers to slight gains or losses basically within the same stratum.

The comparison between parents' social rank and that of their children is called intergenerational mobility ("inter-" = between). In contrast, status change within a person's lifetime is called intragenerational, or career, mobility ("intra-" = within). The Great American Dream is based on a belief in both types of upward mobility through hard work and clean living, the essence of the work ethic.

Mobility in the United States

There is some truth in the dream of continued upward movement, although it is not unique to the United States. Between 1945 and 1965, most modern industrial societies experienced similar mobility patterns because of a massive shift from manual to nonmanual occupations—a shift that automatically enhances status because white-collar employment is more prestigious than manual labor and usually requires more education. Most of this movement was intergenerational, with sons exceeding their fathers' status; it is correct for the authors to speak here only of sons and fathers because almost all historical mobility data were gathered for men. It was assumed until quite recently that a woman's status was determined by that of her father and then that of her husband, marriage being her primary avenue of upward mobility.

The fact that mobility patterns for industrial societies are basically similar, with some cultural differences, strongly suggests that *the structure of the economy* is the major determinant of mobility rates. In other words, most occupational mobility can be explained by societal-level variables rather than by individual factors.

Structural Mobility

Structural, or demand, mobility refers to those societal-level variables that affect mobility rates: (1) the number and types of jobs available at any historical moment, and (2) the number and types of people available to fill them. The distribution of jobs reflects changes in the economy as a whole, such as the sharp reduction in the need for farm labor since 1900, as machines replaced workers, or the growth of the manufacturing sector from 1900 to 1960, and the current increase in both high- and low-skill service occupations. The number and quality of competitors for these jobs depends on variations in birth rates and on educational opportunity.

These processes are illustrated in Figure 5.4, which shows the proportion of American workers in different occupational levels from 1900 to 1998. These triangles show the dramatic shift in occupations over this century, off the farm and into the factory, and then out of the factory and into offices, automatically creating upward mobility in the hierarchy of occupational prestige. With each shift, educational qualifications rose, so that each generation moved up a notch or two in the educational hierarchy.

The number and type of job openings were not the only structural factor accounting for the spurt in upward mobility between 1945 and 1965. Of equal importance were the extremely low birthrates, especially for middle-class families, during the Great Depression of the 1930s and World War II in the early 1940s. This meant that managerial jobs were opening up at a faster rate than the children of the middle class could fill them, creating a vacuum into which young people from the working class could move and thus move up. Furthermore, if they were veterans of World War II, men (and a few women) from the working class could take advantage of the GI Bill, which provided a full college education financed by a grateful nation. This was an option open primarily to whites, as few African-American veterans could afford to remain out of the labor force for another four years. In other words, the upward mobility enjoyed by so many American families in the 1950s was the product of social forces that advantaged some segments of the population.

Absolute and Relative Mobility

As they surpassed their fathers in education, occupational prestige, and income, sons experienced *absolute mobility,* moving upward on all these hierarchies. But, as you can see from the asterisks in Figure 5.4, there is not much difference in the location of fathers and sons relative to everyone else. This is so because the entire occupational structure was upgraded. In terms of *relative mobility,* within the stratification system as a whole, there has not been a great change. It is this process that gives the impression of great upward mobility in industrial societies while at the same time preserving the advantage of the top strata and obscuring the high level of **class immobility,** the tendency for relative status to be reproduced from generation to generation. In other words, it looks as if each generation has done better, and it probably has in absolute terms, but so have most others in that stratum, which leaves the relative distribution of status unchanged.

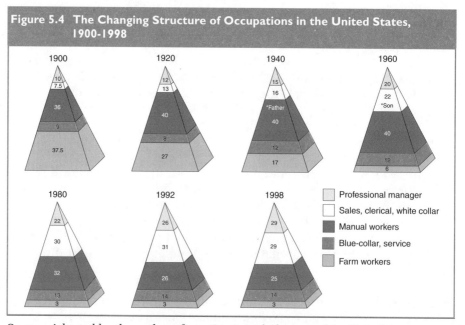

Figure 5.4   The Changing Structure of Occupations in the United States, 1900-1998

Source: Adapted by the authors from *Statistical Abstract of the United States,* 1999; *Historical Statistics of the United States, 1975.*

What, then, you may be asking, are your mobility chances? Here, you may face two problems: (1) job growth in the service sector is uneven, with more positions opening up at the bottom than at the top; and (2) college students in the early twenty-first century follow two decades of baby boomers who entered the labor force between 1965 and 1985 and who will clog avenues of job advancement for many years to come. Your best bet is to stay in school as long as possible; the more you know, the fewer competitors and the better able you will be to adapt and take advantage of new opportunities.

Status Attainment

Success in the United States and other industrial societies remains profoundly influenced by ascribed characteristics such as race, ethnicity, sex, and social class at birth. It helps to be white, male, and of Northern European ancestry, and although religion is less important than in the past, most business and political leaders still come from the more liberal branches of Protestantism.

Children of the middle class begin life with a number of advantages associated with high achievement in school and work. In chapter 3 you learned how a parent's occupation affects child-rearing behaviors, with middle-class parents using techniques that reward self-direction, intellectual curiosity, and **deferred gratification**, the ability to put off instant pleasure in order to pursue a distant goal. Middle-class children also benefit from smaller family size, older parents, and the probability of spending one's childhood in a two-parent household. The middle-class household is usually more likely than working-class households to offer **cultural capital** in the form of an interest in literature, art, classical music, and a general knowledge of current events that impresses teachers.

The basic model of status attainment is shown in Figure 5.5. In this model, a daughter's or son's original social position, based on father's occupational status, is directly related to the length and quality of schooling. In addition, parents also have **social capital**, in the form of friendship and influence networks that can be tapped to help the son or daughter find that all-important first job. The child's own input, educational level, and success in his or her first job then predicts subsequent jobs and ultimate position in the stratification system.

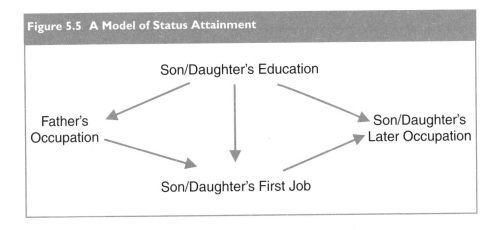

Figure 5.5 A Model of Status Attainment

Son/Daughter's Education

Father's Occupation

Son/Daughter's First Job

Son/Daughter's Later Occupation

Although family background is a powerful predictor of social mobility, it is not all-determining. There are always individual skills that lead to different outcomes, even for children in the same family. And then there is sheer luck, unpredictable chance events—being in the right place at the right time, getting a tip from a friend, following a hunch. But motivation and attitude will get you only so far. Inequality is structured when the wealthy transmit advantages and assets to their children, regardless of the children's ability.

Nonetheless, the American dream of unlimited individual achievement remains a powerful vision, especially with the instant fortunes to be made in new high-tech ventures. At some point, however, reality has to intrude; there are not that many slots at the top. How do people deal with the gap between early high hopes and their actual achievements? Most will lower aspirations to fit reality, but surrendering the dream is very difficult, which may account for the anger expressed in the popular music that appeals to working-class youth with limited mobility potential.

Social Status in Everyday Life

From the interpretive perspective, at the level of face-to-face interaction, social status is a crucial aspect of how you see yourself and how you present that self to others, what sociologists call *impression management*. The trick is to manipulate the image you project in order to protect the "self" and gain recognition for what you consider your better traits. At the same time, role partners are trying to manipulate your perception of them. Each interaction becomes a game to see who controls the situation.

In this game, **status symbols**, or **cues**, the outward signs of social rank, are crucial for locating people in the prestige hierarchy. Think of how differently you address people whom you see as social superiors from those perceived as equals or status inferiors—e.g., "sir," "old buddy," or "hey, you." And you are really quite skilled at picking up the cues that tell you the social location of others. Sex and skin color are immediately visible, but other traits take a bit of effort to identify, such as speech patterns, clothing, or hair styles. Observe yourself the next time you go to a party where you meet people for the first time and notice how quickly you pick out those features that allow you to locate them in the stratification system, and how anxious you are until you can place them.

Status symbols or cues are outward signs of social rank and help locate people in the prestige hierarchy.

Status symbols also serve to advertise a person's sense of importance while putting inferiors in their place. "Keeping up with the Joneses" refers to the scramble for status recognition in the neighborhood—the larger home, more expensive car, fancier patio, and the in-ground swimming pool. Such displays of conspicuous consumption are the ultimate in impression management. The advertising industry is devoted to stimulating ever-higher levels of demand in order to signify success and earn the respect of others, thus keeping the economy humming and the work ethic fulfilled.

In this, Americans are not much different from the Kwakiutl tribes of the Pacific Northwest who periodically hold a feast, the potlatch, in which the host heaps gifts upon his guests and then throws the leftovers on a fire. "How wasteful," you may be saying. But this is how the pecking order there is created and maintained; all those guests are inferior to their host until they, too, can throw a grand potlatch. Think of some event that you may have attended recently—a wedding, perhaps, or confirmation, or Bar/Bat Mitzvah—where sheer wastefulness was the subtext.

Figuring out the social location of role partners is relatively easy when the person sends out clear and consistent cues. In modern society, however, many people occupy incompatible positions in ascribed and achieved hierarchies. Status consistency occurs when an individual occupies similar positions in different stratification systems: the ascribed hierarchies of race, religion, ethnicity, sex, and social class at birth, and the achieved hierarchies of education, income, and occupation. A white, Anglo-Saxon, Protestant, male Harvard-educated executive with a six-figure income is as status consistent as they come. So, too, is the dark-skinned Hispanic woman who cleans his office for the minimum wage. In contrast to the castelike nature of these extremes, most Americans present a mixed picture, or status inconsistency.

Status-inconsistent people—the woman doctor or African-American lawyer, for example—create cognitive dissonance, an uncomfortable feeling in one's mind caused by incompatible perceptions (Festinger 1957). How can we reconcile low ascribed status with high achieved status? To which cue do we respond? Some role partners will resolve the dissonance by assuming that the woman or person of color is less qualified but got there through affirmative action, thus creating consistency in the partner's head.

The status-inconsistent person has the problem of being accepted at his or her higher status when other people respond to the lower one in order to maintain control of the interaction. This often leads the person to overemphasize his or her achievements in a way that others describe as "pushy" or "uppity."

At the other extreme of status inconsistency are people who rank high in ascription—males, whites, persons of European background, and Protestants—but low in education, occupational prestige, and income. School dropouts with a history of employment problems, feeling entitled to better treatment by virtue of their ascribed statuses, can come to resent the success of those they perceive as their inferiors—women, blacks, Jews, and gays. It is precisely among these status-inconsistent men—white, underemployed, high school educated—that organizations like the Ku Klux Klan or American Nazi Party, with their emphasis on racial purity and male superiority, find most of their recruits. This is a basically *structural* explanation of recruitment to organizations. Attitudes are shaped by social locations, and resentment is a logical outcome of occupying statuses that should bring a person greater rewards than are actually received.

❖ ❖ ❖ ❖

❖ ❖ ❖ ❖   ## Conclusion

This emphasis on social locations is basic to the sociological perspective. In this chapter, you have seen how a person's location in various stratification hierarchies affects attitudes and behaviors, life choices and chances. Ascribed statuses have a profound impact on achievement opportunities that, in turn, are transmitted as social capital to the next generation.

All societies that are more complex than a gathering band are stratified, with some individuals or groups entitled to more of the collective resources than are other members of the society. The unequal distribution of power, prestige, and property produces a hierarchy of social worth. In modern societies, differences in educational attainment, occupational esteem, and income are typically used to measure socioeconomic status (SES), which is an index of social class. Although the myth of classlessness remains part of the American belief system, the United States is a highly stratified society, with a small but powerful upper stratum, a large and fluid middle class, and, for a modern society, a relatively large segment of disadvantaged.

You have learned about the processes of social mobility and the crucial importance of the structure of occupations in determining a person's chances of upward movement. While personal characteristics do play an important role, overall rates of mobility are dependent on the number and type of jobs available as well as the opportunity to receive the training required to fill the occupational slots.

At the micro-level of everyday life, you have seen how status positions affect your evaluation of self and others. Locating people along various dimensions of social rank—by their appearance, language, and other status cues—is crucial to your knowing how to respond to them. In many ways, each encounter is an exchange of status presentations.

The bottom line is that, as difficult as it often is to acknowledge the importance of social class, it remains one of the most powerful variables in sociology, along with race and gender. Where one begins in the hierarchy has much to do with where one ends up.

Surfing the Sociological Internet

 1 Almost any information on the economy is easily accessible from a variety of government sites:
For economic indicators go to: http://www.whitehouse.gov.fsbr/esbr.html
The Department of Labor address is: http://www.dol.gov
Federal Reserve Board: http://www.federalreserve.gov/ The U.S. budget figures are at: http://www.whitehouse.gov/OMB/
Congressional Budget Office can be found at: http://www.cbo.gov/

2 SES indicators can be found at http://census.gov
Work force statistics can be found at: http://stats.bls.gov
For more employment data: http://bls.gov/cesprog.htm

🖳3 Poverty guidelines, research, and measurement: http://
aspe.os.dhhs.gov/poverty/poverty.htm

🖳4 For statistics on the economic health of families, see: http://
www.census.gov/
The Joint Center for Economic Research's site has information
on welfare issues: http://www.jcpr.org

🖳5 Who are the richest 400 people in America? Go to: http://
www.forbes.com/tool/toolbox/rich400/

Glossary

Aid to Families with Dependent Children (AFDC) Provided monthly benefits to unemployed single parents.

Apartheid The former South African policy of segregation and political and economic discrimination against people of color.

Block Grants Lump sum payments by the federal government to individual states to be used to lower welfare rolls and reduce unmarried pregnancies.

Caste System A social hierarchy in which everyone's social status is fixed at birth.

Class Consciousness Occurs when class awareness becomes the central organizing point of self-definition and political action.

Class Immobility The tendency for relative status to be reproduced from generation to generation.

Cultural Capital A style of talking and thinking, as well as knowledge of music, art, and literature, that prepares individuals for membership in the dominant strata.

Cognitive Dissonance An uncomfortable feeling caused by an individual's experiencing incompatible perceptions.

Deferred Gratification The ability to put off instant pleasure in order to pursue a more distant goal.

Demand Mobility See Structural Mobility.

Downward Mobility Status loss in the stratification system.

Food Stamps A federally funded program available to very poor households and the unemployed for the purchase of food.

Hierarchy A set of ranked statuses from high to low.

Horizontal Mobility Slight gains or losses basically within the same stratum of a hierarchy.

Human Capital The abilities, training, and social networks in which individuals have invested.

Ideological Hegemony Control over the production of ideas and cultural symbols.

Intergenerational Mobility Comparison between parents' social rank and that of their children.

Intragenerational, or Career, Mobility Status changes within a person's lifetime.

Medicaid A federally funded and state-administered health-care system that reimburses doctors and hospitals for services to the poor.

Meritocracy The rule of the best and the brightest.

Net Worth The value of all of an individual's assets less outstanding debts.

Open Class Systems A class system based mostly on achieved rather than ascribed statuses; it permits individuals and groups to cross class boundaries.

Potlatch A feast held by members of the Kwakiutl tribes of the Pacific Northwest in which the host heaps gifts upon his guests as a sign of prestige.

Prestige The honor and respect given by others.

Professions Top-ranked occupations requiring many years of education and training.

Property Material goods.

Social Capital Friendship and influence networks that can be used to help gain entry into schools, jobs, and other positions.

Social Classes Societal divisions based on ownership and control of the means of production.

Social Mobility Movement upward or downward across stratification lines.

Social Stratification The distribution of individuals and groups on the basis of their command over scarce societal resources.

Socioeconomic Status (SES) A summary measure of social rank based on occupational prestige, income, and education.

Status Consistency An individual occupying similar positions in different stratification systems.

Status Inconsistency An individual occupying different positions in different stratification systems.

Status Symbols, or Cues The outward signs of social rank that help locate people in the prestige hierarchy.

Structural, or Demand, Mobility Societal-level factors that affect mobility rates.

Supplemental Security Income (SSI) A program that provided cash assistance to the elderly and the disabled.

Upward Mobility Improving one's position in the stratification system. ✦

The American Mosaic: Racial, Ethnic, and Religious Minorities

A **mosaic** is an object composed of many pieces of different colors and shapes. In many ways, the United States resembles a mosaic in its mix of persons of different races, national origins, and religious preferences. This chapter examines the history and experience of various **minority groups**, the pieces of the mosaic, including such topics as:

- Defining a minority.
- The social construction of race and ethnicity.
- Immigration trends.
- Processes of inclusion and exclusion.
- The enduring significance of race.
- Ethnic groups in America.
- Religious minorities.

What Is a Minority Group?

A **minority group** is defined in contrast to a society's **dominant group**, those who control the major sources of power and who set standards of social worth and beauty. The dominant group does not have to be a numerical majority, as in the case of the United States today, where white males of Northern European (Anglo-Saxon) ancestry and Protestant faith (WASPs) are a small fraction of the population, but compose the vast majority of political and economic leaders, with powerful influence on our culture, language, laws, and beliefs. Thus, in our society, people who differ from the WASP ideal have characteristics that set them apart and that often become cues for special, unequal treatment.

Sociologically, minority group status involves four elements:

1. A *visible* ascribed trait by which group members can be recognized.
2. *Differential* (unequal) treatment on the basis of that trait.
3. *Organizing a self-image* around this identity.
4. *Awareness of a shared identity* with other similar people.

For example, people with red hair are not a minority group by this definition, but if red hair came to be seen as a sign of the devil and if redheads were sent to separate schools and given only low-paying jobs, they might soon define themselves in terms of their hair color and join with other redheads in protest.

In our society, and most others, the most visible traits leading to differential treatment are sex (discussed in chapter 7) and skin color. Country of origin **(ethnicity)** is less obvious but continues to be the basis for unequal access to education and jobs. And for most of U.S. history, Catholics and Jews were excluded from some colleges and residential areas. The stress of minority group status produces subcultures, which then provide a supportive social network as well as an alternative viewpoint in which the ascribed trait becomes a positive rather than negative feature. Over time, in the United States, ethnicity and religion have lost their castelike power to limit entry into positions of prestige and power, but race, or more accurately, blackness, remains a stubborn barrier to mobility, as discussed in this chapter.

Societies vary in the number of minority groups they contain. Most simple societies and many modern ones such as Sweden are **culturally homogeneous** (*homo* = similar; *gens* = people) in that the great majority of citizens are of the same race and share a common language and religion. In contrast, the United States and such populous societies as China and India are **heterogeneous** (*hetero* = different), composed of many distinct subgroups. Sometimes, even in a homogeneous society, if there is no visible physical trait to set them apart, a certain subgroup will become a "virtual minority," as in the case of Gypsies (Roma) in Central Europe and the Burakumin of Japan, who look exactly like other Japanese but who are nonetheless shunned (Rhim 1993).

In addition, the movement of populations across national boundaries throughout the world today has made it difficult to retain racial and ethnic homogeneity. The mixing of populations has caused outbursts of hostility and terrorism in all regions, including such modern societies as Austria, France, and West Germany, where attacks on foreign laborers are increasingly common. This chapter examines the history and experience of minority groups in the United States. That history is both unique and universal: unique in the variety of groups and depth of divisions, universal in illustrating general processes of separation and integration. 🖥 1

The Social Construction of Race and Ethnicity

From the sociological perspective, minority group status is a social construction, that is, a matter of cultural definition (who is "in" or "out" of the dominant group) and of treatment by others in the society.

Race

Although you probably have an idea of race as a set of readily identifiable physical characteristics, race is actually impossible to define in scientific terms. Human populations have become so intermixed that racial classifications are more arbitrary than not. The most obvious traits—skin color, eye shape, hair texture—appear in bewildering variety both within and between populations. Most such physical characteristics developed as responses to particular environments during the thousands of years of recent human evolution. But the most important point is that these traits have no built-in relationship to any capacity or ability, intellectual or athletic. *All innate human abilities, including intelligence, are distributed in much the same way within any racial category*; that is, you will find roughly the same percentage at the high and low ends of the distribution, with the great majority clustered around the middle or mean.

Nor are there any crucial *genetic* differences among the races. One of the most important lessons of the recently deciphered human genome is the extreme homogeneity of our species, with less variation among individuals than among mice or even other primates. Ninety-nine percent of genetic matter is distributed similarly across racial groups. The other one-tenth of 1 percent appears to be associated with skin color and hair texture (Owens and King 1999). In other words, from a genetic perspective, racial differences are

❖ ❖ ❖ ❖ literally only skin-deep. There is no basketball gene for blacks or comedy gene for Jews or police gene for Irish Americans (Marks 2000).

But when whiteness or darkness is associated in the public mind with certain abilities, and treated accordingly, race does indeed become a factor in achievement. Remember the *definition of the situation*, that what people believe to be real is real in its consequences? If most Americans, throughout our history, perceived blacks as less evolved or competent than whites, the consequences for schooling and employment were very real indeed. As disadvantages accumulate over time, it appears that the original perception was correct—another example of the *self-fulfilling prophecy*.

Notice that when people talk about race, it is often with reference to American blacks and Asians, but white people also have "race." It is simply that white people are rarely conscious of it. By not acknowledging that whiteness is a racial characteristic, people overlook the extent to which it confers advantages on those who have it (Kincheloe et al. 2000; Hitchcock 2000). Just being white is a privileged status that gives some people a better chance at most jobs, allows them to move to any place they can afford, keeps them from being pulled over by state troopers, guarantees that their children will not be teased about their skin color, makes it more likely that they can get a home improvement loan, and on and on and on. Also overlooked is the extent to which whites act to preserve their racial privileges, as when the claim that rules should be "race-neutral" actually solidifies the advantages they

already enjoy. For example, generations of being denied entry into trade unions or higher education have led to accumulated disadvantages that cannot be easily overcome by declaring that the playing field is now level (Sugrue 1996).

Being white is a privilege and status that gives some people a better chance at jobs, allows them to live anywhere they can afford, and guarantees that their children will not be teased about their skin color.

Ethnicity

Ethnicity refers to cultural variables, primarily language and customs, associated with common ancestry or country of origin. The sense in which ethnicity is socially constructed has to do with how it is perceived by the dominant groups and how it becomes part of one's self-image. In general, the closer to Northern Europe a person's country of origin is, the easier it is to fit into the American mainstream. Ethnicity also gets mixed in with race, with skin color usually being more important than country of origin, as when employers prefer to hire lighter-skinned immigrants who do not speak English rather than offer jobs to American-born blacks willing to work for lower wages (Massey and Denton 1993).

The importance of ethnicity to your identity varies greatly by (1) how long your family has been in the United States; (2) the degree to which your ethnicity is positively or negatively valued in the society; and (3) how often family members have married someone from a different ethnic group. Over time, as the group fits into the dominant culture, as barriers to education and employment fall, and as intermarriage rates rise, the sense of being defined by your ethnicity declines. Rather than "being" a hyphenated American, ethnic identity is voluntary, a "feeling" of being attached to a particular heritage and being able to select or discard specific aspects of that tradition (Bakalian 1993; Alba 1998). 🖥 2

Coming to America

It is still not clear how or when the first Americans reached this continent, but it seems likely that about 20,000 years ago, some hunter-gatherer bands crossed a land bridge from Asia to Alaska, gradually moving down the Pacific coast to the tip of South America and eastward to the Atlantic. By 1492, several million Native Americans, divided into dozens of tribes, were scattered across North America, and many millions more had created very sophisticated cultures in South and Central America.

The first European settlers came in the 1600s, mostly from England, Scotland, and Ireland, plus a few from Holland, France, and Spain. Throughout the next two centuries, immigrants from North and West Europe arrived, some driven by a desire to worship as they pleased, others by a sense of adventure, and still others sent to the colonies as punishment. Immigration flows are the outcome of factors that "push" people out of one country (poverty, persecution) and that "pull" the migrants toward another society (freedom, jobs). As shown in Figure 6.1, at the time of the founding of the United States, 95 percent of the population was of North and West European ancestry.

In the 1880s, as industrialization picked up steam, outpacing the supply of American-born workers, immigration from Southern and Eastern Europe increased, in response to the need for unskilled factory labor. Millions of immigrants flowed into the country in the early 1900s, until the outbreak of World War I in 1914. At the end of that war, another large wave of newcomers, mostly Catholics and Jews from Southern and Eastern Europe, managed to reach American shores before 1920, when an attack of xenophobia (fear of foreigners) gripped the nation. Restric-

Native Americans remain one of the poorest and most disadvantaged racial and ethnic groups in the United States. Currently, Native Americans are reclaiming their rights and traditions and urging the U.S. government to honor the many treaties signed in the past. There has also been a revival of cultural pride and increasing interest in preserving the diversity of tribal history, customs, and crafts.

tive immigration laws in effect between 1920 and 1968 ended most of the flow from Asia and Africa, and reduced the entry of Europeans, but not of Latin Americans. Since the late 1960s, new immigrants have come primarily from Latin America and Asia.

The fact that most recent immigrants are young persons of color from high fertility regions has spurred a renewed debate on American immigration policy (Martin and Midgley 1999). On one side are a majority of Americans (over 70 percent in 1998) who believe that it is time to shut the gates again. They worry that European whites will be a numerical minority in the near future and that the new immigrants will overburden the welfare and health systems. On the other side are those who see immigration as a source of diversity and vitality throughout our history, part of the American heritage

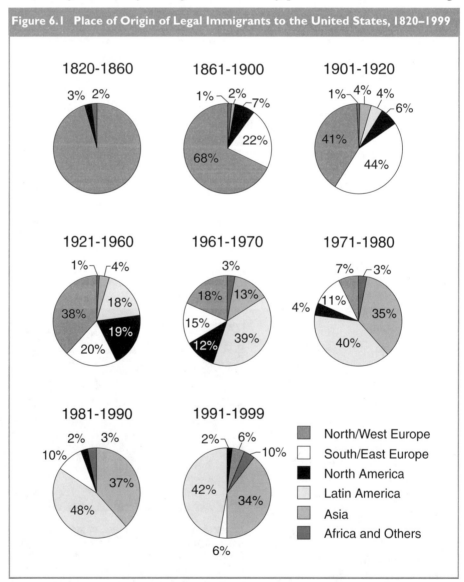

Figure 6.1   Place of Origin of Legal Immigrants to the United States, 1820–1999

Source: *Statistical Abstract of the United States*, 2000: Table 8; *Historical Statistics of the United States*, 1975: 105–109.

as a haven for the persecuted and needy, including the grandparents of most people who want to restrict immigration today.

In reality, the United States was always very choosy about which "poor and huddled masses" have been let in; applicants have been screened for health status and for political views. Immigration laws and quotas have been stacked in favor of migrants from Northern and Western Europe, and only reluctantly extended to the rest of Europe, much less Asia, Africa, and South America. In the late 1930s, for example, Jewish refugees from Nazi Germany were turned away. Much also depends on the employment picture. When workers are needed, the barriers go down; when unemployment is high, the barriers go up. Thus, the most recent immigration debate reached a fever pitch in the early 1990s, when it was argued that Latino (Hispanic) and Asian immigrants willing to work for low pay were taking jobs away from native-born Americans. By the end of the decade, however, full employment and a shortage of entry-level workers moved that issue off the front burner. Xenophobia, however, lurks just under the surface of most societies, so do not be surprised if anti-immigration feelings erupt again.

Whites' fears of being outnumbered by nonwhites are based on population projections into the middle of the twenty-first century. As Figure 6.2 indicates, given current immigration trends and racial/ethnic differences in fertility rates, only a slim majority of the American population will be non-Hispanic white in 2050. The African-American population will rise slightly from 13 to 15 percent, while the Asian-American population will double from

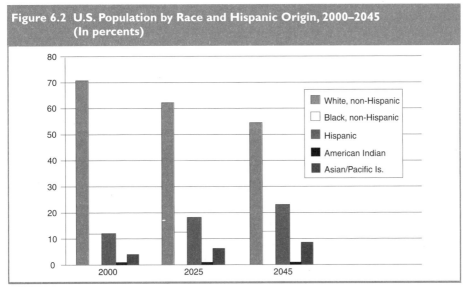

Figure 6.2 U.S. Population by Race and Hispanic Origin, 2000–2045 (In percents)

Source: Population Projections Program, U.S. Census Bureau, Washington, DC: January 13, 2000.

4 to over 8 percent, and almost one in four Americans will be of Hispanic origin, 90 percent of whom are also classified as "white."

The positive side of these numbers is that Asian and Latino immigrants and their children will keep the United States population from declining (see chapter 15 for a discussion of population dynamics). The influx of younger workers will also ease the strain on the Social Security system. The downside

❖ ❖ ❖ ❖   is that like all immigrant waves, the first generation will have relatively low incomes and high poverty rates. But there is no reason to believe that educational and occupational levels will not rise over time, and fertility rates decline, in the same pattern experienced by earlier immigrant groups. 3

Models of Americanization

As a nation of immigrants, a major issue since 1850 has been how to turn diverse waves of foreigners into Americans. From a functional perspective, social stability depends on a shared set of values and on bringing newcomers into the ongoing systems of control—schools, workplaces, political structures. From a conflict perspective the focus of research was on how the WASP elite was able to maintain its hegemony (pronounced "heh-gem-oh-nee"), a word that means dominance or leadership.

The 'Melting Pot' Model

For much of American history, the basic model for absorbing immigrants was that of the melting pot, in which cultural differences would melt away through exposure to the common language and customs. It was assumed that the newcomers would throw off all traces of their former identity and eagerly embrace the dominant standards of behavior and beauty. It was even hoped that Catholics and Jews would gradually renounce their strange practices. Color, however, was seen as an unmeltable trait.

The public schools were the major mechanism for socialization to the American Way, and the children and grandchildren of immigrants became strongly attached to its values and institutions. Indeed, second- and third-generation ethnic Americans are among the most vocal patriots and at the forefront of the movement to restrict further immigration. To ease their way into the mainstream earlier in this century, many changed their names to disguise their ethnic or religious origins. This was necessary because elite universities were known to have quotas for Jews and applicants whose names ended in a vowel. And many housing developments had "restrictive covenants," or rules forbidding sales to colored people, Jews, Catholics, Italians, or any other minority in the region. Up until the 1950s, few ethnic or racial group members could hope to win public office or be accepted into the higher ranks of corporate power. Most people would have laughed at the idea of a Catholic president, a man named Lee Iacocca heading a major company, or a Jewish Secretary of State, much less a black on the Supreme Court.

For the first two generations at least, many minority group members never "melted" totally, maintaining feelings of cultural uniqueness and of the importance of religion and ethnicity as sources of identity and community. By the 1960s, when ethnic and religious background had ceased to be major barriers to upward mobility and when the most successful minority members had moved to the suburbs and intermarried, keeping the "old culture" had become largely voluntary and selective. Thus, while a lot of the surface differences have melted away, there remains a bedrock of personal identity (Alba 1999).

Cultural Pluralism

Recognizing that many differences are unmeltable, especially race, and that tensions among minority groups are inevitable, especially if the groups are competing for the same jobs and living space, critics of the melting pot ideal have proposed a different goal. Rather than trying to erase differences, why not encourage and welcome them? The **cultural pluralism** ideal celebrates the special contributions of each minority group. If the melting pot ideal can be likened to a plate of hash, where all the ingredients have been blended together, the pluralists' meal is a stew, where each ingredient keeps its distinct color and flavor. But cultural pluralism has its limits. It is one thing to accept differences in personal matters such as family relationships, religious customs, and community activities, but quite another to tolerate demands for separation of the races or ethnic groups.

Pluralist ideals have been tested over recent decades as one minority group after another, previously barred from full participation, has claimed its rightful place. The road to self-respect began with a renewal of ethnic/racial pride and a rejection of the WASP standards of worth and beauty. When carried far enough, the separatist element in the pluralist model provokes a backlash, as seen in the current spate of "English only" laws. Pluralism is more than allowing minorities to express themselves; the other side of the coin is that members of the dominant culture should make a serious effort to understand and appreciate the values and lifestyles of minority cultures.🖥4

Processes of Inclusion and Exclusion

Minority groups are attached to the larger society along a *continuum*, a line that represents degrees of difference between two extremes, from near isolation (segregation) to complete blending (amalgamation), as shown in Figure 6.3.

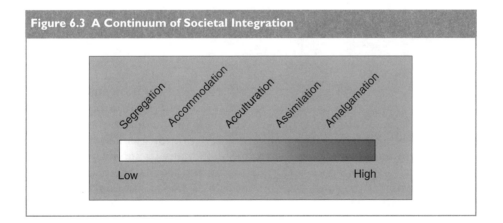

Figure 6.3 A Continuum of Societal Integration

Segregation

One way of dealing with a minority group is to isolate it from contact with other members of the society. Gypsies have been kept outside the city walls; Jews have been restricted to special areas within the city (*ghettos*); South African blacks and Native Americans were sent to reservations; and American blacks were separated from whites by laws and customs in the South. Once the group is isolated, there is no threat of intermarriage or cross-group friendships; education and job opportunities can be carefully controlled. The main problems, from a sociological perspective, are that (1) it takes a lot of policing and deployment of resources to maintain a system of apartness (or **apartheid**, as practiced in South Africa and the American South), and (2) the system ultimately dehumanizes both populations, as the dominant group becomes convinced of its vast superiority and continues to define the "other" as innately inferior.

Segregation can be either *de jure*—a matter of law—or *de facto*—a matter of fact. In the American case, for example, *de jure* segregation was only declared unconstitutional by the Supreme Court in 1954, in a famous decision about school district boundaries, *Brown v. the Board of Education of Topeka, Kansas*. It took many more decades before the structures of *de jure* segregation were finally dismantled. But in the meantime, whites were moving from the cities into the suburbs, so schools and residential areas became resegregated, but this time the process was *de facto* and not a violation of the Constitution. Indeed, the ability to move as you wish is a protected right.

Nonetheless, as discussed in chapter 15, residential segregation by race is strongly associated with lowered job opportunities and incomes, and is thus a major factor in continued racial inequality. Racial segregation protects whites not only from black neighbors but from close knowledge of what it is like to be non-white, which is another privilege of being a member of the dominant group.

Accommodation occurs when members of a minority group become aware of the dominant norms yet keep their distinct culture and language.

Accommodation

The next step toward integration into the general culture occurs when members of the minority group become aware of the dominant norms yet adapt just enough to deal with mainstream institutions while keeping their distinct culture and language. For example, in many Latino or Asian neighborhoods, adults can negotiate the job market and see that their children stay in school, while at the same time maintaining a very traditional home life.

Acculturation

Awareness of the dominant culture is one thing (accommodation); accepting it is quite another, what sociologists call **acculturation**. Acculturation occurs when the American way replaces the ancestral one, and when minority group members participate fully in the economic, political, and educational systems, but—and it is a big "but"—are still refused entry into more intimate groupings such as clubs, private schools, or charitable organizations. For example, Jews who are directors of major American companies are rarely invited to the exclusive eating and country clubs of the WASP elite.

Acculturation often creates the condition of marginality, a group's being on the fringe, caught between two cultures, no longer fully at home in the one or accepted in the other. The upside is that marginality often provides a place from which the individual can see into the society from both inside and outside. Many of the most insightful analyses of American culture have come from people occupying marginal statuses—Jews, gays, and women.

Assimilation

To assimilate means to "incorporate," literally to swallow up. Sociologically, assimilation takes place when minority group members are accepted into the informal as well as formal structures of the dominant group. The outsider gets to come inside. Ease of assimilation depends on how closely the individual resembles members of the dominant group—in color, culture, and faith. Sometimes, even being white and speaking English do not help, as in the case of early Irish immigrants, called "uncivilized barbarians" by the leading newspapers. Only in contrast to later, darker immigrants did the Irish become "white" (Ignatiev 1996).

Amalgamation

The ultimate in assimilation is full integration, or amalgamation, when almost all traces of difference are erased, typically through intermarriage. In general, marriage between people of different ethnic backgrounds has become very common in the United States, as long as it is within the same race and religion. There was a time, not so long ago, when this was not the case, because ethnicity was more strongly linked to social class than it is today. Ask the oldest member of your family what happened when, for example, an Irish aunt wanted to marry an Italian bricklayer.

Religious intermarriage has also increased since the 1970s, but interracial marriage rates remain extremely low. You may read a headline that says "interracial marriages up by 50 percent this year," but if you start with a very small number, any increase is going to look big. In addition, most of the 3 percent of American marriages across racial lines today involve Asians rather than blacks. This is where all those earlier barriers to interaction—residential, educational, and occupational segregation—have their ultimate effect: If you do not meet people, you do not marry them. And if you do not intermarry, the two groups stay apart and retain their differences and their hostilities.

But even low rates accumulate, so that over time in the United States a growing number of children of biracial marriages find it impossible to "check one" Census category when ask to identify themselves by race (Korgen 1998). In addition, an unknown number are the great- or great-great-grandchildren of unions between white masters and slave women, many of whom have "passed" for white over several generations, as in the case of some descendants of President Thomas Jefferson and his servant, Sally Hemmings.

Mechanisms of Resistance to Integration

A lot of energy and resources are spent on maintaining the barriers to full integration of minority groups, especially when contact might have a negative impact on property values or social status. Over time, however, getting an education and making money will go a long way toward "normalizing" members of minority groups.

Historically, the fate of immigrant groups depends on (1) how close to the WASP ideal they look and act; (2) the job skills brought with them; and (3) the state of the American economy when they landed here. Often, when comparing their own family history to that of African Americans, third-generation ethnic Americans ask, "If we made it out of poverty and the inner city, why can't they?" Part of the answer is that most immigrants were permitted entry because their labor was needed; that they arrived during a period of expansion of the public school system; and that, however difficult their experiences, they were never the objects of as much unrelenting, dehumanizing hatred and physical violence as that directed toward blacks over the entire history of this society (Patterson 1998). On all three barrier traits—appearance, skills, job opportunities—the deck has been stacked against blacks, legally in many ways and places until just a few decades ago, and as a matter of habit and custom in other cases.

The major mechanisms of resistance to integration are prejudice, discrimination, and institutionalized racism. As seen in Table 6.1, prejudice and discrimination are two separate dimensions of relating to minority groups. **Prejudice** refers to attitudes, literally pre-judgments, about the "other." **Discrimination** refers to actual behavior. When the two variables are cross-tabulated, as in Table 6.1, four categories can be identified.

Table 6.1   The Relationship Between Attitudes and Behavior

	Attitude	
	Prejudiced	**Accepting**
Discriminatory Behavior	1. Not only hates having strangers next door but actively tries to prevent it.	2. Has no negative feelings but joins in excluding strangers.
Nondiscriminatory Behavior	3. Does not want strangers next door but will not do anything to prevent their moving in.	4. Does not object to and may even welcome diversity in the neighborhood.

(1) Some people both hate and show it; (2) other people will discriminate without necessarily disliking the targets of their actions; (3) still others have strong negative feelings yet never act on them; and (4) some neither dislike nor discriminate. You probably know several people who fit into the first and last boxes, whose attitudes and behavior are in sync. It is the two other

❖ ❖ ❖ ❖

types—where attitudes go one way and behavior the other—that are most interesting sociologically. Under what conditions would a very prejudiced person tolerate a black or Hispanic workmate or neighbor? Answer: when the costs of discrimination outweigh the advantages, and this is most likely where the law forbids it and is enforced, and where the public temper discourages acts of hostility.

By the same token, under what circumstances would a nonprejudiced person act in a discriminatory manner? Answer: when the costs of not doing so are high. Pretend, for example, that you are a real estate agent in an office with a plaque on the wall saying it is an equal housing agency. You have just been asked by a young, well-to-do black couple to show them a house in the nicest part of town. Without a prejudiced bone in your body, you may find yourself behaving like many real estate agents and "steering" the couple toward a different area, one in which some nonwhite families already live. You do this because if you get a reputation for showing homes in exclusive neighborhoods to "them," you will soon be out of work; other agents will not show the homes you have listed, and homeowners will not give you their homes to list. You have a mortgage to pay and children to feed—what would you do, honestly?

This is an example of **institutionalized racism**, behavior patterns built into the way business is done: how banks make loans; how stores treat different kinds of customers; how police deal with suspects; how schoolchildren choose playmates; and so on. Therefore, if your goal is to end discrimination, the way to do it is *not* by trying to change attitudes but by raising the costs of the behavior, such as enforcing the laws and fining violators.

One of the more striking examples of institutionalized racism is the practice of "racial profiling" by police on interstate highways, based on the belief that drug trafficking is primarily a minority activity. For example, in one Illinois district, in which about 7 percent of the area motorists were African American, they compose 31 percent of those stopped by the highway drug unit (Lamberth 1999). By targeting cars with dark-skinned drivers, highway patrols will find some drug runners, whose arrests will then reinforce the original perception—another example of the *self-fulfilling prophecy*. The only offense committed by the vast majority of drivers who are pulled over is "DWB," or "Driving While Black." And who knows how much cocaine was being transported in cars with light-skinned drivers, on its way to the middle-class suburban home of the typical user? 💻 5

The Enduring Significance of Race and Ethnicity

Although many scholars believe that social class is more important than race in explaining inequality, there is no doubt that the history of race relations in America has had long-term consequences.

Native Americans

The tribes that populated North America before the arrival of European explorers and colonists were quickly defined as biologically and morally "inferior" to the new arrivals, who managed to convince themselves that they were doing God's work in trying to convert the heathen. Despite the great variety of Native American cultures, the tribes were all called "Indians" and treated with equal contempt.

Ethnocentric assumptions followed the westward migration of white settlers, who absorbed the best farm and grazing lands on the basis of treaties that were not intended to be taken seriously. In the late 1800s, entire tribes were relocated to reservations in sparsely settled areas with few natural resources. By the century's end, wars, relocation, and disease had effectively destroyed most native cultures and social systems. But an unknown number, probably over half of all Native Americans, found their way to factory towns, intermarried, and disappeared into the industrial labor force.

Today, after several generations of intermarriage, the Census counted 2.4 million people who consider themselves Native Americans, including the Eskimo and Aleuts of Alaska. About one-third live on reservations or other areas administered by the Bureau of Indian Affairs (BIA), where, according to the treaties, they were to receive adequate housing, education, health care, and economic opportunity. In reality, the history of the BIA has been one of total neglect, corruption, and goal displacement, in which billions of dollars allocated to the tribes have gone to maintaining the BIA bureaucracy. Meanwhile, back on the reservations, life is marked by high rates of unemployment, alcoholism, disease, school failure, family violence, and infant mortality—the outcome of internal colonialism, whereby the native population is treated as if it were a foreign colony.

Not one of the 300 treaties between the tribes and the United States has been fully honored (Richardson 1993). But in the past several years, a number of tribes have gone to court and won back either their land or other compensation, causing friction between Native Americans and other residents. When the treaties were used to take resources from the tribes, no one spoke up; now that the treaties are being used to reclaim lost property, a loud backlash has emerged (Egan 2000).

The major factor in improving the economic status of tribal members has been the introduction of gambling casinos on the reservations. The original treaties guaranteed to the tribes full rights to local resources and freedom from control of state governments. These conditions had earlier brought great wealth to the Oklahoma reservations sitting on vast oil deposits. Now, claiming full sovereignty over their land and therefore not bound by state regulations about gambling, tribal leaders have built huge casino complexes that provide jobs to thousands and bring in millions in nontaxable revenues. Today, Native Americans are a growing political power in states such as Connecticut and Wisconsin. 💻6

African Americans

The legacy of slavery.   How can one group of people treat another group as if they were not human? Only by defining the "other" as so different as to be not only "not us" but "not human." This process is easiest when "they" do not look like "us," which is why race and especially blackness remains a caste-like barrier to mobility long after religion and ethnicity have lost much of their power to determine life chances in America. The enduring strength of these barriers for blacks, in comparison to Asian and Native Americans, suggests that a particular streak of *racism* is a fundamental aspect of our society and perhaps the American character, rather than being just a temporary condition (Shalom 1998).

Of all Africans brought to this hemisphere as slaves, 90 percent were sold to owners in South America, with only about 10 percent or 650,000 sent to North America. Although importing slaves was banned in 1808, this relatively small population grew so rapidly that by 1860 most of the 3 million blacks in America were native-born. Racial stereotypes had changed accordingly, with the slaves being thought of as children needing fatherly guidance (paternalism) rather than as untamed savages, but still without the rights accorded any other American-born person (Pinkney 2000). In response to these conditions, the slaves developed a unique subculture, blended from native elements and those imposed by their owners, in which some self-direction could be exercised. The subculture of slavery, developed and maintained in large part by the women, provided generational continuity, protected and supported, offered hope and the strength necessary for survival (Dill 1998). Ironically, Christianity, which the owners introduced in the hopes of converting the "heathen," was eventually used to challenge the system of slavery itself and, a century later, to bring down the lingering legal obstacles to equality.

Some African Americans occupy high positions in the U.S. government. Dr. David Satcher (on left) was the U.S. Surgeon General, responsible for the overall health care of the American public.

Not all African Americans lived in the South or in slavery; many made their way to the North and West, where they also endured difficulties but were at least legally free. In the South, however, after legal freedom was assured following the Civil War, the states constructed a new set of barriers—called "Jim Crow" laws—that effectively kept blacks from holding political office, living in certain neighborhoods, or going to the same schools as their white age peers. And if the laws did not keep blacks in their place, a public lynching would serve as a reminder of who made the rules (Patterson 1998). Some elements of this system lasted until the 1960s, a full hundred years after the official end of slavery.

African Americans today. The black population in the United States today consists primarily of descendants of Southern slaves and Northern freemen, plus a few million immigrants from the Caribbean region and a small but steady flow of immigrants from Africa. In general, despite dramatic gains for some subpopulations—blacks from the West Indies and those descended from early migrants to the North—African Americans remain disadvantaged along many dimensions of social stratification and personal well-being (Hughes and Thomas 1998; Pollard and O'Hare 1999). In many respects, current drawbacks, especially in educational attainment and occupational status, reflect a long history of neglect and open hostility. In addi-

❖ ❖ ❖ ❖   tion, many of the gains in income and employment between 1965 and 1980 were reversed in the next decade and a half. Only the historically high employment rates of the late 1990s have kept the racial income gap from widening any further.

Although the black population accounts for 13 percent of the U.S. population, blacks represent less than 2 percent of elected officials, primarily in the South, and an equally small proportion of high-level corporate executives. In a pattern similar to that for women in big business, African Americans in middle management tend to be found in positions dealing with personnel and community relations rather than with production and corporate finances, which are the royal rungs to the top of the ladder.

Ironically, just as large numbers of African Americans were finally admitted into high-paying unionized jobs, in the 1970s, that sector of the economy began to decline. In addition, the entry-level manufacturing jobs in big cities that had been there for earlier generations of immigrants were also being moved out—either to low-wage Southern states or out of the country altogether. But because it was extremely difficult for blacks to follow the flight of whites into the newly developed suburbs, the resulting separation by race has closed off many avenues of upward occupational mobility for blacks.

A growing proportion of African-American households consist of college-educated professionals who are succeeding in the American economy.

Racial separation not only keeps blacks and whites apart, it also increases the social and physical distance between the disadvantaged blacks in the central cities and the growing proportion of African-American households classified as middle class—the college-educated white-collar workers and employers who have managed to find housing outside the urban center. Forgotten in the focus on the very poor and the relatively successful are the majority of black households, solidly blue-collar, stable working-class families (Horton et al. 2000).

But no dark-skinned person in America is free of the burdens of blackness, which include humiliations both large and small: schoolyard hazing, difficulties in the workplace, reduced likelihood of promotion, being ignored by cab drivers, denied entry into shops, kept under surveillance, and constantly being stopped by police on the trail of villains. Black women must cope with all this in addition to the extra harassment that goes with gender (St. Jean and Feagin 1998). And even in the military, the most racially integrated and officially color-blind institution in America, African-American personnel find themselves subjected to hate speech and discrimination (Holmes 1999).

At this moment, however, black gains in any area of social power are being successfully challenged by conservative legal foundations on the grounds that favoritism by race is a form of "reverse discrimination" that violates the equal-protection clause of the Fourteenth Amendment. As a result, election districts drawn to increase the likelihood of a minority winner have been struck down by the courts, as have college admission formulas that take race into account, as well as attempts to steer some government contracts to minority firms. In addition, minority group members are disproportionately affected whenever American taxpayers demand cuts in government programs, not only as recipients of benefits but as job holders, because government bureaucracies are more willing employers of minorities than are private businesses. 🖥 7

Box 6.1

The Enduring Significance of Symbols

As a reminder that the Civil War never ended in the hearts and minds of some Southerners, the twenty-first century dawned in South Carolina with a battle over flying the Confederate flag from the statehouse. The flag had first flown there *not* in 1862 but in 1962, as a symbol of resistance to the federal government's efforts to desegregate the public schools. The refusal of the state legislature to remove it, despite pleas from the governor and business leaders fearful of losing Northern firms on the verge of relocating, provoked the National Association for the Advancement of Colored People (NAACP) to call for a boycott of the state by professional groups holding annual meetings.

To the one group, the flag represented a proud heritage of Southern honor; to the others it signified the oppression of slavery. The issue was finally, but only partially, resolved when the State legislature voted in 2000 to remove the flag from atop the statehouse and place a smaller version next to a Civil War memorial on the statehouse grounds. The compromise, like the flag itself, was a symbolic gesture, in this case pleasing neither most of the white legislators nor the NAACP.

Asian Americans

Asian Americans—or people of the Pacific Rim—are a very diverse racial minority, representing dozens of different cultures and language groups. As you can see in Figure 6.4, there were major changes between 1970 and 1997 in the composition of the Asian-American population, with persons of Chinese and Philippine descent now outnumbering those of Japanese ancestry.

Although the roughly 11 million Americans of Asian origin compose about 4 percent of the population today, that proportion will double by 2050 as a result of continued immigration from Southeast Asia and relatively high fertility. Despite these small numbers, the Asian influence on American society will be strengthened by their high income and education levels, as well as their high rates of intermarriage (Lee 1998). In this sense, various strands of the Asian-American population are thought to be perfect examples of a model minority, fulfilling the great American Dream of upward mobility through good habits, hard work, and respect for family.

These overall patterns, however, hide great variations among Asian subgroups in terms of history and their experience in this country. A few very brief summaries should give you the flavor of these varied histories.

Chinese Americans. The story of Chinese Americans begins with the thousands of young men lured onto ships bringing them to North America to work on the transcontinental railroad. Isolated in work camps, forbidden to become citizens or to send for their family in China or to marry here, they

❖ ❖ ❖ ❖   were expected to return to Asia once the railroad was built. But many stayed, moving to almost all-male communities within the major cities of the West

The Asian influence on American society has been strengthened by its high income and educational levels. Many are fulfilling the American dream of upward mobility through hard work and respect for the family.

Coast, where they were the targets of periodic mob violence. The rampages were inflamed by "yellow peril" scares, right up to the bombing of Pearl Harbor in 1941, when the Chinese suddenly became the "good Asians" in contrast to the "evil Japs."

Since the 1940s, the Chinese-American population has grown in numbers and wealth. Educational attainment is very high, reflecting a traditional respect for learning. A crucial influence on achievement, however, was the example of family-owned small businesses, where everyone pitched in—beginning with the thousands of laundries and restaurants that dot the urban landscape. Such businesses provided the first step up the mobility ladder.

Minority group success often depends on the degree to which a group has carved out a special place, residentially and economically, within the larger urban scene—an **ethnic,** or **racial, enclave**—where group members control local commerce and create a protective subculture. America's Chinatowns are a perfect example of the minority enclave, where local banks and savings societies offer loans for businesses and homes, and where grandparents help out with the children while the parents work. Ironically, success within the enclave gives a young couple the push it needs to move upward economically and outward to the suburbs. Over time, then, the enclave will

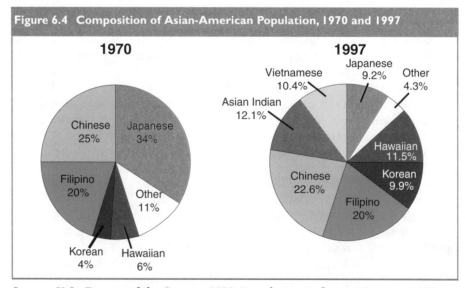

Figure 6.4 Composition of Asian-American Population, 1970 and 1997

Source: U.S. Bureau of the Census, 1973; Population Reference Bureau, 1999.

contain many older people and newer immigrants, who live in poverty. Recently, also, many Chinatowns have experienced the emergence of illegal businesses and youth gangs, in the grand tradition of both Chinese criminal groups ("tongs") and the succession of ethnic groups associated with organized crime in America (chapter 13).

Japanese Americans.   Without the numbers or resources to establish an enclave, Japanese settlers gravitated toward small communities where they could find work as farmers and gardeners; the Japanese gardener was a status symbol for wealthy Californians. Although forbidden to own land or to become citizens, the first generation were able to immigrate as wife and husband, and because their children were born in the United States, the second generation had American citizenship.

Citizenship did not protect them, however, from the anger of their neighbors and the fears of the government following the outbreak of war with Japan in 1941. All Japanese Americans living on the West Coast were rounded up, as a matter of "national security," and sent to detention camps until the end of the war in 1945. Their property was immediately grabbed by envious neighbors, without compensation. Only in 1988 did Congress apologize and award $20,000 each to the survivors of the camps—very little and extremely late. Curiously, in Hawaii, where there were real national security interests, no attempt was made to isolate people of Japanese descent, largely because they were so closely integrated into the economic, political, and social systems of the island, in contrast to their relative isolation and powerlessness on the West Coast (Parrillo 2000).

In addition to a legacy of bitterness, the detention camp experience had other long-term effects, the most important being an erosion of the power of husbands over wives and of elders over their adult children. In addition, many of the younger men were allowed to leave the camps for military service, and other young people were sent to schools elsewhere in the country. This weakening of traditional authority and controls actually helped speed up the process of upward mobility once the camps were emptied.

New Asian immigrants.   Immigration policy changes in the 1960s and 1980s lifted restrictions on Asian immigration, especially if the immigration reunited family members. The result has been a large influx of people from Korea, Southeast Asia, and the Indian subcontinent, representing dozens of cultural and language groups. The mosaic has become much more varied since 1980. These newest immigrants also run the gamut from rural peasants to urban professionals.

The most fascinating aspect of this newest wave is the variety of occupational specialties—or **economic niches**—that come to be associated with the minority group. A niche (pronounced "neetch") is a particular small space carved out of the larger whole. Once some members of an immigrant group master a particular occupation, they open the way for others to follow, leading to ethnic clustering. Thus, Vietnamese refugees have found success (and racism) as fishermen in Texas; Koreans own a large number of grocery shops in large cities; many Pakistanis operate gas station franchises in New Jersey; Philippine nurses staff most large hospitals; and Indian scientists are a major part of the work force in pharmaceutical laboratories.

The children of these Asians, however, will be fully Americanized through the school system, where they excel at mathematics and sciences, and they can be expected to enter the mainstream occupational structure at a rela-

❖ ❖ ❖ ❖ tively high level. The ethnic enclave for many of the newer groups is no longer the neighborhood in a large city but a section of a suburb (Osborne 2000). As more racial/ethnic families move into an area, it becomes easier for others to buy a home in that community, and gradually the neighborhood takes on the characteristics of the urban enclave, with stores, civic associations, restaurants, and other local businesses. 8

Americans of Hispanic Origin (Latino/Latina)

The Census categories of *Hispanic* and *Spanish origin*, and the more recently preferred *Latino/Latina*, are umbrella terms that cover a diverse, largely Catholic, population. Table 6.2 summarizes important sociological differences among the four major subgroups: Mexican, Puerto Rican, Central/South American, and Cuban.

Table 6.2 Hispanic Population of the United States, Selected Characteristics, 1999			
Country of Origin	% Total	% College Graduates	% Families in Poverty
Mexico	65.2	7.1	24.4
Central/South America	14.3	18.0	18.5
Puerto Rico	9.6	11.1	26.7
Cuba	4.3	24.8	11.0
Other	6.6	15.0	18.2

Source: U.S. Bureau of the Census, *Current Population Reports*, Series P20-527, February 2000.

Overall, the population of Hispanic origin accounts for about 12 percent of the U.S. total today but is expected to rise to 24 percent by 2050 as a result of continued immigration and relatively high fertility among a young population, at the same time that non-Hispanic white birthrates will decline. Although, as noted before, while 90 percent of the Hispanic population is racially classified as white, Latinos/Latinas are often treated as if they were a racial category.

Box 6.2

My Land Is Your Land—Maybe

In many affluent suburbs in the Northeast, where there are wide lawns to be cared for, stone walls to be built, and gutters to be cleaned, Latino men provide an army of day laborers, waiting on local street corners for contractors to pick them up. Their presence has stirred up considerable commotion, as witnessed at a meeting of Putnam County, New York, Board of Legislators in December, 1999. The Chair of the Board made the following statement:

> . . . There's a cultural difference between Americans and Latinos. We don't stand on the street looking for work. The average person will wake up at 8 o'clock and go to work. *They* wake up and stand on the street corner and look for work. I call it visual pollution.

He offered legislation to urge federal authorities to get rid of those he called illegal immigrants and a plague on the community. Other participants arrived at the meeting with a "Say No to Hate" petition, and a lively debate took place, with ☞

✦ ✦ ✦ ✦

☞ immigration officials agreeing to meet with local office holders. The last word, however, went to Lone Hawk, a Native American, who reminded the audience that this was really his land, where the tribes had lived in peace until the white man came. As the reporter noted, "Mr. Hawk was generous enough not to ask everyone to leave" (Purdy 1999).

Mexican Americans (Chicanos/Chicanas).   Almost two-thirds of Latino/a Americans are of Mexican origin. Some are descendants of people who settled the Southwest long before it was annexed by the United States in 1848; others have lived there for several generations; and a few will have entered only yesterday, looking for jobs in American factories intentionally built close to the border. And although the great majority of Chicanos/Chicanas are legal residents, the social construction of "illegal alien" is often applied to all Americans of Mexican descent.

Most Mexican Americans live in urban areas, where the men find work as laborers or machine operators while the women become domestic servants and office cleaners. The areas in which Chicanos/Chicanas are concentrated are often referred to as "barrios," suggesting the degree to which language and culture isolate them from the Anglo majority. Skin color also matters; the darker or more Indian-like your features, the lower will be your earnings, even at the same level of education and skill as more Anglo-looking peers (Telles and Murguia 1990).

In general, upward mobility has been a slow process, due to job discrimination and residential isolation from the outside and from within the group, due to the conservative forces of tradition and religion and fear of leaving the protective environment of the barrio. In time, however, many do move up and out, although family income and educational attainment remain below the U.S. average.

For Mexican Americans, upward mobility has been a slower process due to job discrimination, residential isolation, and the protective environment of the barrio.

Living in the United States has also brought slow but powerful changes in family relationships. It is difficult for the men to maintain the kind of respect and power they exercised in Mexico, because they lose so much control over their lives as low-skill, low-income workers in a foreign land. In addition, when their wives earn money on their own, maneuver in the world outside the home, make their own friends, and learn English, they become less and less dependent on and subservient to their husband (Segura 1993). Similarly, when the children come home from school, speaking English and showing their familiarity with American culture, the parents feel powerless. Parental power is further diminished when young women and men follow the American pattern of choosing a husband or wife rather than having the marriage arranged (see chapter 8). In this way, as other minority groups have found, success in America also means the end of the traditions and closeness of the ethnic community.

Puerto Ricans. We do not speak of "Puerto Rican Americans" for the simple reason that residents of the Island have been American citizens since 1917, free to move to and from the mainland as they wish. Migration to the mainland was particularly heavy in the 1950s when the Island's sugar industry collapsed, with large numbers settling in the New York/New Jersey area, where they found a niche in low-end service jobs.

Puerto Ricans have not yet established enclaves like those of Asian Americans, with opportunities for self-employment and self-help, perhaps because of frequent moves between the mainland and the Island and the belief that eventually they will return to their homeland, even though they have higher achievement expectations than Puerto Ricans who have not migrated. At the same time, the urban economy of the Northeast has not produced the kinds of jobs that are springboards to upward mobility.

In comparison with other Hispanic groups in the United States, Puerto Ricans rank last in education, income, employment, and two-parent families. Low SES translates into residential segregation, which in turn, reduces labor force opportunities and family stability (Santiago and Galster 1995). Nonetheless, educational attainment is rising, political influence is growing, and representation in the arts has increased.

Cuban Americans. The Cuban-American experience is a perfect example of the importance of when you come to America, why you come, and what resources you bring with you. The Cubans who fled their island when Fidel Castro came to power in the mid-1950s were a well-educated and wealthy elite, many of whom were descended from European Spaniards. Politically conservative, they settled in Miami, where they established a very successful enclave and became a powerful force in local and national politics. In the five decades since Castro came to power, no American president has dared to suggest normalizing relations with Cuba for fear of angering Cuban Americans, until they appeared on television burning American flags and defying federal authorities in the case of Elián Gonzales, the child whose mother died in her immigration attempt and whose father wanted to take his son back to Cuba.

Box 6.3

Whose Child Is This?

American history offers many examples of prejudice and discrimination on the basis of race, class, religion, and ethnicity, but there is one incident that combines them all—the "Great Arizona Orphan Abduction" (Gordon 1999). In 1904, a Catholic hospital for orphans sent 57 abandoned children of Irish immigrants all the way to foster families in mining towns in Arizona. The problem arose when the Anglos in the towns realized that the foster families were Mexican American and therefore not really "white." Under intense pressure from their wives, Anglo men, both laborers and middle class, united to preserve their racial/ethnic pride and kidnapped most of the children, claiming that Mexicans, because of their race and beastly habits, were unfit to raise a white child. The Catholic church and the courts chose not to dispute the outcome. And this is how the Irish became officially "white" and a group of Catholic children came to be raised by Protestant mining families in the wild, wild West at the turn of the century.

More recent waves of Cuban immigrants, many expelled by Castro in the 1980s, are much poorer and less educated than the rest of the community and have provoked considerable hostility. In the city of Miami and south Florida in general, opposition to the Spanish-speaking minority comes from Anglos resentful of their political and economic clout and from African Americans, who feel that authorities have favored Latino immigrants over native-born blacks. 9

Middle Easterners

The newest piece in the mosaic consists of recent immigrants from the Middle East: Egypt, Syria, Jordan, Lebanon, Iran, and Iraq. Many are joining relatives who came much earlier; others are escaping turmoil in their homelands; some are students; but all expect to be upwardly mobile (Parrillo 2000). Relatively light-skinned, they represent a variety of language and culture communities. Some are ethnic Arabs, others are not; most are Muslim, but not all. The size of this minority group was about 4 million in 2000, but because it is a largely young adult population from high-fertility cultures, its numbers could soon exceed 6 million, surpassing the Jewish population in the United States.

Assimilation has been made difficult by the demands of the Muslim religion, especially the need to stop work and pray several times a day. Patterns of family life and the role of women also set the Middle Easterners apart from the mainstream, at least for the first generation. In addition, few Middle Easterners have escaped American hostility generated by the hostage crisis in Iran from 1979 to 1981, the war against Iraq in the early 1990s, and the fear of "Arab terrorists" that still lingers and bursts forth whenever an airplane crashes or a building is bombed (Ansari 1992).

In reality, many Middle Eastern subgroups fit the "model minority" pattern of establishing economically successful enclaves, with low unemployment and poverty. Their goal, however, may not be full assimilation but, rather, keeping their cultural and religious traditions intact in the face of modernizing pressures. It remains to be seen whether the old ways can withstand the influence of Americanization, as the children become better educated than their parents and as the women experience the world outside the enclave. 10

Religious Minorities

The sociology of religion is examined in detail in chapter 12, but something should be said here about religion, the immigrant experience, and stratification outcomes. Although the nation was founded by people deeply concerned with religious freedom, reflected in the First Amendment to the Constitution, in practice this concern often extended only to varieties of Protestantism. Catholics were feared on the grounds that their first loyalty was to the Pope in Rome; Jews were hated for their presumed betrayal of Jesus; and Native American religions were dismissed as savage throwbacks. But it may not have been religion that bothered the native-born Protestants as much as ethnicity: the Catholics were portrayed as drunken Irish or illiterate Italians, and many of the Jews were even stranger, from odd-sounding places in Eastern Europe.

Over time, however, education, intermarriage, and moving out of the enclave have eroded the sharp lines that once isolated Catholic and Jewish minorities from the mainstream and from one another. Yet, within each major religious group, there is a stratification hierarchy that reflects when the group immigrated, from where, with what skills, and its subsequent history in the New World.

Protestants

Numerically and ideologically, the United States is a Protestant nation. Protestants compose 65 to 70 percent of citizens, compared with 25 percent Catholic, 2.5 percent Jewish, and 1.5 percent Muslim. Yet it is a majority composed of many minorities, or *denominations*, autonomous faith communities within the Protestant umbrella. These denominations can be arranged in a hierarchy of prestige, based on the social class of worshipers, ranging from Episcopalian Wall Street brokers at one extreme to National Baptist tenant farmers at the other. The placement of other denominations reflects the overall stratification system, plus ethnicity and color.

Intermarriage rates are highest between denominations closest to one another in the hierarchy and within the same race. Although the effect of ethnic background, with the exception of Hispanic, has become blurred over time, religious intermarriage rates have increased slowly, and primarily with Catholics rather than Jews. If there is a fault line in American Protestantism today, it is no longer rooted in the immigrant experience but in contemporary concerns between the more "liberal" (Northeastern), high-status denominations and the more "conservative" fundamentalist denominations of the South and Midwest "Bible Belt" (chapter 12).

Catholics

The deep mistrust of Catholics carried to America by the Protestant settlers lasted almost 300 years, and it still slips into the literature of the militant Christian Right (chapter 16). Unlike Protestantism with its self-governing denominations, the Catholic Church is a single entity, a hierarchically structured organization in which power flows from the Pope downward. But, like Protestantism, the Church embraces social class extremes, from the Kennedys to the most recently arrived Chicano family.

The internal stratification system of American Catholics is based on time of arrival, closeness to Northern European ancestry, and skin color. Some French Catholics have been here since colonial times, but the great waves of Catholic immigration date from the mid-nineteenth century. For most of the past 150 years, the Catholic community was dominated by the Irish, who monopolized the top positions in the religious hierarchy, Catholic educational institutions and charities, and Catholic-American politics. Only in the last three decades have they been replaced by men (and it remains overwhelmingly men) with Italian, Polish, and Latino names.

The social class divisions that separated Catholic ethnic subpopulations have gradually eroded as non-Irish Catholics have caught up in terms of education and occupational status. Today's high rates of intermarriage among Catholics of different ancestry testify to the blurring of ethnic differences. Although they might not be asked to join an elite country club, American Catholics face few barriers to integration and upward mobility. The emphasis on community fostered by the parish church and the close family ties of Southern and Eastern European Catholic immigrants probably lowered the motivation for individual achievement among second-generation American Catholics. Since the 1960s, however, the ethnic communities have dispersed to the suburbs, college attendance has soared, and upward mobility is now the norm.

At the same time, the Church remains a powerful source of identity and primary group ties. Most marry within the faith, and many continue to send their children to Church-run schools. But in terms of personal behavior, it is a much more "optional" religion than in the past, less bound to tradition and official Church positions on matters of everyday conduct. Current issues in American Catholicism are discussed further in chapter 12.

Jews

Prejudice and discrimination—*anti-Semitism*—are nothing new or unusual for Jews, the eternal minority. With the exception of the State of Israel since 1948, Jews have stood apart, *in* but never *of* the host society. In the United States, Jews have avoided the extreme hostility they faced in Europe, in part because of the Constitutional guarantee of freedom of religion and in part because, outside of a

Descendants of Eastern European Jews took advantage of public and private higher education in the United States and entered the occupational structure, enjoying upward mobility. Many American Jews return to their roots by visiting Israel.

few major cities, Jewish communities were few and far between and sparsely populated. Nonetheless, anti-Semitism is a continuing underground theme in American history, among both conservative Southern Christians and the Eastern Protestant elite.

The internal stratification of American Jewry follows the pattern for other religious groups, based on time of arrival, closeness to the Northern European ideal, and occupational achievements in America (Sachar 1992). At the top of the hierarchy are the descendants of families fleeing the Spanish Inquisition, who settled in the Carolinas and Virginia before the Revolutionary War. By the 1860s, the Jewish population in America was 150,000, soon increased by many highly educated immigrants escaping from an outbreak of anti-Semitism in Germany. The German Jews soon found a very prosperous niche in areas of finance and banking that the WASP elite felt beneath their dignity. Never very religious and eager to assimilate, German Jews tried to be as American and WASPish as possible, even moving Sabbath services from Friday night to Sunday morning.

These early arrivals were followed by the major wave of Jewish immigration, between 1890 and 1920, when tens of thousands of European Jews, mostly from rural villages in Poland, Lithuania, and Russia, fled to the United States a few steps ahead of armed mobs. Compared to the acculturated German Jews, the new arrivals were very strange indeed—Yiddish-speaking, deeply superstitious, relatively uneducated, and very poor. For many decades, the German Jewish elite had little direct contact with the newcomers, other than providing charitable support. Intermarriage between German and East European Jews was treated with the same hostility as if the children had married Gentiles.

Eventually, the children of Eastern European peasants took advantage of the public system of higher education, and they entered the occupational structure when the white-collar sector was expanding, enjoying instant upward mobility. Today, in comparison to their numbers in the population, Jews are vastly overrepresented among college graduates and high-income earners. Still prohibited from joining the elite dining and country clubs, they formed a parallel system of exclusive private clubs and organizations.

The unintended consequence of Jewish success is that the children and grandchildren of immigrants moved out of the urban enclaves into the suburbs and went to schools where they met non-Jews. Intermarriage rates have reached historic highs, involving perhaps one-half of Jewish men today. Also, given the high educational attainment of both Jewish women and men, birthrates are at a historic low. All these factors threaten the survival of the Jewish-American community (Klaff 1998).

The exception to these trends is the small subgroups of extremely traditional Orthodox Jews who have been able to retain their unique way of life by isolating themselves from both mainstream American Judaism and the dominant culture. They can do this by living in closely knit neighborhoods, sending their children to religious schools, and taking jobs that do not conflict with religious obligations. Orthodox fertility is very high, but given the small size of the population to begin with, this may not be enough to keep the number of American Jews from declining even further.

Muslims

The newest and fastest-growing religious minority in the United States consists of followers of the Islamic faith, known as **Muslims**. This population is enormously varied in terms of race, ethnicity, culture, and language, united only by its religion. The earliest Muslim immigrants came from Lebanon and Syria in the 1920s and settled in the Midwest, where the first mosques were built in North Dakota and Iowa. Relatively light-skinned, they found a niche selling household goods and clothing to farmers and villagers, and, despite their unusual religious practices, they were eventually assimilated into the local communities.

In the 1990s, however, large numbers of Muslim immigrants, primarily from Iran and Pakistan, settled in major urban areas such as New York, Los Angeles, and Chicago, where they established supportive ethnic and religious enclaves centered on the mosque (Parrillo 2000). Women from these cultures remain largely under the influence of men; they receive limited education and have little power outside the household, although these factors are likely to change as their daughters move into the school system and become Ameri-canized and as the mothers enter the labor force. At the moment, however, tending their relatively large families is a full-time job for many of these women.

In comparison with earlier Muslim immigrants, these newer groups are darker skinned, and they are subjected to considerable hostility, job discrimi-nation, and residential isolation, although it is difficult to separate what is triggered by skin color and what is caused by a general dislike of "Arabs," although neither the Pakistanis nor Iranians are ethnically Arab.

The American Muslim community has also grown through the conver-sion of several hundred thousand African Americans, including prizefighter Muhammad Ali, basketball player Kareem Abdul-Jabbar, and an early leader of the Black Muslims, Malcolm X. The appeal of Islam to African Americans lies in part in its extreme difference from the American society already expe-rienced as oppressive and dangerous; here is an altogether new way to build community, untainted and pure. Others are attracted to Islam's demands for personal and sexual discipline, rather like the Protestant work ethic in its emphasis on achievement through self-control.

❖ ❖ ❖ ❖

Conclusion

Although this chapter has focused on the history and experiences of minority groups in America, most intergroup processes are universal. Domi-nant groups will always feel threatened by "strangers," and the newcomers will always face obstacles of varying strength and duration. In the United States, as in many other parts of the world today, the public has been periodi-cally aroused by fears that foreigners will soon outnumber the native born and destroy their unique culture. America has always been a land of cultural diversity, but a combination of declining white fertility and the entry of darker-skinned populations has revived the historic xenophobic streak in our country. At the local level, some cities have tried to enact "English Only" rules for official business, but these have been struck down by the courts. The movement against bilingual education has had more success. At the national level, Congress continues to struggle with immigration rules, while Western states attempt to stop the flow of undocumented workers from Mexico.

The debate over immigration is also an argument over the virtues or dan-gers of multiculturalism, or the celebration of diversity. In reality, your school most likely has a more diverse student body than in the past, and your neighborhood and workplace will be less homogeneous in the future. Your children will have friends of various colors and cultures. Some of your neigh-bors will lament the death of Western Civilization; others will see the revital-ization of American ideals of tolerance. Will the United States become a model for the rest of the world as all nations are increasingly linked by the continual movement of trade, ideas, and populations? The answer will depend on your generation's response to the American mosaic, whether to encourage cultural differences or to insist on rapid acculturation. Welcome to America in the twenty-first century.

❖ ❖ ❖ ❖   ## Surfing the Sociological Internet

🖥 1   For numerous links for resources on race and ethnicity, see:
http://www.mosaicweb.com/interrac.html
http://eserver.org/race/default.html

🖥 2   For an interactive discussion of racial and ethnic identities go to:
http://members.aol.com/Jakajk/Oneworld.html

🖥 3   On Immigration:
http://library.thinkquest.org/26786/en/home/help.php3
http://www.ercomer.org/wwwvl is The WWW Virtual Library
on Migration and Ethnic Issues
Reach the INS at: http://www.ins.usdoj.gov/

🖥 4   Living in a Multicultural Society:
http://racerelations.about.com/newsissues/
Teaching about diversity:
http://create.familyeducation.com/topic/front/0,1156,33374,
00.html

🖥 5   On racial stereotypes in the media:
http://www.media-awareness.ca/eng/issues/minrep/
getinvolved/kidtalk.htm
On reducing prejudice and discrimination:
http://www.hatewatch.org/index1.html
http://www.adl.org/

Websites for racial and ethnic groups in the United States:

🖥 6   Native American websites:
http://www.pitt.edu/~lmitten/indians.html
http://www.nativeweb.org/
The U.S. Bureau of Indian Affairs can be found at: http://
www.ios.doi.gov/bureau-indian-affairs.html

🖥 7   African Americans:
http://www.africana.com
http://www.blackplanet.com
http://www.blackfacts.com
Association for the Study of African-American Life and History:
http://www.artnoir.com/asalh
Africans in America: http://www.pbs.org/wgbh/aiaold/
home.html

🖥 8   Asian Americans:
http://www.AsianAvenue.com/
http://www.mit.edu:8001/afs/athena.mit.edu/user/i/r/irie/
www/aar.html
http://www.seacaef.org/
http://asiapacificuniverse.com/

🖥 9   Latinos:
http://www.latino.com/

http://www.ozemail.com.au/~ecuapita/latam.html and http://www.latinworld.com/index.html

💻 10 Middle Easterners:
   http://wizard.ucr.edu/~skiasatp/mideast.html
   http://commhum.mccneb.edu/mpaul/newpage1.htm
   http://www.peachnet.edu/galileo/internet/area/mid-east.html

For website links for Religious Minorities, see chapter 12.

Glossary

Accommodation Occurs when members of a minority become aware of the norms and values of the dominant culture but do not replace traditional ways of life with new ones.

Acculturation Occurs when minority members adopt the dominant culture and participate in major institutions but are nonetheless refused entry into intimate social groupings.

Amalgamation Loss of minority group traits through social acceptance and intermarriage.

Apartheid System of rigid separation between whites and people of color.

Assimilation Occurs when minority group status is no longer a barrier to full integration into the dominant group.

Culturally Homogeneous Society One in which the great majority of citizens are of the same race and share a common language and religion.

Culturally Heterogeneous Society One in which there are many subgroups which differ in language, race, religion, and national origin and culture.

Cultural Pluralism A model that emphasizes the special contributions of each minority group to the diversity of American society.

De facto Segregation Segregation that occurs but is not necessarily supported by law.

De jure Segregation Segregation created by laws.

Discrimination The practice of treating people unequally; it refers to actual behavior.

Dominant Groups Those who control the major sources of power and who set standards of social worth and beauty.

Economic Niche An occupational specialty that comes to be associated with a minority group.

Ethnicity Cultural identity derived from common ancestry or country of origin.

Ethnic/Racial Enclave An area within a city where group members control local commerce and create a protective subculture.

Hegemony Dominance or leadership by a given group.

Institutionalized Racism Systematic discrimination against a racial or ethnic group that is built into social structures.

Internal Colonialism Occurs when a native population is treated as if it were a foreign colony.

Marginality A group's being on the fringe, caught between two cultures, no longer fully at home in the one or accepted in the other.

Melting Pot The basic model for absorbing immigrants, in which cultural differences would melt away through exposure to the common language and customs.

Minority Group Not belonging to the dominant group and identified by visible traits, differential treatment, shared identity, and self-image.

Model Minority A minority group that fulfills the American Dream of upward mobility through good habits, hard work, and respect for the family.

Mosaic An object composed of many pieces of different colors and shapes.

Multiculturalism The celebration of diversity.

Muslims Followers of the Islamic faith; the fastest-growing religious minority in the United States.

Prejudice Attitudes, literally "pre-judgments," about others.

Race A social construction influenced by the meanings assigned to a skin color by a given society.

Segregation Keeping a minority isolated from contact with other members of the society.

Xenophobia Fear of foreigners. ✦

Chapter 7

Drawing Distinctions:
Gendered Inequality

Social notes from around the world in the year 2000:

- Egyptian women were finally given the right to divorce (Sachs 2000).

- A few Afghani girls were allowed to attend a makeshift school, but only up to age 11 (Bearak 2000).

- The head of the Czech government explained the absence of women in his cabinet by saying that "men were just better problem solvers" (*New York Times*, February 27, 2000).

- In Japan, the birthrate has fallen so low that officials are debating giving bonuses for having babies, but the women said they would prefer a husband who would help raise the children (Sims 2000).

Across the globe, ideology, law, custom, and institutions have for so long been dominated by men that it is easy to forget how much all of these have been shaped by men's interests rather than reflecting any "natural" order. This condition is called **gendered inequality**, relationships of male superiority and female inferiority in a stratification hierarchy that reflects and affects the distribution of all types of social resources. This chapter is primarily concerned with the dramatic changes that have occurred in the lives of women as the structures of gender stratification have come under analysis and challenge. The chapter covers the following topics:

- Defining gender.

- Becoming gendered.

- Systems of gendered inequality.

- Gendered worlds.

- Winds of change.

What Is Gender?

Defining "gender" is no easy task, mostly because it is so often used interchangeably with "sex." As you saw in chapter 4, sociologists use "sex" to refer to male and female as biological categories, even though there is not always a clear-cut distinction. "Gender," in contrast, refers to socially constructed realities, such as feminine or masculine, that vary greatly across cultures and within a society by class, race, and ethnicity (Lorber and Farrell 1991). But gender is more than identity; it is an aspect of social structure—in the language that makes religion masculine, in the atmosphere that feminizes grammar school, in the division between private (her home) and public (his job), in assumptions about sex-based abilities, and so on. The list is endless because there is no part of social structure that does not have a gender dimension. Can you think of any social system in which you take part where women and men are expected to think and act in the same way and to have the same power over the situation?

We act and think like women and men because our language and social structures divide us, on the basis of biology, into two distinct categories, as when you say, "He is a man; therefore he must have such and such abilities

and feelings." Then, when you observe the expected differences, you assume
they are biologically or psychologically programmed (Kramer 2001).

The Nature of Sex Differences

Most of the literature on biologically based sex differences—from brain size to evolutionary drives—appears to be a cross between wishful thinking and overgeneralizing (Angier 1999). This is so because there are very few basic differences that cannot or have not been altered by culture, social structure, and unique experiences. The bottom line is that humans are enormously adaptable, and behavior is the outcome of complex interactions of body, mind, and the environment. In this view, sex does not necessarily determine gender, and gendered expectations have a lot to do with what are assumed to be the effects of biological sex.

Yet arguments for male superiority based on biological traits continue to influence people's thinking. Many still believe that men's greater *body size* and *aggressiveness* account for their greater social power. But size has nothing to do with intelligence, and highly aggressive individuals usually end up in prison. Nor do *hormones* explain much, since most research has found only a weak link between hormone levels and specific behaviors (Sapolsky 1997). Most recently, scholars have explored the *evolutionary psychology* argument that certain sex-linked traits are coded in the human psyche as a result of millions of years of survival pressures (Buss 1999). In this view, males are driven to spread their sperm and females to make themselves attractive to males, but there are very powerful *social* reasons for these behaviors in societies where a man's power is measured by the number of children he sires or where women are judged by the success of their husbands. Note that in the United States today, a man's prestige depends less on having a lot of children and much more on having a beautiful woman on his arm. No neurological hard-wiring is needed to explain these patterns.

The problem with all reductionist models is that they cannot account for the wide variability in whatever behavior they try to predict. Even among primates, there are great differences in patterns of competition and cooperation and sexuality. For example, our closest animal cousins, the chimpanzees, are more egalitarian and less aggressive than other primates and members of many human groups (Jolly 1999).

For sociologists, then, it is most useful to see sex and gender differences as primarily influenced by culture and social structure rather than by genes, hormones, or the evolutionary past (Kimmel 2000a). It is also important to understand that sex differences are not absolute. When researchers report, for example, that boys are more active than girls or that girls are more gentle than boys, they are actually describing *group differences*. Some girls and boys will not fit the description and others will behave exactly like the other sex. Whatever trait is being measured, the findings are likely to resemble Figure 7.1 for, say, acts of nurturance among kindergarteners, with lots of overlap and general clustering around the middle.

Note also that the difference between the highest- and lowest-scoring boys and girls (10 and 0) is five times greater than the difference between the group averages (2). As with most traits that researchers have measured, males and females differ more among themselves than they do from each

❖ ❖ ❖ ❖

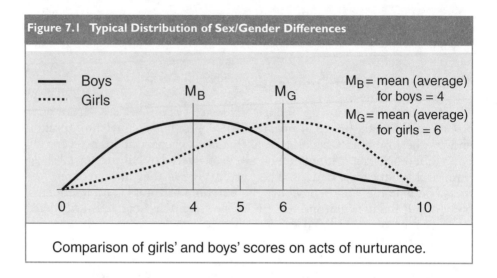

Figure 7.1 Typical Distribution of Sex/Gender Differences

Comparison of girls' and boys' scores on acts of nurturance.

other. Indeed, basic research on IQ, various aptitudes, and achievement in children has found few or no consistent sex differences, yet boys and girls are raised to see themselves as different (Maccoby 1998).

A Sociological View

The sociological perspective on **male dominance**, or **patriarchy** (the rule of men), looks at characteristics of culture and social structure to explain historical trends and differences among societies. As shown in Figure 7.2, the degree of gender stratification is variable, higher in some kinds of societies than in others. Because hormones, genes, and evolutionary drives do not suddenly change with the introduction of new technology, we must ask why a herding tribe differs from an agricultural society in a way that affects power differences between women and men.

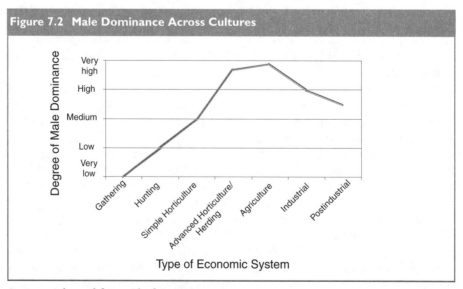

Figure 7.2 Male Dominance Across Cultures

Source: Adapted from Chafetz 1990.

❖ ❖ ❖ ❖

Power differences are lowest in hunting and gathering societies because both men and women are responsible for the food supply and for the care of children. As societies grow more complex in terms of division of labor, women and men become specialists in different tasks and skills, and what men do is invariably considered more important than what women do. In herding and agricultural societies, where owning cattle and land are of supreme importance and where inheritance passes from fathers to sons, male dominance is at its highest. Some men will be more powerful than others, but all men are more powerful than women because control of women is the best way to ensure that the children who inherit your resources are biologically yours. Women and children are considered part of the family's wealth. Male dominance is reduced in traditional societies where women have their own economic resources and are able to own property in their own name (Chafetz 1990).

With industrialization, the power of families declines. Land, cattle, and kinship are less important than learned skills, intelligence, and luck. Eventually, most industrial societies also become democracies, although it took a very long time to include women in the electorate and the college population. Modern families (see chapter 8) tend to be small, with girls and boys given similar opportunities. Thus, although men remain dominant, the trend is toward greater equality, or egalitarianism. However, it is important to distinguish between formal equality, as in most written constitutions, and actual practices. Even in the most self-consciously egalitarian societies such as Sweden, official equality is not reflected in the division of household labor and other crucial institutions (Acker 2000).

Gender inequality is reinforced by practices at all levels of social structure: (1) in the micro-level interactions, where gender identities are formed and continually validated; (2) in the meso-level arrangements of the workplace, school, and household; and (3) in the macro-level institutions of politics and religion. The message is the same throughout: to be male is to be privileged and powerful; to be female is to be dependent and less effective. In other words, gender is about power (Connell 2000). 💻 1

Becoming Gendered

Learning a gendered identity is similar to any other socialization experience. You are rewarded for appropriate behavior and negatively sanctioned for inappropriate acts. The same agents are at work: parents, peers, teachers, and the media for young people, and your spouse, friends, bosses, and co-workers as an adult. No society leaves this process to chance. And since there are only two recognized sexes in this society, behaviors must be squeezed into one of two boxes, with the male box often narrower than the female one.

Socialization Processes

Most parents have gendered expectations of their children, even before birth. In one classic study, when asked to describe their newly born infants, fathers saw their sons as tough and husky and daughters as soft and cuddly, although there were no significant physical differences between the two sets of infants (Rubin et al. 1979). Even parents committed to gender equality will

❖ ❖ ❖ ❖   have difficulty counteracting the influences of school and the peer cultures of young children (Carlton-Ford and Houston 2001; Thorne 1993). The local toy store is influenced by and influences gender expectations, when the cover for a Lego set for girls features a female child in a frilly pink dress and patent leather shoes playing with pink and white Lego pieces, building "her honeymoon cottage" complete with heart-shaped windows. If a girl is interested in computers, Mattel has a new Barbie version, loaded with Fashion Designer and Detective Barbie software. The company's version for boys, Hot Wheels PC, is filled with educational software and logic-learning games. 💻2

Differential socialization has an effect on **cognitive structures**, that is, how children process information. When daughters are kept closer to home while sons are given greater leeway to explore the big world outside, they develop different skills and competencies: girls learn to manipulate with words, boys, by doing. These experiences also have an effect on self-image. In general, girls have lower self-esteem than do boys, especially in pre-adolescence. However confident a girl may have been in childhood, by the time she reaches high school, her self-image has become less positive and more filled with doubt, especially among white, middle-class young women (Pipher 1994). There is some evidence that black and working-class girls have greater resilience to these pressures to conform to gender stereotypes and are more willing to express their anger (Brown 1998).

All but a very few positions of substantial power in the United States are occupied by white men. Even though dress in business has become more casual, these three men are the top executives of a major U.S. corporation.

Developing a positive self-image does not become easier in adulthood. Women and men both think less of a woman's achievement than of a man's. Socialization is only partly responsible for such judgments. Inequality is a structural factor, and low self-esteem is a logical outcome of occupying statuses of little power or social worth (Howard and Alamilla 2001). Lower self-esteem no doubt accounts for the fact that the great majority of cosmetic surgery patients are women (Weitz 1998).

Micro-Level Interactions

From the interpretive perspective, gender identities and inequality are reflected and recreated in everyday interactions (Ridgeway and Correll 2000). How people talk to one another, how they use space, who opens doors for whom—these are all acts with deep symbolic meaning. The key variable is power, which is easy to see in teacher-student or employer-worker interactions but is less obvious when looking at casual male-female encounters. Listen carefully to conversations between women and men and see if you can uncover the gender dynamics—for example, who controls the interaction, opens and closes a conversation, interrupts or changes the subject? Notice also how status differences are reflected in patterns of speech such as hesitations or tentative statements (O'Barr 2001).

Space itself is gendered (Spain 1992). There are men's places and women's places in all societies. Indeed, one measure of gender equality is the degree to which such spaces overlap. In some Islamic countries today, women are forbidden to leave the home unless escorted by a close male relative. In contrast, in the United States today, formerly all-male places such as the pool hall, the military, or the locker room are now open to women, although all-female places such as child-care facilities are rarely invaded by men. If American women do not go out alone at night, it is not because it is forbidden but because it is dangerous. The fear of sexual violence effectively limits the range of women's space.

It is in the small but telling details of everyday life that gender is continually being constructed. Unlike other systems of inequality such as race and class, where people do not necessarily have to interact across stratum lines, men and women are in constant contact, at home, at work, at school, on the streets. As one leading social psychologist has put it:

> What is interesting about the gender system is not that it never changes, but that it sustains itself by continually redefining who men and women are while preserving the fundamental assumption that whatever the differences are, they imply that men are rightly more powerful. (Ridgeway 1999, 89–95)

Systems of Gendered Inequality

An umbrella term such as the *status of women* covers a lot of variation. There are the various dimensions of stratification—power, prestige, and property—plus the different institutional spheres such as family, politics, economy, religion, and education. Then, too, women will vary in their opportunities by race, ethnicity, and social class. Although in general women are subordinate to men, some have greater economic and social power than do others, as when women in the middle and upper strata hire Latinas and African Americans as domestic servants (Romero 1992). Thus, in the United States, women of color must deal with multiple systems of inequality, making it extremely difficult to talk about "the status of women" without specifying the women's locations in stratification hierarchies. Nonetheless, some generalizations are possible.

The Power Dimension

All but a very few positions of great power in America—in politics, business, education, the media, and religion—are occupied by white men. This situation is usually explained as being a result of women's lack of driving ambition or leadership qualities. Other personal shortcomings are put forth to explain the absence of blacks and Latinos. In contrast to this emphasis on *human capital*—the abilities that individuals bring to the job market—sociological research focuses on the structural factors that make it more or less difficult to move to the top. These structural conditions include informal social

❖ ❖ ❖ ❖   networks (shared friends, clubs, fraternity membership), support from senior colleagues, and help with child care. The barriers are in the situation rather than the person, although when faced with such obstacles, many women will lower their expectations. The most powerful obstacle for women is having primary responsibility for children, especially if the woman wants to get ahead in an occupation that requires an extraordinary investment of time (Maume 2001). Nonetheless, the number of women seeking top jobs in politics and business continues to rise.

Politics. Women have always made up a majority of campaign workers, stuffing envelopes and making phone calls. In the past three decades, they have also made dramatic gains in being elected to local offices, which is where people gain the credentials and credits essential to running for higher office. As Table 7.1 shows, there has been a slow increase in the number of women governors and members of Congress.

Table 7.1 Women in Political Office, 1980–2000 (in percents)			
	1980	1990	2000
U.S. Senate	1%	2%	13%
U.S. House	4	5.8	12.9
State Legislature	12	18.2	22.5
Statewide Office	11	18	28.5

Source: National Information Bank on Women in Public Office, a service of the Center for the Study of Women in Politics, Eagleton Institute, Rutgers University, 2000.

Clearly, a woman politician is no longer a rarity, although she will have more trouble than her male peers in raising money and having her ideas taken more seriously than what she is wearing. 🖥3

Business. Getting ahead in the world of big business has been equally difficult for women. In 1999, women comprised 11.2 percent of board of directors members of major American companies; only 2 percent were women of color, and typically one to a company. Becoming a chief executive officer (CEO) remains the most unusual accomplishment—only six women for the 1,000 largest firms in 2000 (Catalyst 2000). These numbers will undoubtedly change, as women who are now flocking to graduate schools of business (where they comprise about 40 percent of the student body) work their way up the corporate ladder.

Once within the corporation, women's careers tend to veer in a different direction from those of men. Women executives are typically located in "people-oriented" departments, such as personnel, public relations, and human resources (diversity issues). In contrast, male executives are in production and financial management posts—the royal roads to the very top. In addition, women executives are concentrated in low-prestige sectors of the economy, such as book publishing, retail sales, fashion, and cosmetics, in contrast to big-money, high-power fields such as investment banking, transportation, and oil and chemicals, which remain almost exclusively male.

The introduction of one or two "outsiders," employees not like those already there—especially when it is done for display rather than substance—has been labeled **tokenism**. Tokens feel extremely self-conscious because they have to carry the burden for their entire sex or race. But as tokens accumulate and master the corporate culture, they can begin to mentor newer employees. A series of small gains in work practices and cultural norms appears to be a more effective strategy for dealing with sex or race discrimination than are company-wide efforts from the top down (Myerson and Fletcher 2000).

At the moment, it is still lonely at the top for females, and doubly stressful if they have family obligations. As a result, many female executives bump against the **glass ceiling**, where they can see through to higher positions but never reach that level of authority. However, recent research suggests that the ceiling is most difficult to break through at the early stages of a woman's career rather than as she moves up the ladder (Baxter and Wright 2000). For women of color, the "glass" becomes a "concrete" ceiling very early in her organizational experience (Catalyst 2000).

In contrast, male tokens—men in predominately female occupations—are on a **glass escalator**, better paid than women and encouraged to apply for administrative posts. However, the number of men entering female-dominated jobs—nursing, noncollege teaching, and flight attendants—has declined since 1998, even with the earnings and promotion advantages (Bureau of Labor Statistics 2000).

The corporate "fast track" is very demanding—60 hours a week or more, weekend meetings, constant travel, and unexpected crises that interfere with stable child care. Because most employers have not made the changes that would lighten a woman's burden, staying on the fast track often involves delaying childbearing or forgoing motherhood altogether. Most choose the "mommy track" and lower their goals in order to find a balance between work and family (Schwartz 1989). Others will leave corporate America and start their own businesses, a risky proposition but at least allowing control of working conditions. Women-owned firms are a fast-growing sector of the economy, but most are small scale, with only a few employees, such as beauty parlors, retail stores, and real estate offices. Retail stores and personal service businesses also have the highest rates of bankruptcy (Dun & Bradstreet.com 1998). Nonetheless, although the presence of women in positions of political and economic power is only slightly higher than a decade ago, the idea of their being there has become taken for granted. 🖥 4

Prestige

If prestige is measured by occupational rank, few American women qualify. Yet, despite lower rewards for high occupational achievement compared to their male peers, women are earning graduate degrees in predominately male professions in ever-increasing num-

Women executives are typically located in people-oriented departments, such as human resources and public relations. Why is that so?

❖ ❖ ❖ ❖   bers, as shown in Table 7.2.

Table 7.2	Professional Degrees Earned by Women, 1960–1999	
	(as percent of total)	
	1960	1999
Medicine	5.5	41
Law	2.5	44
Dentistry	0.8	36
Theology	—	25.2

Source: *Statistical Abstract*, 1999: 206; U.S. Department of Education, National Center for Education Statistics, 2000d.

In two other previously all-male professions—pharmacy and veterinary medicine—over half the new degrees were earned by women in 1997: 62 percent in pharmacy, now that self-owned drug stores have given way to supermarket departments; and 57 percent of veterinarians, now that most patients are household pets rather than farm animals.

Women who pursue the high-status occupations of medicine and law receive less encouragement from family or friends than their brothers, and consequently face fewer penalties when they drop out of school or work part-time. Those who finish graduate school and work full-time are, therefore, highly self-selected for ambition and skill. Yet, like women in business, they tend to be clustered in low-prestige specialties: in pediatrics rather than surgery, or family law rather than corporate mergers (Lorber 2001). They are also more likely than their male classmates to take jobs in the public rather than the private sector—in district attorney or public defender offices in the law, and in health departments and clinics in medicine. Pay and prestige are often lower in these jobs, but so is discrimination and harassment. Compared to private companies, the public sector has been more willing to hire and promote women and persons of color (Gornick and Jacobs 1998). By the same token, any cutbacks in government services will adversely affect minority and female professionals as well as their clients.

In higher education, the proportion of women faculty in a department is inversely related to the prestige of the department; the more women, the lower the prestige. Technical areas or "hard science" rank highest and "soft" subjects such as the arts, humanities, and social sciences, lowest. In addition, the higher the academic rank, from instructor to full professor, the fewer women, and the more elite the school, the fewer women faculty (see chapter 11).

Of special concern are the very low numbers of women in engineering and the more traditional technological fields, especially those with links to the military (Fox 2001). The process begins much earlier, with girls doing less well than boys on math tests and being discouraged from science courses. Even if some of this difference is due to innate cognitive factors, the performance gap can be dramatically closed with access to training and jobs. In newly emerging fields such as the Internet.com firms, where there has not been time to establish an "old boy's" network or a masculinized corporate culture, women now hold 45 percent of top management posts (Kaufman 2000).

With the exception of the new Internet sector, the entry of women into an occupation typically makes that field less attractive to men. The presence of women lowers the prestige ranking; men flee and pay scales plummet. Being a bank teller, for example, was once a young man's entry into a banking career, but when more attractive white-collar work became available after 1945, the men left and the banks were forced to hire women; being a bank teller then became mostly a dead-end job, filled by women (Cohn 1985).

It is also the case that when women and persons of color get a toehold in some well-paying blue-collar occupation, these types of jobs are about to disappear, as in automobile and steel production in the United States in the 1980s. The last to be hired is the first fired, and the last to be hired is most often a minority woman for whom the concrete ceiling has been replaced by the "sticky floor" that locks her into the lowest levels of the occupational hierarchy (Berheide 1992).

Property

It will come as no surprise that wealth and income are heavily skewed by sex. Of the *Forbes'* listing of the 400 wealthiest people in America in 2000, only a very few were women, and most of those had inherited their fortunes from a father or dead husband. Estée Lauder, the cosmetics queen, and Oprah Winfrey, of media fame, are the only ones who made it on their own. Had *Forbes* been counting earlier in this century, the black businesswoman, Madam C. J. Walker, would surely have made the list.

For the other 99.9 percent of U.S. households, the wife's income, although lower than that of equally skilled men, is often enough to lift the family into the middle or upper-middle class. For nonmarried women who support themselves and their children, however, median income is less than half that of a married couple. If the female householder is black or Latina, the difference is even greater, as you saw in chapter 5. In terms of property, then, to be female is to be relatively disadvantaged unless your earnings can be added to those of a male breadwinner.

Gendered Worlds

In the sociological perspective, gender is more than a personal characteristic or description. It is built into the very structure of social institutions. Religions are gendered and so are the organizations that embody the faith, as discussed in chapter 12. Also, as discussed in chapter 8, families are so deeply gendered that it is often difficult to separate the natural from the constructed. Everyday encounters carry gendered messages about appropriate femininity and masculinity. This section briefly reviews two of the most important institutional settings for the creation and maintenance of gender inequality: work and education.

Work

The key to personal independence is participation in the labor force. Like most workers, women have "jobs" with limited autonomy rather than "careers" with clear promotion ladders. But a job of her own, however routine, is an opportunity for a woman to leave the house, make new friends, and have money that she can spend as she chooses. All this makes her less dependent on a male wage earner and reduces the power differences within a mar-

❖ ❖ ❖ ❖   riage. In other words, labor force participation is a powerful factor in reducing gender inequalities (Bianchi and Dye 2001).

Today, about two-thirds of American women between ages 16 and 65 are in the labor force, and 80 percent of these are full-time, year-round workers. Sixty-one percent of married women with children age 3 and under are in the labor force, as are almost 80 percent of married women with adolescent children. As shown in Figure 7.3, not only have participation rates continued to rise, but also women now compose close to half

Women have historically done work with limited autonomy, receiving low wages. These women in Bangladesh are rolling incense for export to the West.

the civilian labor force. This means that when you imagine "the American worker," that person is almost as likely to be female as male.

Immigrant women, African-American women, and women of the working class have always had high labor force participation rates—in factories, stores, laundries, and the homes of the wealthy. In addition, many women have earned money by working at home, as dressmakers, cooks, taking in paying guests, or doing farm chores, but because the Census classified them as "housewife," the number of women workers has consistently been

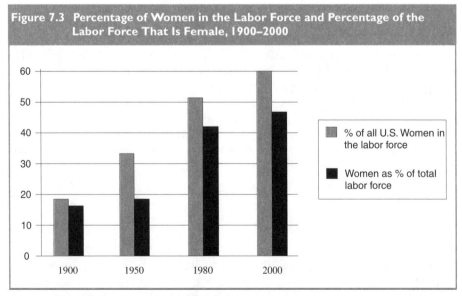

Figure 7.3   Percentage of Women in the Labor Force and Percentage of the Labor Force That Is Female, 1900–2000

■ % of all U.S. Women in the labor force

■ Women as % of total labor force

Source: *Historical Statistics of the United States, Vol. 1, 1975*: 132; Bureau of Labor Statistics, *Statistical Report*, June 2000.

undercounted (Bose 1987). Full-time motherhood has typically been a luxury of the households that could live on the husband's income alone. Yet even during the Baby Boom years from 1948 to 1968, one-third of women remained in the paid labor force.

Most married women who are not in the labor force are nevertheless working, though not for pay. They provide a range of services for other household members—shopping, food preparation, laundering, chauffeuring, and care of the frail elderly. In a society where people are judged by their labor value, housewives are greatly undervalued, which may be one source of their higher rates of emotional distress compared to employed women (Rosenfeld 1992).

As you see every day, the labor force is thoroughly gendered, with female-dominated jobs at the bottom of the skill and pay ladders. This pattern of **sex-segregated jobs** is the major reason why the **gender wage gap** has remained fairly steady since the 1950s, with full-time women workers earning between 65 and 73 cents for every dollar earned by a man, even in the same type of job (Bose and Whaley 2001). Some of the earnings gap can also be traced to family responsibilities that inhibit women from working overtime or relocating for a better job. And some of the gap is due to wage discrimination by employers, both conscious and unconscious (Reskin 2000). Although sex and race discrimination in hiring and wages is illegal, employers can always find some other reason for preferring one type of employee over another.

In practice, the great majority of male and female workers are in occupations dominated by members of their own sex, with male wage scales and fringe benefits consistently higher, even when similar levels of training and skills are involved. The concept of **pay equity**, or **comparable worth**, in effect in many government jobs but not in the private sector, is based on the principle that people who do work that requires similar levels of training and responsibility should be paid similarly (Steinberg 2001). 🖥 5

Education

As you saw in chapter 5, years of education is a powerful determinant of social status. A college diploma is the entry card to the middle class, and it is increasingly required for even low-prestige white-collar employment. Cross-culturally, a prime index of gender equality is the rate at which girls are permitted to attend school and women are allowed in universities. Limiting female education to what is needed to run a household is a powerful form of social control. Thus, the great majority of the world's women remain illiterate, without political power, and more likely than men to live in poverty (Parikh and Shane 1998).

Even in industrial societies, gaining equal access to education for females has not been a simple task. For most parents, until quite recently, schooling was more of a priority for sons, who would eventually have to earn a living and support a family, than for daughters, who needed only to learn the arts of homemaking. For this, though, some education was necessary, at least through grammar school. Later in the twentieth century, high school attendance was made mandatory for girls as well as boys, although married or pregnant female students (and teachers) were expelled before they could contaminate innocent children with their sexual knowledge.

In terms of gender, in this century at least, elementary school is a "feminized" environment. Most teachers are women; students are expected

Box 7.1

Dying to Learn

When the Taliban Islamic traditionalists took control of Afghanistan in 1996, they enacted laws that banned women from employment and girls from school. On the rare occasions when a woman could leave her home, she had to wear a heavy cloth garment that covered her from head to toe, with only a mesh slit around the eyes. Unable to be treated by a male doctor, poorly fed, and often abused, women's life expectancy in Afghanistan is among the lowest in the world, and infant mortality rates are among the highest (Population Reference Bureau 2000).

Yet the thirst for an education has somehow survived, and illegal schools for girls have been opening in the country's few urban areas, without desks, books, or writing materials, but always with more students than can fit on the cold floors (Bearak 2000). Many are daughters of illiterate mothers who want a better life for the girls; others had spent years disguised as boys in order to attend regular school. All the students, and especially the teachers, live in fear of a crackdown by officials, leading to beatings, arrests, and even a public execution.

to be neatly dressed, to sit still and wait to be called on, and to display other female virtues. All of these expectations are very difficult for boys, whose nervous systems are less mature than those of the girls and who are used to the rough and tumble of boys' play. Things get a little better for the boys in high school, which is a more masculine environment. There are more male teachers; a "jock" culture brings rewards to many students, while others begin to excel in academics. Where girls had outperformed boys in the lower grades, the boys now catch up and get serious about their education. The hidden curriculum here is socialization to gendered adulthoods (Spade 2001).

Men do better than women on the SATs, though the gap has narrowed somewhat; they win more academic as well as athletic scholarships, and they are more likely to apply to college, regardless of school grades. Families with limited financial resources are still more likely to spend more on a son's college education than on that of a daughter, which means that the women will probably attend a less prestigious school. Women are more likely than men to attend a public rather than private college, a two-year rather than four-year school, and to have problems financing their education (American Council on Education 2000).

In some Islamic countries today, such as Afghanistan, women are forbidden to leave home unless escorted and are expected to veil their faces.

Despite less encouragement and financial support, the percentage of women high school graduates going on to higher education has doubled—from 38 percent in 1960 to over 70 percent today (compared to 63 percent for men). From 1988 on, the proportion of women entering college has exceeded that of men by a widening margin, so that today, women comprise 60 percent of all college students. Even though the degree will bring a woman fewer economic rewards than for her male peers, she is increasingly likely to be awarded a bachelor's degree and to enter graduate school.

Even more so than high school, colleges and universities are masculine places—founded by men for the training of men who will lead the nation. Privilege and hierarchy were built into the earliest colleges and remain the guiding principles of elite schools today. Just as boys were uncomfortable in the lower grades, women often find the university a chilly place, where their presence is tolerated at best and resented at worst.

By their sheer numbers, however, women students are bringing change to their colleges and universities. Sexual harassment and interpersonal violence have been made visible and are less tolerated than before. Women's Studies courses and degree programs are now offered on many campuses, sparking intellectual interest and stimulating research. Clearly, it is no longer the same campus as that of your grandparents or even your parents. 💻 6

Winds of Change

As a result of all these trends—in occupations, education, and income—today's woman has more independence and status opportunities than in the past. For many young women, this new reality is taken for granted. It is easy to forget that today's trends toward greater equality are the result of active organizing by a small number of women in the late 1960s. The New Feminist Movement, a curious combination of young campus activists and older professional women, chal-lenged gender inequal-ity in every major institutional sphere: family, work, schools, politics, health care, religion, and the law (Ferree and Hess 2000). The challenge extended even to local car dealerships, where women had been denied credit without the joint signature of a father or husband.

International Feminism

Today, the movement for women's rights is worldwide, at work in developing nations as well as postindustrial societies. The basic goals essential to gender equality anywhere and everywhere are: the right to vote, to exercise reproductive choice, to receive an education, and to control one's own earnings and property. By these standards, the societies of Northern Europe rank highest, with much of Africa and the Muslim world lowest. Yet even in the most traditional cultures, these ideals

Women students are bringing change to their colleges and universities, and even institutions that have long resisted women, such as the Citadel, have recently graduated the first women cadets.

have activated small groups of women, at great personal risk, to challenge custom and confront male authorities (Ferree and Subramaniam 2001). At the very least, issues that once escaped attention, such as the surgical mutilation of girls or the killing of widows, have been widely publicized. In early 2000, the United Nations endorsed a campaign to end homicidal violence against women in societies where customs encourage it and the law fails to protect them (Crossette 2000). The condemned practices included "acid attacks" by rejected suitors in Bangladesh; "bride burnings" in India, when the bride's dowry was less than that desired by the groom's family; the death of female infants; and general lack of access to health care. Unfortunately for all citizens of these countries, keeping women down has a price in delayed economic development (Moghadam 1999). The Third World countries with the healthiest economies are those where girls are as well cared for as boys, and where women can control fertility, vote, enter the labor force, and end an unhappy marriage (United Nations 1999). 💻 7

Not surprisingly, the far-ranging agenda of modern feminism has unleashed a powerful backlash, in the United States as well as the Third World (see chapter 16). Opposition comes from the many women and men who are quite content with existing gender relations, from employers who would have to change the way they do business, and from people with firm beliefs about the proper place of women. From their perspective, there is much to lose and little to gain from change. And while many speak of a "post-feminist" generation, research data indicate that the goals of the movement remain strongly supported by both men and women: reproductive choice, equal pay, and sharing household responsibility. It is safe to say that vast and probably irreversible changes have taken place, although much remains to be done to ensure gender equity (Vannoy 2001).

Changes in Men's Lives

As the statuses of women change, so, too, do those of the men with whom they share their lives. In comparison to the deep and broad sweep of the feminist revolution, it is more difficult to chart the changes in cultural images and social practices of men—however, their world is certainly not the same as it once was. Although people often use the term "masculinity" as if there were a single universal set of behaviors and feelings that define "real men," this, too, is a social construction that has varied historically and cross-culturally. The only universal is that maleness is more highly valued and rewarded than femaleness. Thus, just as whites tend to overlook their racial privilege, men often fail to appreciate the advantages conferred by just being male. Indeed, many men feel overburdened by the demands of gender, especially those who see themselves as relatively powerless at work and at home (Johnson 1997).

In American society today, the components of masculinity vary by race, religion, ethnicity, social class, sexual preference, and stage of the life course (Kimmel and Messner 1998). Thus, the social construction of manhood for African Americans will differ from that of whites because their life circumstances are so very different. Even here, however, there are also class differences and situational factors. Upwardly mobile black men find that race is a more important consideration than social class when police officers or store personnel confront them and expect them to act in a subservient manner. In contrast, many famous black rock stars and sports figures adopt a "gangsta" attitude, complete with in-your-face clothing, jewelry, and speech patterns that are then adopted by the very much less famous boys and men left in the neighborhood. Being a man is most difficult for those who have few resources other than their toughness (Majors and Bilson 1992; Springwood and King 2000).

Yet among this diversity of masculinities there are some core elements that explain the slow pace of changes in behavior and concepts of manliness. First, maleness is defined in opposition to femaleness, a very negative identity. To appear to be anything less than a "real man" is to leave yourself open to the total humiliation of being called a "wuss." As many a drill sergeant has discovered, there is no more effective tool for reducing new recruits to putty in his hands than to refer to them as "ladies." At a more basic level, a boy's need to establish his identity by separating himself from his mother (and rejecting all things feminine) often leads to a compulsive masculinity that makes it difficult to be fully comfortable with women in adulthood. These tendencies are reinforced by socialization in school and peer groups. Although parents may no longer fret over a tomboy daughter, they remain extremely anxious about unconsciously encouraging "feminine" traits in their sons, as you can easily observe on any trip to a clothing or toy store.

The second core issue is the link between maleness and power, which few people ever give up willingly. To the extent that women become less dependent on men and actually compete with them for jobs, many men will feel threatened. Much harassment and violence against women at home and in the workplace is designed precisely to "keep her in her place" (Rundblad 2001). Another way to deal with an increasingly independent wife or girlfriend is to try to be nicer while retaining control, which is the agenda of the Promise Keepers movement (Kimmel 2000b). At the movement's high point in the mid-1990s, tens of thousands of men would gather at mass rallies and renew their masculine roots, pray together, and promise to go home and be better husbands, more sensitive and helpful, but also to uphold their traditional role as head of household. Financial problems have reduced the mass rallies, but local Promise Keeper groups remain active throughout the country (Bessel 2000).

Getting in touch with one's "inner man" in the new era of sensitivity became a minor industry in the early 1990s, with the publication of books with titles like *Iron John* (Bly 1990) and the popularity of male-bonding groups spending weekends in wilderness survival camps or playing at war games with paint guns. The basic idea is that men need a place where they can open up emotionally and help one another, while at the same time giving

Laundry day on the Ivory Coast finds both men and women doing the family wash. Is doing the laundry men's or women's work? How do gender expectations influence the work we do and the careers we choose?

❖ ❖ ❖ ❖   voice to their wild man impulses in a world that has rendered them powerless at work and at home. Earlier in the twentieth century, in response to the growing suffrage movement, a similar need to find an all-male haven led large numbers of men to join fraternal organizations such as the Elks and Kiwanis, while their sons became Boy Scouts (Kimmel 1994). In both eras, the emotional closeness among men did not extend to the relationships with women, where traditional assertive masculinity is required.

A very different type of men's movement has also emerged, consisting primarily of academic and professional *profeminist* men. Though vastly outnumbered by Promise Keepers and "wild men," members of profeminist organizations have been influential through their research and advocacy, especially on campuses and in the social sciences. Viewing masculinity as a social construction, they see feminism as liberating them from having to equate manliness with violence and uncontrollable sexuality. In this view, the link between maleness and violence is learned and not written on the male chromosome or carried in male hormones. Only a small number of boys and men are street fighters; few carry a weapon more powerful than a pocketknife; and although they might talk a good game, most do not prey on their female classmates or colleagues. To see boys and men as repressed animals is insulting (Kimmel and Messner 2000c; Messner 1997).

Yet this is exactly how many antifeminists do see them. Several best-selling books in the past few years claim that the feminist movement has declared "war against boys" and that it is boys, not girls, who are the endangered sex (Gurian 1996; Sommers 2000). These authors note that, compared with girls, boys have higher rates of suicide, mental illness, learning disabilities, and victimizations of all kinds. The root of these problems, in their view, is that boys are no longer allowed to be boys. Propelled by hormonal surges and hard-wired for aggression, boys are now expected to meet feminine norms of behavior in school, constantly on guard lest they offend with a stupid but well-intentioned remark or action. They can look forward to an equally restrictive adulthood, fearful of being sued as a harasser, and without their old refuges from the world of women—the pool hall, men's bar, even the military (Gutmann 2000). 🖥 8

The counterarguments are that feminized schools are nothing new, nor are the sex differences in rates of suicide, mental illness, and learning disabilities. Another set of observers of the condition of American boys concludes that many of their problem behaviors can be traced to the difficulties of living up to the learned expectations of "real manhood" (Kindlon and Thompson 1999; Pollack 1999). In this view it is the cruel pressure of the peer group and the fear of expressing emotions that are crippling youths. It is not the aggressive impulses that are being repressed but the loving, cooperative ones. In either case, raising sons today is probably more difficult than raising girls, who now have greater leeway than before in exhibiting the varied facets of self. 🖥 6

What is most sociologically interesting is the revival of theories of absolute, biologically based differences between the sexes as part of an antifeminist backlash to the movement for gender equality. If sex differences are written in our genes, if there is a female or male "essence" that guides us, then it is not only futile to try to change behavior and social structures but absolutely harmful, especially for boys and men, who must then repress their true

selves, with all the physical and emotional turmoil this involves. In intellectual circles today, the war of the sexes is currently being waged between
"essentialists," who maintain that gender differences reflect biological realities, and the "constructionists," who emphasize the way in which culture and
social structure produce gender differences.

Conclusion

This chapter has examined the concept of gender and the process of
becoming gendered. Structures of gendered inequality were described, along
with the changes brought about by the modern feminist movement. Yet we
still live in gendered worlds that affect men and women differently. What the
future holds depends largely on the choices you make about work and family
and child rearing. If gender is written in your genes, there are limits to the
changes that can be made or sustained. If gender is largely a social construction, you can remake the world.

Surfing the Sociological Internet

1 http://www.inform.umd.edu:8080/EdRes/Topic/
   WomensStudies/GenderIssues/ is a Women's Studies database
   on gender with links to every issue discussed in this chapter and
   more.
   Sociologists for Women in Society with links to other websites:
   www.socwomen.org

2 On Toys, Colors, and Invisible Sexism: http://ucs.orst.edu/
   ~huj/512/

3 Women in Politics: http://www.rci.rutgers.edu/~cawp/ and
   http://www.ipu.org/iss-e/women.html

4 Women and Employment: http://gatekeeper.dol.gov/dol/wb

5 Women in Business: http://www.womenconnect.com/
   Loclink/ and http://www.catalystwomen.org

6 Women and education: http://www.aauw.org/2000/re-
   search.html

7 Global activism: www.womenswire.net or www.womens-
   wire.org
   Women and International Development: http://www.isp.
   msu.edu/WID/
   Women of color: http://www.hsph.harvard.edu/grhf/WoC/

8 Men's issues: http://www.vix.com/pub/men/index.html
   NOMAS: The National Organization for Men Against Sexism:
   http://www.nomas.org

❖ ❖ ❖ ❖   ## Glossary

Cognitive Structures Shape how the mind processes information.
Comparable Worth   See Pay Equity.
Gender Wage Gap The discrepancy between average earnings of women and men.
Gendered Inequality Differences between men and women in the distribution of power and prestige.
Glass Ceiling Blocks the way to the very top jobs for women and minorities.
Glass Escalator Takes men in predominantly female occupations on the fast track to promotions.
Patriarchy The rule of men, or male dominance.
Pay Equity, or Comparable Worth The principle that people who hold jobs requiring similar levels of training, skill, and responsibility should receive similar wages.
Sex-segregated Jobs Concentration of men or women in a given occupation or in particular jobs within an occupation.
Tokenism The appointment or promotion of one or two "outsiders" to visible positions, done for display. ✦

Part III
The Institutional Order

Chapter 8

Mating and Marrying: Contemporary Families

❖ ❖ ❖ ❖ Every society must deal with two major survival issues: controlling sexual impulses and pairing off members for orderly reproduction. The solution to both problems is the set of rules and roles that govern mate selection and marriage—the **family system**. Groups which devised norms that most people could follow survived, while groups that failed to regulate sexuality or ensure marital stability disappeared. The result is a world with hundreds of different family systems, each of which claims to be the one normal, natural, and sacred way of mating and marrying. In other words, family life is neither divinely ordained nor biologically programmed. The family is a socially constructed institution, as much a product of culture and history as political or economic systems (Farrell 1999; Coltrane 1998). This chapter examines such central aspects of marriage and family as:

- Cross-cultural and historical variations.
- Mate selection in modern societies.
- Modern marriage.
- Family diversity in America.
- The new family life cycle.

Family Systems Across Space and Time

The human family differs from the ties that link our primate cousins because of the unique qualities of culture such as language and norms, and the human qualities of foresight and self-control. The first and most powerful norms were those that directed sexual attraction into socially helpful patterns, namely the **incest taboos** that forbid sexual relations among blood relatives or kin. Although the taboo is found in all existing societies, there is great variation as to which relatives are covered. Sometimes the taboo involves only parents and children and brothers and sisters; in other societies individuals even remotely related are forbidden to mate. In a few instances, members of a ruling elite were expected to marry a close relative in order to keep the family property intact.

By forbidding sexuality within the kinship group, three important social goals are accomplished: (1) jealousy among people who live together is reduced, (2) doubt about how members are related to one another is eliminated, and (3) young people are forced to look elsewhere for marriage partners. A fourth benefit was accidental, namely, a lowered incidence of mental and physical disorders caused by inbreeding. The most important immediate consequence of incest taboos, in the earliest human societies and right up to modern times, was to forge alliances between kinship groups. There is a sense in which the 1960s bumper sticker, "Make Love, Not War," represents one of the earliest social insights: It is better to establish ties of mutual obligation than to create enemies.

The exchange of sons and daughters as marriage partners illustrates another important principle of social life: the **rule of reciprocity**, whereby to receive a gift is to be obligated to return something of equal value. If you give your daughter to my son in marriage, we are forever mutually obligated. The giving of presents before and during a marriage, today as well as in the past, serves to link the families and the couple to one another and to the larger community.

A third cultural foundation of marriage is based on the **principle of legitimacy**, or **social fatherhood**, whereby one man, the husband, is responsible for his wife's children, whether or not he is their biological father. Having a social father ensures that the child will be looked after materially. This is important in societies where a father's status determines the social location of his children. Where there is little to inherit, it matters little whose child you are, which is why illegitimacy rates are higher among the poor than the wealthy—not because the poor have looser morals but because legitimacy confers few advantages. For people with property, it makes a big difference who inherits it.

Polygamy is an extended household composed of a man with more than one wife and his offspring.

Kinship in Cross-Cultural Perspective

Kinship, or relationships based on descent and marriage, was the central organizing principle of most societies before the rise of the nation-state. In the days before centralized governments could guarantee social order, people depended on their kin for protection, and when most people made a living on the land, the kinship group was an economic unit. It was crucially important for family honor and wealth that your child marry someone whose family connections could benefit the kinship group. The last thing you want as a family elder is to have your careful plans upset by a child who falls in love with an inappropriate partner. For these reasons, in many societies even today, daughters are kept under tight supervision, and the choice of a marriage partner for both sons and daughters is made by the parents. You may not have to go too far back in your own family history to find an example of an arranged marriage. 🖥 1

As you can see in Table 8.1, mate selection is only one dimension on which traditional and modern societies differ. The variations on these essential elements, along with patterns of child rearing, divorce, and widowhood, mean that no two family systems are exactly alike. The only common thread in preindustrial societies is the supreme importance of the kinship group rather than the individual members. In modern societies, where your eventual position in the social world is not totally dependent on that of your parents, you have more room to negotiate your own choice of mate. If you are not waiting for your father to die in order to inherit the farm, you do not have to be quite as obedient.

Table 8.1 Kinship in Cross-Cultural Perspective		
	Traditional Societies	**Modern Societies**
Number of spouses at one time	One (monogamy) or plural (polygamy) Polygyny—two or more wives Polyandry—two or more husbands	One (monogamy)
Choice of spouse	Choices made by parents to enhance family power	Relatively free choice
Line of descent (inheritance)	From males (patrilineal) From females (matrilineal)	Both equally (bilateral kinship)
Couple's home	With groom's family (patrilocal) with bride's family (matrilocal)	Place of one's own (neolocal)
Power relationships	Various degrees of male dominance (patriarchy)	Greater equality (egalitarian)
Functions of family	All-embracing, to protect the kinship group as a whole	Specialized to provide a stable environment for child rearing and emotional support
Structure	Extended	Nuclear
Focus of obligation	Blood relationships	Marriage tie and children

The Family in Historical Context

The kinship group that so dominates its members is often described as an extended family, a unit composed of related households sharing economic tasks and providing support in illness and old age.

In contrast, the modern family is one in which the emphasis shifts to individuals, to the well-being of the couple and that of their children in the nuclear family. Industrialization erodes the power of family elders; young adults leave the village for the city and make their own way in the world. There are police forces to protect you, schools to educate you, and places of worship that you share with nonrelatives. The ties that bind the generations are no longer based on duty but on affection, which must be earned rather than commanded. The functions of family are reduced to those related to physical and emotional well-being within the privacy of the nuclear household (Waite 2000).

It is this separateness and self-sufficiency that distinguishes the modern family from nuclear units of the past. The central relationship is the marriage rather than the bloodline. If, for example, two messengers arrived simultaneously at the door of today's young wife, one with word that her father was gravely ill at hospital X and the other with news that her husband had had an accident and was at hospital Y, where would she go first? Most likely to the

✦ ✦ ✦ ✦

side of her spouse; in contrast, someone from a traditional society, particularly a son, would probably go to his father's bedside.

Unfortunately, the same emotional bonds that are the strength of the nuclear family system are also a source of weakness. Remember Georg Simmel's description of the essential fragility of the dyad (chapter 1)? When the affection that holds it together is lost, what is left? The modern family is an extremely vulnerable institution, but not many young people today would prefer the extended family alternatives.

The vision of generations of happy kin living together—the "family of Western nostalgia" (Coontz 1992)—is more wishful thinking than historical reality. In America, and in much of Western Europe from the eighteenth century on, most people lived in nuclear units, perhaps joined temporarily by a widowed grandparent. There is no reason to believe that past generations of parents and children desired to live together any more than they do today. As told in the Greek plays of 2,500 years ago and throughout the Bible, family relations have always been marked by fear, jealousy, sibling hostility, and murders of parents by children and children by parents.

Mate Selection in Modern Society

When the goal of marriage is personal fulfillment and emotional well-being, then you must be free to select your mate on the basis of personal attraction. Thus, the ideal of *romantic love* emerged as the only legitimate rationale for mate selection in modern societies. Think how difficult it would be to justify your choice of marriage partner with any reason other than "I love him/her," even if you were doing it for the money or social status. True, there are tales of romantic love from olden times, but usually tragic ones: Romeo and Juliet do not ride off into the sunset, nor did Tristan and Isolde live happily ever after. Perhaps the poor could marry for love, but not the powerful and wealthy.

Marrying for love has its hazards. Few of us are perfect judges of character. The excitement of the moment can blind us to destructive faults. A lifetime of bliss is probably more than should be expected of any relationship. Indeed, it is precisely the difficulty of achieving personal fulfillment through marriage that accounts for the high divorce rates in modern societies. If you married only out of duty to kin, your expectation level might be low enough to enable you to endure situations that would be unacceptable to you today. But when you marry for love, just "getting by" is not enough.

The Pool of Eligibles

Even though you are essentially out there on your own in search of a partner, your parents have not been powerless. They have already influenced your choice in a number of ways: by where they lived, what church they joined, and which extracurricular activities they encouraged. Your parents are also inside your head; think of the last person to whom you were strongly attracted before a little voice told you that this was not someone you could bring home to dinner. To the extent that your parents serve as role models, you will look for similar qualities in a prospective mate—someone of the same race, religion, ethnicity, and social class. People who are like you in

❖ ❖ ❖ ❖   terms of background characteristics will have shared similar socialization experiences, which means that you will agree on a lot of issues. And surely you have noticed that people who agree with you are smarter and nicer than those who disagree.

For all these reasons, although you are theoretically free to marry anyone who catches your fancy, your selection is generally limited to those you meet and can confidently introduce to relatives and friends. These considerations automatically reduce your "pool of eligibles" to those who are not all that different from yourself. The tendency to pick a partner who shares your ascribed characteristics—race, religion, ethnicity, and social class—is called **homogamy** (from "homo"= "same" and "gamy"= "marriage").

At the same time, young people today are able to travel a lot farther from home, at an earlier age, and more frequently than in the past, so the chances of meeting someone different from yourself have increased. As a consequence, in terms of ethnicity and religion especially, an increasing number of marriages are **heterogamous** ("hetero"= "different"). The risks in heterogamy are value conflicts and misunderstandings arising from different socialization experiences. The plus side is that the partners are exposed to other ways of thinking and behaving, which should expand their range of tolerance and adaptability.

An increasing number of American marriages are heterogamous with respect to ethnicity and religion. Why is this happening?

Although the importance of religion and ethnicity have diminished, race remains a powerful factor. For example, black/white marriages comprised only three of every 1,000 U.S. marriages in 1980 and only six in 1998—a 100 percent increase but still not very many people. In any event, as shown in Table 8.2, most interracial marriages involve "others," primarily Asian-Americans. 🖥 2

Table 8.2 Married Couples of Same or Mixed Races, 1980 and 1998		
(Number per 1,000 marriages)		
	1980	1998
White/white	903.4	869
Black/black	67.5	70
Black/white	3	6
White/other	9	17
Black/other	1	1
All other couples	16.1	37

Source: *Statistical Abstract of the United States, 1999*, p. 58.

The Marriage Market

When marriages are not arranged, women and men must make the best bargain they can. The word "bargain" is used intentionally because mate selection has many characteristics of the marketplace, where sellers advertise their best qualities and buyers look for the best value. Your market value is based on what others are willing to pay for, and despite all the changes of recent decades, that is still youth and beauty in women and earning ability in men, as illustrated in the market for donor eggs and sperm described in chapter 4, or the "Personals" column in your local newspaper. This means that a woman's market value declines over time, while a man's typically increases. The process was perfectly illustrated by the smash-hit TV program *Who Wants to Marry a Multi-Millionaire?*, in which 50 young women in bathing suits competed for a marriage proposal from a middle-aged millionaire. The man and the woman he chose met and married in front of the cameras in prime time. Unfortunately for the producers, the groom had been less than honest about his background, and the couple split as soon as they returned from the honeymoon.

Social class is another major determinant of market value. Although most people will marry within their class level, a man can "marry down" since it is his achieved status that locates the couple in the class hierarchy. A woman, however, is under great pressure to marry at the same level as her father or to try to move up; otherwise, she will lose social status. Those of you with a sibling of the opposite sex know this very well. When a daughter announces that she has just met the nicest guy, her mother probably asks, "Where does he live, dear?" because it really matters and the mother has a social-class map of the community engraved in her head. The son who has just met the nicest gal is usually asked, with a wink, "What does she look like?"

The market is especially difficult for a woman with high educational and occupational statuses; there are not many unmarried men at her class level and the men can always marry down. By the same token, men at the lowest ranks of the educational and occupational hierarchies will have difficulty finding a woman willing to marry them. This is why high-ranked women and low-status men are overrepresented among the never-married.

In the highly rated television program Who Wants to Marry a Multi-Millionaire?, *the groom was able to choose one wife from 50 contestants who were competing for his attention. The marriage lasted less than a week.*

The mate market is also sensitive to numbers. Where there is a shortage of one sex or the other, people will marry across lines of age and even race. For example, a shortage of young white women in the Western states in the nineteenth century led to many marriages between young men and older women or between white men and Native American women. Today, in African-American communities where women outnumber men yet have few opportunities to marry across racial lines, many will remain single. In other words, that black women are twice as likely as white women to be unmarried is primarily related to a shortage of marriageable men (Franklin 1997).

Nevertheless, over 90 percent of American men and women somehow manage to find a mate—for a longer or shorter period. Marriage certainly has not gone out of style.

The Modern American Family

The modern family differs in both structure (the private nuclear household) and function (emotional well-being) from the family of traditional societies. Indeed, the structure is essential to the function. In addition, contemporary American families also differ from the nuclear models of the 1950s and 1960s along such crucial dimensions as age at first marriage, power relationships, and risk factors for divorce and remarriage. 🖥 3

Age at First Marriage

The most dramatic change is the increasing age of first marriage for both women and men over the past half-century, as seen in Figure 8.1.

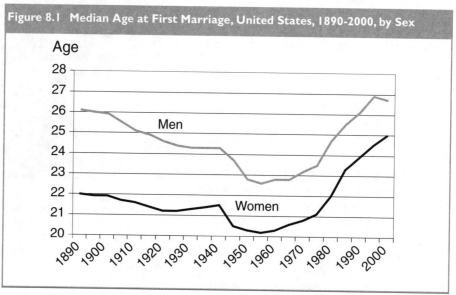

Figure 8.1   Median Age at First Marriage, United States, 1890-2000, by Sex

Source: U.S. Bureau of the Census. Internet release, January 1999.

Until World War II, marriage was typically delayed until the husband-to-be could support a family. By the late 1940s, however, young men could be supported by parents or the GI Bill for veterans while completing their education. Even college educated women were marrying before or right after graduation. Others went directly from high school to the altar. In the 1950s, close to half of all American women were married by age 20!

The nation was drowning in domesticity. Low-cost veterans' mortgages led to the development of suburban housing tracts (chapter 15); the birthrate shot up; and functional theorist Talcott Parsons (see chapter 1) could marvel at the harmonious division of labor in the modern nuclear family. Television shows featured mothers in aprons, fathers of infinite wisdom, and adoring children, not to mention the dog and cat, and the house with a picket fence and one-car garage.

In the 1960s, some of the glow had worn off. Divorce rates were creeping upward; the college-age children were experimenting with pot and alternative life-styles; and mother was marching for women's rights. By 1980, the median age at first marriage had risen two years, up to where it had been in 1890. In 1998, by age 25, only half of American women were married, while the median age at first marriage for men reached a historical high of 26.7 (Bureau of the Census, 1999).

The basic factor in this dramatic shift was the feminist movement and the new world of possibilities opened to women. Families were increasingly willing to pay for a daughter's college education; occupational choices opened up; independence was within reach; and marriage could be delayed, especially since the availability of effective contraceptives took much of the risk out of sexual relationships. As a result, young women were entering college, staying to graduate, taking jobs, seeing the world, and living on their own for several years before marriage (Kramer 2001).

Egalitarianism

Another way in which the contemporary family differs from that of a generation ago is in the reduction of power differences between husband and wife and between parents and children. To some extent, this trend toward egalitarianism is also a product of modern feminism, but a more basic factor is that the goal of mutual respect is incompatible with relationships of superiority and inferiority—superiors tend to get arrogant, and inferiors tend to lose self-respect. It is doubtful that slaves love their masters as much as the masters like to believe. What this means is that marriage partners and children and parents must earn rather than demand respect and affection.

Modern Marriage: Rewards and Risks

In general, married people are happier and healthier than the nonmarried (Waite and Gallagher 2000). Although people tend to think of men as less in need of marriage than women, husbands derive somewhat greater benefits than do wives in terms of physical and mental health, sexual satisfaction, and occupational success. Compared with their nonmarried peers, married men are very much better off (Nock 1998). Married men live longer than the unmarried and are far less likely to commit suicide, be homicide victims, die in accidents, or end up in mental health institutions. For women, the difference in death rates and health status between married and unmarried is much smaller than for men. The major problems for nonmarried women are financial. These trends are magnified by race, with black men particularly vulnerable to early death and black women overrepresented among the poor.

Yet for all the benefits of marriage, the closeness of the nuclear family can make it an emotional hothouse. People who are intensely dependent on one another for all their interpersonal needs are also very vulnerable.

Violence

As there are no accurate data from before the 1970s, it is impossible to say whether family life has become more or less violent. It can be argued that the lack of family privacy in the past made it easier for relatives and others in the community to intervene in cases of physical assault. But it is just as likely that the great power imbalances between husband and wife and parents and children encouraged abuses. What can be said for certain is that a lot of what was once acceptable disciplining in families is no longer tolerated.

This change in the public temper is due to the work of advocates for women and for children's' rights over the past three decades (Straus 2000). Although men are often targets of abuse from wives or girlfriends, the more common and most serious incidents involve women as victims (Kurz 2001). Both women and children are prime targets because outbursts of violence in the home are typically related to threats to authority. Men who feel powerless (especially at the hands of a woman) and parents who think they are being mocked can lose their cool very quickly. Despite claims that family violence cuts across class lines, it is strongly associated with low educational and occupational status, early marriage, and unplanned pregnancy (Gelles 1997). The incidence of physical abuse of women and children is also relatively high among members of groups that demand absolute obedience, such as the military and extremely religious communities (Schmidt 1994).

The most common and serious incidence of violence involves women as victims. Women are increasingly speaking and acting out against such violence.

Does violence in the home matter? Very much, for children. Being the target of an abusive parent has a number of negative consequences—from a higher probability of becoming a juvenile delinquent to being violent with one's own wife and children (Swinford et al. 2000). It is safe to say that nothing good comes from hitting children, even with the best of intentions. The boys tend to become brutalized and the girls to be depressed (see chapter 3).

The low esteem of abused daughters can make them unwitting targets for later violence. However, a girl need not have grown up in a violent home to feel that, as a woman, she is responsible for the emotional well-being of her husband or boyfriend, so that when anything goes wrong, she blames herself for whatever is driving him to violence. For many women, just having a man in her life is an affirmation of femininity. Here are some of the reasons that women typically give for staying with someone who hits them: "He's O.K. when he doesn't drink," "I really should stop nagging," "He's awfully sorry afterward," and "What are my choices?" They cannot go home to parents who will say "We told you so." There are not many shelters, and those are only for temporary use. Taking children out of school is difficult. Thus, many will stay and hope things will change, although they rarely do (Kurz 2001).

Increasingly, however, women are taking steps to leave abusive relationships, to become self-sufficient, and to use the police and courts to protect themselves. In addition, law enforcement agencies are being trained to be more sensitive to the dynamics of family violence and to be more helpful to the victims, female or male, young or old. 🖥4

Divorce

Much that has been written about the American divorce rate is not accurate. The rate at which marriages break up has *not* risen for at least three decades. As you can see in Figure 8.2, there was a sharp upturn in divorces in the late 1940s, most likely due to hasty wartime marriages or marriages that could not survive a long separation. Then came two decades of low divorce rates, with another up-tick in the late 1970s before leveling off and even dropping in the late 1990s.

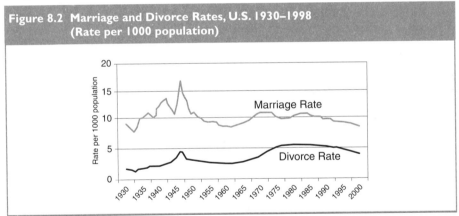

Figure 8.2 Marriage and Divorce Rates, U.S. 1930–1998 (Rate per 1000 population)

Source: *Monthly Vital Statistics Report*, Vol. 43(1), 1994; Vol. 48(5), 2000.

Predictors. The answer to questions of why divorce rates have remained stable or even declined since 1970 is contained in Figure 8.1: *Median age at first marriage*. This is the single most powerful predictor of marital stability. When half the women in America were married before age 20, you could predict that a lot of them would not have made a wise choice or have been mature enough to handle marriage and early motherhood. By the late 1960s, for many, that home in the suburbs seemed as confining as it had seemed liberating in the late 1940s. Among men who had married in the postwar years and who were upwardly mobile, many found that the young woman they had married out of high school did not fit their new lifestyle.

Other risk factors for divorce include low income and education, premarital pregnancy, husband's unemployment, and frequent residential moves (Shelton and Deen 2001). In general, employed wives are more likely than the unemployed wives to leave an unsatisfying marriage. Conversely, factors tending to preserve the marriage include participation in religious services and later age at first marriage, which is associated with shared decision making, planned pregnancies, adequate income, and emotional maturity.

Once married, the most powerful predictor of continued stability is, quite simply, the number of years already married. As is the case for most roles, the longer you stay, the more of your self is invested in the role's success and the harder it is to walk away and admit that you have wasted all that time. Most divorces occur very early in the marriage, in the first five years, and contrary to popular belief, there is no second peak when the children have left home; rates decline steadily with the length of the marriage. The presence of children does not appear to hold a troubled marriage together, although having a son attaches a father more closely to the family than does the presence a daughter (P. Schwartz 1994).

The American divorce rate is somewhat higher than that for other modern societies, but so, too, is our marriage rate, and, as you see in Figure 8.2, the two tend to move together. When assessing divorce rates, it should be kept in mind that, in the past, many marriages were terminated by the death of a spouse. It cannot be assumed, of course, that the couples who did not divorce in the past were happy in their marriage. Probably quite the opposite was true, but the costs of leaving the marriage were simply too great for women— instant poverty as well as a kind of social death in many communities.

Consequences. Although the social stigma has largely disappeared, the economic consequences of divorce for women remain strongly negative (Smock, Manning, and Gupta, 1999). About 15 percent of former wives are awarded *alimony*, and only half of them receive the full amount from their ex-husbands. There are also a few men who receive payments from an ex-wife. The dollar amounts of the awards averaged $5,000 a year in the late 1990s, which does not go a long way toward paying the rent.

Women with children may ask for *child support*, but only half the eligible mothers in 1997 were awarded anything, and only half of those collected the full amount, which, again, averaged only a few thousand dollars a year. When paid in full, however, child support can be crucial in lifting a family above the poverty line. At the same time, arguing over payments can escalate the existing conflict between parents. Many ex-husbands and fathers are themselves low-income earners, and many have a second family to support. Most give no material assistance to their children other than support payments. And although over half were given visitation rights, not all took advantage of the opportunity. It appears that for many children of divorce, their father becomes a shadowy figure (Garfinkel et al. 1998).

There are many negative outcomes of divorce for children, although it is difficult to separate the effects of divorce from those of the turmoil that preceded it (Hanson et al. 1998). For children living with their mother, the most common result is a loss of economic security, often requiring a change in residence that disrupts friendships and schooling. If the mother is a full-time employee, adequate supervision becomes a problem, as does her ability to help with homework and monitor school performance. Compared with their peers in two-parent households, children living with only their mother are more likely to drop out of high school, get into trouble with the police, and have spells of unemployment in adulthood (McLanahan and Sandefur 1994).

Women who spent part of their childhood in a single-parent home are more likely than other women to marry early, have a premarital pregnancy, and ultimately to experience divorce themselves (Wolfinger 1999). Many of these negative consequences also characterize children from intact families where the parents are continually fighting.

When the family income is adequate, when the custodial parent has satisfying work, and when the noncustodial parent is in frequent contact, the children do as well as most from two-parent households. But these are not the typical conditions for American children of divorce. In contrast, in most European countries, social welfare policies protect all types of families from poverty and isolation. It is not the end of the marriage as much as the lack of supportive services that makes divorce a social problem in the United States (Goode 1993).

Thus, although divorce is the solution to many problems, it creates others. There is little evidence that ending a marriage is taken lightly by the vast majority of unhappily married couples. Nonetheless, the hope of fulfillment through marriage remains strong, and most divorced men and women venture into the marriage market once again. 💻 5

Remarriage

Because divorces usually take place early in a marriage, before children are present, most men and women will remarry, the men sooner and at a higher rate than the women. The older and better educated the divorced woman, the lower her chances of remarriage because the pool of eligibles—divorced, widowed, or never-married educated men—is not very large. Men seeking to remarry can dip into a larger pool, filled with younger and less educated women.

As in the case of first marriage, just being married benefits men in terms of physical and mental health, although not necessarily economically (Nock 1998). Women gain immediately in terms of financial security, with remarriage as the most important factor in raising a family out of poverty. In comparison with first marriages, however, the risk of failure is somewhat higher the second (or third) time around—not for any deep psychological reasons but because there are not as many people to choose from so that more compromises have to be made between your ideal and what is available. For example, a woman may decide that a much older husband is better than none at all. Or a man may marry an attractive woman with several children rather than someone less attractive with no children.

When divorced parents remarry, they create a blended family composed of her children, his, and perhaps theirs. Despite all the difficulties in adjusting to a stepparent and to one another, the children will gain the financial and care-giving advantages of a two-parent family (Morrison and Rituolo 2000). Compared with only a few decades ago, American children and their parents live in increasingly varied types of households.

Family and Household Diversity in Contemporary America

When Americans think of "the family," the image is of a nuclear household composed of two parents and their young children, with the husband as major breadwinner; against this ideal other family forms appear "deviant." In reality, as seen in Table 8.3, the traditional pattern accounts for only about 7 percent of all households. Children are as likely to be living in a household with dual earners as with a single parent. What you see is a range of household types that meet people's needs at various points in the life cycle or that are forced upon them by circumstances. In Census terms, a "family" is a unit composed of two or more persons related by blood, marriage, or adoption. A mother and child is a family; so is a childless couple or two brothers sharing living quarters. "Households," in contrast, can be composed of one person or unrelated individuals living together (Demo, Allan, and Fine 2000).

Table 8.3 U.S. Households, 1999 (By Percentage)	1970	1999
Married couple, children, one earner	24%	7%
Married couple, children, dual earners	16	17.5
Married couple, no children under 18	30	28
Single parent	11	16.5
One person household	17	26
Two or more nonmarried persons	2	5

Source: U.S. Bureau of the Census, Series P-20-527, 2000e.

The married couple/no children category includes both older couples whose children have grown as well as younger marrieds with "dual incomes/ no kids," or DINKs. Similarly, the single-person household category lumps together young never-married adults and elderly widows, as well as divorced persons of any age (most of whom will remarry and be replaced by the newly

When divorced families remarry they create a blended family composed of her children, his children, and perhaps theirs.

divorced). It is possible that at different points in your life, you will be a member of each of these types of household. 🖥6

Distribution of Household Types

The distribution of household types will vary by race/ethnicity. For example, Asian-American households are most likely to have two earners and children; whites to be DINKs, Hispanic families to fit the traditional one-earner pattern; and blacks to have a single householder. In addition, immigrant households may include other relatives, both for cultural and economic reasons. As noted in chapter 6, however, by the second and third generations, acculturation will also affect family structure and relationships.

The interplay among race, ethnicity, social class, gender, and immigration status is illustrated by the experience of many Latino families. Despite the important educational and income differences between Puerto Rican, Chicano, and South American subgroups, the general pattern for the first generation is to retain fairly traditional family structures and processes. Compared to all American women, Hispanic fertility rates are high and labor force participation is low. A reliance on the extended kinship system ("familism") has often been linked to cultural factors, but a more sociological analysis views these characteristics as logical responses to residential and economic segregation (Roschelle 1999).

Immigration and the flow of generations have also challenged traditional family power dynamics, as children become Americanized through schooling and wives enter the labor force. For Puerto Rican men, especially, low-status employment can erode one's ability to control other family members. At the intersection of ethnic, generational, and racial stratification systems, the class and gender dynamics of contemporary Latino families are in the process of rapid change (Kivisto and Runblad 2000).

African-American Families

From slavery to current welfare policies, structural forces have shaped the formation and functioning of many African-American families (Franklin 1997; Paterson 1998). Residential segregation and employment discrimination have created pockets of extreme poverty in urban and rural areas alike, while negative stereotypes of black women drive welfare policies that further impoverish the lives of women and children. As a consequence, compared with other racial and ethnic subgroups, black Americans are more likely to postpone marriage or never marry; to experience divorce, separation, and desertion; and to forgo remarriage. Fewer than half of African-American households are composed of a married couple, compared to about 80 percent for both whites and Asian Americans, and 70 percent for Hispanic households. In addition, almost half of black family households are headed by a mother, in contrast to about 15 percent for white households.

The shortage of marriageable men in inner-city black communities has already been noted. Large numbers are periodically unemployed as jobs move out of cities and into residentially segregated suburbs. Others are victims or perpetrators of crimes, filling American prisons. Many join the armed forces. The most successful quickly move out of the neighborhood. Those who stay face innumerable difficulties in providing for and protecting their families.

Young black women are faced with a tough choice: to take whatever affection is offered, however fleeting, or do without and hope that something permanent will come along. Most will end up raising children on their own. The prevalence of female-headed households has led some critics to speak of a *matriarchal* family system, but these are not women with much power in society, or even in their own communities. Nor are the households always without a male presence—a relative or boyfriend. The more accurate description is **matrifocal**, or woman-centered. Female kin—whether real or honorary—help one another, care for children, and try to negotiate the agencies and authorities that regulate so much of their lives (Hill Collins 1990). Although often perceived as "deviant," the matrifocal family has survived two centuries of slavery, segregation, and discrimination in America. There is some doubt, however, if even the kinship network of grandmothers, mothers, sisters, daughters, and "aunts" can survive the current period of diminishing welfare services, deteriorating housing and schools, and crime-ridden streets.

At the opposite end of the spectrum, almost two-thirds of high-income black men and women are in long-term marriages. These families typically have two adult wage earners, similar to one another in terms of education and occupational status. In other words, the middle-class African-American marriage is likely to be more egalitarian than its white counterpart because the partners are themselves more equal in status characteristics. In this sense, the black middle class marriage may be the pattern for all college-educated couples in the future. An alternative scenario notes that the wife's labor force participation is necessary to maintain middle-class status because wage and job discrimination have lowered the husband's earning power. It takes two wage earners to equal one white male's salary at the same level of education and skill (Toliver 1998).

In the middle, and often overlooked, are the majority of African-American households, firmly rooted in the working class (Horton et al. 2000). Family patterns among working-class blacks appear to be little different from their white educational and occupational peers, even though wages are typically lower.

Cohabitors

The word **cohabit** means to "live with." While cohabitors account for about 5 percent of American households today, 40 percent of Americans will have cohabited at some point over the life course. In 1999, the Census counted slightly over five million "persons of the opposite sex sharing living quarters" or POSSLQs ("possel-kews")—up from 1.5 million in 1980. Although one tends to think of cohabitors as being college-aged, most are over age 25, with only a high school education. It is estimated that close to half of American children will spend some part of their childhood living with one parent and her or his live-in partner (Smock 2000).

Are cohabitors different from couples who marry? Most will eventually marry, but many will not. Given the dramatic increase in age at first marriage, the availability of contraceptives, and greater public tolerance, it is probably too much to expect that all those young people will remain virginal until marriage. In the meantime they share living quarters for relatively short periods of time. The one characteristic that distinguishes younger cohabitors from noncohabitors is *religiosity*. The more religious the young person, the less likely he or she is to engage in premarital sex (Thornton 1992).

Does cohabitation have an effect on subsequent marriage? There are indications that divorce rates are higher for cohabitors who subsequently marry one another, but it is not clear what this means. People who cohabit may simply be less inclined than others to remain in an unhappy marriage. Many of the cohabitors are themselves divorced and unlikely to remarry, an effect that carries over to their children, who have lower marriage rates than children from intact families (Smock 2000). 7

Domestic Partnerships

Not all cohabitors are heterosexual. Some small percentage of nonmarried-couple households will be composed of lesbian or gay male partners. Contrary to popular beliefs, homosexual couples do *not* usually recreate the stereotyped heterosexual pattern of dominant male and submissive female. Rather, because the couple tends to be very similar in educational and occupational statuses, homosexual relationships are typically characterized by mutuality and equality (Sullivan 1996). The educational and income levels of homosexual Americans tend to be higher than the American average, and high proportions have been in relatively long-term relations, at least as long as many heterosexual unions (Black et al. 1999).

In addition, many gay and lesbian couples have children from an earlier heterosexual relationship, adoption, or *in vitro* fertilization. As for the potential problems in raising children, the research on lesbian and gay male parenting has found "no differences on any measures between the heterosexual and homosexual parents regarding parenting styles, emotional adjustment, and sexual orientation of the children" (Allen and Burrell 1996, 19).

If couples could be evaluated on the basis of the quality of their commitment and depth of caring, rather than by the sex of partners, many homosexual unions would be judged healthier (or at least less destructive) than some heterosexual marriages. Conversely, there are violent and exploitive gay relationships, just as there are among heterosexuals. The great difficulty for a gay person is that as much as he or she may long for a lasting relationship, the pool of potential partners is so small that success becomes much more problematic than for heterosexuals.

Nonetheless, the idea of acknowledging the validity of marriage-like unions between people of the same sex is no longer as far-fetched as only a decade ago. Increasingly, businesses, local governments, and academic institutions are recognizing the rights of **domestic partners**, people who live together in a committed relationship, to be covered by the same benefits as married employees. The French government, in 1999, recognized a "civil pact of solidarity" by which a homosexual couple is officially registered as responsible for one another and entitled to the same treatment as their heterosexual married peers. As with a marriage, the civil pact can be terminated by another official process.

In North America, an 8–1 decision by the Supreme Court of Canada in mid-1999 struck down the law that defined

A gay couple, living as domestic partners, celebrate their commitment to each other following a "holy union," a marriage-like ceremony, in a Protestant church.

"spouse" as applying only to heterosexuals. This decision opened the way for widespread changes in federal statutes to eliminate any differences in the legal standing of heterosexuals and homosexuals (*New York Times*, May 21, 1999). It is expected that most Canadian provinces will also amend their laws.

Across the border, in December 1999, the Supreme Court of Vermont ruled unanimously that the state must extend the same benefits to gay and lesbian couples that are afforded to heterosexual spouses. To ensure that such legal protections are provided, the Court gave the state legislature the choice of recognizing gay marriage or enacting the most sweeping domestic partnership law in the nation (Goldberg 1999). The legislature responded in mid-2000 with a domestic partnership law that could eventually be a model for other states. 🖥 8

It is unlikely that other states will follow soon. Under enormous pressure from religious and political conservatives, back in 1996 when it appeared that the Supreme Court of Hawaii might sanction same-sex unions, a majority of state legislatures proposed laws to bar homosexual marriages and deny recognition to those performed in any other state. There may be a constitutional difficulty here, as one of the basic underpinnings of the U.S. system is the "full faith and credit" clause that mandates recognition of marriages and divorces from one state to another. To deal with this problem, Congress passed the Defense of Marriage Act of 1996 that releases the states and other territories of the United States from an obligation to recognize same-sex marriages under the laws of another state. The Act will ultimately be challenged in the U.S. Supreme Court. 🖥 9

Single-Parent Households

As a result of divorce and nonmarital childbearing, only 68 percent of children under 18 years old live with both parents today, compared with 77 percent in 1980. Twenty-three percent live with their mother, 4 percent with their father, and another 4 percent with neither parent. While 75 percent of white children live with both parents, this is true for only 36 percent of black youngsters. The Census data, however, obscure the extent to which there may be a cohabiting adult in the household. It is estimated that 40 percent of the children born to unmarried mothers are raised in homes with two adults, at least for part of the time (Bumpass and Lu 2000).

As noted earlier in this chapter, the major problem for the single-mother family is lack of money. Not all single mothers are equal; much depends on whether the mother is widowed, divorced, or never married, largely because each has different economic consequences. The less financially secure the household, the more problematic the outcomes for children in terms of education, occupational status, and personal happiness in adulthood (Biblarz and Gottainer 2000). In general, widowed mothers are more financially secure than divorced mothers, and the divorced are better off than the never married.

Over half of children in mother-only families live below the poverty level, compared to 10 percent in two-parent households. The 1996 law that ended federal welfare payments makes it even harder for the mother to count on steady income. The jobs available to her often pay less than the poverty level, while state agencies have made it difficult to receive health and other benefits. Finding adequate child care is extremely difficult, even for women with money.

At the other end of the single-mother spectrum are the Murphy Browns—white, middle-class, college-educated women who choose to bear and raise children without the benefit of marriage. For these women, who have chosen motherhood and who are financially secure, the link between marriage and maternity has become optional.

Today, about 20 percent of single-parent households are headed by a father, double the proportion in 1980. Compared to single mothers, the fathers tend to have higher incomes, to have household help, and to remarry within a few years. How do they behave in the parent role? Just like a mother (Risman et al. 1999). It is not the sex of the parent but the demands of the situation that shape feelings and actions. Balancing home and work responsibilities, for both single-parent fathers and mothers, is greatly aided by supportive employers and coworkers. 🖵 10

In single-parent households that are not financially secure there may be more problematic outcomes for children in terms of education, occupational status, and opportunity.

Dual-Earner Families

Today, a majority of two-parent households also have two employed adults. Seventy-two percent of married mothers are in the labor force, including 77 percent of those with children between ages 7 and 16, and 64 percent of mothers of children age 6 and under.

It is the two incomes that lift some families out of poverty and that keep others firmly planted in the middle class. With the exception of men in the top occupational brackets, the family income for dual-earner households is double that of single earners at similar skill levels. This fact alone makes it unlikely that women will leave the labor force in large numbers any time soon. In addition to the independence gained by earning one's own money, employed women also derive benefits in self-esteem and the friendship network of colleagues (Prather 2000). Indeed, the trend is toward an increasingly earlier return to work after childbirth, for all these reasons in addition to ensuring continued health benefits (Orenstein 2000). For some working women, however, low pay and low job satisfaction, combined with full responsibility for housework and child care, can erase the benefits of employment (Spade 1994). For others, when domestic chores seem endless and unsatisfying, paid work can be a less demanding and more rewarding refuge (Hochschild 1997).

There is little evidence that children are harmed by a mother's labor force participation and much to indicate that her sense of well-being plus the added income are beneficial to the children, especially if she has help with household chores (Chira 1998; Deutsch 1999). Recent research also suggests that the image of a generation of "latchkey" children is vastly overdrawn. Only 12 to 14 percent of children aged 5 to 12 spend any time on their own at home between the end of school and the arrival of a parent; the average time spent alone is one hour. Most of these are older children, many of whom value their "down time" alone (Hofferth and Jankuniene 2000).

The effects of a wife's employment on her husband's well-being are complex (Coltrane and Adams 2001). Many men are relieved at sharing economic responsibilities and having the added income. Others feel emasculated, and some even lower their share of housework. Not surprisingly, then, divorce rates are higher for dual-earner than for single-earner couples, but this higher rate could simply reflect an employed woman's greater ability to leave an unhappy marriage. Nonetheless, working out compatible schedules and learning to share breadwinning and home and child-care tasks will be a major challenge for all but a few American couples in the future (Deutsch 1999).

Variations on the dual-earner model include: (1) **Dual-career couples**— careers differ from a job in requiring a deeper commitment of time and

---

Box 8.1

Daddy's in the Kitchen: The New Division of Family Labor

The key to success for dual-earner couples is a division of labor that both partners consider fair. It does not have to be equal, just perceived as fair enough to relieve a working mother of constant worry and role overload, but not so much as to cause a father's resentment. Data on men's contributions to homemaking and child care are difficult to interpret because as the wife/mother reduces the time she spends on these tasks, his share of the total will rise for the same number of hours. In addition, the division of household labor tends to be gender-typed: The outside is his, the inside hers, which is why the garbage is such a bone of contention—it is generated inside but gets disposed of outside.

The area of greatest change is men's involvement in child care. However, a number of barriers remain. One problem for many men is the ridicule they face from employers and coworkers. You can imagine the reaction to a colleague who said he was leaving early to take his daughter to dancing class. In addition, most workplaces are not flexible enough to allow employees to come and go at different times. Men on an upward career path take great risks when they appear to value family responsibilities over loyalty to the firm.

Unlike many European countries, the United States does not a have a program that provides income and social services to workers who need to take time off to care for a newborn or ill child, spouse, or elderly parent. The U.S. Family Leave Act of 1993, which covers less than 30 percent of the labor force, only says that you can not be fired or lose a promotion or benefits because you chose to take *unpaid* time off to care for a newborn or ailing family member. As a result, very few women and even fewer men have taken advantage of the opportunity.

Despite these barriers, it does appear that married men are spending more time with their children than did their own fathers, beginning with the birth itself (Levine 2000). For one-fifth of preschool children, their father is the main caregiver while mommy is at work, either because the couple works split shifts or because he can work at home. An additional 8 to 10 percent of men are not looking for work because of "home responsibilities"—up from 4.6 percent in 1991. And a national organization of "At-Home Dads" now runs its own website. Clearly, the division of household labor is more varied than in the past, and the long-term benefits of a nurturing father for the emotional development of daughters and sons are increasingly apparent (Warner and Steel 1999).

energy, but the pay-off is a higher salary. Thus, while the difficulties of a dual-earner family are magnified by the demands of a career, the added income can buy a lot of services. (2) **Commuter marriages**—there are career opportunities that require a couple to live in different places, working apart during the week and spending weekends and long vacations together (Gerstel 1999). Some marriages thrive when the partners are not together all the time, but it is difficult when children are involved. As a result, commuter arrangements are most common among couples who choose to remain childless or whose children have left the nest. 🖥 11

The New Family Cycle

The convergence of many of the trends covered in this chapter—age at marriage, mate selection, divorce, and remarriage—plus those covered in other chapters, such as increased life expectancy (chapter 15), greater independence for women (chapter 7), and reproductive choices (chapter 4), have created a "modern family life cycle" different from that of even a generation ago. 🖥 12

1. At the beginning of the cycle, there is the decade or more between sexual maturity and marriage, during which young people experiment with intimacy and narrow down the pool of eligibles.

2. Once married, the couple typically has two children born within a few years of one another, so that even with later age at marriage, childbearing is completed by the time the mother is in her mid-thirties.

3. The children begin to leave home while the parents are still relatively young, creating a new phase in the life course: *the empty nest*. For couples who have survived all the difficulties of child rearing, satisfaction in marriage at this phase rises to the level of the newlywed stage.

4. Because middle-aged Americans today can expect to live well into their 80s, the nest stays empty for quite a while—except for periods of housing a "boomerang baby," a grown child who returns to the nest for refueling. Can you figure out why sons are far more likely than daughters to come home for months at a time? The middle-aged wife or mother, however, must also cope with aging parents. Despite all the changes in her life, she is still the one expected to do all the "kinkeeping," not only for her parents but for her husband's as well.

5. The added years bring widowhood to most women, due to higher death rates for men plus the fact that husbands are typically older than their wives.

Thus, the family life cycle ends where it began, with a single-person household.

Although children will have fewer siblings and may live with only one parent for part of their growing up, they will know more of their grandparents and even great-grandparents and spend more time with them than in the past. If you think about it, a child whose parents divorce and remarry could have four or more sets of grandparents. It is not uncommon today for grandparents to continue to stay in touch with grandchildren even after the parents have split.

In some cases, the grandparents take over the parent role. In the late 1990s, close to 4 million children were living in homes maintained by a grandparent—double the proportion in 1970 (Bryson and Casper 1999). Grandparents also provide about 16 percent of child care for working mothers, either in their own home or in that of the child.

What is most striking about contemporary families is their great diversity. Critics and politicians who call for a return to "traditional family values" are idealizing what was a temporary adaptation to historical conditions (Coontz 1997). It is doubtful that many of you would willingly return to an extended family system in which your needs would be sacrificed to those of the kinship group. Since there are no laws against multigenerational living, we assume that the spread of nuclear households is evidence that married couples do not want to live with their parents or other relatives. And since women are not being forced to wait for marriage or to have only two children or to enter the labor force, it seems likely that these decisions represent their wishes (Demo, Allen, and Fine 2000).

The diversity of family structures today appears to be an adaptive response to the postmodern world: to changing needs across the life course, extended life expectancy, the decline of patriarchy, the emancipation of women and children, and, above all, the emphasis on self-fulfillment and the privacy of intimate relationships (Gerson 2000). For many, the choice may be between the "new family" of egalitarian flexibility or "no family," by forgoing marriage and/or parenthood (Goldscheider and Waite 1991). But short of forcing couples to stay together, there really is not any viable alternative to letting them dissolve a miserable union. Nevertheless, much could be done to strengthen families through public programs that provide income supports for all households with children, day-care facilities for preschoolers and the frail elderly, paid family leave, housing assistance, and counseling services.

The downside to the modern emphasis on individual happiness is that you can become so self-centered that you forget your responsibilities to others and the community at large. The most difficult task of your adulthood will be to find a balance between the demands of self and others. The good news is that both women and men can choose among a range of family forms in order to realize Freud's formula for the good life: To be fulfilled in love and work.

Conclusion

This chapter has examined the family as a social construction across cultures and through history. You have seen how the modern family differs from the traditional types, in both form and function. The contemporary nuclear family is specialized for the early socialization of children and the emotional well-being of all members. You are essentially on your own in choosing your life partner(s) and establishing a supportive environment for personal growth, and while the failure rate is high, so are the rewards of success. Modern conditions have led to a diversity of households, with or without children or marriage. The chapter closed with a description of the changing family life cycle.

Surfing the Sociological Internet

1   Kinship: http://daphne.palomar.edu/kinship/

2   Family Resources:
     http://osiris.colorado.edu/SOC/RES/family.html
     http://www.familydiscussions.com/ http://www.aacap.org/
     publications/factsfam/index.htm
     http://www.nimh.nih.gov/publicat/baschap6.cfm#marr

3   Household Statistics: http://www.census.gov/
     Latino Families: http://www.elclick.com/
     Asian-American Families: http://www.cacf.org/
     African-American Families:
     http://www.blackfamilies.com
     http://www.blackparenting.com/main.shtml

4   Family Violence:
     http://www.famvi.com/
     http://www.silcom.com/~paladin/madv/

5   Divorce: http://www.divorcenet.com/
     Children and divorce:
     http://www.muextension.missouri.edu/xplor/hesguide/
     humanrel/gh6600.htm

6   Worldwide summary on domestic partnerships, cohabiting, and
     marriage:
     http://www.iglhrc.org/news/faqs/marriage_981103.html

7   Cohabiting:
     http://hometown.aol.com/cohabiting

❖ ❖ ❖ ❖

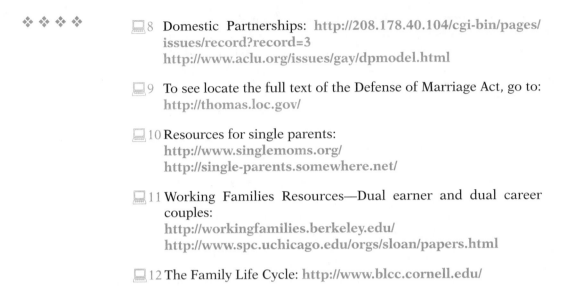

💻8 Domestic Partnerships: http://208.178.40.104/cgi-bin/pages/ issues/record?record=3 http://www.aclu.org/issues/gay/dpmodel.html

💻9 To see locate the full text of the Defense of Marriage Act, go to: http://thomas.loc.gov/

💻10 Resources for single parents: http://www.singlemoms.org/ http://single-parents.somewhere.net/

💻11 Working Families Resources—Dual earner and dual career couples: http://workingfamilies.berkeley.edu/ http://www.spc.uchicago.edu/orgs/sloan/papers.html

💻12 The Family Life Cycle: http://www.blcc.cornell.edu/

Glossary

Blended Family Unit created when divorced parents remarry and are joined by her children and his children.

Cohabitation Nonmarried persons sharing living quarters.

Commuter Marriages A couple whose career opportunities require them to live in different places.

Domestic Partners Persons who live together in a committed relationship recognized by the state.

Dual Career Couples Both partners have a career.

Dual Earner Families Both partners are in the labor force.

Egalitarianism The reduction of power differences between husband and wife and between parents and children.

Extended Family A unit composed of related households (often involving three or more generations) sharing economic tasks and providing support in illness and old age.

Family System A society's set of rules and roles that govern mate selection and marriage.

Heterogamy The tendency to select a marriage partner of a different race, religion, ethnicity, or social class.

Homogamy The tendency to select a marriage partner who shares your characteristics, such as race, religion, ethnicity, and social class.

Incest Taboos Rules that forbid sexual relations among blood relatives.

Matrifocal Families centered on the woman.

Nuclear Family A unit composed of a married couple and their dependent children.

Principle of Legitimacy (social fatherhood) Principle holding one man, the husband, responsible for his wife's children, whether or not he is their biological father.

Rule of Reciprocity Principle of social life dictating that if a gift is received, the receiver is obligated to return something of equal value. ✦

Who Wants to Be a Millionaire? Economic Factors

❖ ❖ ❖ ❖   Not only will you spend most of your adulthood at work or thinking about it, but, as Karl Marx so forcefully pointed out, the economic sector of any society is basic to all the other institutions. So, although eyes tend to glaze over when reading about economics, this is a very important chapter for understanding the trajectory of your own work life as well as the structure of American society.

This chapter covers the following major topics:

* The nature of economic systems.

* Capitalism and socialism.

* Work in modern industrial society.

* The American labor movement.

* Corporate life.

The Nature of Economic Systems

The roles, rules, and structures that we call "the economy" involve three separate activities: (1) the *production* of goods and services; (2) how these are *distributed*; and (3) how goods and services are *consumed*. As you learned in chapter 5, unequal distribution of societal resources produces stratification systems of varying degrees. That chapter also describes how consumption patterns serve to reinforce class distinctions. This chapter concentrates on the productive processes and organizations, and the work life of contemporary men and women.

The basic productive process involves taking things from the land, such as growing crops and gathering them. It's harvest time in Slovakia.

The most basic productive processes involve taking things from the land, gathering fruits and berries, growing crops, hunting, and digging things from the ground. As shown in Figure 2.1, these kinds of economies characterized most of human history and are still common throughout the world.

During the Industrial Revolution of the past 250 years, the economic base of most Western nations and Japan was transformed from agriculture to manufacturing. In the space of only a few decades in Europe, landless young people moved from farms and villages to the towns and cities, where factory work was available. In the sparsely populated

United States, the factories were filled by a steady stream of immigrants—women and men, children and adults (chapter 7). Gradually, the children were pushed out of the labor market, less from humanitarian motives than as an attempt to raise the pay of adult workers. As employment in shops and offices opened up for women, many chose these more "genteel" occupations over work on an assembly line. Once married, women tended to leave the official labor force, although they often did productive work in the home, such as taking in boarders, laundry, or sewing (Bose 1987).

The last three decades have seen another major shift in production, from an economy based on manufacturing goods to one in which most of the labor force is engaged in providing services. Service work includes the production of information, medical care, government administration, legal assistance, banking, teaching, hairdressing, law enforcement, and all the paperwork in the office buildings that line America's major highways. This shift in employment can be seen in Figure 9.1.

But there are service jobs and service jobs. For every physician added to the labor force, there will be several hundred nursing home attendants, nurse's aides, and home health aides. Preschool workers, prison guards, and restaurant workers will also be in great demand, as shown in Table 9.1. As you can see, with the exception of computer specialists, most of the fastest growing employment sectors are not very prestigious or well rewarded. And many are "pink-collar" occupations, employing women in dead-end jobs. Ironically, just as the educational level of the labor forces has risen, the skill gap has widened, and many workers will be *underemployed* in jobs for which they are overqualified. In other words, the "education-jobs gap" is not that workers are poorly trained, as employers suggest, but that there is shortage of jobs at decent pay scales with opportunities for upward mobility (Livingstone 1998).

Figure 9.1 Number of Workers in Selected Occupations, 1972–2005

Source: *Statistical Abstract, 2000.*

Table 9.1 Change in Employment, 1992–2005	
Occupation	**Percent Increase**
Registered nurses	42
Computer scientists and system analysts	111
Homemaker and home health aides	136
Nursing aides and psychiatric aides	44
Preschool workers	65
Guards	51
Teacher aides	43
Human services workers	136
Restaurant and food service managers	46
Corrections officers	70

Source: *Statistical Abstract, 2000,* 427.

What are your prospects? Job growth at the high-status end will continue to increase, although at a lower rate than less prestigious occupations. The very best jobs require the ability to think abstractly, to express oneself articulately, to view problems in context, and to be creative and flexible—exactly the skills learned in college. Your best bet is to stay in school, not just for the diploma but to sharpen your mind. As seen later in this chapter, the jobs of the future will have less security and a shorter career trajectory than in the past; few of you will spend your work life in the same company, so adaptability will be essential.

Table 9.2 Occupations With Largest Projected Job Growth, 1996–2006, and Education/Training Category	
Occupations	**Education/Training Needed**
Cashiers	Short-term on-the-job training
Systems analysts	Bachelor's degree
General managers, top executives	Bachelor's degree or higher, work experience
Registered nurses	Associate's degree
Salesperson, retail	Short-term on-the-job training
Truck drivers, light and heavy	Short-term on-the-job training
Home health aides	Short-term on-the-job training
Teacher aides	Short-term on-the-job training
Nursing aides, orderlies	Short-term on-the-job training
Teachers, high school	Bachelor's degree
Child care workers	Short-term on-the-job training
Clerical supervisors, managers	Work experience in related field
Database/computer specialists	Bachelor's degree
Marketing and sales supervisors	Long-term, on-the-job training
Food servers/preparers	Short-term on-the-job training
Teachers, special education	Bachelor's degree
Computer engineers	Bachelor's degree

Source: Bureau of Labor Statistics, *Monthly Labor Review*, November 1997.

Contemporary Economic Systems

For most of human history, economic activity was shared by members of a family, clan, or tribe. Exchanges of goods and services were governed by the **rule of reciprocity**, whereby giving a gift obligates the receiver to return something of equivalent value at a later time. Gift exchanges not only distribute surplus goods but also create social ties. Even today, in our society, if you came back from class and found a gift package at the door, your first thought, after wondering who sent it, would be "What do I have to do in return?" There are no free gifts!

In modern societies, the distribution of goods and services is based on the **market system**, in which the worth of any item is what someone is willing to pay for it, a process governed by laws of supply and demand rather than by obligations of kinship or the needs of the group. In other words, economic activity is separated from the web of personal relationships. But this does not mean that either the market or the technology that drives it is as impartial or self-directing as economists claim. Various types of work and workplaces are shaped by history and culture and are deeply influenced by not-so-rational forces, including gender practices and ideology (Acker 1998; Tilly and Tilly 1998)

Capitalism and Socialism

There are two basic models for a modern economic system, based on the degree to which market forces are regulated by government agencies representing the **public interest** or are left to the **private interests** of individuals, families, and corporations. In reality, these are end points along a continual line (or continuum) representing degrees of difference, as shown in Figure 9.2.

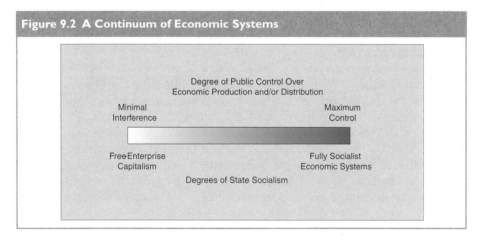

Figure 9.2 A Continuum of Economic Systems

At one extreme is free enterprise **capitalism**, with minimal public supervision or intervention. Business decisions are made on the basis of what is in the best interests of owners or stockholders. The goal of the corporation is to make a profit that enhances its value to potential investors. The underlying theory is that over the long run, under conditions of perfect competition, everyone will benefit from the most efficient use of economic resources such as raw material, labor, and investment capital. As the head of a major Ameri-

❖ ❖ ❖ ❖   can corporation so famously put it: ". . .what's good for General Motors is good for the country" (Wilson 1952).

Yet, as one eminent economist observed, "In the long run we are all dead" (Keynes 1923), and actions that might be very good for General Motors may not be all that positive for particular workers or cities in which GM has closed factories. To cushion the impact of impersonal market forces and to reduce capitalism's inevitable drift toward inequality (chapter 5), most modern industrial societies have instituted mechanisms for protecting the public interest, such as antitrust legislation.

Socialism is the name given to government attempts to minimize the negative effects of economic inequality. At the most extreme, as in the former Soviet Union or the People's Republic of China, the central government tried to control both the production and distribution of goods and services. This kind of central planning, however, turned out to be very inefficient, leading to widespread famine and material shortages. It also turned out to be very expensive in terms of subsidies to failing industries in order to maintain employment.

But some elements of socialism can be found in all industrial societies, in the form of social welfare programs such as old age pensions, family allowances, national health insurance, and unemployment benefits. As noted in chapter 5, the United States has the fewest and least generous programs. In contrast, Denmark, Norway, and Sweden have the most extensive and generous welfare systems, while the ownership of production remains in private hands, a situation referred to as state socialism (Esping-Andersen 1990).

The trade-off is between the economic efficiency of capitalism, on the one hand, and socialism's more equal distribution of health care, education, housing, and family supports, on the other hand. As a consequence, while tax rates are higher and productivity lower in the Scandinavian countries than in the United States, there is much less poverty, homelessness, childhood hunger, untreated illness, domestic violence, and crime.

The difference between the United States and other industrial societies is rooted in ideology and power. The ideological aspect is the fierce belief in individual salvation and the promise of upward mobility. The power aspect— the political dominance of business interests and wealthy donors—has worked against the mobilization of working-class discontent. The consequence is that, with the exception of old age income, Americans see such services as health care or higher education as a private rather than as a public responsibility; that is, as a privilege rather than a right of citizenship. Attempts to expand public services are met by the charge of "creeping socialism," which is usually enough to ensure their defeat in Congress. Recent efforts to develop a national health insurance system met such a fate. In the United States, you get what you can pay for, thus reinforcing the stratification system, with the willing agreement of many members of the working class.

It is easier to maintain an extremely limited social welfare system when the most needy are of a different race or nationality from those with the power to provide assistance, as in the United States. In contrast, a Norwegian or Swede will look at an ill and unemployed person and see someone just like one's self, someone who can evoke sympathy and a sense of shared fate. The downside is that extensive social welfare systems are expensive, and in times of slow economic growth may need to be reduced. Despite such cutbacks, in striking contrast to the United States, no European welfare state has backed out of its commitment to provide basic services and to reduce inequality.

What is the future of the welfare state in the United States? At this writing, American leaders are prepared to curtail even the minimal public obligation to the elderly and the poor. In addition to the changes in welfare described in chapter 5, the newest trend is privatization, hiring profit-making companies to run schools, prisons, immigration centers, highway systems, public hospitals, parks, and other activities traditionally under control of local, state, and the federal government, including Medicare and Medicaid. Even Social Security is under challenge by politicians who claim that people could better provide for their old age by investing in the stock market. The basic assumption behind this trend is that the private sector is more efficient and perhaps less expensive. The counterargument is that there are some things that ought to be considered the responsibility of the society as a whole, a communal obligation. In this view, even if privatization saved tax dollars, something would be lost in terms of social solidarity. Indeed, the Social Security system also provides for the disabled and the widows and children of deceased workers.

In a market system the value of items such as vegetables and fruits is whatever people are willing to pay for them.

Postindustrial Economies

Will a service economy make so much difference in people's lives that it deserves a name of its own? Some theorists see the postindustrial economy, with its emphasis on knowledge over mechanical skills (at least in the upper reaches of the occupational structure) as profoundly liberating. They predict a decline in inequality based on ascription, a heightened awareness of self and concern for the quality of life, with an emphasis on consumption in this world rather than devotion to the work ethic (Block 1990). The basic theme is that workers will move from one type of job to another, that the life course will be more flexible, and that roles will be less narrowly defined. Already, the Internet and e-mail make it possible for some employees (19 million in 1999 compared to only 4 million in 1990) to work at home or anywhere but the office (Stainback and Donato 1999; O'Brien 2000).

Other observers take a darker view. There is something to be said for a predictable work life, for steady employment in a stable workplace (Sennett 1999). Loyalty to an employer, commitment to one's job, sinking roots in a community, and being able to plan for the future are what anchor people in social worlds—the closest we come to *Gemeinschaft*. Without these, we drift aimlessly, turned inward, unable to make long-term commitments.

The temping of the labor force. Both views take account of the fact that employment in the twenty-first century is likely to be less continuous and secure than in the past. The new labor force will be increasingly contingent, with workers hired on a temporary basis and other services "outsourced" to independent contractors. Today, about half of new employees are "temps" and other part-time workers (including many instructors in your school). The advantages to an employer are many: relief from fringe benefits and tax withholding; a flexible workforce; and the upper hand in negotiations. Advantages to workers are less obvious: some parents may prefer part-time employment; other workers might enjoy the independence of freelancing. But most will be working for less pay and fewer fringe benefits than comparable full-time, in-house employees (Kalleberg et al. 2000). These developments further divide the working class into factions, with full-timers resentful of the temps and fearful for their own jobs (Smith 1998).

Even white-collar employees are affected as firms cut their costs by "downsizing," a nice-sounding word for reducing the managerial staff. Since those let go are most likely to be middle-aged workers, finding comparable employment will be difficult. Some will become independent contractors, working out of their homes; others will change employers; and still others will opt for early retirement. Some shifts are made necessary by the obsolescence of technology or of a particular product (typewriters, for example). Overall, however, in the booming economy of the late 1990s, more jobs were created than eliminated, leading to a high turnover—13 million American workers each month entering or exiting the labor force, or looking for new work (Bureau of Labor Statistics 1999).

Despite the considerable "churning" caused by job losses and openings, between 30 and 40 percent of the labor force has been with the same employer for at least a decade, which may not be much lower than in the past. These data are not easily collected, and measurements are often not comparable from one economic era to another. In any event, you will most likely experience more job shifts than did people entering the labor force twenty years ago, if only because of the rapid pace of technological change. This is a powerful argument for using your college years to develop such abilities as critical thinking and intellectual flexibility rather than narrow vocational skills.

Will the decline of traditional workplace discipline bring liberation or produce such anomie that people will flock to a religious or political agitator? Maybe both, as high-status workers enjoy greater freedom of choice while the less skilled become increasingly angry and resentful. Nor is it clear whether Americans are "overworked" (Schor 1992). Some workers, especially in the Internet field, will find their work so fascinating that they willingly put in long hours, while others may need to take on two jobs in order to support a family. In addition, American employers offer much shorter paid vacation periods than is common in other industrial societies. For whatever reason, American workers spend more time on the job (almost 2,000 hours a year) than workers in other industrial societies (e.g., Norway, with 1,400 hours).

Paradoxically, data from time diaries suggests that men and women may actually have *more* free time than they did in the 1970s, even when household labor is counted (Robinson and Godby 1999). Furthermore, workers are entering the labor force at older ages and leaving at younger ages than in the past, which suggests a major increase in leisure time before and after the decades of intense commitment to work.

The underground economy. Another economic sector that is impossible to measure is the underground economy, or informal labor force of people who work "off the books," for cash, with no paper trail. This category includes those engaged in illegal activities (the drug trade being the largest and most lucrative) but also a large number of people whose only crime is not reporting income, such as moonlighting police officers, independent contractors, home-based workers, and the officially unemployed (Pozo 1996). This sector will undoubtedly continue to expand as the postindustrial economy makes lifetime single-employer careers increasingly problematic. For many inner-city youths, the underground economy remains one of the few options available (Anderson 1998). Although they remain twice as likely as their white age peers to be jobless, the employment rate for young black men has risen with the booming job market, reducing the lure of the underground economy (Nasar and Mitchell 1999).

About the only certainty for the future, at all skill levels, is that you must be prepared for anything, be able to shift gears, learn a new technology, and keep an open mind. This may be the real postmodern mentality: flexible, adaptable, able to tolerate uncertainty. Fortunately, sociology is a great way to develop these abilities.

The Organization of Work

While waiting for the postindustrial transformation, most work organizations are still characterized by extreme division of labor, in which tasks are divided into distinct parts, each part to be performed by the same person. Think of an assembly line, the ultimate in efficient labor, with each station performing the same set of actions over and over again. In this way, as Marx prophesied, workers themselves become like a machine part, dehumanized and alienated. Alienation refers to a sense of powerlessness, of being cut off from one's labor, from others, and eventually from oneself (Erikson and Vallas 1990). The same argument can be extended to office work, where most employees perform only a few specialized tasks.

It appears, however, that this fine division of labor is a double-edged sword. Some work can indeed become "deskilled," as when cashiers need only swipe a bar code, but other jobs can be upgraded, as when the departmental secretary is the only one who knows how to use a complex computer program. Although automation will displace some factory labor with a machine, the workers who service that machine have a monopoly on scarce knowledge.

Despite the routine dullness of most jobs, about 85 percent of American workers are generally satisfied with their current jobs, though they are not totally enthusiastic (Saad 1999). Some will have lowered their expectations to fit reality; others will find pleasure in workplace friendships and the things they can buy with that paycheck. The most satisfying jobs are those that allow you to make decisions about the pacing and sequence of work with minimal supervision. The freedom of such job autonomy is most often found in high-pay and high-prestige occupations that already provide intrinsic (built-in) satisfactions. The lower the occupational status, the more heavily supervised you are and the fewer decisions you can make on your own. Nonetheless, when asked what was "very important" when taking their current job, Americans tend to cite features of the workplace, coworkers, skills utilized, and family-related factors, with pay and promotions at the bottom of the list (Galinsky 1999).

Because satisfied workers tend to be more productive, many American companies have developed some form of employee involvement, such as quality circles, where groups of workers and supervisors meet to talk about production problems. But decision making power remains with the bosses, even though one can now call them by their first names (Manley 2000). In any event, there is little evidence that worker morale is greatly improved. To the contrary, researchers suggest that such efforts at harmonious labor relations are often used to cushion the stresses associated with the latest fad in manufacturing—lean production. Designed to cut costs, lean production involves minimal inventory, with raw materials shipped just in time and only in the needed quantity, using the fewest workers, who are continually moved around so that no time is lost (Rinehart et al. 1997).

The ultimate in employee participation are those few cases of workplace democracy, where the workers actually own and manage the business; since these are generally firms that the capitalist owner has abandoned as unprofitable (with good cause), success is problematic. Even in Europe, where the conditions for workplace democracy are more favorable, highly successful examples are few and far between (Whyte and Whyte 1988; Cheney 2000).

Short of any meaningful role in management, the closest that American workers come to ownership is through ESOPs (employee stock ownership programs), in which shares in the company are part of the benefit program. The catch is that ownership of the stock is deferred until the employee leaves, so that management continues to have voting power, as well as tax advantages. In sum, the new industrial workplace looks a lot like the old one, with a few cosmetic touches, and much less worker security or privacy.

Box 9.1

Abandon Privacy, All Who Enter

Curiously, at a time of very tight labor markets, employers have increased their surveillance and monitoring of employees, white and blue collar alike. Seventy-one percent of major U.S. firms require some form of medical examination and psychological testing, not only for new hires but also for current employees, and two-thirds engage in some form of electronic tracking (American Management Association 2000). Checking on employees' use of the Internet (54 percent) and the telephone (44 percent) is most common, followed by reading employees' e-mail messages (38 percent) and looking into their computer files (31 percent). Drug testing, however, has declined slightly, from 74 to 68 percent, but still extends to a wide variety of jobs where safety is not a consideration.

Smaller firms are equally zealous in their control of the workplace, checking the purses of female employees, regulating the time spent on toilet breaks, and limiting the number of people who can congregate around the water cooler (Ehrenreich 2000). Such oversight can extend beyond the workplace, even to monitoring behavior in the community. Just as the Ford Company did in its factory towns in the early 1900s, when they removed drinkers and lapsed churchgoers, contemporary employers have fired employees for activities during nonwork hours, such as organizing for a union or appearing in a sexually explicit home video on the Internet (Ali 2000). ☞

✦ ✦ ✦ ✦

Legally, unless the employee can prove a violation of antidiscrimination laws, a private employer has great leeway in hiring, firing, and setting working conditions. Given the weakness of American unions, there is little that the employee can bargain with, except the threat to quit, which immediately marks the worker as an expendable "troublemaker." As a practical matter, however, constant surveillance is not a very effective way to enhance performance. Compared with other workers, electronically monitored employees have lower morale, higher levels of depression and anxiety, and lowered productivity (Rosen 2000). Nonetheless, employers apparently feel that they have more to gain in weeding out people who might incur high medical costs or use paid time for personal business, or do something to blacken the company's reputation.

If history and the European experience are any guides, the best bet for workplace democracy lies in the power of organized labor. In Western Europe, the economic interests of the working class have been represented by a distinct political party, usually called "Labor" or "Social Democratic," in a system of other class-based political parties (Western 1998). In the United States, with its myth of classlessness, the fact that capitalists tend to vote Republican and organized labor to support Democratic candidates is rarely defined as class-based behavior. To speak of "class interests" is to challenge the dominant ideology, as if only the poor acted out of status concerns in contrast to the wealthy who think only of the common good. 💻 3

Because they have no political party of their own, American workers have had their interests represented largely by self-governing labor associations, on those occasions when workers and their labor leaders can agree on what goals to pursue.

The American Labor Movement

From its origins in the late 1860s, the movement to organize workers in America was fiercely resisted by employers and all levels of government. In 1886, Chicago police fired on marchers supporting the radical idea of an eight-hour workday. Just over a century ago, Pinkerton guards hired by the Carnegie Steel Company fought an open battle with strikers, and the state militia joined in protecting the mill. These are only two examples of how attempts to organize workers were crushed by the combined forces of business and government (McCammon 1993). Public opinion began to shift after a fire at the Triangle Shirtwaist factory in New York City in 1911 killed 146 girls and young women, mainly recent Jewish and Italian immigrants, because doors to the fire escape were locked in order to keep the workers from sneaking out for a breath of air. The top wage for a six-day, 52-hour week at the factory was $3.00 (Kaufman 1999).

It took more than two decades after 1911 before unions won the right to bargain collectively on behalf of members, and then only in return for getting rid of their more radical elements. Because the most successful early efforts at unionization involved skilled craft people, the result was a labor movement more often opposed to immigrants, women workers, and racial minorities than to management (Stepan-Norris and Zeitlin 1991).

The unionization drive was further hampered by internal struggles for power between the American Federation of Labor (AFL), representing the largely white and male trade unions such as plumbers or electricians, and the Congress of Industrial Organizations (CIO), representing a more diversified workforce in a given industry, steel or garment workers. Only in 1955 did they join ranks to form the AFL-CIO, but by then organized labor was already in decline, from a high of 35 percent of the workforce in 1945 to about 14 percent today. In addition, the proportion of private-sector employees who are unionized has dropped to under 10 percent. Most union strength today is in the public sector, where over one-third of government workers are unionized. The public sector, however, is a shrinking part of the economy as the rush to privatization continues. One of the reasons why privatization can be seen as a "money saver" is precisely because these firms do not have to pay union wages or benefits.

Ironically, then, even though unionized workers are much better off than similarly skilled nonunion workers in terms of wages, health coverage, vacations, and pensions, membership continues to decline. The causes for this decline are diverse, partly because of changes in the U.S. economy since 1980, and partly because the steadfast opposition of employers and the power they can exert over the media and politics (Hirsch and Macpherson 1988) Some of the reasons are listed below.

- The loss of jobs in the highly unionized "smokestack" industries such as steel and automobiles.

- Reagan-Bush policies in the 1980s that were openly hostile to unions

- Failure of union leadership, until recently, to organize the service sector with its large numbers of women and minority workers

- Employers' relocations abroad or to states in the U.S. South with "right to work" laws that make union organizing extremely difficult

- Negative public image arising from highly visible cases of union corruption

Not all attacks on unions come from the political right. Liberals have criticized the labor movement for failing to become a class-based force in opposition to the overwhelming power of employer interests. Critics also note that union leaders have been coopted, becoming more interested in maintaining their own perks and high salaries than in organizing new members. A final criticism is that those who benefited most from unionization—high-skill white male "blue- collar aristocrats"— have turned their backs on the original goals of the movement, which were to improve the status of all workers and to reduce

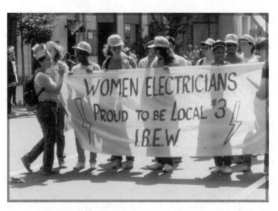

The International Brotherhood of Electrical Workers was one of the AFL unions which originally only admitted male workers. Today, women are members of the IBEW and other unions.

inequality in the society. In the 1980s, the voting preference of these workers shifted from Democratic to Republican, thus contributing further to the decline of organized labor.

Yet another factor in the failure to attract new members is the reality that all American workers have shared in the hard-won triumphs of organized labor: the eight-hour work day, five-day work week, sick leave and unemployment insurance, the minimum wage, and a safer, more sanitary workplace. But as labor power declined throughout the 1980s, workers lost ground in wage settlements and fringe benefits, often agreeing to "givebacks" of previously won gains. Only the very tight labor market of the late 1990s has slowed these trends. 💻 4

The Future of American Unions

If they are to survive, America's unions must attract workers in previously nonunionized occupations, including both high-tech white-collar and low-wage service personnel (Clawson and Clawson 2000). Organizing white-collar employees is difficult because they do not see themselves as similar to people who carry lunch pails to work. Organizing low-skill service workers is difficult because employers can easily replace "trouble makers." The fate of the labor movement today may rest in the hands of the largest pool of unorganized workers—women, in both offices and factories.

Historically, organized labor in the United States has been a white male fellowship, even though the early factories were filled with women and children. From the 1880s to the 1930s, women workers were among the most militant supporters of the unions, but once the right to collective bargaining was won, union leaders did their utmost to get women out of the labor force, or at least out of leadership positions. Even today, as women comprise 40 percent of union members and two out of three new recruits, only eight of the 50 top officers of the AFL-CIO are women. 💻 5

Labor's Unfinished Business

Although American unions have improved the status of their members and have won victories on behalf of all working people, the labor movement has failed to reduce inequality within the society or even within the working class. Societal inequality in the United States, as you saw in chapter 5, is rooted in profound ideological and historical forces, reinforced by the weakness of organized labor and, most recently, by the shrinking of the public sector. Inequality in modern indus-

The dual economy includes a peripheral sector composed of labor-intensive, low-profit businesses such as clothing manufacturing. These workers toil for long hours, yet receive very low wages. Why is this so?

trial societies is reduced when most workers are unionized and when government plays a major role in providing services, neither of which is true for the United States today (Gustafsson and Johansson 1999).

Inequality *within* the working class, however, reflects the stratification of the economy itself. The dual economy refers to the distinction between a core sector of major capital-intensive industries (automobiles, pharmaceuticals) and a peripheral sector composed of labor-intensive, low-profit businesses (clothing manufacturing, retail stores). The two sectors draw from different labor pools. In this split, or segmented, labor market, core workers are drawn from a pool of white males while the peripheral labor force is largely female, minority, and/or immigrant. Therefore, workers' wages, benefits, and chances of upward mobility depend less on their personal qualities than on their location in the labor market. At similar levels of education or skill, core and peripheral workers receive very different rewards. These conditions are compounded when, within a given firm, employers channel workers into different career paths on the basis of sex and race, a double problem for black women (Reskin and McBrier 2000).

Box 9.2

Affirmative Action and Reaction

Few policies are as little understood and more mocked than affirmative action, the federal government's attempt to reduce sex and race discrimination in the workplace (Reskin 1998). The term derives from an executive order signed by President Lyndon Johnson in 1965 that requires firms with federal contracts to take "affirmative action," that is, to do something positive and proactive to ensure that workers are hired and dealt with "without regard to race, color, or national origin." Sex was added to the list in 1967, and Congress later included Vietnam veterans and the disabled. In other words, employers were asked to make a good-faith effort to avoid future discrimination; they were asked to draw up reasonable goals and a timetable for achieving greater diversification in the workplace, based on the local supply of qualified personnel. There is nothing in the legislation about quotas or allowing unqualified applicants to jump to the head of the line. An employer simply had to show an effort to reach out to previously overlooked populations and show that pay and promotion policies were based on objective criteria.

Without affirmative action, most workforces were all-white, with the exception of janitors and cleaning women, while pay and promotion policies systematically worked against female employees. Following the executive order, from 1965 to 1985, modest gains were realized by minority and women workers, partly closing the great gaps in hiring, pay, and promotion, without negatively affecting pay and promotion prospects for the vast majority of white males. How, then, did "affirmative action" come to symbolize such evil in the public mind?

The answer lies, once again, in the interaction between political and economic interests. Conservatives in general and business owners in particular have always fought government intervention in the workplace. The Republican Party saw an issue that would resonate to working-class discontents over pay and promotion. And the media continually confused affirmative action with the Civil Rights Act, under which judges could order firms that had willfully violated antidiscrimination laws to hire previously excluded workers. But even here, class action discrimination suits were extremely rare. In any event, federal enforcement came to a halt with the election of Ronald Reagan in 1984, and affirmative action became associated in the public mind with the vision of white male employees being replaced by blacks and women of inferior abilities.

The claim of "reverse discrimination" was successful in every way. The working class was split: Minority workers were made to feel unqualified; white workers had   ☞

❖ ❖ ❖ ❖

☞ something to blame for lack of success; and no one blamed employers. No politician would touch the issue, except as a "red flag" to arouse emotions·

In its place, many companies have instituted "diversity management and training" programs to develop and supervise a more inclusive workforce. Because these programs lack the standards and government oversight of affirmative action, they are extremely diverse in quality and results. Some programs are very well designed, while others rely on material that often reinforces the very stereotypes that lead to discrimination in the first place (Stein and Korgen 2000). Many consumer-oriented businesses have hired women and minority employees as a means of reaching new markets, with little expectation that they will be integrated into top management (Reskin 1999). The result is a more diverse workplace than in the 1960s, though far from the ideal of hiring, pay, and promotions on the basis of ability rather than ascription. 💻6

Employment in the periphery is uncertain. Workers are hired when needed and let go when demand slackens. Largely nonunionized, these employees are less likely than core workers to have health coverage, unemployment insurance, and retirement benefits. The disadvantages experienced early in one's work life accumulate over time, and, as Table 9.1 indicates, the periphery is where most new jobs are being created.

Even as previously excluded subgroups have found employment, the number of new jobs and their earnings remain well below the levels needed to revive the inner city and stabilize impoverished families (Pollin and Luce 1998). In some cases, even when suitable work is right around the corner, inner-city minority youth do not get the jobs because hiring is typically done through interpersonal networks, the "social capital" that is so important for finding employment (Kasinitz and Rosenberg 1996). Contrary to the belief that a rising tide lifts all boats, the economic growth of the 1990s floated a lot of yachts while leaving many of the unskilled to sink or swim.

Box 9.3

Goodbye to Gadsden

One of the first manufacturers to go South in search of cheap labor, the Goodyear Tire and Rubber Company moved from Ohio to Gadsden, Alabama, in 1929, where its plant became the leading employer and source of income for the area. Over seven decades, however, the plant lost its technological edge and overseas markets dried up. The employees eventually unionized and won decent wages and fringe benefits, but when it appeared that Goodyear was no longer investing in upgrading the factory, the workers agreed in the early 1990s to "givebacks" that they hoped would keep the plant competitive. Their efforts were to no avail, and the plant closed. Goodyear expects to save tens of millions of dollars; several thousand workers are on the job market, but most of the available jobs are nonunion; and all the surrounding businesses—shops, restaurants, places of entertainment—are hurting for clients. The town has lost millions in tax revenue as a result of the plant closing's "multiplier effect" on the rest of the town's economy.

Gadsden is offering a variety of tax incentives to new industries. A community college was built to train workers and the downtown area was renovated—all at taxpayer expense, with no success. Soon, skilled workers and their families will move to where the jobs are. Thus, the same process that emptied the "rustbelt" cities of the North earlier in the century is now being repeated in parts of the South (Firestone 1999; Milkman 1997).

The Corporate World

Economic sociology also covers the study of business organizations as social actors and as mini-societies, with particular structures and cultures. Research in this area covers a range of topics from macro analyses of world trade to micro-level observations of the boardroom and shop floor. There are studies of how the community context affects a business and also of the impact of corporations on their community, as well as how the age and sex composition of an organization affects its structure and, conversely, of how an organization's structure influences the kinds of people that are hired.

At the *macro-level*, one could ask why is modern industry organized into large-scale corporations rather than small private firms? The traditional answer has been "for the sake of efficiency," but one recent study suggests that in the United States it was a mix of political, financial, and economic power by lawmakers, bankers, and larger firms that drove smaller enterprises to sell out or merge (Roy 1997). And although some large corporations (railroads, for example) started out with government assistance in the form of land and tax relief as providers of public services, they were soon transformed into privately owned companies with minimal government oversight. The point is that economic activity is embedded in a complex web of social forces and cannot be explained simply by other economic variables, which is why economists have been notoriously unsuccessful in accurately predicting anything, including the Great Depression. Corporations are not closed systems but are dependent on their external environment for material, personnel, and customers.

At the micro-level, sociologists observe the inner workings of business organizations such as stores, including high-end department stores such as Harrod's in London. The biannual storewide sales attract shoppers from many countries who queue up hours before the store opens.

At the *meso-level*, researchers examine the actual composition and operation of organizations, asking, for example, if the number of women in corporate management makes a difference in the company's culture and structure. The answer is "yes," at least for start-up technology companies, where researchers found that firms with a higher percentage of women in the first year of operation subsequently were less bureaucratized than otherwise similar businesses (Baron and Burton 1999).

At the *micro-level*, sociologists have observed the inner workings of management as well as of the steno pool, typically through participant observer studies. How, for example, do employers control workers such as temps and others not under their direct immediate supervision (Gottfried 1991)? What are the power dynamics between male bosses and female office workers? One participant observation of Japanese corporations found that the status difference between the all-powerful male managers and the subservient Office Ladies (OL) actually worked in the women's favor (Ogasawara 1998). The women were so powerless that they had nothing to lose by disregarding the corporate rules, while their bosses were totally dependent on the OLs to do their assigned tasks. In addition, the managers would lose face, a very serious problem in Japanese culture, if it appeared that they had lost control over their subordinates.

The bulk of research at all levels shows that American corporations have demonstrated a remarkable ability to adapt to broad changes in the economy and society. Specific firms emerge and disappear, whole industries rise and fall, former competitors merge, local stores are swallowed by national chains, recessions come and go, and through it all, the power and prestige of business leaders increases steadily, along with their share of the wealth of the nation.

Corporate Power and Pay

In 1999, out of a total labor force of about 136 million, over 100 million workers were employed in the private sector's 6.6 million businesses. Eighty-six percent of these firms have fewer than 20 employees, and the great majority are single-owner—America's "small business" component. But real economic and political clout are concentrated in the 10,000 companies with 500 or more employees—"big business." The sheer size of operations and amounts of money involved make big business something different from, not simply larger than, small business. For example, if your local stockbroker makes bad guesses and goes bankrupt, it will cause a lot of suffering to a few people, but you cannot expect the federal government to reimburse you. If, however, an elite investment firm, with millionaire clients and staffed with Nobel Prize economists betting billions on small shifts in the value of foreign currency, makes a mistake, the potential consequences for the world banking system are so destabilizing that the U.S. Treasury Department arranges for a loan from other American financial institutions to cover investors' losses. Large companies cannot be allowed to fail with the same ease as your corner hardware store.

In addition to big business's economic clout, corporate leaders and trade organizations are heavy contributors to political campaigns. Since the Supreme Court ruled that campaign donations are a form of speech protected by the First Amendment, it has been difficult to get Congress to set any limits on funding, especially since most members of Congress owe their election victory to unlimited contributions. In return for their support, large contributors gain access to lawmakers and expect favorable treatment from them, especially when rewriting tax laws.

Other examples of corporate welfare include subsidies to wealthy ship owners for the use of their vessels during wartime, which last occurred 50 years ago; millions of dollars paid to American food companies so they can advertise overseas; tax breaks to sugar producers; price supports for tobacco growers; and a loosening of the rules for cleaning up toxic dump sites (Common Cause 1999).

The most expensive and well-documented example of corporate welfare was the great savings & loan (S&L) bailout of the 1990s. S&Ls were originally chartered by Congress to provide housing loans to low-income families, but under great pressure from the industry in the 1980s, Congress removed many controls on banking activity. The S&Ls then extended unsecured loans to friends, relatives, and powerful local interests; the result of years of such questionable and risky practices was a wave of bank failures. Hundreds of billions of dollars were lost or unaccounted for, and much of the loss was ultimately made good by the federal government with your tax dollars. Only a handful of bank executives were brought to court and only a few million dollars in fines were assessed. In the final analysis, ordinary taxpayers subsidized the risky behavior of wealthy bankers to the tune of at least 300 billion dollars, and very few homes for low-income families were financed (Glasberg and Skidmore 1997). 🖥 7

Corporate Actors

A **corporation** is a formal organization that is a legal actor in its own right. Corporations can enter into contracts, accumulate assets or debts, and go bankrupt without individual owners, managers, or employees being held responsible. That is, you can sue the company but not its personnel for flawed products. And if enough people sue, the company can declare bankruptcy, leaving the plaintiffs, minor creditors, and investors to fight over the remaining assets. In the meantime, the corporation reorganizes, with new personnel and new financing, as in the case of the National Gypsum Company when faced with asbestos-related claims.

Ownership in American corporations is widely held—about 40 percent of U.S. families own some securities, typically through a pension plan. Although this might suggest that corporate profits are spread lavishly across the stratification system, the great majority of stockholders are in the upper income brackets, and over 90 percent of all shares are held by other corporations, banks, and company executives, in addition to pension funds.

One of the defining features of the corporation in a capitalist economy is the separation of ownership (stockholders) from management (corporation officers), but this line has become blurred as executives are increasingly rewarded with stock and stock options as part of their benefit package. Because executive salaries doubled and tripled while most workers' pay barely kept pace with inflation in the 1980s and 1990s, corporations have chosen to avoid negative publicity by increasing executive bonuses and stock options rather than salaries. At the same time, compensation in stock options serves as a motivation for the CEO to enhance the value of the corporation. In any event, America's top executives are very well rewarded (Frank 1995).

The corporation is a formal organization that is a legal actor in its own right—it can enter into contracts, accumulate assets or debts, or go bankrupt.

The bottom line for a corporation is pleasing stockholders, which is done by increasing the value of the company's stock. Until the 1970s, profits were geared to production and marketing operations, and corporate leaders were drawn from these specialties. Over the past several decades, however, companies have found that they can manipulate the value of their shares through mergers, buyouts, takeovers, and acquisitions—paper profits and losses—a trend that has elevated financial experts to the top of corporate leadership (Fligstein 1990).

The very top of the corporate hierarchy is 95 percent white and male, rather like an elite fraternity. Until the 1960s, the fraternity was closed to Jews and Catholics, as well as to women and persons of color. Much business is done in informal settings—a golf course, country club, private eating club—where nonWASPs in general and women and African Americans in particular are not members. We all feel most comfortable dealing with people who share our view of the world and who have had life experiences similar to ours. Thus, no matter how smart and skilled they may be, women and nonwhites disturb the equilibrium of both the boardroom and the shop floor (Martin and Collinson 1999). When business leaders speak of a "gentleman's agreement," they mean precisely that, a promise based on a sense of trust in one another because of their shared identity as members of a privileged brotherhood. 🖥8

Middle management today is more diverse than the top, with a handful of women, a sprinkling of darker faces, and a host of outside consultants (some of whom are former full-time employees). Yet within management ranks, women and minority employees tend to be channeled into particular areas where it is presumed they have special talents—especially personnel and public relations—hardly the fast tracks to corporate power.

But even if more women were to reach high positions in a variety of departments, most business organizations would remain deeply *gendered*. The very idea of an organization as an impersonal set of job slots to be filled by the best qualified persons tends to obscure the fact that the ideal employee is really thought of as a man, or at least someone who does not get pregnant, breast-feed, or need child care (Acker 1990). The way in which business leaders behave is also deeply gendered, as seen in struggles for status—the need to avoid humiliation, to prove oneself as cool, to be the "alpha" male. 🖥9

Corporate Cultures

Corporations are also characterized by all the familiar elements of **culture** described in chapter 2: beliefs, values, norms, rituals, artifacts, and symbolic representations. As in any society (and the French word for a business firm is *societé*), these elements of culture define the collectivity, establish both boundaries and links between it and the external world, and invest daily activities with meaning. For example, the company logo and colors are intended to be as distinctive as the flag of any nation. In many corporations, dress codes vary by level of responsibility, as does the food served in separate dining areas. Rank is signified not by facial paint but by the size and location of your office. Company rituals such as the employee picnic or the executive fishing trip serve the same purpose as a totem pole or rain dance—they bring people together to celebrate the corporate gods. There are taboos (no dating a subordinate) and sacred texts (the sayings of the founder).

In general, well-established firms such as International Business Machines (IBM) or General Electric (GE) have relatively old-fashioned corporate cultures. Indeed, until recently, trainees at IBM sang and marched together much like a military unit, wearing their uniforms of dark suit, white shirt, and striped tie. In contrast, the new technology start-ups that depend on the intellectual brilliance of former high school nerds have a very laid-back culture. Sandals, blue jeans, Mickey-Mouse T-shirts, long hair, unshaven faces, and granny glasses are the uniform of the day. Employees come and go at will, bringing their pets with them, pulling all-nighters or disappearing for a few days. There are often no time clocks to punch or fixed traditions to follow.

The culture of new high-tech firms is less blatantly sexist than that of older established corporations; in part, this is because displays of aggressive masculinity to boost one's ego are not very helpful in a business that requires brain power and collaboration. In part, also, new businesses of whatever nature have not yet established the "old boys' networks" that exclude women and minority candidates. And finally, today's young men are much more sensitive to gender-related issues than are their elders. As a consequence of all these trends, in addition to greater gender and race diversity, newer firms are also more democratic and less hierarchical—perhaps a productive model for all businesses in the future (Rothschild 2000). 🖥 10

Corporations and the Community

In the early stages of the Industrial Revolution, the link between factory and community was organic; each fed the other. Long into the twentieth century, even as local factories were replaced by national corporations, plants and offices remained in the same place for a long period, with owners and top executives living in the area. But as business ownership becomes increasingly concentrated in fewer corporate hands, and as the quest for short-term profits leads to mergers and takeovers and plant relocations, the bond between the corporation and community is broken. Today's top executives may never have seen the local plant or office, or even know where it is, because the property is just that, something owned by the company that can be kept or sold according to whatever increases the book value of the corporation, regardless of the ripple effect on entire communities such as Gadsden.

At the same time, public good will is an asset, especially for firms producing consumer goods. Well-publicized corporate gifts to national and local charities or subsidies to artistic productions serve important corporate goals; the publicity is free and so is the warm, fuzzy image, as in the example of Ronald McDonald Houses. Most giving, however, is local, with hospitals being especially attractive, but here, too,

A majority of American corporations require some form of medical examination and psychological testing for new hires and two-thirds engage in some forms of electronic tracking, such as checking employees' use of the Internet and the office telephone.

❖ ❖ ❖ ❖

mergers and closings have limited corporate involvement at the same time that smaller firms are being taken over. Another form of *philanthropy* (gift-giving) is practiced by the foundations established by the most successful early capitalists—Carnegie, Rockefeller, Ford, and Russell Sage, for example. Andrew Carnegie, the man who ordered the Pinkertons to break strikes, was also a great benefactor of public libraries in New York City. And the Ford, Rockefeller, and Sage Foundations have been at the forefront of funding for programs to reduce the consequences of inequality in education and health care.

Gift giving by *individuals* at the top of the corporate hierarchies, however, as noted in chapter 5, serves primarily to reinforce the unequal distribution of advantage. Most gifts go to the executive's local place of worship and the private schools and universities that gave him a leg up in the first place. Such gifts confer great prestige among peers, similar to the potlatch. Having a building named after you is the new ultimate status symbol, and a major source of leverage for university fund-raisers. How many buildings or labs on your campus carry the donor's name? This pattern may be broken by the relatively young new Internet millionaires, who are less concerned with leaving a monument to themselves than to funding programs that have a long-term impact on the society (Verhovek 2000). For example, Microsoft billionaire Bill Gates has established a foundation that funnels money to schools and libraries in relatively needy communities. 🖥 11

Conclusion

This chapter has introduced the concepts essential for a sociological analysis of economic systems at the macro-level, the nature of organizations at the meso-level, and workplace interactions at the micro-level. Historically, the structure of occupations has shifted from agricultural to industrial to the postindustrial emphasis on information and services that characterizes the American economy today.

You have examined the essential differences between capitalism and socialism, although most economic systems in industrial societies combine elements of both, for efficiency and fairness. Economic systems do not operate in a vacuum; rather, politics and ideology combine to shape a society's mechanisms for production and consumption of goods and services.

The American experience is unique among modern industrial societies in the organization of work and its meaning, in the relative powerlessness of organized labor, and in the consequent dominance of corporate interests over all sectors of social life.

Surfing the Sociological Internet

🖥 1–2 Find out information on job growth at the Department of Labor's website: http://www.dol.gov/
Employment statistics can be found at: http://www.bls.cesprog.htm

🖥 3 Information for workers: www.workers.gov

❖ ❖ ❖ ❖

💻4 Organized labor websites:
AFL-CIO: http://www.aflcio.org/
International Labor Organization: http://www.ilo.org
For links to other labor organizations, see: http://www.michaelmoore.com/newlinks.html

💻5 Women and labor unions: http://www.aflcio.org/women/

💻6 Affirmative Action facts and myths: http://www.essential.org/ussa/foundati/aamyths.html
http://www.feminist.org/other/ccri/aafact_menu.html
Gender Diversity in the work place: http://www.analytictech.com/mb021/gender.htm
Women and minority-owned business information: http://www.census.gov/csd/mwb/1992/

💻7 On corporate welfare: http://www.corporations.org/welfare/

💻8–10 For an example of corporate culture, go to IBM's employment website: http://www-3.ibm.com/employment/us/

💻11 Bill and Melinda Gates Foundation website for and example of corporate philanthropy: http://www.gatesfoundations.org/Default.htm

Glossary

Affirmative Action Policies adopted by the federal government in an attempt to reduce race and sex discrimination in the workplace.

Alienation A worker's sense of powerlessness, of being cut off from his or her labor, from others, and eventually from oneself.

Automation The replacing of workers with machines.

Capitalism An economic system based on free enterprise with minimal public supervision or intervention.

Contingent Labor Force Workers hired on a temporary basis and other services outsourced to independent contractors.

Core Sector The part of the economy consisting of major industries, large investments in plants and equipment, unionized labor, monopolies, and high profits.

Corporate Welfare Financial supports, subsidies, and tax breaks given to corporations by the government.

Corporation A formal organization that is a legal actor in its own right and that can enter into contracts, accumulate assets or debts, and go bankrupt without individual owners, managers, or employees being held responsible.

Division of Labor Work organization in which tasks are divided into distinct parts, each part to be performed by one person or a group of people.

Dual Economy Economic system that contains both a core sector of major capital-intensive industries (automobiles, pharmaceuticals) and a peripheral sector composed of labor-intensive, low-profit businesses (clothing manufacturing, retail stores).

ESOP Employee stock ownership plans, in which workers own shares in the company as part of a benefit program.

Job Autonomy The ability to make decisions about the pacing and sequencing of one's work, with minimal supervision.

Lean Production A recent trend in manufacturing that involves minimal inventory, raw materials shipped just in time and only in the needed quantity, and use of the fewest workers, who are continually moved around so that no time is lost.

Market System Economic system in which the value of goods and services is determined by supply and demand factors.

Peripheral Sector The part of the economy composed of smaller, competitive, low-profit firms, employing low-pay, nonunion manual workers.

Postindustrial An economy characterized by an expanding service sector and the importance of knowledge over mechanical skills.

Private Interests Market forces that are primarily guided by individuals, families, or corporations.

Privatization The turning over of previously public or governmental functions to private, profit-making businesses.

Public Interest Market forces that are primarily regulated by government agencies for the benefit of all.

Quality Circle Groups of workers and supervisors who meet and talk about production problems.

Rule of Reciprocity Norm that obligates the receiver of a gift to return something of equal value at a later time.

Services Economic activity that includes information processing, medical care, government administration, banking, teaching, law enforcement, etc.—as opposed to the production of goods.

Socialism An economic system in which the means of production are collectively owned and the distribution of goods and services is guided by public needs.

Split, or Segmented, Labor Market The pool of workers differentiated by race and gender, with core workers being white men and peripheral workers being primarily women, minorities, and immigrants.

State Socialism An economic system with extensive and generous welfare systems while the ownership of production remains in private hands.

Underground Economy Informal labor force of people who work "off the books" for cash, with no reporting of income.

Workplace Democracy Where the workers actually manage, and in some cases own, the business. ◆

Who Rules? Power, Politics, and the Military

❖ ❖ ❖ ❖   Unlike the Biblical story of Moses and the Ten Commandments, norms do not come to us from on high, fully formed and written in stone. Rather, the rules that govern social life emerge through trial and error, the product of struggles for power within the group, shifting over time. As the old saying goes: Laws are like sausage; you really do not want to know how they are made. But it is important that you understand power, how it is distributed and exercised. The following will be examined in this chapter:

- Power—what it is and who has it.

- Political systems.

- Civil rights.

- The iron law of oligarchy.

- Political participation.

- The contemporary American political scene.

- The military and militarism.

Power Defined

Max Weber (1922), defined power as the probability of achieving one's goals regardless of the wishes of others. The ability to impose your will on other people is one of the three major societal resources that is always unevenly distributed—some people will have more of it than others. By definition, power is *relational*, not something you have all by itself; it is yours only when other people acknowledge it. Power is an aspect of all social relationships, from a dating couple to a meeting of the United Nations.

Weber distinguished two kinds of power: One is informal, interpersonal influence, based largely on persuasion. Some people are better con artists and others fall for it, a process we authors leave to the psychologists to analyze. As sociologists, we are primarily concerned with socially legitimated power or authority, exercised by virtue of occupying a particular status. Weber distinguished three bases of legitimacy: traditional, charismatic, and legal-rational authority.

Traditional authority is based on custom and the force of habit—"this is the way it has always been done." Traditional leaders often claim that their authority is also blessed by the gods, that they have a "divine right" to power. Thus, the first-born son succeeds his father, husbands rule over wives, and religious leaders guide their flocks.

Charismatic authority attaches to those rare individuals who have personal magnetism or embody some stirring ideal and who therefore attract a wide and loyal following. Among such leaders are the founders of the world's great religions—Moses, Jesus, Mohammed, Buddha. More recent examples include Mahatma Gandhi of India, the German Nazi Adolf Hitler, and Evita Peron of Argentina. In American history, an excellent example is Martin Luther King, Jr., the civil rights leader of the 1960s, who combined a forceful speaking style with a powerful message and commanding physical presence.

Weber saw both traditional and charismatic authority as "irrational," because followers are motivated by emotion rather than by reason and because there is no limit on the use of power. If the leader told them to jump off a cliff, the true believers would leap. Traditional authority is further suspect because the person who inherits the position may not be competent or even sane. The king's first-born son could as easily be a stupid fool as a wise ruler.

Irrationality may have been tolerated in earlier historical periods but in modern industrial societies, with their emphasis on technical skills, it is crucial that people who occupy positions of great power have the ability to do the job. In addition, it is also necessary to guard against unrestrained power and the pressures of immediate emotions, which is why Weber placed special value on the third legitimate basis of authority.

Legal-rational authority rests on: (1) laws that limit the exercise of power, as in the United States Constitution, and (2) an election process that allows citizens to choose their leaders, preferably on rational grounds.

Traditional, charismatic, and legal-rational are not mutually exclusive categories. Charismatic figures have become elected officials, and some traditional leaders have also been charismatic.

Historical Trends

Political systems develop out of the need to maintain order within a society and to defend it from outside enemies. Order depends on group members' willingness to follow the rules, and defense ultimately depends on some members' willingness to sacrifice their lives for the group. For most of human history, the thousands of years of hunting-gathering bands, decision making was a fairly egalitarian process, with all adults joining in, so that the norms reflected a basic *consensus* (agreement). Once a group grows so large that it is difficult to get everyone together or to agree on everything, leaders emerge to make decisions for the collectivity. Over time, these leadership positions tended to become hereditary, legitimated by tradition and ever more absolute in their power.

Legal-rational authority is a very recent development, only a few centuries old, and is the defining characteristic of the modern nation-state that gradually took shape in Europe in the late eighteenth century. But the rule of law is always threatened by the rise of a charismatic political or religious leader who throws out the Constitution, dissolves Parliament, and rules as an absolute monarch.

The distinction between representa-

Modern nation-states are based, for the most part, on legal-rational authority. Each nation's flag symbolizes the nation's autonomy.

❖ ❖ ❖ ❖   tive government and absolutism is a matter of degree, as illustrated in Figure 10.1, a continuum on which political systems can be arranged from the most to the least democratic. 1 The key variable that makes for democracy is the *right to oppose the government and its decisions*. The term **totalitarian** describes a system in which this right does not exist, where the government tries to control all aspects of social life and even personal behavior. Current examples include the rule of religious leaders in Afghanistan, of military figures in Central Africa, and the civilians who control the government of China.

It does not matter whether the system is called *fascist* (ruling in the name of an ethnic or religious elite) or *communist* (ruling in the name of the masses) or *theocratic* (ruling in the name of God), the structure is the same. Power is in the hands of a few leaders who answer only to themselves, rule by force, and repress all shades of dissent. This control extends to cultural products such as books, music, art, theater, and the mass media. Today, the Internet may become the major channel for resistance to totalitarianism.

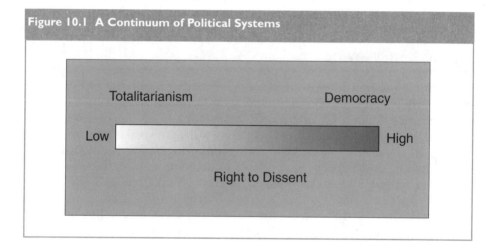

Figure 10.1 A Continuum of Political Systems

At the other extreme is a **democratic** system, where the right to organize in opposition, is protected by law. It is not simply being able to vote—totalitarian systems have a huge voter turnout—but of being able to choose among candidates. In the United States, the right to dissent, to organize in opposition, is guaranteed by the second clause of the First Amendment to the Constitution:

> Congress shall make no law respecting an establishment of religion, or prohibiting the free exercise thereof; or abridging the freedom of speech, or of the press; or the right of people peaceably to assemble, and to petition the government for a redress of grievances. 🖳 2

Civil Liberties

The rights protected by the First Amendment—to speak, to publish, to gather together, and to protest—are called **civil liberties** because they belong to you as a member of the society. But you must be eternally vigilant, because there are always pressures to keep some people from talking or writing or meeting. You may not be one of those directly under threat, but you do have a stake in everyone's rights, even the most loathsome. You can be arrested for breaking the law if you destroy property or attack someone, but you cannot be punished for your beliefs or stopped in advance because the authorities think you might do harm (*prior restraint* is totally unconstitutional). So, yes, the Klan can march down Main Street, advocates for and against abortion can wave signs, gays and hardhats can shout abuse at one another, adults may watch dirty movies in the privacy of their home, and you could have your very own flag-burning. 3

Spinning Public Opinion

No matter how many limits are placed on those in power, certain processes are set in motion whereby those who make decisions for others need to have their actions approved and supported. This goes for the dominant parent in the household as well as for the boss at work and the heads of government. Once a decision is made, all sorts of pressures are put on subordinates, not only to go along willingly but also to endorse the good judgment of the leader.

At the level of government, manipulating public opinion, or "spinning," takes many forms, all of which are easier to achieve in a totalitarian system but nonetheless appear on the American scene with amazing regularity. Some are listed below.

Propaganda is the selective release of information favorable to your cause, as when the government announces how many people were cut from welfare rolls without telling you where they went for housing, food, or income.

Censorship is the selective withholding of unfavorable information, as when documents that detail government mistakes are stamped "top secret." At the local level, politicians continue to try to censor art exhibits or books in school libraries. 4

"Chilling" refers to government tactics that make you think twice about voicing dissent. The fear of being wiretapped or having the FBI interview your boss is enough to scare most people away from organized protests.

Coercion involves the use of force to eliminate opposition. House arrest, imprisonment, public trials, and executions are common in totalitarian societies, but the United States has also seen the prosecution of teachers of evolution and the imprisonment of Americans of Japanese ancestry in the early 1940s.

The ultimate in coercion is **genocide**, the intentional systematic killing of an entire population, or currently, **ethnic cleansing**. This is what happened to 6 million Jews, Gypsies, communists, homosexuals, and other "undesirables" in Nazi Europe. And it has taken place in the 1990s in the former Yugoslavia, where Serbs wipe out Moslem villages in Kosovo, and the Kosovars massacre Serbian farmers in return.

The Iron Law of Oligarchy

After defeating the corrupt, unpopular, and American-backed General Chiang Kai-shek in 1949, the victorious Chinese Communist leader Mao Zedong declared, "Let a thousand flowers bloom!" By this, he meant to unleash the creative energies of his people, including "constructive criticism" of his own regime. Yet when the criticism came, he was not pleased, and a decade of violent suppression of "non-Maoist" thought followed. Only in the late 1990s have any fragile shoots of opposition appeared, also to be quickly quashed by the new leaders.

It is not only totalitarians who seek to suppress dissent; they just have more power to succeed at it. All leaders have a deep and abiding ("vested") interest in having their choices approved. They hear only favorable opinions ("What a beautiful suit of clothing you have on, Emperor"), while negative information is screened out by those who surround them—who wants to be the messenger who gets beheaded? Up until the moment he withdrew from the 1968 election, Lyndon Johnson thought he could win the Vietnam War, that protesters were kooks, and that the public was behind him (Caro 1982).

This process whereby leaders are shielded from contact with the public is known as the **iron law of oligarchy** (Michels 1911/1962). "Oligarchy" means rule of the few, and Michels' iron law states that because decision makers need approval of the governed, they manipulate information to gain that support, while their closest aides shield them from any negative feedback. Even in organizations formed to represent the masses, such as trade unions, the leadership becomes cut off from the followers. The few who rule have a full-time commitment to the task; the masses are only periodically activated. A gap grows between the rulers and the ruled. Eventually, the gap becomes so large that a mass movement emerges to overthrow the ruling elite, but the iron law suggests that the new leaders will, in time, behave very much as the old ones did. For example, the revolutionaries who overthrew the Shah of Iran in 1979 have become every bit as totalitarian as he had been.

As noted by the British political theorist Lord Acton (1878/1985): "Power tends to corrupt and absolute power corrupts absolutely." Having power feeds arrogance, a feeling of superiority coupled with contempt for the less powerful. You may have observed how inequality erodes respect and trust in families and at work, which is a powerful argument for egalitarian relationships between women and men. But governments are rarely egalitarian institutions; someone has to make the difficult decisions and take responsibility. The beauty of democracy is precisely this: Every two or four or six years, your leaders must justify themselves in competition with other candidates. You can replace one set with another, so even if the iron law cannot be repealed, you can see to it that no one stays in office long enough to become fully corrupted.

It is important, therefore, that you become an informed citizen and exercise the right to vote. Every vote does count, if only to remind candidates that someone is paying attention. The best guarantee against official corruption is an

The minimal act of political participation is voting. Only slightly more than half of all registered voters participated in the 2000 presidential election between Albert Gore and George W. Bush.

open election, but even that will not work unless you show up. 5 ✦ ✦ ✦ ✦

Political Participation

In a democracy, you can do more than just show up for an election. You can run for office or work on behalf of other candidates. You can sign petitions and buttonhole (*lobby*) elected officials on behalf of your chosen causes. In rare moments, you can even take part in a recall movement, removing corrupt or inept officials before the legal end of their term.

Running for Office

The typical path to becoming a candidate is by working your way up the party ladder, beginning at the local level. It also helps to be male, tall, and the same race as the people in your district. Today, however, it is possible to buy one's way to the top, which immediately screens out everyone except a handful of the very wealthy such as Ross Perot and Steve Forbes.

Campaign Activity

Only a few people become campaign workers, usually less from ideological commitment than because they were brought in by friends. Contributing money, however, is something that millions of people do. And some of these contributors give millions. Since the Supreme Court's 1976 decision (*Buckley v. Valeo*) that political contributions are a form of speech protected by the First Amendment, few serious attempts to limit and regulate such spending have succeeded, in part because the legislators already in office have an advantage in raising money over their challengers.

As a consequence, the presidential election of 2000 was awash with dollars—hundreds of millions of them. Although the maximum for a single contribution to a presidential candidate is $1,000, you, your spouse, parents, and adult children can each donate. Then, you can all give unlimited amounts of "soft money" for issue-oriented ads by the political action committees (PACs) that support your candidate's positions, and so can your employer and professional organizations or unions. Furthermore, if your candidate can afford to decline federal matching funds, she or he is immune from state spending caps during the primaries. Money does talk. And to that extent, people without money are relatively voice-

Big money spoke in the elections of 2000. Hundreds of millions of dollars were spent by special interest groups and, despite a lot of talk about limiting the size of contributions, no such laws were passed. How do such huge contributions by special interest groups limit democracy?

❖ ❖ ❖ ❖   less in setting the political agenda. In other words, class and race or ethnic differences in political power are reinforced by the American system of campaign financing. Although labor unions have raised millions for their favored candidates, business elites have had an overwhelming advantage in money and influence (Lo and Schwartz 1998), as well as ownership of most of the mass media (Frankel 1999).

Campaign contributions give the donors access to legislators as well as some influence over what gets enacted into law. For example, two of the most generous contributors to Congressional candidates—the National Rifle Association and the tobacco industry—were very successful throughout the 1990s in blocking controls on guns and cigarettes. Of greater effectiveness today, however, may be the special-interest PACs' ability to shape public opinion through issue-oriented ads (television, print media, direct mail) paid for with an endless stream of soft money. In 1992, for example, the health care industry used a massive advertising campaign to turn public opinion against a proposed health plan that would have regulated the industry's practices and reduced profits. Within months, the Clinton proposal for a universal health insurance system was buried in ridicule (chapter 14).

In addition to funding candidates and PACs, interest groups can use friendship and business networks and other channels of persuasion, as seen in the battle over the North American Trade Agreement (NAFTA) in the early 1990s. In this case, an unusual degree of unity within corporate America produced the USA-NAFTA coalition that was able to mobilize an array of resources to influence public opinion and pressure Congress to pass the legislation (Dreiling 2000). The class-based interests of big business in opening up markets in the Western Hemisphere outspent and outmaneuvered efforts by organized labor to defeat the treaty and keep jobs from leaving the United States. 💻6

Voting

The minimal act of political participation is voting. As you can see from Table 10.1, not everyone comes to the ballot box, which gives those who do vote a lot of power. These data are for presidential election years, when turnout is higher than for nonpresidential years; then only 35 to 40 percent of eligible citizens bother to vote. 💻7

Table 10.1 Voting in Presidential Elections, Selected Years 1964–1996 (Percent of voting-age population)						
		1964	1972	1980	1988	1996
	Percent voting	69.3	63.0	59.2	57.4	54.2
Race	Black	58.5	52.1	50.5	51.5	50.6
	White	70.7	64.5	60.9	59.1	56.0
	Hispanic	—	37.5	29.9	28.8	26.7
Gender	Male	71.9	64.1	59.1	56.4	52.8
	Female	67.0	62.0	59.4	58.3	55.5
Age	18–24	50.9	49.6	39.9	36.2	32.4
	25–44	69.0	62.7	58.7	54.0	49.2
	45–64	75.9	70.8	69.3	67.9	64.4
	65+	66.3	63.5	65.1	68.8	67.0

Source: U.S. Bureau of the Census, *Current Population Reports* P20-504, July, 1998.

As you can see, voting rates have steadily declined, by year, race, sex, and among all but the oldest voters. If you were a politician running for national or statewide office, how much attention would you pay to the interests of Hispanic American or college-age voters? Although the black-white voting gap has been cut in half, African Americans compose slightly under 12 percent of the voting age population. But you had better start listening to the women.

The Political 'Gender Gap'

The most interesting data in Table 10.1 are those on sex. Although both women and men are less likely to vote now than they were in 1964, the proportion of female to male voters has shifted, from a 5 percentage point gap in favor of men in 1964 to a 4 point advantage for women today. When you consider that adult women outnumber men in the general population, those 4 percentage points translate into a large number of voters. Although not yet fully available, the data for the 2000 elections appear to follow the same patterns.

In addition, the gender gap extends to party preference, with women favoring Democratic candidates, while men are more likely to vote for Republicans. In the 2000 presidential election, for example, men split 53/42 in favor of George W. Bush, while women split 54/43 in favor of Al Gore. In terms of gender politics, the Republican image is "hard" and masculine: pro-military, pro-guns, anti-abortion, and anti-welfare. In contrast, Democratic concerns are seen as "soft" and feminine: education, social welfare, healthcare, reproductive choice, and minority civil rights (Brooks 2000). As long as women outnumber men at the voting booth, Republicans seeking national office will tone down the toughness, as in George W. Bush's "compassionate conservatism." 🖥️8

Table 10.2 Percent Voting by Education, Occupation, and Income, 1996		
Education	Less than high school	38.8
	High school graduate or GED	51.7
	Some college/Associate's degree	63.1
	Bachelor's degree	74.1
	Advanced degree	83.3
Occupation	Manager, professional	73.1
	Technical, sales, administration	60.9
	Farming, forestry, fishing	57.4
	Service (all types)	48.8
	Crafts, repair, precision work	47.5
	Operators, laborers	43.1
Annual Family Income	Under $5,000	37.9
	$5,000–9,999	38.3
	$10,000–14,999	46.7
	$15,000–24,999	52.0
	$25,000–34,999	56.6
	$35,000–49,999	62.6
	$50,000–74,999	69.4
	$75,000–over	76.2

Source: U.S. Bureau of the Census, *Current Population Reports* P20-504, July, 1998b.

❖ ❖ ❖ ❖   ## Class Differences in Voting

As shown in Table 10.2, for the presidential election year of 1996, voting percentages rise with education, income, and occupational prestige. People with a college education are twice as likely to vote as those who did not graduate from high school, and people with family incomes of $50,000 and over are almost twice as likely to vote as those earning less than $12,000. When so many voters are in the upper levels of the stratification system, you would think twice as a candidate before favoring massive programs for the redistribution of wealth.

Nonvoting

What can one say about the 21 million registered voters who chose not to show up for the 1996 presidential election? The Census Bureau (1998) did ask why they failed to vote and found that the most often mentioned reasons were "no time off/too busy" (22 percent), "not interested" (17 percent), and "ill, disabled" (15 percent). Whatever the reasons people give, American voting rates are so far below those of any other modern democratic society that one must also look at structural factors. The most important of these is probably that, unlike Europe, where elections are held on weekends, ours take place on a weekday, when it is difficult to find baby-sitters or to take time off from work, especially for hourly workers (Beegley 1986). Also, unlike other democracies, we make it difficult for people to register and stay enrolled when changing residence. Only in 1993 did Congress reluctantly agree to allow people to register to vote at the same time they apply for driving licenses or welfare benefits, or by mail. As a consequence, registration has increased significantly since 1995.

Between April and October 2000 the authors tried to obtain a photo of the 100 U.S. Senators. We sent letters, faxes, e-mails, and made numerous phone calls, but no such picture was available at press time. Why? Some of the senators were absent the day the photo was taken, and their pictures had to be individually superimposed in the composite photo, and then the new photo has to be approved by each of the 100 senators. With such inaction, who needs to filibuster?

In all U.S. elections since 1920, the year women were first allowed to vote in national elections, the proportion of nonvoters exceeded the percentage that elected the president. This means that every man who has held the highest office has been placed there by between 25 and 35 percent of all potential voters! And, before 1920, they were elected by less than 15 percent of adult citizens. In other words, very few presidents can claim to have had an overwhelming mandate to govern.

Political Socialization

How is it that you end up being, in the words of Gilbert and Sullivan, "a Little Liberal or a Little Conservative"? Political socialization, like any other type, begins at home, and most of you will follow the path of your parents, in large part because you inherit their social position and its preferences.

For many of you, however, the college experience can be either liberalizing or conservatizing, depending on your friendship networks and your field of study—business majors tend to become more conservative, while liberal arts majors become more liberal. In addition, your work experiences and friendships can further reinforce or lead to changes in your political orientation. The result is often a mixture, with people in the upper middle class being conservative on economic issues (taxes and wages) and liberal on social ones (abortion, sexual preference), while those in the working class are liberal on economic issues but conservative on social ones. Or, are these distinctions now obsolete?

New Fault-Lines and Alignments

Some political sociologists argue that the United States, along with other postindustrial societies, is undergoing a shift in political culture—away from material concerns such as housing and pay and toward a *postmaterialist* emphasis on lifestyle issues such as the environment, gay rights, and self-expression (Clark and Hoffman-Martinot 1998). Others suggest that the old cleavages in American society, by class, race, and region have been replaced by a cultural divide over values and morals—a "culture war" between orthodox traditionalists and progressive modernists that cuts across class, sex, race, region, and religions (Hunter 1991, 1994).

The evidence for such a deep cultural divide remains limited (Brooks and Manza 1997; Williams 1997), although most researchers can agree that it is increasingly difficult to put American voters into simple categories such as liberal or conservative. Not only do individuals vote one way on some issues and the other way on different questions, but they are also influenced by their ascribed statuses. Bread-and-butter issues still mean a lot to those without a surplus of food and income, while lifestyle concerns are an upper strata luxury. Sometimes, also, both low- and high-status voters will find themselves on the same side of an issue but for different reasons, as in North Carolina today (see Box 10.1).

Box 10.1

Tar Heel Politics

For most of the twentieth century, North Carolina was governed by an alliance of landowners, businessmen, and members of the social elite who managed to keep out unions, limit the political power of blacks, and lure Northern industries with the promise of cheap labor and low taxes. But now, according to sociologist Paul Luebke (1990, 1998), two very distinct North Carolinas have emerged. There is the North Carolina of affluent, well-educated, urban "modernizers," and the North Carolina of dirt-poor rural white "traditionalists." The modernizers are willing to raise taxes to improve the educational system and make gestures toward racial and gender equality that would encourage industrial growth. The traditionalists are fearful that relocated Northerners will lower moral standards. They are also aware that, as with most Southern states, the tax system is highly regressive and would affect them disproportionately (chapter 5).

> Where the two North Carolinas come together is in their opposition to labor unions and to government programs that might redistribute resources, even though the white rural poor would benefit. Since both traditionalists and modernists are found in both the Democratic and Republican parties, the struggle is taking place within rather than between the major political divisions in the society as a whole. But it is not a very energetic struggle, since both North Carolinas are profoundly conservative in their low-tax, anti-labor, business-friendly orientations, with the modernizers only marginally more liberal on social issues.

The Structure of Political Power

Who rules America? Is it a relatively small subset of white college-educated males, drawn from the middle and upper classes? Or is power more widely distributed among groups and organizations at various levels of civic life?

The Power Elite

The **power elite model**, as illustrated in Figure 10.2, takes its name from a 1956 book by sociologist C. Wright Mills, in which he traced the social-class background and ideology of leaders in business, government, and the military and found that they talked the same language in the sense of sharing values and a vision of what is good for America. 🖥 9 There is no conspiracy here; they do not have to know one another, but they will make decisions that are mutually beneficial and that reinforce their own high status. And today, if you look at who runs the government, major corporations, universities and foundations, the media, and the judicial system, it might seem as if it is the same set of faces, a "national upper class" (Domhoff 1998). And sometimes it really is the same people, moving from one top spot to another, such as business leaders who go into politics or politicians who become university presidents.

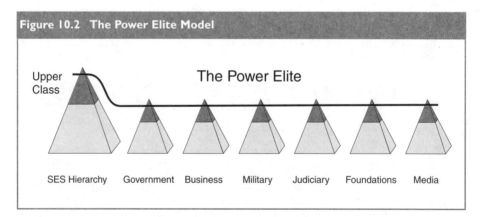

Figure 10.2 The Power Elite Model

The Pluralist Model

A contrasting view of the distribution of political power assumes that elite interests are not always complementary and that there are many ways in which ordinary people can become politically effective. Business and the mil-

itary compete for scarce resources and trained personnel; what is good for
General Motors may not help smaller companies; government power is
spread out among federal, state, and local agencies; and many Americans
participate in community and neighborhood organizations.

In the **pluralist model**, as depicted in Figure 10.3, this diversity of interests and diffusion of power assures that no one group can control decision
making throughout the society. Each power sector serves as a potential buffer
against the uncontrolled expansion of the others, as when government regulations set limits on business monopolies.

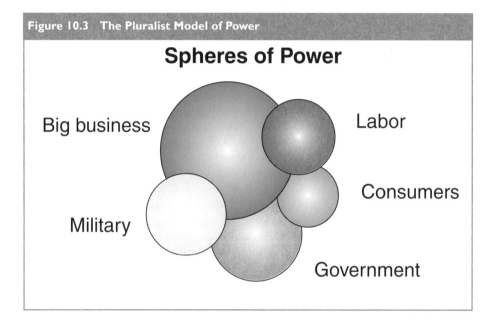

Figure 10.3   The Pluralist Model of Power

Spheres of Power

Big business

Labor

Consumers

Military

Government

Although the two models are often presented as mutually exclusive, they
can best be seen as alternative ways to analyze power systems. The power
structure of your home town probably fits the elite model, with local leaders—the mayor, businessmen, newspaper editor, zoning board chair—drawn
from the same social stratum, meeting regularly (that Monday lunch at the
best restaurant in town), and making mutually beneficial decisions.

In contrast, the power structure of your university looks very much like
the pluralist model, with several strong competing sectors—administration,
faculty, staff, and students. Administration and faculty are continually testing the limits of each other's powers; staff members can go on strike; students
have been known to protest policies and personnel decisions; and when students get out of hand, the administration can activate campus police.

Pluralists and elitists can agree on one point: The great mass of citizens
remain politically passive, so power holders are rarely challenged. Although
there appears to be a revival of community and neighborhood organizing to
empower "ordinary" people to protect their interests against city hall or corporate powers, these attempts are difficult to sustain. People who live in
threatened neighborhoods typically have a lot of other problems to attend to,
with little time for meetings and demonstrations. Yet, on those rare occasions
when a "community identity" emerges, success is possible (Gotham 1999).

❖ ❖ ❖ ❖   Democratic Dilemmas

Democracy has been described as the most inefficient form of government because lawmakers must act slowly and seek widespread support (Marks and Diamond 1992). They cannot demand obedience or lock up perceived enemies. There is always the possibility that citizens will become impatient and look for someone to make instant decisions—the "man on horseback," typically a military figure, a Napoleon or General Douglas MacArthur—who will deliver them from the incompetence of pointy-headed intellectuals and incompetent bureaucrats.

An additional dilemma, especially in a society with low levels of political interest and participation, is "creeping totalitarianism" through loss of privacy (G. Marx 1986). In their eagerness to catch a thief, arrest a drug dealer, plug an information leak, or uncover a terrorist, citizens become willing participants in the gradual erosion of legal barriers to wiretapping, mail intercepts, and searches without a warrant. Then there are all those surveillance cameras in stores and public street corners, lie detector testing by employers, drug testing by schools, and all the reams of information on your shopping and entertainment habits being gathered daily by credit card companies and law enforcement agencies. Banks that are supposed to maintain client privacy find it difficult to do so when they also serve as credit bureaus. And just wait until your health records are added to the data banks. An attempt in 1999 by Congress to protect the privacy of medical records was abandoned under pressure from insurance companies, health care businesses, and law enforcement officials. In 2000, however, President Clinton's last act was to sign an executive order to safeguard medical records.

An additional threat to democracy, or more broadly, to the modern nation-state, is the gradual loss of functions performed by the national government. This trend is especially marked in the United States today, the result of three currents that gained strength in the 1990s. The first of these is economic globalization. Decisions that once could be made on the basis of supply and demand factors within a society are now hostage to the global trading system (chapter 16). Large international corporations, operating above or outside the laws of any one society, call the tune. Freedom from government regulation is the essence of capitalism, and free trade on a global basis will have effects that national governments cannot control. Impersonal market forces halfway around the world can cost you your job, and there is not much that federal agencies can do about it. The question then becomes: "How does a sovereign nation govern itself effectively when politics are national and business is global?"(Garten 1999).

The second trend, very strong in the United States under Republican administrations, is toward shifting responsibilities from the federal to the state level. This process of devolution drains power from national leaders and agencies. Advocates of this shift claim that it brings government "closer to the people." But it is often the case that the degree of incompetence and corruption is highest at the lowest level of government—towns and cities. Although you may not have much respect for the people in the White House and Congress and the various federal departments, they are on the whole a bit smarter and more honest than their counterparts in state capitols and town halls (Geoghegan 1999).

The third trend, which also affects state government is **privatization**, turning over previously public, or governmental, functions to private profit-making businesses (Quadagno 1999). The claim here is that private is more efficient, that market pressures squeeze out waste and inefficiencies. At the moment, some states are experimenting with private prisons, profit-making educational companies, and even private companies to manage welfare cases. The counterarguments are that (a) the main goal is probably to replace unionized labor with less expensive personnel, and (b) some functions—health care, education, crime control, and social welfare—ought to be public responsibilities both to promote and symbolize social solidarity.

These three trends taken together spell the end of national politics, as business interests look outward and political power shifts ever downward and into the private sector. While globalization is irreversible, devolution and privatization are not inevitable. But resisting these pressures depends on an informed and active citizenry.

One last area of potential threat to democratic values and institutions in any society is the military.

The Military

A basic characteristic of the nation-state is its monopoly over the use of force. Political positions were created in the first place to settle disputes within the group and, later, to protect it from outside enemies. For the first function, you needed wise elders; for the second, brave warriors. In hunting and gathering bands, all adult males served as protectors. In larger societies, a distinct caste of military figures emerged, although the mass of foot soldiers were ordinary peasants pressed into service when required.

At the founding of the United States, the very wise men who drew up the Constitution were well aware of the dangers of a military that could not be controlled by civilian leadership. For this reason, the president, a civilian, serves as commander-in-chief. Military personnel who run for elective office must first resign their commissions and appear in civilian clothes.

The United States was also unique among modern nations, until very recently, in having a relatively small class of professional warriors.

The Citizen-Soldier

The ideal throughout our history, until 1973, was the **citizen-soldier**, a civilian who could be called upon to join the armed forces only when necessary and who would be returned to civilian life as soon as possible. When volunteers were in short supply, citizens could be forced (*conscripted*) into service for temporary duty, as happened during the Civil War, World War I and II, and the Korean and Vietnam wars. The citizen-soldier ideal is perfectly exemplified by the TV series *M*A*S*H*, in which the members of the unit go to great lengths to maintain their civilian identities—in clothing, behavior, and attitude toward military authority. They saw themselves as civilians first and only temporarily as soldiers.

Because the Vietnam War became so unpopular and also revealed obvious inequities in conscription, when college youth and anyone with influence could avoid being drafted, the citizen-soldier model was abandoned in 1973.

❖ ❖ ❖ ❖   ## The All-Volunteer Force

The citizen-soldier ideal was replaced by a new concept, the *economic man* model of military service. In this model, serving in the armed forces is a job like any other, to which recruits would be attracted by competitive pay, a chance to travel, educational opportunities, and health and retirement benefits. The all-volunteer force (AVF) would be small but more professional than the citizen-soldier force, and because volunteers would be making a career out of military service, the higher pay would be offset by lower turnover and training costs. In other words, the AVF is something very different ideologically and organizationally than its predecessor. 🖳10

Race and ethnicity. The AVF has a higher proportion of black and Hispanic personnel than did the conscripted forces—about 30 percent—which makes the military the most integrated institution in our society, at least at the lower ranks. The proportion of minority officers, 15.3 percent, while double that of two decades ago, remains disproportionately low. Even so, the armed forces offer greater opportunities for training and promotion to minority youth than does the civilian labor force (Moskos and Butler 1997). Yet, as in civilian life, minority personnel are clustered in the lower prestige areas, which makes later career moves difficult. According to a recent Department of Defense survey, a majority of black enlisted persons have experienced racially offensive encounters (Holmes 1999), and although segregation is minimal on duty, off-duty socializing tends to be racially exclusive. 🖳11

Education. Because the AVF can be selective, its recruits are better educated and from a higher socioeconomic status than in the past. But when the civilian labor market is tight, both enlistments and reenlistments drop, and then the military has to offer added inducements such as a signing bonus or it has to dip into a less educated pool of recruits and accept a higher proportion of women.

Today about 14 percent of active-duty personnel, both enlisted and officer corps members, in the United States military are women. Here a U.S. Army captain is the company commander of a military intelligence unit on their way to Bosnia.

Women in the military. In World War I, the Navy and Marine Corps established women's auxiliaries to handle office-type jobs, while other women enlisted in the Army Nurses Corps. All were disbanded at the end of the war in 1918. In World War II, women served in all branches of the armed forces, mostly in health care and administration but also as mechanics and weapon instructors, and several hundred ferried aircraft from the United States to war zones. These women were also released from service at war's end in 1945.

Pressures to open the armed forces to women on a regular basis increased with the emergence of the Women's Movement in the

mid-1960s and grew even stronger with the introduction of the AVF and its
need for qualified personnel. Today, the proportion of women in the United
States military is the highest of any modern nation; 14 percent of active-duty
personnel, both enlisted and officer corps, are women (Bourg and Segal
2001).

Originally, women were barred from a large number of military jobs, out
of traditional views of their abilities and fears for their safety. These jobs happen also to be the specialties that lead to higher rank. Gradually, however, all
but direct combat, armored units, and submarine service have been opened
up. Since the Air Force has fewest restrictions, it has the highest percentage
of women: 18 percent of enlisted personnel and 16 percent of officers. Conversely, the Marine Corps has the most off-limits jobs and hence the smallest
proportion of women—5 percent of enlisted persons and 4 percent of officers. For the Army, comparable numbers are 15 percent and 13 percent, and
for the Navy, it is 12 and 14 percent. In contrast to the situation of black and
Hispanic men, the proportion of female officers reflects their presence in the
lower ranks. In fact, racial and ethnic minority women join the armed forces
at a higher rate than their male counterparts; they currently comprise over
one-third of all enlisted women and 15 percent of women officers. 💻 12

Military families. Formerly, only officers' families were allowed to live
on base; it was a highly stratified society in which the husband's military rank
determined the family's social position. But if the goal is to have enlisted personnel make the military their life's career, the military post will have to
become more like a civilian community. With the AVF, then, the families of
enlisted personnel also came on base, and the unit commander must now
worry about schools, health care, and social services, including support for
families whose mother is fighting a war halfway around the world. Indeed,
the military's child-care system has become a model for civilian employers,
providing quality care at affordable fees, as a necessity for retaining personnel (Becker 2000). 💻 13

Militarism and Masculinity

Militarism refers to a glorification of war and an emphasis on military
ideals and virtues, a warrior image that is deeply masculinized in our culture.
Militarism and manhood are closely linked, especially among white southerners, for whom military schools and service are badges of honor (Mangold
2000; Kimmel 2000b). Having women in the military is disturbing to many
men (and women), the barracks being the last refuge of real manhood, a
world in which men can offer proof of their strength and courage. Critics of a
gender-neutral military claim that the presence of women erodes the ability
of fighting men to bond fully to one another and to make the sacrifices necessary to winning battles (Gutmann 2000). The counterargument is that very
few armed troops see any sort of combat these days and that women are as
capable as men of handling the high-tech devices that have replaced face-to-
face warfare.

If sharing their world with women is so stressful, you can imagine how
some servicemen feel about homosexuals in their midst. Masculinity for military men is profoundly (some would say exclusively and compulsively) het-

❖ ❖ ❖ ❖   erosexual, essentially defined in contrast to both women and gays (Herbert 1998).

Homosexuals in the military. For many reasons, the military has tried to exclude gay men and lesbians, officially banning them in 1950. Nonetheless, an unknown (and obviously unknowable) number of homosexual service personnel have served with distinction during wartime and are currently valued members of their units, as long as they remain closeted.

Attempts to lift the restrictions on homosexuals have met fierce resistance. The most recent effort, by President Clinton in the early 1990s, ended with some minor changes to the policy of instant removal of gay personnel. In the new arrangement, commanders cannot ask and service persons need not tell about their sexual orientation. Yet, under the "Don't Ask, Don't Tell" policy, the number of discharges for homosexuality has almost doubled (Bourg and Segal 2001). Personnel can be discharged for engaging in homosexual acts (unless they can convince their superiors that this was a one-time mistake by someone essentially heterosexual); for trying to marry someone of the same sex; and for making a statement about their sexuality, whether or not they commit any overt act. Ironically, this policy results in heterosexuals who have had same-sex relations remaining in service, while celibate gays can be discharged. 🖥 14

Militarism refers to a glorification of war and a warrior image that is deeply masculinized in American culture. The number of casualties and deaths suffered by American soldiers in Vietnam and the domestic opposition to that war challenged the glory of combat.

Sexual harassment. One powerful technique for enforcing the code of heterosexual masculinity on both women and gays at the level of informal interaction is sexual harassment by teasing, stalking, sabotaging equipment, refusing to obey orders, and generally making life difficult for targets. To maintain group cohesion, women and homosexual personnel find themselves conforming to standards that deny their basic selfhood (Herbert 1998). 🖥 15

For the moment, however, the military must deal with widespread antigay bias across all branches and units. Following the killing of a gay serviceman by members of his own unit, the Department of Defense undertook an extensive survey of attitudes and behaviors (*New York Times*, March 25, 2000). The researchers found that 80 percent of respondents had heard antigay remarks, and 37 percent had witnessed some form of harassment, often in the presence of supervisory personnel. Redoubled efforts to explain the policy and train officers and unit leaders are now underway.

Militarism and Democracy

Militarism has always been a problem for a democratic society because, by its nature, the military is a totalitarian institution. It is a rigid hierarchy in which absolute obedience is required. You cannot fight a war by consensus or by letting the troops decide for themselves when and where to do battle. The citizen-soldier ideal and the President as commander-in-chief were designed as counterweights to the military hierarchy. An army of civilians is not likely to plot against the government. The AVF, however, is a body of professionals, and there is always the slimmest chance its leaders just might consider themselves above the law if they felt the nation was being endangered. There is some evidence that military leaders are more conservative, less trustful of civilian institutions, and more rigid in their values than nonmilitary leaders (Kohn and Feaver 1999).

The Military-Industrial State

In 1961, in his Farewell Address, President Eisenhower, a former Army general, warned of a new threat to democracy: the **military-industrial complex**. The combination of a large military establishment and an immense defense industry with its legislative supporters, he felt, could become an independent power in setting national spending priorities. And he was right. The military build-up for the Korean Conflict, Vietnam War, and the "Cold War" with the Soviet Union sent military budgets skyrocketing, at the cost of spending on domestic problems. The defense industry has enormous influence on Congress; it poured over 50 million dollars into lobbying and campaign contributions in just one decade (Wayne 2000).

The manufacture of weapons and military vehicles provides well-paid jobs and the entire local economy is boosted, regardless of the usefulness of the product. The Osprey fighter plane, for example, is an item that the Defense Department never wanted and has tried to cancel for over a decade, but Congress loved the idea of a craft that could lift off and land like a helicopter but cruise like an airplane, and particular Congresspersons were even more delighted with the money that the 37 *billion* dollar program would bring to their districts (Weiner 2000). To date, the Ospreys remain grounded after continued failures and two deadly crashes with 23 servicemen aboard.

Box 10.2

Lost in the Stars

The power of the military-industrial complex and the interplay between strategic and political decision making is well illustrated by the "Star Wars" project. The story began in 1983 when President Ronald Reagan proposed that the United States build a defense system that could shield the nation from a Soviet-launched nuclear attack by intercepting the incoming missiles. At that time there was no technological basis for the program, only some vague ideas and movie clips, but it caught the public attention and was so politically appealing that 60 billion dollars have already been spent on research and development of a Strategic Defense Initiative (SDI).

Despite the collapse of the Soviet Union and our country's signing of an Antiballistic Missile Treaty, Congress has continued to fund work on the SDI in a scaled-down version, now designed to protect the United States from missiles launched by "rogue states" such as Iraq or North Korea. Although the system would not be fully operational for many more years, and despite the failure of test rockets to tell the difference between a nuclear warhead and a balloon decoy, election-year politics and the need to appear strong on defense issues have kept the program alive, at the cost of additional tens of billions of dollars (Fitzgerald 2000).

Today, a decade after the collapse of the Soviet Union, spending on national defense remains at an all-time high—$309,000,000,000 (that's 309 *billion*) a year, or about 17 percent of the total U.S. budget. This is as much as the federal government spends on everything else in the budget except Social Security, Medicare, and interest on the national debt. In fact, the 1999–2000 budget included billions more than the Pentagon requested, including the Osprey and similar projects.

Once in place, a weapons program takes on a life of its own. No matter how poorly the plane or tank performs, it keeps getting funded because someone in the military has a reputation at stake and because to close down the operation would put thousands of workers out of a job. Of course, other jobs would be created if the money were spent on needy children, for example, or school construction and health insurance, but these jobs are not equivalent to the ones lost, nor would they generate as much political benefit for the sponsors. Ironically, these improvements in the education and health of poor children would be of greater ultimate benefit to the military than another wing of nonfunctional B-1 bombers, because as adult recruits, the beneficiaries would be better equipped to handle the complex weapons systems of the twenty-first century (Shanahan 1999).

Another irony is that each new weapons system immediately makes the existing ones obsolete. The old material is then sold to Third World countries, where it can be bought or stolen by the very terrorists who are the targets of our new weapons (Greider 1998). In other cases, war material is sent to friendly countries that subsequently end up on our "enemies list," for example, the Taliban of Afghanistan, who received billions of dollars in training and weapons from the CIA to fight communists but who now harbor suspected anti-American terrorists.

The selling of munitions on the international market by both private companies and the U.S. military is a major source of income for both. The United States has become the weapons warehouse of the world, accounting for one-third of all global sales in 1999 (Myers 2000). These armaments are shipped primarily to less developed nations, where despite widespread poverty, the military absorbs the bulk of public funds that do not go directly into the pockets of corrupt officials. All of this drives the country deeper into poverty, stirring unrest and creating such regional instability that United States and United Nations forces are eventually called upon to intervene.

In the four decades since Eisenhower's parting warning, successive Congresses and American presidents have found it difficult if not politically suicidal to resist the military-industrial complex. And because national defense represents such a large proportion of the budget, it affects how much is left over to do anything else in the public sector. A final consideration is that once a complex weapons system is in place, the temptation to use it grows. The world today is filled with powerful munitions and a host of local wars—in Asia, Africa, and the Near East. Although only a few countries admit to having a nuclear arsenal, many others could be well on their way. Secrets can be stolen and transmitted with relative ease today, and the technical know-how of former Soviet scientists is often for sale.

It took a while for the destructive implications of these developments to sink into the sociological imagination. Who wants to contemplate being wiped out by a nuclear weapon, whether by accident or design? But to study such possibilities, the Sociology of War and Peace has recently been recognized as a legitimate subfield. Research topics include much of what you have learned in this chapter: manipulation of public opinion, the military-industrial complex, the world trade in armaments, militarization of society, and the dynamics of international cooperation and conflict, not to mention the potential devastation of the planet (Grimshaw 1992).💻16

Conclusion

This chapter has covered some of the major issues and areas of political sociology: the concept of power and its application, the historical development of political systems, and the distinction between democratic and totalitarian regimes. You were reminded of the crucial role of civil liberties in maintaining a democracy, and the need for eternal vigilance against oligarchal tendencies. Aspects of political participation and voting patterns were discussed, along with models of the distribution of power in America. The chapter ended with an extended discussion of the military, its structure, ideology, and contemporary problems and possibilities, including the power of the military-industrial complex and the spread of nuclear weapons in an increasingly unstable world.

Surfing the Sociological Internet

💻1 Websites on various governmental forms:
For information on democracy to communism, see: http://www.cyberenet.net/~lking/
On democratic socialism: http://socialist.org/base.html

💻2 For the core documents of American democracy, see: http://www.access.gpo.gov/su_docs/locators/coredocs/index.html

💻3 The American Civil Liberties organization has a website with information on First Amendment Rights at: http://www.aclu.org/

💻4 Issues related to censorship can be found at: http://www.ala.org/bbooks/
http://digital.library.upenn.edu/books/banned-books.html

💻5 Get information and go vote: http://govote.speakout.com/index.asp

💻6 See the Common Cause website, a PAC watchdog: http://www.commoncause.org/
A directory of Federal PACs can be found at: http://www.pacfinder.com/afp2000/
PAC political campaign donations are listed at: http://www.opensecrets.org/pacs/

💻7 The Democracy network run by the League of Women Voters provides election information: http://www.dnet.org/

❖ ❖ ❖ ❖

💻8 On the gender gap in voting: http://www.feminist.org/research/report/84_seven.html
http://www.rci.rutgers.edu/~cawp/

💻9 Excerpts from C. Wright Mills' *The Power Elite*: http://www.thirdworldtraveler.com/Book_Excerpts/PowerElite.html

💻10 United States military websites:
The Department of Defense: http://www.defenselink.mil/
Home pages of the American Military Forces:
The Army: http://www.army.mil/
The Air Force: http://www.usafa.af.mil/
The Navy: http://www.navy.mil/
The Marines: http://www.usmc.mil/
The Coast Guard: http://www.cga.edu/
Military Families:
resources: http://www.nmfa.org/
research: http://mfi.marywood.edu/

💻11 Racial/ethnic groups and the military:
http://www.redstone.army.mil/history/integrate/CHRON1.html
http://www.coax.net/people/lwf/aa_mh.htm
http://www.mosaicweb.com/afric_military.htm
http://www.africana.com/tt_235.htm
http://www.americanpatrol.com/DUALCITIZENSHIP/armygedcaldera011499.html

💻12 Women in the military: http://www.au.af.mil/au/aul/bibs/women/womtoc.htm
http://www.gendergap.com/military.htm
http://www.minervacenter.com/

💻13 Military families: resources: http://www.nmfa.org/
research: http://mfi.marywood.edu/

💻14 Gays in the military: http://www.sldn.org/scripts/sldn.ixe?page=article_0003
http://members.aol.com/co501boy/BGL.htm
http://www.california.com/~rathbone/links001.htm

💻15 Sexual harassment in the military: http://www.au.af.mil/au/aul/bibs/sex/haras.htm

💻16 The Military Industrial Complex: A Report, at: http://www.foreignpolicy-infocus.org/papers/micr/

Glossary

All-Volunteer Force (AVF) Military service composed of people who enter as a full-time career.
Authority Socially legitimated power.

Censorship A government's selective withholding of unfavorable information from the public.

Charismatic Authority Power based on some extraordinary quality of the leader or some stirring ideal that attracts a wide and loyal following.

"Chilling" Government tactics designed to limit dissent.

Citizen Soldier A civilian who can be called upon to join the armed forces only when necessary and who will return to civilian life as soon as possible.

Civil Liberties Rights protected by the First Amendment—to speak, to publish, to gather together, and to protest.

Coercion The use of force to induce compliance.

Democratic System Government in which the right to oppose leaders is protected by law.

Devolution The shifting of responsibilities from the federal to the state level.

Ethnic Cleansing See Genocide.

Genocide The intentional systematic killing of an entire population.

Globalization Economic trend seen as a threat to the modern nation-state, as large international corporations operate above and outside the laws of any one society.

Influence The ability to impose your will on others.

Iron Law of Oligarchy The tendency for leaders to drift apart from the masses and to be corrupted by power.

Legal-Rational Authority Based on laws that limit the power of office holders, and on an election process allowing citizens to choose their leaders.

Militarism A glorification of war and an emphasis on military ideals and virtues.

The Military-Industrial Complex The combination of a large permanent military establishment and an immense defense industry with its legislative supporters.

Pluralist Model Assumes that there are many different and competing bases of power in the United States, with no one group dominating the other.

Power Elite Model Views decision-making as concentrated in the hands of a few members of the same social class sharing similar values and interests.

Privatization The turning over of previously public or governmental functions to private profit-making businesses.

Propaganda A government's selective release of information favorable to those in power.

Totalitarian Describes a political system in which the government tries to control all aspects of social life and personal behavior.

Traditional Authority Power based on custom and the force of habit. ✦

Multiple Choices:
Educational Systems

❖ ❖ ❖ ❖   Which of the following best describes the American system of public education?

(please use a #2 black lead pencil)

    (a) The best in the world in terms of openness.

    (b) The worst in the industrial world in terms of test scores.

    (c) A dangerous place for children's imaginations.

    (d) In need of daily prayer and posting of the Ten Commandments.

Answer: Any of the above, depending on who is talking. And many people are talking about education in the United States today, mostly about what they perceive as its failures. Most commentators, however, speak without much knowledge of the sociology of education. This chapter should give you a strong head start in understanding how the system actually works, its short-term goals and long-range effects, what can be improved, and what ought not to be touched by politicians. Here are its major themes:

- The functions of public education in America.

- Schools and stratification hierarchies.

- Structure of the American educational system.

- Quality and equality.

- Vouchers and vendors.

- Higher education.

Public Education: Ideals and Realities

The United States has the most extensive system of public education in the world. 🖥 1 That is, a higher proportion of young people attend school for more years than in any other society. **Public education** refers to tax-supported schools that are open to all but the most disabled children in a given district. From its beginning in the nineteenth century, public education in America has been a local responsibility; that means that funds are raised in each district and the schools are supervised by an elected school board. It also means that schools in the 16,000 separate districts will differ widely in what is taught, how, and by whom—which is why state education departments have recently tried to impose general standards on the districts. Federal attempts to set educational policy have been fiercely resisted by state and local authorities, although they gratefully accept funding for special needs.

Ideally, the public system was seen as the great unifier of the nation, the one place in which children from all walks of life and backgrounds could meet one another, be exposed to the same vision of America, and could be given an equal opportunity to succeed. The urban school, especially, was envisioned as a great "melting pot" (see chapter 6), where children of immigrants (and the parents themselves through night school) could learn English and become Americanized.

As the pace of industrialization picked up, so did the need for skilled workers, and the years of mandatory (demanded by law) schooling were extended. In addition, getting children out of the labor force, both for human-itarian reasons and to open up jobs for adults, meant that an alternative activity was needed to occupy the children's time and energies. Today, with the shift from manufacturing to service industries, additional emphasis is being placed on basic skills such as the old three R's, plus computer literacy.

For all these reasons, then, the public school system has expanded in terms of the numbers of students and years needed to educate them. The schools have also increased the range of activities that take place under their supervision, including sports, preschool, driver training, health and sex education, parenting classes, and drug avoidance programs. As a consequence, schools are frequently blamed for failing to deal with both educational needs and the problems that students bring with them into the classroom.

Schools teach more than pure academics and the activities just cited. Long after you have forgotten who fought in the War of 1812, you probably remember the most important lessons, the **hidden curriculum**, of the early years of schooling, such as obedience to authority, patriotism, the necessity of competition, who really runs the school, the importance of being male, and the superiority of whiteness and white-collar work (Dreeben 1968). "Fitting in" is the most important activity because being different might make you a target for teasing and physical abuse. You probably also learned that teachers have their own jobs to protect. Above all, you found out whether or not you had the "right stuff" to succeed in the occupational system.

Schools and Stratification

The Functional View

Ideally, also, the public schools were to be the great levelers—an even playing field offering equal opportunity to all students. If the school is an impersonal and impartial testing ground, then those who do best must be especially talented. From this perspective, school grades measure innate abilities, and the ultimate ranking of students represents a hierarchy of the most worthy, or a **meritocracy**, a viewpoint strongly supported by those who have been most successful. As for the less talented, the school system will help them find their "natural" place, which meritocrats claim is much kinder than

Schools function to prepare children for adult roles in the community, the workplace, and as citizens, whether in India or the United States.

letting them operate under the illusion that they are better than they really are.

The Conflict Perspective

But suppose the tests measure developed (learned) rather than innate abilities and that scores are strongly affected by your teacher's skills, the resources provided by your parents, the influence of friends, and characteristics of your neighborhood? The conflict perspective emphasizes the struggle for scarce resources and the ability of the more powerful to dictate the terms of the competition. In this view, the schools, as gatekeepers to the occupational system, are not neutral at all but are actively engaged in sorting students into winners and losers at an early age (Gittell 1998).

Researchers in this tradition point out that a student's race, sex, and social class have a strong effect on teachers' perceptions (Ferguson 1998). In most schools, the assignment of children to ability groups (*tracking*) tends to reflect the distribution of students in terms of race and parents' social status, and once children are placed in a track, the quality of education varies accordingly. In other words, the process is far from impartial.

Social Class Reproduction Through Schooling

Thus, whether because they are truly superior or simply blessed with resources, children from the middle and upper social strata score much higher than other students on standardized tests, and they stay in school longer regardless of test scores. This is so for a number of reasons, one of which may be innate ability, but it is difficult to isolate this from all the other effects of social class, beginning with health status at birth and continuing throughout life.

In part, just having more money helps. Preschool programs and tutors can be purchased. The local schools in middle-class neighborhoods are well-funded and filled with many other achievement-oriented students. Families can afford to have children remain out of the labor force past high school graduation, while college costs can be covered for all their offspring. But money is not everything; there are many other advantages to growing up middle class as set out in the following paragraphs.

Cultural capital. Cultural capital refers to lifestyle variables. College-educated, white-collar parents transmit a way of thinking, talking, and behaving that allows their children to feel comfortable in educational settings and in the wider world as defined by dominant elites (Bourdieu 1984; DiMaggio 1982). Familiarity with classics of literature, music, and painting go a long way to impressing teachers. In fact, children with cultural capital are so attractive that some are singled out as particularly "gifted," a category found almost exclusively in upper-income school districts (Margolin 1993).

Social capital. Another type of resource is social capital, a student's networks of supportive relationships and social contacts (Schneider and Coleman 1993). At the individual level, being able to call on people who are in a position to help you is an enormous advantage. Social capital is also a characteristic of social structures, of neighborhoods and schools—for example, where the parents of students are friends of one another and reinforce achievement norms (Sampson et al. 1999; Morgan and Sorensen 1999). Parental involvement in school activities is another resource that appears to benefit upper-status students to a greater extent than their lower-status peers (McNeal 1999). 📃2

Achievement expectations. As noted in chapter 3, the use of psychological rather than physical punishments in middle-class homes leads to internalized guilt and high achievement motivation in the children.

Control over their environment. Middle-class parents are in a position to reward their children for **deferred gratification**, putting off immediate pleasures for the sake of getting good grades. Children know whether their parents can make deferred gratification pay off, and working-class youth are well aware of their parents' relative powerlessness in the world outside the home. Middle-class parents can also make things happen at school (Lareau 1989). The parents are usually status superiors to the school administrators, and when they demand that their child be put in a higher track, chances are that the child is transferred. In contrast, school principals, who are typically recently upwardly mobile themselves, can assume a superior position in dealing with working-class parents, whose children then stay in the assigned track (Useem 1992).

Family size. Although there is continuing debate over the strength and cause of the relationship, it appears that the fewer and more widely spaced the children in a family the higher a child's academic achievement (Guo and VanWey 1999; Downey et al. 1999). Also, in general, the higher the family income, the fewer children to educate.

Household composition. It helps to have two adults in the household. They can provide income security, as well as supervision and help with homework (McLanahan and Sandefur 1994). Single parents are under enormous time and money pressures. In addition, teachers may have differing expectations of children from one- or two-parent homes. For these and other reasons, children in single-parent households tend to have more academic and behavioral problems in school than do children from two-parent households. But the difference is not as great as commonly assumed, once the mother's own education and involvement in her children's schooling are taken into account (Heiss 1996; Phillips et al. 1998).

Neighborhood effects. The unique viewpoint of sociology, remember, is to see people in their social *context*. One of these contexts is location in stratification systems. Another context is geographic location. It does matter where you live and who else lives in the neighborhood. Independent of other influences, the income level of your neighbors has a direct effect on your test scores and the likelihood of staying in school (Brooks-Gunn et al. 1997). White children are more likely than black or Hispanic youths to live in well-to-do neighborhoods.

For all these reasons, then, middle- and upper-class youths have a better chance of success in school, regardless of their innate abilities. The longer that you stay in school, the higher will be your eventual income. The higher your lifetime income, the better your own children will do in school. The relationship between years of schooling and income—which is both cause and effect—is shown in Table 11.1. As you see, women, blacks, and Latinos do not receive the same income returns from education as do men and whites. 📃3

❖ ❖ ❖ ❖

Table 11.1 Earnings by Highest Degree Earned, by Race and Sex, in 1998 Dollars						
	Black		White		Hispanic	
	Female	Male	Female	Male	Female	Male
Not HS Graduate	10,607	15,423	10,700	20,071	10,503	17,447
HS Graduate	15,789	22,440	17,166	29,298	15,747	22,253
Some College	18,346	26,743	18,083	32,294	16,258	24,807
Associate's Degree	23,416	29,099	24,059	37,362	21,705	29,627
BA Degree	29,091	35,792	30,041	51,678	29,173	37,963
Master's	37,425	46,729	38,426	65,421	35,790	54,790
Professional	*a*	*a*	63,450	110,977	*a*	*a*
Doctorate	*a*	*a*	54,587	89,110	*a*	*a*

a = Base figure too small for statistical accuracy.

Source: *Statistical Abstract, 1999,* p. 170.

Structural Features of the American Education System

Local Control of Primary and Secondary Schools

The American education system differs from that of other modern societies in several ways. First, as already noted, primary (grammar school) and secondary (high school) education is a local responsibility. The federal Constitution says nothing about education, so it was left largely to the fifty states to set guidelines. By the 1970s, however, some federal legislation was required to ensure equal access to educational opportunity for minority, female, and, disabled children in the school district. Most state constitutions now contain a section guaranteeing a "thorough and efficient" (the New Jersey wording) education to all children in the state, with consequences discussed in the last section of this chapter.

Inclusiveness

American public education continues through high school graduation. In many other countries, examinations are used to determine which children can go on to a college-preparatory high school and which are directed to vocational training. In this sense, the American system is far more open and democratic—*inclusive* rather than exclusive—providing an extended avenue of upward mobility for all youth.

Where the United States lags behind many other industrial societies, however, is in the provision of early childhood education through publicly funded preschool programs. It is up to the state or the local district to offer prekindergarten, although it is of great importance to working mothers and to children whose home environment may be less stimulating than needed for optimal cognitive growth. Unfortunately, the federally funded **Head Start** program for disadvantaged preschoolers has no basic curriculum or standards for improving cognitive skills (Farkas 2000). As originally conceived,

Head Start was to include health exams and hot meals, but these are tempting targets for cost-cutters, so the program is chronically underfunded and poorly staffed, reaching only a fraction of eligible children and for only part of one year. As a result, the children are soon overwhelmed by all the other effects of poverty, which wipe out the preschool gains (Entwisle, Alexander, and Olsen 1994). This failure to provide early education is most unfortunate, since a carefully designed, concentrated program to improve cognitive skills of preschoolers will do more than any other policy initiative to reduce class and race inequality in the long run (Jencks and Phillips 1998; Farkas 2000).

Postsecondary Choices

The number and variety of choices of where to go after high school is far greater in the United States than in any other country. American colleges and universities are discussed later in this chapter, but there is something after high school for almost everyone: apprenticeship programs, vocational schools, adult education classes, and distance learning or correspondence courses. Post-secondary education is paid for by the students, but every state has a number of low-cost colleges and universities, so a larger proportion of American young people are enrolled than in other modern nation.

As a consequence, Americans are among the most schooled (in terms of years in the classroom) in the world, with about 85 percent graduating from high school, and over 25 percent receiving college degrees. The proportion of women in higher education beats all other countries. Unfortunately, years of schooling do not necessarily translate into high test scores, but when comparing American youngsters with their European counterparts, you have to keep in mind that our student body can include everyone in the mandated age group, while the European systems are far more exclusive, especially after tenth grade, when testing determines which youngsters are channeled into vocational training rather than the college preparation curriculum.

Public and Private Schools

As in many other societies, private schools operate as an alternative to the public system. While all parents pay taxes that fund the public schools, since it is in the interests of all citizens that children be educated, parents can also, if they choose, pay for a private school. In 2000, slightly over 11 percent of primary and secondary students attended private schools, over 75 percent of which are church-related, or **parochial** (the word means "of the parish").

Parochial schools. The most extensive parochial school system in the United States is operated by the Catholic Church, with about 3 million students in over 8,000 primary and secondary schools. This is a much-reduced system from its peak in the 1950s, before Catholic families left their city parishes and scattered into the suburbs and before the number of nuns and brothers in teaching orders declined sharply. The number of Catholic schools and students continues to shrink as expenses mount, due to the costs of busing students and of paying competitive wages to lay teachers.

The fastest-growing parochial systems today are those operated by Orthodox Jews and by conservative Protestant churches. The Orthodox Jews live close together, within walking distance of the synagogue, have large fami-

❖ ❖ ❖ ❖

lies, and, as a matter of their faith, must bring up their children in a religiously sanctioned manner. The conservative Protestants today are like the Catholics earlier in the century who turned to parochial schools as a way of protecting their children from the corrupting influence of nonbelievers. Parents who send their children to parochial school—Catholic, Protestant, Jewish, or Muslim—are also doing more than preserving tradition or insulating their children from exposure to competing values; they are limiting their children's friendship choices and, ultimately, the people whom they are likely to date or marry.

One of the fastest growing parochial systems today are those operated by Orthodox Jews. Here, a student choir performs.

Preparatory schools. With the exception of a few hundred schools for children with special needs, "prep" schools are places where the daughters and sons of the upper strata are groomed for success and are taught what they need to enter elite colleges and occupations. At the very top of the hierarchy are the exclusive WASP boarding schools covering grades 9 through 12, typically single-sex, where children of wealth develop cultural and social capital and the confidence that equips them for leadership. The social class system is also literally reproduced when prep school friendship networks define the pool of eligibles for dating and marriage.

There are also private day schools that cover the elementary grades as well as high school. These **independent** schools are less exclusive than in the past, typically coed, and with increasing numbers of scholarship students from minority and working-class families. Even so, the link between family income and attending private school remains quite high. For example, less than 3 percent of children from low-income families are in private school, mostly parochial, in contrast to 12 percent of children from higher-income households (National Center for Educational Statistics 1999).

There are now a number of private **pre-kindergartens** that are as difficult to get into as the Harvard Medical School. Private nursery schools stressing cognitive development and social skills are the first stepping-stone in an elite educational career. In New York City in 1999, tuition in one high-quality pre-kindergarten ran about $20,000, but do not rush to sign up your daughter or son; the waiting lists are already full. In fact, there is a waiting list just to get a tour of the school and an interview. Yes, the interview is for the three-year old as well as the parents (Kelley 1999).

Questions of Quality and Equity ❖ ❖ ❖ ❖

Private Versus Public

Do private schools do a better job of educating children than public schools? It depends on which private and which public schools you are comparing. Public schools in wealthier suburban districts are probably comparable to most preparatory or independent schools in terms of student performance and acceptance to top-ranked colleges, while urban parochial students perform no better than most public school youngsters. A recent survey of test scores among New York State fourth graders found little difference between private and public schools outside of the larger cities (Hartocollis 1999). Yet as long as people believe that public schools are inferior, private schools will attract the more motivated parents and their children, thus boosting the schools' performance ratings.

It is impossible, however, to separate out the academic aspects of private education from all the other meanings attached to attending a preparatory or independent school—such as wealth, prestige, and social power. The hidden advantages of parochial schooling include a sense of being special in God's eye, and close contacts between parents and teachers and among the parents—a form of social capital (Bryk et al. 1993). In both types of private school, classes are small, everyone is on the college track, and parents have already shown an interest in their child's performance. Most importantly, private schools can pick and choose who enters and who stays. Low performers and troublemakers need not apply, at least not without a hefty endowment contribution from parents. The public school, on the other hand, must take and keep all but the most disabled or uncontrollable.

Yet, despite all their advantages, private school students do not do notably better on standardized tests than their peers in suburban school districts. Still, most Americans appear to believe that when given a choice, parents would flock to the private alternatives. In reality, private school enrollments have risen only slightly in the past two decades, while the numbers in public schools continue to increase by 15 percent or more (U.S. Department of Education 2000). For every upwardly mobile urban professional family that has chosen to send its children to private schools, an even larger number have solved their schooling problem by moving to suburbs with high-ranking public systems (Rothstein 2000).

Nonetheless, most Americans do have a sense that the public schools are not doing a good job. In a recent Gallup Poll, for example, over 60 percent of respondents expressed dissatisfaction with public schools, yet when asked about the quality of education being received by their own chil-

Independent schools are less exclusive than in the past, usually coed, and with increasing numbers of scholarship students from minority and working-class families.

dren, almost 80 percent report being satisfied (Gallup 2000). Sizeable majorities gave their local schools an "A" or "B," and most would continue to send their sons and daughters to their neighborhood school even if the government paid for a private alternative (Rose and Gallup 1999). As seen in the presidential election campaign of 2000, much of the discontent with public schooling and support for vouchers comes from conservative critics ideologically opposed to government services in general and teachers' unions in particular. In this, they are often supported by parents in low-performing urban districts.

When a school system does fail to educate its students, it is difficult to divide responsibility among the various elements—students who are not interested in learning, overburdened parents, how the school is organized, ineffective administrators, or poorly prepared teachers—but many schools (especially in cash-starved urban areas with large minority populations and also in some suburbs) are indeed failing their students.

Suburban Schools

All the factors that give an advantage to middle-class students—concerned parents, adequate funding, neighborhood supports, high achievement expectations—also benefit suburban school systems, at least in the lower grades. High schools, however, draw from a larger geographic area and therefore contain students from a variety of backgrounds. Although most students graduate on time and go on to postsecondary education, the suburban high school has been described as a place where boredom rules and the student body is divided into subcultures of nerds, jocks, skins, trendies, and headbangers. This splitting up probably helps administrators maintain order, at least until the fighting and teasing get out of hand. Apparently, one of the conditions driving two boys at Columbine High School in Colorado in 1999 to shoot their classmates was their feeling of being disrespected by the dominant jock in-group (Applebome 1999).

Nonetheless, suburban schools typically have a core of motivated students with the cultural, social, and financial capital often lacking in today's inner-city schools.

Urban Schools

Unlike in the past, city schools today must take in more children of the poor and keep them longer and send them into a disappearing labor market. As examined in chapter 15, urban school districts cannot raise much money through local property taxes, nor can they count on suburban legislators to provide state funding. Federal assistance has primarily been used in the 1990s to reduce local and state contributions, leaving the needy districts no better off (Farkas 2000). The result is that buildings continue to deteriorate; experienced teachers leave for better pay and working conditions in the suburbs; neighborhoods are terrorized by unemployed youth; and powerless parents have difficulty convincing their children that it is worth their while to stay in school. These problems are magnified when the atmosphere within the school breeds failure.

Despite a shortage of cultural and social capital, inner-city youngsters can nevertheless do very well indeed when there is a climate of expectation that no one will be allowed to fail; when the school itself and the classes are small; and where discipline is fair—the very things that make for success in suburban and private schools (Bryk 1999). Unfortunately, most urban schools are overcrowded and understaffed. Of special importance is convincing the students that hard work in school will pay off in a decent job, which is extremely difficult when entry-level livable-wage jobs have disappeared.

Knowing how limited their chances are, many youngsters will take the easier route to survival and peer prestige: drop out and live on the streets. Drop-out rates in the inner city are extremely high: between one-third and one-half of high school students either leave or are pushed out. This clears out the troublemakers and improves the environment for the remaining students, but the ones that need most help are out in the cold.

Box 11.1

College Dreams

In 1981, the principal of an inner-city school in New York City invited one of the school's most successful graduates, a wealthy industrialist named Eugene Lang, to come and talk to the sixth grade class. When Lang had attended the school, 50 years earlier, the neighborhood was home to white ethnic immigrants. The sixth grade this day, however, was African American and Latino, survivors of extreme poverty. Lang threw out his prepared remarks and made a promise to the children: If you stay to graduate from high school, I'll see to it that you have the counseling and financial help to attend college.

Ten years later, in a school with a 75 percent dropout rate, almost three-fourths of Lang's students had completed high school and half were in college. Similar programs have been financed by other wealthy individuals and businesses, also with high success rates. The bottom line: Once assured of a payoff, children from all kinds of backgrounds will stay in school and do well. It is the *structure of opportunity* that determines behavior.

The major objection to such programs is that some children are favored over others as a matter of luck or whim. Your chances of attending college should not depend on what side of the bed some wealthy person got up on that morning. This type of opportunity should be there for all students, but that would involve higher taxes and diverting resources from other districts.

Equity

Equity, remember, means "fairness." And the question of equity in relation to the public schools is one of fairness in financing. Because public schools are financed by local property taxes, districts differ in how much they can raise for each pupil. Districts with a thriving business sector and expensive homes can raise a lot of tax dollars, in contrast to an inner-city district with few taxable buildings. If the state constitution guarantees every child a thorough education, and it can be shown that $14,000 per student buys a more thorough education than $1,600, then the property tax is not only unfair, it is unconstitutional at the state level. By 1996, a dozen states were under court orders to come up with a more equitable school funding mechanism (Reed 1997), with new lawsuits filed yearly. Since equalizing funding

❖ ❖ ❖ ❖   today will do little to redress the gaps that have built up over decades, the most recent challenges focus on equalizing programs such as Advanced Placement courses and on providing resources such as up-to-date textbooks, science laboratories, and even enough classrooms (Purdum 2000).

Few states, however, have obeyed the courts in findings ways to equalize school funding, and the legal maneuvering drags on and on while children in low-income districts continue to fall further behind. For example, only in 2000 did the New Jersey legislature vote full funding for school building repairs as ordered by the state supreme court two years earlier, in accordance with a 1985 decision in a suit originally filed in 1973—a 27-year struggle—and then not before trying to reduce the number of school districts covered by the decree (Carter 2000).

The most obvious solution to reliance on the local property tax is a state-wide income tax, but this, as noted several times, is politically impossible in today's climate. In addition, as an alternative to improving all schools in a district, many lawmakers have embraced the concepts of *vouchers* and *charter schools*, which would actually siphon resources from the district as a whole.

Vouchers. Politicians in a majority of states are currently debating the use of **vouchers** as a no-cost solution to the perception of failing schools. The voucher is like a gift certificate that a parent can use to pay for private schooling. It is worth a certain amount of money to be paid for out of the public school budget. Some cities and states are currently experimenting with various versions, some of which include parochial schools. Several state courts have ruled these plans unconstitutional, while other jurisdictions have been given the green light.

Supporters emphasize the aspect of "choice," allowing parents to use their tax monies as they choose in order to find the best possible education for their children. They also claim that the competition should spur the public schools to do a better job and that no children should be forced to attend a school where they are in danger of bodily harm and mental stagnation. It is further argued that the availability of voucher money will encourage the creation of small specialized schools, enlarging the range of parental options.

The counterarguments are that vouchers will take money away from the larger schools, that they will also skim off the better students whose parents are savvy enough to take advantage of the program, that public money for parochial education violates the doctrine of separation of church and state, and that the program does nothing to help all students in the district, but rather increases inequality and reduces diversity in each school.

This is one of those "hot button" issues that you will probably be voting on every time you enter the booth in the foreseeable future. At the moment, however, most voucher programs have targeted students in districts with a high failure rate, with the hope that success there will legitimate the program elsewhere. 💻4

Charter schools. Yet another educational innovation intended to enlarge parental choice and spur competition is the **charter school**. The "charter" in question is a license to run a school, using public school money but accountable to some state agency rather than to the local board of education. Just who gets a charter and what rules are imposed, what is taught, and how the schools are to be evaluated have yet to be fully worked out. Charter schools enjoy support from liberals as well as conservatives, with several having proven very effective in inner-city neighborhoods (Schorr 2000). At the moment, about 1 percent of American students are enrolled in charter schools, each with a unique emphasis—environmentalism, arts and music, various learning techniques, or racial/ethnic themes. 💻5

Home schooling. A third alternative to public education is home schooling. In 2000, about 3 percent of primary and secondary students were being taught at home under supervision of parents. Originally a choice highly favored by religiously conservative families worried about the lack of discipline in public schools, home schooling has recently been favored by parents looking for just the opposite—a more individualistic and less regimented educational experience for their children than offered by public schools (Kilborn 2000). Thus far, home-schooled children are doing very well on standardized tests and are having little difficulty adjusting to college (Nussbaum 2000). 💻6

Does choice make a difference? It is still too soon to evaluate the long-term effects of expanded school choice on the students or on the public system. The evidence to date is mixed. On the one hand, test scores among children in some voucher programs showed improvement, thanks to smaller class size, individualized attention, and high expectations among parents, teachers, and students (Wyatt 2000). On the other hand, ten years after allowing all parents freedom of school choice, the government of New Zealand is rethinking the policy. What happened was that under conditions of full competition, a few elite schools competed for the best students, social class divisions increased, and the native Maori children who were supposed to benefit from the program found themselves increasingly isolated in schools with declining resources (Fiske and Ladd 2000). In the United States, as well, there is evidence that school choice has widened racial divisions.

In the Schools

The sociology of education also covers micro-level phenomena such as what goes on in the classroom. How do teachers treat students? How do students get along with one another? How is student achievement measured? Here, again, social class, gender, and race are all very important. Teachers tend to develop expectations based on ascribed characteristics and, consciously or not, treat the children differently (Ferguson 1998). You probably knew early on just what to wear and how to act in order to please or annoy your teacher.

Gender

Few classroom differences are better documented than those based on gender (Kimmel 2000a; Spade 2001). Teachers continue to make very traditional assumptions about the differing abilities of girls and boys. One of the most powerful lessons in the hidden curriculum is that girls and boys are different and that the boys are superior (Rhode 1997). Although, as noted in chapter 7, there are some scholars who feel that boys are being damaged by the demands of a feminized classroom, most research indicates that boys receive more attention in the classroom—in part because they are noisier—and that teachers tend to take their contributions more seriously than those of girls, even though the girls will outscore the boys, at least through middle school. Then, around ninth grade, there is a rather abrupt turn-around: the girls' grades decline and those of the boys begin to rise. The girls have learned that being popular is more important than being smart. In contrast, the boys realize that they had better pull themselves together and get decent grades if they want to be successful economically.

Despite lingering stereotypes and various levels of sexual harassment, there are signs that girls' high school test scores are improving, although they are still well below those of boys in math and science. For the girls who persist, there is now national recognition and scholarship money available. For example, in 1999, young women won 45 percent of National Merit Scholarships and the year's most prestigious award for a high school science project, both unheard-of accomplishments before the 1990s. 💻 7

In other areas—especially sports and extracurricular activities—girls and young women in public schools have benefited from Title IX of the Education Act Amendments of 1972, which forbids discrimination in school resources on the basis of sex. Although there are probably only a handful of districts in which the resources are actually divided evenly, what the girls get is considerably more than in the past—when they got the playing field after the boys were finished and received a plaque instead of a varsity jacket. Even though many parents still feel that it is more important for their sons than for their daughters to be engaged in competitive sports, especially if it leads to a college scholarship, the past three decades have given many girls a chance to develop the skills and satisfactions of athletic accomplishment. Because sport is also a major arena for the social construction of gender, the girls had the additional burden of overcoming the perception of being too masculine, but increasing numbers have done just that (Dworkin and Messner 1999). Whereas only 4 percent of girls played high school sports in 1971, one-third do so today. While the number of boys participating in high school athletic programs is about the same as in 1972, girls' participation has gone from about 300,000 in 1971 to over 2.6 million in 1998 (*Statistical Abstract of the United States 1999*, 272). 💻 8

Race

Success in sports, however, will do little to change the educational disadvantage of black youth. The consistent and persistent racial gap in test scores and school performance has led some observers to conclude that the causes must be biological and therefore resistant to social intervention (Herrnstein and Murray 1996; Rushton 1999). Yet, the most exhaustive study of test score differences by race states: ". . . despite endless speculation, no one has found genetic evidence indicating that blacks have less innate intellectual ability than whites." (Jencks and Phillips 1998, 2). As you know by now, even if there were such evidence, it would be impossible to disentangle what is built-in from what is influenced by the environment, since each affects the other (Korenman and Winship 2000). It is equally difficult to figure out what might be traceable to race *per se*, assuming that race could be accurately measured, and what comes out of the social construction of whiteness and blackness (see chapter 6). In addition, family disadvantage translates into children being assigned to schools that reinforce the deficiencies that result in lower test scores (Roscigno 2000).

Nonetheless, for whatever set of reasons, the test score gap is real and has real consequences when used by college admissions officers and employers to predict success. Reducing the gap would go a long way toward reducing other forms of racial inequality (Jencks and Phillips 1998). But reducing the gap requires very early intervention—a preschool program designed to develop cognitive skills and to help parents use the kind of techniques that encourage a child to learn. Talking to the child, constructing a stimulating environment, answering questions, and avoiding physical punishments are all as important to predicting school achievement as is whether or not the parent is single (Phillips et al. 1998). Within the school, small classes and trained teachers are essential. In the broader society, it is essential to convince other Americans that the test score gap is not genetic in origin and that all citizens would benefit from reducing racial inequality. Yet, when the tests are seen as impartial measures of intellectual achievement, they support the myth of the school as a meritocratic playing ground while "hiding from view the very uneven practice fields we have" (Ferguson 1998, 318).

Testing—1, 2, 3

At the moment, testing is all the rage across the nation, as part of a general mood of "getting tough" with children and holding teachers "accountable." Although testing has some virtues as a diagnostic tool in telling the schools where students need more help, it also has some grave drawbacks. Not the least of these is that no one is sure what the tests measure beyond memorized factoids. Another major problem is that teachers and schools will concentrate on test preparation rather than on the more difficult tasks of cultivating curiosity, encouraging critical thinking, and developing a love of learning (Kohn 1999); these are the lessons that will last a lifetime, long after the last SAT is taken.

Setting precise standards for all children in a given grade—a "one-size exam fits all" approach—goes against everything we know from developmental psychology, namely, that children, especially at the lower grades, develop different abilities at different times (Gardner 1999). Children are like snowflakes; no two are quite alike. Preparing the entire class for their tests means that teachers cannot treat the children as individuals, which may be a very important aspect of the hidden curriculum: You are no longer a unique person but someone who must meet precise standards every day in every way, and if you should fail, it means you did not try hard enough.

As currently used, the tests discriminate against students unfamiliar with the middle-class world, denying high school diplomas to children who may have never been taught the subjects being tested. Nor is there any evidence that using the tests to determine who gets promoted or held back has a positive effect on the retained students, who are at high risk of dropping out completely (Hauser 1999; Ohanian 1999).

When teachers and administrators are also judged by the students' test results, those in low-performance schools will leave at once for greener pastures, and for those who stay, the temptation to cut corners, even to cheat, will become almost irresistible. In other words, the unintended consequences of testing, especially in urban school districts, may be to further disadvantage the students. 🖥 10

How Do Children Learn?

The focus on tests and a standard curriculum runs against most of the current research on how children learn, which is by following their curiosity and by helping one another (Kohn 1999). The individualistic emphasis in both testing and tracking reinforces and reflects the competitiveness of the society as a whole, which is probably a very useful lesson, even though it increases inequality. But if you wanted to help all students in the class to improve their skills, you could replace tracks with heterogeneous study groups in which the better students serve as peer tutors. Under some circumstances, **cooperative learning** actually helps both fast and slow learners (Oakes 1994). 🖥 11 Another arrangement that benefits both high- and low-performing students is to maintain heterogeneous classrooms, with ability groupings within the classroom (Ferguson 1998). The public school could also follow the lead of private schools and place all students on a college preparatory track, which usually leads to improved grades for "the forgotten half" (Nyberg et al. 1997). The problem with these arrangements is that the parents of high-performing students will leave the school system if they feel that their children are not receiving special inputs (Jencks and Phillips 1998).

Historically, in America, educational policies have fluctuated between the more permissive, child-centered approach and a hierarchical, discipline-oriented mode, depending largely on the general mood of the public. Today, the pendulum has swung sharply toward the "get tough" side. Many schools have returned to the use of corporal punishments. Others have adopted a "zero tolerance" policy toward any violation of rules, expelling pupils who have carried anything remotely resembling a weapon. There are renewed calls for prayers in the schools, and several states have legislated the posting of the Ten Commandments—as a "historical document"—in each classroom, although there are no data to suggest that either prayer or the Commandments inspire better behavior (Johnson 2000a).

The strong political emphasis on testing and a standard curriculum goes against current research on how children learn by following their curiosity and helping one another. Cooperative learning helps all learners.

The Selling of the Schools

Whatever they may not be learning, the children are receiving a full education in the virtues of capitalism (Manning 1999). What could be more tempting to a local board of education than the offer of a corporate gift, even if it means having the firm's logo all over the school? It beats raising property taxes. And does it really matter whether the children get Pepsi or Coke from the vending machine if one of the companies is willing to pay for exclusive rights to sell their product in your school? Why cannot children learn to count by adding and subtracting Tootsie Rolls as well as any other item when the candy company supplies books free? And surely the billboards advertising Speedo products are nicer-looking than the standard yellow on the school bus? It is never too early to establish brand loyalty, especially since children between 4 and 12 now spend about $25 billion per year (*American Demographics* 1998).

In addition, there is Channel One. Over a decade ago, Channel One offered to give public schools all the equipment needed to wire up the school and install television in each classroom in return for the rights to broadcast a daily 12-minute current events program complete with commercials. Today, Channel One can be found in about one-fourth of the nation's schools, with a captive audience of 8 million students in grades six through 12. Among the advertised items are candy bars, acne medication, and the U.S. Army (Hays 1999). The new management of the company is planning to expand its operations in states and districts that have previously opposed commercial TV in the classroom, largely through a massive lobbying effort to convince legislators to change their minds. Stay tuned.

Upward and Onward: Higher Education in America

In 1975, about half of high school graduates went directly on to a two- or four-year college or university. Today, that figure is two out of three. Plus, an increasing number of "nontraditional" (older) students are sitting in college classrooms alongside recent high school graduates. There are a number of cross-cutting trends at work here: (1) By 1999, enrollment of male high school graduates had declined slightly, thanks to a tight labor market providing decent-paying jobs for young men not overly interested in higher education. (2) Older workers and downsized white-collar employees returned to college to update and upgrade their skills. (3) Young women continued to increase their presence on campuses, much to the dismay of trustees fearful that their institution would lose prestige. (4) Employers continued to use educational requirements as a screening device. Overall, going to college, at least for a few years, is now an expected stage in the life of most American youth.💻12

As you might expect, enrollment is directly related to family income and parents' educational level—the higher one is on either of these variables, the more likely one is to attend college and to attend a high-prestige institution.

The Stratification System of Higher Education

You will not be surprised to learn that there is a clear hierarchy of American colleges and universities. One dimension of stratification is public versus private.

Private higher education. As in the lower grades, private includes both religious and secular institutions, with the latter a continuation of the process that began when a child was admitted to that elite nursery school. Private colleges and universities are funded through student tuition, alumni contributions, and the interest on endowment investments. Because the graduates of elite private colleges typically began life with a lot of money and end up earning much, much more, endowment drives bring in hundreds of millions of dollars. This secure financial base allows the schools to offer generous scholarships and grants to attractive applicants. Although graduates of elite universities will earn more than graduates of less selective institutions, they would have been just as successful regardless of which school they attended; that is, the income effect reflects selection bias, with top-ranked schools accepting the students most likely to succeed under any circumstances (Kreuger and Dale 2000).

Public higher education. Each state has a system of publicly funded universities and colleges, most of which began as land-grant colleges in the mid-nineteenth century as a democratic alternative to the elite Eastern schools. Admissions are less selective and tuition is lower than for private schools. Funding is primarily from tax money allocated by the state legislature, alumni gifts, student tuition, and, for a few, television revenues from sports broadcasts. A winning sports team does more than bring TV money, it loosens the pocketbooks of alumni and legislators. For example, the University of Connecticut's basketball teams so delighted state residents that the school's budget was increased. A winning team also increases student applications, up 30 percent for Virginia Tech in 1999 thanks to "Hokie-Mania" for its undefeated football team.

A second dimension of stratification is the distinction between a university and a liberal arts college. Universities can award master's degrees and the doctorate. Colleges confer only the baccalaureate, or bachelor's, degree. This distinction is increasingly blurred as state colleges try to enhance their prestige and attract better students by instituting a few master's programs and calling themselves a university. For ease of writing, however, the authors will use the term "college" to refer to any institution of higher education.

College students today are more diverse in terms of gender, race, ethnicity, and country of origin than in the past. What is the ratio of women to men on your campus? What ethnic and racial groups are represented at your college? What portion of students are 'nontraditional'?

At the top of the hierarchy are a handful of "Ivy League" institutions: private universities (e.g., Harvard, Yale, Princeton, Stanford), followed by elite private colleges (e.g., Dartmouth, Vassar, Amherst), and major research-oriented public universities such as the University of California at Berkeley. Scattered through the middle are second-tier private universities and state universities, followed by state colleges, and at the base of the pyramid, the community colleges. The higher the rank of the institution, the more selective its admissions, the higher its fees, and the fewer women and blacks on the faculty. Thus, the hierarchy of higher education both reflects and reinforces the basic stratification system of the society. 🖥 13

Community colleges. Despite being at the base of the hierarchy of institutions of higher education, the public two-year community colleges may actually be the best academic value in America. Classes are typically small, the price is right, and your chance of being taught by an instructor with a graduate degree is actually greater than at many universities (who use graduate students as teachers). Today, over 40 percent of undergraduates are enrolled at community colleges, with a higher proportion of women (58 percent), nontraditional, and minority students than at other campuses. Almost half of all minority students in the country are at a community college. 🖥 14

The mix between academic and vocational courses will vary with the location of the school. Those in urban areas emphasize skills required by the local job market, while those in the suburbs function as a college-transfer station primarily for their white, middle-class students. Even at the suburban campuses, a majority of students will be enrolled in "career" courses such as office management, business, and technology. Part-time enrollment and evening courses make the community college especially valuable to employees seeking to retrain or to make up for lost opportunities earlier in life.

The great accomplishment of the community colleges is to have kept open the door to higher education for many who would not otherwise have the chance to learn the very same things they teach at Harvard. This they have done, with honors.

The faculty. Faculty are stratified three times over: (1) on the basis of where their school stands in the hierarchy; (2) on their academic rank, ranging from instructor to full professor; and (3) on whether they teach full or part time. Part-timers—or **adjuncts**—are hired to teach one or two courses for a few thousand dollars each. Obviously, hiring four adjuncts to cover the course load of a full-time teacher saves the institution tens of thousands of dollars in salary and benefits. Adjuncts can be hired and fired at will and have no guarantee of academic freedom. Little wonder that today nearly half of all college teaching is done by part-timers, who must be continually traveling from one school to another to earn all of $10,000–15,000 per semester. But if the schools are saving money through the employment of adjuncts, this has not slowed the continued rise in tuition and other student fees.

College costs. As you can see in Table 11.2, college costs vary considerably. Fortunately for applicants from less wealthy families, financial aid is available from the government (primarily low-interest loans) and the colleges (scholarships, grants). In addition, a majority of college students, particularly those who live off campus, supplement their aid package with part-time work. Nonetheless, many families will find themselves priced out of the four-year market, especially if they need the earnings of their adult children. At the other extreme, the top scholastic prospects are in such high demand that they can shop around for the best package, much like professional athletes.

Table 11.2 Average Fixed Charges for Undergraduates, for the Academic Year, 1999–2000 (Includes tuition, fees, and room and board if residential)	
Elite 4-year private	$30,000
Average 4-year private	21,340
State university	8,086
State college	3,670
Community college	1,627

Source: College Board, 1999.

Is it worth it? You bet. As you saw in Table 11.1, the longer you stay in college, the higher your earnings. But income should be only one consideration and maybe not the most important. Being an educated person is associated with feelings of control and competence, with cognitive complexity and problem-solving abilities, with good health and a long life, and with overall life satisfaction (Reynolds and Ross 1998).

Getting In

With the exception of a few hundred highly selective schools, most of the nation's 3,700 institutions of higher education are open to anyone with ambition, a high school diploma, and enough money. And even among the top-ranked colleges, a diverse student body is an important goal. In addition to SATs and high school transcripts, admissions officers are looking for geographic distribution, artists as well as athletes, students from varied backgrounds with unusual skills (Kane 1998). Your best bet for getting into an Ivy League school, however, is to be the daughter or son of a graduate—called "legacies"—with the expectation that parents will be generous supporters of the endowment fund (Karen 1991). Without such a "legacy," an applicant would be wise to minimize the competition by moving to Utah, learning to play a Renaissance instrument, taking up an obscure sport, working on the high school paper, running for school office, and spending Sundays at a soup kitchen. All this is a far cry from only a generation ago when there were quotas for Jews and Catholics at the elite schools, blacks were few and far between, and women were considered too frail.

Between 1970 and 1995, the link between family income and attending a private college had weakened, but since 1995, Congress has steadily cut back on student loan programs and other forms of federal assistance. At the same time, middle-class incomes have remained somewhat stagnant, resulting in "middle-income melt," whereby students who might have attended a private college enroll in the public university, and others take their first two years at a community college (Miller 1999).

College admissions policies have recently become embroiled in the politics of race and gender, as seen in the issues of open admissions and affirmative action.

Open admissions. If the historic mission of public colleges is to provide an educational opportunity for the masses, then admission should be open to anyone who meets minimal academic qualifications regardless of income.

Historic missions, however, tend to fade over time. In the 1970s, in its heyday as the most admired and comprehensive state system, the University of California offered an appropriate place in one of its four- or two-year schools to any high school graduate. Then came a taxpayer revolt, with a huge loss of revenue and subsequent cuts in the budget for higher education, and an effective end to educational aspirations for many impoverished youth. Only recently, thanks to added revenues from the economic boom, have state systems, including California, replaced some of the lost funding. But no state system since has come any closer to realizing the ideal of tuition-free, universal educational opportunity.

Open admissions also became highly politicized in the 1990s, with the City University of New York (CUNY) as the poster child for opponents of the policy. Historically, CUNY had been the path of upward mobility for ambitious children of primarily European immigrants, offering a low-cost top-grade education to selected high school graduates. In 1970, an open admissions policy opened the door much wider, and large numbers of the new urban minorities, mainly black and Latino, walked through. Many had not been adequately prepared, resulting in a high dropout rate; many who stayed needed costly remedial courses. Large numbers also had to hold down a job in order to pay for tuition and books, so it took more than four years to graduate. In a situation that required additional resources to help these students, the city did the reverse and cut the CUNY budget, which meant that faculty and courses were also cut, making it harder to get the courses needed to graduate. Today, the open policy has been replaced by tighter standards for admissions to the four-year colleges, cuts in remedial programs, and greater control over the community colleges. 💻 15

Affirmative action. There are only a limited number of ways the student body can be made racially diverse if the number of white applicants with high test scores will always be larger than that of high-scoring blacks and Latinos. You can set aside a certain number of seats to be awarded as a matter of discretion—but "quotas" are both bad politics and bad policy. You can have two sets of standards, but be prepared for lawsuits. You can seek out especially good prospects and encourage them to apply, which is what **affirmative action** is all about—taking positive steps to expand the pool of applicants.

Because affirmative action has been confused with quotas and double standards, it, too, has fallen under heavy political and legal attack, on grounds of reverse discrimination against better-qualified white applicants. The result is that some public college systems have been forced by the courts or voter referendums to end race-sensitive admission policies. The immediate effect was a dramatic drop in the number of black and Latino applications. So dramatic was the decline that states such as Texas and Florida quickly moved to Plan B: a statewide policy of automatic admission for applicants from the top 10 or 20 percent of each high school graduating class. Ironically, the more segregated the high school, the better the chance of a minority applicant, so their presence on campus is now close to what it was before the end of affirmative action. In the meantime, the more academically gifted black and Hispanic students in Texas and California have been heavily recruited by out-of-state schools.

Asian-American students have benefited greatly from the opening up of higher education. Although they constitute only 4 percent of the American population, Asian Americans currently comprise about 20 percent of students at elite universities where many are enrolled in technology and science programs. The academic success of Asian-American students can be traced to a combination of high parental expectations and socioeconomic factors such as high median household income and small families (Goyette and Xie 1999).

Because private universities have greater leeway in their admissions policies than do public institutions, they have been able to admit students from racial or ethnic minorities whose test scores have been lower than those of white applicants. One recent study of graduates of elite private and public universities found that although such special-admissions students received slightly lower grades and graduated at a lower rate than other students, they achieved notable successes after graduation (Bowen and Bok 1998). They earned advanced degrees at the same rate as their white classmates, became more active in their communities, and realized considerable upward mobility. The authors conclude that had these students been denied admission solely on the basis of test scores, both the schools and the society would have lost something of great value.

As a result of all these trends in the wider society and in the college admissions office, today's student body is much more diverse than ever in terms of sex, race, age, ethnicity, social class, and foreign birth. With or without affirmative action, the proportion of minority students will continue to rise, as seen in Figure 11.1.🖳16

Going Into Business

As schools continue to add to their course offerings, upgrade and expand their physical plant, and increase their scholarship aid packages, many are feeling a financial pinch. Not surprisingly, as federal and state funding drops, the schools are forced to look elsewhere. Enter the business community, selling everything from exclusive rights to the soda machine to the uniforms with

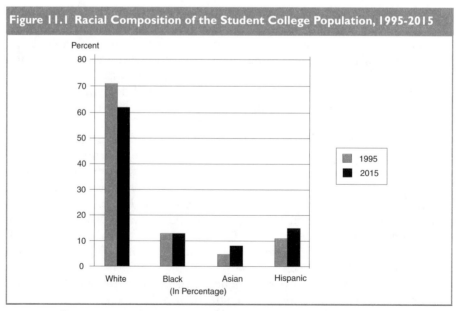

Figure 11.1 Racial Composition of the Student College Population, 1995-2015

Source: Education Testing Service, 2000.

a swoosh. But the links between the corporate world and academe go even deeper.

Box 11.2

Goodbye, Mr. Chips; Hello, Mr. Chip

Who owns a professor's lecture notes? The school that has hired her? Or are they her intellectual property? This was not a very important question when authors of textbooks sold a few thousand copies, but suppose you could make your lectures available to millions of people on the Internet and charge everyone who logs on? At a minimum of $5.00 a shot, there is a great deal of money involved, and the employing institution is increasingly likely to ask for a share.

This is only one of the major issues created by the dramatic growth of **distance learning** programs, once confined to "Sunrise Semesters" via television and remote hook-ups from school to home. Today, however, the net can link a potential student body of millions with thousands of faculty. A college education is within the reach of a mouse for any American adult. Why sit in a cold and ugly classroom when you can learn at home at a fraction of the cost? By 2002, it is estimated that 80 percent of American colleges and universities will be on-line (Steinberg and Wyatt 2000).

Colleges and universities, of course, offer more than lectures. There is the social life, the clubs, concerts, athletic events, and the sheer pleasure of being away from home. Going to a residential school will probably remain an important *rite of passage* for middle-class young adults, but for students who are older, less affluent, employed, and/or raising a family, distance learning is a lifeline to knowledge. To the degree that higher education determines social class location, distance learning can provide a new avenue of upward mobility for excluded subgroups. 🖳17

Football and basketball are not the only sources of outside revenue for institutions of higher education. There are faculty grants for research from government agencies and foundations, but the big money-makers for major research universities are contracts for research from private corporations, especially in pharmaceuticals (see chapter 14), and high-tech engineering and science projects.

This relationship—several billion dollars worth in 1999—raises several ethical questions. Are private profit-making companies taking advantage of research facilities in public institutions built by taxpayers? If the corporation controls the data, what does this mean in terms of the university's mission of open inquiry? As a researcher, you may be torn between loyalty to the company that is paying you, on the one hand, and your responsibility as a scientist to share your data with peers, on the other hand. These are all dilemmas that have emerged in recent years as the level of university-based research rises and the schools enter into commercial arrangements with private corporations (Aronowitz 2000). If research is fudged or delayed or kept secret, the entire ethical base of science is threatened, but there is a lot of money at stake, some of which can make the researchers instant millionaires through patents on commercial processes and some of which can keep the school well in the black.

Another ethical dilemma arises when a wealthy person offers a university millions of dollars to institute a specific program—in Western Civilization, for example, or Hispanic Studies—with professors of the donor's choice. These are decisions that are typically the responsibility of the faculty and that are made on strictly academic grounds. Some schools have taken the money

❖ ❖ ❖ ❖   and have done as the donor asked; others have refused and seen the money go elsewhere. Other donations come with nonacademic strings, such as naming a building or building a new stadium. One college in New Jersey even changed its name to comply with the request of a donor offering a large gift.

Is there nothing left of the ideal of education as the pursuit of pure knowledge? Is it all politics and money? It would certainly appear that from preschool to postgraduate, nonacademic considerations dominate our educational system. The trick for you will be to find and cherish those nuggets of truth and beauty hidden in the pursuit of higher education. The life of the mind is a glorious adventure, worth pursuing for its own sake. Enjoy!

Conclusion

This chapter has surveyed several crucial aspects of the contemporary educational scene. Important topics include the continuing debate over whether the system is a true meritocracy or a means of reproducing the social class hierarchy; the relative advantages of private and public schools; and the potential effects of enlarging educational choice through vouchers and charter schools. Another long-term issue involves the tension between quality and equality in educational opportunities and outcomes. Many of these same concerns are found at the level of higher education, itself a highly stratified system of schools and faculties. And at all levels, from preschool to postgraduate, increasing commercialism raises fundamental questions about the integrity of the educational system.

Surfing the Sociological Internet

1   General education informational sites:
Department of Education: http://www.ed.gov/
For research and statistics on education in America: http://www.ed.gov/stats.html
Data from the Census: http://www.census.gov/population/www/socdemo/education.html
Educational Resources Center: http://www.accesseric.org/
The American Educational Research Association: http://www.aera.net/
National Education Association: http://www.nea.org/
The United States Student Association: http://www.essential.org/ussa/ussa.html
To follow educational policy in the news nationally and locally: http://www.edweek.org/

2   National Coalition for Parental Involvement in Education: http://www.ncpie.org/

3   Center for Educational Reform: http://edreform.com/
The National Education Goals Panel (NEGP) is a unique bipartisan and intergovernmental body of federal and state officials created in July 1990 to assess and report state and national progress

toward achieving the National Education Goals. For their
website go to: http://www.negp.gov/

❖ ❖ ❖ ❖

💻 4 School vouchers—for and against: http://www.infidels.org/library/modern/church-state/vouchers.html
http://www.rethinkingschools.org/Links/vouclink.htm

💻 5 On charter schools: http://eric-web.tc.columbia.edu/digests/dig119.html

💻 6 On home schooling: http://www.caro.net/~joespa/ and http://www.n-h-a.org/

💻 7 Gender and education: http://www.aauw.org/2000/research.html

💻 8 Gender equity in sports and Title IX: http://bailiwick.lib.uiowa.edu/ge/

💻 9 Race and education:
For reports on minorities and educational experiences and issues see: http://resi.tamu.edu/publications.html
On blacks in higher education: http://www.pbs.org/wgbh/pages/frontline/shows/race/economics/
The dynamics of race in higher education including issues on testing and use of test scores for admissions: http://www.aacc.nche.edu/services/MRC/dynamics_of_race_in_higher_educa.htm

💻 10 Testing: The Educational Testing Service which administers S.A.T.s is located at: http://www.ets.org/

💻 11 On cooperative learning: http://www.clcrc.com/

💻 12 For higher education news, see the Chronicle of Higher Education at:
http://www.chronicle.com/
http://www.acenet.edu/ is the website of the American Council on Education, an advocacy group for higher education.
For information and resources related to higher education, go to ERIC:
http://www.eriche.org/main.html

💻 13 See http://www.usnews.com/usnews/edu/college/corank.htm for a popular ranking of American colleges and universities.

💻 14 For information and resources on community colleges: http://www.mcli.dist.maricopa.edu/cc/ and http://www.aacc.nche.edu/

💻 15 On the open admissions controversy, see:
The Report to the Mayor of New York City, 1999: http://www.ci.nyc.ny.us/html/cuny/html/admissions.html
Study on open admissions and consequences for ending it: http://www.soc.qc.edu/ufs/Lavin.htm

❖ ❖ ❖ ❖

16 For affirmative action myths and facts: http://www.essential.org/ussa/foundati/aamyths.html
Report to the President on Affirmative Action: http://www.whitehouse.gov/WH/EOP/OP/html/aa/aa-index.html

17 For a site promoting distance learning K-12 and in higher education, see: http://www.usdla.org/

Glossary

Affirmative Action Attempts to reduce race and sex discrimination by expanding the pool of eligible students or workers.
Adjuncts Part-time college instructors hired to teach one or two courses for a modest sum, usually with no benefits and no job security.
Charter School A school licensed to use public school money but accountable to some state agency rather than to the local board of education.
Cooperative Learning Students pooling their talents and helping one another.
Cultural Capital Ways of thinking, talking, and behaving that make middle class children comfortable in educational settings.
Deferred Gratification The ability to put off immediate pleasure to pursuit a long-term goal.
Distance Learning Programs that are electronically transmitted via television and remote hook-ups from colleges to homes.
Equity In Education Equity refers to fairness in financing.
Head Start A federally funded program for disadvantaged preschoolers.
Hidden Curriculum Attitudes learned in the early school years, such as ethnocentrism and obedience to authority, that are not part of the official curriculum.
Home Schooling Students taught at home under the supervision of parents.
Independent Schools Private day and boarding schools that include elementary, middle, and high school grades.
Meritocracy A hierarchy in which the most worthy are ranked higher.
Parochial Schools Private schools operated by religious organizations.
Preparatory Schools Privately operated schools designed to prepare upper-strata children for entry into elite colleges.
Public Education Tax-supported schools that are open to all but the most disabled children in a given district.
Social Capital Supportive relationships and social contacts.
Voucher Allows a family to spend a given sum of tax money for private schooling. ✦

Believing and Belonging: Religious Institutions

❖ ❖ ❖ ❖   You probably did not need Sigmund Freud to remind you that to be human is to be anxious—sometimes, very anxious—about almost everything, including your identity, right and wrong, and the meaning of it all. Because humans are not born with the answers to such questions, they spend a lifetime seeking some degree of certainty. The most crucial and universal sources of certainty are those systems of beliefs and rituals that we call **religion** when based on the concept of a divine power or **secular ideology** when based on worldly rather than supernatural forces. In this chapter, the term "religion" will also include secular belief systems. In addition to the personal benefits of religion, when members of a group share a set of beliefs that gives them an identity and significance in the world, they are prepared to assume responsibility for one another and to sacrifice for the good of the collectivity. In other words, belief systems give meaning to individual lives while also holding the group together, which is why they are found everywhere, even though the precise content varies greatly from society to society. This chapter covers the most important aspects of the sociological study of religions and secular beliefs:

- Theoretical perspectives.
- The structure of belief systems.
- Varieties of religious experience through history.
- Organized faith in the United States.
- Contemporary trends.
- Cults and New Religious Movements.

Theoretical Perspectives

Durkheim

The sociological perspective on religion is rooted in the crucial insights of Emile Durkheim. For Durkheim, beliefs, like any other aspect of culture, emerge out of the history of the society—this is who we are, where we came from, how we should behave, and where we are going. At the same time, the society is experienced through the shared faith and rituals, reinforcing the ties that bind group members together. In this view, *all* religions, regardless of content, fulfill the same functions everywhere and are of equal validity. As Durkheim put it:

> There are no religions that are false. All are true in their own fashion; all answer, though in different ways, to the given condition of human existence. . . .
> A religion is a unified system of beliefs and practices that unite into one moral community all those who adhere to them. (1912/1961, 17, 62)

As sociologists we do not ask whether any particular set of beliefs is true or false—that is not a question that can be answered empirically. All religions are true to the faithful. Cannibalism, Calvinism, and Communism are of equal validity if they reduce individual anxiety, offer hope, and unite the community of believers. Only when the belief system fails to satisfy these needs can we make a value judgment—not that it was "false" but only that it "did not work."

We do ask questions that can be researched, such as: How did the beliefs arise? Do they meet individual and group needs? How is the religion organized? And how do the beliefs, rituals, and organizations fit in with other structures of the society?

Weber

This last question was of great interest to Max Weber. As you learned in chapter 2, it was Weber who pointed out how the ideas of early Protestantism created a psychological and political context for the development of capitalism and the extreme individualism that still characterizes the American value system. In contrast, Confucianism, the traditional religion of China, emphasized ascribed statuses and obedience to elders, thus supporting centuries of rule by emperors and bureaucrats.

Marx

The link between religion and economic/political power structures was central to the work of Karl Marx. He noted that if the poor and powerless could be convinced that their lowly status was the will of God or other higher authority, they would not rebel, especially if they were also convinced that their rewards would come in the next world, where "the last shall be first." It is in this sense that Marx described religions as the "opium" (painkiller) of the masses (1844/1975); He saw religion as an agent of oppression of credulous workers by the ruling elites.

Realizing the functional necessity of belief systems for personal and societal needs, Marx's followers attempted to construct a **secular ideology** based on their interpretation of historical reality and the actual conditions of everyday life. "Secular" means "of this world." Marxism ultimately had its own idols, holidays, life course rituals, hymns, and myths, just like any religion but based on historical events and secular ceremonies. Ultimately, the demand for blind faith in the Communist leadership was not that different from the total obedience called for by many religions, a situation that would probably have appalled Marx.

The Structure of Belief

Although the specific content of belief systems varies greatly, there are certain universal aspects, at all three levels of sociological analysis (Yinger 1969). The religion originates in people's awareness of problems in daily life (individual level), which leads to the development of explanations and rituals to reduce the anxiety created by that awareness (cultural level), and finally moves to the creation of specific roles for maintaining the rituals and meanings (social structural level). 🖥 1

There are also universal elements in the content of the belief system:

1. An origin story such as the biblical account of Creation or the Tiwi's emergence from the waters or the secularist's belief in human evolution.

2. Rules of behavior in this world, such as the Ten Commandments, and similar codes whose divine origin gives the norms a sacred dimension.

3. A vision of the future and of belonging to some grand sweep of history. The idea of an afterlife or the return of the Cave God or the triumph of Communism gives meaning to a person's brief time on Earth.

4. Life-course ceremonies to help individuals and groups deal with the unknown, such as the baby's future, the fate of the marriage or the flight of soul from the body. These are the moments that most often bring us to a house of worship or personal prayer.

Sectarian Conflict

These structural similarities and their universality testify to the functional necessity of belief systems. When all members of a society share the same faith, its benefits are clear. Yet this very strength becomes a potential drawback when there is more than one religious community within the society. Because the essence of faith is that one's religion is the only true and good way, there is the potential for conflict with others who also possess the one and only true word. With so little room for compromise, religious wars have been among the longest and bloodiest in history. The ideals of mercy and brotherhood that unify the faithful tend to divide them from nonbelievers.

When there is more than one religious community within a society, believers may be divided from nonbelievers and adherence to one's faith can turn to conflict with those of other faiths. Religious wars have been among the longest and bloodiest in history—the conflict between Catholics and Protestants in Ireland continues into the twenty-first century.

Thus, rather than serving as a unifying force, belief systems often lead to internal struggles. **Sectarian conflict** refers to open violence between religious groups. The United States has avoided sectarian conflict by making religious freedom a legal principle, even though Catholics, Jews, and atheists have been subjected to periodic attacks from the Protestant majority. Elsewhere in the world today, Catholics and Protestants are working at a shaky peace in Northern Ireland, but Hindus and Muslims are still shooting one another in parts of India; Jews and Muslims trade rocks and rockets in the Mideast; and two sets of Christians engage in ethnic cleansing in parts of the former Yugoslavia. More often than not, these conflicts are less about religion than about political and economic inequality, issues that are exploited by religious leaders. In this way, the shared faith that promotes in-group solidarity may be dysfunctional for the society as a whole when two or more religious communities attempt to co-exist.

The Sacred and the Profane

A fundamental structural aspect of religions is the distinction between (1) behaviors and objects that are **sacred**, invested with supernatural force, set apart, and literally awe-inspiring, and (2) the everyday world of the **profane**, earthy and understandable in its own terms. Sacredness is not built in; it emerges from the history of a people and becomes endowed with holiness. The Christian cross is simply two pieces of wood to nonbelievers, and the sacred burial places of Plains Indians are so much pasture land to Midwest farmers.

In all societies, some people are in charge of maintaining and protecting sacred things and places. **Religious roles** were among the first to emerge in human history. When these roles are combined with political leadership, the result is **theocracy**, the rule of the clergy, as in the Vatican or Iran today, where religious rules also govern everyday life.

Varieties of the Religious Experience Across Time and Place

Although religion must have emerged with the earliest human bands, the first traces of ritual date from Neanderthal graves of close to 100,000 years ago in which the bodies were placed in a ceremonial position amid offerings of seeds and flowers to accompany the departed into the afterlife. Then, about 30,000 years ago, carvings and figurines of pregnant women appear throughout Europe suggesting that the early religion of *Homo sapiens* linked the fertility of women and nature. 💻2

With the emergence of agriculture, 10,000 to 15,000 years ago, came the need to conquer nature (and all things female) and a new religious imagery appeared. The image of the powerful father who rules through his chosen sons reflected the real-life patterns of inheritance of land and cattle in the Near East, birthplace of Judaism, Christianity, and Islam. With the triumph of these world religions, an all-male religious leadership replaced whatever feminine influences may have characterized the earlier faith or ritual. Indeed, because of their assumed closeness to nature and hence to the profane, women were specifically excluded from religious places and roles—to this very day in many traditions.

As can be seen in Figure 12.1, followers of Christianity, Islam, and Hinduism constitute two-thirds of all believers (and nonbelievers).

Priests and Prophets

Because religions claim to deal with the eternal—either truth is everlasting or it cannot be The Truth—most organized religions also tend to be conservative and supportive of the existing political and economic order. Yet, belief systems are always changing, and many have been agents of social change. New movements are continually being generated from within estab-

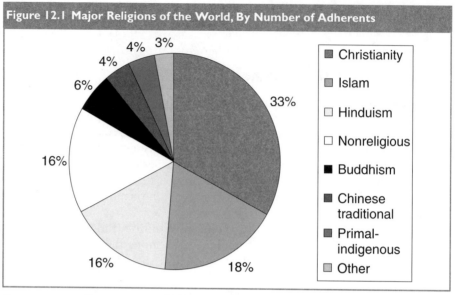

Figure 12.1 Major Religions of the World, By Number of Adherents

4% 3%
4%
6%
16%
16%
18%
33%

- Christianity
- Islam
- Hinduism
- Nonreligious
- Buddhism
- Chinese traditional
- Primal-indigenous
- Other

Source: www.adherents.com, 1999.

lished religions, typically led by a charismatic figure such as Jesus, Muhammad, Martin Luther, or Joseph Smith, founder of the Church of Jesus Christ of Latter-Day Saints (Mormonism).

The dual nature of religions—as support for the status quo and as agent of social change—is captured by Weber's distinction between priests and prophets. **Priests**, whether rabbis, ministers, ayatollahs, bishops, or vestal virgins, are the keepers of the holy traditions and places, the protectors of all things sacred. **Prophets**, in contrast, are disturbers of the peace. Think of Biblical prophets, charismatic figures who challenge the status quo, inveigh against corruption, and beseech sinners to repent.

Charismatic leaders attract a loyal following, but also arouse fierce opposition, often meeting an early and violent death or exile. If the prophet's message is to last longer than a lifetime, there has to be a nuts-and-bolts organization to carry on the crusade—a process that Weber called "the routinization of charisma," whereby the sacred mission is transformed into an effective institution, under control of priests. For example, would the life of Jesus have been the foundation of a world religion without the Disciples to record events and rally the faithful? In time, the newly established religion may become the kind of oppressive system described by Marx, and the ground is prepared for the rise of a new prophet.

Secularization

The most powerful challenge to organized religion comes out of the historical process of **modernization**—the replacement of family-based work units by factories, the flow of young people off the land into cities, increased reliance on science and technology, and a focus on this world rather than the next. The **secular spirit** celebrates the individual and the pleasures of the senses. Ever since August Comte, sociologists assumed that the march of science and rationality would eventually replace religion as the guide to behavior and meaning, and in many ways, for many people, that has happened. But religions have not faded away; some have made their compromise with modernity; others remain relatively unchanged; and new forms keep emerging.

Although the power of religious authorities to regulate everyday life has diminished greatly in modern societies, the need for ultimate answers remains. There is always one more question that science cannot answer, such as "What about the moment *before* the Big Bang?" Nor can a laboratory provide the support that comes from shared worship. People must still deal with joy and pain, blessings and losses. The world remains filled with famine, pestilence, death, and destruction.

Not only has religious faith survived its encounter with modernization, but a particularly militant form—fundamentalism—has emerged across the globe, from Arkansas to Afghanistan.

Fundamentalism Revived

Fundamentalism refers to a rigidly traditional set of beliefs and practices, based on unchanging sacred principles in which the world is divided into clear-cut forces for good or evil with no middle ground (Marty and Appleby 1993). As a response to the imperfections of secular society, fundamentalism offers a firm anchor to the bewildered and uprooted (Armstrong 2000).

Throughout Asia and Africa, the failure of both civilian and military governments to control corruption, reduce poverty, and end civil wars has provided fertile ground for fundamentalists of all religious traditions, but especially in Muslim countries. In contrast, most European countries are firmly secularized, even the predominately Catholic nations of Spain and Italy. It is only in the United States, among modern societies, that religious fundamentalists have become important players in the political system. Let us take a closer look at the contemporary American scene.

Belonging and Believing in Twenty-First Century America

In what many think of as the most modern of industrial societies, it is difficult to find anyone who does not believe in God. A full 80 percent believe that after they die, a part of them lives on in heaven or in a next life, and 38 percent personally know someone who will end up in hell (*New York Times,* May 7, 2000).

Over 40 percent of survey respondents say that they attend religious services on a monthly basis, although other data suggest that the actual rate of attendance is much closer to 25 percent (Hadaway et al. 1998; Chaves et al. 1999). In addition, contrary to claims of a religious revival in America, there is evidence that weekly attendance at religious services has been declining since the 1970s (Presser and Stinson 1998). Two-thirds of respondents have joined a congregation, down slightly from the mid-1980s but still higher than for most industrial nations. The Americans most likely to belong and attend reg-

❖ ❖ ❖ ❖ ularly are women, African Americans, Southerners, and low-income earners (Religion News Service 2000).

It is not easy to count religious affiliation in America. The census does not ask; survey data tend to overstate membership; and information from the churches is incomplete and not comparable—some count children, others only adults. The best estimate is that about 60 percent of American adults are Protestant (including Mormons), 26 percent are Catholic, with Jews, Muslims, and followers of Eastern religions each accounting for 2 to 3 percent, and 7 percent without a religious preference. (Religious Research Center 1999). 💻 3 Although overwhelmingly Christian, there is no "official" religion in the United States. To the contrary, the First Amendment to the U.S. Constitution specifically states that:

> Congress shall make no law respecting an establishment of religion, or prohibiting the free exercise thereof. . .

Notice that there are two different parts to this injunction: (1) an "establishment clause" that forbids the government from favoring any one faith over another and (2) a "free exercise clause" that forbids government from interfering in religious affairs. For this reason, church property and most income are not taxable; in the words of Chief Justice John Marshall (1819), "the power to tax involves the power to destroy." In addition, the financial arrangements of the churches and behavior of the leaders, short of their committing a crime such as embezzlement, are of no concern to law enforcement.

Notice, also, the possibility of conflict between the establishment and exercise clauses. When the courts forbid using public school facilities for meetings of religious groups on grounds of separation of church and state (the establishment clause), some organizations have charged that this interferes with their ability to practice their faith (the exercise clause). Over the past several years, as a result of increased legal activism on the part of conservative churches, each Supreme Court term has been presented with new cases with slightly different issues to be dealt with by the Justices, including a number of variations on having nondenominational prayers recited by public school students, as well as the posting of the Ten Commandments in the classroom.

In the Bronx, New York City water flows from the feet of an image of the Madonna of Lourdes. Santeria followers stand in line to present gifts of thanksgiving to Obatala for favors received and to collect the water which they believe holds curative properties. Santeria is a slave religion which originated among the Yaruba in Africa and was transported to the Caribbean where it was influenced by Catholicism.

The First Amendment also leaves open the definition of a "religion": Can you declare that God has just commanded you to establish a church? Yes, if you can convince the Internal Revenue Service that your organization is a serious attempt to meet spiritual needs. In practice, this means that American believers have their choice of many different varieties of the religious experience—a virtual bazaar of offerings from the most conservative Muslim mosque to the most recent witches' coven.

Box 12.1

Vocabulary Lesson

Church—At the macro-level, the entire religious grouping, as, for example, the Catholic or Protestant or Mormon Church.

Mainstream churches—Formally organized religious bodies that are recognized as legitimate and that support the dominant culture and social structures.

Denomination—Some churches have branches, or *denominations*, that vary in doctrine and/or practice, yet fit under the same umbrella. American Protestantism, for example, is really a collection of dozens of denominations, each with its own organizational structure. American Judaism can also be thought of as having three major denominations: Orthodox, Conservative, and Reform; all are Jews, although with minimal contacts across denominational boundaries. Islam, throughout the world, is divided by deep and long-standing denominational differences that often lead to open conflict. In contrast, the Mormon and Catholic Churches are unitary, composed of one body of believers.

Denominations typically come into being when a group of believers splits off from a main church because of some dispute over scriptural interpretations or the conduct of church leaders, but does not leave the mother church altogether.

Sect—Some differences about doctrine or practices result in a small group of believers moving to the very fringe of the Church, where they develop their unique version of the faith in partial isolation—a sect. Often led by a charismatic figure, sects appeal to people already marginalized by poverty or race or ethnicity. Many sects are characterized by highly emotional forms of worship, such as talking in tongues, snake handling, and personal witnessing. In Orthodox Judaism, a number of sects, related to the towns in Eastern Europe from which their leaders came, practice a similar kind of ecstatic spirituality. Over time, some sects move toward the mainstream and become recognized denominations, as did Seventh Day Adventists and Jehovah's Witnesses.

Cults—Cults are similar to sects in their small size and charismatic leadership, but they are not associated with any recognized (legitimated) Church or denomination. Cults consist of a body of believers whose beliefs may be deeply religious or purely secular or some unique mixture of both. Followers tend to be fiercely devoted to their leader, often turning away from the rest of the world, including their family and former friends.

There is, as always, an element of social construction in these categories; one person's sect may be another's denomination, and a "cult" is usually something of which the definers disapprove. For example, in size and organization and complexity, the Unification Church of the Reverend Sun Myung Moon (hence "Moonies") is a Church, yet some see it as a Protestant denomination, others as a sect, and still others as a cult, depending on how threatening it appears.

The Civil Religion

With such a variety of legitimate religious groups, are there any beliefs that unify Americans? Some sociologists (Bellah 1975) have found the functional equivalent of a common faith in the **American civil religion**, in which the nation itself and its institutions (including religious pluralism) become sacred objects, seen as divinely blessed, with a mission in this world and a glorious destiny.

❖ ❖ ❖ ❖   The civil religion is functional in adding a moral dimension to the social order and uniting an otherwise diverse population. The mixing of religion and everyday life can be seen in both (1) how we Americans give a sacred dimension to secular holidays such as Thanksgiving and the Fourth of July and (2) how we transform sacred holy days into commercial orgies, as at Christmas.

A more unusual example of the mixing of religion with everyday life can be seen in the sign on the back of this bus.

Critics of the civil religion argue that it is simply a watered-down version of authentic faith and can be easily co-opted by politicians who wrap themselves in religion and the flag and by business leaders who join a prayer breakfast before closing down a factory. The line between sacred and profane is surely blurred when athletes on both sides of a game hold locker-room services to ask God's help in scoring touchdowns.

African-American Churches

Faith in eventual justice has always been a resource for oppressed people. For African Americans, churches were especially important as the only basic institution not under white control. In black communities before and after the Civil War, the church served as the center of communal life, providing social services on behalf of or in place of governmental agencies, and organizing for change (Patillo-McCoy 1998). The churches serve to unify the black community while also forming a bridge to the mainstream.

The great majority of African Americans are Protestant, members of Baptist denominations, with a blend of African and Southern cultures, and an emphasis on music and personal participation. A small percentage are Roman Catholic, in Louisiana and among recent Haitian immigrants, and a growing number are converts to Islam.

Because the church was the primary avenue of upward mobility for talented and ambitious black men excluded from high-status positions in the wider society, it will be no surprise to learn that all but a few leaders of the Civil Rights Movement came from the clergy. Today, however, when men and women of color can pursue careers in high-paying professions, proportionately fewer have entered religious work.

The role of women in the black churches has historically been more visible than that for white women, as participants and leaders if not as ordained ministers. To the extent that the church is the heart of the black community, women have been its lifeblood (Gilkes 1985; Higginbotham 1993). As long as racism limits involvement and achievement in the mainstream, black women will continue the tradition of spiritual uplift and social service, especially as sources of outside support dwindle in the era of declining government assistance. 💻 4

Contemporary Trends

The big story is that from a peak in the 1960s, mainstream Protestant churches in America have lost members (and influence), while marginal denominations and sects have experienced rapid growth. The Catholic Church has held its own, thanks to Hispanic immigrants, while the Mormon population has more than doubled, as a result of high birthrates and aggressive recruitment.

Protestantism

The decline of mainstream Protestant churches and the rise of smaller, more conservative denominations reflects the growing division *within* American society and its institutions between social liberals and conservatives— the "culture wars" discussed in chapter 10. Throughout most of our history, the upper classes belonged to the more established Protestant denominations, with Episcopalians at the very top, followed by Presbyterians and Methodists, with some regional variations such as the high status of Congregationalists in Boston or Quakers in Philadelphia. The major mainstream churches were led by graduates of theological seminaries, men of learning and relatively high social status. In general, the established churches and their leaders remained above politics, except at rare moments such as the Abolition Movement in the 1850s and the Civil Rights Movement in the 1960s. The challenge to those who had proclaimed a concern for justice and equality from their own pulpits was clear: Put your body where your words are. The religious establishment, led by younger clergy, responded in strength. There were few early civil rights demonstrations that were not headed by rows and rows of priests, nuns, ministers, and rabbis (Guth et al. 1997).

The problem back home, however, was that many congregants resented the fact that their leaders were in an Alabama jail rather than in their pulpits. The pews gradually emptied and contributions fell off. A new emphasis on serving one's own flock replaced concerns for social justice for many church leaders, but other changes were also reducing the power of the mainstream churches, including a general population shift from the Northeast to the South and Southwest; the decline of political liberalism; and the emergence of television preachers in the evangelical tradition.

Throughout the first half of the twentieth century, the denominations and sects that ministered to the relatively poor and less educated believers of the "Bible Belt" had been pushed into the margins of American Protestantism. In the rural South and Midwest, the Pentecostal movement took root as a reaction to the secularization of mainstream churches. Believing that God's spirit could be tapped by anyone of pure faith, the Pentecostals spoke in tongues, laid on hands to cure illnesses, and waited for the Second Coming. This highly individualistic and egalitarian tradition became the basis for the spread of Evangelicalism, a movement based on a personal commitment

❖ ❖ ❖ ❖

(being "born again"), following Biblical commandments, and spreading the gospel. Most Evangelical denominations have accommodated to the secular world and moved to the center of religious life in America. Evangelicals today are highly educated, upwardly mobile, politically involved, and urbanized, while also adhering to the strict demands of their faith and the call to convert others (Smith 1998).

Many conservative congregations, however, remained unwilling to adapt to modernity, insisting that the Bible is the very word of God and without error, and maintaining traditional practices, including a refusal to permit women to serve as pastors. In the words of one leader, "Southern Baptists are engaged in a battle against modernity, earnestly contending for the truth and authority of an ancient faith" (Mohler 2000). Ironically, many of these **fundamentalist** churches enjoyed a wave of popularity and power in the 1980s precisely by entering the modern age with a vengeance, through the new information technologies and political activism.

With the mainstream success of the televised ministry of evangelist Billy Graham in the 1970s, the path was cleared for a host of newer, more colorful and controversial figures: Jim and Tammy Faye Bakker, Jimmy Swaggert, Jerry Falwell, and Pat Robertson. These men (and a few women) were products of bible schools, students of preaching, masters of immediate emotionality, in contrast to the cool, distant Northern speech of mainstream religious leaders. Most created their own congregations, unaffiliated with any recognized denomination. They were also extremely successful in raising money from the faithful. Their audiences wanted a highly personal experience, a direct communion with the Holy Spirit, and that is precisely what the televised revivals provided. The number of religious radio stations has also mushroomed, filling American airwaves with music, sermons, and stories of personal renewal. Most recently, hundreds of websites keep the faithful in touch with one another. Thus, religions that once spread the Good Word through interpersonal networks have harnessed modern technology.

Falwell and Robertson also led the march into electoral politics. Fundamentalist sects had long been the strongest supporters of the separation of church and state, fearful that government would forbid some of their practices, such as snake handling. By 1980, however, such fears were overcome, and the congregations became part of the "Christian Right," a coalition of socially conservative organizations and political interest groups linked to the Republican Party. The coalition promotes a "pro-family" agenda characterized by opposition to abortion and the Gay Rights Movement and support for men as family head and the rights of parents to raise their children as they see fit (Diamond 1998). Although Soviet Communism is no longer the great evil, the new targets for Christian activism are liberalism, feminism, the federal government, and "secular humanism." → next pg

reaction to secularization

Another response to the perceived dangers of modernity and a general feminization of society has been a revival of "muscular Christianity," attempts to make religious commitment more acceptable to men (Messner 1997). The Promise Keepers movement is one manifestation of this trend, as are the various groups of Christian athletes who hold prayer meetings before and after contests. 💻5 The Christian Sportsmen's Fellowship, founded in 1994, is designed to use hunting and fishing themes to illuminate religious messages. The Fellowship's best fund-raiser is the *Camouflaged Bible*, a pocket-sized edition with a green, tan, and black cover (Yellin 2000).

❖ ❖ ❖ ❖

Box 12.2

The New Satan: Secular Humanism

For many fundamentalists, the most dangerous trend in American society is the denial of a divine power in everyday life, or secular humanism, a belief system based on rational understanding and a commitment to improving lives in this world. For people who believe that only God can solve personal problems, the idea that you can overcome difficulties through your own effort is close to heresy. On this basis, fundamentalists have called for the removal from school libraries of books such as *The Wizard of Oz*, the Harry Potter series, and those that promote self-help because they teach children to depend on their own skills rather than acknowledging the superiority of a sacred presence. More is at stake here than banning a few books: If fundamentalists can convince school boards that secular humanism is being taught in the schools and that it is tantamount to a religion, then other views, such as Creationism, should be given equal consideration.

The American Humanist Association⬚6, however, has only a few thousand dues paying members. Their *Humanist Manifesto* (1988) is based on the following tenets:

- A faith in human intelligence and abilities.

- A commitment to democracy and civil liberties.

- A belief in the importance, if not divine origin, of the Ten Commandments.

- A commitment to gender and racial equality and world peace.

- A compassionate concern for all human beings.

Catholicism

The Catholic Church in America also has its extremely traditional, fundamentalist elements, resisting the modernizing influence of the Second Vatican Council in the mid-1960s (Cuneo 1997). Indeed, under Pope John Paul II, the church leadership has become profoundly conservative, leaving the more liberal clergy on the fringe. As a hierarchical and patriarchal institution, the Catholic Church defies the major trend of modern societies toward democratic participation and gender equality, yet it remains a powerful force in individual lives and American politics. The problems for American Catholics stem from two sources: (1) a lack of fit between official church doctrine and the actual behavior of congregants and (2) the declining numbers of men and women entering religious orders.

The Catholic Church in America enjoyed enormous power over its congregants in the early years of the twentieth century, when the major cities of the Northeast contained large communities of immigrants from Italy, Ireland, and Poland. By the third generation, however, these communities had all but disappeared, as children moved out to suburbs and up the social-class ladder. In the process, younger Catholics began to resemble other Americans in their private behavior, especially in the use of

The largest proportion of parochial schools is operated by the Catholic Church. Why do some parents choose the parochial schools instead of public ones?

❖ ❖ ❖ ❖ contraception. Large numbers today disagree with the church hierarchy on a range of issues in addition to birth control: premarital sex, women as priests, allowing priests to marry, and permitting divorce and remarriage. Nonetheless, most remain in the Catholic Church and hope for eventual changes (Dillon 1999). Any erosion in membership because of such differences or through intermarriage has been made up by large numbers of recent immigrants from Latin America and Asia.

Although the Catholic population remains stable, the number of men and women in religious orders has declined sharply since the mid-1960s. Among women, the number of nuns has dropped from a high of 180,000 in 1965 to about 83,000 today, and most of those who are left are in their retirement years. Reasons for this dramatic shift include (1) smaller Catholic families, with fewer unmarried younger daughters, and (2) the daughters who seek a calling in social services now have a choice of secular occupations.

Smaller families and a larger range of job opportunities for the sons of immigrants also account for the decline in the numbers of men entering Catholic seminaries in the United States—from over 8,000 in 1967 to about 3,500 today. As a result, the number of active priests has also dropped, from close to 60,000 in the early 1970s to about 47,500 today. A slight upturn has recently taken place, primarily in the more conservative seminaries, as a result of an influx of immigrants from Vietnam and Mexico (Neibuhr 1999). Nonetheless, the overall shortage of priests remains severe and is not likely to improve soon, which puts pressure on the hierarchy to use the talents of women and of former priests who left to get married, and possibly to relax the rule of celibacy for the priesthood. Thus far, the church leadership has resisted these pressures, leaving many pulpits officially empty or having one priest serve a number of parishes.

Islam

Islam is the religion of almost 20 percent of the world's population and of an increasing number of Americans, close to 4 million by 1999. The religion was founded by the prophet Muhammed in the 7th century, and its holy book, the *Koran*, incorporates both the Old and New Testaments, plus the words of Allah (God). Although men and women are theoretically equal, the reality is that Muslem men have many more privileges than women, including the right to drive a car, to vote, and to divorce by saying so three times. Male believers are held to a strict religious discipline: to pray five times a day, to fast during the month of Ramadan, and to make a pilgrimage to Mecca.

The problems faced by America's Muslims include finding occupations where the men can follow religious rules; trying to maintain traditional power relationships when children and wives become Americanized; and deal-

Islam is the religion of almost 20 percent of the world's population and an increasing number of Americans. Here the faithful pray at a mosque in Sumatra, Indonesia.

ing with the public perception that they are "Islamic fundamentalists," short-hand for militant fanatics. Like Orthodox Jews, who also must engage in daily prayer, Muslims tend to find jobs where they can control their work hours. And also like Orthodox Jews, they have found that the best way to preserve tradition is to live near one another, in communities centered on the place of worship (the *mosque* for Muslims, *synagogue* for Jews). For many American Muslims, these attempts at preservation appear to be temporary steps on the way toward acculturation, as the children go to public schools, the women enter the labor force, and everyone watches television. (Parrillo 2000).

The Nation of Islam is not just an American religion but is an international movement. In London's Hyde Park, a gathering to attract new converts to the Nation of Islam.

Judaism

America's six million Jews are the nation's largest category of non-Christians, although both the Muslim and Buddhist populations are catching up quickly. The major problem for assimilated Jews in America is the loss of congregants through intermarriage. This is a great irony because it stems from Jews' very success in becoming fully Americanized. Jews are disproportionately represented among college graduates, the occupational elites, and highest income earners; the more successful you are in mainstream activities, the more likely you are to meet people of other religions, to fall in love, and to marry outside the faith.

The Orthodox denominations have avoided this problem by staying in their closed communities, educating their children in religious schools, and encouraging large families. Indeed, the Orthodox may soon outnumber other American Jews. In response to these developments, the more liberal denominations have adopted many of the Orthodox rituals and traditions, such as reading the Bible in Hebrew, wearing a *yarmulka* (skull cap) and prayer shawl, and attending daily services—obligations that are available to women as well as men in Reform and Conservative congregations. It remains to be seen whether these accommodations to tradition will stem the loss of congregants.

Women and the Churches

In their origins, Judaism, Christianity, and Islam were patriarchal; the image of God or Allah was male, as were the founders, prophets, and early disciples. Indeed, the argument against women in the Catholic priesthood and Southern Baptist ministry is precisely that all Jesus' disciples were men. Obedience to a male God was translated into obedience to the priest/father as head of the church and the husband/father as head of the family. With few exceptions, it was a woman's duty to be obedient and raise the next generation of believers—until the 1960s, that is. The New Feminist Movement and its ideal of gender equality has transformed all but the most traditional churches (Chaves 1997). Among those swimming against the tide, the Southern Baptists Convention in 1998 declared that women should submit to their husbands, according to the word of God as written in the Bible.

Today, over one-third of all theology school students are women, a figure that rises yearly. As shown in Figure 12.2, the proportion of women in the clergy has more than doubled since 1983. This figure will most likely increase as, following the example of other once male-dominated occupations, the rapid feminization of the clergy will make the profession less attractive to men (Nesbitt 1997). In the meantime, women ministers and rabbis have less prestigious positions, lower incomes, and less job security than male clergy at a similar point in their careers (Zikmund et al. 1998; Nesbitt et al. 2001). Three decades has not been long enough to erase doubts about women in the pulpit even among denominations that have opened the ministry.

Another way in which the Women's Movement has affected religious thought in America is through new scholarship. When traditions, doctrine, and sacred scriptures are reviewed through a feminist lens, a different reality emerges (Kamienkowski and Rosenblaum 2000). You may have noticed the introduction of inclusive language and rituals in your place of worship. 🖥7

Despite a lengthy resistance to change, the mainstream Protestant churches, as well as reform and conservative branches of Judaism, have begun to ordain women. Cathy Roskum is one of 11 women bishops in the Episcopalian Church of the United States.

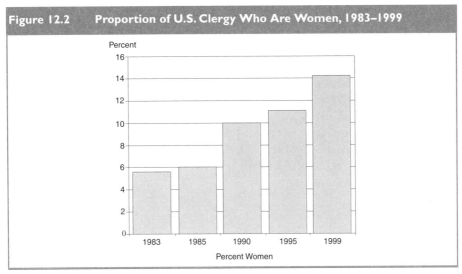

Figure 12.2   Proportion of U.S. Clergy Who Are Women, 1983–1999

Source: McClain 2000.

A third direction in which women's religious interests have taken them is toward the rediscovery of ancient female-dominated belief systems, including wicca or witchcraft (Capek 1989). The Covenant of the Goddess, for example, has been incorporated as a nonprofit religious organization since 1975 and operates a very informative web site. Like patriarchal religions, the Goddess faith links women to the Earth and the life-force of nature, but with a positive rather than negative twist. Through oneness with Mother Nature, each individual in the group contributes to the spiritual rebirth of all. These groups have also revived interest in herbal medicine and other alternative remedies. 8

In sharp contrast to the patriarchal command to subdue the earth, the ecofeminist movement seeks to empower women as the protectors of nature (Capek 1989). In this view, it is women's unique role to preserve the environment and to restore a oneness with the natural world as the means of achieving physical and emotional health (Ruether 2001). The *Women's Spirituality Movement* is one example of the contemporary trend to find the ultimate answers outside the established churches—what might be thought of as pushing the religious envelope.

The New Religious Movements

New Religious Movements (NRM) is an umbrella term that cov-

For India's Hindus, the Ganges River is sacred and its waters are spiritually purifying.

ers a range of organizations and practices that fall within the broad definition of a belief system as involving a search for transcendent (outside one's self) meaning, shared rituals, and a commitment to a code of conduct. The liberating currents of the 1960s in the United States challenged all established institutions and provided a fertile base for new forms of believing and belonging, especially on the part of young people. Some of the NRMs were based on Eastern religions such as Buddhism, or a mix of East and West; others were glorified self-improvement businesses (est and Scientology); many involved dabbling in other-worldly phenomena (seances, healing rocks); and still others are part of the antigovernment white supremacy Christian militia movement.

Eastern-Oriented Cults

The late 1960s saw a groundswell of interest in religions of the Far East, based on the search for perfect bliss, of escaping materialistic desires, and of becoming one with all humankind. Hare Krishna followers and dozens of similar groups which appeared on the streets of America were composed of people who abandoned their previous identity in order to live together under the tutelage of a wise leader, or guru. The supply of gurus was greatly increased by the repeal in 1965 of the Oriental Exclusion Act that had limited the number of Asians admitted to the United States.

Some gurus became very wealthy, for example, the late Bhagwan Shree Rajneesh, who brought his group of educated middle-class followers to the backwoods of Oregon, where they built a new city and competed with local businesses. The Bhagwan, along with his personal fleet of Rolls Royces, was eventually deported as an illegal alien. The Rajneesh cult is an example of the blending of Eastern mysticism and contemporary commercial activities that characterize many self-invented religions, the most successful of which is the Unification Church of the Reverend Sun Myung Moon.

The Unification Church

Led by a Korean businessman who claims to be the new Messiah, the Unification Church mixes Christian and Buddhist beliefs, is allied with the political right while practicing a communal way of life, and preaches simplicity while amassing great wealth through the money-making activities of followers. These contradictions do not appear to bother the mostly young recruits who live in group homes and work full time for the Church. So deep is their commitment to the Reverend Moon that they allow him to choose their marriage partners.⌨9

Parents of recruits find it difficult to believe that their children could so coldly cut themselves off from family and friends and follow a middle-aged Asian who claims to have talked to Jesus, Moses, and Buddha. The only logical explanation for the parents is that the child must have been duped and brainwashed, held against his or her will, and weakened by lack of food and sleep. Under such circumstances, the parents feel that it is perfectly legitimate to re-kidnap and "deprogram" the child.

Brainwashing or Normal Conversion?

The brainwashing issue has split sociologists of religion. Some scholars claim that recruits are subjected to mind-control techniques similar to those used by totalitarian governments (Allen 1999). Other academics point out that most newcomers to cults leave very quickly and that those who stay go through the same process as any convert to a new faith (Anthony and Robbins 1997). People who leave one belief system for another are often even more committed than those born into the religion, in order to justify their switch.

The career of a typical joiner follows a fairly common scenario. Most at risk are young people who are *structurally available* for recruitment: freshmen, transfer students, someone between jobs or relationships. Befriended by a sympathetic listener, they are introduced to the group of seemingly happy age peers. Seeking community and acceptance, they find it. Without necessarily believing the ideology of the NRM, a young person will become fully committed through a series of small tasks such as selling paper flowers on a street corner. Once you have done something as strange as that, you either have to admit it was a dreadful mistake—and get out fast—or make up some powerful reasons why it makes sense. This is not "brainwashing" in the technical sense, but the process operates at high speed to attach the convert to the new faith. The longer you stay, the deeper the investment of your self in the role and the harder it is to get out. This is true of most roles—your job or intimate relationship or marriage.

Scientology and the Technological Fix

The Church of Scientology illustrates all the conflicting currents in defining a religion. In 1993, the Internal Revenue Service finally granted the organization religious status and all the tax advantages and freedom from oversight that follow, primarily in order to avoid the costs of another decade of law suits and harassment of agents (Frantz 1997). Yet, is it a religion? Some would call it a cult, others a profitable business, and the German government has banned it as a danger to public safety. What is undeniable is that the organization is very wealthy and has a roster of famous members, including John Travolta, Tom Cruise, and Lisa Marie Presley.

Founded by L. Ron Hubbard in 1954, with his book *Dianetics* (1950) as the sacred text, the Church of Scientology has spread across the globe. Membership numbers are debatable, with the Church claiming 8 million members, but most other students of religious movements suggesting no more than 200,000, one-fourth of whom are in the United States (Bainbridge 1997). Much depends on who gets counted. If it is anyone who has had any contact with the Church over the past 45 years, it will be several million.

What the organization offers is a program that is a cross between therapeutic counseling and self-improvement—but at a price of several thousand dollars (Hall 1998). The basic idea behind the therapy is that a part of your mind records unconscious "engrams" that interfere with rational thoughts. To rid your mind of engrams, you pay for "auditing" sessions with a Church minister, hooked up to an E-meter that registers the mind's energy. When the engrams have been eradicated, you are "Clear," that is, in the highest state of awareness as a spiritual being (Bromley and Bracey 1998). As long as mil-

❖ ❖ ❖ ❖   lions of people continue to buy Hubbard's books and thousands pay for auditing sessions, the Church of Scientology will remain a powerful new player in
the religion sweepstakes of contemporary America. 10

The 'New Age' Movement

The fastest-growing spiritual trend in the United States at the beginning
of the twenty-first century embraces a variety of beliefs generally referred to
as "new age" or "out-of-this-world" phenomena: contacting the dead, consulting angels, near-death experiences, astrology, reincarnation, psychic
healing. That these ideas have become a national obsession is reflected in the
number of new movies and television programs that deal with angels, dead
people come to life, paranormal experiences of all kinds, from *The X-Files* to
alien abductions. If you wish to contact friends or family members after your
death, you can check into the web at <finalthoughts.com> and store those e-
mail messages.

Some New Agers are into alternative healing, herbs, and nonmedical
treatments such as meditation and yoga. As part of the *holistic health* movement, they emphasize the oneness of body and mind, of self and the natural
world—an echo of the Eastern religions and the ecofeminist concerns noted
earlier. Other New Agers seek guidance from entities from the beyond
through a process called *channeling*. A channel puts you in contact with this
source of wisdom. And while the channels and their clients are predominately female, the entities from beyond are typically male, an indication that
although channeling may be a reaction to women's marginality in mainstream religions, the sound of authority remains masculine (Brown
1997). 🖥 11

Christian Militias

At the other end of the spectrum from the New Agers and their belief in
spiritual oneness and world peace are the semi-military groups of Christian
patriots, who see their duty as restoring the nation to its white Christian heritage (Barkun 1997). The enemies are gays, feminists, Jews, and blacks.
Located primarily in the Midwest and Mountain states, members may number only a few thousand, but their influence is much stronger, through their
loose alliance with other white supremacist organizations and through their
talk radio programs that cover the entire South and Midwest. The militias
have taken up the cause of religious sects and cults under attack by the United
States government, such as the remaining polygamists of Utah and the
Branch Davidians in Waco, Texas.

The Waco episode raises a number of issues in the study of religion, sects,
cults, and church-state relations. In 1993, on their home television screens,
Americans could see agents of the Bureau of Alcohol, Tobacco, and Firearms
(ATF) launch an attack on a compound occupied by a breakaway sect of Seventh Day Adventists (itself a sect a generation earlier). Calling themselves
Branch Davidians, the group had taken on some of the characteristics of a
cult, led by a charismatic figure, David Koresh, who claimed to be the Messiah. Prior to the attack, the ATF had carried on a 51-day siege of the compound, which it justified on the grounds that the Davidians were hoarding

illegal weapons (not unusual in that part of Texas), although the more immediate reason appeared to be that four of its agents had been killed in an earlier botched raid.

❖ ❖ ❖ ❖

Because the Davidians believed that the end of the world was near and would take the form prophesied in the Bible, the ATF attack with fire and bullets fulfilled their worst fears, and a bloody massacre was the result; those who were not killed by the ATF committed suicide. The anniversary of this event is remembered by the Christian militias, not so much out of sympathy with Davidian beliefs as out of fierce opposition to the government attack on civilians.

Cults Demystified

The deaths at Waco and other well-publicized incidents of mass suicide by cult members in the United States and Japan raise the question of how otherwise "normal" people can follow their leader to such a bloody end. All evidence suggests that the followers were indeed quite ordinary citizens, and while the leaders were somewhat strange, as charismatic figures often are, they were not madmen. The answer, for sociologists, lies in the *structure of the situation* that the leader creates.

If you wanted to create a cult that would follow you without question, your first step would be to isolate the group from contact with outsiders, so that the close interactions within the circle of believers would reinforce their sense of togetherness and dependence on the leader. As with all **total institutions** (those that control you 24 hours a day), the needs of the organization overwhelm those of the individual (Goffman 1961). Then make sure that you are the only source of information about the outside world, which doubles the group's dependence on you. You could also insist that existing relationships be broken and that both women and men depend on you for emotional support and, often, sexual satisfaction. And if your followers also endow you with superhuman qualities, then your word is their command.

Most American cults, however, stop well short of such total control, have a limited life span, and are relatively harmless. Even the coming of the millennium failed to generate the expected number of cults and sects prophesying the end of the world, although a few groups did sell off their possessions and move to Israel in late 1999 to await the apocalypse, and others committed suicide while waiting for the spaceships that never came to transport them to the next world (Balch 1995). The eventual fate of most cults and sects is that history passes them by. For those that survive, compromises with the secular world take away the strangeness, public hostility declines, and the faith becomes another choice in the "religious marketplace" (Hammond 1992).

This pluralism and variety of established and new religious movements is a defining characteristic of contemporary America. Under the protection of the Constitution, belief systems compete for the allegiance of an increasingly individualized population. At the moment, the more expressive and personally empowering faiths appear to be the winners. There is something here for everyone who searches for meaning and community, who seeks believing and belonging.

Conclusion

This chapter has discussed the theoretical foundations of the sociological perspective on religion and has looked at the central concepts and universal aspects of belief systems. You have been introduced to the varieties of religious experiences across time, with a focus on the history of religion in the United States. Contemporary trends, including the particular problems of established churches, were examined. The chapter ended with an extended examination of New Religious Movements, from Eastern mysticism to New Age conversations with angels. The United States is unique among nations in the richness and diversity of religious activity. Not all new sects and cults have been welcomed or tolerated—the Mormons, for example, were driven out of the Northeast and Midwest right over the Rocky Mountains. Yet, in the long run, you may have more to fear from those who would narrow the definition of "true faith" than from those seeking to expand the boundaries of belief. 💻12

Surfing the Sociological Internet

💻1 Some general sites with links for information on many religious traditions:
http://home.about.com/religion/index.htm?PM=59_0239_T and
http://www.edunet.ie/resources/religion.html which give data and statistics on membership in world religious traditions with links to official sites such as the Vatican, at: **http://www.vatican.va/** and the World Council of Churches at: **http://www.wcc-coe.org/wcc/english.html**
http://www.religion-online.org/ is a site giving access to hundreds of sacred texts and links to other sites on religion.

💻2 For a site on early earth goddess religions, go to: **http://www.mothergoddess.com/**

💻3 For an archive for studying American religion: **www.arda.tm**
A religion news service can be found at: **http://www.religionnews.com/**

💻4 For African-American, Afro-Caribbean, and African religious traditions:
http://afroamculture.about.com/culture/afroamculture/msub23.htm

💻5 The Promise Keepers: **http://www.promisekeepers.org/**

💻6 The American Humanist Association is at: **http://www.infidels.org/org/aha/** and the Council for Secular Humanism is at: **http://www.secularhumanism.org/**

💻7 On women and religion: **http://www.academicinfo.net/religwom.html**
For an extensive bibliography on women and religion online, go

to: **http://www.newvision-psychic.com/bookshelf/
womenspirit.html**

💻8 On Wicca: **http://www.cog.org/general/iabout.html**

💻9 The Unification Church's website is at: **http://unification.org/**

💻10 Scientology's official site can be found at: **http://www.scientol-
ogy.org/home.html**

💻11 On New Age Religions: **http://members.aol.com/theloego/
welcome/index.html**

💻12 **http://www.religioustolerance.org/welcome.htm#new** is a
site promoting religious tolerance by providing unbiased information about religion and religious groups.

Glossary

American Civil Religion A common faith in which the nation itself and its
institutions become sacred objects, seen as divinely blessed.

Ecofeminism Feminist theory emphasizing interdependence of all living
things and the relationships of social oppression and ecological domination.

Fundamentalism A rigidly traditional set of beliefs and practices, based on
unchanging sacred principles.

Guru In Eastern religions, a wise leader.

Modernization Historical process in which family-based work units were
replaced by factories; young people left the land and went to cities; reliance
on science and technology increased and focus shifted to this world rather
than the next.

New Religious Movements (NRM) An umbrella term that covers a range of
organizations and practices that fall within the broad definition of a belief
system as involving a search for transcendent meaning, shared rituals, and a
commitment to a code of conduct.

Priests Keepers of holy traditions and places and protectors of all things
sacred.

Profane Behaviors and objects that are earthly and understandable in everyday terms.

Prophets Charismatic figures who challenge the status quo.

Religion A system of beliefs and rituals.

Religious Roles Sets of behaviors involved in the supervision of sacred objects, places, and ceremonies.

Routinization of Charisma Transformation of a sacred mission into an effective institution under the control of priests.

Sacred Behaviors and objects that are invested with divine or supernatural
force.

Sectarian Conflict Open violence between religious groups.

Secular Humanism A belief system based on rational understanding and a
commitment and a commitment to improving lives in the world.

Secular Ideology A belief system based on worldly rather than supernatural
forces.

Secular Spirit Celebrates the individual and the pleasures of the senses.

Theocracy The rule of religious authorities.

Wicca Practice of witchcraft within the framework of women's spiritual identity; term also used for wise woman healers who were often accused of witchcraft during the witch hunts of the Middle Ages. ✦

Chapter 13

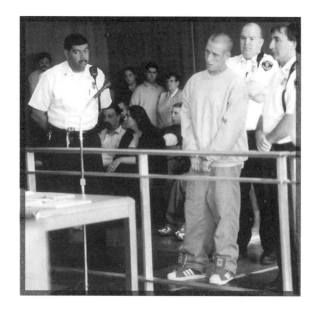

Crimes and Punishments:
The Criminal Justice System

❖ ❖ ❖ ❖   As the Mikado in the Gilbert and Sullivan operetta sang, while claiming to be among the more humane of leaders:

> My object all sublime
>
> I shall achieve in time—
>
> To let the punishment fit the crime—
>
> And make each prisoner pent
>
> Unwillingly represent
>
> A source of innocent merriment!

Not much has changed since 1885. Devising a punishment to fit the crime and possibly reduce its repetition is still a bit of a puzzle, while as a source of innocent merriment, one of the hottest toys of the year 2000 was Death Row Marv, who comes strapped to an electric chair and convulses when a switch is thrown. This chapter looks at issues of criminality and the justice system, namely:

- The criminals.
- The police.
- The courts.
- The prisons.

Criminals

What is a crime? Anything that violates the laws. Who makes the laws? The people with authority to do so. As you learned in chapter 3, what is considered normative, and by the same token what falls outside the norms, is a matter of social definition. Because laws are norms that cover behavior essential to the survival of the group, their violation brings harsh sanctions. Laws change over time, however, and they are seldom applied in the same way to each subgroup. In this sense, criminality is a social variable—not a characteristic of the individual but a judgment of that person's behavior.

Laws often cover activity that only some people are likely to do; who, after all, is affected by vagrancy statutes or by curfews? As the writer Anatole France (1894/1917) put it: "The law in its majestic equality forbids the rich as well as the poor to sleep under bridges, to beg in the streets, and to steal bread." At the same time, the law does not criminalize other actions that could be considered dangerous to public safety, such as performing unnecessary surgery, building faulty bridges, or failing to test new drugs adequately— although all of these can lead to law suits and fines in the civil rather than criminal courts.

Theoretical Perspectives

The major sociological perspectives on crime build on the models of deviant behavior mentioned in chapter 3: *blocked opportunity, differential association, inequality,* and *anomie.* 1 In plainer language, criminals tend to be people who do not have much going for them, who hang out with people who break the law, who are poor and poorly educated, and who do not feel much attachment to the rest of society. There is little to tie them to the law-abiding world, such as a job, a stable marriage, religious commitment, or community roots. At some point, when it appears that the gains from criminal activity outweigh the potential costs, people will make a rational choice among alternatives—or a choice that seems rational when the person is under the influence of alcohol or drugs. From the viewpoint of the actor, as shaped by experience and community norms, and in the context of the situation, the acts of a criminal, even violent ones, make sense (Athens 1997). 🖥 2

Not all violators of the law fit this description, just the ones who are likely to be caught, processed through the justice system, and sent to prison. These are the ones who commit street crimes.

Crime in the Streets

When Americans think about "crime," they probably visualize being attacked on the street by a dark stranger. In fact, despite widespread fears, rates for street crimes have been declining for more than twenty years, as shown in Figure 13.1. The data for Figures 13.1a and 13.1b come from a yearly sample survey of over 40,000 households and 80,000 individuals age 12 and over conducted by the U.S. Department of Justice; those surveyed are asked about all incidents in which a household member was the victim of a crime or an attempted crime, whether or not reported to the police.

As you can see, victimization rates have fallen sharply over the past decade, especially for property crimes. Violent crimes, those that involve a physical assault, rose sharply in the early 1990s, largely as a result of the crack cocaine epidemic in low-income areas, when homicide and robbery rates soared as sellers fought over turf and buyers scrounged for money.

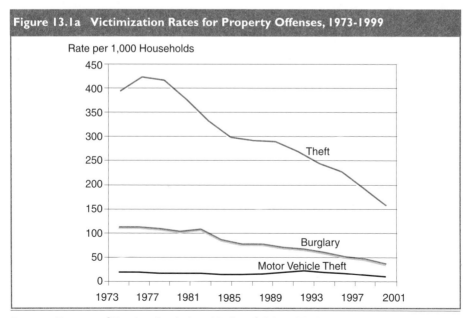

Figure 13.1a Victimization Rates for Property Offenses, 1973-1999

Source: Bureau of Justice Statistics, *National Crime Victimization Survey, 2000.*

Figure 13.1b   Victimization Rates for Violent Offenses, 1973-1999

Rate per 1,000 Persons

(Graph showing Simple Assault, Aggravated Assault, Robbery, and Rape rates per 1,000 persons from 1973 to 2001)

Source: Bureau of Justice Statistics, *National Crime Victimization Survey, 2000.*

When the popularity of crack declined and neighborhoods united to stop the scourge, the rates for both violent and property crimes fell.

IN ONE YEAR FIREARMS KILLED 19 CHILDREN IN GREAT BRITAIN, 153 IN CANADA, 0 IN JAPAN, 57 IN GERMANY AND 5,286 CHILDREN IN THE UNITED STATES.

PERHAPS WE SHOULD CHANGE THE SCHOOL DRESS CODE.

A major reason for the high rate of homicides in the United States is the easy availability of handguns. In one year firearms killed 5 children in Japan, 19 children in Great Britain, 57 in Germany, 106 in Canada, and 9,390 in the United States. Which groups favor the control of handguns and which groups oppose control? Why?

Other factors behind the drop include: (1) the aging of the baby boomers beyond the crime-prone years; (2) police efforts to stop gun violence; (3) more sophisticated security devices in homes and businesses; (4) the increase in legitimate employment in the late 1990s; and (5) an increase in the prison population, although imprisonment rates had been rising for three decades and cannot explain the jump in crime between 1989 and 1993, followed by an abrupt drop in 1995. Some researchers have even suggested that the decline in crime is a delayed effect of the legalization of abortion in 1973 that reduced the number of children growing up under high-risk circumstances (Donahue and Levitt 2000). For whatever causes, American streets are much safer today than in the 1970s, although they are still a bit more dangerous than in most modern societies. 🖥 3

Victims and perpetrators. Because most street crime is committed by young men in their own neighborhoods, the perpetrators and victims are demographically similar: disproportionately black and Latino, male, and relatively poor. If you are worried about your grandmother being attacked, rest easy; she is the least likely target, having little to offer an attacker. Ironically, while white suburbanites list crime as a serious problem, they are relatively immune from its occurrence. Concern about crime is most intense where it is a visible problem day after day, namely inner-city neighborhoods in which the proportion of minority poor rises as crime rates drive out anyone who can afford to move (Liska et al. 1998).

Index crimes. In addition to the Department of Justice's National Victim-ization Survey, crime statistics are also gathered by the Federal Bureau of Investigation (FBI) from reports filed by state and local law enforcement agencies. These data count only crimes that have been reported to the police, or roughly 40 percent of all victimizations. 🖥 4 The more violent the crime or the greater the money loss, the more likely it is to be reported. From these reports, the FBI tabulates an **index** of the seven most serious offenses: (1) vio-lent crimes such as murder, rape, robbery, and aggravated assault, and (2) property crimes such as burglary, larceny, and motor vehicle theft. Of these, the most closely watched and analyzed is the murder, or homicide, rate, although homicides are relatively rare.

Homicide. From a recent high in early 1993, the number of murders per 100,000 Americans has declined for all age groups in each subsequent year until a slight rise in early 2000. The 1990s drop was most dramatic for 14- to 17-year-olds—the very age group once predicted to become a generation of "superpredators" (Bennett et al. 1996).

Figure 13.2 shows the fluctuations in homicide rates since 1950, espe-

Figure 13.2 Homicide Victimization, 1950–2000 (Rate per 100,000 population)

Source: Federal Bureau of Investigation, *Uniform Crime Reports*, various years.

cially the dramatic increases in the 1970s, as Baby Boom children reached their late teens.

Young men between ages 18 and 24 continue to commit most murders, as well as being a majority of the victims. Homicide is the leading cause of death among young black men, with a rate of almost 150 per 100,000 aged 20 to 24,

❖ ❖ ❖ ❖   compared to 16 per 100,000 for young white men. In most cases, the victim and attacker were known to one another (U.S. Department of Justice 1999). Women are most likely to be murdered by a husband or boyfriend; men by another man with whom they have quarreled.

Even at its current low of 6.5 per 100,000 population, the U.S. homicide rate is higher than that for other modern societies. A number of reasons have been given for America's historically high murder rate: (1) a frontier/macho mentality; (2) availability of handguns; (3) economic inequality; (4) residential segregation; and (5) lack of a social welfare safety net. All these factors increase the likelihood that young people have little to link them to the social institutions that promote conformity—family, school, work, and neighborhood. 5 What they do have is a gun.

The gun debate. Gun ownership in the United States is so widespread that it is difficult to show a statistically significant relationship between having a gun in the house and becoming a murderer or a victim (Kleck and Hogan 1999). Some researchers even claim that the more guns there are in circulation, the lower the crime rate because if potential victims are armed, it raises the "price" of the crime to the potential offender (Lott 1998). Other sociologists have marshaled equally compelling evidence of the crucial role of guns in the level of violence in the society. Comparing the high U.S. homicide rate with the very low one in Canada, for example, researchers concluded that the primary difference between the two societies is the ready availability of guns in the United States (Hagan and Foster 2000). Of those killed by guns, the rate was ten times higher in the United States than in Canada. 6

American gun makers and organizations such as the National Rifle Association form a powerful political lobby; they donated millions of dollars to candidates and political parties throughout the 1990s in their successful effort to limit gun control legislation. Despite public concern over school shootings in the late 1990s, gun manufacturers and distributors are reaching out to the youth market, as illustrated by articles and advertisements in gun culture magazines.

Box 13.1

'Stick 'Em Up!'

In one of the few studies of actual street criminals (Wright and Decker 1997), the researchers found that the men committed only a few robberies a month, mostly to get money for drugs or gambling or to build their street reputation. They picked targets that could provide a lot of cash with minimal effort, which is why liquor stores or people who have just cashed checks are especially attractive. Another common target is other criminals, such as drug dealers, who carry wads of cash and are not likely to call in the police. By the same token, though, the street robbers themselves become tempting victims.

All but a few of the robbers had been caught by the police and had served time, but this rarely deterred them from planning their next crime. Apparently, the immediate pleasures that could be purchased with stolen goods outweighed the fear of getting caught or hurt or robbed. In this sense the criminals are acting rationally, given their limited calculation of costs and benefits. What would it take for you to decide to lift the wallet of some prosperous-looking man on the street?

At the moment, the schools are actually less violent than the homes or neighborhoods of many children, and may be no more violent than they ever were. At least through 1997, the percent of ninth- to twelfth- graders reporting that they carried a weapon to school declined steadily. But since the number of schoolchildren has increased and so have the number of weapons in their homes, the potential severity of school violence may have risen (Kingery et al. 1999).

❖ ❖ ❖ ❖

'Quality of Life' Crimes

A new element in the fight against crime in urban areas is a campaign to improve the quality of life by closing down pornography shops, getting rid of the "squeegie men" who demand money for cleaning your car windshield, locking up school truants, giving tickets to jaywalkers, and impounding the cars of illegal parkers. Some of these offenses apply to middle-class citizens as well as to the poor, but the ones who end up in jail are not the men or women in business suits.

The idea behind the crackdown on minor offenses (the *broken window* theory) is that when people get away with little violations of the law, they soon graduate to more serious offenses (Bennett et al. 1996). Effective law enforcement, then, depends on stopping the minor offenses before things get out of control, a policy that was adopted by New York mayor Rudy Giuliani with dramatic results. The streets are cleaner and safer, and ordinary people feel that they can walk out without fear. Crime rates are down for all types of offenses, but this was also true of almost every large American city in the late 1990s (Federal Bureau of Investigation 1999).

Female Criminals

Although violent crime remains an almost exclusively male pursuit, property crimes involving females have risen over the past two decades. In addition, the courts are more likely than in the past to sentence women to prison. As a consequence, the female prison population is increasing at a slightly faster rate than that for males. Nonetheless, females still comprise only about 7 percent of prison inmates, and most are there for drug-related offenses (Belknap 2001). Prisons for women, however, are very expensive; there is not the same economy of scale as with a men's prison. An added cost to the incarceration (the word means "put behind walls") of a mother is the expense of providing foster care and other services to her children. As a result, there is pressure to

Property crimes involving women have risen over the past two decades with courts more likely than in the past to sentence women to prison.

❖ ❖ ❖ ❖   find alternatives for dealing with female offenders.

Most crimes committed by women are an extension of their female roles, as mothers, wives, and girlfriends. Typically, they steal to feed their children; run drugs or become prostitutes to please a boyfriend; and turn violent after years of abuse from a husband or lover. Also, it is they who are left to fend for themselves and their children when the men in their lives are murdered or jailed (Miller 1997; Girshick 1999).

For the most part, when women erupt in violence, it consists of simple assaults directed at someone they know, and often under the influence of alcohol or drugs (U.S. Department of Justice 1999). For many, the pattern of violence and abuse is a continuation of childhood experiences. As with male prisoners, the proportions that say that they were physically or sexually abused as children is double that of the population in general: 36 percent of women in prison compared to 17 percent in the population. The comparable figures for men are 14 percent in prison versus 5 to 8 percent outside (*New York Times,* April 12, 2000). 💻 7

Juvenile Offenders

A juvenile (the word means "youth") is whatever the law says, and the designation can vary from year to year, state to state, and from crime to crime, making comparisons unreliable. In addition, juveniles can be charged for acts that are not crimes if done by adults. These **status offenses** include running away from home, skipping school, drinking alcoholic beverages, and being out of control (*incorrigible*). As trivial as some of these offenses may seem, youth delinquency does have long-term negative impacts on educational attainment and occupational success for both males and females (Tanner et al. 1999). In part, these effects reflect a risk-prone social environment, but they are also greatly influenced by how authorities deal with the delinquent.

The creation of a separate system of justice for young people was based on the belief that a juvenile cannot have the same awareness of right and wrong, or as much control over behavior, as does an adult, and therefore should be dealt with differently. Juvenile courts were designed to keep young offenders out of the adult criminal justice system, and judges were given great leeway in devising alternatives to young people being officially labeled as criminals.

This trend was abruptly reversed in the early 1990s when rising juvenile crime rates created public pressure for the criminal prosecution of young

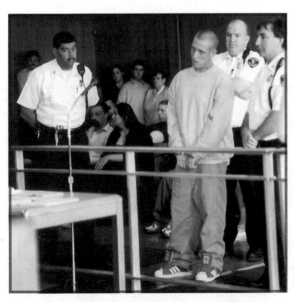

Juveniles can be charged for acts that are not crimes if committed by adults, such as running away from home, skipping school, drinking, and being out of control.

people. "Commit the crime, do the time" was the rallying cry, and every state now has at least one provision for trying a youthful offender as an adult. Even though all forms of juvenile crime have declined since 1993, a few highly publicized cases revived public fears, and 1999 saw a number of teenagers sentenced to from 25 years to life, escaping the death penalty only because they were under age 16 when the crime was committed. One boy who was 11 at the time of his crime will spend the rest of his childhood with adult offenders, and would have remained much longer had the judge not "stunned prosecutors and disappointed lawmakers" by limiting the sentence to seven years (Bradsher 2000, 1). Since 1997, between 7,500 and 8,000 juveniles have been sent to adult prisons each year, over half for crimes of violence, but also several hundred for motor vehicle theft (Strom 2000). 🖥 8

Even though most of the high-profile homicides by juveniles involved white youths, the harshest penalties have been imposed on black and Latino youngsters. Some of the difference in sentencing is due to stereotyping by court personnel, and some is due to the fact that minority youth and their families lack the resources necessary to avoid imprisonment—good lawyers, psychiatric services, or the money to attend alternative schools, for example (Bridges and Steen 1998). Just recently, a student at an elite preparatory school who carved an anti-gay slur into the back of another student was given a suspended sentence of two and a half years (Goldberg 2000). How do you think the episode would have been defined if the knife-wielder had been a 17-year-old African American?

Indeed, racial disparities are found at every level of the juvenile justice system, from being under suspicion to the length of the prison sentence. The result is that, although black youth comprise only 15 percent of the population under age 18, they account for 26 percent of juvenile arrests, 33 percent of cases sent through the courts, 45 percent of young people in detention, 66 percent of the inmates of secure juvenile facilities, and 58 percent of juveniles in adult prison (U.S. Department of Justice 2000). Of all cases of juveniles transferred to the adult system for every type of offense, black youths were more likely than white to be sent on to the criminal courts (U.S. Department of Justice 2000b).

Juvenile prisons. There are dangers for juveniles sent to an adult facility, but things may not be much better in juvenile institutions. Overcrowding and understaffing, tough inmates and poorly supervised guards are a recipe for brutality and violence. In 1999, for example, abuses in the California juvenile correctional system ranged from forcible injections of sedatives to leaving boys handcuffed to urine-soaked beds all night (Whitaker 1999). The grand prize, however, has to be shared by the Jena and Tallulah Correctional Facilities in Louisiana, which the state had turned over to a profit-making company. A state judge removed inmates after finding that they had been brutalized by guards, kept in solitary confinement for months without cause, and deprived of adequate food, clothing, recreation, schooling, and medical and psychiatric care, even though several hundred of the boys suffered from mental illness or retardation (Butterfield 1999, 2000). Indeed, nationwide, it is estimated that between 50 and 75 percent of incarcerated juveniles suffer from physical and emotional disabilities (Burrell and Warboys 2000). Finally, in late 2000, the state of Louisiana agreed to a court order to abandon its private youth prisons and to provide adequate health and mental health care

(Butterfield 2000b). The private company, however, still operates juvenile facilities in a dozen other states.

Louisiana is not an exception. Other privatized juvenile systems have been sued on the basis of "cruel and unusual punishment," and some companies have been closed down; the federal Department of Justice has recently investigated reports of abuses in public facilities, as well. Nonetheless, the money-saving appeal of privatization is far stronger than any fears about the well-being of the inmates, and over one-third of the states have contracted out some of their custodial responsibilities.

Boot camps. One of the hot ideas of the 1980s was to take juveniles and treat them like military recruits, on the assumption that strict discipline would shape up the delinquent youth. Despite a decade of data from the U.S. Department of Justice showing that "boot camps" not only failed to reform but also had negative effects, state politicians continued to fund the facilities. In actuality, the boot-camp paramilitary model encourages brutality, and unless the boys are provided with employable skills and followup social services, they commit additional crimes at the same rate as comparable youth not sent to the camps. Because the recruits were selected for success—first-time nonviolent offenders with community ties—the failure of the camps is even more striking (Zachariah 1999). It took a series of adolescent deaths and newspaper exposés of widespread physical abuses finally to get the attention of state legislators; some states are consequently phasing out their camps while others continue to expand the program. The belief that harsh discipline is good for the soul dies hard, but the real lesson is one that you learned in chapter 3: Physical punishment is not an effective teaching tool.

Many of the same problems are also found in another popular program with surface plausibility, *Scared Straight*. It seems logical to assume that if young people heard directly from convicts, in horrifying detail, about how crime messed up their lives, the listeners would be frightened out of any impulse to misbehave. Yet there is little empirical evidence to support this claim. One carefully designed study found that in addition to not deterring youngsters from delinquency, the program probably encouraged deviance (Finckenauer 1999).

Organized crime has flourished in Russia since the breakup of the Soviet Union. Here several suspects are being arrested for the illegal purchase of property.

Organized Crime

A more seasoned set of criminals consists of the adults who belong to "criminal families," organizations engaged in illegal activities. The best-known example is the network of real and fictional kin, originally from Sicily, lumped together in the popular mind as The Mafia. But organized crime in America is not some exotic import from Italy. In the 1880s, the organizations were run by Irish and German immigrants, and in the Prohibition years of the 1920s, your neighborhood supplier of liquor was as likely to be Jewish as Catholic. Today, most of the low-level or "dirty" work—prostitution, drugs, loan sharking—has been spun off to African-American, Latino, and Asian gangs. As Merton's model of deviance and anomie predicts (chapter 3), members of racial and ethnic groups who are denied access to legitimate means of success will find illegal activities very rewarding. And so it has been throughout our history (O'Kane 1992).

Organized crime groups prosper when (1) they supply goods and services not legally available, such as drugs, prostitutes, or risky loans; (2) public officials are easily corrupted; and (3) members are willing to use force. Today, many of the older crime families have been broken up by law enforcement agencies, and others have matured to the point that they can take over legitimate businesses and milk them for cash before selling out. By the third generation, also, the children and grandchildren of criminals have been able to achieve upward mobility through respectable channels. 🖥9

Some of these generational dynamics are played out in the television series *The Sopranos*, with Tony Soprano poised between the old-time mobsters and his own violent business interests, on the one hand, and the yearning for respectability of his wife and college-bound children, on the other. The distance between the two worlds is conveyed in the opening sequence of each episode as Tony drives from the mob's headquarters in an Italian neighborhood of a North Jersey city to his newly built mansion in a classy suburb.

Crime in the Suites

As frightening as street crime is, it involves far less money and harm to public health and safety than the crimes committed by many businessmen and businesswomen. It is also likely that there are more criminals in the office suites than in the streets, but the very nature of their crimes makes it difficult to uncover the offenses and pursue the offenders (Coleman 1998).

White-collar crime refers to illegal acts committed by respectable persons for their own gain, in the course of their employment. Embezzlement, theft, kickbacks, and trading securities on the basis of insider information are common forms of white-collar crime. Most cases involve low-level employees and small sums taken by people under temporary financial stress because of gambling losses or because they cannot make child support or credit card payments; these people plan to put it back as soon as possible. They usually get away with it because they can slip under the radar—no one is looking, the amounts are not glaring, and law enforcement personnel have few resources for following paper trails (Freidrich 1996).

But there are also some very big cases; for example, multimillion-dollar stock market scams that take years to unravel and are extremely difficult and expensive to prosecute, because the accused file appeal after appeal. Perhaps the most astounding instance of white-collar criminality involved hundreds of executives of American savings and loans associations in the 1980s who took advantage of a change in the law that allowed them to make unsecured loans to friends and relatives—which they then did to the tune of *$500 billion* in unpaid debt, ultimately covered by American taxpayers at a cost of about $4,000 each (Glasberg and Skidmore 1997). Only a few of these executives have been prosecuted; the one conviction was later overturned on appeal; and little of the money has been recovered.

White-collar crime is not confined to the corporate sector. Government employment, especially at the city level, also affords opportunities to line one's pockets. There are kickbacks to building inspectors, rigged auctions of confiscated property, and full-time public employees receiving welfare benefits—all three of these stories appeared on the same page of the *New York Times* for June 12, 1999.

As the economy shifts from manufacturing to services and electronic commerce, opportunities for white-collar crime will multiply, while the technology needed to keep everyone honest will lag well behind. A "worst case" scenario is being played out in Russia, where the government is powerless to control the excesses of free enterprise unleashed by the fall of the Soviet Union; the result has been corruption and criminal activity that have siphoned off billions of dollars that end up being laundered across the globe (Bonner 1999).

Organizational crime is also committed in the course of a person's employment but for the good of the business itself rather than for one's self. When pharmaceutical companies fail to disclose negative test results, when defense contractors fill out dummy invoices, when insurance companies inflate Medicare claims, when city employees falsify records, and when cigarette makers shred documents, employees are committing crimes in the routine discharge of their jobs. Because nobody is mugged, and because the criminals look just like the people who run the country, it takes something dramatic to alert the public to the fact that a crime has been committed, and even then, the details are usually so complex that the response is often a huge shrug. Even if the company should be indicted, its officers are usually protected from personal responsibility.

Government officials have also broken the law, destroyed documents, and given false testimony when they thought it necessary for the good of the nation. Only in 1994, for example, did the U.S. Department of Energy release records of experiments conducted in the 1950s, when prison inmates, mental hospital patients, and nursing home residents were exposed to low-level radiation to test its effects on civilians (Hilts 1996). These particular civilians, however, could not give informed consent; nor could the 400 African-American men in the rural South who were intentionally inoculated with syphilis and left untreated for 25 years in the government Tuskegee experiments of the 1970s (Yoon 1997). 🖥 10

Victimless Crimes

A third category of crime cuts across both the street and the suites. **Victimless crimes** are those in which the victims have willingly participated. No one is forced to visit a prostitute or is likely to go to the station house and complain that he did not get his money's worth. The same is true for illegal gambling, borrowing money at very high interest, and buying cocaine. When something that is highly desirable is forbidden by law, someone will step in to provide it, typically an organized crime family.

Some victimless crimes depend on extremely gullible or greedy victims—those who think you can get something for nothing. *Confidence games* depend on winning the trust of the "marks" and setting them up to hand over their money with the promise of greater riches to come. "Gifting clubs" are the latest variation on the ever-popular **pyramid scheme**, in which newcomers provide the funds to pay off those who entered earlier. You are told that your $2,000 "gift" to the club may eventually be worth $16,000 if you get two more people to join and they each get two more and so on. The first ones in the club will get out with their $16,000, but at each subsequent stage the numbers needed to pay out will increase geometrically, so that after 15 rounds you would need eight million new members—and the pyramid collapses (Hanley 1999). It is such an inviting scheme, though, that a new club will open tomorrow and thousands of people will line up to join.

Victimless crimes have an additional public cost in that they place law enforcement personnel in a very vulnerable position. The police are asked to enforce morality, never an easy task, but when your commanding officer says, "Today, let's clear the streets of the floozies," and there are more of them than can fit into your van, which ones will you arrest? The ones whose looks you don't like? The ones whose pimp hasn't given you a holiday turkey or information? And what about that stash of drugs just sitting there waiting to be logged into the evidence room—who would miss a few bags? Why raid one poker game rather than another? It is in these moments, when the police have choices in cases of victimless crimes, that doubts can find a toehold, which is why it is so often the morals or vice squad that is involved in cases of police corruption.

Drug-Related Offenses

The victimless crime with the greatest impact on law enforcement today is illegal drug use. Prescription medications are legal, but the production and ingestion of heroin, cocaine, marijuana, peyote (from mushrooms), and of synthetic substances such as Ecstasy are forbidden by law. Being forbidden guarantees that a thriving market will emerge, so that law enforcement resources devoted to the problem need to be increased.

It appears that the habitual use of marijuana and powder cocaine by adults dropped dramatically between 1986 and 1991 and has since leveled off. The use of crack cocaine (the kind that is smoked in contrast to the powdered form that gets sniffed) has remained steady: about one-half of 1 percent of the population uses it (Department of Health and Human Services 1999). Among teenagers, pot smoking increased during the 1990s before leveling off in 1997, while the use of Ecstacy

The federal war on drugs has not reduced the use of crack cocaine because when one dealer is put away, it creates a vacancy chain soon filled with another supplier.

Roll Out the Barrels

The line between deviance and criminality is written in the sands of politics. Although criminal penalties for opiates and narcotics are increasingly harsh, the most deadly drugs in America —alcohol and tobacco—are perfectly legal and freely available in most of the nation. Deaths attributed to drinking and smoking are five to 20 times higher than those linked to illegal drug use (U.S. Department of Health and Human Services 1998). Clearly, the difference in legal status among drugs has little to do with actual public health hazards and much to do with the political clout of tobacco interests and the widespread public demand for alcohol.

The one national attempt to regulate alcohol, the Eighteenth Amendment in 1919, was repealed in 1933, but not before a vast criminal network emerged to provide the forbidden fruit. Today, while a few Midwest counties remain "dry" (alcohol sales forbidden), the rest of the nation is awash in beer, wine, and hard liquor. Over 32 million Americans in 1997 engaged in binge drinking, defined as five or more drinks at one sitting, and 11 million, primarily white and male, are estimated to be heavy drinkers (U.S. Department of Health and Human Services 1999). As traditional home to the great breweries of America and of a large German-American beer-loving population, Wisconsin has the most bars and highest proportion of binge drinkers, 23.2 percent, compared with Maryland, the lowest at 6.3 percent (Johnson 2000b).

Drinking and bingeing are alive and well on college campuses, most notably on fraternity row, despite efforts by school administrators to control alcohol use, especially among underage students (Weschler 2000). Arrests for alcohol and drug-related offenses at the nation's colleges rose sharply in the late 1990s, although this may reflect tougher enforcement rather than heavier use (Nicklin 2000). Not surprisingly, the University of Wisconsin ranked number one in drinking arrests in 1997. In contrast, most religiously affiliated colleges and universities have banned alcohol altogether. How would you describe the drinking scene on your campus?

rose from about 6 to 8 percent of high school seniors, along with a slight increase in heroin use among white suburban teenagers (University of Michigan 2000).

Although rates of illegal drug use among adults had already peaked and were on the decline, fear of a major crack cocaine epidemic in the late 1980s led Congress and the states to pass very strict laws, with long mandatory prison terms for even minor offenses. There was strong evidence that crack use in the inner cities contributed to high rates of homicide and other violent crimes, and the same was feared for other communities. As it happened, crack cocaine never spread to the suburbs, and it created such havoc in urban areas that its use fell there, too. By the time the epidemic faded, however, the new laws led to a dramatic increase in drug arrests, as shown in Figure 13.3.

Although the national Household Survey on Drug Abuse found that the typical drug addict was a white suburban male in his twenties, that is not who gets arrested and sent away. Because most drug sweeps by the police take place where blacks live, blacks now comprise 60 percent of prisoners doing time for drug offenses, even though they constitute only 12 percent of the population and 16 percent of regular drug users (Human Rights Watch 2000). In Columbus, Ohio, for example, where black males are about 11 percent of the population, they account for 90 percent of drug arrests (Cole 1999). In the meantime, the suburban sniffers of powder cocaine go relatively untouched; they are subject to minor penalties if caught and are rarely shown

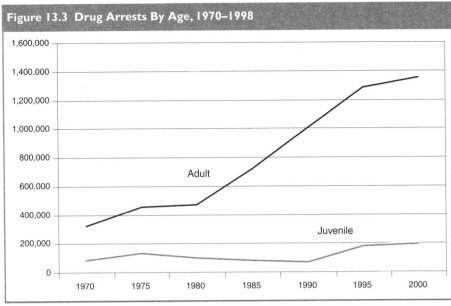

Figure 13.3 Drug Arrests By Age, 1970–1998

Source: Federal Bureau of Investigation, 1999.

on the late night news programs, so that the public continues to perceive drug abuse as a minority problem.

The federal "war on drugs" has failed to reduce the use of crack cocaine because when one dealer is put away, it creates a *vacancy chain* that soon gets filled with another supplier. The war's emphasis on stopping the supply has led to billions of dollars spent on reducing the flow of heroin from other countries, with minimal success. But the war cannot be called off because too many politicians are fully invested in get-tough rhetoric and because there is a lot of money to be made in the antidrug business, including programs for schools such as D.A.R.E. (also ineffective) and especially the booming industry of building and staffing prisons, which is discussed later in this chapter (Perrucci and Wysong 1999).

Efforts to control the demand rather than the supply, however, remain greatly underfunded and politically unpopular ("coddling criminals"), even though such policies would lower crime rates by reducing the number of addicts who need to commit crimes to pay for their habit. There is evidence that the methadone treatment program initiated in the 1970s was very effective in controlling a heroin epidemic and reducing drug-related crime (Massing 1998). There is also agreement among criminal justice experts that treatment of addicts, in the community or in prison, would be more cost effective than the current dependence on incarceration. Thus, even as the number of drug-related offenders rises, treatment programs are cut because the corrections budgets are eaten up by the costs of building and maintaining the prison system (Butterfield 1999).

Another approach from the demand side involves **decriminalizing**—removing criminal penalties—from minor forms of drug use, without actually legalizing it. On the plus side, taking the profit out of the drug trade should reduce crime and the cost of more prisons; on the minus side, the numbers of users might increase and overwhelm the health care system.

❖ ❖ ❖ ❖   Here is another tough social issue for you to grapple with in the years ahead. ⌨11

The Police

As formal agents of social control, with responsibility for on-the-spot decisions about how to maintain public order, police officers have a lot of discretionary power. This power is directed most often at the people who are thought to present the clearest danger to public safety. Without immediate supervision on the job, officers react to stereotyped expectations, leading to disproportionate arrest rates of poor people and persons of color (Cole 1999). Sometimes police behavior reflects deeply held prejudices, as with the New Jersey State Police, whose decades-long harassment of minority colleagues and "racial profiling" in arrests finally led the federal government to intervene (Hennelly 1999).

Occupational Strains

Police work has a number of built-in contradictions and strains (Barker 1999). Although an officer may have discretionary power on the street, the organization of police work is a strict hierarchy, just like the military. An officer is king of the streets but also dependent on public trust and assistance. When out of uniform, the officer must enact ordinary civilian roles. In many cases, the people drawn to police work as an avenue of upward mobility are from the same ethnic or racial groups as the criminals they are chasing. For example, in New York City in the early 1900s, Irish and German cops dominated the departments; in the 1920s, Italians and Jews entered the force in large numbers; and today increasing numbers of blacks and Latinos, women as well as men, are pounding the beat.

Police work involves a number of strains on family life. Workers in any occupation with irregular hours and split shifts have high rates of marital break-up. In addition, the fact that the officer shares the dangers and triumphs of work with a partner, to the exclusion of a husband or wife, can cause problems in a marriage. "What did you do today?" the spouse asks. The officer answers: "Nothing much" or "You wouldn't understand" or "I don't want to talk about it." How long before the husband or wife storms out of the house?

Especially frustrating to a police officer may be the realization that nothing you do on the job seems to have a lasting effect (Barker 1999). The war on drugs has diverted a lot of resources from dealing with the basic causes of crime that lie in the social and economic disintegration of urban centers. You deal with dirt and violence all day long. There is not much respect from the public or the press. The pay is low, especially compared with what the criminals are stashing away. It is truly a jungle out there. And when you lose your cool, there are only your fellow officers to protect you. ⌨12

Private Police

Today, many men and women who feel drawn to police work can find ready employment in the private sector. Guard and security work is one of the fastest-growing occupations, ranging from patrolling the gated communities of the wealthy to collecting fines for regular police departments. Private security now employs three times as many people as are engaged in official police work. Many college campuses have a private police force as large as that of the surrounding town.

There are limits on how much regular police work can be farmed out to private companies. In theory, only the state can use force to secure compliance with the laws, and the state is run by elected officials, ultimately responsible to the voting public. In contrast, private security forces are responsible only to their employers and do not have to meet the same legal standards of fairness as do the regular police. For example, one study of department store detectives found that shoplifters were treated differently on the basis of social class; the relatively well-off were assessed damages, while the poor were referred to the local police (Davis et al. 1991).

These considerations have not kept state governments from trying to save money by privatizing their jails and prisons, as discussed in the section on juvenile facilities. By the year 2000, almost every state had contracted out some correctional responsibilities to profit-making companies, who can hire nonunion guards, can shift prisoners from one state to another, and can pretty much run their facility outside the supervision of public authorities. Public authorities insisted on tightened safeguards only after some well-publicized violent incidents, but the private corrections lobby has managed to minimize outside controls (Belluck 1999). Thus, it has fallen to the courts to deal with potential abuses within the criminal justice system, even as the courts are overwhelmed by other judicial responsibilities.

The Courts

In the United States, an accused person must be told the nature of the charge, have legal assistance if requested, and be tried by a jury of peers (status equals). 💻 13 In reality, most cases are settled by a guilty plea or by release of the suspect because of lack of evidence. Of the few cases that do go to trial, most defendants prefer to appear before a judge without a jury. At each stage

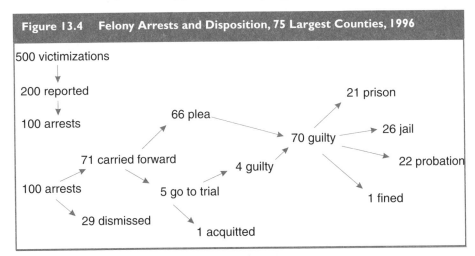

Figure 13.4   Felony Arrests and Disposition, 75 Largest Counties, 1996

500 victimizations

200 reported

100 arrests

66 plea

70 guilty

21 prison

26 jail

22 probation

1 fined

71 carried forward

4 guilty

100 arrests

5 go to trial

29 dismissed

1 acquitted

Source: *Sourcebook of Criminal Justice Online*, 2000.

of the process, cases are lost or dropped, so that the people who end up in prison are typically very unlucky or very poor. The flow of offenders through the criminal justice system is shown in Figure 13.4.

Justice: Ideal and Real

You may have seen a statue of Justice at your local courthouse. She holds a sword in one hand, a set of scales in the other, and wears a blindfold. The symbolism is powerful: (1) the sword for swift justice—"justice delayed is justice denied;" (2) the scales for fairness—giving the accused all the legal rights needed to protect an individual from the overwhelming force of the state; and (3) the blindfold for impartiality—not seeing race, sex, or class. In practice, however, she is rarely swift, is much more fair to the rich than to the poor, and is very much aware of race and gender.

The slowness comes from an overloaded docket (schedule of cases), as longer and harsher penalties are being imposed for more kinds of crimes while little money has been added for more courtrooms, judges, and court personnel. It is not unusual for cases to take a year or more to be heard and to have someone sitting in jail for all that time, unable to raise bail. The unfairness is a result of the differing resources available to defendants in terms of quality of legal help and ability to hire private investigators and to provide character witnesses. Race and gender play a role in how judges and juries perceive the defendant and the victim. Can you imagine the attorney for a homeboy telling the judge, "Your honor, the negative publicity surrounding this case has been punishment enough for my client and his family"? The end result is that even when convicted, white middle-class defendants receive shorter terms and are more likely to be sentenced to community service, left in the care of their psychiatrist, or otherwise kept out of prison than are other defendants. Thus, the prisons are increasingly filled with darker, poorer, and more violent prisoners, and the darker the prisons become, the less likely are judges to send white defendants there even after conviction.

The upshot is a dual system of justice in which money and skin color make all the difference at every stage: being caught, being processed, being tried, being found guilty, and being sentenced to a prison term. Twenty-eight percent of black males will enter prison at some point in their lives, compared to 4.4 percent of white males (Bureau of Justice Statistics 2000).

Plea Bargains

One way in which the quality of your legal help can have an impact is in negotiating with prosecutors for a reduced charge. **Plea bargains**, whereby a suspect agrees to confess to a lesser charge, is how most criminal arrests are resolved. Why would you plead to a crime? If you thought that you might be convicted on the greater charge and do not have the resources to fight it out in court. Why would the district attorney's office agree? If it had a backlog of cases, little time to prepare, not much evidence, and a staff shortage that could jeopardize the chance of a conviction. The costs of going to court—in terms of money, time, and risk of failure—are very high for both parties. The plea bargain is a "win-win" situation for everyone except the wrongfully accused and the arresting officers who see their work go up in smoke.

Thus, when politicians call for "no more plea bargains" without also providing funds for expanding the court system and the district attorney's office, they risk creating such a backlog that minor suspects will be let go before they even need to plead.

Punishments

How does a society make the punishment fit the crime? Does that mean a punishment proportional to the social costs of the crime? Or a punishment that will reform the criminal? Or a punishment that makes law-abiding citizens feel that justice has been done? Should judges be able to tailor the punishment to the specific case? Or should there be clear guidelines that ensure comparable treatment of similar cases? There are many such questions and very few solid answers.

At this writing, the public favors long and mandatory sentences (Rossi and Berk 1997). Yet there is no strong evidence to suggest that harshness of punishment has much of an effect on crime rates. True, locking up a person ensures that that individual will not commit a crime for the length of the sentence, yet all but a few inmates will eventually be released back into society. The exceptions are those sentenced to life or to death.

Capital Punishment

Capital punishment (literally, to be beheaded) refers to the death penalty. The history of capital punishment in America is a fascinating case study of the influence of the public temper. Up until 1967, executions by firing squad, hanging, or the electric chair were an accepted part of the justice system, although we were the only modern capitalist society with a death penalty. The public temper of the late 1960s was one in which state-sanctioned violence came into question, and in 1972 the death penalty was challenged in the courts on two grounds: (1) that it violated the Eighth Amendment ban on cruel and unusual punishment, and (2) because it was used so overwhelmingly against poor minority males, that it violated the Fourteenth Amendment guarantee of equal protection of the law.

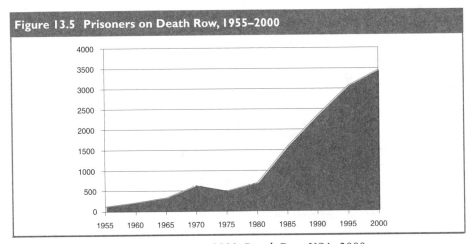

Figure 13.5 Prisoners on Death Row, 1955–2000

Source: Bureau of Justice Statistics, 2000; Death Row USA, 2000.

The Supreme Court did not rule on the constitutional issues but ordered a temporary ban on executions until the states could come up with procedures for the uniform treatment of defendants. The states rushed to enact new laws and, finally, in 1976, succeeded in having the death penalty reinstated. Executions were resumed in 1976 and have increased each subsequent year, as seen in Figure 13.5.

Today, there are over 3,700 men and a few women awaiting their deaths in state prisons, primarily in Florida, Texas, and California. Almost half are black, most are between 24- and 54-years-old; only a few have gone beyond twelfth grade, and a large number are mentally ill or handicapped (Death Row USA 2000). Almost by definition, the people who end up on death row have few resources; most have had to depend on poorly paid, court-appointed defense lawyers with little experience in criminal law. The trials are often highly publicized, and prosecutors cannot afford to lose a conviction. The chance of error is quite high. In January, 2000, the governor of Illinois ordered a halt to executions after reporters discovered that half of all death penalty convictions in the state since 1977 were overturned on appeal because of flaws in the prosecution, incompetent defense lawyers, or unfair trial tactics. Another study of all capital cases between 1975 and 1997 found that in seven out of every 10 appeals, the courts found serious, reversible errors (Liebman et al. 2000). The three major causes were: (1) incompetent defense attorneys (37 percent); (2) prosecutorial misconduct, such as suppressing evidence (12 percent); and (3) faulty instructions to jurors (20 percent). In a few of these cases, newly available DNA testing techniques have helped to free the unjustly condemned (Scheck et al. 2000).

At the federal level, Congress has added several dozen offenses to the list of capital crimes than can be prosecuted in the federal courts. Although the federal caseload is relatively small, it, too, shows distinct regional and racial disparities. Most of the prosecutors who have sought the death penalty come from a few, mostly Southern, states, and the defendants in 75 percent of all capital cases have been minority group members (U.S. Department of Justice 2000).

The U.S. Supreme Court has not been much help to those on death row. In 1987, the Court rejected the last major challenge to the death penalty—that it was still being applied arbitrarily, but on the basis of the race of the *victim* rather than the offender. If you kill a white person, you are over four times more likely to be tried as a capital case and sentenced to death than if

The United States Supreme Court is the final court of appeals, and through their decisions the nine Justices interpret and shape American law. Capital punishment, privacy, racial and sexual discrimination, and which votes should be counted in the Presidential election of 2000 were some of the legal issues considered in recent decisions.

you murder a black or Latino (Death Penalty Information Center 2000). The Court, however, did not see these data as evidence of systematic bias. Since then, the Court has approved the execution of mentally retarded and juvenile offenders and has taken steps to shorten the appeals process.

Although the most powerful argument for retaining the death penalty is that it deters crime, there is no evidence that executions have a strong or long-term deterrent effect on other criminals, and they may even lead to an increase in the homicide rate (Sorenson et al. 1999; Thompson 1999). Large majorities of Americans nevertheless continue to support capital punishment, although the number has declined since the recent publicity over possible flaws. Thus, the United States and Japan remain the only modern industrial societies with the death penalty, but the Japanese execute only a few convicts each year and do so in almost total secrecy. The leader in executions is China with 1,067 in 1998, followed by Congo with 100, and the United States with 68, compared with six for Japan (Amnesty International 2000). 🖥 14

If harsh prison sentences and capital punishment have only a small impact on crime rates, what purpose do they serve? Here one must return to one of Durkheim's great insights: Punishment reaffirms the norms of the society and unites us in shared condemnation of evildoers. When punishments were moved from the town square to behind the prison walls, they lost some of their solidarity-producing impact, but the revival of capital punishment allows us to unite once again in righteous anger and to draw the line between us, the law-abiding, and them, the criminal. Thus far, although there are many people in favor, the executions have remained untelevised.

Life Behind Bars: Prisons and Jails

In February, 2000, the United States pulled ahead of Russia to become the world's imprisonment rate leader, with over two million men and women behind bars. Another four million were under criminal supervision, in probation and parole programs. As shown in Figure 13.6, the imprisonment rate rose sharply in the 1990s, with two-thirds of the new inmates being convicted of nonviolent offenses, primarily drug-related. They are there because of mandatory sentencing laws, including decades-long sentences, even life imprisonment, for persons convicted of three felonies ("three strikes and you're out"). But most of the increase in the prison population has happened because those already inside are serving longer terms as a result of "no early release" laws. Therefore, although the number of inmates increased by 70 per-

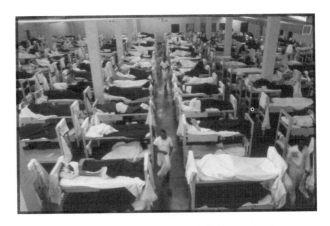

U.S. prisons are increasingly overcrowded due to mandatory sentencing laws and the fact that those already inside are serving longer terms. Are prisons the solution or part of the problem?

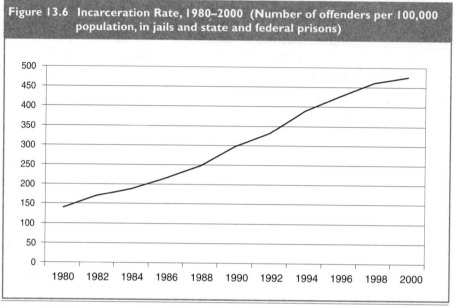

Figure 13.6 Incarceration Rate, 1980–2000 (Number of offenders per 100,000 population, in jails and state and federal prisons)

Source: U.S. Department of Justice, *Prison and Jail Inmates*, various years.

cent, the number of new prisoners rose only 20 percent. ⌨ 15

Moreover, while fewer and fewer suspects are being arrested for violent crimes, in part because so many potential offenders are already behind bars, more of those arrested are given long sentences (Bureau of Justice Statistics 1999). In addition, the penalties for minor offenses keep getting upgraded and more behaviors are criminalized. In some states, the penalty is enhanced if it can be shown that the motive for the crime was hatred on the basis of religion, race, or sexual orientation (Jenness and Grattet 2000).

In other words, the growth of the prison population reflects changes in sentencing policy rather than any big surge in villains or vastly improved police work. There are regional as well as racial differences, as you might expect. If you want to minimize your risk of being locked up, stay out of the South and head to the far North. In Louisiana, for example, the incarceration rate was 1,025 persons per 100,000 population in mid-1999, compared with 203 per 100,000 Vermonters.

Not only are the prisons brimming with untreated drug abusers, it appears that at least 16 percent of the inmates also suffer from mental illness, moving from homelessness to jails to prisons and out again and then in again. Because their behavior is so erratic and because their conditions go untreated, the mentally ill get in fights in prison and end up staying a year or more longer than other convicts. Thus, America's jails and prisons have become the mental hospitals of the poor (Butterfield 1999).

About one-third of new inmates are the kind of violent criminals we think of when picturing life behind bars. In contrast with the typical prisoner of the past, the new inmates are younger, darker-skinned, and likely to be members of a street gang that gets reconstituted in the prison. These are tougher inmates for the guards to handle than in the past, when a convict subculture and social system emerged whereby old-timers maintained order among the inmates in return for favors from the guards (Hunt et al. 1993). Now, the guards have to keep the gang members from fighting one another.

The mix of violent and nonviolent, youthful offenders and old-timers, and those in need of treatment for substance abuse or mental illness—all locked up in facilities that are filled to capacity and a half—make American prisons extremely volatile and very expensive. If you take a look at your state's current budget, you will find that the allocation for corrections far exceeds that for higher education. Prison spending has increased 60 percent over the 1990s while that for higher education remained unchanged. In California, a prison guard makes about $51,000 per year, compared to $41,000 for a first-year college professor; tuition at the state universities has been raised in order to pay for the construction of a dozen new prisons (Egan 1999).

Corrections today is a $40-billion-dollar industry that includes the building and staffing of various facilities, the costs of private prison contracts, and the manufacture and selling of products such as handcuffs and riot gear. Increasingly, prisons are being built in rural areas with high unemployment, so the facility soon becomes the largest employer in the county. To close it down would create economic havoc in the region. Therefore, between meeting the public temper for long and harsh penalties and voting for programs that bring jobs to impoverished rural communities, lawmakers are not likely to pull the plug on prison construction very soon. The result is that black and Hispanic men from the city are being imprisoned in rural areas, far from family visitors, and watched over by rural whites.

Not only is it good politics to put more offenders in prison, it also pays to support harsh treatment while they are behind bars—no frills such as TV, weight lifting, smoking, prison libraries (especially those with law books), or educational programs. The major exception is if there is something that the inmates can manufacture for the pay of a dollar an hour (Leonhardt 2000). The latest limitation on prisoners comes in the form of state statutes that remove inmates from the protection of civil rights laws, so prisoners can no longer sue for abuses and cruel and unusual punishments. In 1999, Michigan went so far as to eliminate retroactively a suit filed on behalf of women prisoners who had been sexually assaulted by guards (*New York Times*, December 21, 1999). At the federal level, Congress passed a Prison Litigation Reform Act in 1999 designed to protect state prisons from court-ordered remedies to overcrowding and custodial brutality (Sullivan 2000).

Although these punitive measures are very popular, they do little to rehabilitate the inmate, who will leave the prison more antisocial than when he or she entered. The harsher the routine, the more tense and dangerous the place becomes for the guards as well as the prisoners.

Prisons as Total Institutions

Prisons share a peculiar social system with mental hospitals, nursing homes, convents and monasteries, military bases, boarding schools, and many cults. They are all **total institutions**, enclosed spaces where the residents are under full-time control of authorities (Goffman 1961). Because the goal of the institution is to maintain order and to socialize inmates into its culture, activities are strictly scheduled and are carried out in full view of everyone else. Civilian identities are erased by the use of uniforms, shaved heads, and numbers or nicknames. All these tendencies are exaggerated in the prison context. There is nothing in this experience to prepare a person for successful living in the real world, to which most prisoners return within five to seven years.

Costs and Benefits

Has putting people behind bars reduced crime and drug use?

Benefits. Certainly, removing a lot of felons has made the streets safer, although several other factors are at work, including fewer young men in their crime-prone years in the population, containment of the crack epidemic, community-oriented police work, more private guards, and improved employment opportunities in the late 1990s.

The effects of imprisoning large numbers of low-level drug dealers and users on the overall rate of drug use are less clear. The major drop came before the rush to imprisonment, and the demand for most illegal substances has remained unchanged since 1992, with crack down but heroin up. Once you have locked up all the usual suspects, the dragnet catches increasingly less-important offenders, so that the impact on crime and drug-use rates also diminishes.

Costs. The costs of incarcerating two million people are extremely high, in terms of: (1) the tens of billions of dollars that are not available for other government functions, (2) broken families and wasted lives, and (3) a general coarsening of the public temper. In addition, the heaping on of penalties is self-defeating, because, for most states, the corrections budget is all used up on building cells and paying the guards, with little left for health care, education, job training, or drug treatment. Because nothing is done to make the inmate any more capable of surviving on the outside, the prison experience will probably reinforce existing antisocial attitudes. And since all but a few will eventually be released, they will emerge more dangerous than when they went in. Thus, the more people who pass through the system and the longer their stays, the greater the likelihood of becoming a repeat offender, or recidivist. **Recidivism** literally means "to fall back," an echo of the Puritan Ethic to refer to someone who sins again.

Recidivism rates are difficult to interpret because there are so many factors to take into account, and solid

Prisons are total institutions, enclosed spaces where the inmates are under full-time control of authorities. In some states, like Alabama, inmates are chained from morning to sundown.

national data have not been collected since the early 1980s. One carefully designed 20-year follow-up study of New Jersey offenders found that although those who had been imprisoned were more likely to be rearrested than offenders not sentenced to confinement (82 percent to 70 percent), when all the relevant variables were factored in, there was no statistically significant difference in recidivism between the two groups (Gottfredson 1999). In this study, the likelihood of being arrested again was not affected by the length of time served, where it was served (jail, youth facility, or prison), or what type of fine or terms of probation were imposed. In other words, there is nothing in this research to support the idea that long and harsh punishment will lower the recidivism rate.

In recognition of all these costs, and of the fact that between 50 and 85 percent of inmates are there because of drugs or alcohol abuse, federal officials recently proposed an extensive program of drug testing and treatment for anyone who gets caught in the criminal justice system (Wren 1999b). The additional cost of treatment is a lot less than the national average of $20,000 to $25,000 per year to keep someone in a cell. If your typical new inmate is in his mid-twenties and can expect to live another 50 years, the cost to taxpayers of a life sentence without parole will be $1,000,000–1,500,000 at today's rate. Even greater savings can be realized by keeping someone out of jail in the first place, as found out in Arizona, where a program of probation and mandatory treatment for nonviolent drug offenders has helped over 77 percent of the probationers to stay drug-free (Wren 1999a).

In addition to drug treatment, job training is essential to reducing recidivism. And not just any old job—making license plates is not going to save many souls—but "quality jobs" with decent pay, intrinsic satisfactions, and promotion opportunities (Uggen 1999). However, before many inmates can begin job training, they need to learn to read and write; yet these are the first programs to be cut as "frills" by a cost-conscious legislature.

It also helps to keep a convict in touch with his or her family, which is why building a new prison in some remote area is self-defeating in terms of reintegrating the inmate. Anything that makes it difficult for spouses, friends, and children to visit on a regular basis adds to the risk of recidivism.

Here is another lively issue to debate in class: What is it worth to feel safer? Will fear win out over the pocketbook? 🖥 16

Conclusion

This chapter has examined the criminal justice system and the dilemmas of assuring public safety in a modern democratic society. Although crime in the streets has declined dramatically over the past decade, the more complex and elusive range of white-collar and organizational crimes has increased. Recent trends in female and juvenile offenses and imprisonment were reviewed. From the point of view of law enforcement, the chapter discussed the built-in tensions of police work, as well as the problems confronted by prosecutors and judges in an overburdened court system.

Although the great majority of convicted offenders serve only a few years in prison, the experience does little to rehabilitate. Nonetheless, the American prison system has expanded to accommodate several million inmates, many of whom are serving mandatory sentences for drug-related offenses.

❖ ❖ ❖ ❖   The chapter also took a close look at the death penalty and the current controversy surrounding its application at the state and federal levels.

Surfing the Sociological Internet

💻 1–2 For crime theories see: **http://www.crimetheory.com/**

💻 3 **http://www.geocities.com/CollegePark/Quad/5889/index.htm** This web site is that of the National Criminal Justice Research Service. This is one of the world's largest sources of criminal and juvenile justice statistics. Here you will find information on the criminal justice system, courts, crime, and corrections: **http://www.ncjrs.org/homepage.htm**
American Society of Criminology: **http://www.asc41.com/**
This site shows how to access and use crime statistics: **http://www.crime.org/**

💻 4 The FBI can be accessed at: **http://www.fbi.gov/**
Uniform Crime Reports on the FBI site are at: **http://www.fbi.gov/ucr.htm**
For the U.S. Department of Justice statistics with links to other sources, go to: **http://www.ojp.usdoj.gov.bjs**
For more links, organizations, and journals:
http://www.runet.edu/~lridener/DSS/crimedev.html
For criminology links, including types of crime and statistics:
http://www.middlebury.edu/~sa288s97/crimlks.html

💻 5 The Treasury Department's Alcohol, Tobacco, and Firearms site on guns and gun use in the United States is at: **http://www.atf.treas.gov/firearms/index.htm**

💻 6 For a guide to gun laws, federal and state, see: **http://jurist.law.pitt.edu/gunlaw.htm**

💻 7 For a Justice Department report on female criminals and women in prison, see: **http://sun.soci.niu.edu/~critcrim/prisons/wom93** and **http://www.ojp.usdoj.gov/bjs/abstract/wopris.htm**

💻 8 National Center on Crime and Delinquency reports on juvenile crime: **http://www.nccd-crc.org/**

💻 9 For a site which tracks global organized crime, see: **http://www.csis.org/goc/taskfina.html**
For consequences of global organized crime: **http://www.american.edu/projects/mandala/TED/hpages/crime/text3.htm**
This Department of Defense site gives access to information on international organized crime and the drug trade: **http://www.dso.com/**

🖥 10 The National White Collar Crime Center provides information and statistics as well as advice on prevention of white-collar crime: http://www.iir.com/nwccc/default.htm

❖ ❖ ❖ ❖

🖥 11 Drugs, drug use, and the war on drugs: http://www.usdoj.gov/dea/
In addition to the above governmental sites, see:
http://www.drugfreeamerica.org/
http://www.nida.nih.gov/NIDAHome1.html
http://www.drugsense.org/
http://www.csdp.org/

🖥 12 Sites for and about police and policing issues:
http://www.officer.com/
http://police.sas.ab.ca/
http://www.aclu.org/issues/criminal/bustcardtext.html also contains information on abuses by private police.
http://www.leolinks.com/ is a directory of law enforcement sites.

🖥 13 Website for the U.S. court system: http://www.uscourts.gov/

🖥 14 On capital punishment: http://www.amnesty.org/ailib/intcam/dp/

🖥 15 On prisons: http://www.bop.gov/
For sites related to the debate over prisons and prison conditions:
http://www.hrw.org/advocacy/prisons/
http://www.prisonactivist.org/
http://www.cjlf.org/
http://www.ojp.usdoj.gov/ovc/

Glossary

Capital Punishment The death penalty.

Decriminalizing Removing criminal penalties from minor forms of drug use without actually legalizing that use.

Index Crimes FBI tabulation of violent crimes—murder, forcible rape, robbery, and aggravated assault—and property crimes—burglary, larceny, and auto theft.

Organizational Crime Committed by white-collar employees in the interests of their employing organization.

Organized Crime Committed by members of organizations engaged in illegal acts.

Plea Bargain Negotiating with prosecutors for a reduced charge.

Pyramid Scheme A type of confidence game in which newcomers provide funds to pay off those who entered earlier.

Recidivism To become a repeat offender.

Status Offenses Acts that are illegal for juveniles but are not crimes if done by adults, such as running away from home.

Total Institutions A setting in which residents are monitored and controlled in all aspects of behavior, 24 hours a day.

Victimless Crimes Illegal acts in which participants engage willingly.

White-Collar Crime Illegal acts committed by respectable persons in the course of their employment for their own personal gain. ✦

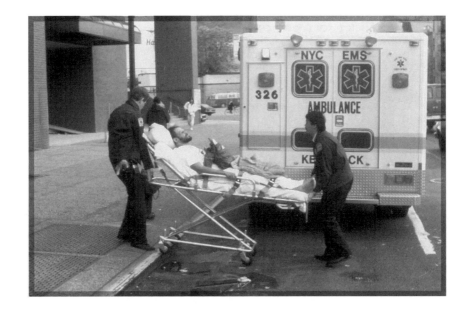

A Sound Mind in a Sound Body: Health, Illness, and the Delivery of Care

❖ ❖ ❖ ❖ Surely, you may be thinking, being sick is a biological reality; the health of your mind and body are empirical facts. Yes, but illness and wellness are also culturally defined and socially constructed. What might be an acceptable disability in one society is a matter of grave concern in another. Within a society, a person's health status can vary greatly by all the usual sociological suspects: sex, age, income, education, occupation, race, ethnicity, and even religion. Historically, fads in illness and wellness come and go—how many upper-middle-class women today suffer from "the vapors," a common ailment in the late 1800s? Why was no one diagnosed with "chronic fatigue syndrome" in the days when most workers engaged in manual labor? Finally, the organization of health care in America is just as structured by race and gender as is its education system. This chapter covers the following topics:

- Patterns of health and illness.
- The sick role.
- History of American medicine.
- Public and private hospitals.
- Models of health care delivery.
- Contemporary dilemmas: cost, coverage, and quality.

Patterns of Health and Illness

Some illnesses strike at random, but most are clearly patterned, that is, rates will vary systematically by some of the sociological variables with which you are now familiar. **Social epidemiology** is the study of these patterns, of how illnesses are distributed within a population. The most powerful of these variables are age, sex, social class, and race.⌨ 1

Age

The clearest indicator of the health status of an entire population is **life expectancy**, the number of years you can expect to live, depending on your year of birth. On the one hand, increased life expectancy is a sign of societal well-being; on the other hand, an aging population presents medical and financial burdens to a society. In the United States, as in most modern societies, there has been a dramatic increase in life expectancy over the twentieth century, from about 47 years in 1900, on average, to about 76.5 years today. This does not mean that people suddenly keeled over on their 47th birthday in 1900, but if half the people born in 1900 died in childhood and the rest lived 100 years, you would have an average of around 50. In other words, the data for 1900 reflect high infant and childhood death rates; getting through the first 15 years of life was the key to living to old age. Over the century, improvements in public health, such as sewers, pasteurized milk, and indoor plumbing, as well as advances in medical practice, including vaccinations and the use of sterilized instruments, made it increasingly likely that babies would reach adulthood.

Once assured that their children will survive infancy, couples typically have fewer babies. The combination of increased life expectancy and lowered birthrates means that the population as a whole gets older, with more people in the older age ranges and fewer in the younger. When the population itself ages, a different set of health problems emerges. In 1900, two of the leading causes of death in the United States were epidemics of influenza and intestinal infections—short-term, acute illnesses that strike young and old alike and run quickly through the population. In contrast, the major causes of death today are chronic illnesses, the types of heart disease and cancer that take a long time to develop and that get progressively worse. It should be no surprise, then, that health care would become a major concern for the nation and individual families in modern societies. The older the population, the more doctors' visits, medications, hospitalizations, and nursing care there are to be paid for. Acute conditions come and go; chronic is forever—and expensive. 📖 2

Sex and Gender

Some health issues are unique to women or to men by virtue of biological sex differences, primarily related to reproduction. Most sex differences in health status and life expectancy, however, are gender-related, due to how men and women behave and are treated by others. As you can see in Table 14.1, there is a striking difference in life expectancy by sex today that was not obvious in 1900.

Table 14.1 Life Expectancy at Birth, United States, 1900 and 2000, by Race and Sex (in years)				
	Females		Males	
	White	Black	White	Black
1900	48.7	35.0	46.6	32.5
2000	80.5	74.7	74.2	64.6

Source: Bureau of the Census, *Statistical Abstract of the United States, 1975, 2000.*

The sex differential in life expectancy reflects both biological and gender influences: (1) Biologically, males are at greater risk than females for diseases of the heart and respiratory system. This vulnerability is related in part to male infants, with their slightly broader shoulders, being born at an earlier and more fragile stage in their physical development, when they can get through the narrow birth canal. There is also evidence that female hormones protect against some forms of heart disease, a protection that is lost in menopause, when heart problems increase sharply for women. Another factor with a biological base that affects women's life expectancy is the risk of dying in childbirth. The big change between 1900 and 1990 for a woman is that instead of being pregnant seven or eight times and giving birth to six or more infants, she now will typically have two pregnancies and two routine births, and a much longer life. (2) The two most powerful gender influences on life expectancy today are differences in *lifestyle* and in *health-related behaviors*. Regarding lifestyle choices, men are more likely than women to smoke, drink too much, eat the kind of food that clogs the arteries, drive carelessly, and place themselves in risky situations. Regarding health-related behaviors,

❖ ❖ ❖ ❖   women are more likely than men to know when their body is not working as usual, more willing to see a physician and to take medication, and more likely to take time off work to recuperate (Zimmerman and Hall 2001).

Just imagine a breakfast conversation between a wife and husband, when

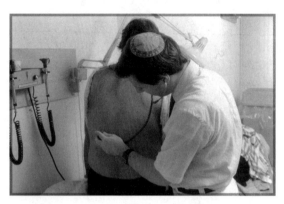

Social epidemiology is the study of how illnesses vary in a population by age, sex, social class, and race.

she says, "Dear, you don't look too well, shouldn't you see the doctor?" His first three responses are likely to be "No time," "I feel just fine," and "Can't leave the job." By the time he finally arrives at the doctor's office, he is at a more advanced stage of an illness than his wife would have been. Also, because many women visit a gynecologist once a year, they come in direct contact with the health care system. Unlike her husband, she is not afraid of feeling powerless before a medical authority, and she probably realizes that her workplace will survive her absence. 💻 3

Box 14.1

A Tale of Two Pills and the Politicians

Sex and gender affect what kind of medications are researched and produced by pharmaceutical companies, approved by government agencies, and reimbursed by medical insurers. Viagra, a male potency enhancer, won rapid approval from the Federal Drug Administration (FDA), even before all clinical trials were completed. It can be prescribed by any physician, whether or not an expert on urology or sexual dysfunction. The Pentagon budgeted $50 million in the first year of availability, which adds up to over $200 million by 2001. Many insurers were willing to cover the costs until the demand became too great. In addition, the FDA has also approved an alternative to Viagra, despite evidence of harmful side effects (*New York Times*, April 11, 2000).

Contrast this speed with the decades-long delay in making available to American women a drug treatment, RU 486, clinically tested over many years in Europe with few side effects, that terminates a pregnancy in its earliest stages without the need for surgery. Not only have potential manufacturers and distributors been intimidated by religious groups opposed to abortion, but the FDA has attached regulations for its administration that limit the number of physicians likely to prescribe it.

Similarly, Japanese politicians, who typically take years to approve new drugs, granted immediate acceptance to Viagra while continuing to refuse distribution of many contraceptives (WuDunn 1999). In Israel, a religiously dominated parliament quickly added Viagra to the "basket" of pharmaceuticals covered by national health insurance, while leaving contraceptives out.

Race and Ethnicity

There are a few diseases that are unique to one racial or ethnic group, for example, sickle-cell anemia among Africans and African Americans and Tay-

Sachs disease among Jews of European origin. Most race or ethnic differences in epidemiology, however, reflect differences in living conditions and
health behaviors. The very low life expectancy of Native Americans can be
traced to high rates of diabetes and infectious diseases on the reservations.
Immigrant Latino construction and factory workers have a large number of
work accidents because they are more likely than native-born workers to be
employed on sites with substandard safety arrangements. Lack of adequate
prenatal care increases the risks of physical and mental disability among
infants of poor African-American women. Unbalanced diets, smoking,
overdrinking and drug use are common responses to the stresses of residential isolation and unemployment.

Yet, as Table 14.1 indicates, when living conditions and access to health
care improve, so does life expectancy, which has doubled in this century for
blacks. Nonetheless, death rates for blacks are over half again as high as those
for whites for all but a few illnesses, in part as a result of differences in education and income that are also associated with knowledge of and access to
health care, as shown in Table 14.2 (Howard et al. 2000). The racial gap is
especially wide for infant mortality, with African-American infants over twice
as likely as white infants to die in their first year of life (National Center for
Health Statistics 1999). 🖥4

Table 14.2 Ratio of Male to Female and Black to White Deaths From the 15 Leading Causes of Death, United States, 1998

Rank		Male to female	Black to white
—	All causes	1.8	1.5
1	Diseases of heart	1.8	1.5
2	Malignant neoplasms (cancers)	1.4	1.3
3	Cerebrovascular diseases (stroke)	1.1	1.3
4	Chronic obstructive pulmonary diseases	1.4	0.8
5	Accidents and adverse effects	2.4	1.2
	Motor vehicle accidents	2.2	1.1
	All other accidents and adverse effects	2.7	1.4
6	Pneumonia and influenza	1.6	1.4
7	Diabetes	1.2	2.4
8	Suicide	4.3	0.6
9	Kidney diseases	1.6	2.6
10	Chronic liver disease and cirrhosis	2.3	1.1
11	Septicemia (blood poisoning)	1.2	2.7
12	Alzheimer's disease	0.9	0.7
13	Homicide and legal intervention	3.5	5.7
14	Atherosclerosis	1.3	1.0
15	Hypertension with or without renal disease	1.1	3.8

"Deaths: Final Data for 1998." *National Vital Statistics Reports, National Center for Health Statistics,* July, 2000:5.

Box 14.2

Health Care: Separate and Unequal

It will come as no surprise to students of sociology that there are at least two health-care systems in the United States and that the difference between them is a function of race. Not only do physicians make different diagnoses of the same condition depending on the race and sex of the patient (Rathore et al. 2000), but patients also receive different treatments for the same disease (Sheifer et al. 2000). With regard to race, white patients were typically thought to be more in need of treatment and then given more intensive care than were blacks with identical symptoms. Although it might help if black patients were seen by a doctor of the same race or ethnicity, this is not likely since minority enrollments at medical schools have dropped steadily since 1994, when affirmative action programs were scaled back (Noble 1998). Recent cuts in loan programs for medical students who would repay by working with the poor after graduation have also reduced the number of minority physicians in low-income areas (Winter 2000).

Early and correct diagnosis is crucial. So is the type of treatment. One study of over 11,000 elderly early-stage lung cancer patients found that blacks were less likely than whites to be referred for life-saving surgery, even when the patients were similar on SES, insurance coverage, and complicating medical conditions. This leaves unconscious racial bias as the major explanatory variable (Bach et al. 1999). Similar findings have been published for the treatment of kidney failure: black patients are much less likely than whites to be referred for a transplant, the most effective treatment (Garg et al. 1999). Even when the preferred treatment is inexpensive and covered by Medicare—something as basic as beta-blockers to reduce the risk of death from heart attack—physicians are less likely to recommend it when the patient is black, female, or poor (American Heart Association 2000). For minorities in the inner city, the situation is extremely difficult. Not only do few physicians practice in the area, but also the neighborhood clinics and hospital emergency rooms on which the poor depend are closing down, as discussed later in this chapter.

Social Class

Race and ethnic differences in death rates are in many ways a proxy for

Years of research indicate that smoking is related to a high incidence of lung cancer and other respiratory diseases. In the light of such information, why do so many Americans continue to smoke?

the most powerful variable of all in predicting health status and life expectancy—social class. It is more than just money and education. It is the ability to avoid or deal with stress and to develop a sense of control over your life, to live in safe communities and stable neighborhoods, and to be imbedded in social networks. It also helps to be able to afford all necessary health care, to eat well, and to have a room of your own.

The classic study in this regard involved a 25-year longitudinal study of about 18,000 men in the British civil service—a perfect bureaucracy with a clear chain of command (Marmot and Shipley 1996). The researchers found that death rates varied strongly and consistently with a man's rank in the hierarchy: The higher the man's rank, the lower the risk of death. This was true for both smokers and nonsmokers, and for other risky conditions. In other words, even among people with college degrees, good jobs, high pay, and full health insurance, each degree of rank adds to your sense of mastery and security, and therefore to your health and life.

Playing the Sick Role

Not only do sociological variables predict the distribution of illness, but social factors affect how a person "does" sickness—that is, how he or she behaves as a sick person and how other people respond. Being sick means that you cannot perform your ordinary tasks and that ongoing social systems will be disrupted. To preserve social order, some limits must be set on how long a person can avoid responsibilities. The sick role, as described by Talcott Parsons (1951), gives you a legitimate excuse for dropping out of everyday obligations, but for only so long. In return, you must try to get better, see a doctor, and take your medications. If you linger in illness (*malingering*), you run the risk of exhausting the good will of the people who cut you some slack and even offered their sympathy and attention. Notice how quickly you stop feeling sorry for someone that you thought should have been better by now and back at the job.

Notice, also, that the socially constructed "patient" is essentially female—passive and trusting—which may be why boys and men have more difficulty in playing the sick role than do girls and women. In addition, there are ethnic differences in how pain is experienced and expressed. As one classic study discovered among patients suffering from the same condition, Italian-Americans tended to play the sick role with great emotion, while the New England Yankees maintained a stiff upper lip (Zola 1966). Similar cultural influences affect the way in which members of different ethnic groups acknowledge and cope with emotional distress (Agbayani-Stewart et al. 1999).

Mental Illness

Difficulties in defining what is sick or healthy are compounded in the case of mental disorders because there are few clear-cut standards. As noted in chapter 3, the contents of the *Diagnostic Manual*, which is the Bible for mental health specialists, change with each edition: Conditions that had passed for relatively normal (gambling) become medicalized, while others (homosexuality) have been removed from the list of pathologies (Kutchins and Kirk 1997). In addition, race, ethnicity, sex, and social status are associated with differential exposure to stressful conditions, and, in general, the greater the adversity and stress in your life, the less control you have over events, and the more likely you are to experience emotional distress (Dohrenwend 2000). Thus, although almost half of respondents in a national study reported symptoms of a mental disorder at some point in their lifetimes, the rates are highest for those with fewer resources or less social power (Kessler et al. 1994).

Race, ethnicity, sex, and social class also affect how professionals diagnose and treat a patient's emotional problems. In the nineteenth century, Afri-

❖ ❖ ❖ ❖   can Americans were said to suffer from a peculiar condition called drapetomania if they sought to escape slavery (Kreiger 1987). Even today, racial stereotypes continue to influence the clinical judgments of mental health professionals (Abreu 2000). The sex of a patient also triggers differential diagnoses. Women are more often considered in need of therapy than similarly afflicted males, and they are also more likely than men to be institutionalized and to be given more radical treatment. In many mental hospitals, for example, until the 1960s, difficult male patients were restrained with belts and straitjackets, while difficult female patients were treated surgically, through operations on the brain or sexual organs (Braslow 1997).

Clearly, defining who is mentally ill is not an exact science. Even more difficult, however, is providing the appropriate treatment. The people who are most in need of mental health services are those least able to recognize their condition or to afford treatment. Conversely, the relatively wealthy, who present minimal danger to themselves or others, have access to unlimited psychiatric services and private hospitals. This imbalance is heightened by the fact that mental health care has traditionally been a responsibility of local and state government and has been perhaps the most poorly administered of all public services. State mental hospitals have historically been underfunded, poorly staffed, and filled with patients who have no alternatives (Grob 1991).

In the 1960s, however, several developments reshaped the mental health scene. One was the introduction of extremely effective drug treatments for controlling most symptoms of distress. The other was the failure of the federal government to include mental health treatment in Medicaid, the insurance program for the poor. At the same time, the Mental Health Centers Act of 1963 did offer limited funding for small, community-based treatment facilities. Together, these developments encouraged state governments to close down many of their expensive state hospitals, releasing patients by the tens of thousands; the number of patients decreased from 500,000 in 1965 to about 60,000 today (Purnick 1999). Few of the states, however, chose to use the millions of dollars saved through deinstitutionalization to create small, community-based group homes, which were also strongly opposed by local residents. As a result, thousands of former patients left their hospitals with little more than a handful of prescriptions and no follow-up services. Large numbers joined the growing ranks of homeless that still populate American cities. For many, the psychiatric emergency room at a public hospital is the only facility available today, but the hospital can only provide temporary care before discharging the patient. For example, the man who pushed a woman under a subway train in New York City in 1999 had been hospitalized 13 times since 1997, often for violent episodes and often at his own request, but, without resources or insurance, there was no place where he could receive long-term treatment (Winerup 1999).

One does not need to be impoverished to have difficulty finding and affording appropriate mental health care. Because some forms of psychiatric treatment can continue for years, with weekly sessions costing $100 or more, few employers and health insurance companies offer full coverage (Carrasquillo et al. 1999). Some insurers may cover short-term therapies, while others require large out-of-pocket payments by the patient. In recent years, some states have ordered health insurance companies to cover mental health care at the same level of reimbursement as other health services, which may only drive some insurance companies out of the state. Yet even with financial help, many people will fail to seek treatment for emotional distress because of the stigma attached to the label of "mentally ill" (Link et al. 1999). As a result, most cases go unacknowledged and untreated for many years, with untold costs for individuals, families, and the society. 💻5

The Development of the American Health Care System

Although physicians and even hospitals have been with us since ancient Greece, it is only in the past hundred years that they have come to dominate the provision of health care in modern societies. Throughout the nineteenth century in America, doctors were held in relatively low esteem, poorly trained or supervised, peddling all kinds of tonics and elixirs (healing potions), and applying dangerous treatments. Hospitals were few and far between and so unsanitary as to infect as many patients as were cured, especially when physicians moved from autopsies to maternity wards without washing their hands (Lorber 1997).

The Rise of Medical Dominance

The professionalization of medicine in America dates from the early 1900s, when it became clear that such haphazard and hazardous practices were unsuitable for the new century of science and progress. In 1910, the *Flexner Report* established rigorous standards for the education, licensing, and supervision of doctors. Diploma mills were replaced by medical schools, the quality of care improved, and the power of physicians over the entire health field was firmly established (Starr 1982). The medical establishment—in the organizational form of the American Medical Association (AMA)—determined how many medical schools were built, who and how many people would be admitted to the schools, what they would learn, and how they should practice in the community. Medicine was now very special knowledge, given only to a selected few, and those few could be judged only by their peers—the hallmark of a true profession. 💻6

Up until the 1950s, the AMA operated as "an old boy's club" of like-minded members who resembled one another in terms of race, sex, religion, ethnicity, and social class. Many of the more prestigious medical schools stopped admitting women and blacks; the new medical training was considered too difficult for their frail constitutions or limited mental capacities. Women, who had composed 20 percent of physicians in many cities in 1900, were now channeled into nursing or social work. It was not until the late 1960s that medical schools were forced to adopt nondiscriminatory admissions policies (Lorber 1997). Although 80 percent of American doctors today are white males, the proportion of women is bound to rise as they comprise over 40 percent of entering medical school students. The number of Asian-American physicians, both men and women, will also increase sharply. 💻7

The outlook for African Americans and Hispanics, however, is less optimistic. The costs of a medical education and the added years of training keep many motivated students from poor families from entering the field in favor of other well-paying occupations that require less of an investment of time and money. Nonetheless, Meharry Medical College and the medical schools at Howard University and Morehouse College have continued to train the majority of black physicians for over a century. ⌨8

Gender and Race in the Practice of Medicine

Although women will eventually make up close to half of the medical profession, they will not be distributed in the health care system in the same way as men. Women physicians, like women lawyers, will be disproportionately employed in the public sector, where hours and working conditions are more compatible with child-care responsibilities, and in the lower-status specialties (gynecology, pediatrics, and family medicine), where they can more easily find mentors and internships (Lorber 2001). A similar pattern holds for minority physicians, for whom attracting white patients is an additional problem.

The differential distribution of women and minority physicians reflects the internal stratification system of medical specializations, with heart and brain surgery at the top and family-related practices at the bottom. There is a "halo effect" at work whereby the practitioner takes on the prestige of clients or patients. Treating high-status white men, a majority of heart patients, is simply worthy of greater respect than dealing with nauseated children and overworried mothers.

The Doctor Is in—Business

The absolute power of the American doctor to control the profession and the care of patients is being challenged today from a number of directions. In many parts of the country, individual and small-group practices are being bought out by profit-making chains that operate clinics, hospitals, and nursing homes, with the doctors as salaried employees. In return for giving up decision-making power to corporate officials, the doctor receives a fully equipped office, support staff, steady income, and perhaps some corporate stock. ⌨9

In other cases, medical people compete among themselves for control of health-care profits. For example, a group of physicians will invest in medical support facilities, such as testing labs or diagnostic centers, to which they can refer their own patients, typically more often than other doctors and at much higher fees (Eichenwald and Kolata 1999b). Although the federal government forbids such double-dipping for the treatment of Medicare and Medicaid patients, it has little control over private providers and insurers.

The scramble for profits is partly fueled by an increase in the number of physicians competing for patients who are insured or who can pay in full. Thus, despite the relative glut of doctors—260 per 100,000 Americans today compared with 150 in 1960—very few are practicing in the inner city, rural America, or places with a concentration of low-income elderly. The big money and high prestige belong to specialists rather than to the old-fashioned family doctor. Specialists need to be where there are a lot of potential paying patients, namely the wealthier sections of large cities or suburbs. New York's Park Avenue is home to hundreds of psychiatrists, cosmetic surgeons,

❖ ❖ ❖ ❖

and heart specialists, while entire counties in the Midwest are without a single doctor of any kind.

Another area in which physicians-as-businesspersons may have a conflict of interests is in their links to drug companies and to manufacturers of medical devices (instruments and equipment). Because the Food and Drug Administration (FDA), which must approve prescription drugs and devices before they are put on the market, does not have the money or staffing to do the testing in government labs, it must depend on the manufacturers to conduct careful studies and report all results. The drug companies, in turn, pay doctors to enroll their patients in these tests; testing has become a multibillion-dollar industry involving thousands of private physicians. The physicians, of course, are under pressure to report positive results so that the drug company will continue to hire them (Eichenwald and Kolata 1999a). When researchers in the pay of a pharmaceutical company publish their findings, these invariably present a positive picture of the drug's effects, downplaying negative outcomes or the effects of competing products. Nevertheless, these data are all that the FDA has to go on when deciding whether to approve the drug for sale (Rennie 1999).

With regard to medical devices, many doctors are themselves the inventors of new techniques and instruments, for which they can either set up their own production company or sell the rights to another manufacturer. Ethical questions arise when the doctors conduct their own research, claiming to be objective experts while having a large financial stake in the device being adopted by other physicians. The practice is so widespread today that personal interests often outweigh scientific evidence in the evaluation of medical devices (Eichenwald and Kolata 1999b).

The FDA has had some success, however, in catching the drug companies in misleading advertisements, but there is not much it can do other than complain loudly. The pharmaceutical industry is one of the most powerful lobbying groups in Washington, DC, and employs tens of thousands of workers in many states. In 1998 and 1999, almost every major drug company was warned about its advertising claims for a wide range of products (Pear 1999). Before the rules were changed in the mid-1990s, drug companies could advertise prescription products only in professional medical journals. Now they can appeal directly to the public, urging you to ask your doctor about miracle products X, Y, and Z. In one sense, the advertisements empower the patient by providing information that was once the secret knowledge of professionals. The downside is that patients may insist on prescriptions that are not medically necessary, thus driving up the total cost of health care. During this week, keep count of the number of newspaper and TV ads to which you are exposed that extol the virtues of one or another prescription product— especially hair restorers, nasal decongestants, and potency enhancers. 💻10

Today, the most serious challenge to a physician's full control over treatment choices, however, comes from the health insurance industry, discussed in a later section. First, you need some background about the rise and decline of hospitals as primary sources of care.

❖ ❖ ❖ ❖   ## The American Hospital

The emergence of the hospital as the major center for health care parallels the growth of physician dominance of medical practice. In 1870 there were only 100 general hospitals in the United States, and they were owned by local or state governments or by religious charities. After 1910, however, there was a great need for a place for newly trained professionals to hone their skills and to treat patients with serious illnesses. Physicians then became the dominant voice in setting hospital policy because only they could admit the patients that filled the beds. This monopoly over health care was strengthened when the AMA persuaded politicians to limit the number of free clinics serving city populations and to forbid public health offices from providing direct care (Starr 1982).

The hospital system grew to 7,000 facilities by 1980 but has shrunk to about 6,000, as earlier treatment, insurance limits, and more sophisticated outpatient procedures have reduced the need for overnight stays. About 5,000 of these facilities are general hospitals, in contrast to those for specialized treatments (e.g., psychiatric, cancer, long-term care). Hospital ownership falls into three broad categories: (1) privately owned for-profit, or **proprietary**; (2) nonprofit private; and (3) public (see Table 14.3). 🖥11

Proprietary Hospitals

In 2000, about 40 percent of American acute-care hospitals were part of an investor-owned, profit-making chain—a medical Walmart. The chains began by buying up local community hospitals that were in financial trouble—and almost all were losing money, with empty beds and patient fees that failed to cover costs. By centralizing purchasing and administrative tasks, the

Proprietary hospitals serve patients who can afford private suites, gourmet food service, fresh flowers, and a staff of well-paid doctors.

proprietary chains claim to be able to lower costs while introducing businesslike efficiency. Most of the cost savings have actually come from spending relatively less on nursing care and from hiring nonunion workers (Woolhandler and Himmelstein 1997).

The private hospitals do for health care what private schools do for education—skim the cream off the top of the client population. Proprietary hospitals can pick and choose their patients, typically those who are fully insured and have uncomplicated conditions. For patients who can afford the extra expense, there are private suites for family members, gourmet food service, fresh flowers, and a staff of well-paid doctors. Marketing and overhead expenses, including executive salaries, absorb most of the profit in the for-profit sector.

Although private hospitals must provide first aid to anyone who shows up at the door, they are under no obligation to do more than stabilize emergency patients before sending them off to the nearest nonprofit or public facility.

Private Nonprofits

The majority of American hospitals are owned and operated as tax-exempt nonprofit institutions by a board of local civic leaders. A private nonprofit hospital can make money, but the money has to be plowed back into the institution rather than being distributed to individuals. In most communities, being on the hospital board is a high-profile status symbol.

The costs of operating a hospital have risen sharply: cost to the institution for an average stay was $500 in 1970 but over $6,500 today (Health Care Financing Administration 2000). This increase reflects investments in complex technology, expansion of the range of tests and services available, and the need to pay a living wage to hospital workers (now also likely to be unionized). At the same time, public financial support and patient fees have not increased as rapidly, and insurance companies take their time, often several months, to cover patient bills, while the hospital staff must be paid weekly.

A community nonprofit hospital enjoys a tax-free status as long as it continues to serve the community, which means caring for uninsured patients. To make up for those who cannot pay out-of-pocket, most nonprofits add a surcharge onto the bills of insured patients, which is another factor in the high cost of hospital stays. There is pressure, then, to provide the minimum of care to the uninsured and to try to fill hospital beds with paying consumers, even as the length of average hospital stays has declined, thanks to more powerful treatments and outpatient services. It is when there are empty beds that the proprietary owners come into town and offer to buy the facility and promise to keep it open for community residents, a promise that is not always honored.

The nonprofits that remain financially and medically sound are those that are located in wealthy suburbs or well-populated urban areas and that have diversified their services to provide outpatient surgery and clinics for everything from drug rehabilitation to problem pregnancies. But few are so sound that they are not at risk of a takeover. You might want to take an inventory of hospitals in your hometown over the past two decades and see how many are still there and what services are offered.

Public Hospitals

Owned and operated by the federal, state, or local government, public hospitals today are typically in great financial trouble because they serve a primarily poor, uninsured, and often very ill patient population. Especially hard hit are the hospitals located in major cities. In a political climate where to increase taxes is to commit electoral suicide, state and local government officials not only refuse to raise the funds needed to operate the public hospitals but are actually cutting health care outlays by changing the rules for who is eligible for subsidized care—and this is in a decade of relative prosperity for the states. One can imagine what will happen during the next recession.

The hospitals are forced to cut staff and services and continually have to beg the state legislature for money to cover the uninsured (Steinhauer 1999). In New Jersey, a relatively wealthy state, every year, after months of wrangling, the legislature passes a stopgap measure involving considerably less money than the hospitals have already spent on charity cases.

Table 14.3 Types of American Hospitals

Type	Funding	Operating procedures	Client base
Proprietary Hospitals	Investor-owned for-profit chains	Centralized purchasing and administrative tasks to reduce costs	Focusing on private patients who can afford the high costs with extra "perks" such as private suites and gourmet food
Private Nonprofits	Tax-exempt nonprofits, operated by local communities or religious organizations	Profits are poured back into operating expenses, and costs are also covered by insurance reimbursements. Diversification of services helps defray costs	Operating in and for the local community, these hospitals also take the uninsured along with private and insured patients. A surcharge on insured patients helps to defray the costs of the uninsured
Public Hospitals	Owned and operated by federal, state, or local governments—taxpayer supported	Usually operating at a loss because of high demand and cutbacks in tax supports	They primarily serve the poor, often uninsured and seriously ill patients, including Medicare and Medicaid recipients

At the Congressional level, the Balanced Budget Act of 1997 made sharp cuts in subsidies to the university teaching hospitals that serve many of the nation's charitable cases. If there is a medical school on your campus, find out how it is financed, and what types of patients are served, and what might be the impact on the community if it were to shut down.

The result of all these trends is a three-tiered hospital system in the United States that parallels the social class hierarchy: excellent private care for those who can afford it; adequate service to the ordinary employed person whose employer provides a health insurance benefit; and bare-bones treatment for the poor. And, although many Americans object to a national health insurance program on the ground that it would ration health care, that is exactly what the country already has: doctors and hospitals that ration care on the basis of ability to pay.

The Hospital as a Social System

❖ ❖ ❖ ❖

The hospital is a social system, with its sets of patterned statuses and roles (including the sick role for patients), several stratification systems, and a particular culture in which it is assumed that all personnel contribute to healing. This belief in their own therapeutic powers, plus fears of malpractice lawsuits, combine to create a veil of secrecy over mistakes. Thus, it came as a shock when the National Academy of Sciences (1999) reported that tens of thousands of hospital patients die annually because of preventable errors. What is sociologically interesting about the report is that the most common mistakes were not the fault of incompetent personnel but products of the systems in which they worked. Since part of that system was the failure to report errors, the dangers remained uncorrected. For example, several surgeons made the same mistake when reaching for a drug that was in the same colored vial as another medication and picking the wrong one. Had knowledge been shared, simply changing the color of the lids could have prevented additional deaths. Another factor was the illegibility of many doctors' handwriting, leading to pharmacists' mistakes. Errors in dosage, because of the varying strengths in which pills are manufactured, were quite common, by both nurses and pharmacists. The report was a sad but illuminating example of how the structure and culture of a workplace has an effect independent of the skills of the workers.

The stratification systems within the hospital consist of overlapping hierarchies of medical staff and administrators. If you have had occasion to visit a hospital recently, you are probably aware of many of the fine distinctions within and between medical and administrative personnel. The length of their white coats distinguishes medical residents from interns, while admitting physicians wear street clothes. The nursing staff is similarly divided by rank and responsibility, though not necessarily by uniforms, from Nurse Administrator to Registered Nurse (RN) to Practical Nurse to Nurse's Aide. The lower down the status hierarchy, the higher the number of minority employees.

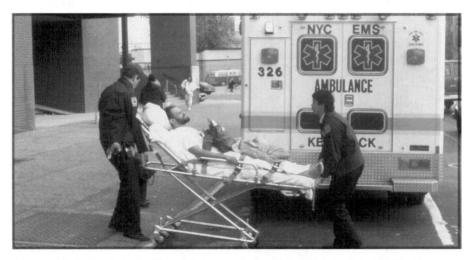

Many public hospitals in the United States are in financial trouble because they tend to serve poor, uninsured, and very ill patients. This patient is being transported by EMS in New York City to one such public hospital. Why are public hospitals underfunded and overcrowded?

Box 14.3

Women in White

The field of nursing offers many examples of how nonmedical factors, such as gender, prestige, and finances, affect the delivery of health care. Throughout most of human history, healers were women steeped in the knowledge of herbs and home remedies, attending births and deaths. With the rise of modern medicine, women's traditional contributions were dismissed as "folklore" and "witchcraft," and the midwives and herbalists were replaced by men with scientific training. If women were to have a role in medicine, it would naturally be as handmaidens to the physicians (Roberts 1995).

Nursing increasingly competes with other career choices open to women, including becoming a doctor. Why are nurses' salaries significantly lower than those of physicians?

The history of modern nursing dates from 1854, with the well-to-do women recruited by Florence Nightingale to care for British soldiers wounded in the Crimean War. Nightingale was the first to define nursing as respectable paid work rather than as charity or women's natural duty. In the United States, by the 1920s, the growing number of recently trained physicians (almost all men) and the hospitals built to care for their seriously ill patients generated a demand for nursing staff. Nursing soon became a popular career choice (there were few others) for the upwardly mobile daughters of first-generation immigrants. By the 1950s, however, the field had lost much of its luster; pay and prestige were relatively low; doctors treated nurses as servants; and hospitals wanted a cheap and controllable labor force. Nursing training typically consisted of two years at a school attached to the hospital. The work itself was hard, often dirty and dangerous, involving frequent displays of subservience to male authority (Melosh 1982).

To transform nursing into a profession, its leaders had to redefine the role as that of a medical specialist, upgrade training to require a bachelor's degree, and turn the American Nursing Association into a real trade union willing to fight for better pay and working conditions as well as for a degree of decision-making authority. Most of these goals were achieved in the 1970s and 1980s, but by this time, nursing had to compete with other career choices open to women, including becoming a doctor. Yet the image of a nurse as selfless servant persists. Notice how, on the few occasions that nurses have gone out on strike, the first question a newsperson asks is not, "Why are you striking?" but "How could you leave all those poor sick patients?" 💻 12

Models of Health Care Delivery

A society's values will determine how health care needs are met and how scarce resources are allocated. Such seemingly neutral acts such as performing an organ transplant or advising a pregnant woman are deeply influenced by nonmedical factors such as insurance coverage (the poor rarely get new hearts) or religious beliefs (Catholic hospitals refuse to provide a full range of family planning information). In our society, the power of business interests and a lingering mistrust of government have combined to produce a structure in which each citizen is on his or her own in negotiating the insurance

and health care systems, and in which profits for private providers are fully
protected. As a consequence, the United States is the only modern state without some kind of publicly funded health insurance with universal coverage.
What Americans do have is the ". . . most wasteful, costly, and inequitable
health care system in the industrialized world" (Light 2000), as indicated in
Table 14.4. Nor does it appear that the situation will change any time soon, as
all proposals for change continue to rely on private-sector solutions, in keeping with the history of health care in America.

Table 14.4 Comparative Health Care Expenditures as Percent of Gross Domestic Product,* 1980 and 1998		
	1980	1998
United States	9.1	14.0
Canada	7.3	9.3
United Kingdom	5.6	6.9
Japan	6.4	7.4
Ireland	6.7	6.1
Germany	8.8	10.6

* The Gross Domestic Product (GDP) is the value of all goods and services produced in
the country.
Source: *United States Statistical Abstracts, 2000.*

In 1945, when President Harry Truman proposed a very modest national
health insurance program, the American Medical Association and employer
groups waged a very successful lobbying and media campaign to persuade
Congress and the public that this would be the entering wedge for socialism
in America. It took another two decades before the words "national health
insurance" could be heard in the land. By 1965, however, the growing number
of old people with large medical bills reached the point where the elderly and
their adult children were overwhelmed. Congress heard their pain and finally
passed a limited program of health insurance for people 65 years of age and
older.

Medicare is funded by payroll deductions from workers and employers,
is administered by federal agencies, and reimburses health-care providers for
services rendered. But not all services are covered. The most-used ones, such
as a yearly check-up, eyeglasses, hearing aids, most dental care, and all prescriptions must be paid for by the patient. Older people who want to be covered for visits to a doctor's office must pay an additional monthly premium,
and many will also purchase supplemental insurance in the private sector.
Over time, costs have risen and the range of covered services reduced, so that
out-of-pocket expenses by the elderly are proportionately the same today as
before Medicare.

At the same time, in 1965, Congress also passed a federally funded and
state-administered program of reimbursements for health care services to
the poor, **Medicaid**. 🖳 13 But because the health needs of the poor are enormous and costly, the program has been in trouble from the beginning. Fewer
than 40 percent of eligible Americans are enrolled, and the states have little
interest in finding the rest. Indeed, a majority of states have reduced reimbursement rates, and the lower the repayments, the less likely it is that a doctor or hospital will accept Medicaid patients, most of whom are children and

their impoverished mothers. At the same time, millions of dollars have been siphoned from the program by consultants and state governments (General Accounting Office 2000).

An additional obstacle for low-income parents is a byproduct of the welfare system changes of 1996 (see Chapter 5) that made it easier for officials to deny all kinds of benefits. Although the law specifically provides for continuation of food stamps and Medicaid coverage, state and local welfare agencies have routinely made it difficult for poor parents to meet application standards (Pear 1999). One assumed money-saver for some states has been to convert Medicaid from a reimbursement for services program to a managed care system (see below), but the savings quickly evaporated and costs rose, so the states began cutting benefits and raising premiums, leaving the very poor and very sick once again without coverage or care. But, as Tennessee's health care director explained to a reporter, the poor could help pay for their care if they stopped spending money on cell phones and cigarettes and demanding everything for free (Kilborn 1999, 1).

These two programs—Medicare and Medicaid—are all the United States can show for government-sponsored and government-funded health care. There is no overall policy; implementation varies from state to state; funding is never quite secure; powerful interest groups such as doctors and insurers exert their pressure; and politicians are unlikely to offend campaign donors (Kronenfeld 1997). The most recent effort to construct a comprehensive national policy, with a major role for nonprofit organizations, was in 1993, during President Clinton's first term; it turned into a fiasco when the proposal proved too detailed to be easily understood and was fiercely attacked by physicians and insurance companies, who revived public fears over "socialized medicine." Especially effective were radio and TV ads featuring a couple named Harry and Louise who scared up a storm with their images of patients being herded like cattle into doctors' offices—you could hear the mooing in the background.

Thus, as the United States enters the twenty-first century, all people, other than the elderly and the poor, are on their own in a health-care system that was once exclusively based on the professional model but that is increasingly dominated by managed care companies.

Health is influenced by genetics, nutrition, and one's lifestyle. These women, playing in a basketball tournament, lead an active lifestyle.

The **professional model** refers to the system before the 1980s, when physicians made all the major decisions about health care—whom to see and where, which treatments to order, and what to charge. Payment was on the basis of *fee-for-service*, with the doctor setting the fee and the patient paying only for what was done on each visit. By the 1980s, however, these fees were rising faster than the patients' incomes, and while many Americans were able to afford private health insurance policies, and others had their insurance paid for in full or in part by an employer, a large proportion paid out-of-pocket, if they bothered to see a doctor at all.

As physician fees and the cost of hospital stays escalated, many people with private policies could no longer afford the premiums, and employers began to cut back on what they could offer. The combination of high costs and shrinking coverage created a "health care crisis" that was met in part by the emergence of **health maintenance organizations (HMOs)** and other forms of **managed care**.

Managed care is based on the concept that health-care providers—primarily physicians and hospitals—will contract with employers to cover the health-care needs of employees for a fee agreed upon in advance. In the spirit of the competitive marketplace, both providers and employers will bargain for the best deal—employers in order to save money, providers in order to earn it. By spreading the risk over a large number of people, including workers who are young and in good health, the plan can pay for the ones who get sick and can still make a profit. Doctors and hospitals give up some of their income in return for having patients in their waiting rooms and hospital beds.

In some cases, providers will join together and bargain directly with employers, but this involves a lot of overhead expense and record keeping. The more common solution is a *third-party payer*, an insurance company or HMO that negotiates between providers and employers, and between providers and patients. Some third-party payers are nonprofit organizations, often operated by unions or religious groups, but the great majority are for-profit, privately owned corporations, whose shares are traded on the stock exchange and whose value, therefore, depends on profits and earnings. The primary goal of these organizations is to remain attractive to investors. Although all the current research indicates that for-profit HMOs offer lower-quality care at higher cost than the nonprofits, all current proposals for changing the system reinforce the position of the for-profits (Himmelstein et al. 1999; Light 2000). 🖥14

Box 14.4

The Doctor's Dilemma

The doctor's dilemma today, in essence, is how to make money when managed-care fees are lower than what you could otherwise charge. If you refuse to join a managed-care system, you lose patients. If you do join, you may find that you need to see more patients for shorter sessions in order to maintain your income, or you could earn outside income by enrolling your patients in drug company trials. A growing number, however, are giving up their regular practice and becoming specialists in *lifestyle medicine*, the type of elective procedures that that are not medically necessary but that make people look more attractive and feel better about themselves.

Most insurers do not cover liposuction, wrinkle removal, teeth whitening, or elective laser eye treatments, which means that the surgeons can charge whatever patients are willing to pay, up front, with no red tape. With so much new wealth in the nation, plus the American obsession with youthful appearance, there is no shortage of customers (Steinhauer 2000). Plastic surgery, once a low-status medical specialty, is now the lifeblood of many hospitals that can realize hundreds of thousand of dollars a day in immediate cash for operating room charges, although many procedures could as easily be performed in the physician's private office.

❖ ❖ ❖ ❖   Although there are variations on the basic managed care model, the dominant form is the HMO, whose enrollment has increased from 9 million in 1980 to almost 77 million in 1998 (National Center for Health Statistics 2000).

Managed Care

The Health Maintenance Organization is a peculiarly American invention. Although a few are nonprofit organizations, the majority are profit-making corporations. Individual doctors, hospitals, and any other eligible health-care providers sign on with as many HMOs as possible, agreeing to charge only so much for various treatments. The HMO markets its collection of providers to employers and sometimes to individual clients, who pay a monthly premium plus a minimal co-payment when the service is provided. Once signed up with the HMO, you are limited to its roster of providers, although you could pay on your own to go outside the network. Some plans also cover prescriptions, although this has become so expensive that many HMOs now cover only a limited set of relatively inexpensive versions of popular medications.

The HMO is a big money-saver for the patient, unless it refuses to cover the cost of some new or "experimental" treatment, in which case you might be able to pay for it yourself, or do without, or exhaust your savings and try to enroll in Medicaid. Even so, many of the complaints against HMOs are made by people who forget what it was like without managed care, when most Americans could not afford basic, much less the state-of-the-art, treatment for everyone in the family and when a catastrophic illness could wipe out a lifetime's savings.

In addition to their loss of income because of caps, or ceilings on reimbursements, physicians and hospitals also fault the HMOs for reducing their decision-making power, for example, by setting limits on the number of hospital days they will pay for, or by second-guessing a doctor on the need for diagnostic tests. The HMO is in the business of cutting costs, which often translates into cutting services, but some of the services may have been unnecessary and unnecessarily expensive in the first place—yet, who is to say? 15

These are some of the dilemmas about managed care currently being debated, as government is under pressure to curb the power of the managed care companies. But with each new mandate, costs will rise, and employers will cut coverage or ask employees to pay higher premiums. In addition, bankruptcies and mergers have reduced to a handful the number of national HMOs competing for large employers, thus increasing their bargaining power. At the moment, over 85 percent of insured workers are in some form of managed care. The other 15 percent have traditional fee-for-service coverage from an insurance company, the premiums for which run into several thousand dollars per year.

Not all workers are insured. Many small businesses do not offer any plan; other employers offer limited coverage; and many employees would rather opt out, take the added weekly income, and pray that they stay healthy. In 1998, almost 44 million Americans, or about 18 percent of the nonelderly population, were without any health insurance, a figure that rises to almost

one-third for poor persons (Employee Benefit Research Institute 2000). As
you might expect, coverage increases with income, education, and size of
employing firm. Most likely to be uninsured are single men, people between
ages 18 and 24, Hispanic Americans, immigrants, and full-time workers
whose incomes still fall below the poverty line. Many of these low-income
workers are former welfare recipients who have taken jobs with no health
benefits or who cannot pay their share of employer-sponsored plans, and
who were illegally dropped from Medicaid (Pear 2000).

Box 14.5

Home Is Where the Heart (or Lung or Liver) Is

Now that organ transplants are a multibillion-dollar industry, with prestige as
well as profit at stake for doctors and hospitals, a new set of turf wars has broken
out. The old conflict was about who goes to the head of the waiting list, typically
won by people with the most "socially valuable" characteristics (Friedman et al.
1992). The big battle today is over which facility gets to perform the surgery. In the
era of managed care, there are not many opportunities to get approval for procedures that cost hundreds of thousands of dollars, plus expenses for blood, medications, psychiatric counseling, and postoperative rehabilitation. In addition, because the need for organs far exceeds the number of donors, transplant surgeons
are competing fiercely with one another for bodies and prestige (Stolberg 1999).

Until 1999, donor organs typically went to the nearest transplant center, which
meant that a large number of smaller facilities were able to stay in business and
also that local patients would receive transplants regardless of their level of need.
Thus, different regions of the country had widely diverse waiting times. However,
when President Clinton proposed that organs be distributed nationally on the basis
of need rather than geography, open warfare broke out. Congress was heavily lob-
bied by the local medical facilities, many of which were owned by physician
groups. States passed laws requiring that organs be offered locally before crossing
state lines. Eventually, the local interest won out. The moral of this story is either
stay very healthy or move to where the hearts are.

There are no free lunches. For every cost-cutting effort by the third-party
payers, there will be a firestorm of negative comments from doctors, politicians, and the affected patients. But without regulating services and reimbursement rates, the nation will be back to the "health care crisis" of two
decades ago: trying to find a balance between coverage, cost, and quality of
care. There is a solution, not quite a free lunch either, but it is politically
impossible in the United States—namely, to eliminate the third-party payers,
take the savings, and shift to some form of a single-payer plan as in every
other modern industrial society.

Single-Payer Systems

The single payer is the government, and the funds primarily come out of
general taxes. Although people in countries with this plan are taxed at a
higher rate than Americans, Americans end up actually paying much more
for their health care when you add up co-payments, prescriptions, and insurance premiums (the share paid by your employer, which eventually comes
out of your wages). To the argument that you do not want government
bureaucrats deciding what treatment they will pay for, critics of our current

❖ ❖ ❖ ❖   system would answer: Are you any more comfortable with an employee of Blue Cross making that judgment? These are not easy choices. Everyone cannot have all the treatments available, immediately, and at no charge. At the moment, in the United States, decisions about who has access to what level of care are made by the size of your wallet.

Under a single-payer system, and there are a number of variations on the basic model, costs are controlled by putting a cap on providers' fees and by budgeting for entire geographic areas, with local officials deciding how to allocate the money. The closest example would be that of Canada, where health-care expenditures are lower than in the United States but life expectancy is higher and infant mortality lower. The system is funded through federal taxes, and the money is distributed to the various provinces (comparable to our states), provided that the province has a plan to cover every aspect of health care for every citizen and has a public nonprofit agency to administer the program. The downside is that unless the program is well-financed, there will be a shortage of doctors, nurses, and hospital beds, so patients may have to wait many months for elective (nonemergency) surgery; because of the wait, some Canadians cross over to the United States and pay out of pocket (Brooke 2000). At the same time, thousands of Americans take day trips to Canada to buy prescription drugs at considerably lower prices than in the United States.

The single-payer system could save much of the money now going to the insurance companies. Ideally, the savings would then be used to expand public health programs and prevention services that reduce the need for medical intervention later on. But these very virtues are precisely why Americans will not see a single-payer system any time soon. Not only would unhappiness with managed care need to reach unbearable levels, but also politicians would have to take on the AMA, the pharmaceutical industry, and the insurance companies. Health care would have to be redefined as a public responsibility, which appears to be a long way off.

On the one hand is the argument for letting the problems be solved by private enterprise, based on the claim that public bureaucracies breed inefficiency, that physicians are best equipped to make medical decisions, and that consumers are perfectly capable of deciding how much care they are willing to pay for. On the other hand is the argument that unless coverage is universal, the insurance companies will "cherry-pick" the healthiest and wealthiest, generating ever-greater inequalities in the society. The Netherlands, Denmark, and Sweden have health-care delivery systems that are fair, efficient, and effective and that deliver state-of-the-art medicine to the entire population at half the per-capita cost of the American system (Light 2000). This is a

Among proposals for controlling the cost of health care in the United States is the single-payer system which could be used to expand public health programs and prevention services that reduce the need for medical intervention later on. There is agreement that loving and caring parents are necessary for the health of all children.

debate that will not go away soon—and it is one on which your very life depends.

    The other development to watch carefully is the changing nature of the AIDS epidemic, no longer as great a killer in the United States as in the past but increasingly a clear and present danger in the developing nations of Africa and Asia.

❖ ❖ ❖ ❖

Box 14.6

HIV: A Modern Pandemic

A *pandemic* is an especially widespread disease, a word that well describes the spread of HIV (human immunodeficiency virus) across the world today. The HIV virus is a direct cause of AIDS (acquired immunity deficiency syndrome), although not all people who are HIV-positive will develop AIDS. What happens medically is that the virus destroys the ability of the body's immune system to resist infections that might otherwise have little effect. It is these infections that are the immediate cause of death. The virus is spread through the exchange of bodily fluids (namely, blood and semen). At special risk are people who engage in sexual intercourse without using a barrier device, share infected intravenous syringes, or receive blood transfusions. Because it takes many years for full-blown AIDS to develop, many people infected during adolescence or young adulthood, when unprotected sex is most common, will continue to spread the virus.

    When AIDS was first recognized in the United States, several decades ago, its effects were most obvious among white gay males. Once alerted, activists organized to reduce risky behaviors, lobby for research funds, and establish support services for victims. By 1999, due to the introduction of complex combinations of medications, the death rate from AIDS among white men, gay or not, had stabilized and even declined. In contrast, the number of new HIV cases among minorities has continued to rise. For African-American men and women between ages 25 and 44, AIDS is now is a leading cause of death (National Center for Health Statistics 1999; Altman 2000), partly because community activists failed to acknowledge the problem and to mobilize effectively against the disease. As long as poor women engage in the sex trade to make a living and drug addicts continue to share needles, the infection will spread, passed on to later sex partners and to infants in the womb, many of whom will be born with the virus.

Figure 14.1 World's HIV/AIDS Cases

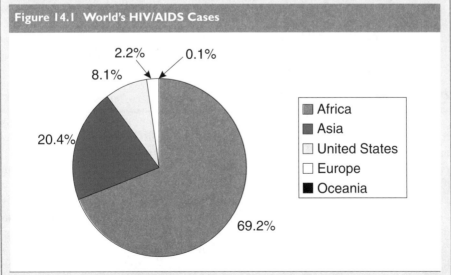

Source: Population Reference Bureau, *World Population Data Sheet*, 2000.

Nonetheless, North America accounts for a small proportion of HIV infections across the globe. As shown in Figure 14.1, two-thirds of all reported HIV cases are found in the African nations below the Sahara Desert, and another 20 percent in South and Southeast Asia, almost all as a result of heterosexual sex (United Nations 1999). In South and Southeast Asian countries, especially Thailand, "sex tourism" is a major source of foreign currency. Men from Japan and Korea and other highly traditional Asian societies travel to where they can enjoy all kinds of otherwise forbidden sexual pleasures, particularly involving children, girls and boys alike (Seabrook 1997). The governments of these countries have only recently tried to control the sex trade, as a matter of national reputation and public health.

In the African countries, the spread of the virus follows the truck routes over which almost all trade moves; the drivers, away from their home communities for long journeys, engage in unprotected sex with prostitutes, and both of them pass the infection on to their next sex partners, including, ultimately, the driver's wife (Herdt 1997). Another contributing factor is the disruption caused by civil wars and the massive movement of refugees: women are raped, family ties are broken, communities are destroyed. In the cities, AIDS has spread to the middle class, as white-collar workers can now afford prostitutes. From the cities, the disease moves rapidly to the countryside, where poverty and lack of proper sanitation have already taken their toll on the immune system (United Nations Food and Agriculture Organization 2000).

For decades, the problem was ignored; governments did not want to admit that a sexually transmitted disease was spreading rapidly; families were embarrassed; rural folk were completely baffled by the illness. So the epidemic turned into a pandemic, with catastrophic effects. Just when many of these countries were finally realizing a drop in infant mortality and an increase in life expectancy, the AIDS epidemic wiped these out gains. Botswana, a relatively stable country, has lost 20 years in life expectancy since 1994. The United Nations has estimated that almost half of 15-year-olds in the most affected parts of Africa will eventually die of the disease (United Nations Development Program 2000b). Since 1981, 13 million African children have been orphaned by AIDS. No longer protected by other kin or villagers, the orphans roam rural areas and towns, work as child labor, or join a semi-military gang when old enough to hold a gun. Given the rapid spread of both HIV and AIDS, the number of orphans may climb to 40 million by 2020.

The pandemic has also strained the economy of African nations. In countries where between 10 and 25 percent of the population are HIV positive, 2 percent of the work force dies of AIDS each year. Few individuals can afford the expensive treatments; the countries' health care systems cannot absorb the cost. With so many people ill, productivity declines, economic growth stalls, more people starve, families disintegrate, workers and refugees migrate, and more women go into the sex trade. The only solutions for these countries are large-scale education programs and vast cultural change—in a deadly race against time. ▣ 16

Conclusion

As you have seen throughout this chapter, health and illness have a powerful social and cultural dimension, from epidemiological patterns to individual behavior in the sick role. The history of the practice of medicine in America, the emergence of professional dominance in a market economy, and the current shift of power to managed care have all been guided by nonmedical forces. The nature and functions of hospitals and their personnel, similarly, have shifted with other social tides. Questions of cost, coverage, and quality remain unanswered and often unasked. The quality of American medicine is extremely high, technologically superb, but distributed unevenly across subgroups. Managed care has brought some control over medical expenses, but at the cost of limiting treatments. And, one in six Amer-

icans remains without insurance coverage, while many others have only partial protection. Health care is one of those issues that will require your closest
attention in the decades ahead.

Surfing the Sociological Internet

1   The following is an excellent source for epidemiological statis-
    tics: http://www.cdc.gov/nchs/nhis.htm

2   For health and health care in the United States: http://
    www.os.dhhs.gov/ and
    http://www.whitehouse.gov/fsbr/health.html
    For a fact sheet from the CDC on life expectancy and mortality
    rates, go to: http://www.cdc.gov/nchs/releases/98facts/
    98sheets/finmort.htm
    For children's health status contributing to higher life expec-
    tancy:
    http://www.childstats.gov/ac2000/hlthtxt.asp

3   Gender and mortality rates:
    http://www.4woman.gov/
    http://www.snowcrest.net/freemanl/women/atlas/in-
    dex.html#home

4   Minority health:
    http://www.omhrc.gov/
    Statistics on African-American population, health, and mortal-
    ity rates: http://www.afroamerhealthdata.com/vital.html

5   Mental health: http://www.nmha.org/

6   The American Medical Association can be found at: http://
    www.ama-assn.org/

7   The American Women's Medical Association is at: http://
    www.amwa-doc.org/
    Their journal site can be found at: http://www.jamwa.org/
    top.htm which includes articles on health issues for women and
    minorities.

8   http://www.aabhs.org/welcome.htm is the site for the Associa-
    tion for the Advancement of Blacks in the Health Sciences.
    For reports on minorities in medicine: http://www.aamc.org/
    about/progemph/diverse/releases.htm

9   Medicine as business: http://www.managedcaremag.com/

10 The Food and Drug Administration is at: http://www.fda.gov/

11 For hospital information, see: http://www.aha.org/default.asp

12 The American Nursing Association can be found at: http://
    www.ana.org/

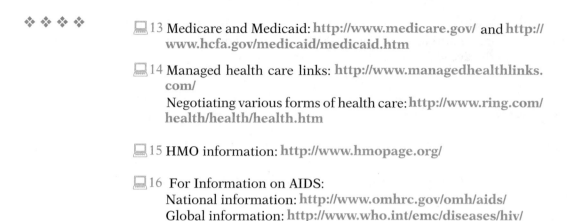

❖ ❖ ❖ ❖

🖥 13 Medicare and Medicaid: http://www.medicare.gov/ and http://www.hcfa.gov/medicaid/medicaid.htm

🖥 14 Managed health care links: http://www.managedhealthlinks.com/
Negotiating various forms of health care: http://www.ring.com/health/health/health.htm

🖥 15 HMO information: http://www.hmopage.org/

🖥 16 For Information on AIDS:
National information: http://www.omhrc.gov/omh/aids/
Global information: http://www.who.int/emc/diseases/hiv/

Glossary

Acute Illness   A short-term condition.

Chronic Illness   A condition that takes a long time to develop and that gets progressively worse.

Halo Effect   In medicine, reflects the stratification system of specializations whereby the practitioner takes on the prestige of patients.

Health Maintenance Organization (HMO)   A form of managed care based on prepayment for health care by patients who agree to use member physicians and hospitals.

Life Expectancy   The number of years a person can be expected to live depending on the year of birth.

Managed Care   A medical system in which physicians and hospitals contract with employers to cover the health care needs of employees for a fee agreed upon in advance.

Medicaid   A federally funded and state administered health-care system that reimburses doctors and hospitals for services to the poor.

Medicare   A federally administered insurance program, funded by workers' and employees' contributions, to reimburse providers for certain services given to older patients.

Private Nonprofit Hospital   Hospital owned and operated as a tax-exempt nonprofit institution by a board of local civic leaders, with money being plowed back into the hospital.

Professional Medical Model   System in which physicians make all major decisions about health care and charge fees for service.

Proprietary Hospitals   Hospitals owned for profit, typically serving patients who are fully insured and have uncomplicated conditions.

Public Hospitals   Hospitals owned and operated by federal, state, or local governments.

Sick Role   A set of rights and obligations attached to the status of being ill.

Single-Payer Medical System   Health-care system with the government as the single payer, using funds from general tax revenue.

Social Epidemiology   The study of patterns of occurrence of illness within a population. ✦

Part IV
Modern Dilemmas

Demography as Destiny: Populations and Their Environments

❖ ❖ ❖ ❖   Demography (from *demos* = people) is the study of populations, their size and composition (by sex, age, race, etc.), and their movement from one place to another. As you will soon see, many of your life choices and chances are influenced by how many people are in your society and their ages. In addition, the size and distribution of the world's population will have an impact on many events during your lifetime. **Human ecology** refers to the interactions between populations and their physical environment, such as the use of resources and the causes of climate change. This chapter examines aspects of both populations and environments:

- World population.
- Population dynamics.
- Life expectancy and age pyramids.
- Environmental concerns.
- From farm to city to suburbs.
- The crisis of American cities.

World Population: Six Billion and Counting

Throughout all of prehistory and right up to the sixteenth century, the population of the world, as best we can estimate, stayed pretty much in balance. High birthrates and high death rates canceled each other out, and populations remained stable. But around the middle of the eighteenth century in Europe, the proportion of children surviving to adulthood began to rise, as shown in Figure 15.1. Over the past two centuries, throughout the world, populations have doubled and tripled in the space of decades. The world population today is six billion, up from three billion in the 1960s, and expected to be close to nine billion around 2050. But while the numbers will increase, the rate of growth has slowed, for reasons to be discussed throughout this chapter. 💻 1

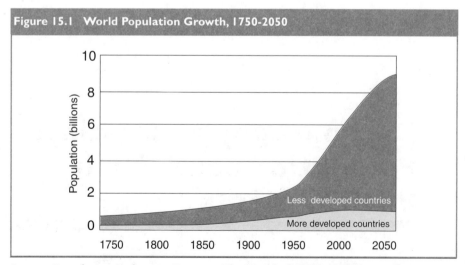

Figure 15.1 World Population Growth, 1750-2050

Source: Population Reference Bureau, *The World of Child 6 Billion*, 1999.

The primary cause of the population explosion in eighteenth-century Europe and in much of the world today was a dramatic decline in death rates, especially in infancy. This decline was due to the spread of such public health measures as boiled water and covered sewers, followed in the nineteenth century by pasteurized milk, sterilization of surgical instruments, and vaccinations. In fact, the covered sewer may be one of the great inventions of human history, keeping insects from picking up germs from filthy drains and then spreading disease to humans. Yet if birthrates remain high even as death rates drop, the world's population will increase, as it has over the past two hundred years.

Once assured that infants will live, couples can have fewer but healthier children, so eventually birthrates also drop. This is called the **demographic transition**—a shift from populations kept in check by high birthrates and high death rates to those stabilized by low birthrates and death rates. This transition characterizes modern industrial societies, where families no longer need many children to use as farm labor or to exchange as marriage partners; where women have some degree of social and personal power; and where the authority of religious and political leaders over private life is limited. Success in modern societies requires long periods of education, so the fewer the offspring, the better off they will be. In addition, urban living reduces the space available to a family. For all these reasons, industrialization typically brings a rapid decline in birthrates.

Throughout much of the world today, however, these modern conditions still do not apply. Children are needed for whatever they can produce and to provide old age security. Girls and women are denied the education and jobs that might make them independent. High fertility is seen as a sign of national strength and male potency. In other societies, efforts are being made to control population growth, but until families can be assured material security, the programs will have limited success. 🖥 2

Current and future population growth will take place almost entirely in the less developed regions, which will be home to almost eight of the nine billion people on the planet after 2050, as shown in Figure 15.2. This estimate is slightly lower than earlier projections because of (1) further declines in birthrates as family planning services take hold, and (2) higher-than-expected death rates in parts of Africa and Asia ravaged by AIDS. 🖥 3

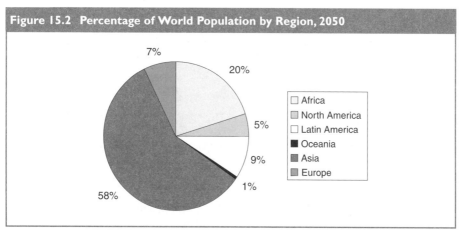

Figure 15.2 Percentage of World Population by Region, 2050

Legend:
- Africa
- North America
- Latin America
- Oceania
- Asia
- Europe

7%, 20%, 5%, 9%, 1%, 58%

Source: Population Reference Bureau, *World Population Data Sheet*, 2000.

❖ ❖ ❖ ❖   ## Population Dynamics

Not only does it make a difference how many people share the planet with you, it also matters how they are distributed by age. If there are a lot of children relative to adults, then education and housing are a major concern, as in Mexico. If the population contains a lot of old people, health care and retirement income will absorb a large part of the public budget, as in the United States today. Although all those Baby Boomers are blocking channels of upward occupational mobility for young adults today, their children will have a clearer shot at the top simply because they were born when the birthrate was low.

The raw materials for demographers are three variables: (1) birthrates, (2) death rates, and (3) net migration (the difference between the numbers leaving and those entering a society). Each of these is strongly influenced by government policies, religious beliefs, economic factors, and the influence of surrounding societies. In other words, birth, death, and migration take place in social context, and one that is highly gendered. Taken together, the three variables produce specific age structures. 4

Table 15.1 Commonly Used Demographic Terms	
Birthrates	**Life expectancy**
The number of births per 1,000 population of a particular society for a given year. For example, the birthrate in the United States is 15 births per 1,000 people.	The average number of years a person can expect to live given current mortality rates.
Death (mortality) rates	**Net migration**
The number of deaths within a given time period as a proportion of the entire population.	This is measured by subtracting people who moved out from the number who moved into a particular area over a given period of time.
Demographic transition	**Overpopulation**
A shift from populations kept in check by high birth and high death rates to those stabilized by low birth and death rates.	A relative term signifying that a society lacks sufficient resources to provide an adequate standard of living to its citizens.
Demography	**Population pyramids**
The study of populations, their size and composition, and their movement from one place to another.	The structural representation of the combined data on birth, death, and net migration, called the age structure of society.
Fertility rate	**Zero population growth**
The average number of children born to a woman between ages 15 and 49.	When fertility reaches the level of 2.1 offspring required to replace the parental couple.

Birthrates

✧ ✧ ✧ ✧

Although the decision to have children or not is made by each couple, the sum of these decisions is a social fact: the birthrate—the number of births per 1,000 population—of that society for a given year. If having babies was instinctual behavior, birthrates would not fluctuate, but they do, quite wildly, from one country to another, from one historical moment to the next, and within a society by religion, education, business cycle phase, and the degree to which women can choose when and how many children to have. Wherever women have been able to control the timing and spacing of births, the rate declines, often dramatically. For example, Spain and Italy, two of the most Catholic nations in Europe, where the Church and political authorities supported high birthrates up to the 1970s, now have the lowest rates in the world, largely because modernization has given women political and personal power. Conversely, where women are without power, birthrates remain high, as in most of Africa and the Islamic world.

The vast differences in fertility—the average number of children a woman will have between the ages of 15 and 49—among the nations of the world is shown in Table 15.2. Fertility rates vary from a high of 7.5 live births (not counting pregnancies that did not carry to term) in sub-Sahara Africa to a low of 1.2 in Hong Kong and Spain.

Table 15.2 Total Fertility, Selected Countries and Regions, 2000
(Average number of children for women age 15–49)

World	2.9
More Developed Countries	1.5
Less Developed Countries	3.2
Africa	5.6
Niger	7.5
South Africa	2.9
North America	2.0
Latin America	2.8
Asia	2.8
Yeman	6.5
China	1.8
Hong Kong	1.2
Europe	1.4
Albania	2.2
Spain	1.2

Source: Population Reference Bureau, *World Data Sheet,* 2000.

Since 2.1 children are needed to replace the parental couple (the point-one is to correct for infant deaths), anything close to 2.0 is zero population growth (ZPG) for that society. 🖥 6 As you can see, the industrialized world is experiencing population declines.

Death Rates

The great demographic story of the twentieth century, throughout the world, has been the enormous increase in life expectancy—the average number of years a person can expect to live. As you saw in chapter 14, life

Box 15.1

When the Population Is Political: Controlling Fertility

The struggle for control over women's bodies must be the most long lasting in human history and is far from over, as these three cases illustrate.

Case Number 1—*Romania (1945–1989)*

When the Communists came to power in 1945, as good Marxists, they passed laws that gave women greater control over their lives, especially in the area of marriage and reproduction. The result was a plummeting birthrate, as the women chose to dissolve unsatisfying marriages or not to marry at all. Because population size is often equated with national strength, the government became alarmed. So, out with Marx and in with laws that lowered the age for marriage, made divorce all but impossible, banned contraceptives, gave tax advantages to large families, and opened clinics to which women had to report to explain why they were not pregnant or to ensure that they did not terminate a pregnancy. The birthrate rose a bit for a short time, and when the Communists were overthrown in 1989, women joyously trashed the clinics.

Case Number 2—*The People's Republic of China (1949–present)*

Another Communist nation, but with the opposite problem—too many births; 1.26 billion, or almost 21 percent of all the people in the world today, live in a country not yet fully industrialized. How could they lower the birthrate? Why, of course, by raising the age of marriage, easing divorce, showering couples with contraceptives, giving tax advantages to one-child families, and opening clinics to help women avoid or terminate a pregnancy. This program has been most successful among educated urban professionals, who would probably have followed the Western pattern of small families anyway. In the countryside, however, and among traditional subgroups, it has been difficult to implement the program. The claim of a 1.8 fertility rate is probably an exaggeration, but the trend is clearly and sharply down.

Case Number 3—*United Nations International Conference on Population and Development (1994)*

This international conference was the first to acknowledge that world population growth was not going to be slowed by distributing condoms and that the surest way to lower birthrates is to empower women. This point aroused such a strong negative response from some Catholic and Moslem leaders that little was accomplished by the conference. At a follow-up meeting in 1999, however, delegates finally reached consensus on a document that called for the education of girls, access to family planning methods, reproductive rights of adolescents, and other health needs of girls and women. Although it is up to each country to implement these policies, it was a major victory for women's rights advocates simply to have the United Nations on record as supporting the human rights of girls and women.

The moral of the story: Population is political, a matter of national pride, political power, religious authority, and male dominance, all played out on the bodies of women.🖥5

expectancy in the United States rose dramatically over the twentieth century. Similarly, throughout the industrialized world, death typically comes at later and later ages. Table 15.3 shows life expectancy at birth for selected countries.

Low death (*mortality*) rates, although a sign of national good health, are not without problems, as when large numbers of elderly, many with chronic diseases, become a burden on the health care system and on their families. In Japan, for example, where elder care is a family responsibility, a combination of low pension benefits, a large number of frail elderly widows, and typically small houses have placed adult children caregivers under great stress (Strom 2000).

Table 15.3 Life Expectancy at Birth, Both Sexes (in Years), Selected Countries	
Japan	81
Switzerland, Hong Kong	80
Sweden, Norway	79
Italy, Spain	78
United States	77
Russia	67
Haiti	49
Afghanistan	46
Niger	41
Rwanda, Swaziland	38

Source: Population Reference Bureau, *World Population Data Sheet,* 2000.

Conversely, high mortality signals a different set of problems for a society. In Africa today, life expectancy has declined largely because of civil wars and the AIDS epidemic. In Russia, the average life expectancy of men dropped from 63 years in 1985 to 59 years in 1993, primarily as a result of deadly health habits—smoking, alcohol abuse, and accidents (Haaga 2000). Thanks to a strong anti-alcoholism campaign, Russian men today have a life expectancy of 61 years , compared to 73 years for Russian women—a 12-year differential that means large numbers of unmarried or widowed older women.

Net Migration

The third major demographic variable is migration. Since people who move from one country to another tend to be young and single, the place they come from will experience a drop in births, while the country they enter will see its population increase by both the immigrants and their children. For example, in the mid-1800s, when famine in Ireland forced young people to leave the countryside and move to England and the United States, the out-migration immediately lowered the birthrate in Ireland and relieved the effects of the famine, while it increased the fertility of the receiving countries for many decades. Today in the United States, it is young Latin-American and Asian newcomers who are keeping fertility rates from dropping below 2.0.

On the global scene, migration is at an all-time high (Martin and Widgren 1996). One stream consists of men from high-unemployment countries who have moved to where the jobs are, in the Middle East or the industrial West. Such **guestworkers** are tolerated because they do the "dirty work" that local residents no longer perform. Yet, when they

Tombstones provide information about family history and insight into how demographic transitions impact on family lives. This grave is the final resting place of three generations of a family, living from 1856 to 1986.

bring their families and settle down in the guest country, they are often met with violence (chapter 6).

The second major stream of migrants, across borders and within nations, consists of refugees from war and ethnic cleansing in Southeastern Europe, Western Asia, and sub-Sahara Africa. In 1999, the United Nations estimated that there were over 13 million transnational refugees and another 30 million displaced from homes and villages in their own country (www.refugees.com 2000). Civil wars destroy the food supply, disrupt orderly government, and produce waves of homeless wanderers. The refugees endure starvation, lack health care, strain the local economy, and add to international tensions. Abandoned widows and children roam the countryside, as refugee camps soon become overcrowded and unsanitary. With populations so in flux, it is difficult to predict the ultimate outcome, other than continued high mortality. 🖳 7

Population Pyramids

When combined, the data on birth, death, and net migration produce the *age structure* of the society. This structure is typically presented in the form of a **population pyramid**, as shown in Figure 15.3 for the more developed countries of Northern Europe and the less developed nations of Asia and Africa. 🖳 8 These pyramids show exactly how many males and females there are in each age category. The people born in a given set of years are called an **age cohort**, and successive age cohorts produce the peculiarly shaped pyramid for any society. The contrast between the pyramids for the more and less developed regions is dramatic—a great number of babies in the one and a growing proportion of old people in the other, producing a very different set of social and economic problems.

Indeed, the narrowed base, almost an inverted pyramid, for Western European societies constitutes a **second demographic revolution**, in which

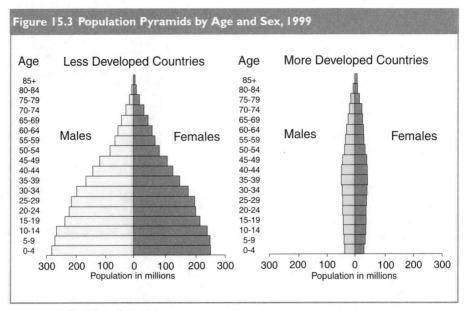

Figure 15.3 Population Pyramids by Age and Sex, 1999

Source: Gelbard et al., 1999.

declining birthrates outstrip falling death rates, with a net population loss. But short of removing women from schools and jobs, withdrawing all contraceptives, forbidding divorce, and forcing teenage girls to marry, there is little that can be done in a modern democratic nation other than to offer extended maternity, child care, and family benefits (Kent 1999) or to encourage larger families through a public relations campaign. In the United States, conservative voices warn of the dangers when selfish women pursue personal gratification at the expense of traditional values and future generations (Fox-Genovese 1996). Among the more militant Christian Identity groups (chapter 16), the fear is that unless white women have more babies, Western civilization will be doomed in a world increasingly populated by Asians and Africans.

Large numbers do not necessarily indicate that a country is overpopulated. **Overpopulation** is a relative term, signifying that the society lacks sufficient resources to provide an adequate standard of living to its citizens. Just what is "sufficient" and "adequate" are also relative, but widespread starvation, disease, and homelessness are pretty clear signs of inadequacy. By these criteria, many countries are overpopulated even though there are fewer persons per square mile than in wealthier societies.

In the second phase of the demographic transition, when fertility remains high while death rates fall, the population could outpace its resources. Overpopulation refers to an imbalance between the number of people born and the ability of the society to support them.

Overpopulation typically occurs in the period between the lowering of death rates and eventual reductions in fertility—the demographic transition gap. Throughout much of the world today, however, fertility has *not* declined; it remains high at the same time that traditional support systems have collapsed and nothing has taken their place. Kinship groups have scattered as new leaders assume ownership of the land and keep for themselves whatever local crops earn on the world market. Individuals must then look for jobs in cities, which have become vast slums. In Gaza, half the population is under age 15 and most of their parents are unemployed. In Afghanistan, where education and health care for women are denied, the infant death rate is 150 in every 1,000 live births (compared to 3.5 for Finland). In Bangladesh, with limited fertile land, where the population continues to grow while the stock of food and shelter declines, there are roughly 2,500 people per square mile (compared to 76 for the United States).

Much of the misery of starvation and homelessness in the less developed regions is the result of internal politics. For example, the governments of Pakistan and India, where tens of millions are without adequate food and shelter, nonetheless find the millions of dollars required each day to keep their troops sniping at one another atop the uninhabited mountains of Kashmir. In addition, as noted earlier in this chapter, bloody civil wars throughout Africa and Asia produce the millions of refugees whose gaunt faces haunt us from the printed page and television screen. 🖥9

❖ ❖ ❖ ❖   ## Human Activity and the Environment

In the process of securing food and shelter, humans have always brought changes to their environment, from the first group to deplete a region of its fruits and berries to the loggers who are currently stripping the Amazon River Valley of its natural resources. The difference is that what used to take decades to destroy can now be done in days. At the same time, technological advances have increased crop production and distribution. Nonetheless, the continual pressures of population growth in the less developed nations and rising living standards in modernizing societies will increase the demand for basic foodstuffs (Brown et al. 1998; Pinstrup-Anderson et al. 1999). 💻10

Food Supply

The most immediate and pressing problem is the balance between a region's population and its food supply. Back in 1798, English economist Thomas Malthus predicted that because populations grow in a geometric ratio (2,4,8,16, and so on) while food supplies increase arithmetically (1,2,3,4 . . .), starvation and disease would eventually reduce the population to manageable size. Fortunately, Malthus underestimated the ingenuity of agricultural scientists. While world population has increased six times over since 1800, the food supply has kept pace, thanks to fertilizers, crop rotation, farm machines, and development of new strains of rice and wheat. The major problem in many countries is not the production of food but how it is distributed (Sen 1999). When people cannot buy the food, they starve. In addition, at some point, the fertilizers lose their effectiveness and contaminate the earth. In much of the Third World today, overplanting and overgrazing have led to erosion of farmland, so the desert creeps up, soil clogs streams, waste material flows into rivers, and the water gets saltier.

In Northern China today, what was once a fertile farming and herding region is now covered with several feet of sand. The thin layer of topsoil was destroyed by grazing herds; farmland eroded; earth and water dried up after three years of drought; and the desert soon reached the tops of houses (Eckholm 2000).

Deforestation. Farmland is also lost when trees and shrubs are cut down for firewood or for building homes and furniture, destroying the roots that kept soil from running off during a rainstorm or from being swept away by winds. In some developing countries, lumber cutting is a major economic activity, bringing needed dollars from foreign companies (often right into the

Deforestation occurs when trees are cut down to build homes and furniture, destroying the roots and the topsoil, which then has a negative impact on the adaptability of the entire ecosystem. A vital portion of the Mayan land in Mexico has been destroyed by cutting 4.7 million acres of forest land.

pockets of corrupt officials). Once the timber is gone, so, too, are the foreign investors, along with the topsoil, the thousands of different plants, animals, and birds that lived in the forests, and the marine life that inhabited the streams and rivers. This loss of **biodiversity**—nature's many varieties of living things—has a negative impact on the adaptability of the entire ecosystem. In general, the more species of animals and plants there are in the environment, the greater the probability that some will survive natural or human-made disasters.

Endangering indigenous people. It is not only the plants and animals that are displaced when farmland is lost and the forests stripped. Native (**indigenous**) peoples lose their place in the world; they are scattered to less productive areas or absorbed into the economy as common laborers. The loss of cultural diversity diminishes the richness of the world as a whole and limits our understanding of the human condition.

Consumption

Even if all the food needed could be produced, not everyone will benefit. The bigger problem today is the uneven distribution of all kinds of resources. Starvation is widespread in the Third World, in part because of climate changes and natural disasters and in part because of political violence that disrupts food production and leads to mass migrations of refugees. The uprooted cannot grow food, and the impoverished cannot buy it. Children are especially vulnerable because poor nourishment in those crucial growing years has long-term negative consequences for mental and physical health. In addition, in many traditional societies, because sons are more valued than daughters, the health and nutrition of girls is neglected, leading to higher than expected mortality. If girls were treated as well as boys in rural China, parts of India, and throughout North Africa, there would be 100 million more women in the world than there are today (Sen 1999).

At the other end of the spectrum, modern industrial societies account for most of the consumption of the world's resources, although these, too, are unevenly distributed within each society (see chapter 5). Not only do wealthy societies and individuals consume most goods and services, they also produce most of the world's waste. For example, the United States, with 5 percent of the world's population, uses up 25 percent of the world's supply of fossil fuel while producing 72 percent of the world's supply of hazardous waste (Population Reference Bureau 1997).

In this section we have looked at human ecology primarily in terms of the people part of the equation: Is there enough to go around, and does it go around? The basic question is one of **carrying capacity**—the size of the population that Earth can support. Estimates range from a few billion to over 40 billion, but there are so many variables involved that it is difficult to give a figure here. There is, for example, a big difference between staying alive and living with dignity. When the quality of life is factored in, the carrying capacity will be much smaller than when one simply estimates how much food it takes to avoid starvation. 🖥 11

In addition, there are interactive effects—ways in which human activity changes the environment and, conversely, how environmental change affects societies and individuals. The next section examines the process from the

❖ ❖ ❖ ❖   standpoint of the environmental impact of industrialization, urbanization, and population growth. 12

Environmental Concerns

In addition to farmland loss, deforestation, and the threats to biodiversity, ecologists point to other worrisome trends that could ultimately reduce Earth's carrying capacity and the quality of life for all its inhabitants.

Global warming refers to a rise in Earth's temperatures as a long-term result of human activity and the accumulation in our atmosphere of carbon dioxide and other gases that act like the glass in a greenhouse, keeping moisture and heat inside. This *greenhouse effect* is difficult to measure, but there appears to be a consensus that Earth's atmosphere is warming (Stevens 2000). There is less agreement among scientists about how much of the warming is due to human activity and how much to natural causes, or what the ultimate impact will be; some regions may benefit from higher temperatures; others could be flooded by rising sea levels. Most experts, however, point the finger at human activity. One major study of climate changes over the past 1,000 years concluded that natural causes like volcanic disturbances and variations in sunshine probably were the major factors before 1900, but that in the twentieth century such natural events could account for only 25 percent of the warming over the past hundred years (Crowley 2000). Far more important today are the effects of human activity, especially the burning of fuels that release carbon dioxide and other heat-trapping gases.

As you may well expect by now, politics also plays a part. Both conservatives opposed to government intervention and business leaders concerned that environmental protection mandates would raise their production costs tend to downplay the concept itself as well as the alleged causes and effects of global warming. There is little doubt, however, that the sustained drought of the late 1990s that turned Northern China into a desert has also affected the United States, reducing crop yields, limiting recreation as the water levels fall in lakes, and raising the risk of wildfires (Stevens 2000b).💻 13

Ozone depletion occurs when industrial carbons erode the layer of ozone that protects us from the sun's cancer-producing ultraviolet rays. This, too, is an issue hotly debated by business interests, especially those in the heavy manufacturing sector where most carbons are emitted. The question that the corporate interests ask is what is an "acceptable risk," weighing possible health deficits against the benefits of jobs and lower costs for consumers. No one knows yet the full long-term consequences of increased exposure to radiation; perhaps there will be more cases of skin cancer and eye problems for humans, as well as loss of the plankton at the base of the fish food chain. For the workers in these sectors, the costs would be real and immediate—their jobs and family security.

Air pollution refers to the release of toxic (illness-producing) material into the atmosphere. Billions of tons come from U.S. industry alone, not to mention emissions from the millions of automobiles on our roads. The current popularity of extra-large sports-utility vehicles (SUVs), encouraged by the low cost of fuel in the United States and by the SUV as status symbol, only adds to the carbon level. In the rest of the world, smog-filled cities, where much of the future population growth will take place, are jammed with small cars burning leaded gasoline (Carty 1999). In addition to automobiles, both large and small, other major sources of air pollution are the East European, Russian, and Chinese factories that burn the cheapest available fuel, soft coal and peat, leaving entire regions covered with soot, a black cloud that envelops people, crops, cattle, and houses. 💻 14

Water resources are also endangered by many kinds of human activity. Ever since the first farmers diverted water from a stream into their fields, the course of rivers has been changed by ditches, dams, and reservoirs. In some cases, entire lake beds have dried up as the water is siphoned off for other uses. In addition to the pollution caused by silt run-off and deposits of fertilizer salts, fresh water can be contaminated by household and industrial waste—not only in the Third World but also close to home. In West Virginia, for decades, waste matter from strip mines has been dumped into streams; yet when a federal judge banned the practice in 1999, the mining industry threatened to close down, and the state governor called the ruling "devastating to state and local budgets" (*New York Times*, October 24, 1999). When the choice is between jobs, profit, and tax revenue, on the one hand, and cleaner rivers, on the other, environmental forces are typically outnumbered.

In the never-ending search for food and jobs in developing nations, coastal areas have become overpopulated, destroying marine environments, polluting the wetlands, and eroding the soil. Survival needs overcome concern for the future; why should your child starve in order to ensure adequate fisheries for the future? Coastal degradation is a growing problem in the United States as well, partly because of acts of nature but also because of the instant gratification and status needs of wealthy landowners who are building beach homes of 5,000 square feet or more (Brozan 2000).

❖ ❖ ❖ ❖

Water resources become contaminated by industrial waste.

Box 15.2

The Tragedy of the Commons

This tension between immediate needs and long-term interests has been called "The Tragedy of the Commons,"(Hardin 1968). The Commons, or Green, was an area in the center of a village where all the townspeople could graze their cattle. It is in your interest to feed as many of your cattle as possible on the common land because part of your costs will be borne by everyone else, while you get to keep all the proceeds from the sale of an animal. As long as the number of cattle remains within the carrying capacity of the common land, all goes well. Eventually, though, each herder will try to add more animals, and the Commons becomes overgrazed. Townsfolk with few other resources lose their herds, the earth is ravaged, and the village ceases to be a community. "Freedom in the Commons brings ruin to all." What benefits individuals will eventually destroy the collectivity, if not checked by law or a sense of communal obligation.

Energy Sources

Few events have only one outcome. Even the most positive developments have unanticipated and often undesirable consequences. Industrialization—the process that has produced enormous benefits and raised the standard of living for hundreds of millions—has caused much of the damage to the Earth's atmosphere and its water. In addition, industrial development diminishes the supply of energy sources, especially the coal and oil deposits that took tens of millions of years to fossilize.

Coal and *oil* are unrenewable resources; once used, they are gone forever. After the easily tapped supply is extracted, wells and mines must be dug ever deeper, spoiling the natural environment. Burning coal also produces sulfur particles that linger in the air and come down to earth in the form of acid rain. Although oil is cleaner to burn, transporting it carries risks of leaks and spills. Renewable resources such as wood, water, and nuclear power also have their own risks.

Hydroelectric power, produced by harnessing the energy of falling water, is the cleanest, safest, and most common renewable resource. Yet, in order to increase water flow, large dams have been built, with many unintended outcomes: soil erosion, silted rivers, flooded farms and pasture land, and the displacement of local populations. The proposed dams on the Yangtze River in China, designed to prevent periodic disastrous floods, will require the relocation of millions of peasants.

Nuclear energy, the resource of the future, already has a checkered past, including the

Coal and oil are unrenewable resources which, once used, are gone forever. Industrialized countries, particularly the United States, are major consumers of these nonrenewable resources. As Americans face increases in oil prices, these truckers are seeking governmental support to offset growing diesel fuel costs.

1986 meltdown at the Chernobyl plant in Russia that sent clouds of radioactive material across northern Europe. Problems of safety and of the disposal of radioactive waste have delayed the production of nuclear energy in the United States and have even caused some plants to close. No new reactors are being built, even though the existing ones are producing more energy than before at a much lower risk of radiation exposure (Wald 1999). In Europe, in contrast, nuclear power now provides between 40 and 80 percent of the energy in many nations, compared to 20 percent for the United States.

Some research is now being carried out on nonpolluting and renewable alternatives such as *wind power, solar heat,* and *underground steam,* but these have not attracted much popular or political support in the United States, especially when opposed by powerful oil and gas industries. Some European countries, however, are investing in pilot projects. Another new technology uses *fuel cells* that operate by a chemical process rather than by burning fossil fuel; it is clean, safe, and more reliable than the electrical grid that links the country and which is subject to massive failure during natural disasters.

The issue for people in developing nations, however, is much more immediate and severe: how to stay warm and cook food. In the absence of money of their own or help from their government, they will cut down trees and dig up wads of peat, even if the long-term effect is to degrade the land. The "tragedy of the commons" updated!

An additional hazard is the possibility that a scarcity of energy will lead to continued violence in the developing world, both civil wars and struggles between countries over control of waterways, farmland, forests, and mines. Inevitably, the Western nations get drawn into these conflicts in order to protect their own sources of oil and other raw materials. Few world leaders can afford to take seriously the environmentalists' claim that everyone has a stake in seeing that the world's resources are distributed more fairly across and within nations. 🖥 15

Environmental Justice

The fair distribution of resources is a goal that is probably unrealizable. It is hard enough getting Americans to donate a dollar or two to famine relief, and few of us are ready to give up driving a car in order to reduce the number of asthma deaths in the nation. Within many societies, consumption patterns are a display of social status—the "potlatch principle" that power goes to the one who can throw the most lavish feast and then throw away the leftovers. Waste equals wealth. This raises the issue of where to put the waste, particularly the toxic kind.

The obvious answer is "where the powerless live." In general, exposure to ecological hazards is *inversely* related to social status: the greater the wealth of a community, the lower its exposure to environmental risks. In the United States today, three out of four people living near a hazardous waste landfill are poor African Americans or Hispanics (Bullard 2000). Among the favorite locations are rural areas in the South and Native American reservations, where poverty is so pervasive that any income source appears better than none. **Environmental racism** is the practice of locating hazardous waste in places where people are least able to protest, and of dumping garbage from

❖ ❖ ❖ ❖   white households into facilities located in minority neighborhoods. You might want to know where your local dump and incinerator are located.

Few government agencies are powerful enough to limit the practice, which is not illegal—corporations are acting in their stockholders' best interests by finding cheap disposal sites. Business interests and conservative law centers have spent decades and millions of dollars fighting the Environmental Protection Agency; lawsuits can linger for years in the courts, while substantial contributions are made to politicians.

Nonetheless, a grassroots *environmental justice movement* has been formed out of a diverse set of people concerned with any or all of the issues discussed in this section; members range from professional ecologists to neighborhood mothers (Glazer and Glazer 1998). Although they lose more often than not to powerful political and commercial interests, they have managed to stop the dumping of nuclear waste in the Mojave Desert and to delay the building of a nuclear incinerator near Yellowstone National Park (Janofsky 1999). Such victories, however, are few and far between, and if the United States keeps producing nuclear waste, it has to go somewhere and that somewhere is most likely to be where there is the least opposition. 🖥16

In the United States today, three out of four people living near a hazardous landfill are poor African Americans or Hispanics. This is called environmental racism.

Nuclear colonialism is a particular form of environmental racism, whereby military bases engaged in the testing of nuclear devices are located in areas occupied by relatively impoverished Native American tribes in the American Southwest—the "tainted desert" (Kuletz 1998). Pyramids of waste material from commercial uranium mining operations now dot the landscape.

Internal Migration in the United States: From Farm to City and Back

The first American Census, in 1790, counted 3,929,214 individuals, almost all located on farms or in small villages.

Rural America

Two hundred years later, out of a population of 248,709,873, less than 3 percent of the labor force was engaged in farming; while 25 percent lived in rural areas, only 7 percent of those households were working farms. Where did all the rural folk go? The young ones went to where the work and fun were, to the towns and cities, with their factories and shops, places of recreation and entertainment, bars and restaurants. By the 1930s, as machines replaced hand labor, tenant farmers and sharecroppers were forced off the land, and owners of small, inefficient farms sold out to larger landholders and ultimately to the handful of corporations that now dominate American agriculture (agribusiness).

Government programs to aid farmers today often benefit the few high-tech companies that account for almost 75 percent of agricultural sales, a form of corporate welfare costing American taxpayers several billion dollars a year. In the meantime, the remaining family farmers are deep in debt, unable to keep up with payments on machinery or the mortgages on their home and land, as property values drop (Barboza 1999).

Village life. In addition to farms, "rural places" (defined as incorporated areas with fewer than 2,500 inhabitants) include villages that serve as social and economic centers, with a post office, general store, church, and gas station. In the 1950s, as the young folk continued to move out, and as the interstate highway system bypassed most of small-town America, the villages were left isolated and depopulated, without even the occasional income from passing tourists and nightly lodgers.

With the loss of its economic vitality, rural America is marked by widespread poverty, especially in the South and among minority groups. Government agencies find it difficult and expensive to provide services to such a widely scattered client population. Health services are nonexistent in many areas; schools are few, far between, and poorly staffed and funded. The story is the same in other rural areas such as Appalachia, where villages have been turned into ghost towns as rising costs forced owners to abandon the mines that had provided work to generations of men from the backwoods hollows. The geographic isolation of the region and its difficult terrain discourage other economic activity, leading to increased poverty and the continued outflow of young people.

The 'rural rebound.' The past two decades, however, have seen a repopulation of rural areas, primarily on the outskirts of metropolitan areas, but as an extension of the suburbs rather than a revival of village life (Johnson 1999). The rural/urban fringe is the new frontier in industrial and office development by corporations seeking cheap land. The offices are then followed by modest housing, perhaps a trailer park, and convenience stores that provide employment to the long-term residents.

Beyond this fringe, in the *ruburbs,* farmland is being replaced by large retirement communities and by "McMansions" for the upwardly mobile young executives who can keep in touch with the big world through faxes, e-mail, and cell phones. It remains to be seen whether the newcomers will become countrified or whether the countryside will soon resemble a small city, with school overcrowding, traffic congestion, and general sprawl. 💻 17

Urban America

The process whereby villages become towns and towns grow into cities is called urbanization (from "urbs" the Latin word for "wall," since most early

❖ ❖ ❖ ❖   cities were circled by some sort of fortification). Cities differ from towns in the sheer size, density, and diversity of their population and by a complex division of labor. The city also offers a variety of services—health care, schooling, libraries, and so forth—and extensive opportunities for socializing. In contrast to the village (an example of *Gemeinschaft*), the city is a true *Gesellschaft*, marked by impersonal, formal, and instrumental relationships,

The urban spirit reflects sophistication, literacy, and a strong interest in art.

greater privacy, and more choices—a way of life referred to as **urbanism**. Also in contrast to the village, where everyone knows your family's social position, city dwellers must emphasize the external trappings of status (houses, cars, clothing) to announce their identity. While the move to the city weakens old social ties, people quickly make new friends. There is little evidence that city dwellers are any more alienated or isolated than their rural counterparts (Freudenberg 1992).

Urbanism is not necessarily confined to city-dwellers but can be considered a characteristic of a modern society at a high level of technological development. The urban spirit is also **urbane**—sophisticated, literate, dynamic, and secular, nurturing artistic impulses, stimulating the mind through contrasts, and encouraging tolerance of differences. These influences can spread beyond the city via the mass media. Television, movies, video tapes, CDs, and the Internet can today bring you into instant contact with urban culture, some of which may be far from uplifting but is typically at the cutting edge.

The great benefit of cities and urbanism is the creativity unleashed by the presence of many different kinds of people. Great art is rarely produced in a social vacuum. Writers, painters, and musicians typically need a supportive subculture and appreciative audiences, and the stimulation of new ideas and perceptions, all of which are most often found in urban areas. The city's concentration of universities, theaters, and concert halls provides a critical mass of people who appreciate new work and provide networks of influence and funding (Martorella 1996). American cities such as New York, Boston, Philadelphia, Chicago, and San Francisco will remain important centers of culture and commerce, and others are emerging as leaders in the new era of global trade (Miami) and the Internet (Seattle). Yet for many older cities, once vital hubs of business and locally nurtured artistic institutions, such as Cleveland, Detroit, and Buffalo, the term "crisis" is not an overstatement.

The Rise and Fall of American Cities

The story begins in the mid-nineteenth century when the first factories were built along the banks of rivers or seashores, where boats could provide transportation for people and material. The factories served as magnets for rural youth. With the influx of workers, some kind of housing was necessary, typically blocks of rented rooms or tenements, owned by the factory, with rents deducted from wages. Workers could shop at the company store, and by the end of the month, the factory owners probably got back most of what they had given out in wages.

Once the workers and housing were in place, other businesses followed, **amenities**, or niceties of urban life, such as barber shops, taverns, vaudeville halls, and eating places. These establishments provided more jobs, drawing more workers into town, necessitating more housing, and so on. Each successive wave of workers displaced tenement residents who could now afford homes of their own, though still within walking distance of work. The owners and other well-off families, in the meantime, had moved as far out of town as their horses and carriages could take them.

The concentration of workers and amenities attracted more factories and businesses, and when the local labor supply was used up, by the mid-1800s, the nation opened it doors to immigrants, preferably white and English-speaking (see chapter 6). At the same time, a second migrant stream had been moving northward from the rural South—displaced white tenant farmers and black sharecroppers, who moved into the oldest housing near the factories. The rural stream northward continued through the early decades of the twentieth century. The Great Depression of the 1920s and 1930s filled city streets with the jobless and homeless, overwhelming local resources and services. Only with the federal relief programs of the 1930s, known as the New Deal, and the wartime economic revival of the early 1940s were the cities pulled out of near-bankruptcy.

The next big development came at the end of World War II, when returning veterans became upwardly mobile, thanks to the GI Bill's provisions for a free college education and low-cost home mortgages, coupled with the creation of jobs in the white-collar managerial sector (see chapter 5). Both developments were of special benefit to white men. Blacks and other nonwhite service personnel could not afford another four years out of the labor force and so rarely took advantage of the GI Bill. As for managerial jobs, only those whose skin matched their collar need apply. But before white families could move out of the city, several other trends had to converge. One of these, beginning before the war but accelerated immediately after, was the mass production of automobiles at affordable prices. The cars would have had limited usefulness if the government had not also embarked on a massive program of highway construction to keep the postwar economy rolling.

With the cars, the highways, and the home mortgage loans generating pressure, residential development of the area beyond the city limits, the **suburbs**, produced huge housing tracts, with what some people laugh at today as "cookie-cutter" homes for the newly mobile young couples. That suburban home was the American Dream come to life: a private place, with its own yard and garage, cared for by a wife-mother-homemaker whose husband left each day to work in the city, the ideal family of functional theory. It is important to note, as sociologists of the time did not, that this ideal family was typically WASP. The new housing developments had *restrictive covenants* in their articles of incorporation, forbidding sales to certain categories, most particularly blacks, but often also Jews and Italians (Sugrue 1996).

The suburban Dream House and its occupants, including the 3.5 postwar children, needed to be furnished and fed and entertained. The solution was to move retail stores from the cities, whose populations were getting poorer and darker, to the suburbs, where income and consumer needs were rising

✦ ✦ ✦ ✦

✦ ✦ ✦ ✦   sharply. The 1960s saw an enormous expansion of suburban shopping centers and the flowering of a "mall culture."

Meanwhile, back in the city, the exodus of white-collar workers opened up housing for successful blue-collar workers, whose previous homes were then occupied by more recent immigrants. But by the 1960s, major problems surfaced, most importantly, the decline of manufacturing jobs and the movement of service businesses to the suburbs, where their managerial employees lived and where the air was nicer, crime rates lower, and schools better. When businesses and high-income people leave the city, the tax base (or *ratables*) declines, and the city can no longer raise money for the services that make it livable. More people then move across the city limits, especially when the city raises tax rates to make up for the revenue shortfall. When the paying public goes, so, too, do the amenities. Stores are abandoned, restaurants close, shops are boarded up.

"White flight" to the suburbs accelerated in the 1970s, as a reaction to the early successes of the Civil Rights Movement in changing zoning laws and school assignment formulas. Even today, white families with young children are three to six times more likely to move if they live in a neighborhood with at least 6 percent blacks than if they are in a more segregated community, regardless of socioeconomic variables (Harris 1999a). In other words, it is not the income but the race of one's neighbors that motivates the flight of white families with young children.

Those left in the urban area have difficulty finding jobs and paying the rent, and without rental income, landlords cannot maintain their properties. At this point, it is cheaper for landlords to abandon the property than to pay back taxes, so the city takes it over but has no means of keeping up services, and the slums spread. No jobs, no ratables, no tax income, and no help from the state or federal government. No help from the state because the balance of power in the state legislature has shifted from the cities to the suburbs. Just how long do you think you could stay in office representing a suburban district if you voted to raise state taxes in order to help the inner-city schools? And no help from the Congress in the late 1990s, partly for the same reason but also because Republicans do not get many inner-city votes.

Throughout this process, the racial composition of the central city becomes increasingly nonwhite. This shift also began in the 1940s and 1950s, when black workers were frozen out of blue-collar unions and most white-collar employment. It took a decade of civil rights activism in the 1960s to reduce discrimination in employment, but by then African-American families had lost decades of opportunities for upward mobility (Sugrue 1996). Not only are whites more likely than minority workers to have the jobs and money that make it possible to leave the city or live on its fringe, they are also more likely to be welcomed (Bullard et al. 2000).

Although restrictive covenants are now illegal, even when minority families can afford to move to a better neighborhood, they often find that they are not wanted. Homes that they have contracted to buy are defaced and firebombed. Real estate brokers direct them to a different and inferior set of houses than those shown to white house hunters with comparable income and occupational credentials (Massey 2000). Mortgages or home repair loans are difficult to get because banks do not readily give loans to people who live in rundown or transitional areas (Woodstock Institute 1999). This practice is called **redlining**, for the way these areas are marked on the bank's maps (Squires 1997).

The end result of a half-century of intentionally excluding persons of color from decent housing and well-paying jobs has produced the current **urban crisis** of decaying inner cities, for which the poor themselves are frequently blamed. The process whereby the suburbs became white and the cities dark can also be viewed as an example of the unanticipated outcome of a series of mutually reinforcing events and trends: the GI Bill of veterans' benefits, Henry Ford's mass-produced automobiles, subsidized highway construction, the growth of suburban housing developments and shopping malls, the shift from manufacturing to a service economy, population moves that change the political balance of power, all played out on a strong undercurrent of racism (Cummings 1998). Certainly, today, residential segregation, or "American apartheid," coupled with the loss of entry-level jobs in the cities, accounts for widespread unemployment and underemployment among young minority males, failure to form stable families, and the resulting social disorganization (Massey and Denton 1993; Krivo et al. 1998). These conditions make it increasingly difficult for the majority of black and Hispanic families, stable working-class households, to raise their children successfully; yet most do manage, often against great odds (Furstenberg et al. 1999).

Can the cities be saved? Probably, if anyone with the ability to make a difference cares. The presidential election campaigns of 1996 and 2000 were notable for their resounding silence on urban policy. Congress continues to cut whatever federal programs are still on the books for housing and transportation. States refuse to obey court orders to increase funding for inner-city schools (see chapter 11). The logical steps are politically impossible. For example, erasing the city boundaries and folding the urban center into an area-wide political entity would meet instant resistance from the suburban communities. So, too, would any plan to raise state taxes and redistribute the money to assist the urban poor.

At the moment, urban assistance comes in the form of programs initiated by business interests, faith-based organizations, and some self-help groups (Donnelly and Majka 1998). There is no master plan or secure funding and no evidence that a ballpark or gambling casino alone can reverse the decades of decline (Noll and Zimbalist 1997). Among the more successful efforts have been those that restore waterfront areas with restaurants and shops that at least bring the affluent into the area for a few hours while providing service jobs for the locals. But the profits from these ventures do not go into the pockets of the poor. 🖥 18

Gentrification

The most systematic attempts to bring the white middle class back into the city involve low-cost housing loans for renovations, street-by-street clean-up, beautification, and increased safety measures. These efforts at **gentrification** ("gentry" are property owners) have been successful in parts of many cities. Once the housing is upgraded, amenities follow: shops become boutiques, restaurants replace fast-food outlets, and so forth. Tax revenues increase, services are expanded, and more middle-class families are encouraged to move back. The major drawback is that very few cities have built addi-

❖ ❖ ❖ ❖   tional housing for the people displaced by the gentry. Indeed, displacement of minorities is often equated with "making the city safe again," an exercise in internal colonialism whereby the unruly natives are pacified by their superiors and the disputed territory is taken back, block by block (Smith 1996).

Sometimes city governments do not wait for the gentry to arrive, as when thousands of row houses in poor neighborhoods of Baltimore were torn down, with no plans for replacing them or for using the empty space (Rozhon 1999).

Gentrification proceeded rapidly in the late 1990s as younger families with high incomes chose to live in urban centers. Rents and prices soared, luring buyers into once ignored neighborhoods. Low-cost housing units were razed or renovated. Single-room occupancy hotels became classy condominiums. The poor who had once occupied these spaces either doubled up with other family members or stayed on the streets, but they did not stay in the newly gentrified areas, where quality-of-life laws forbid sleeping in public places and other unsightly behaviors such as pushing overloaded shopping carts.

Gentrification refers to the renovation of formerly run-down neighborhoods and involves upgrading housing and increasing local amenities such as boutiques and trendy restaurants.

The Suburbs

Beyond the city limits lie the suburbs, as stratified by class and color as the rest of the society. A growing number of minority families have followed their white counterparts out of the city, typically into the areas just vacated by an earlier wave of the upwardly mobile. Indeed, the proportion of blacks in suburban areas is growing at a faster rate than the urban populations, yet these moves have not brought integration—90 percent of both blacks and whites live in basically segregated communities—or the same level of benefits in terms of school quality and civic services (Beveridge 2000).

The appeal of the suburbs—safer streets, better schools, slower pace, closer to nature—tends to fade over time, as traffic builds up, green space gives way to asphalt, teenagers have no place to go after school, and the streets become less safe. Because there is always the next suburb to move out to, a series of concentric rings emerges beyond the city limits. In general, the closer the ring is to the city, the lower the SES of its residents and the more racially integrated the neighborhoods. Conversely, the further out the ring, the less integrated and the higher the occupation and income level of its residents, as reflected in the amount of space taken up by each home, from a quarter-acre in the immediate suburbs to three- or four-acre lots in the further suburbs.

Although many people view suburban life as dull and conformity ridden, the residents themselves express considerable neighborhood satisfaction (U.S. Bureau of the Census 1998a). Some current researchers have found that a sense of community is alive and well in the suburbs (Baxandall and Ewen 2000), although this unity is often mobilized in the interests of resisting changes that appear to threaten their way of life. In addition to the NIMBY ("not in my back yard") reaction to low-cost or group housing, critics have added such acronyms as LULU ("locally unacceptable land use") and BANANA ("build absolutely nothing anywhere near anyone"), among many others, to characterize suburbanites' attitudes (Herszenhorn 2000).

As for the truly wealthy, they have moved to the rural fringe on extensive estates from which they can stay in touch by Internet or reach their offices via helicopter or chauffeur. Others live in gated communities, literally walled off from the less affluent. The gates are both a security mechanism and a status symbol. Those within the fortress walls develop a sense of *gemeinschaft*, but at the cost of excluding and withdrawing from democratic engagement with the rest of society (Blakely and Snyder 1997). In the Rocky Mountain states such as Montana, wealthy landowners own tens of thousands of acres for a vacation retreat, where they have fenced off grazing land, streams, and access roads used by the local residents, while also fighting local school tax assessments and going to court to stop lower-cost housing developments (Janofsky 1999).

Thus, what may once have been a tale of two cities (the rich and the poor) is today a tale of two societies—the exclusive world of the few and the great mass of Americans who struggle to make ends meet.

Box 15.3

You Can't Go Home Again ... or Can You?

Is it possible to design a housing development for an urban area that can recreate the self-sufficiency of a small town? This is the goal of the **New Urbanists**, architects of several hundred planned communities in the United States (Duany and Plater-Zyberk 2000). These Traditional Neighborhood Developments (TNDs), are laid out in such a way that shops and amenities are within walking distance, housing is mixed and is varied to accommodate all age groups, with many public places for socializing and relaxation.

One of the earliest TNDs, Seaside, is a Victorian-style village in Florida built in the early 1980s and still flourishing. Others are located on the urban fringes of northern cities in an attempt to reverse the unregulated sprawl that has turned so many suburbs into ugly and polluted mini-cities. A well-known TND, Celebration, is a Disney-backed planned community with the emphasis on "planned," since every detail of architecture and lifestyle is carefully regulated. Despite its artificial traditionalism, Celebration has also prospered. 🖳 19

Maintaining community closeness while avoiding pollution and sprawl depends largely on reducing automobile traffic. As long as work and shopping are within reach of walkers or public transportation, the TND will come very close to resembling the nineteenth-century village of American nostalgia. Yet, even when the TND is only partially successful, it has great appeal to those who can afford it (Ehrenhalt 2000).

Conclusion

In this chapter, you have been introduced to several subfields in sociology dealing with populations, their physical environments, and their geographic

❖ ❖ ❖ ❖ locations. The size and distribution of the world's population has clear consequences for global well-being, in the developed as well as the developing
nations. Within a society, the number of people in each age group will affect
how resources are allocated, to children and their parents or to the elderly.
Population pyramids can tell you a great deal about any society.

Each society is located within a particular physical environment, subject
to climate changes and other natural events, but, at the same time, human
activity transforms that environment, consuming its natural resources and
producing toxic effects. While it may not be easy to follow how the flapping of
a butterfly's wings in one part of the globe has a powerful effect in another
place, it does matter to all of us whether the Amazon River basin is denuded
of its trees.

Finally, population migrations change the face of entire regions. Migrations between nations are a powerful engine of social change. So, too, are
migrations within a society. In the United States, the flow of farm workers to
towns and cities transformed the country, as did the post-1945 exodus to the
suburbs. The history of American cities illustrates many of the basic themes
of this textbook, of the unintended consequences of social action, of the
depth and breadth of racism, and of growing income inequality—in the
world and here at home.

Surfing the Sociological Internet

 1   For the latest numbers, see the world population clock at the U.S.
Census Bureau:
http://www.census.gov/cgi-bin/ipc/popclockw

2   For more information on world population and demographics:
http://www.prb.org/
For links to demographic sites and journals on demography, go
to: http://dir.yahoo.com/Social_Science/Sociology/Demogra-
phy/
The United Nations statistics on population can be found at:
http://www.popin.org/pop1998/
For population control issues, see: http://www.popcouncil.org/
and
The UNICEF site tracks fertility rates at: http://www.unicef.org/
pon95/fami0005.html

3   For AIDS and population issues, see: http://www.popin.org/
pop1998/6.htm

4   A virtual demography library can be found at: http://demogra-
phy.anu.edu.au/VirtualLibrary/

5   The ZPG site can be found at: http://www.zpg.org/

6   POPLINE allows you to do your own research on population,
health, and family planning issues: http://db.jhuccp.org/
popinform/index.stm
For an overview of the United Nations' Cairo Conference on is-

sues related to population growth and development, see: http://www.iisd.ca/linkages/cairo.html

🖥 7 For information on refugees, go to: http://www.unhcr.ch/

🖥 8 The following site allows you to build your own population pyramids: http://www.census.gov/ipc/www/idbpyr.html

🖥 9 http://www.xist.org/ allows you to explore the demographics of many different countries and their development, wealth, natural resources, etc.

🖥 10–12 For a discussion on issues of consumption, go to: http://www.enviroweb.org/issues/enough/enough02.htm

🖥 13–14 Facts and figures on global warming can be found at: http://www.globalwarming.net/
The World Meteorological Association, which monitors air pollution and ozone depletion, is at: http://193.1a35.216.2/

🖥 15–16 http://library.envirolink.org/ has links related to all the issues discussed in the environmental section.
http://www.balance.org/ is a grassroots organization in the United States devoted to issues of environmental justice.

🖥 17 For rural life and development, see: http://www.ers.usda.gov/epubs/pdf/rdp/rdp.htm

🖥 18 Can we rebuild urban areas? See: http://www.brook.edu/pa/policyupdates/gore/gore.htm

🖥 19 See: http://celebration.nm1.net/ for Disney's idea of an old/new town, Celebration.
For an assessment of Disney's new town, Celebration, go to: http://www.e-architect.com/pia/rudc/celebra.asp

✤ ✤ ✤ ✤

Glossary

Age Cohort People born in a given set of years.
Agribusiness A type of farming in which a few high-tech corporations produce most of the food consumed domestically and abroad.
Air Pollution The release of toxic (illness-producing) material into the environment.
Amenities Niceties such as movie houses, restaurants, and shops.
Biodiversity Refers to the many varieties of living things on Earth.
Birthrate The number of births per 1,000 population of a society for a given year.
Carrying Capacity The size of the population that Earth can support.
Demographic Transition A shift from populations kept in check by high birthrates and high death rates to those stabilized by low birthrates and low death rates.
Demography The study of populations, their size and composition, and movement from one place to another.

Environmental Racism The practice of locating hazardous waste in places where people of color live.

Fertility The average number of children a woman will have between the ages of 15 and 49.

Gated Communities Communities walled off from the less affluent for security and as a status symbol.

Gentrification The migration of middle- and upper-income people into urban centers, their displacement of lower-income residents, and the renovation of existing housing.

Global Warming A rise in Earth's temperatures as a long-term result of human activity and the accumulation of gases that act like the glass in a greenhouse, keeping moisture and heat inside.

Guestworker A person from a country with high unemployment who moves to an industrial society and does the work local residents do not perform.

Human Ecology Study of the interactions between populations and their environments.

Indigenous Native population.

Life Expectancy The average number of years a person can be expected to live.

New Urbanists Designers of planned communities.

Nuclear Colonialism A form of environmental racism whereby military bases engaged in the testing of nuclear devices are located in areas occupied by impoverished Native Americans in the Southwest.

Overpopulation Indicates that a society lacks sufficient resources to provide an adequate standard of living to its citizens.

Ozone Depletion The erosion of the layer of ozone protecting people from the sun's cancer-producing ultraviolet rays.

Population Pyramid A graphic representation of the age and sex distribution of a society's population.

Redlining Banks' refusal to give loans and mortgages to people or businesses in rundown or transitional areas of a city.

Second Demographic Revolution When declining birthrates outstrip falling death rates to the extent that there is a net population loss.

Urban Crisis The decay of inner cities, stemming from the exclusion of persons of color from decent housing and well-paying jobs.

Urbane Adjective to describe the modern spirit, which is sophisticated, literate, dynamic, and secular; nurtures artistic impulses; stimulates the mind through contrasts; and encourages tolerance of differences.

Urbanism A way of life marked by impersonal, formal, and instrumental relationships, greater privacy, and more choices.

Urbanization The process whereby villages become towns and towns grow into cities.

Zero Population Growth Fertility of about 2.1 offspring, that is required to replace the parental couple. ✦

2001.com: Technology and Social Change in a Global System

❖ ❖ ❖ ❖ No society is really quite the same from one generation to the next, although the rate of change will be slowest for groups that live in relative isolation, but there are very few of these left in the world. Today, loggers are hacking in the deepest Amazon jungles, military outposts occupy the polar ice caps, Mount Everest is climbed daily, and cell phones are everywhere. New ideas that used to take decades to work their way through a society are now yours at the stroke of a keyboard, and they are potentially available to all, not just the elites. This chapter examines the basic processes of social change and how these affect societies in an increasingly interdependent global economy. The chapter closes with some thoughts about the postindustrial, postmodern information age in which you will spend the rest of your life. Included are the following topics:

- Processes of social change.

- Theoretical perspectives.

- Master trends: modernization and globalization.

- Social movements and collective behavior.

- 2001—here already.

Processes of Social Change

Social change is the process through which values, norms, institutions, stratification systems, social relationships, and even the self are altered over time. The process can cut both ways. Macro social developments, such as economic or political system changes, will affect how institutions function at the meso-level and how people relate to one another and see themselves at the micro-level. Conversely, individuals and groups can become agents of social change, engaging in actions that ultimately have an impact on culture and institutional structures. ⌨ 1

Change originates either outside or within a society. The most important external sources are (1) environmental events, (2) invasion and warfare, and (3) contacts with other societies and cultures. Internal sources include (1) innovation, (2) population shifts, (3) cohort flow, (4) new technologies, and (5) political and ideological revolutions.

External Sources of Change

Environmental events such as earthquakes, floods, or crop failure can wipe out a society or force its people to flee elsewhere. When the accustomed patterns of everyday life are disrupted, social order collapses, and individuals experience *anomie* as accustomed norms no longer apply.

Invasion and warfare remain common sources of change throughout the world. The major difference today is that modern weapons can kill many more people, both military and civilian, and can do so from a distance. Yet, in the closing days of the twentieth century, murderous face-to-face rampages were reported around the globe—in Southeast Asia, Eastern Europe, and Central Africa—in full sight of TV cameras and even shown on the combatants' websites.

Wars and invasions have a number of different goals. Colonialism is the name given to the forcible conquering of traditional societies by Western nations in search of cheap raw materials and/or political pride. Most colonies were returned to local control beginning soon after World War II, but the colonial rulers had redrawn tribal boundaries in such a way that even today, in Africa, civil wars continue. The last colony, Portuguese Macao, was turned over to China only in the final days of 1999. *Economic colonialism* refers to the more recent practice of using military forces to protect commercial interests, such as American interventions in Latin America on behalf of the United Fruit Company.

Still other conflicts represent the bubbling up of centuries-old resentments, as in Northern Ireland or Serbia today, where militants recall victories and defeats of four centuries ago, although it is difficult to disentangle the historical and religious issues from those of current economic and political inequality. Still, whatever the source or goal, wars by definition generate change on all sides. Villages and cities are destroyed, economies disrupted, governments overthrown or reinforced, land transferred from one nation to another. Effects linger long after the last soldier has left the battlefield. When millions of young men die, millions of young women are left without a husband, leading to lowered birthrates for a generation or more.

Throughout history, also, attempts have been made to destroy a population on the basis of race, religion, or ethnicity. Genocide literally means to kill ("cide") an entire group of people ("gens"). The most shocking modern example of genocide—the Holocaust—involved the mass extermination of six million Jews, another five million "genetically inferior" people (gays, Gypsies, and the mentally retarded), and political enemies of the Nazi regime in Germany between 1941 and 1945 (Clendinnen 1999). More recently, ethnic cleansing is the phrase used to describe similar attempts to wipe out an entire population, as in the former Yugoslavia, where Bosnian Muslims, Serbian Eastern Orthodox, and Croatian

Throughout history, attempts have been made to destroy a population on the basis of race, religion, or ethnicity. The latest example of genocide occurred in Rwanda in Africa. These refugees escaped the slaughter and are trying to survive in refugee camps in Zaire.

Catholics took turns killing and raping and setting fire to entire villages. Being European and religious is no guarantee of civilized conduct. 💻 2

Culture contact is the primary means by which cultural artifacts, norms, and values are spread (diffusion) from one society to another. Most contact is relatively peaceful, usually for the purposes of trade and the exchange of marriage partners. Some of the most important discoveries and inventions, such as fire or the wheel, were made in one or two places and then diffused. Artifacts are easier to accept than ideas because you can see their advantages

❖ ❖ ❖ ❖   immediately. It is much easier to demonstrate the superiority of your fire-arms than that of your religion. Today, Coke and blue jeans have traveled the world much faster than ideas about a free press or equality for women.

Internal Sources of Change

Innovation refers to new items of culture—discoveries or inventions—that produce something not known or seen before. Discoveries involve awareness of some aspect of the natural world, such as the phases of the moon or the law of gravity, while inventions involve combining existing items of culture in a new way. Not all innovations are immediately accepted. Some new ideas may upset existing belief systems, as any heretic has discovered; others threaten established economic interests, as seen in the slow development of nonpolluting automobiles; and some will remain forever hidden in an inventor's basement for lack of funding.

Some of the most important innovations of prehistory, such as the introduction of agriculture, spread from one place to another as groups of humans migrated, over thousands of years, from Africa to Asia and Europe, bringing their knowledge and technology with them (Cavilli-Sforza 2000).

Population shifts include major changes in birthrates or death rates or in the numbers of people who migrate in or out of the society. As discussed in chapter 15, trends that affect the size of different age groups will influence family formation and economic development. For example, the United States will still be dealing with the consequences of the Baby Boom of 1947–1967 well into the twenty-first century.

Cohort flow is the term used to describe the movement through history of people born at the same time. For example, the birth cohort of 1980 to 1985, to which many of you belong, will have a different set of life experiences than the cohort of 1960 to 1965, simply because the society itself has changed in terms of educational opportunities, occupational openings, courtship norms, and gender relationships. At the same time, as you move from home to school to work to marriage and parenthood to retirement and old age, your cohort will leave its imprint on various institutions and ideologies. That is, both people and social structure are always affecting one another in new ways. No society is the same from one generation to the next, although the rate of change will vary greatly.

At various historical moments, major innovations and the cohorts embracing them can change the entire course of history through *new technologies*. The Industrial Revolution would have been impossible without dozens of major technological leaps. Think of all the elements that had to be in place in order to mass produce the automobile and how that one product changed the residential distribution of Americans. Later in this chapter, the impact of computers and the Internet on American culture and the world economy is examined. 💻 3

The Pace of Change

Sometimes change is *incremental* (gradual). Many changes are part of a broad historical trend whose final form emerges over time. Small changes that may go unnoticed will accumulate until—lo and behold!—a major transformation has taken place. For example, today's revolution in the status of women is the product of over a century of incremental changes in attitudes and behaviors, small steps forward, some backsliding in the face of resistance, then another advance, and so forth (Ferree and Hess 2000). The broad trends—or "silent revolutions"—in modern societies, and increasingly across the globe, are toward more inclusive political participation, higher education, gender equality, personal privacy, and sexual openness.

In contrast, the overturn of an existing regime by its political and ideological enemies brings instant, *revolutionary change*. The best modern example is probably the overthrow of the Shah of Iran in 1979, which replaced a Western-oriented dictator with the rule of very traditional religious leaders. The new rulers imposed controls on culture (no Western music or movies or TV), on the dress of women, on the activities of young people in general, and on the economy. As the "iron law of oligarchy" (chapter 10) would predict, the dictatorship of the Islamic mullahs (priests) has proven as oppressive as that of the Shah, so that 25 years later, the Iranians elected more liberal leaders. As another recent example, the collapse of the Soviet Union and other communist governments in 1989 brought instant changes to much of Central and Eastern Europe, in the direction of cultural and political openness, although the economic consequences are mixed, with some systems flourishing and others in ruins (Burawoy and Verdery 1999).

Most change—incremental or revolutionary—will meet resistance from those who benefit from the status quo (things as they are) or who fear losing whatever they do have. The word "sabotage" comes from the name for wooden shoes (sabots) that French workers threw into the new machinery that they feared would replace them in the early days of the factory system. Most recently, American workers, fearful of losing jobs to Third World sweatshops, have protested against reducing barriers to free trade.

Resistance also comes from the powerful, as in the American Medical Association's 20-year battle against medical insurance for the elderly (see chapter 14). Yet those already in high positions are best able to control, contain, and take advantage of innovations. Thus, by the time Medicare was enacted in 1965, the legislation protected the power and profits of the medical establishment.

Theories of Social Change

Is there an inner logic to human history? Does it point in one direction, either upward to progressive perfection or downward, as a fall from an earlier Golden Age? Or does change occur in cycles, as civilizations rise and fall? Or is it all a matter of chance and historical accidents? These questions have produced several theoretical models.

Evolutionary models from the eighteenth and nineteenth centuries saw human history in unidirectional terms—an upward path from savagery to civilization. This model served to rationalize colonialism, since the savages (i.e., members of simple societies) needed to be saved from their ignorance and barbarism by the agents of higher civilization (i.e., European colonists). It was a sacred task, the "White man's burden," to bring the blessings of Christianity and Western rule to the natives. Presumably, God also approved their removing natural resources and taking over the best farmland.

Cyclical theories, which flourished in the early twentieth century, saw history as a succession of civilizations that, like any organism, are born, grow, reach maturity, and then decline. According to the "rise and fall" model, European civilization had reached its high point with the colonial expansion of the nineteenth century, and its decline had begun with World War I, even before the massive destruction of World War II. Although comparing a society to a biological organism is no longer in vogue, it could be argued that the era of American dominance began in the ashes of World War II and is currently at its peak, to be replaced some time in the twenty-first century by China (which had been the dominant civilization in Asia two thousand years earlier).

A variation on the cyclical model of change sees an alternation *within* each society between periods dominated by conservative values and those more focused on creativity and personal liberation (Sorokin 1941). In this view, the current American "culture wars" make perfect sense, being a continuation of the pattern whereby periods of artistic and sexual liberation such as the 1920s and 1960s are followed by attempts to restore traditional values and behaviors.

Neo-evolutionary models are based on the idea that the cumulative direction of historical change is toward increasing structural complexity but that the actual history of any given society is a matter of chance. Wars, accidents, climate changes, even a crazy person with a gun can abruptly alter the social landscape. From the small bands of prehistoric gatherers to the technologically sophisticated societies of today, the overall trend is toward new ways to exploit the environment, larger populations, increased specialization, more coordinating mechanisms, and greater institutional elaboration. What this means, in plain terms, is that (1) as groups learn new ways to supplement their food supply, more people can be supported; (2) then, in a larger society, there are many new ideas and different things people can do; (3) with all the new ideas and activities, it becomes difficult to coordinate everything; and (4) these difficulties lead to more rules and ways to enforce them, as shown in Figure 16.1.

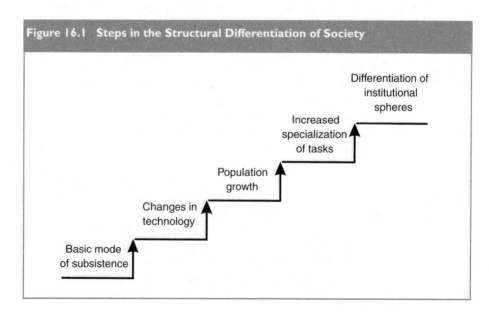

Figure 16.1   Steps in the Structural Differentiation of Society

The process is one of increasing specialization, or differentiation, in which the social world becomes divided into ever more separate parts, a far cry from the all-embracing kinship group or village. Social change also tends to be *cumulative*, continually building on past innovations; each innovation enlarges a society's knowledge and culture base and therefore increases the likelihood of further discoveries and inventions.

Master Trends: Modernization and Globalization

Modernization

Modernization refers to the process whereby nonindustrial societies come to resemble more economically powerful nations. As the trend unfolded in the Western world, it had three main components: secularization (see chapter 12), urbanization (chapter 15), and industrialization (chapter 9). Today, in other parts of the globe, the paths to modernity are more varied, as each country or region has to deal with its unique culture, history, and legacy of colonialism (Inglehart and Baker 2000). Although modernization sounds like a desirable goal for a developing nation, there are many drawbacks: local communities are destroyed, families dissolve, and young people move to overcrowded shantytowns on the urban fringe. Foreign investors want to see profits, and ruling elites are often corrupt. Nonetheless, the overall trends are toward increased urbanization, extended education, and expansion of the global economy. Eventually, these societies may also develop a free press, democratic politics, and gender equality.

In many countries that used to be part of the Soviet Union or Yugoslavia, a particularly violent form of nationalism has emerged. Nationalism involves fierce loyalty to one's place of origin, even at the risk of war and destruction. It is these strong feelings that create nations, just as the nation, once in existence, generates patriotism (Calhoun 1998). During the communist era, the different ethnic groups were held together by a strong central government. When those governments collapsed in 1989, the parts went their separate ways, each constructing a national identity out of its past history. Now there are a dozen individual countries where there once were two, and several of these are engaged in bloody wars.

A different form of nationalism can be found in some of the industrialized nations of Europe, where resentment of foreign workers, darker skinned and from less modern societies, has led to riots and house burnings. In Austria in 2000, a political party with the goal of controlling immigration won close to 30 percent of the vote. Similar political parties in France, Italy, and Switzerland have also attracted large followings.

At the same time, the nations of Europe have moved in the direction of overcoming geographical divisions and forming a single union for purposes of trade, with one currency and open borders. The European Union has thus become competitive in the new global economy. It remains to be seen which European citizen embodies the future—the ethnocentric nationalist or the citizen of the world.

❖ ❖ ❖ ❖   Globalization

Despite the reemergence of nationalism, the world has actually been moving in the direction of increased cooperation and trade among nations. Today, information technology links every nation to every other, and every person with any other who has a computer or a cell phone. The flow of money and trade and people (workers and refugees) has created a **world social system**, in which the exchange of information and material goods erases many of the barriers that protected cultures in the past.

Globalization involves the exchange of information and material goods, erasing many of the barriers that protected cultures in the past. Businesses, such as McDonald's, can be found all over the world, including Korea.

Although it may seem that American products are swamping the rest of the world, you may be overlooking the extent to which most of what you are wearing, including shoes and backpack, was made somewhere else. A glance at the labels on your clothing will probably read like a Third World atlas. The transition to a world economy has an uneven effect on American workers. Those in export industries do well, while garment workers are competing with Indonesian children being paid pennies a day. The anger of many unionized workers and student activists was evident in street protests in 1999 and 2000, designed to disrupt meetings of the World Trade Organization (WTO), the World Bank, and the International Monetary Fund (IMF).

These organizations were founded and funded by political and economic leaders of the wealthy nations, originally to help the economic recovery of Europe following World War II, but more recently they operate to establish and enforce rules of international development and trade. The organizations embody many of the public fears about globalization—their members are unelected and unaccountable, consisting of a handful of appointed diplomats and economists with the power to make decisions that affect tens of millions of poor people. Until very recently, these organizations have shown little concern for environmental degradation, the exploitation of child labor, or the ramifications of their actions on local communities (Held et al. 1999). For example, the World Bank or the IMF often makes a loan to a developing nation contingent on that nation's cutting spending on social programs and raising interest rates in order to attract foreign capital. The cost in human misery of following such orders is enormous—and unnoticed by world leaders.

The major beneficiaries of IMF, WTO, and World Bank actions have been the transnational corporations (TNCs) that increasingly dominate world trade in pharmaceuticals, publishing, and automobiles, among other products. TNCs are businesses with global markets and branches, often formed by mergers of companies in different countries. The TNCs become a power in their own right, beholden to no one government, with the sole goal of maximizing profitability. Thus, although political colonialism has ended, economic domination continues. Not only do the TNCs set prices and control markets, but they have also become ideologically dominant, spreading the gospel of "free trade" as the salvation of the entire world (Evans 2000; Dreiling 2000).

Thus, a new division of labor has come to characterize the relationship between the industrialized First World (the "North" in a global sense) and the developing nations of the Third World (the "South"). In addition to the usual flow of raw materials from the South to the North, the countries of the South increasingly specialize in labor-intensive industries, while the postindustrial nations of the North develop the high-technology service sector—especially financial services and information processing.

As a consequence, although many Third World countries have enjoyed economic growth, the basic situation is a high level of inequality in the global economy, with wealth flowing to the North and poverty increasing in many parts of the South. Much of the poverty is caused by corrupt politicians and civil wars as well as pressures from international agencies (World Bank 2000; United Nations Development Program 2000a). The dream of a world of interdependent nations—the global community—remains a distant ideal at the beginning of the twenty-first century. Indeed, some see increasing anarchy as world order collapses under the weight of poverty, overpopulation, corruption, armies of youthful mercenaries, and TNCs pursuing profit at any cost (Kaplan 2000). Optimists hope that these problems are only temporary setbacks in the growth of democratic institutions, greater personal freedom, and higher living standards (Sen 1999). For better or worse, your future is now global.

❖ ❖ ❖ ❖

Social Movements and Social Change

When examining how social change takes place within a society, apart from the basic processes noted at the beginning of this chapter, one must look at intentional efforts to promote or resist specific changes—various forms of collective behavior, ranging from fads and fashions to mass membership organizations.

Collective Behavior

The term "collective behavior" covers the range of activities undertaken by groups or collectivities that fall outside the expected and accepted norms of behavior. Collective behavior includes such relatively unscripted phenomena as mass hysteria at the spontaneous end, organized social movements at the other end, and various types of crowds in between, as shown in Figure 16.2.

Mass hysteria, panics, and *crazes* are unpredictable short-term behaviors that appear irrational but that usually have a method to their madness. What is the current craze at your school—the thing that everyone has to have or to

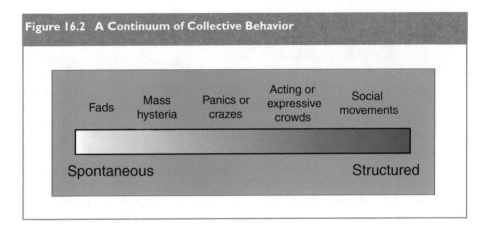

Figure 16.2 A Continuum of Collective Behavior

wear? Why would you be tempted to follow the trend? It really does not matter what the object is, it is the having it that counts. For example, in 1636, Europe was swept by a craze for Dutch tulip bulbs, and prices rose as speculators outbid one another for the flowers (Dash 2000). One year later, the tulip market crashed as spectacularly as it had risen, rather like some offerings on the New York Stock Exchange today.

Similarly, *fads*, or off-base behaviors, such as swallowing goldfish or piling into a phone booth, that spread quickly from one campus to another, often represent a youthful last fling of silliness before having to settle down.

Was there an incident in your grammar school when, for example, the sixth graders suddenly felt dizzy and nauseous and were sent to rest on cots in the gym, where they were examined by local medical emergency teams? Chances are that tests of the air ducts and food turned up no pollution or harmful bacteria. This is a classic case of mass hysteria, in which the suggestion of illness sweeps through the group, and people really do begin to faint and throw up. The effects are physical, but the causes are social and psychological (Altman 2000). What is most interesting about cases of mass hysteria is that they typically involve schoolchildren or women factory workers—two populations that share powerlessness and boredom. Remember the concept of the *sick role* in chapter 14? The attack of illness places the afflicted at the center of attention of concerned teachers, parents, bosses, and medical staff, and provides release from boring work for at least a day.

Sociologists have also analyzed *fashion* as collective behavior, asking such questions as: Who determines what is fashionable, or what clues do you use to determine social status from what people wear? Body decorations, used in many traditional societies to indicate a person's social rank, have become in modern societies almost exclusively a means of enhancing sexual attractiveness.

Urban legends (Brunvald 2000) are rumors that have become so widespread that they can be thought of as folklore—it is the story that your classmate's sister heard from a friend of a friend who knows the next-door neighbor of the family whose baby ended up in the microwave or who found the mouse tail in a hamburger. The list also includes sexy green M&Ms, razor blades in Halloween candy, widespread satanic rituals, and aliens from outer space (Best 1990; Glassner 1999). Although none of these has yet been proved, many of these tales resonate to cultural anxieties—about the vulnerability of children, corporate greed, evil in the everyday world, and fears of the

❖ ❖ ❖ ❖

unknown. Other urban legends have an element of humor, as in the story of the children's TV character (you can name any one) who uses a curse word when the microphones are open. 🖵 4

Crowds. A crowd is more than a loose collection of individuals but not as structured as an authentic group (people linked in a division of labor). Crowds are temporary gatherings of people who share a common focus and awareness of one another. A *casual crowd* is the most temporary, an accidental coming together of witnesses to an accident, for example, who look to one another for information and clues as to how to respond. *Conventional crowds* are bound by the rules or conventions of their location—at a concert or religious service, for example.

The sociologically fascinating aspect of crowd behavior is that how it ends up is not always clear at the beginning. That is, there is an **emergent quality**—the possibility of a number of different outcomes. The crowd could just break up or it could turn nasty, get dispersed by police or riot out of control. An *expressive crowd* will show strong feelings, favorable or unfavorable. You have probably been

The fears and fantasies that become the making of urban legends are exploited in the headlines of sensationalist publications. What are some urban legends you have heard?

at events where the performers were booed off the stage or drowned in cheers. And you may even have been there when emotions got out of hand and the *acting crowd* stormed the stage or brought down the goalposts. At this point, the crowd becomes a mob. Not all acting crowds are out of control. Some are organized into *demonstrations* for or against a specific goal, although these, too, can become unpredictable.

Here are the common elements of crowd behavior that open the door to emergent possibilities:

1. A lack of certainty about what to do next.

2. The spread of a feeling that something should be done.

3. The creation of a certain mood based on uncertainty.

4. Openness to suggestions about what to do.

5. Relaxation of customary norms.

Theoretical views. Early social-psychological models of collective behavior focused on individuals, "lost in the crowd," freed of normative restraints, and vulnerable to suggestion (LeBon 1895/1960). A more sophisticated view (Blumer 1951) saw the crowd as an evolving set of relationships in which members influenced one another in a spiral of **emotional contagion**.

In order to predict what kind of action a crowd would take and to examine its emergent nature, a more detailed theoretical framework was needed. The **value added model** (Smelser 1968) proposed a series of steps through which collective behavior becomes increasingly focused.

1. First, the government has to permit protest, which does not happen in many societies even today.

2. There has to be something to protest about, some perceived wrong or inequity that is felt by a large constituency.

3. An explanation for the problem crystallizes and spreads.

4. Some dramatic event confirms the beliefs and sets the protest in motion, as when neighbors learn that a minority family is moving in or inner-city residents hear of police brutality.

5. A leader emerges who can mobilize the protesters and direct their actions.

6. Finally, success or failure depends on how the authorities respond. Political leaders can meet the demands of protesters, duck the issues, or fight back by sending in troops.

These models may help you understand some types of collective behavior and protest activities, but they do not tell us much about serious efforts to promote or resist societal change. Why do particular causes emerge when they do, who joins, and how is commitment maintained for the long haul?

Social Movements and Resource Mobilization

A more sociological approach emphasizes organizational variables, namely the resources—money, influence, people—that need to be activated ("mobilized") to promote or resist change. In this **resource mobilization model**, the success or failure of the social movement depends more on its organizational capacities than on the virtue of the cause. If social protest succeeded on the basis of moral claims, African Americans could have had seats at a Woolworth's lunch counter in the 1860s, and women would have voted in the election of 1789.

Although beliefs do matter when attracting followers and gaining public support, social networks matter just as much if not more (Passy and Giugni 2000). People who become active participants in a social movement are typically recruited by friends. If you have ever spent time on a picket line or at a protest meeting, chances are you got there because someone you knew asked you to come along. It also helps to have had politically involved parents and socialization that encouraged activism rather than passive obedience (Sherkat and Ellison 1994). In addition, some American campuses have a history of political activism, which attracts the type of student most likely to become an activist (Van Dyke 1998). Where would you place your campus on a scale of student protest activity?

The influence of peers and colleagues can overwhelm personal values, as when doctors who were quite neutral on the issue of abortion joined a Right to Life campaign because they were afraid of being isolated from other physicians and potential patients (Eckberg 1988). This example illustrates once again the power of the situation to determine behavior, regardless of your attitudes. Remember those real estate agents described in chapter 6, who were not in the least prejudiced yet refused to show certain homes to African Americans in order to stay in business?

Once you have been identified as a potential supporter, the next hurdle for the social movement is keeping you interested and involved over months and years. This usually requires some kind of formal organization with funding, mailing lists, newsletters, and a pipeline to the media. Organizing a demonstration every now and then serves to reinforce the commitment of followers, bringing the true believer together with thousands who feel the same way, while also providing pictures for newspapers and TV in order to influence public opinion. 💻5 Even so, keeping people mobilized over time is extremely difficult.

Types of Social Movements

Social movements are generally classified according to their goal, from limited changes to a complete transformation:

Reform movements advocate changes within the existing system, such as extending the Fourteenth Amendment's guarantee of equal protection of the laws to persons of color. The most effective tactics are the ones that influence politicians and the general public: lawsuits, demonstrations, mobilizing voters, and media events.

Revolutionary movements aim at overturning the existing system, a radical goal that is used to justify extraordinary tactics such as hijackings and other acts of terrorism.

Resistance or *countermovements* are formed to protect traditional values and institutions. Countermovement groups use the full range of tactics—from normal electoral politics to firebombing family planning clinics.

Utopian movements seek an ideal society, with a select group of believers serving as an example. The word "utopia" means "no place," a recognition of the impossibility of worldly perfection even as one strives for it. There is a strain of utopian idealism in America that periodically produces communities of the faithful, from the religious sect of Shakers in the nineteenth century to the young "hippies" of the 1960s. 💻6

Phases in the Development of a Social Movement

Most models of the life course of a social movement distinguish four phases: (1) vague unrest and personal discontent within the society; (2) a focusing of concern, "naming" the problem, and constructing information networks; (3) emergence of formal organizations; and (4) eventual success or failure, or, more often, a mix of the two. As seen in Table 16.1, each phase has its challenges, typical structural forms, and leadership type.

No matter how righteous the cause or deep the discontent, the social movement can succeed only to the extent that its leaders make alliances with other groups, avoid internal conflicts, and maintain the commitment of its members; those tasks are not easy, especially over years or decades. In addi-

❖ ❖ ❖ ❖   tion, the fate of the movement is only partly in the hands of its members; much depends on how the opposition mobilizes its resources.

Table 16.1	Phases in the Development of Social Movement			
Phase	**1** Preliminary	**2** Focusing of concern (Crystalization)	**3** Organization (Mobilization)	**4** Institutionalization
Character-istics	Widespread but isolated feelings of discontentand deprivation	Recognition that others share feelings	Centralization of power Mass membership	Public recognition and acceptance of ideas
Challenges	Media access Grass-roots organizing	Ideological development Communications network	Organization survival Avoiding internal conflicts Maintain members commitment	Organizational legitimation Benefiting members Resisting co-optation
Structure	Informal	Local units (cells)	National organizations Alliances with other groups	Bureaucratic formal structures
Leadership	Prophet or agitator	Charismatic leader	Managers (statespersons)	Bureaucrats (priests)

The most positive outcome would be to have the movement's goals realized in policy and practice, as when the Abolition Movement won the passage of the Thirteenth Amendment prohibiting slavery in America in 1865. At the other extreme, the goals can be repudiated in law and behavior, as in the case of the Temperance Movement, which saw victory with the Eighteenth Amendment prohibiting the manufacture and sale of alcoholic beverages in 1919, only to see it resoundingly repealed in 1933.

Sometimes, however, success also breeds defeat. Partial victories can take away much of the enthusiasm needed to maintain mobilization. For example, when the Suffrage Movement won the right to vote for American women in 1920, the broad-based coalition behind this one issue could not agree on other goals. It took another four decades for a New Feminist Movement to emerge and pursue the rest of the agenda (Ferree and Hess 2000).

An effective way to neutralize a social movement is co-optation, when establishment institutions claim to embrace movement goals and even bring some activists into leadership roles in the establishment. The Latino presidential advisor and the feminist corporate official become part of the power elite they once fought from the outside. A few visible acts of co-optation can reduce support for further activism by giving the impression that the war has been won, thereby thinning the ranks of opposition leaders.

Success can also derail a social movement through the process of goal displacement, whereby simply maintaining the organization—its offices, payroll, and perquisites—replaces the movement's original goals. As you saw in chapter 9, goal displacement has been a major problem for the labor union movement.

Finally, movement activism can simply be crushed by the power of the state, as has happened often in United States history (Amenta and Young 1999). The movement for workers' rights met with official resistance for decades; anarchists and communists have been imprisoned; and the antiwar protests on college campuses in the 1960s ended abruptly after students were killed by National Guard troops at Kent State and Jackson State Universities in 1970. Yet despite the overwhelming power of established institutions to resist and co-opt change, social movements never leave the social scene quite the same as it was before. New voices have been heard, interest groups have been created, and memories have been kept and passed on to the next generation of activists. 💻7

The 1960s: A Decade of Protest

Social movements typically appear in clusters. Once one set of grievances has been aired, others follow. The resources helpful to organizing for one cause are available to others. Often, the same subgroups are active in a number of movements. There have been a few such periods of extraordinary social movement activity in American history, the most recent being the 1960s. 💻8

One of the most unusual features of the 1960s, from the Free Speech Movement at the University of California, Berkeley, in 1960, to the gunshots at Kent and Jackson State Universities in 1970, was the extent to which college students were involved, not a common sight in American history. Students were at the center of the New Left and Antiwar movements and marched alongside their elders in the Civil Rights and Feminist movements. The spurt of student activism has been linked to a desire to break out of the smug complacency of the 1950s, as well as to the legacy of affluence that gave young people the freedom to drop out of the race for survival for a short period. By the mid-1970s, however, the scene within and outside the campuses had changed, and most students returned to their studies and career goals. Their experience as student protesters did have a lasting effect on many, who continued to be active in liberal causes throughout the following decades (Jamison and Eyerman 1994).

Of all the social movements of the 1960s, the two most socially significant and long-lived are the Civil Rights Movement (CRM) and the New Feminist Movement (NFM). Today, also, the Gay Rights Movement (see chapter 4) has had a measurable impact on social policy and practices. All three movements have provoked a powerful countermovement of organizations on the conservative end of the political spectrum, often referred to as the New Christian Right (NCR). 💻9 The interplay of movement and countermovement has brought some successes, some failures, and much unfinished business. Battles are won but wars lost, and vice versa. These pro-

The Gay Rights Movement has had an impact on social policy and practices as it seeks to develop protective legislation for gay men and lesbians and to provide personal support.

cesses can be seen in three current movements—the CRM, NFM, and the new supremacists.

The Civil Rights Movement (CRM)

Most of you were born after the major events of the 1960s and you have grown up in a society greatly altered by the legacy of the CRM. Yet it was only four decades ago that, throughout the American South, black and white children could not go to school together; adults of different races could not eat in the same restaurants or live in the same neighborhood, much less marry one another. Although lynchings were no longer common, the threat of violence kept many blacks, particularly in the South, from voting or protesting the lack of public services such as roads, water, or electricity for their neighborhoods.

All this began to change in the mid-1950s, when Northern blacks, taking advantage of enhanced educational and occupational opportunities, mobilized the resources needed to support collective protests. The resources included leadership from the churches, financing from a growing middle class, a community base of support in both North and South, and a network of college students primarily at minority schools in the South (Barnett 2000; Morris 1993). At the same time, the old Southern elites were being replaced by a new business class more interested in attracting Northern investment and factories than in maintaining racial segregation and flying the Confederate flag.

The legal basis for CRM activity was established in 1954 when the Supreme Court decided that racially segregated schools violated the Fourteenth Amendment's guarantee of equal protection of the laws. By extension, all other government-sponsored "separate but equal" arrangements were also unconstitutional. So when, in 1955, Rosa Parks was asked to step to the back of the bus, she refused to give her seat to a white man; the driver then called in the police to remove her; and the black community responded with a boycott of the bus system and white-owned businesses in Montgomery, Alabama. The courts eventually ruled that public transport could no longer be segregated. The protesters took on one target after another—lunch counters, movie houses, and hotels—meeting stubborn resistance every step of the way. It took federal marshals and troops to enforce school integration in Arkansas and Alabama, where the governor himself blocked the school door, declaring "segregation now and forever." Finally, in 1964, a Civil Rights Act passed Congress, 102 years after the Emancipation Proclamation.

By the mid-1960s, CRM demonstrations had mobilized the great mass of African Americans and large numbers of white sympathizers, many of whom were jailed or assaulted, put upon by police dogs, pushed with cattle prods, and even murdered. These events only increased media coverage and public outrage. Although financial and moral support from Northern whites were important, the CRM's own strengths, built up over decades, were the key to success (Morris 1993).

CRM goals remain reformist—to extend to all races the same life choices and chances enjoyed by whites. This is not possible, however, without redressing the advantages enjoyed by whites from three hundred years of privilege. For example, when rioting whites shot or burned alive hundreds of blacks and destroyed thousands of homes and businesses in Tulsa, Oklahoma, in 1921, the effects multiplied over two and three generations, with one set of citizens enjoying accumulated benefits—land, jobs, decent schools—and the other set progressively losing ground (Yardley 2000). No amount of reparations to the survivors today can make up for all the lost time and opportunities.

Nonetheless, leaders of the CRM sought to occupy the moral high ground, under the charismatic leadership of the Reverend Martin Luther King, Jr., by adopting the tactics of nonviolent civil disobedience perfected by Mahatma Gandhi in India. **Civil disobedience** involves a peaceful refusal to obey an "unjust law." When authorities then react with violence, public opinion is deeply affected. The most massive—and totally peaceful—civil rights demonstration took place in Washington, DC, in 1963 (attended by one of the authors of this book), and is best remembered for Dr. King's "I Have a Dream" speech, but this high point was the product of a decade of local organizing in black communities.

Five years later, in 1968, the CRM was greatly weakened by the assassination of Dr. King. As Max Weber would have predicted, when charisma is not "routinized," that is, supported by a nuts-and-bolts organization, a leadership vacuum follows the death of the charismatic figure. To this day, no one person or group can speak for the many different parts of the CRM. A second blow to the cause of civil rights was the urban riots of the late 1960s that provided a pretext for many whites to withdraw ideological and material support. Politically, the nation began to retreat from a federal commitment to civil rights, a direction confirmed with the election of a conservative Congress from 1994 to 2000. At the state level, one state after another has ended affirmative action programs, reduced funding for urban areas, and defied court orders for educational equity.

Where to go from here? Without strong national leadership or widespread public support, the CRM today can be described as in a state of *abeyance*, of suspended animation, waiting for something or someone to remobilize the troops. In the meantime, the battles are being fought at a lower level of power or awareness—in neighborhoods, churches, Congressional caucuses, charitable organizations, and election booths. 💻 10

The New Feminist Movement (NFM)

The social movement with the greatest staying power and potentially strongest effect on every aspect of society is the struggle for gender equality (Ferree and Hess 2000). Four decades after the collapse of the broad-based coalition that fought for women's suffrage, a New Feminist Movement emerged in the 1960s. In terms of the model in Table 16.1:

1. Personal discontent was widespread, especially among two groups of women: politically active middle-aged professionals and radical college students. Both resented being treated either as children ("We can't give you a credit card without your husband's permission") or as second-class citizens ("We're not interested in your opinion, go make the coffee"). Clearly, being able to vote had not ended visible discrimination or subtle pressures to conform to traditional expectations. The unrest generated by other social move-

❖ ❖ ❖ ❖   ments of the 1960s striving for equality and justice provided the basis for claiming the same goals for women.

2. In the second phase, women had to be made aware of how many others shared their feelings and to realize that the causes of their discontent were in the social system and not in some personal failing. The term "sexism" helped to focus the issues and to define the cause as one of basic civil rights. Newsletters, campus grapevines, and media attention were used to publicize demonstrations and to spread the new ideas swirling around the movement. This phase was also characterized by a new type of structure: the "consciousness-raising group" that linked participants in shared awareness of their common experiences and needs.

3. The third phase involved mobilizing resources and coordinating the energies of movement members. The emergence of mass membership organizations such as the National Organization for Women (NOW) was paralleled at the local level by groups with more specific goals, such as workplace problems or educational opportunities. In higher education, women's caucuses were formed in every discipline from accounting to zoology. The sociological caucus, Sociologists for Women in Society, for example, was founded in 1971 with three goals: to protect the interests of women in the profession (hiring, pay, promotion, and tenure), to spur research on gender, and to support changes in the society that would benefit girls and women as well as boys and men.

4. The final phase—institutionalization of the movement goals—is a record of great triumphs and ultimate failures. The triumphs, as you saw in chapter 7, have literally changed the face of the nation, so much so that young people today take it for granted that women can try out for just about anything. Attitudes and behaviors have changed dramatically in all social strata. In the academic world, no field of study has been left untouched by feminist scholars. If you were to read a sociology book from the 1970s, you might wonder what society was being described.

Yet these very successes have bred an equally long-lasting and deeply felt opposition. As noted in other chapters, levels of violence against women remain high, discrimination in work and pay persists, glass ceilings are cracking slowly, and talk radio hosts have a bottomless well of crude and cruel jokes. The term "feminist" has become a negative epithet, especially among young women who say, "I'm not a feminist but—I want equal pay, or whatever." The intellectual backlash proclaims a *postfeminist* era in which women will gladly return to their true calling of homemaking and child rearing. Scholars produce volumes claiming that biological sex differences account for men's unfaithfulness as well as for women's need to be forever sexually attractive. Even the struggle for reproductive choice that seemed settled in 1973 is no longer a certainty.

The basic lesson is that what the political system gives, it can also take away. Unless the movement has produced fundamental changes in every institution and in the hearts and minds of citizens, all gains are temporary. At the moment, the national organizations remain in place, though without the influence in the media they once enjoyed. Most women feel that they can make it on their own, a "feminism without feminists" (Ferree 2000). Whether or not there will be a Third American Feminist Movement some time in the twenty-first century depends on whether women interpret the barriers to equality that still impede their progress as evidence of personal failure or as socially constructed obstacles that require another mobilization. 🖥 11   ❖ ❖ ❖ ❖

For both the CRM and NFM, the outcome of further struggle may depend less on the resources they can mobilize than on the strength of opposition movements. Most of these countermovement organizations, the bulk of the New Christian Right, are in the political and religious mainstream, representing traditional beliefs and institutional arrangements. There are, however, a growing number of groups on the extreme fringe of the anti-feminist, anti-minority spectrum that together constitute the New Supremacists.

The New Supremacists

Minority gains coupled with deteriorating mobility opportunities have produced a sense of **relative deprivation** for many working-class families—strong feelings that they are not receiving the rewards to which they are entitled and that less deserving people are getting them instead. As you saw in chapter 5, feelings of resentment are fueled by the lack of fit between high-status ascribed traits—being a white, Anglo-Saxon, Protestant male—and low-achieved educational and occupational statuses. These resentments form the basis for recruitment to various subgroups under the general banner of White Separatism (Diamond 1998).

Christian Patriots. A number of fundamentalist sects, loosely linked in the Christian Patriot or Christian Identity movement, are engaged in "the politics of righteousness," a war to be waged against those who oppose God's will: Jews, feminists, gays, blacks, communists, abortionists, and gun-control liberals (Barkun 1997). These groups are often heavily armed and consider themselves a military force ("militia")

At some Ku Klux Klan rallies there appear to be more police officers and protestors than Klan members. The 'new' KKK is trying to develop a family-friendly image, appealing to blue- and white-collar families.

divinely ordained to save the nation. Literature from these groups was found in the belongings of Timothy McVeigh, convicted of killing 168 people in the bombing of a federal office building in Oklahoma City in 1997. Government offices have been a prime target for activists, who believe that black helicopters, jack-booted agents of the FBI, and even bar codes on grocery items are part of a conspiracy to deprive Americans of their individual freedoms (Hardisty 1999).

The New Ku Klux Klan. It is a "new" Klan in the sense that it has developed a family-friendly image, replacing the burning crosses with a savvy media campaign appealing to blue- and white-collar men and women who see themselves as overtaxed, underappreciated, and victims of reverse discrimination (Blee 1996). Its motto "equal rights for all; special privilege for none"—a veiled reference to legislation that protects the civil rights of blacks, gays, and women—has broad appeal among people who might not otherwise see themselves as members of the KKK (Berbrier 1998).

Neo-Nazis. The neo-Nazis or Aryan Nation share the Patriots' contempt for Jews and the Klan's fear of blacks. The link is *Aryan purity*—the need to maintain the Northern European bloodline of blond, blue-eyed Christians. Much of their effort is aimed at encouraging higher fertility among its women in order to counter that of "mud people" and "Christ killers." Some members are rootless teenagers who enjoy the uniforms and all-male companionship; others are older true believers in the superiority of their race and ethnicity (Ferber 1998).

Skinheads. Drawing from the vast reservoir of rootless, resentful working-class youth with limited job prospects in a postindustrial society, the "skins" provide an outlet for pent-up energies through their mix of music and metal, leather, and loudness. Not all young males with shaved heads and Doc Marten boots are attracted to neo-Nazi hate groups. Some skinhead groups have mixed-race membership, and others are composed of angry blacks and Hispanics, which only heightens the fears of the supremacists.

WAR: White Aryan Resistance. Founded in 1983, WAR claims to be the coordinating body for the supremacy movement. Its major goal is to alert the general public to the dangers of an international Jewish-led conspiracy to impose a "New World Order." Members are encouraged to engage in acts of justified terrorism to prevent the "mongrelizing" of America (Dobratz and Shanks-Meile 1997).

What makes such organizations much more powerful than they were a decade ago are the technological developments that permit instant communication—namely, the Internet and talk radio stations. At the same time, the supremacist movement encourages "leaderless resistance," urging members to act on their own. For example, the bombings of government facilities and family planning clinics have been the work of "lone wolves," wandering avengers with guns and explosives, whose actions cannot be easily predicted (Thomas 1999).

But you do not need to join any of these groups to find out what they believe; just turn on your computer or your radio. The Internet is filled with several thousand websites eager to inform you, as are hundreds of AM and FM stations, largely in the South (Political Research Associates 2000). These outlets reach millions of Americans every hour of every day, so although the number of active members in supremacist organizations is probably only a few hundred thousand, there is no way of counting the individuals who have been influenced by their ideology. 🖥 12

2001.com: Here Already

It was only a few decades ago that "2001" symbolized a distant future, where robots operated complex machinery, space capsules hurtled through the universe, and people communicated through wireless screens. And now, we are there. What do these developments mean for societies and individuals? Your guess may be as good as those of the experts, who have proposed a number of conflicting scenarios.

At the micro-level of face-to-face interaction and the construction of identity, sitting in front of a computer console can either isolate you from contact with family and friends or put you in touch with a "virtual community" through interactive sites, chat rooms, and bulletin boards. On the one hand, some scholars deplore the trend away from community involvement in general—a retreat into the self, evidenced by shorter marriages, smaller families, lower voting rates, declining membership in voluntary associations, and more time on your own in cyberspace. The book title *Bowling Alone* (Putnam 2000) says it all. A recent national survey found that the more time people spent on-line, the less time they spent with "real human beings" or the mass media, leading researchers to predict a wave of social isolation sweeping the nation (Nie et al. 2000).

On the other hand, reading newspapers and watching TV are not nec-

The growth of internet cafés like this one in London makes staying in touch with a virtual community easier when you're away from home. You can also have a cappucino if you like.

essarily more social than getting your news and entertainment on-line. Not everyone has a lot of family and friends at hand; one in four American households, remember, consists of one person. In contrast, cyberspace is filled with millions of potential acquaintances. With the latest technology, you can even speak directly to them, which is not all that different from shouting upstairs to a family member. With regard to staying in touch with family members, another recent study found that e-mail was strengthening family ties, especially for women, who now comprise a majority of on-line browsers (Pew Research Center 2000).

In addition, not only can you connect with many different kinds of people, but you yourself can also become many different persons (Turkle 1999). You can construct a "virtual self" for each Internet encounter; an entire world of identities is open to you, expressing all facets of your personality under conditions of anonymity. Plus, you can claim a piece of cyberspace with your very own website and home page.

Several sociologists have recently argued that in an era of rapid change and abbreviated work and family relationships, the networked society frees individuals from reliance on the few persons with whom they come into physical contact (Wellman and Hampton 1999; Pescosolido and Rubin 2000). Entire new worlds open up, multiple links allow greater flexibility, while the loss of any one relationship is less catastrophic than in the past.

At the macro-level of societal institutions, new industries have developed around the Net; shopping habits have been altered; distance education is transforming the university; patients in underserved areas can receive health care information; and instant political mobilization is possible. These trends should put more power into the hands of ordinary people, bypassing elitist barriers to services and products. In other words, many see the Internet as a democratizing machine. 🖥 13

At the moment, however, there is a widening gap in owning and using computers between the higher and lower education and income categories, and between white and minority households at all income levels (U.S. Department of Commerce 1999). Thus, in the United States, the new technology has reinforced inequality by race and class and, to a lesser extent, by gender. Gender differences are most pronounced in the production and use of software, especially in the area of computer games. Check out any arcade. There are also striking differences by age, but this really reflects generational differences in familiarity and should lessen with each new age group (National Public Radio 2000).

Box 16.1

The Digital Divide

Does it matter that there are wide race and income differences in access to computers at work or at home? You bet. Those who lack computer literacy and ready access lose out in a number of ways (Downs 2000):

- Job skills—occupations of the future will increasingly require familiarity with computers.
- Purchasing—families can save money by shopping on the Internet.
- Distance learning—a college degree is at your fingertips at a fraction of the time or cost of attending in person.
- Health information and home care assistance—especially important for those who live in underserved areas or who are uninsured.
- Schoolwork—a home PC is an invaluable help for homework and other projects. Children with PCs gained in self-esteem, improved grades, greater interest in learning, and pride in producing nice-looking papers.
- Government services—most agencies are now on the web, where they can be contacted at all hours. Saves a lot of time on the phone or waiting in line and losing a day's pay.
- On-line voting—the "next big thing" that will add to the political power of people with computer access.

In all these ways, and others we have not yet realized, the digital divide will widen the gap between haves and have-nots. The gap begins in school, where students in low-income districts lack both teachers and computers

---

Another potentially antidemocratic factor is government itself (Hurwitz 1999). In their zeal to protect children—and adults—from pornography and hate material, politicians from local library boards to the White House appear ready to impose restraints on what computer users can see or do. This is precisely that "slippery slope" (once you are on it, it is hard to stop) from which the First Amendment should protect the public. At what price do we shield one another from information and activities that are potentially dangerous?

There are also questions of privacy, in terms of eavesdropping or the sharing of presumably private information by both law enforcement and commercial interests. Somewhere out there, your entire life may be on a floppy, to be bought and sold.

Some people feel that the most powerful antidemocratic factor of all is the *commercialization* of cyberspace. What many original "cybernerds" had envisioned as a great freeway, a space for free expression, open to all, has become one huge billboard. Thus, it was no surprise that in early 2000 several coordinated attacks were made on commercial sites, disrupting service for several hours by simply overloading their capacity with more information than they could handle. These attacks exposed the vulnerable underside of the Internet. Sometimes, the more technologically sophisticated things get, the easier it is to disable them. 💻14

This brief discussion illustrates one of the basic principles of sociology: Little in this world has only one outcome. There are always unintended, unforeseen, and often undesirable consequences of any social arrangement. Thus, 2001.com will bring great benefits to some and leave others out, open new worlds of beauty and of ugliness, liberate individuals while making it easier to keep tabs on them, and bring citizens together while encouraging the development of narrow interest groups.

Conclusion

In this chapter, you have looked at the various ways in which social change enters and affects cultures, social structures, and individual lives. Among the many sources of change are the organized efforts called social movements. If the goals of a social movement involve widespread or radical changes, a countermovement is likely to emerge. In the United States today, the Civil Rights, Feminist, and Gay Rights movements have produced a powerful backlash, often referred to as the "culture wars" of the 1990s and early twenty-first century.

Another source of change is the increased globalization of everything, from technology to culture. For better or worse, all nations are linked by trade and telephones. The new world economy will be dominated by communication technologies that also have implications within each society. The computer/Internet culture has profound consequences for individuals and societies, but these effects are neither clear nor consistent. The rest of this chapter—indeed, the story of American society and world systems—will be written by you and your generation as you move through social structures that are only dimly visible now. Bon voyage!

Social change includes Russia's aging MIR space station, which was going to be transformed into an orbiting business park and vacation resort for high flyers. However, when the funds for the repairs and renovation did not materialize, the project was abandoned. The MIR will be destroyed.

❖ ❖ ❖ ❖   ## Surfing the Sociological Internet

For links to sites on and about social movements and social change, see: http://sg.yahoo.com/social_science/sociology/collective_behaviour/

Sites related to the Holocaust:
The U.S. Holocaust Memorial Museum:
http://www.ushmm.org/
http://www.academicinfo.net/histholo.html is an academic site on holocaust studies with links to other related sites.
The Simon Wiesenthal Center for Tolerance has links to other sites dealing with other genocidal events and ethnic cleansing along with links about hate groups in the United States and internationally: http://www.wiesenthal.com/
Data on the Romany people (Gypsies) and the Holocaust can be found at: http://198.62.75.1/www2/gypsies.net/RemDG.html and http://www.geocities.com/Paris/5121/holcaust.htm which has links to other sites.
For information on "ethnic cleansing" see Amnesty International's site: http://www.amnesty.org/ailib/intcam/kosovo/

3 For a trip to the Industrial Revolution to see how it changed society, go to: http://members.aol.com/mhirotsu/kevin/trip2.html
This site gives a chronology of the Industrial Revolution and links to other technological changes that affected modern society in profound ways: http://campus.northpark.edu/history//WebChron/WestEurope/IndRev.html

4 The latest urban myths and legends can be found at: http://www.urbanmyths.com/

5 Social movements and mass communications: http://www.geocities.com/CollegePark/Quad/5889/

6 For information on the Shakers, see: http://www.shakers.org/ and for hippies, go to: http://www.therumbles.net/hippies/

7 Go to: http://www.stile.lboro.ac.uk/~gyedb/STILE/t0000270.html for information on and links to sites about the histories of various kinds of social movements.

8 For another "blast from the past," go to: http://www.slip.net/~scmetro/sixties.htm

9 For news on social change, the religious right, and other social movements, go to: http://www.igc.org/datacenter/culture.htm

10 For the history of the Civil Rights Movement: http://www.fred.net/nhhs/project/

and http://www.cr.nps.gov/nr/travel/civilrights/intro.htm—both with links to many other sites.

🖥 11 The Women's Movement: http://www.now.org/ and http://www.feminist.org/
Go to: http://eserver.org/feminism/activism/activism.html for links to other groups in the women's movement.
For an extensive list of links to women in history, go to: http://info-s.com/history-w.html
For resources on the Second Wave of the Women's Movement: http://www.nau.edu/wst/access/2ndwav/2ndwavsub.html

🖥 12 For information on hate groups and links to websites, see: http://www.publiceye.org/

🖥 13 For a history of the development of the Internet, see: http://www.gseis.ucla.edu/iclp/hp.html
For an atlas of cyberspace, go to: http://www.cybergeography.org/atlas/atlas.html

🖥 14 To find out about cyberspace law and policy, see: http://www.gseis.ucla.edu/iclp/hp.html

❖ ❖ ❖ ❖

Glossary

Civil Disobedience Peaceful refusal to obey an "unjust law."
Cohort Flow The movement of people born in a given time period across their life course.
Colonialism The forcible conquering of traditional societies by Western nations in search of cheap raw material and/or political pride.
Co-optation A way to neutralize a social movement where establishment institutions claim to embrace movement goals and bring activists into leadership roles.
Cyclical Theories Theories of social change based on the view that society resembles a living organism going through phases of growth and decline.
Differentiation Increasing specialization; a basic process in the development of cultural complexity.
Diffusion The process by which cultural norms and values are spread from one society to another.
Emergent Quality The possibility of a number of different outcomes of crowd behavior.
Emotional Contagion Early theoretical view of how the intensity of crowds develops.
Ethnic Cleansing See Genocide.
Evolutionary Models Theories of social change that see human history as a unidirectional upward path from savagery to civilization.
Genocide The systematic, intentional killing of an entire population.
Goal Displacement Displacement of a movement's original goals by the goal of simply maintaining the organization.

Holocaust The mass extermination of six million Jews and another five million people designated "genetically inferior" or who were political enemies of the Nazi regime in Germany between 1941 and 1945.

Innovation Refers to new items of culture, discoveries, or inventions.

Modernization A master historical trend involving industrialization, urbanization, and secularization.

Nationalism A consciousness of shared identity among the members of a politically distinct territory.

Neo-evolutionary Models Theories of social change that see increases in cultural and societal complexity but do not make value judgments about the superiority of one society over another.

Relative Deprivation A sense that one is being unfairly treated in comparison to others thought to be one's equals.

Social Change The process through which values, norms, institutions, stratification systems, social relationships, and even the self are altered over time.

Resource Mobilization Model Emphasizes the organizational supports required for social movement success.

Value Added Model A detailed theory of the emergent nature of crowds; specifies six conditions that are necessary and sufficient to produce collective behavior.

World Social System Increased cooperation and trade across national boundaries and a rapid spread of information and technology. ✦

Photo Credits

Unless otherwise acknowledged, all photographs are the property of Roxbury Publishing Company.

Cover Photos

Clockwise from top: Youth being arrested—Reuters/Shaun Best/Archive; barnraising—Paul Solomon/Woodfin Camp & Associates; truckers—Reuters/Archive Photos; blind runner—Reuters/Gary Hershorn/Archive Photos; Washington, DC, Baptist church—Catherine Karnow/Woodfin Camp & Associates; protesting mothers—Sylvia Johnson/Woodfin Camp & Associates.

Chapter 1

Page 3—Catherine Karnow/Woodfin Camp & Associates; page 6—Peter J. Stein; page 12—Catherine Karnow/Woodfin Camp & Associates; page 13—Reuters/Shaun Best/Archive Photos; page 14—Reuters/Win McNamee/Archive Photos; page 16—Dwight Cendrowski/FocuSing Group Photography; page 21—Peter J. Stein.

Chapter 2

Page 31—Paul Solomon/Woodfin Camp & Associates; page 33—Dana Lichty; page 35—Reuters/Mike Segar/Archive Photos; page 42—Reuters/Gary Hershorn/Archive Photos; page 45—Peter J. Stein; page 50—Paul Solomon/Woodfin Camp & Associates; page 53—Photodisc.

Chapter 3

Page 57—Courtesy of the Masters School; page 59—Dana Lichty; page 61—Courtesy of the Masters School; page 64—Peter J. Stein; page 68—Rosanne Anello; page 73—Mark C. Ide; page 76—Photodisc.

Chapter 4

Page 83—Bettina Chavanne; page 85—Dana Lichty; page 92—Photodisc;—page 96—Photodisc; page 101—Photodisc.

Chapter 5

Page 107—William U. Harris; page 110—William U. Harris; page 116—William U. Harris; page 121—William U. Harris; page 126—William U. Harris.

Chapter 6

Page 131 Cont/J. B. Diederich/Woodfin Camp & Associates; page 134—William U. Harris; page 135—Cont/J. B. Diederich/Woodfin Camp & Associates; page 140—William U. Harris; page 145—Reuters/Juda Ngwenya/Archive Photos; page 146—Geoffrey Clifford/Woodfin Camp & Associates; page 148—James D. Wilson/Woodfin Camp & Associates; page 151—Stephanie Maze/Woodfin Camp & Associates; page 155—Miryam Wahrman.

Chapter 7

Page 161—Shehzad Noorani/Woodfin Camp & Associates; page 166—Reuters/Jeff Christensen/Archives Photos; page 169—William U. Harris; page 172—Shehzad Noorani/Woodfin Camp & Associates; page 174—Roland and Sabrina Michaud/Woodfin Camp & Associates; page 175—Reuters/Archive Photos; page 177—B. Press/Woodfin Camp & Associates.

Chapter 8

Page 183—Peter J. Stein; page 185—Dana Lichty; page 188—Peter J. Stein; page 189—Reuters/Archive Photos; page 192—Photodisc; page 196—Peter J. Stein; page 199—Jeffrey R. Halvorsen and George F. Cisneros; page 201—Mark C. Ide.

Chapter 9

Page 207—William U. Harris; page 208—Eva Momatiuk and John Eastcott/Woodfin Camp & Associates; page 213—Dana Lichty; page 218—William U. Harris; page 219—Catherine Karnow/Woodfin Camp & Associates; page 222—Peter J. Stein; page 224—Reuters/Peter Morgan/Archive Photos; page 226—Dwight Cendrowski/FocuSing Group.

Chapter 10

Page 231—Reuters/Pete Silva/Archive Photos; page 233—William U. Harris; page 236—Reuters/Jim Bourg/Archive Photos; page 237—Photodisc; page 246—Reuters/Pete Silva/Archive Photos; page 248—William U. Harris.

Chapter 11

Page 255—Courtesy of the Masters School; page 257—Dana Lichty; page 262—Miryam Wahrman; page 263—Courtesy of the Masters School; page 270—Courtesy of the Masters School; page 272—William U. Harris.

Chapter 12

Page 281—Rev. Catherine S. Roskum; page 284—Reuters/Jeff Mitchell/Archive Photos; page 288—Emily Mahon; page 290—William U. Harris; page 293—A. Ramey/Woodfin Camp & Associates; page 294—Michael S.

Yamashita/Woodfin Camp & Associates; page 295—Peter J. Stein; page 296—
Rev. Catherine S. Roskum; page 297—Dana Lichty.

Chapter 13

Page 305—Mark C. Ide; page 308—PAX; page 311, A. Ramey/Woodfin
Camp & Associates; page 312—Mark C. Ide; page 314—Reuters/Pierre Virot/
Archive Photos; page 317—Digital Stock; page 324—Supreme Court Histori-
cal Society; page 325—A. Ramey/Woodfin Camp & Associates; page 328—A.
Ramey/Woodfin Camp & Associates.

Chapter 14

Page 333—William U. Harris; page 336—William U. Harris; page 338—
Digital Stock; page 344—Peter J. Stein; page 347—William U. Harris; page
348—William U. Harris; page 350—A. Ramey/Woodfin Camp & Associates;
page 354—William U. Harris.

Chapter 15

Page 361—Peter J. Stein; page 367—Peter J. Stein; page 369—Dana
Lichty; page 370—Reuters/Daniel Aguilar/Archive Photos; page 373—Ron
Brazil/Archive Photos; page 374—Reuters/Archive Photos; page 376—
Photodisc; page 378—Peter J. Stein; page 382—Peter J. Stein.

Chapter 16

Page 387—Dana Lichty; page 389—B. Press/Woodfin Camp & Associ-
ates; page 394—Dana Lichty; page 397—William U. Harris; page 401—
Photodisc; page 405—Digital Stock; page 407—Peter J. Stein; page 409—
Reuters/Archive Photos. ✦

Bibliography

Abma, Joyce, Anne Driscoll, and Kristin Moore. 1998. "Young Women's Degree of Control over First Intercourse: An Exploratory Analysis." *Family Planning Perspectives* 30: 12–18.

Abreu, Jose M. 2000. "Conscious and Unconscious African American Stereotypes: Impact on First Impression and Diagnostic Ratings by Therapists." *Journal of Consulting and Clinical Psychology* 67: 387–394.

Acker, Joan. 1990. "Hierarchies, Jobs, Bodies: A Theory of Gendered Organizations." *Gender and Society* 4: 139–158.

——. 1998. "The Future of Gender and Organizations: Connections and Boundaries." *Gender, Work, and Organizations* 5: 195–196.

——. 2000. "A Contradiction in Reality: Feminism in Sweden." *SWS Network News,* Spring, 17: 16–18.

Acs, Gregory and Megan Gallagher. 2000. "Income Inequality Among America's Children." *Urban Institute*, January.

Acton, J.E.E.D. 1878/1985. "The History of Freedom in Antiquity." In *Selected Readings of Lord Acton*, Vol. 1. Indianapolis, IN: Liberty Fund.

Adler, Patricia A. and Peter Adler. 1998. *Peer Power: Preadolescent Culture and Identity.* New Brunswick, NJ: Rutgers.

Agbayani-Siewart, Pauline, David Takeuchi, and Rosavinia Pangan. 1999. "Mental Illness in a Multicultural Context." In Carol Aneshensel and Jo Phelan, Eds., *Handbook of the Sociology of Mental Health,* pp. 19–36. New York: Plenum.

Alan Guttmacher Institute. 2000. "Induced Abortion." *Facts in Brief.* February.

Alba, Richard. 1999. "Immigration and the American Realities of Assimilation and Multiculturalism." *Sociological Forum* 14: 3–26.

Ali, Sam. 2000. "The Naked Truth." *The Star-Ledger*, July 10, 27–29.

Allen, Charlotte. 1999. "Brainwashed: Scholars of Cults Accuse Each Other of Bad Faith." *Lingua Franca*. December/January: 27–36.

Allen, Mile and Nancy Burrell. 1996. "Comparing the Impact of Homosexual and Heterosexual Parents on Children: Meta–analysis of Existing Research." *Journal of Homosexuality* 32: 19–35.

Altman, Lawrence K. 1998. "Dismaying Experts, H.I.V. Infections Soar." *New York Times*. November 24.

——. 2000. "Mysterious Illnesses Often Turn Out To Be Mass Hysteria." *New York Times,* January 18.

Amenta, Edwin and Michael P. Young. 1999. "Democratic States and Social Movements: Theoretical Arguments and Hypotheses." *Social Problems* 46: 153–168.

American Council on Education. 2000. *The American Freshman: National Norms for Fall 1999.* New York: ACE.

American Demographics. 1998. "Establishing Brand Loyalty in Schools." November.

American Heart Association. 1999. "New Study Finds African Americans Less Likely to Receive Stroke-Saving Surgery." *American Heart Association Journal*, July, 1.

——. 2000. "Low-cost Treatments for Heart Attack Underused in Blacks, Women, and the Poor." *AHA News Release*, August 7.

American Humanist Association. 1988. *Humanism is the Best Way of Life.* Amherst, NY: AHA.

American Management Association. 2000. Press releases on 1999 Survey on Workplace Testing, Surveillance, and Monitoring. June 14. New York: AMA.

American Psychiatric Association. 1994. *Diagnostic and Statistical Manual, IV.*

Amnesty International. 2000a. "Countries with Most Executions in 1998."

——. 2000b. "Capital Punishment Around the World."

Anderson, David C. 1998. *Sensible Justice: Alternatives to Prison.* New York: New Press.

Angier, Natalie. 1999. *WOMAN An Intimate Geography*. Boston: Houghton-Mifflin Co.

Ansari, Maboud. 1992. *The Making of the Iranian Community in America*. New York: Paradis Press.

Anthony, Dick and Thomas Robbins. 1997. "Religious Totalism: Exemplary Dualism and the Waco Tragedy," In Thomas Robbins and Susan J. Palmer, Eds. *Millennium, Messiahs, and Mayhem: Contemporary Apocalyptic Movements*, pp. 261–284. New York: Routledge.

Applebome, Peter. 1999. "Alma Maters: Two Worlds Behind the Massacres." *New York Times*, May 2.

Armstrong, Karen. 2000. *The Battle for God*. New York: Knopf.

Aronowitz, Stanley. 2000. *The Knowledge Factory: Dismantling the Corporate University and Creating True Higher Education*. Boston, MA: Beacon.

Astone, Nan Marie. 1997. "Review of 'The Personal Responsibility and Work Opportunity Reconciliation Act of 1996.' " *Contemporary Sociology* 26: 413–416.

Athens, Lonnie. 1997. *The Creation of Dangerous Violent Criminals*. Urbana, IL: University of Illinois.

Bach, Peter B., Laura D. Cramer, Joan L. Warren, and Colin B. Begg. 1999. "Racial Differences in the Treatment of Early-Stage Lung Cancer." *New England Journal of Medicine* 341: 1198–1205.

Bainbridge, William Sims. 1997. *The Sociology of Religious Movements*. New York: Routledge.

Bakalian, Anny. 1993. *Armenian/Americans: From Being to Feeling Armenian*. New Brunswick, NJ: Transaction.

Balch, Robert. 1995. "Waiting for the Ships: Disillusionment and the Revitalization of Faith in Bo and Peep's UFO Cult." In James R. Lewis, Ed., *Gods Have Landed: New Religions from Other Worlds*, pp. 137–166. Albany, NY: State University of New York.

——. 1998. "The Evolution of a New Age Cult: From Total Overcomers to Anonymous Death at Heaven's Gate." In William W. Zellner and Marc Petrowsky, Eds., *Sects, Cults, and Spiritual Communities: A Sociological Analysis*. Westport, CT: Praeger.

Barboza, David. 1999. "Many Can't Survive the 'New Agriculture'." *New York Times*, November 28.

Barker, Joan. 1999. *Danger, Duty and Disillusion: The Worldview of Los Angeles Police Officers*. Prospect Heights, IL: Waveland.

Barkun, Michael. 1997. "Millinarians and Violence: The Case of the Christian Identity Movement." In Thomas Robbins and Susan J. Palmer, Eds., *Millennium, Messiahs, and Mayhem: Contemporary Apocalyptic Movements*, pp. 247–260. New York: Routledge.

Barnett McNair, Bernice. 2000. "Soldiers in the Army: Black Women Civil Rights Activists and Their Resistance Strategies." Paper presented at the Annual Meeting of the American Sociological Association, Washington, DC: August.

Baron, James N. and M. Diane Burton. 1999. "Building the Iron Cage: Determinants of Managerial Intensity in the Early Years of Organizations." *American Sociological Review*, 64: 527–547.

Baxandall, Rosalyn and Elizabeth Ewen. 2000. *Picture Windows: How the Suburbs Happened*. New York: Basic.

Baxter, Janeen and Eric Olin Wright. 2000. "The Glass Ceiling Hypothesis: A Comparative Study of the United States, Sweden, and Australia." *Gender & Society* 14: 275–294.

Bearak, Barry. 2000. "Afghanistan's Girls Fight to Read and Write." *New York Times*, March 9.

Becker, Elizabeth. 2000. "Child Care in Military Is Praised as a Model." *New York Times*, May 17.

Becker, Howard S. 1963. *Outsiders: Studies in the Sociology of Deviance*. New York: Free Press.

Beegley, Leonard. 1986. "Social Class and Political Participation." *Sociological Forum* 1: 496–513.

Beisel, Nicola. 1997. *Imperiled Innocents: Anthony Comstock and Family Reproduction in Victorian America.* Princeton, NJ: Princeton.

Belknap, Joanne. 2001. "The Criminal Processing System: Girls and Women as Victims and Offenders." In Dana Vannoy, Ed., *Gender Mosaics,* pp. 374–384. Los Angeles: Roxbury.

Bellah, Robert N. 1975. *The Broken Covenant: American Civil Religion in a Time Trial.* New York: Seabury Press.

Belluck, Pam. 1999. "As More Prisons Go Private, States Seek Tighter Controls." *New York Times,* April 15.

Benedict, Jeffrey R. 1998. *Athletes and Acquaintance Rape.* Thousand Oaks, CA: Sage.

Bennett, William J., John J. DiIulio, and John P. Walters. 1996. *Body Count: Moral Poverty and How to Win America's War Against Crime and Drugs.* New York: Simon & Schuster.

Berbrier, Mitch. 1998. " 'Half the Battle': Cultural Resonance, Framing Processes, and Ethnic Affectations in Contemporary White Separatist Rhetoric." *Social Problems* 45: 431–443.

Berger, Peter L. and Thomas Luckmann. 1966. *The Social Construction of Reality.* Garden City, NY: Doubleday.

Berheide, Catherine White. 1992. "Women Still 'Stuck' in Low Level Jobs." *Women in Public Service* 3: 1–4.

Berke, Richard L. 1998. "Chasing the Polls on Gay Rights." *New York Times,* August 2.

Bessel, Diane R. 2000. *Re-ordering the Nation: A Case Study Analysis of the Promise Keepers Movement.* Eastern Sociological Society, March.

Best, Joel. 1990. *Threatened Children: Rhetoric and Concern about Child Victims.* Chicago: University of Chicago.

——. 1999. *Random Violence: How We Talk About New Crimes and New Victims.* Berkeley, CA: California.

Beveridge, Andrew A. and Jeannie D'Amico. 1994. *Black and White Property Rates and Other Homeownership Costs in 30 Metropolitan Areas: A Preliminary Report.* New York: Queens College of the City University of New York.

Bianchi, Suzanne and Jane Lawler Dye. 2001. "The Participation of Women and Men in the United States Labor Force: Trends and Future Prospects." In Dana Vannoy, Ed., *Gender Mosaics,* pp. 460–472. Los Angeles: Roxbury.

Bianchi, Suzanne M., Melissa A. Milkie, Liana C. Sayer, and John P. Robinson. 1999/2000. "Is Anyone Doing the Housework? Trends in the Gender Division of Household Labor." Paper presented at the annual meeting of the American Sociological Association, August, 1999, revised 2000.

Biblarz, Timothy J. and Greg Gottainer. 2000. "Family Structure and Children's Success: A Comparison of Widowed and Divorced Single–Mother Families." *Journal of Marriage and the Family* 62: 533–548.

Black, Dan, Gary Gates, Seth Sanders, and Lowell Taylor. 1999. *Demographics of the Gay and Lesbian Population in the United States.* Paper presented at the Annual Meeting of the Population Association of America, March.

Blakely, Edward J. and Mary Gail Snyder. 1997. *Fortress America: Gated Communities in the United States.* Washington, DC: Brookings.

Blee, Kathleen. 1996. "Becoming a Racist: Women in Contemporary Ku Klux Klan and Neo-Nazi Groups," *Gender & Society* 10: 680–702.

Block, Fred. 1990. *Postindustrial Possibilities: A Critique of Economic Discourse.* Berkley CA: California.

Blumer, Herbert. 1951. "Collective Behavior." In Alfred McLung Lee, Ed., *New Outlines of the Principles of Sociology.* New York: Barnes & Noble.

——. 1969. *Symbolic Interactionism.* Englewood Cliffs, NJ: Prentice-Hall.

Bly, Robert. 1990. *Iron John: A Book about Men.* Reading, MA: Addison-Wesley.

Bobo, Lawrence, James Kluegel, and Ryan A. Smith. 1997. "Laissez–Faire Racism: The Crystallization of a 'Kinder, Gentler' Anti–Black Ideology." In S. A. Tuch and J. K. Martin, Eds., *Racial Attitudes in the 1990s: Continuity and Change*. Greenwood, CT: Praeger.

Bonner, Raymond. 1999. "Russian Gangsters Exploit Capitalism to Increase Profits." *New York Times*, July 25.

Bose, Christine E. 1987. "Dual Spheres." In Beth B. Hess and Myra Marx Ferree, Eds., *Analyzing Gender: A Handbook of Social Science Research*, pp. 267–285. Newbury Park, CA: Sage.

Bose, Christine and Rachel Bridges Whaley. 2001. "Sex Segregation in the U.S. Labor Force." In Dana Vannoy, Ed., *Gender Mosaics*, pp. 228–239. Los Angeles: Roxbury.

Boswell, John. 1994. *Same-Sex Unions in Premodern Europe*. New York: Villard.

Bourdieu, Pierre. 1984. *Distinction: A Social Critique of the Judgment of Taste*. Cambridge, MA: Harvard.

Bourg, Christina and Mady Weschler Segal. 2001. "Gender, Sexuality and the Military." In Dana Vannoy, Ed., *Gender Mosaics*, pp.332–342. Los Angeles: Roxbury.

Bowen, William G., and Derek Bok. 1998. *The Shape of the River: Long-Term Consequences of Considering Race in College and University Admissions*. Princeton, NJ: Princeton.

Bradsher, Keith. 2000. "Boy Who Killed Gets 7 Years; Judge Says Law Is Too Harsh." *New York Times*, January 14.

Braslow, Joel. 1997. *Mental Ills and Bodily Cures*. Berkeley, CA: University of California.

Brewster, Karin L. 1994. "Race Differences in Sexual Activity Among Adolescent Women: The Role of Neighborhood Characteristics." *American Sociological Review* 59: 408–424.

Bridges, George S. and Sara Steen. 1998. "Racial Disparities in Official Assessments of Juvenile Offenders: Attributional Stereotypes as Mediating Mechanisms." *American Sociological Review*, 63: 554–570.

Bromley, David G. and Mitchell L. Bracey, Jr. 1998. "The Church of Scientology: A Quasi Religion." In William W. Zellner and Marc Petrowsky, Eds., *Sects, Cults, and Spiritual Communities: A Sociological Analysis*, pp. 141–156. Westport, CT: Praeger.

Brooke, James. 2000. "Full Hospitals Make Canadians Wait and Look South." *New York Times*, January 16.

Brooks, Clem. 2000. "Civil Rights Liberalism and the Suppression of a Republican Political Realignment in the United States, 1972–1996." *American Sociological Review* 65: 483–505.

Brooks, Clem and Jeff Manza. 1997. "Social Cleavages and Political Alignments: U.S. Presidential Elections, 1960 to 1992." *American Sociological Review* 62: 937–946.

Brooks-Gunn, Jeanne, Greg J. Duncan, and Lawrence Aber. 1997. *Neighborhood Poverty, Volume 1: Context and Consequences for Children*. New York: Russell Sage Foundation.

Brown, Lester R., Gary Gardner, and Brian Halweil. 1998. *Beyond Malthus: Sixteen Dimensions of the Population Problem*. Washington, DC: Worldwatch Institute.

Brown, Lyn Mikel. 1998. *Raising Their Voices: Politics of Girls' Anger*. Cambridge, MA: Harvard.

Brown, Michael F. 1997. *The Channeling Zone: American Spirituality in An Anxious Age*. Cambridge, MA: Harvard University.

Brozan, Nadine. 2000. "For Vacation Homes, the Trend Is Bigger." *New York Times*, April 9.

Brunvald, Jan. 2000. *The Truth Never Stands in the Way of a Good Story!* Champaign-Urbana, IL: University of Illinois.

Bryson, Ken and Lynne M. Casper. 1999. "Co-resident Grandparents and Grandchildren." *Current Population Reports*, U.S. Bureau of the Census, May.

Bryk, Anthony. 1999. *Charting Chicago School Reform*. HarperCollins.

Bryk, Anthony, Valerie E. Lee, and Peter B. Holland. 1993. *Catholic Schools and the Common Good.* Cambridge, MA: Harvard University Press.

Bullard, Robert D. 2000. *Dumping in Dixie: Race, Class, and Environmental Quality.* Boulder, CO: Westview.

Bullard, Robert D., Glenn S. Johnson, and Angel O. Torres, Eds. 2000. *Sprawl City: Race, Politics, and Planning in Atlanta.* Atlanta, GA: New Society.

Bumpass, Larry, and Hsien–Han Lu. 2000. "Trends in Cohabitation and Implications for Children's Family Contexts in the U.S." *Population Studies.*

Burawoy, Michael and Katherine Verdery. 1999. *Uncertain Transition: Ethnographies of Change in the Postsocialist World.* Lanham, MD: Rowman & Littlefield.

Bureau of the Census, see U.S. Department of Commerce.

Bureau of Justice Statistics, see U.S. Department of Justice.

Bureau of Labor Statistics, see U.S. Department of Labor.

Burrell, Sue and Loren Warboys. 2000. "Special Education and the Juvenile Justice System." *Juvenile Justice Bulletin,* July. Washington, D.C.: U.S. Department of Justice.

Buss, David M. 2000. *The Dangerous Passion: Why Jealousy Is as Necessary as Love and Sex.* New York: Free Press.

Butterfield, Fox. 1999. "Drug Treatment in Prisons Dips as Use Rises, Study Reports." *New York Times,* January 7.

———. 2000. "Privately Run Juvenile Prison in Louisiana Is Attacked for Abuse of 6 Inmates." *New York Times,* March 16.

Calhoun, Craig. 1998. *Nationalism.* Minneapolis, MN: University of Minneapolis.

Cancian, Francesca, and Stacy J. Oliker. 2000. *Caring and Gender.* Thousand Oaks, CA: Pine Forge.

Capek, Mary Ellen. 1989. *A Woman's Thesaurus.* New York: Harper & Row.

Carlton-Ford, Steve and Paula V. Houston. 2001. "Children's Experience of Gender: Habitus and Field." In Dana Vannoy, Ed., *Gender Mosaics,* pp. 65–74. Los Angeles: Roxbury.

Caro, Robert. 1982. *The Years of Lyndon Johnson.* New York: Knopf.

Carrasquillo, Olveen, David U. Himmelstein, Steffie Woolhandler, and David Bor. 1999. "Going Bare: Trends in Health Insurance Coverage, 1989 to 1996." *American Journal of Public Health* 89: 36–42.

Carter, Kathy Barrett. 2000. "Jersey Must Pay Full Cost of Rebuilding Poor Schools." *Star Ledger,* May 26.

Carty, Win. 1999. "Greater Dependence on Cars Leads to More Pollution in World's Cities," *Population Today,* 27, December.

Catalyst. 2000. *1999 Census of Women Board Directors of Fortune 1000.* New York: Catalyst, February.

Centers for Disease Control, Department of Health and Human Services. 1998. Press Release. "Survey Shows Extent of Violence Against Women." November 17.

Centers for Disease Control. 2000. "Report on AIDS Among Black and Hispanic Men." Atlanta, GA: CDC, January.

Center for the Study of Women. 2000. *National Information Bank on Women in Public Office.* Eagleton Institute, Rutgers University.

Chafetz, Janet Salzman. 1990. *Gender Equity: An Integrated Theory.* Newbury Park: Sage.

———. 1999. *Handbook of the Sociology of Gender.* New York: Kluwer/Plenum.

Chaves, Mark. 1997. *Ordaining Women: Culture and Conflict in Religious Organizations.* Cambridge, MA: Harvard University Press.

Chaves, Mark, Mary Ellen Konieczny, Kraig Beyerlein, and Emily Barman. 1999. "The National Congregations Study: Background, Methods, and Selected Results." *Journal for the Scientific Study of Religion* 38: 458–476.

Cheney, George. 2000. *Values at Work: Employee Participation Meets Market Pressure at Mondragon.* Ithaca, NY: Cornell.

Chira, Susan. 1998. *A Mother's Place: Taking the Debate About Working Mothers Beyond Guilt and Blame.* New York: Harper Collins.

Clark, Terry Nichols, and Vincent Hoffman-Marinot, Eds. 1998. *The New Political Culture*. Boulder, CO: Westview.

Clausen, John A. 1993. *American Lives: Looking Back at the Children of the Great Depression*. New York: Free Press.

Clawson, Dan and Mary Ann Clawson. 2000. "What Has Happened to the U.S. Labor Movement? Union Decline and Renewal." *Annual Review of Sociology* 25: 95–119.

Clendinnen, Inga. 1999. *Reading the Holocaust*. New York: Cambridge University.

Cohen, Albert K. 1955. *Delinquent Boys*. New York: Free Press.

Cohn, Samuel. 1985. *The Process of Occupational Sex-Typing: The Feminization of Clerical Work in Great Britain*. Philadelphia: Temple University Press.

Cole, David. 1999. *No Equal Justice*. New York: The New Press.

Coleman, James S. 1992. "Rational Choice Theory." In Edgar F. Borgatta and Marie L. Borgatta, Eds., *Encyclopedia of Sociology*, pp. 1619–1624. New York: Macmillan.

Coleman, James William. 1998. *The Criminal Elite: Understanding White Collar Crime*. 4th Ed. New York: St. Martin's Press.

College Board. 1999. *Annual Survey of Colleges*. New York: College Board.

Collins, Patricia Hill. 1990. *Black Feminist Thought: Knowledge, Consciousness, and the Politics of Empowerment*. Boston: Unwin Hyman.

Coltrane, Scott. 1998. *Gender and Families*. Thousand Oaks, CA: Pine Forge.

Coltrane, Scott and Michele Adams. 2001. "Men, Women, and Housework." In Dana Vannoy, Ed., *Gender Mosaics*, pp.145–154. Los Angeles: Roxbury.

Comai, Giovanni Andrea and Sheldon Danziger. 1997. *Child Poverty and Deprivation in the Industrialized Countries, 1945–1995*. New York: Oxford.

Common Cause. 1999. "Fight to Eliminate Corporate Welfare." *1999 Issues Agenda*.

Connell, R. W. 2000. "Making Gendered People: Bodies, Identities, Sexualities." In Myrna Marx Ferree, Judith Lorber, and Beth B. Hess, Eds., *Revisioning Gender*. Newbury Park, CA: Sage.

Coontz, Stephanie. 1992. *The Way We Never Were: American Families and the Nostalgia Trap*. New York: Basic Books.

———. 1997. *The Way We Really Are*. New York: Basic Books

Cooley, Charles Horton. 1909. *Social Organization: A Study of the Larger Mind*. New York: Scribners.

Corsaro, William A. 1997. *The Sociology of Childhood*. Thousand Oaks, CA: Pine Forge.

Costa, Paul T., Jr., Alan B. Zonderman, Robert R. McGrae, Joan Cornoni-Huntley, Ben Z. Locke, and Helen E. Barbano. 1987. "Longitudinal Analysis of Psychological Well-Being in a National Sample: Stability of Mean Levels." *Journal of Gerontology* 42: 50–55.

Crosette, Barbara. 2000. "UNICEF Is Fighting Violence Against Women." *New York Times*, March 9.

Crowley, Thomas J. 2000. "Causes of Climate Change Over the Past 1000 Years." *Science* 289: 270–280.

Cummings, Scott. 1998. *Left Behind in Rosedale: Race Relations and the Collapse of Community Institutions*. Boulder, CO: Westview.

Cuneo, Michael W. 1999. *The Smoke of Satan: Conservative and Traditionalist Dissent in Contemporary American Catholicism*. New York: Oxford University Press.

Dash, Mike. 2000. *Tulipomania: The Story of the World's Most Coveted Flower and the Extraordinary Passions It Aroused*. New York: Crown.

Davis, James Allan and Tom W. Smith. 1996. *General Social Surveys, 1972–1997: Cumulative Codebook*. National Opinion Research Center.

Davis, Kingsley and Wilbert W. Moore. 1945. "Some Principles of Stratification." *American Sociological Review* 10, April: 242–247.

Davis, Maradee A., John M. Neuhaus, Deborah J. Moritz, and Mark R. Segal. 1991. "Living Arrangements and Survival Among Middle-Aged and Older Adults in the NHANES I Epidemiologic Follow-up Study." *American Journal of Public Health* 7.

Darroch, Jaqueline E. and Susheela Singh. 1999. "Why Is Teenage Pregnancy Declining? The Roles of Abstinence, Sexual Activity, and Contraceptive Use." *Occasional Report No. 1*. New York: Alan Guttmacher Institute, December.

Death Row USA. 2000. *Execution Update*. Death Penalty Information Center, April.

DeKeseredy, Walter S. and Martin D. Schwartz. 1998. *Woman Abuse on Campus: Results from the Canadian National Survey*. Thousand Oaks, CA: Sage.

D'Emilio, John and Estelle B. Freedman. 1997. *Intimate Matters: A History of Sexuality in America*. 2nd ed. Chicago: University of Chicago.

Denno, Deborah W. 1990. *Biology and Violence: Birth to Adulthood*. New York: Cambridge.

DeParle, Jason. 1999. "Project Rescue Needy Stumbles Against the Persistence of Poverty." *New York Times*, May 15.

Deutsch, Francine M. 1999. *Having It All: How Equally Shared Parenting Works*. Cambridge, MA: Harvard.

Diamond, Sara. 1998. *Not By Politics Alone: The Enduring Influence of the Christian Right*. New York: Guilford.

Dill, Bonnie Thornton. 1998. "Our Mothers' Grief: Racial–Ethnic Women and the Maintenance of Families." *Journal of Family History* 13: 415–431.

Dillon, Michele. 1999. *Catholic Identity: Balancing Reason, Earth, and Power*. Cambridge, England: Cambridge University.

DiMaggio, Paul. 1982. "Cultural Capital and School Success: The Impact of Status Culture Participation on the Grades of U.S. High School Students." *American Sociological Review* 47: 189–201.

Dobratz, Betty and Stephanie L. Shanks-Meile. 1997. *White Power, White Pride: The White Separatist Movement in the United States*. New York: Twayne.

Donahue, John J. and Steven D. Levitt. 2000. Study on relationship of Roe v. Wade to drop in crime 20 years later. *Population Today*. January.

Dohrenwend, Bruce P. 2000. "The Role of Adversity and Stress in Psychopathology: Some Evidence and Its Implications for Theory and Research." *Journal of Health and Social Behavior* 41: 1–19.

Domhoff, G. William. 1998. *Who Rules America? Power and Politics in Year 2000*. 3rd ed. Mountain View, CA: Mayfield.

Donnelly, Patrick G. and Theo J. Majka. 1998. "Residents' Efforts at Neighborhood Stabilization: Facing the Challenges of Inner–City Neighborhoods." *Sociological Forum* 13 (2).

Downey, Douglas B., Brian Powell, Lala Carr Steelman, and Shana Pribesh. 1999. "Much Ado About Siblings: Change Models, Sibship Size, and Intellectual Development." *American Sociological Review* 64: 193–198.

Downs, Stephen J. 2000. *Opportunities Lost: The Cost of the Digital Divide*. Eastern Sociological Society, March.

Dreeben, Robert. 1968. *On What Is Learned in School*. Reading, MA: Addison-Wesley.

Dreiling, Michael. 2000. "The Class Embeddedness of Corporate Political Action: Leadership in Defense of the NAFTA." *Social Problems* 47: 21–48.

Duany, Andres and Elizabeth Plater-Zyberk. 2000. *Suburban Nation: The Rise of Sprawl and the Decline of the American Dream*. New York: North Point Press.

Dun & Bradstreet.com. 1998. "Dun & Bradstreet Creating Database to Identifiy Minority and Women-owned Businesses." Press release 2/2.

Duncan, Greg J. 1994. "Welfare Can Fuel Upward Mobility." *ISR Newsletter* 18: 6. Ann Arbor, MI: University of Michigan.

Duncan, Greg J., Jeanne Brooks–Gunn, W. Jean Yeung, and Judith R. Smith. 1998. "How Much Does Childhood Poverty Affect the Life Chances of Children?" *American Sociological Review* 63: 406–423.

Durkheim, Emile. 1912/1961. *The Elementary Forms of the Religious Life*. New York: Collier Books.

Dworkin, Shari L. and Michael A. Messner. 1999. "Just Do What?" In Myra Marx Ferree, Judith Lorber, and Beth B. Hess, Eds., *Revisioning Gender*, pp. 341–363. Thousand Oaks, CA: Sage, 2000.

Eckberg, Douglas Lee. 1988. "The Physicians' Anti-Abortion Campaign and the Social Bases of Moral Reform Participation." *Social Forces* 67: 378–397.

Eckholm, Erik. 2000. "Chinese Farmers See a New Desert Erode Their Way of Life." *New York Times*, July 30.

Eder, Donna with Catherine Colleen Evans and Stephan Parker. 1995. *School Talk: Gender and Adolescent Culture*. New Brunswick, NJ: Rutgers, 1995.

Edin, Kathryn and Laura Lein. 1997. *Making Ends Meet: How Single Mothers Survive Welfare and Low-Wage Work*. New York: Russell Sage Foundation.

Educational Testing Service. 2000. *College Enrollments, 1995–2015*. Princeton, NJ: ETS, 2000.

Egan, Jennifer. 1999."Why a Priest." *New York Times Magazine*, April 4.

Egan, Timothy. 1999. "War on Crack Retreats, Still Taking Prisoners." *New York Times*, February 28.

——. 2000. "Mending a Trail of Broken Treaties." *New York Times*, June 25.

Ehrenhalt, Alan. 2000. "Suburbs With a Healthy Dose of Fantasy." *New York Times*, *Op-Ed*, July 9.

Ehrenreich, Barbara. 2000. "Warning: This is a Right-Free Workplace." *New York Times Magazine*, March 5: 88–92.

Eichenwald, Kurt and Gina Kolata. 1999a. "Drug Trials Hide Conflicts for Doctors." *New York Times*, May 16.

——. 1999b. "When Physicians Double as Entrepreneurs." *New York Times*, November 30.

Employee Benefit Research Institute. 2000. "EBRI Health Care Research: 2000 Findings." EBRI Online.

——. 1994b. "The Gender Gap in Math: Its Possible Origins in Neighborhood Effects." *American Sociological Review* 59: 822–838.

Erikson, Kai and Steven P. Vallas (Eds.). 1990. *The Nature of Work: Sociological Perspective*. New Haven, CT: Yale University Press.

Esping-Andersen, Gosta. 1990. *The Three Worlds of Welfare Capitalism*. Princeton, NJ: Princeton University.

Esterberg, Kristin G. 1997. *Lesbian and Bisexual Identities: Constructing Communities, Constructing Selves*. Philadelphia: Temple.

Evans, Peter. 2000. "Fighting Marginalization with Transnational Networks: Counter-Hegemonic Globalization." *Contemporary Sociology* 29: 230–242.

Farkas, George. 2000. "Teaching Low Income Children to Read at Grade Level." *Contemporary Sociology* 29: 53–62.

Farrell, Betty G. 1999. *Family: The Making of an Idea, an Institution, and a Controversy in American Culture*. Boulder, CO: Westview.

Fausto-Sterling, Anne. 2000. *Sexing the Body: Gender Politics and the Construction of Sexuality*. New York: Basic.

Feagin, Joe R. and Clairece Booker Feagin. 1994. *Social Problems: A Critical Power Conflict Approach*. 4th ed. Prentice Hall.

Ferber, Abby L.1998. *White Man Falling: Race, Gender, and White Supremacy*. Lanham, MD: Rowman and Littlefield.

Ferguson, Ronald F. 1998. "Teachers' Perceptions and Expectations and the Black-White Test Score Gap." In Christopher Jencks and Meredith Phillips, Eds., *The Black-White Test Score Gap*, pp. 273–317. Washington, DC: Brookings.

Ferree, Myra Marx. 2000. "Looking for Levers in the Policy Machinery Lessons from the Rest of the World." Paper presented at the Annual Meeting of the American Sociological Association, Washington, D.C., August.

Ferree, Myra Marx and Beth B. Hess. 2000. *Controversy and Coalition: The New Feminist Movement Across Four Decades of Change*. 3rd ed. New York: Routledge.

Ferree, Myra Marx and Mangala Subramaniam. 2001. "The International Women's Movement at Century's End." In Dana Vannoy, Ed., *Gender Mosaics*, pp. 496–506. Los Angeles, CA: Roxbury.

Festinger, Leon. 1957. *A Theory of Cognitive Dissonance*. Stanford, CA: Stanford.

Finckenauer, James O. 1999. *Scared Straight: The Panacea Phenomenon Revisited*. Prospect Heights, IL: Waveland.

Firestone, David. 1999. "Search for Efficiency Now Leaves Alabama Town Behind." *New York Times*, February 21.

Fishbein, Diana H. 1990. "Biological Perspectives in Criminology." *Criminology* 28: 27–72.

Fiske, Edward B. and Helen F. Ladd. 2000. *When Schools Compete: A Cautionary Tale*. Washington, D.C.: Brookings.

——. 2000b. "The Invisible Hand as Schoolmaster." *The American Prospect* Vol. 11, 13, May 22.

Fitzgerald, Frances. 2000. *Way Out There in the Blue: Reagan, Star Wars, and the End of the Cold War*. New York: Simon & Schuster.

Fligstein, Neil. 1990. *The Transformation of Corporate Control*. Cambridge, MA: Harvard University Press.

Fonow, Mary M., Laurel Richardson, and Virginia A. Wemmerus. 1992. "Feminist Rape Education: Does It Work?" *Gender & Society* 6: 108–121.

Fox, Mary Frank. 2001. "Women, Men, and Engineering." In Dana Vannoy, Ed., *Gender Mosaics*, pp. 249–257. Los Angeles: Roxbury.

Fox-Genovese, Elizabeth. 1996. *Feminism Is Not the Story of My Life*. New York: Basic.

France, Anatole. 1894/1917. *The Red Lily*. New York Modern Library.

Frank, Robert H. 1995. *The Winner-Take-All Society: How More and More Americans Compete for Ever Fewer and Bigger Prizes*. New York: Free Press.

——. 2000. *Luxury Fever*. Princeton, NJ: Princeton University Press.

Frankel, Max. 1999. "The Information Tyranny." *New York Times Magazine*, June 13: 28–30.

Franklin, Donna L. 1997. *Ensuring Inequality: The Structural Transformation of the African-American Family*. New York: Oxford.

Frantz, Douglas. 1997. "Scientology's Puzzling Journey from Tax Rebel to Tax Exempt." *New York Times*, March 9.

Freudenberg, William R. 1992. "Addictive Economics: Extractive Industries and Vulnerable Localities in a Changing World Economy." *Rural Sociology* 57(3): 305–332.

Friedman, Berhard, Ronald J. Ozminkowski, and Zachery Taylor. 1992. "Excess Demand and Patient Selection for Heart and Liver transplants." *Health Economics Worldwide:* 161–186.

Friedrich, David D. 1996. *Trusted Criminals: White Collar Crime in Contemporary Society*. Belmont, CA: Wadsworth.

Gagné, Patricia and Richard Tewksbury. 1998. "Conformity Pressures and Gender Resistance Among Transgendered Individuals." *Social Problems* 45: 81–99.

Galinsky, Ellen. 1999. *Ask the Children: What America's Children Really Think About Working Parents*. New York: William Morrow.

Gallup Organization. 2000. "Americans Dissatisfied with U.S. Education in General, but Parents Satisfied with The Kids' Schools." *Gallup News Service*. September 5.

Galston, William. 1998. "A Public Philosophy for the 21st Century." *The Responsive Community* 8: 18–36.

Gardner, Howard. 1999. *Intelligence Reframed: Multiple Intelligences for the 21st Century*. New York: Basic.

Garfinkel, Harold. 1967. *Studies in Ethnomethodology*. Englewood Cliffs, NJ: Prentice-Hall.

Garfinkel, Irwin, Sara S. McLanahan, Daniel R. Meyer, and Judith A. Selzer. 1998. *Fathers Under Fire: The Revolution in Child Support Enforcement*. New York: Russell Sage Foundation.

Garg, Pushkal P., Kevin Frick, Marie Diener-West, and Neil R. Powe. 1999. "Effect of Ownership of Dialysis Facilities on Patients' Survival and Referral for Transplant." *New England Journal of Medicine* 341: 1653–1660.

Garten, Jeffrey E. 1999. "Mega–Mergers, Mega–Influence." *New York Times Op-Ed*, October 26.

Gaudio, Rudolf. 1998. "Male Lesbians and Other Queer Notions in Hausa." In Stephen O. Murray and Will Roscoe, Eds., *Boy Wives and Female Husbands: Studies of African Homosexualities*. New York: St. Martin's.

Gelbard, Alene, Carl Haub, and Mary M. Kent 1999. "World Population Beyond Six Billion." *Population Bulletin* 54.

Gelles, Richard. 1997. *Intimate Family Violence*, 3rd ed. Thousand Oaks, CA: Sage.

General Accounting Office. 2000. "Medicaid: Matching Formula's Performance and Potential Modifications."

Geoghegan, Thomas. 1999. *The Secret Lives of Citizens: Pursuing the Promise of American Life*. New York: Pantheon.

Geronimus, A. T. and S. Korenman. 1993. "Maternal Youth or Family Background? On the Health Disadvantages of Infants With Teenage Mothers." *American Journal of Epidemiology* 137: 213–225.

Gerson, Kathleen. 2000. "Resolving Family Dilemmas and Conflicts: Beyond Utopia." *Contemporary Sociology* 29: 180–187.

Gilkes, Cheryl Townsend. 1985. "Together and in Harness: Women's Traditions in the Sanctified Church." *Signs* 10(4): 678–699.

Gilligan, Carol. 1982. *In a Different Voice: Psychological Theory and Women's Development*. Cambridge, MA: Harvard University Press.

Girshick, Lori B. 1999. *No Safe Haven: Stories of Women in Prison*. Boston, MA: Northeastern.

Gittell, Marilyn J. 1998. *Strategies for School Equity: Creating Productive Schools in a Just Society*. New Haven, CT: Yale.

Giuffre, Patti A. and Christine L. Williams. 1994. "Boundary Lines: Labeling Sexual Harassment in Restaurants." *Gender & Society* 8: 378–401.

Glasberg, Davita Silfen and Dan Skidmore. 1997. *Corporate Welfare Policy and the Welfare State: Bank Deregulation and the Savings and Loan Bailout*. New York: Aldine de Gruyter.

Glassner, Barry. 1999. *The Culture of Fear: Why Americans are Afraid of the Wrong Things*. New York: Basic.

Glazer, Penina Migdal and Myron Peretz Glazer. 1998. *The Environmental Crusaders: Confronting Disaster and Mobilizing Community*. University Park: Pennsylvania State University.

Glenn, Evelyn Nakano. 2000. "Creating a Caring Society." *Contemporary Sociology* 29: 84–88.

Goffman, Erving. 1959. *The Presentation of Self in Everyday Life*. Garden City, NY: Doubleday.

——. 1961. *Asylums*. Garden City, NY: Doubleday.

Goldberg, Carey. 1999. "Vermont High Court Backs Rights of Same-sex Couples." *New York Times*, December 21.

——. 2000. "After Dormitory Attacks, Boarding Schools Move to Reduce Risks." *New York Times*, June 17.

Goldhagen, Daniel Jonah. 1996. *Hitler's Willing Executioners: Ordinary Germans and the Holocaust*. London: Little Brown.

Goldscheider, Frances K. and Linda J. Waite. 1991. *New Families, No Families? The Transformation of the American Home*. Berkeley, CA: University of California Press.

Goode, William J. 1993. *World Changes in Divorce Patterns*. New Haven, CT: Yale University Press.

Gordon, Linda. 1999. *The Great Arizona Orphan Abduction*. Cambridge, MA: Harvard University Press.

Gornick, Janet C. and Jerry A. Jacobs. 1998. "Gender, the Welfare State, and Public Employment: A Comparative Study of Seven Industrialized Countries." *American Sociological Review* 63: 688–710.

Gotham, Kevin Fox. 1999. "Political Opportunity, a Community Identity, and the Emergence of a Local Anti–Expressway Movement." *Social Problems* 46: 332–354.

Gottfredson, Don M. 1999. "Effects of Judges' Sentencing Decisions on Criminal Careers." *Research in Brief*. Washington, DC: National Institute of Justice, November.

Gottfredson, Michael R. and Travis Hirschi. 1990. *A General Theory of Crime*. Palo Alto, CA: Stanford University Press.

Gottfried, Heidi. 1991. "Mechanisms of Control in the Temporary Help Service Industry." *Sociological Forum* 8:(1) 699–713.

Gottschalk, Peter and Sheldon Danziger. 1998. "Family Income Mobility: How Much Is There and Has It Changed?," In James A. Auerbach and Richard S. Belous, Eds., *The Inequality Paradox Growth of Income Disparity*, pp 92–111. Washington, DC: National Policy Association.

Goyette, Kimberly and Yu Xie. 1999. "Educational Expectations of Asian American Youths: Determinants and Ethnic Differences." *Sociology of Education* 72: 22–30.

Greene, John. 1999. *Debating Darwin*. Claremont, CA: Regina Books.

Greider, William. 1998. *Fortress America*. New York: Public Affairs.

Grimes, Michael D. 1991. *Class in Twentieth-Century American Sociology*. New York: Praeger.

Grimshaw, Allan D., Ed. 1992. "Special Issue: Needed Sociological Research on Issues of War and Peace." *Sociological Forum* 7(1).

Grob, Gerald N. 1991. *From Asylum to Community: Mental Health Policy in Modern America*. Princeton, NJ: Princeton University Press.

Groneman, Carol. 2000. *Nymphomania: A History*. New York: W.W. Norton.

Gubrium, Jaber F. and James A. Holstein. 1997. *The New Language of Qualitative Method*. New York: Oxford.

Guo, Guang, and Leah K. VanWey. 1999. "Sibship Size and Intellectual Development." *American Sociological Review* 64: 169–187.

Gurian, Michael. 1996. *The Wonder of Boys*. New York: Tarcher/Putnam.

Gustafsson, Bjorn and Mats Johansson. 1999. "In Search of Smoking Guns: What Makes Income Inequality Vary Over Time in Different Countries." *American Sociological Review* 64: 585–605.

Guth, James L., John C. Green, Corwin E. Smidt, Lyman A. Kellstedt, and Margaret M. Poloma. 1997. *The Bully Pulpit: The Politics of Protestant Clergy*. Lawrence: University Press of Kansas.

Gutmann, Stephanie. 2000. *The Kinder, Gentler Military: Can American's Gender-Neutral Fighting Force Still Win Wars?* New York: Scribner's.

Guttmacher Institute. 2000. "Publicly Funded Clinics Provide One-Quarter of All Family Planning Services in United States." *www.agi-usa.org.* October.

Haaga, John. 2000."High Death Rate Among Russian Men Predates Soviet Union's Demise." *Population Bulletin* 28, April.

Hadaway, C. Kirk, Penny Long Marler, and Mark Chaves. 1998. "Overreporting Church Attendance in America: Evidence That Demands the Same Verdict." *American Sociological Review* 63: 122–130.

Hagan, John and Holly Foster. 2000. "Making Corporate and Criminal America Less Violent: Public Norms and Structural Reforms." *Contemporary Sociology* 29: 44–53.

Hall, Deana. 1998. "Managing to Recruit: Religious Conversion in the Workplace." *Sociology of Religion* 59: 393–402.

❖ ❖ ❖ ❖   Hammond, Philip E. 1992. *Religion and Personal Autonomy: The Third Disestablish-ment in America.* Columbia, SC: University of South Carolina.

Hanley, Robert. 1999. "To Authorities, 'Gifting' Is Just a Pyramid Scheme." *New York Times,* June 23.

Hanson, Thomas L., Sara S. McLanahan, and Elizabeth Thomson. 1998. "Windows on Divorce: Before and After." *Social Science Research* 27:329–49.

Hardin, Garrett. 1968. "The Tragedy of the Commons." *Science* 162: 1243–1248.20.

Hardisty, Jean. 1999. *Mobilizing Resentment.* Boston, MA: Beacon.

Harris, David R. 1999a. " 'Property Values Drop When Blacks Move In, Because . . .' Racial and Socioeconomic Determinants of Neighborhood Desirability." *American Sociological Review* 64: 461–479.

——. 1999b. "Driving While Black: Racial Profiling on Our Nation's Highways." *American Civil Liberties Union Special Report.* June.

Harris, Judith Rich. 1998. *The Nurture Assumption: Why Children Turn Out the Way They Do.* New York: Free Press.

Hartocollis, Anemona. 1999. "Private Schools Fare Little Better on New York 4th Grade Tests." *New York Times*, July 1.

Hauser, Robert. 1999. "High Stakes: Testing for Tracking, Promotion and Gradua-tion." Washington. DC: National Academy of Sciences.

Hays, Constance L. 1999. "Channel One's Mixed Grades in Schools." *New York Times*, December 5.

Health Care Financing Administration. 2000. *National Health Expenditures: 1960–1998.*

Heiss, Jerold. 1996. "Effects of African American Family Structure on School Atti-tudes and Performance." *Social Problems* 43: 246–261.

Held, David, Anthony McGrew, David Goldblatt, and Jonathan Perraton. 1999. *Global Transformations: Politics, Economics, and Culture.* Stanford, CA: Stan-ford University.

Hennelly, Robert. 1999. "Arresting Behavior." *New Jersey Monthly,* April 59–139.

Henshaw, Stanley K. 1998. "Unintended Pregnancy in the United States." *Family Planning Perspectives* 30: 24–29.

Herbert, Melissa S. 1998. *Camouflage Isn't Only for Combat: Gender, Sexuality, and Women in the Military.* New York: New York University.

Herdt, Gilbert. 1997. *Sexual Cultures and Migration in the Era of AIDS: Anthropologi-cal and Demographic Perspectives.* Oxford: Clarendon Press.

Hernandez, Raymond. 2000. "Federal Welfare Overhaul Allows Albany to Shift Money Elsewhere." *New York Times*, April 23.

Herrnstein, Richard J. and Charles Murray. 1996. *The Bell Curve: The Reshaping of American Life by Differences in Intelligence.* New York: Free Press.

Herszenhorn, David M. 2000. "Now It's 'Nothing in My Backyard.' " *New York Times,* Op-Ed, April 16.

Higginbotham, Evelyn Brooks. 1993. *Righteous Discontent: The Women's Movement in the Black Baptist Church, 1880–1920.* Cambridge, MA: Harvard University Press.

Hilts, Philip. 1996. "U.S. To Settle for $4.5 Million in Suits on Radiation Testing." *New York Times,* November 20.

Himmelstein, David U., Steffie Woolhandler, Ida Hellander, and Sidney M. Wolfe. 1999. "Quality of Care in Investor-owned vs. Not-for-profit HMOs." *Journal of the American Medical Association* 282: 159–163.

Hirsch, Barry T. and David A. Macpherson. 1998. *Union Membership and Earnings Data Book.* Washington, DC: Bureau of National Affairs.

Hitchcock, Jeff. 2000. *Unraveling the White Cocoon.* Kendall/Hunt Publishing Com-pany.

Hochschild, Arlie Russell. 1983. *The Managed Heart: Commercialization of Human Feelings.* Berkeley: University of California Press.

——. 1997. *The Time Bind: When Work Becomes Home and Home Becomes Work.* New York: Metropolitan/Holt.

——. 2000. "Importing Motherhood," *The American Prospect*, January: 32–36.

Hofferth, Sandra L. and Zita Jankuniene. 2000. "Children's After School Activities." Paper presented at the Biennial Meeting of the Society for Research on Adolescence, Chicago, IL. April.

Holmes, Steven A. 1999. "Survey Finds Race–Relations Gap in Armed Services Despite Gains." *New York Times*, November 23.

Horton, Hayward Derrick, Beverly Lundy Allen, Cedric Herring, and Melvin E. Thomas. 2000. "Lost in the Storm: The Sociology of the Black Working Class, 1850–1900." *American Sociological Review* 65: 128–137.

Howard, G., R. T. Anderson, G. Russell, V. J. Howard, and G. L. Burke. 2000. "Race, Socioeconomic Status, and Cause-specific Mortality." *Annals of Epidemiology*: 214–223.

Howard, Judith A. and Ramira M. Alamilla. 2001. "Gender and Identity." In Dana Vannoy, Ed., *Gender Mosaics*, pp. 54–64. Los Angeles: Roxbury.

Hughes, Michael and Melvin E. Thomas. 1998. "The Continuing Significance of Race Revisited: A Study of Race, Class, and the Quality of Life in America, 1972–1996." *American Sociological Review* 63: 785–795.

Human Rights Watch. 2000. *Punishment and Prejudice: Racial Disparities in the War on Drugs*. Washington, DC: Human Rights Watch, June.

Hunt, Geoffrey, Stephanie Riegel, Tomas Morales, and Dan Waldorf. 1993. "Changes in Prison Culture: Prison Gangs and the Case of the 'Pepsi Generation.'" *Social Problems* 40: 398–409.

Hunter, James Davison. 1991. *Culture Wars*. New York: Basic.

——. 1994. *Before the Shooting Begins*. New York: Free Press.

Hurwitz, Roger. 1999. "Who Needs Politics? Who Needs People? The Ironies of Democracy in Cyberspace." *Contemporary Sociology* 28.

Ignatiev, Noel. 1996. *How the Irish Became White*. New York: Routledge.

Inglehart, Ronald and Wayne E. Baker. 2000. "Modernization, Cultural Change, and the Persistence of Traditional Values." *American Sociological Review* 65: 19–51.

Jamison, Andrew and Ron Eyerman. 1994. *Seeds of the Sixties*. Berkeley: University of California.

Janofsky, Michael. 1999a. "West Virginia Pares Welfare, but Poor Remain." New York Times, March 7.

——. 1999b. "2 Groups Fight Nuclear Incinerator Project Near Yellowstone" *New York Times*, September 17.

Jencks, Christopher and Meredith Phillips. 1998. "The Black-White Test Score Gap: An Introduction." In Christopher Jencks and Meredith Phillips, Eds., *The Black-White Test Score Gap*, pp. 1–55. Washington, DC: Brookings, 1998.

Jencks, Christopher and Joseph Swingle. 2000. "Without a Net: Whom the New Welfare Law Helps and Hurts." *The American Prospect* 4, January: 200–208.

Jenness, Valerie and Ryken Grattet. 2000. *Building the Hate Crime Policy Domain: From Social Movement Concept to Law Enforcement Practice*. Santa Monica, CA: Rand.

Johnson, Alan G. 1997. *The Gender Knot: Unraveling Our Patriarchal Legacy*. Philadelphia, PA: Temple.

Johnson, Dirk. 2000a. "Schools Seeking to Skirt Rules That Bar Ten Commandments." *New York Times*, February 27.

——. 2000b. "Wisconsin Again Leads U.S. in Adult Drinking." *New York Times*, April 25.

Johnson, Kenneth M. 1999. "The Rural Rebound." *Population Reference Bureau, Reports on America* 1 (3), September.

Johnson, Nicholas, Christina Smith Fitzpatrick, and Elizabeth McNichols. 1999. *State Income Tax Burdens on Low Income Families in 1998*. Washington, DC: Center on Budget and Policy Priorities.

Jolly, Alison. 1999. *Lucy's Legacy: Sex and Intelligence in Human Evolution*. Cambridge, MA: Harvard.

Kagan, Jerome. 2000. *Three Seductive Ideas*. New York: Oxford Press.

Kalleberg, Arne, Barbara F. Reskin, and Ken Hudsin. 2000. "Bad Jobs in America: Standard and Nonstandard Employment Relations and Job Quality in the United States." *American Sociological Review* 65: 256–278.

Kamienkowski, Tamar and Mychal Rosenblaum. 2001. "Gender and Biblical Studies," In Dana Vannoy, Ed., *Gender Mosaics*, pp. 397–405. Los Angeles: Roxbury.

Kane, Thomas J. 1998. "Racial and Ethnic Preferences in College Admissions." From Jencks, Christopher, and Meredith Phillips, Eds., *The Black-White Test Score Gap*. Washington, DC: Brookings.

Kaplan, Robert D. 2000. *The Coming Anarchy: Shattering the Dreams of the Post Cold War.* New York: Random House.

Karen, David. 1991. " 'Achievement' and 'Ascription' in Admission to an Elite College: A Political-Organizational Analysis." *Sociological Forum* 6: 349–380.

Kasinitz, Philip and Jan Rosenberg. 1996. "Missing the Connection: Social Isolation and Employment on the Brooklyn Waterfront." *Social Problems*, 43 (2).

Katz Rothman, Barbara, 1999. "Now You Can Choose! Issues in Parenting and Procreation." In Myra Marx Ferree, Judith Lorber, and Beth B. Hess, Eds., *Revisioning Gender*, pp. 399–415. Thousand Oaks, CA: Sage.

Kaufman, Leslie. 2000. "The Dot–Com World Opens New Opportunities for Women to Lead." *New York Times*, March 9.

Kaufman, Michael T. 1999. "Bessie Cohen, 107, Survivor of 1911 Shirtwaist Fire, Dies." *New York Times*, February 24.

Kelley, Jonathan and M. D. R. Evans. 1993. "The Legitimation of Inequality: Occupational Earnings in Nine Countries." *American Journal of Sociology* 99: 75–125.

Kelley, Tina. 1999. "Being Exclusive Draws Big Crowds." *New York Times*, October 15.

Kendall. 1998. " 'When a Woman Loves a Woman' in Lesotho: Love, Sex, and the (Western) Construction of Homophobia." In Stephen O. Murray and Will Roscoe, Eds., *Boy Wives and Female Husbands: Studies of African Homosexualities.* New York: St. Martin's.

Kennedy, Randall. 1998. *Race, Crime, and the Law.* New York: Random House.

Kent, Mary Mederios. 1999. "Shrinking Societies Favor Procreation." *Population Today*, December.

Kessler, Ronald, Katherine McGonagle, Shanyang Zhao, Christoher Nelson, Michael Hughes, Susan Ehsleman, Hans-Ulrich Wittchen, and Kenneth Kendler. 1994. "Lifetime and 12-month Prevalence of DSM-III-R Psychiatric Disorders in the United States." *Archives of General Psychiatry* 51: 8–19.

Kessler, Suzanne J. 1998. *Lessons from the Intersexed.* New Brunswick, NJ: Rutgers.

Keynes, John Maynard. 1923. *A Tract on Monetary Reform.* London: Macmillan.

Kilborn, Peter T. 1999. "Tennessee Talks of Baring Plan for 'Uninsurables'." *New York Times*, May 1.

——. 2000. "Learning at Home, Students Take the Lead." *New York Times*, May 24.

Kimmel, Michael. 1994. *Manhood: The American Quest.* New York: Harper Collins.

——. 1996. *Manhood in America: A Cultural History.* New York: Free Press.

——. 2000a. *The Gendered Society.* New York: Oxford.

——. 2000b. "Saving the Males: The Sociological Implications of the Virginia Military Institute and the Citadel." *Gender & Society* 14: 494–516.

——. 2000c. "The Struggle for Men's Souls." In Michael Kimmel and Michael Messner, Eds., *Men's Lives*. Boston: Allyn & Bacon.

Kimmel, Michael S. and Michael A. Messner. 1998. *Men's Lives*. 4th Ed. Needham Heights, MA: Allyn and Bacon.

Kincheloe, Joe L., Shirley R. Steinberg, Nelson M. Rodriguez, and Ronald E. Chennault, Eds. 2000. *White Reign: Deploying Whiteness in America*. New York: St. Martin's Press.

Kindlon, Dan, and Michael Thompson. 1999. *Raising Cain: Protecting the Emotional Life of Boys.* New York: Balantine Books.

Kingery, Paul M., Mark B. Coggeshall, and Aaron A. Alford. 1999. *Weapon Carrying By Youth: Risk Factors and Prevention.* Thousand Oaks, CA: Sage.

Kinsey, Alfred C., Wardell Pomeroy, and Clyde Martin. 1948. *Sexual Behavior in the Human Male*. Philadelphia: Saunders.

——. 1953. *Sexual Behavior in the Human Female*. Philadelphia: Saunders.

Kivel, Paul. 1999. *Boys Will Be Men*. Gabriola Island, B.C., Canada.

Kivisto, Peter and Georganne Runblad. 2000. *Multiculturalism in the United States*. Thousand Oaks, CA: Pine Forge.

Klaff, Vivian Z. 1998. "Broken Down by Age and Sex: Projecting the Jewish Population." *Contemporary Jewry* 19: 1–37.

Kleck, Gary and Michael Hogan. 1999. "National Case-Control Study of Homicide Offending and Gun Ownership." *Social Problems* 46: 275–293.

Klein, Richard G. 1999. *The Human Career: Human Biological and Cultural Origins*. Chicago: University of Chicago Press.

Kluegel, James R. and Lawrence Bobo. 1994. "Dimensions of Whites' Beliefs About the Black-White Socioeconomic Gap." In P.M. Sneiderman, P. Tetlock, and E. Carmines, Eds., *Race and Politics in American Society*. Palo Alto, CA: Stanford University Press.

Knox, Virginia, Cynthia Miller, and Lisa A. Gennetian. 2000. *Reforming Welfare and Rewarding Work: A Summary of the Final Report on the Minnesota Family Investment Program*. Manpower Demonstration Research Corporation.

Kohlberg, Lawrence. 1981. *The Philosophy of Moral Development*, Vol. 1. New York: Harper & Row.

Kohn, Alfie. 1999. *The Schools Our Children Deserve: Moving Beyond Traditional Classrooms and Tougher Standards*. Boston: Houghton-Mifflin.

Kohn, Melvin and Kazimierz M. Slomczyski. 1990. *Social Structure and Self Direction: A Comparative Analysis of the United States and Poland*. Cambridge, MA: Blackwell.

Kohn, Richard H. and Peter D. Feaver. 1999. "The Gap Between Military and Civilian Society." Paper presented at Research Triangle Park, Durham, NC, December.

Kolata, Gina. 1999. "$50,000 Offered to Tall, Smart Egg Donor." *New York Times*, March 3, 1999.

Korenman, Sanders and Christopher Winship. 2000. "A Reanalysis of 'The Bell Curve': Intelligence, Family Background, and Schooling." In Kenneth Arrow, Samuel Bowles, and Steven Durlauf, Eds., *Meritocracy and Economic Inequality*. Princeton, NJ: Princeton University.

Korgen, Kathleen. 1998. *From Black to Biracial: Transforming Racial Identity Among Americans*. Westport, CT: Praeger.

Kramer, Laura. 2001. *The Sociology of Gender*. Los Angeles: Roxbury.

Kreiger, Nancy. 1987. "Shades of Difference: Theoretical Underpinnings of the Medical Controversy on Black/White Differences in the United States, 1830–187." *International Journal of Health Services* 17: 259–278.

Kreuger, Alan B. and Stacy Dale. 2000. "Estimating the Payoff to Attending a More Selective College." Philadelphia: Andrew W. Mellon Foundation.

Krivo, Lauren J., Ruth D. Peterson, Helen Rizzo, and John R. Reynolds. 1998. "Race, Segregation, and the Concentration of Disadvantage: 1980–1990." *Social Problems* 45 (1).

Krugman, Paul. 1999. "Death and Taxes." *New York Times*, April 13.

Kuletz, Valerie L. 1998. *The Tainted Desert: Environmental and Social Ruin in the American West*. New York: Routledge.

Kulick, Don. 1998. *Travesti: Sex, Gender, and Culture among Brazilian Transgendered Prostitutes*. Chicago: University of Chicago, 1998.

Kurz, Demie. 2001. "Violence Against Women by Intimate Partners." In Dana Vannoy, Ed., *Gender Mosaics*, pp. 205–215. Los Angeles: Roxbury.

Kutchins, Herb, and Stuart A. Kirk. 1997. *Making Us Crazy: DSM: The Psychiatric Bible and the Creation of Mental Disorders*. New York: Free Press.

Lamberth, John. 1999. Cited in "Driving While Black: Racial Profiling on Our Nation's Highways," written by David Harris. June. Published by American Civil Liberties Union, New York.

Lang, Sabine. 1998. *Men as Women: Women as Men: Changing Gender in Native American Cultures*. Austin, TX: University of Texas.

Lareau, Annette. 1989. "Social Class Differences in Family–School relationships: The Importance of Cultural Capital." *Sociology of Education* 60: 73–85.

Laumann, Edward O., John H. Gagnon, Robert T. Michael, and Stuart Michaels. 1994. *The Social Organization of Sexuality: Sexual Practices in the United States*. Chicago, IL: University of Chicago.

LeBon, Gustave. 1895/1960. *The Crowd: A Study of the Popular Mind*. New York: Viking.

Lee, Sharon M. 1998. "Asian Americans: Diverse and Growing." *Population Bulletin* 53. June.

Lefkowitz, Bernard. 1998. *Our Guys: The Glen Ridge Rape and the Secret Life of the Perfect Suburb*. New York: Vintage.

Leland, John. 2000. "Shades of Gay." *Newsweek*. March 20.

Lembcke, Jerry. 1998. *The Spitting Image: Myth, Memory, and the Legacy of Vietnam*. New York: New York University.

Lemert, Charles. 1972. *Human Deviance, Social Problems, and Social Control*. 2nd ed. Englewood Cliffs, NJ. Prentice-Hall.

——. 1997. *Postmodernism Is Not What You Think*. Oxford & Malden, MA: Blackwell.

Lenski, Gerhard and Jean Lenski. 1991. *Human Societies*. 6th Ed. New York: McGraw-Hill.

Leonhardt, David. 2000. "As Prison Labor Grows, So Does the Debate." *New York Times*, March 19.

Lepowsky, Alexandra. 1993. *Fruit of the Motherland: Gender in an Egalitarian Society*. New York: Columbia University Press.

Levine, Suzanne Braun. 2000. *Father Courage: What Happens When Men Put Family First*. New York: Harcourt.

Liebman, James S., Jeffrey Fagan, and Valerie West. 2000. *A Broken System: Error Rates in Capital Cases*. New York: Columbia.

Light, Donald W. 2000. "Fostering a Justice-based Health Care System." *Contemporary Sociology* 29: 62–74.

Link, Bruce G., Jo C. Phelan, Michaeline Bresnahan, Ann Steuve, and Bernice Pescosolido. 1999. "Public Conceptions of Mental Illness: Labels, Causes, Dangerousness, and Social Distance." *American Journal of Public Health* 89: 1328–1333.

Liska, Allen E., Ed. 1992. *Social Threat and Social Control*. Albany, NY: State University of New York.

Liska, Allen E., John R. Logan, and Paul E. Bellair. 1998. "Race and Violent Crime in the Suburbs." *American Sociological Review* 63: 27–38.

Liska, Allen E., and Jiang Yu. 1992. "Specifying and Testing the Threat Hypothesis: Police Use of Deadly Force.". In Allen E. Liska, Ed., *Social Threat and Social Control*. Albany, NY: State University of New York.

Little, Craig B. and Andrea Rankin. 1998. *Why Do They Start It? Explaining Reported Early Teen Sexual Activity*. Eastern Sociological Society Annual Meeting, Philadelphia.

Livingstone, D. W. 1998. *The Education-Jobs Gap: Underemployment or Economic Democracy*. Boulder, CO: Westview Press.

Lo, Clarence T. H. and Michael Schwartz, Eds. 1998. *Social Policy and the Conservative Agenda*. Malden, MA: Blackwell.

Longshore, Douglas. 1998. "A Self-Control and Criminal Opportunity: A Prospective Test of the General Theory of Crime." *Social Problems* 45: 102–113.

Lorber, Judith. 1994. *Paradoxes of Gender*. New Haven, CT: Yale University Press.

——. 1997. *Gender and the Social Construction of Illness*. Thousand Oaks, CA: Sage.

——. 2001. "Hierarchies in the Health Professions." In Dana Vannoy, Ed., *Gender Mosaics*, pp. 436–447. Los Angeles: Roxbury.

Lorber, Judith and Susan A. Farrell. 1991. *The Social Construction of Gender*. Newbury Park, CA: Sage.

Lott, John R., Jr. 1998. *More Guns, Less Crime: Understanding Crime and Gun Control Laws*. Chicago: University of Chicago.

Luebke, Paul. 1998. *Tar Heel Politics 2000*. Chapel Hill: University of North Carolina.

Luker, Christian. 1994. "Dubious Conceptions: The Controversy Over Teen Pregnancy." In A. S. Skolnick and J. H. Skolnick, Eds. *Family in Transition*. 8th Ed. New York: Harper Collins.

Maccoby, Eleanor E. 1998. *The Two Sexes: Growing Up Apart, Coming Together*. Cambridge, MA: Harvard.

Majors, Richard and Janet Mancini Bilson. 1992. *Cool Pose: The Dilemmas of Black Manhood in America*. New York: Lexington.

Mangold, Catherine. 2000. *In Glory's Shadow: Shannon Faulkner, the Citadel and a Changing America*. New York: Knopf.

Manley, Joan E. 2000. "Negotiating Quality: Total Quality Management and the Complexities of Transforming Professional Organizations." *Sociological Forum* 15: 457–484.

Mannon, James M. 1997. *Measuring Up: The Performance Ethic in American Culture*. Boulder, CO: Westview Press.

Marcus, Eric. 1992. *Making History: The Struggle for Gay and Lesbian Equal Rights*. New York: Harper Collins.

Margolin, Leslie. 1993. "Goodness Personified: The Emergence of Gifted Children." *Social Problems* 40: 510–532.

Marks, Gary and Larry Diamond. Eds. 1992. *Reexamining Democracy Essays in Honor of Seymour Martin Lipset*. Newbury Park, CA: Sage.

Marks, Jonathan. 1995. *Human Biodiversity: Genes, Race, and History*. New York: Aldine de Gruyter.

——. 2000. "A Feckless Quest for the Basketball Gene." *New York Times, Op–Ed*, May 8.

Marmot, Michael, and Martin J. Shipley. 1996. *The Whitehall Study*. London: University College.

Marshall, John. 1819. www.tax.org/quotes/quotation from *McCullock vs. Maryland*, March 6.

Martin, Patricia Yancy and David L. Collinson. 1999. "Gender and Sexuality in Organizations." In Myra Marx Ferree, Judith Lorber, and Beth B. Hess, Eds., *Revisioning Gender*, pp. 285–310. Thousand Oaks, CA: Sage.

Martin, Philip and Elizabeth Midgely. 1999. "Immigration to the United States." *Population Bulletin* 54, June.

Martin, Philip and Jonas Widgren. 1996. "International Migration: A Global Challenge." *Population Bulletin* 51.

Martorella, Rosanne. 1996. *Art and Business: An International Perspective on Sponsorship*. Westport, CT: Praeger.

Marty, Martin E. and R. Scott Appleby. Eds. 1993. *Fundamentalism and the State*. Chicago: University of Chicago Press.

Marx, Gary. 1986. "The Iron Fist and the Velvet Glove: Totalitarian Potentials Within Democratic Structures." In James E. Short, Jr., Ed., *The Social Fabric: Dimensions and Issues*, pp. 135–162. Newbury Park, CA: Sage.

Massey, Douglas. 2000. "Housing Discrimination 101." *Population Today* 28 (6) August/September:4.

Massey, Douglas S. and Nancy A. Denton. 1993. *American Apartheid: Segregation and the Making of the Underclass*. Cambridge, MA: Harvard.

Massing, Michael. 1998. *The Fix*. New York: Simon & Schuster.

Maume, David J., Jr. 2001. "Work-Family Conflict: Effects for Job Segregation and Career Perceptions." In Dana Vannoy, Ed., *Gender Mosaics*, pp. 240–248. Los Angeles: Roxbury.

Mazur, Allan, Alan Booth, and James P. Dabbs, Jr. 1992. "Testosterone and Chess Competition." *Social Psychology* Quarterly 55: 70–77.

McCammon, Holly J. 1993. "From Representative Intervention to Integrative Prevention: The U.S. State's Legal Management of Labor Militancy, 1881–1978." *Social Forces* 71: 569–601.

McClain, Dylan Loeb. 2000. "Many Are Called, and More Than a Few Are Women." *New York Times*, April 19.

McCloskey, Deirdre N. 1999. *Crossing: A Memoir*. Chicago: University of Chicago.

McCord, Joan. 1997. *Violence and Childhood in the Inner City*. New York: Cambridge.

McLanahan, Sara and Gary Sandefur. 1994. *Growing Up With a Single Parent*. Cambridge, MA: Harvard.

McNeal, Ralph B. 1999. "Parental Involvement as Social Capital: Differential Effectiveness on Science Achievement, Truancy, and Dropping Out." *Social Forces* 78: 117–130.

Mead, George Herbert. 1934. *Mind, Self and Society*. Chicago: University of Chicago.

Melosh, Barbara. 1982. *'The Physician's Hand': Work Culture and Conflict in American Nursing*. Philadelphia, PA: Temple University.

Merton, Robert K. 1957. "The Self-Fulfilling Prophecy." In Robert K. Merton, *Social Theory and Social Structure*, pp. 421–438. New York: Free Press.

——. 1968. "Manifest and Latent Functions." In *Social Theory and Structure* (Rev. Ed.). New York: Free Press.

Messner, Michael A. 1997. *Politics of Masculinities: Men in Movements*, p. 24–25. Newbury Park, CA: Sage Publications.

Michels, Robert. 1911/1962. *Political Parties*. Translated by Eden and Cedar Paul. New York: Collier.

Milkman, Ruth. 1997. *Farewell to the Factory: Auto Workers in the Late Twentieth Century*. Berkeley, CA: University of California.

Miller, Mathew. 1999. "$140,000 and a Bargain." *New York Times*, June 13.

Miller, Susan L. 1997. *Crime Control and Women: Feminist Implications of Criminal Justice Policy*. Thousand Oaks, CA: Sage.

Mirowsky, John and Catherine E. Ross. 1992. "Age and Depression." *Journal of Health and Social Behavior* 30: 187–205.

Moghadam, Valentine. 1999. "Gender and the Global Economy." In Myra Marx Ferree, Judith Lorber, and Beth B. Hess, Eds., *Revisioning Gender*, pp.128–160. Thousand Oaks, CA: Sage.

Mohler, R. Albert, Jr. 2000. "Against an Immoral Tide." *New York Times Op-Ed*, June 19.

Morgan, Kathryn. 1999. "Factors Associated with Probation Outcomes." *Journal of Criminal Justice* 22: 341–353.

Morgan, Stephen L. and Aage B. Sorensen. 1999. "Parental Networks, Social Closure, and Mathematics Learning: A Test of Coleman's Social Capital Explanation of School Effects." *American Sociological Review* 64: 661–681.

Morris, Aldon D. 1984. *The Origins of the Civil Rights Movement: Black Community Organizing for Change*. New York: Free Press.

——. 1993. "Birmingham Confrontation Reconsidered: An Analysis of the Dynamics and Tactics of Mobilization." *American Sociological Review* 58: 621–636.

Morrison, Donna Ruane and Amy Rituolo. 2000. "Routes to Children's Economic Recovery After Divorce: Are Cohabitation and Remarriage Equivalent?" *American Sociological Review* 65: 560–580.

Moskos, Charles C. and John Sibley Butler. 1997. *All That We Can Be*. New York: Basic.

Murray, Stephen O. and Will Roscoe. 1998. *Boy Wives and Female Husbands: Studies of African Homosexualities*. New York: St. Martin's.

Myers, Steven Lee. 2000a. "Survey of Troops Finds Antigay Bias Common in Service." *New York Times*, March 25.

——. 2000b. "Global Arms Sales Swell to $30 Billion." *New York Times*, August 21.

Myerson, Debra E. and Joyce K. Fletcher. 2000. "A Modest Manifesto for Shattering the Glass Ceiling." *Harvard Business Review*. January/February.

Nanda, Serena. 2000. *Gender Diversity: Cross Cultural Variations*. Prospect Heights, IL: Waveland.

Nasar, Sylvia, and Kirsten B. Mitchell. 1999. "Booming Job Market Draws Young Black Men Into Fold." *New York Times*, May 23.

Nathan, Debbie, and Michael Snedeker. 1995. *Ritual Abuse: The Making of a Modern Witch Hunt*. New York: Basic.

National Academy of Sciences. 1999. *To Err is Human: Building a Safer Health System*. Washington, DC: National Academy News.

National Center for Educational Statistics. 1999. *Digest of Educational Statistics 1998*. May.

National Center for Health Statistics. 2000. "Health Insurance Coverage," NCHS FASTATS, Online, August.

——. 1999. "U.S. Pregnancy Rate Lowest in Two Decades." Washington, DC: Centers for Disease Control, December 15.

National Public Radio. 2000. "The Digital Divide." *Morning Edition*, March 1.

Nesbitt, Paula D. 1997. *Feminization of the Clergy in America: Occupational and Organizational Perspectives*. New York: Oxford University Press.

Nesbitt, Paula, Jeannette Baust, and Emma Baily. 2001. "Women's Status in the Christian Church." In Dana Vannoy, Ed., *Gender Mosaics*, pp. 386–396. Los Angeles: Roxbury.

New American Wellness Group. 1996. *Survey of Health Care Systems*. Atlanta, GA: NAWG.

New York Times. 1998a. "Texas Agency Denies Permit For Waste Site." October 22.

——. 1998b. "Viagra Is a $50 Million Pentagon Budget Item." November 4.

——. 1998c. "A Look at Voting Patterns of 115 Demographic Groups in House Races." November 11.

——. 1999a. "Plan to Build Nuclear Dump In the Mojave Appears Dead." April 4.

——. 1999b. "Canada Court Overturns Definition of 'Spouse' as Heterosexual." May 21.

——. 1999c. "Officials Say Dumping Ban Could Destroy Coal Mining." October 24.

——. 2000a. "Czech Women Take Chisel to Stone Wall of Male Government." February 27.

——. 2000b. "Conclusion on Survey of Gays in Military." March 25.

——. 2000c. "Panel Backs Alternative To Viagra, Despite Side Effects." April 11.

——. 2000d. "36 Percent of Female Inmates Say They Were Abused as Children." April 12.

Nicklin, Julie L. 2000. "Arrests at Colleges Surge for Alcohol and Drug Violations." *Chronicle of Higher Education*, June 9.

Nie, Norman and Associates. *Study on Internet Use*. Washington, DC: Pew Internet and American Life Project.

Nisbett, Richard E. 1998. "Race, Genetics, and IQ." In Christopher Jencks and Meredith Phillips, Eds., *The Black-White Test Score Gap*, pp. 86–102. Washington, DC: Brookings.

Noble, Charles. 1997. *Welfare As We Knew It: A Political History of the American Welfare State*. New York: Oxford.

Noble, Holcomb B. 1998. "Struggling to Bolster Minorities in Medicine." *New York Times*, September 28.

Nock, Steven L. *Marriage in Men's Lives*. New York: Oxford, 1998.

Noll, Roger G. and Andrew Zimbalist, Eds. 1997. *Sports, Jobs, and Taxes: The Economic Impact of Sports Teams and Stadiums*. Washington, DC: Brookings.

NTIA (National Telecommunications and Information Administration). 1999. "American in the Information Age: Falling Through the Cracks." www.ntia.doc.gov/ntiahome/digitaldivide/.

Nussbaum, Debra. 2000. "Home School Graduates Jittery About College at First Are Doing Well Academically." *New York Times*, May 21.

Nussbaum, Emily. 1999. "The Sex That Dare Not Speak Its Name." *Lingua Franca*, May/June.

Nyberg, Kenneth L, J. Daniel McMillin, Nora O'Neil–Rood, and Jane M. Florence. 1997. "Ethnic Differences in Academic Retracking: A Four-Year Longitudinal Study." *Journal of Educational Research* 91 (21): 33–45.

Oakes, Jeannie. 1994. "More than Misapplied Technology: A Normative and Political Response to Hallinan on Tracking." *Sociology of Education* 67: 84–88.

O'Barr, William M. 2001. "Language and Patriarchy." In Dana Vannoy, Ed., *Gender Mosaics*, pp. 106–113. Los Angeles: Roxbury.

O'Brien, Kathleen. 2000. "Taking Advantage of the Mobile Office: Homeward Bound." *New York Times*, April 5.

Ogasawara, Yuko. 1998. *Office Ladies and Salaried Men: Power, Gender, and Work in Japanese Companies*. Berkeley: University of California.

Ohanian, Susan. 1999. *One Size Fits All: The Folly of Educational Standards*. New York: Heinemann.

O'Kane, James M. 1992. *The Crocked Ladder: Gangsters, Ethnicity, and the American Dream*. New Brunswick, NJ: Transaction.

Orbell, John M. and Robyn M. Dawes. 1993. "Social Welfare, Cooperators' Advantage, and the Option of Not Playing the Game." *American Sociological Review* 58: 786–800.

Orenstein, Peggy. 2000. *Flux: Women on Sex, Work, Kids, Love and Life in a Half Changed World*. New York: Doubleday.

Orshansky, Mollie. 1965. *Food Consumption and Dietary Levels of Rural Families in the North Central Region*. Washington, D.C.: Institute of Home Economics.

Orwell, George. 1954. *Animal Farm*. New York: Harcourt, Brace.

Osborne, Lawrence. 2000. "Migration of the Melting Pot." *New York Times Magazine*, April 9: 96–97.

Owens, Kelly and Mary-Claire King. 1999. "Genomic Views of Human History." *Science*, October 15: 451–453.

Parikh, Lina and Barbara Shane. 1998. "Women of Our World 1998." *Population Reference Bureau*, 1998.

Parrenas, Rhacel Salazar. 2000. "Migrant Filipina Domestic Workers and the International Division of Reproductive Labor." *Gender & Society* 14: 560–581.

——. 2000. *Strangers to These Shores: Race and Ethnic Relations in the United States*, 6th ed. Boston: Allyn & Bacon.

Passy, Florence and Marco Giugni. 2000. "Life-Spheres, Networks, and Sustained Participation in Social Movements: A Phenomenological Approach to Political Commitment." *Sociological Forum* 15: 117–129.

Paterson, Orlando. 1998. *Rituals of Blood: Consequences of Slavery in Two American Centuries*. Washington, DC: Civitas/Counterpoint.

Pear, Robert. 1999. "Drug Companies Getting F.D.A. Reprimands for False or Misleading Advertising." *New York Times*, March 28.

——. 1999b. "Health Industry Sees Wish List Made Into Law." *New York Times*, December 6.

——. 1999c. "Poor Workers Lose Medicaid Coverage Despite Eligibility." *New York Times*, April 12.

——. 1999d. "Future Bleak for Bill to keep Health Records Confidential." *New York Times*, June 21.

——. 2000. "Still Uninsured, and Still a Campaign Issue." *New York Times*, June 25.

Pearce, Diana M. 1985. "Toil and Trouble: Women Workers and Unemployment Compensation." *Signs* 10: 439–459.

Perrucci, Robert and Earl Wysong. 1999. *The New Class Society*. Lanham, MD: Rowman & Littlefield.

Pescosolido, Bernice A. and Beth A. Rubin. 2000. "The Web of Group Affiliations Revisited: Social Life, Postmodernism, and Sociology." *American Sociological Review* 65: 52–76.

Pew Research Center. 2000. "Tracking On-Line Life: How Women Use the Internet to Cultivate Relationships with Family and Friends." *Report of the Pew Internet and American Life Project*. Washington, DC.

Phillips, Meredith, James Crouse, and John Ralph. 1998. "Does the Black-White Test Score Gap Widen After Children Enter School?" In Christopher Jencks and

Meredith Phillips, Eds., *The Black-White Test Score Gap*, pp. 229–272. Washington, DC: Brookings.

Pihl, R. O., Jordan Peterson, and Peter Finn. 1990. "Inherited Predisposition to Alcoholism: Characteristics of Sons of Male Alcoholics." *Journal of Abnormal Psychology* 99: 291–301.

Pinkney, Alphonso. 2000. *Black Americans*, 5th Edition. Upper Saddle River, NJ: Prentice Hall.

Pinstrup-Andersen, Pers, Rajul Pandya-Lorch, and Mark W. Rosegrant. 1999. "World Food Prospects: Critical Issues for the Early Twenty-first Century." International Food Policy Research Institute, October.

Pipher, Mary. 1994. *Reviving Ophelia*. New York: Putnam.

Political Research Associates. 2000. "Hard Right Conspiracism and Apocalyptic Millennialism." January 6. Somerville, MA.

Pollack, William S. 1999. *Real Boys: Rescuing Our Sons from the Myths of Boyhood*. New York: Henry Holt.

Pollard, Kelvin, and William P. O'Hare. 1999. "America's Racial and Ethnic Minorities." *Population Bulletin* 54 (3), September.

Pollin, Robert, and Stephanie Luce. 1998. *The Living Wage: Building a Fair Economy*. New York: New Press.

Population Reference Bureau. 1997. *World Population and the Environment Data Sheet*. Washington, DC: PRB.

——. 2000a. *The World of Child 6 Billion*. Washington, DC.

——. 2000b. *World Population Data Sheet*, May. Washington, DC.

Population Today. 2000b. "Teen Birth Rate Continues to Drop." January: 3–4.

Pozo, Susan. 1996. *Exploring the Underground Economy: Studies of Illegal and Unreported Activity*. Kalamazoo, MI: W.E. Upjohn Institute for Employment Research.

Prather, Carole. 2000. "The Dual-Earner Family: Does Employment Always Pay?" *PENpages*. Pennslyvania State University, February.

Presser, Stanley, and Linda Stinson. 1998. "Data Collection Mode and Social Desirability Bias in Self-Reported Religious Attendance." *American Sociological Review* 63: 137–145.

Prieur, Annick. 1998. *Mema's House, Mexico City: On Transvestites, Queens, and Machos*. Chicago: University of Chicago.

Purdum, Todd S. 2000. "Rights Groups Sue California Public Schools." *New York Times*, May 18.

Purdy, Matthew. 1999. "Our Towns; Where Laborers Are Handy but Shunned." *New York Times*, November 21.

Purnick, Joyce. 1999. "Metro Matters; Mentally Ill Are Squeezed by Parsimony." *New York Times*, December 20.

Putnam, Robert D. 2000. *Bowling Alone: The Collapse and Revival of American Community*. New York: Simon & Schuster.

Quadagno, Jill. 1999. "Creating a Capital Investment Welfare State: The New American Exceptionalism." *American Sociological Review* 64: 1–10.

Rathore, S. S., L. A. Lenert, K. P. Weinfurt, A. Tinoco, C. K. Taleghani, W. Harless, and K. A. Schulman. 2000. "The Effects of Patient Sex and Race on Medical Students' Ratings of Quality of Life." *American Journal of Medicine* 108: 561–566.

Reed, Douglas. 1997. "Court Ordered School Finance Equalization." National Center for Educational Services.

Religion News Service. 2000. "Hispanic Catholics Flourish in the Heart of Dixie." Online: August.

Religious Research Center. 1999. "The Religious Preferences of Americans." Online.

Rennie, Drummond. 1999. "Fair Conduct and Fair Reporting of Clinical Trials." *Journal of the American Medical Association*. Vol. 282, 18. November 10.

Reskin, Barbara F. 1998. *The Realities of Affirmative Action in Employment*. Washington, DC: American Sociological Association.

———. 1999. "The Effectiveness of Workplace Diversity and Affirmative Action in Reducing Race and Sex Inequality in the Workplace." Presented at the Eastern Sociological Society, Boston: March 7.

———. 2000. "The Proximate Causes of Employment Discrimination." *Contemporary Sociology* 29: 319–328.

Reskin, Barbara F. and Debra Branch McBrier. 2000. "Why Not Ascription? Organizations' Employment of Male and Female Managers." *American Sociological Review* 65: 210–233.

Reynolds, John R. and Catherine E. Ross, 1998. "Social Stratification and Health: Education's Benefit Beyond Economic Status and Social Origins," *Social Problems* 45: 221–234.

Rhim, Soon Man. 1993. "Untouchables in Japan: the Barakumin in Tokyo." Paper presented at the Annual Meeting of the Eastern Sociological Society.

Rhodes, Deborah. 1997. *Speaking of Sex*. Cambridge, MA: Harvard.

Rice, George, Carol Anderson, Neil Risch, and George Ebers. 1999. "Male Homosexuality: Absence of Linkage to Macrosatellite Markers at Xq28." *Science* 284: 665.

Richardson, Bill. 1993. "More Power to the Tribes." *New York Times*, July 7.

Richardson, Laurel. 1974. "The Changing Door Ceremony: Some Notes on the Operation of Sex Roles in Everyday Life." *Urban Life and Culture* 2(4): 506–515.

Ridgeway, Cecilia. 1999. "The Gender System, Cultural Beliefs, and Intersection." *Sex and Gender News*, November.

Ridgeway, Cecilia L., Kathy J. Kuipers, Elizabeth Heger Boyle, and Dawn T. Robinson. 1998. "How Do Status Beliefs Develop? The Role of Resources and Interactional Experience." *American Sociological Review* 63: 331–350.

Ridgeway, Cecilia L. and Shelley J. Correll. 2000. "Limiting Inequality through Interaction: The End(s) of Gender." *Contemporary Sociology* 29: 110–120.

Rinehart, James, Christopher Huxley, and David Robertson. 1997. *Just Another Car Factory? Lean Production and its Discontents*. Ithaca, NY: Cornell.

Risman, Barbara J. 1998. *Gender Vertigo: American Families in Transition*. New Haven, CT: Yale.

Risman, Barbara, Maxine P. Atkinson, and Stephen P. Blackwelder. 1999. "Understanding the Juggling Act: Gendered Preferences and Social Structural Constraints." *Sociological Forum* 14: 319.

Roberts, Joan. 1995. *Feminism and Nursing: An Historical Perspective on Power, Status, and Political Activism in the Nursing Profession*. Westport, CT: Praeger, 1995.

Robinson, John and Geoffrey Godby. 1999. "The Family Dinner Alive and Well," cited in Karlyn Bowman. *New York Times Op-Ed*, August 25.

Roman, Paul M., Ed. 1991. *Alcohol: The Development of Sociological Perspectives on Use and Abuse*. New Brunswick, NJ: Rutgers Center on Alcohol Studies.

Romero, Mary. 1992. *Maid in the U.S.A.* New York: Routledge.

Roschelle, Anne M. 1999. "Gender, Family Structure, and Social Structure: Racial Ethnic Families in the United States." In Myra Marx Ferree, Judith Lorber, and Beth B. Hess, Eds., *Revisioning Gender*, pp. 311–341. Thousand Oaks, CA: Sage.

Roscigno, Vincent J. 2000. "Family/School Inequality and African-American/Hispanic Achievement." *Social Problems* 47: 266–290.

Rose, Lowell C., and Alec M. Gallup. 1999. "The 31st Annual Phi Delta Kappa/Gallup Poll." *Phi Delta Kappan* 81 (1999): 41–56.

Rosen, Jeffrey. 2000a. "The Lost Promise of School Integration." *New York Times*, April 2.

———. 2000b. *The Unwanted Gaze: The Destruction of Privacy in America*. New York: Random House.

Rosenfield, Sarah. 1992. "The Costs of Sharing: Wives' Employment and Husbands' Mental Health." *Journal of Health and Social Behavior* 33: 213–225.

Rossi, Peter H. and Richard A. Berk. 1997. *Just Punishment: Federal Guidelines and Public Views Compared*. New York: Aldine de Gruyter.

Rothschild, Joyce. 2000. "Creating a Just and Democratic Workplace: More Engagement, Less Hierarchy." *Contemporary Sociology* 29: 195–199.

Rothstein, Richard. 2000. "An Allegiance to Public Schools." *New York Times*, March 15.

Roy, William G. 1997. *Socializing Capital: The Rise of the Large Industrial Corporation in America*. Princeton, NJ: Princeton.

Rozhon, Tracie. 1999. "Old Baltimore Row Houses Fall Before Wrecking Ball." *New York Times*, June 13.

Rubin, Jeffrey Z., Frank J. Provenzano, and Zella Luria. 1979. "The Eye of the Beholder: Parents' Views on Sex of Newborns." In Juanita H. Williams, Ed., *Psychology of Women*, pp. 134–141. New York: W.W. Norton.

Ruether, Rosemary Radford. 2001. "Ecofeminism and Healing Ourselves: Healing the Earth." In Dana Vannoy, Ed., *Gender Mosaics*, pp. 406–414. Los Angeles: Roxbury.

Rundblad, Georganne. 2001. "Gender, Power, and Sexual Harassment." In Dana Vannoy, Ed., *Gender Mosaics*, pp. 352–362. Los Angeles: Roxbury.

Rushton, J. Philippe. 1999. *Race, Evolution & Behavior.* New Brunswick, NJ: Transaction.

Rymer, Gus. 1993. *An Abused Child's Fight From Silence.* New York: Harper Collins.

Saad, Lydia. 1999. "American Workers Generally Satisfied, but Indicate Their Jobs Leave Much to be Desired." *Gallup News Service*, September 3.

Sachar, Howard M. 1992. *A History of the Jews in America*. New York: Alfred A. Knopf.

Sachs, Susan. 2000. "Egypt's Women Win Equal Rights to Divorce." *New York Times*, March 1.

Sampson, Robert J., Jeffrey D. Morenoff, and Felton Earls. 1999. "Beyond Social Capital: Spatial Dynamics of Collective Efficacy." *American Sociological Review.* October: 64,5: 633–660.

Sanday, Peggy Reeves. 1990. *Female Power and Male Dominance: On the Origins of Sexual Inequality.* Cambridge, UK: Cambridge.

Santiago, Anna M. and George Galster. 1995. "Puerto Rican Segregation in the United States: Cause or Consequence of Economic Status?" *Social Problems* 42: 361–389.

Sapolsky, Robert M. 1997. *The Trouble With Testosterone.* New York: Scribner.

Scheck, Barry, Peter Neufeld, and Jim Dwyer. 2000. *Actual Innocence: Five Days to Execution, and Other Dispatches From the Wrongly Convicted.* New York: Doubleday.

Schmidt, Eric. 1994. "Military Struggling to Stem an Increase in Family Violence." *New York Times,* May 23.

Schneider, Barbara and James C. Coleman (Eds.). 1993. *Parents, Their Children, and Schools.* Boulder, CO: Westview Press.

Schor, Juliet. 1992. *The Overworked American.* New York: Basic.

Schorr, Jonathan. 2000. "Giving Charter Schools a Chance." *The Nation*, June 5: 19–23.

Schuman, Howard, Charles Steh, Lawrence Bobo, and Maria Krysan. 1999. "On Survey Data." *ASA Footnotes*, November: 6.

Schwartz, Felice. 1989. "Management, Women, and the New Facts of Life." *Harvard Business Review*, January-February: 65–70.

Schwartz, Pepper. 1994. *Peer Marriage: How Love Between Equals Really Works.* New York: Free Press.

——. 2000. "Creating Sexual Pleasure and Sexual Justice in the Twenty-First Century." *Contemporary Sociology* 29: 213–218.

Schwartz, Pepper and Virginia Rutter. 1998. *The Gender of Sexuality.* Thousand Oaks, CA: Pine Forge.

Seabrook, Jeremy. 1997. *Travels in the Skin Trade: Tourism and the Sex Industry.* New York: Pluto.

Segura, Denise A. 1993. "Chicanos in White Collar Jobs: Gender/Race-Ethnic Dilemmas and Affirmations." Paper presented at the Annual Meeting of the American Sociological Association.

Seidman, Steven, Ed. 1993. *Queer Theory/Sociology*. Oxford: Blackwell.

——. 1997. *Difference Troubles: Queering Social Theory and Sexual Politics*. New York: Cambridge.

Sen, Amartya. 1999. *Development as Freedom*. New York: Knopf.

Sennett, Richard. 1998. *The Corrosion of Character: The Personal Consequences of Work in the New Capitalism*. New York: Norton.

Settersten, Richard. 1999. *Lives in Time and Place: The Problems and Promises of Developmental Science*. Amityville, NY: Baywood.

Shalom, Stephen R. 1998. "Dubious Data: The Thernstroms on Race in America." *Race & Society* 1: 125–157.

Shanahan, Jack. 1999. "The Best Investment the Pentagon Could Make." *New York Times*, September 17.

Shapiro, Isaac and Robert Greenstein. 1999. *The Widening Income Gulf*. Washington, D.C.: Center on Budget and Policy Priorities.

Sheifer, S. E., J. J. Escarce, and K. A. Schulman. 2000. "Race and Sex Differences in the Management of Coronary Artery Disease." *American Heart Journal* 139: 848–857.

Shelton, Beth Anne and Rebecca E. Deen. 2001. "Divorce Trends and Effects for Women and Men." In Dana Vannoy, Ed., *Gender Mosaics*, pp. 216–226. Los Angeles: Roxbury.

Sherif, Muzifer O., Harvey B. White, W. Hood and Caroline Sherif. 1961. *Intergroup Conflict and Cooperation: The Robbers' Cave Experiment*. Norman, OK: Oklahoma.

Sherkat, Darren E. and Christopher G. Ellison. 1994. "The Political Development of Sixties' Activists: Identifying the Influence of Class, Gender, and Socialization on Protest Participation." *Social Forces* 72: 821–842.

Simon, William and John Gagnon. 1998. "Psychosexual Development." *Society*, 35 (2) January-February.

Sims, Calvin. 2000. "Japan's Employers Are Giving Bonuses for Having Babies." *New York Times*, May 30.

Smelser, Neil J. 1968. "Toward a General Theory of Social Change." In Neil J. Smelser, Ed., *Essays in Sociological Explanation*. Englewood Cliffs, NJ: Prentice-Hall.

Smith, Christian. 1998. *American Evangelicism: Embattled and Thriving*. Chicago, IL: University of Chicago Press.

Smith, Neil. 1996. *The New Urban Frontier: Gentrification and the Revanchist City*. New York: Routledge.

Smith, Vicki. 1998. "The Fractured World of the Temporary Worker: Power, Participation, and Fragmentation in the Contemporary Workplace." *Social Problems* 45 (4).

Smock, Pamela. 2000. "Cohabitation in the United States: An Appraisal of Research Themes, Findings and Implications." *Annual Review of Sociology* 26: 1–20.

Smock, Pamela J., Wendy D. Manning, and Snjiv Gupta. 1999. "The Effect of Marriage and Divorce on Women's Economic Well–Being." *American Sociological Review* 64: 79–812.

Sommers, Christian Hoff. 2000. *The War Against Boys: How Misguided Feminism Is Harming Our Young Men*. New York: Simon & Schuster.

Sorenson, John, Robert Winkle, Victoria Brewer, and James Marquart. 1999. "Capital Punishment and Deterrence: Examining the Effect of Executions on Murder in Texas." *Crime and Delinquency* 45: 481–493.

Spade, Joan Z. 1994. "Wives' and Husbands' Perceptions of Why Wives Work." *Gender & Society* 8: 170–188.

——. 2001. "Gender and Education in the United States." In Dana Vannoy, Ed., *Gender Mosaics*, pp. 85–93. Los Angeles: Roxbury.

Spain, Daphne. 1992. *Gendered Spaces*. Chapel Hill, NC: University of North Carolina.

Squires, Gregory D. 1997. *Insurance Redlining: Disinvestment, Reinvestment, and the Evolving Role of Financial Institutions*. Washington, DC: Urban Institute.

Stainback, Melissa and Katharine M. Donato. 1998. "Going to Work but Never Leaving Home." *Population Today*, September: 3–4.

Starr, Paul. 1982. *The Transformation of American Medicine*. New York: Basic Books.

Stein, Arlene. 1997. *Sex and Sensibility: Stories of a Lesbian Generation*. Berkeley: University of California.

Stein, Peter and Kathleen Korgen. 2000. "Sociological Practice and Diversity in the Workplace." Paper presented at the Annual Meetings of the American Sociological Association, August.

Steinberg, Jacques and Edward Wyatt. 2000. "Boola, Boola: E-Commerce Comes to The Quad." *New York Times*, February 14.

Steinberg, Ronnie J. 2001. "How Sex Gets Into Your Paycheck and How to Get It Out: The Gender Gap in Pay and Comparable Worth." In Dana Vannoy, Ed., *Gender Mosaics*, pp. 258–268. Los Angeles: Roxbury.

Steinhauer, Jennifer. 1999. "As Aid Is Cut, Hospitals Prepare for a Tough Year." *New York Times*, February 5.

——. 2000. "Doctors Eliminate Wrinkles, and Insurers." *New York Times*, January 8.

Stepan-Norris, Judith, and Maurice Zeitlin. 1991. " 'Red' Unions and 'Bourgeoise Contracts'?" *American Journal of Sociology* 96: 1151–1200.

Stevens, William K. 1999. "Human Imprint on Climate Change Grows Clearer." *New York Times*, June 29.

——. 2000a. "Global Warning: The Contrarian View." *New York Times*, February 29.

——. 2000b. "Persistent and Severe, Drought Strikes Again." *New York Times*, April 25.

St. Jean, Yannick and Joe R. Feagin. 1998. *Double Burden: Black Women and Everyday Racism*. Armonk, NY: M.E. Sharpe.

Stolberg, Sheryl Gay. 1999. "Iowa Turf War Over Transplants Mirrors Feuds Across the Nation." *New York Times*, December 29.

Straus, Murray. 2000. *Beating the Devil Out of Them: Corporal Punishment in American Families and Its Effects on Children*. 2nd Ed. New Brunswick, NJ: Transaction.

Strom, Kevin J. 2000. "Profile of State Prisoners Under Age 18, 1985–97." (NCJ-176989). Washington, DC: Bureau of Justice Statistics.

Strom, Stephanie. 2000. "In Japan, the Golden Years Have Lost Their Glow." *New York Times*, February 16.

Stryker, Jess. 2000. "Take It to the Bank." *New York Times Magazine*, June 25: 20.

Sucoff, Clea A. and Dawn M. Upchurch. 1998. "Neighborhood Context and the Risk of Childbearing Among Metropolitan-Area Black Adolescents." *American Sociological Review* 63: 571–585.

Sugrue, Thomas J. 1996. *The Origins of the Urban Crisis: Race and Inequality in Postwar Detroit*. Princeton, NJ: Princeton.

Sullivan, John. 2000. "States and Cities Removing Prisons from Courts' Grips." *New York Times*, January 30.

Sullivan, Maureen. 1996. "Rozzi and Harriet? Gender and Family Pattern of Lesbian Coparents." *Gender & Society* 10: 747–767.

Sutherland, Edwin H. 1939. *Principles of Criminology*. Philadelphia: Lippincott.

Swanson, Guy. 1988. *Ego Defense and the Legitimation of Behavior*. New York: Cambridge.

Swinford, Steven P., Alfred DeMaris, Stephen A. Cernkovich, and Peggy C. Giordano. 2000. "Harsh Physical Discipline in Childhood and Violence in Later Romantic Involvements: The Mediating Role of Problem Behaviors." *Journal of Marriage and the Family* 62: 508–519.

Tanner, Julian, Scott Davies, and Bill O'Grady. 1999. "Whatever Happened to Yesterday's Rebels? Longitudinal Effects of Youth Delinquency on Education and Employment." *Social Problems* 46 No. 2: 250–274.

Telles, Edward E. and Edward Murguia. 1990. "Phenotypic Discrimination and Income Differences Among Mexican Americans." *Social Science Quarterly* 57: 682–696.

Thomas, Jo. 1999. "New Face of Terror Crimes: 'Lone Wolf' Weaned on Hate." *New York Times*, August 16.

Thomas, William I. and Dorothy Swain Thomas. 1928. *The Child in America: Behavior Problems and Programs*. New York: Knopf.

Thompson, Ernie. 1999. "Effects of an Execution on Homicides in California." *Homicide Studies* 3: 129–150.

Thorne, Barrie. 1993. *Gender Play: Girls and Boys in School*. New Brunswick, NJ: Rutgers.

Thornhill, Randy and Craig T. Palmer. 2000. *A Natural History of Rape: Biological Bases of Sexual Coercion*. Cambridge: Massachusetts Institute of Technology.

Thornton, Arland, William G. Axim, and Daniel H. Hill. 1992. "Reciprocal Effects of Religiosity: Cohabitation and Marriage." *American Journal of Sociology* 98: 628–651.

Tiemann, Kathleen A. 1999. "Presidential Address: Humanistic Teaching and Technology." *Humanity and Society* 23 (1), February.

Tilly, Charles. 1998. *Durable Inequality*. Berkeley, CA: University of California.

Tilly, Chris and Charles Tilly. 1998. *Work Under Capitalism*. Boulder, CO: Westview.

Toliver, Susan D. 1998. *Black Families in Corporate America*. Thousand Oaks, CA: Sage.

Torr, James D. and Karin Swisher. 1999. *Violence Against Women*. San Diego, CA: Greenhaven.

Turkle, Sherry. 1999. "Cyberspace and Identity." *Contemporary Sociology* 28: 643–648.

Turner, R. J., Blair Wheaton, and Donald A. Lloyd. 1995. "The Epidemiology of Social Stress." *American Sociological Review* 60: 104–125.

Turner, Stephanie S. 1999. "Intersex Identities: Locating New Intersections of Sex and Gender." *Gender & Society* 13: 457–479.

Uggen, Christopher. 1999. "Ex-Offenders and the Conformist Alternative: A Job Quality Model of Work and Crime." *Social Problems* 46 (1): 127–151.

United Nations. 1999. *Human Development Report 1999*. New York: Oxford.

United Nations Development Program. 2000a. *Overcoming Human Poverty: UNDP Poverty Report 2000*. New York: United Nations.

——. 2000b. "HIV/AIDS Epidemic is Shifting From Cities to Rural Areas." Press Release 00/37, June.

——. 2000c. "Report on AIDS in Africa." News Release, June 28.

——. 2000d. Food and Agriculture Administration. *World Data Sheet*. Geneva.

Urban Institute. 2000. "School Lunch Programs Offers Promising Way to Reach Most Uninsured Children." *www.urban.org*. January 4.

U.S. Bureau of the Census. 1975. *Historical Statistics of the United States*. Vol. 1.

——. 1998a. "Neighborhood Pride: Most People Like Where They Live." *Census Brief* 98–3, May.

——. 1998b. " 'Too Busy' to Vote." *Census Brief*, July 9.

——. 1998c. "Voting and Registration in the Election of November 1996." *Current Population Reports*, Series P20-504, July.

——. 1998d. "Health Insurance Coverage: 1997." *Current Population Reports*, Series P60-202. Washington, DC: Government Printing Office, September.

——. 1998e. "Marital Status and Living Arrangement: March 1998 (Update)." *Current Population Reports*, Series P20–514. Washington, DC: Government Printing Office, December.

——. 1998f. "Poverty in the United States: 1997." *Current Population Reports*, Series P60-201. U.S. Government Printing Office, Washington, DC.

——. 1999. *Statistical Abstract of the United States: 1999*. Washington, DC: Government Printing Office.

——. 2000a. *Population Projections Program*. Washington, DC. January 13.

——. 2000b. "Estimated Median Age at First Marriage, by Sex, 1890 to the Present." Internet Release, January.

——. 2000c. "The Hispanic Population in the United States, March 1999." *Current Population Reports*, Series P20–527. Washington, DC: Government Printing Office, February.

——. 2000d. "Transforming Race Relations." March.

——. 2000e. "Money Income in the United State, 1999," pp. 60–209. September.

——. 2000f. "Poverty in the United States, 1999." pp. 60–210. September.

——. 2000g. "The Hispanic Population in the United States, 1999." *Current Population Reports*, Series P20–527. Washington, DC: Government Printing Office.

——. 2000h. *Statistical Abstract of the United States*.

U.S. Department of Commerce. 1999. "Computer Use in the United States, 1997." *Current Population Reports* P20–522, September.

U.S. Department of Commerce, Bureau of the Census. 2000. *Statistical Abstract of the United States*. Washington, DC: Government Printing Office.

U.S. Department of Defense. 2000. "Survey Details Harassment, Cohen Calls for Action Plan." *Armed Forces Information Service Press Release*, March.

U.S. Department of Defense, Office of the Inspector General. 2000. "Gays in the Military."

U.S. Department of Education. 2000a. "Internet Access in U.S. Public Schools and Classrooms, 1994–99." Washington, DC: National Center of Education Statistics, February.

——. 2000b. *Study of Educational Resources and Federal Funding: Final Report*. Washington, DC: August.

——. 2000c. *The Condition of Education 2000*. Washington DC: Government Printing Office.

——. 2000d. National Center for Education Statistics, *Educational Equity for Girls and Women*, NCES 2000-030, by Yupin Bae, Susan Choy, Claire Geddes, Jennifer Sable, and Thomas Snyder. Washington, DC: U.S. Government Printing Office.

U.S. Department of Health and Human Services. 1998. *Substance Abuse and Mental Health Statistics Sourcebook 1998*. Washington, DC: DHHS.

U.S. Department of Health and Human Services, Centers for Disease Control and Prevention. 2000. *Youth Risk Behavior Surveillance System Summary 1999*. Atlanta, GA: CDCP, June.

U.S. Department of Health and Human Services, National Vital Statistics System. 2000. "Births, Marriages, Divorces, and Deaths: Provisional Data for April 1999." Washington, DC: Government Printing Office, June.

U.S. Department of Housing and Urban Development. 2000. *Now Is the Time: Places Left Behind in the New Economy*. Washington, DC: HUD.

U.S. Department of Justice. 1999. *Criminal Victimization 1998*. Washington, DC, July.

U.S. Department of Justice, Bureau of Justice Statistics Bulletin. 2000. *Prison and Jail Inmates At Midyear 1999*. Washington, DC: April.

U.S. Department of Justice, Bureau of Justice Statistics, Online Press Releases. 1999a. "U.S. Violent Crime Rate Fell 7 Percent in 1998, 27 Percent Lower Than in 1993." July 18.

——. 1999b. "About 2.1 Million Violent Female Offenders Annually, Most Commit Simple Assaults Against Other Females." December 5.

——. 2000a. "Number of People Under 18 Sent to Adult State Prisons More Than Doubled Between 1985 and 1997." February 27, 2000.

——. 2000b. "Criminal Victimization 1999." Washington, D.C.: August.

U.S. Department of Justice, Federal Bureau of Investigation. 1999. *Crime in the United States 1998*. Washington, D.C.

U.S. Department of Justice, Office of Juvenile Justice and Delinquency Prevention. 1998. *Trying Juveniles as Adults in Criminal Court: An Analysis of State Transfer Provisions*. Rockville, MD: Juvenile Justice Clearinghouse.

——. 1999. *Juvenile Offenders and Victims: 1999 Annual Report*. Rockville, MD: Juvenile Justice Clearinghouse.

——. 2000a. "Delinquency Cases Waived to Criminal Court, 1988–1997." *OJJDP Fact Sheet* #2 February.

——. 2000b "Self-Reported Delinquency by 12-Year-Olds, 1997." *OJJDP Fact Sheet* #3 February.

——. 2000c. "Children as Victims." *1999 National Report Series*, May.

U.S. Department of Labor, Bureau of Labor Statistics. 1984. *Employment and Earnings*. January.

——. 1997. *Monthly Labor Review*.

——. 2000. *Employment and Earnings*. January.

University of Michigan. *Monitoring the Future Study*. Ann Arbor, MI: Institute for Social Research, various years.

Useem, Elizabeth L. 1992. "Middle Schools and Math Groups: Parents' Involvement in Children's Placement." *Sociology of Education* 65: 263–279.

Van Dyke, Nella. 1999. "Hotbeds of Activism: Locations of Student Protest." *Social Problems* 45: 205–217.

Vannoy, Dana. 2001. "Collapsing the Walls of Patriarchy and Masculine Hegemony." In Dana Vannoy, Ed., *Gender Mosaics*, pp. 507–513. Los Angeles: Roxbury.

Verhovek, Sam Howe. 2000. "Internet's Rich Are Giving It Away, Their Way." *New York Times*, February 11.

Wagner, David. 2000. *What's Love Got To Do With It? A Critical Look at American Charity*. New York: New Press.

Waite, Linda J. 2000. "The Family as a Social Organization: Key Ideas for the Twenty–First Century." *Contemporary Sociology* 29 (3): 463–472.

Waite, Linda J. and Maggie Gallagher. 2000. *The Case for Marriage*. New York: Doubleday.

Wald, Matthew L. 1999. "Reactors: Healthy but Dying." *New York Times*, March 7.

Warner, Rebecca L. and Brent S. Steel. 1999. "Child Rearing As a Mechanism for Social Change: The Relationship of Child Gender to Parents' Commitment to Gender Equality." *Gender & Society* 13: 503–517.

Watts, Jerry. 1997. "The End of Work and the End of Welfare." *Contemporary Sociology* 26: 409–412.

Wayne, Leslie. 2000. "After High Pressure Years, Contractors Tone Down Missile Defense Lobbying. *New York Times*, June 15.

Weber, Max. 1904–1905/1976. *The Protestant Ethic and the Spirit of Capitalism*. Trans. Talcott Parsons. Introduction by Anthony Giddens. New York: Scribner.

Weiner, Tim. 2000. "For Military Plane in Crash, History of Political Conflict." *New York Times*, April 11.

Weitz, Rose, Ed. 1998. *The Politics of Women's Bodies: Sexuality, Appearance, and Behavior*. New York: Oxford.

Wellman, Barry and Keith Hampton. 1999. "Living Networked On and Offline." *Contemporary Sociology* 28: 648654.

Weschler, Henry, Jae Eun Lee, Meichun Kuo, and Hang Lee. 2000. "College Binge Drinking in the 1990s: A Continuing Problem." *Journal of American College Health* 48: 199–210.

Western, Bruce. 1998. *Between Class and Market: Postwar Unionization in the Capitalist Democracies*. Princeton, NJ: Princeton.

Whitaker, Barbara. 1999. "Official Resigns After Charges of Brutality in Juvenile Jails." *New York Times*, December 25.

Whiten. A., J. Goodall, W. C. McGrew, T. Nishida, V. Reynolds, and Y. Sugiyama. 1999. "Cultures in Chimpanzees." *Nature* 399: 682–685.

Whyte, William Foote and Kathleen King Whyte. 1988. *Making Mondragon: The Growth and Dynamics of the Workers Cooperative Complex.* Ithaca, NY: ILR Press.

Wickelgren, Ingrid. 1991. "Discovery of 'Gay Gene' Questioned." *Science* 264: 571.

Williams, David R., James S. Jackson, Tony N. Brown, Myriam Torres, Tyrone A. Forman, and Kendrick Brown. 1999. "Traditional and Contemporary Prejudice and Urban Whites' Support for Affirmative Action and Government Help." *Social Problems* 46: 503–527.

Williams, Rhys H., Ed. 1997. *Culture Wars in American Politics: Critical Reviews of a Popular Myth.* New York: Aldine de Gruyter.

Wilson, Charles E. 1952. General Motors, CEO.

Wilson, William Julius. 1996. *When Work Disappears: The World of the New Urban Poor.* New York: Alfred A. Knopf.

Winerup, Michael. 1999. "Bedlam on the Streets." *New York Times Magazine,* May 23.

Winter, Greg. 2000. "Cuts in Loan Program Squeeze Doctors Who Work With Poor." *New York Times*, July 30.

Witkin, H.A., and Associates. 1976. "A Criminality in XYZ and XXY Men." *Science* 193: 547–555.

Wolff, Edward. 1998. "Recent Trends in the Size Distribution of Household Wealth." *Journal of Economic Perspectives* 12: 131–151.

Wolfinger, Nicholas H. 1999. "Trends in the Intergenerational Transmission of Divorce." *Demography* 36: 415–20.

Wood, Ellen M. and John Bellamy Foster. 1997. *In Defense of History: Marxism and the Postmodern Agenda.* New York: Monthly Review Press.

Woods, James. 1993. *The Corporate Closet: The Professional Lives of Gay Men in America.* New York: Free Press.

Woodstock Institute. 1999. *Two Steps Back.* Chicago, IL: Woodstock Institute.

Woolhandler, Steffie and David U. Himmelstein. 1997. "Costs of Care and Administration at For-profit and Other Hospitals in the United States." *New England Journal of Medicine* 336: 769–774.

World Bank. 2000. *World Development Report 2000/2001: Attacking Poverty.* Washington, DC: World Bank, September.

World Health Organization. 2000. *World Health Report 2000.* New York and Geneva: WHO.

Wren, Christopher S. 1999a. "Arizona Finds Cost Savings in Treating Drug Offenders." *New York Times*, April 21.

——. 1999b. "Top U.S. Drug Official Proposes Shift in Criminal Justice Policy." *New York Times*, December 9.

Wright, Erik Olin. 1985. *Classes.* London: New Left Press.

——. 2000. "Reducing Wealth and Income: Inequality: Real Utopian Proposals." *Contemporary Sociology*: 143–156.

Wright, Richard T. and Scott H. Decker. 1997. *Armed Robbers in Action: Stickups and Street Culture.* Boston: Northeastern University Press.

Wrong, Dennis. 1961. "The Oversocialized Conception of Man in Modern Society." *American Sociological Review* 26: 183–193.

WuDunn, Sheryl. 1999. "Japan's Tale of 2 Pills." *New York Times*, June 27.

www.adherents.com. 1999. "Major Religions of the World and the Number of Adherents."

www.refugees.org. United States Committee for Refugees. 2000. "Principle Sources of Refugees."

www.urban.org. "Welfare Reform: Myth vs. Fact." *Urban Institute,* June 3.

Wyatt, Edward. 2000. "Study Finds Higher Test Scores Among Blacks with Vouchers." *New York Times*, August 29.

Yardley, Jim. 2000. "Panel Recommends Reparations in Long-Ignored Tulsa Race Riot." *New York Times*, February 5.

Yellin, Emily. 2000. "An Evangelical Group for Hunters." *New York Times*, March 26.

Yoon, Carol K.1997. "Families Emerge as Silent Victims of Tuskegee Syphilis Experiment." *New York Times,* May 12.

Zachariah, John. 1999. *An Overview of Boot Camp Goals, Components, and Results.* Topeka, KS: Koch Crime Institute.

Zerubavel, Eviatar. 1985. *The Seven Day Circle: The History and Meaning of the Week.* New York: Free Press.

——. 1997. *Social Mindscapes: An Invitation to Cognitive Sociology.* Cambridge, MA: Harvard.

Zikmund, Barbara Brown, Adair T. Lummis, and Patricia Mei Yin Chang. 1998. *Clergy Women: An Uphill Calling.* Louisville, KY: Westminster John Knox.

Zimmerman, Mary K and Lisa Cox Hall. 2001. "Men and Women: Health and Illness." In Dana Vannoy, Ed., *Gender Mosaics,* pp. 426–435. Los Angeles: Roxbury.

Zola, Irving. 1966. "Culture and Symptoms: An Analysis of Patients' Presenting Complaints." *American Sociological Review* 31: 615–630. ✦

Author Index

Subject Index